History of C

History of Criminal Justice

Fifth Edition

Mark Jones
Peter Johnstone

LONDON AND NEW YORK

First published 2012 by Anderson Publishing

Published 2015 by Routledge
2 Park Square, Milton Park, Abingdon, Oxon OX14 4RN

and by Routledge
711 Third Avenue, New York, NY 10017, USA

Routledge is an imprint of the Taylor & Francis Group, an informa business

Library of Congress Cataloging-in-Publication Data
2011905922

British Library Cataloguing-in-Publication Data
A catalogue record for this book is available from the British Library.

ISBN-13: 978-1-4377-3491-1 (pbk)

Acknowledgments and Dedication

We thank Dr. Herbert Johnson for all his work on the previous editions of this book. We also thank Dr. Michael Braswell, East Tennessee State University, for inviting our participation in this project, for all his good work with Anderson, and for the asset he has been to the study of criminal justice for many years. Thanks to Elisabeth (Biz) Ebben at Anderson Publishing for her patience and help. Thanks to Jason Stephens, graduate student at the University of North Texas, for his assistance. We thank our wives Donna Jones and Christine Pincemin Johnstone for their love and support.

Finally, the efforts of the first author are dedicated to the memory of R. Herbert Jones, Jr. (1924–2008), and to Dorothy Jones.

Contents

Summary 179
References 182
Endnotes 183

CHAPTER 14. Criminal Justice and Terrorism: The Era of
Homeland Security 215
The Real Deal: An Analogy and Overview .... 1... 8
Terrorism Defined 189
Guerrilla and Urban Militancy 990
Terrorism and Allies 191
World War I 185
Michael Collins and the Irish Republican Army 281
The Ulster Brotherhood 192
The Establishment of Israel 390
Guerrilla in the Cold War and Arm Industries 168
The Nationalism 302
The Revolution in Iran 685
Soviet Invasion of Afghanistan 765
The Sabra Amsterdam 799

Gangs and Cooperation in the Squatters:
A European and Pan Asia Perspective 278
Alberti Woman in Resistance 441
The Analysis—Fro the Secret Societies 344
The African Society Again 250
Rhode Vandalism: the 1998 Embassy Bombings 344
Somalia: The Crisis 374
Osama bin Laden 376
The Present and Future for Homeland Security 370
Endnotes 695

CHAPTER 15. People 95

INDEX 391

CHAPTER 1

Introduction

Crime	History	*Mala prohibita*
Deterrence	Incapacitation	Rehabilitation
Divine will	Law Enforcement	Retribution

LEARNING OBJECTIVES

1. Gain a brief understanding of the history of criminal justice as an academic discipline.
2. Learn the reasons for studying and appreciating history.
3. Understand the meaning and application of the term "crime."
4. Gain a brief understanding of the concept of crime being synonymous with sin.
5. Gain insight into the Old Testament view of human nature by learning the story of Cain.
6. Learn the philosophical rationales for imposing criminal sanctions.

Crime and its punishment are among the oldest problems faced by human-kind; however, academic degree programs in criminal justice are relative new-comers to American colleges and universities. Most of these academic programs were launched in response to the federal government's initiative in passing the *Law Enforcement Assistance Act* (LEAA) of 1968. This law stressed federal assistance to state and local governments, as well as to academic institutions, in the hope that increased study of crime, law enforcement, and penology would result in a decrease in the crime rate. Just as the emphasis of LEAA was on the solution of immediate, pressing problems in the law enforcement field, the

1

new academic programs were primarily concerned with the professional subjects essential to graduates who would become law enforcement officers, forensic scientists, and correction officials. The success of criminal justice programs and their general acceptance as part of the university curriculum have begun to modify this emphasis on current problems and practices. The full panoply of humanities and social science techniques are now applied to criminal justice problems. The student of today needs broad education in these fields, as well as in the forensic and legal sciences, if he or she is to function adequately and knowledgeably in the law enforcement profession.

More than professional competence is involved in the liberal education of those who wish to enter the criminal justice field. Our nation and world desperately need informed law enforcement leadership that deals not only with the mechanical "how" criminal justice is operated, but also with the philosophical and moral "why" it should or should not continue to be conducted in a traditional manner. What is perhaps the major problem in human existence—criminal activity and its suppression—requires creative and innovative thought from those in professional leadership positions. Graduation from a criminal justice degree program cannot be the end of study for the professional; it can only be the beginning of a lifetime of hard study, applying good judgment, and communicating ideas by articulate speech and writing.

HISTORY TODAY

Some students say that they see little or no relevance in studying courses outside their major. Besides falling back on the cliché of being a "well-rounded" person, consider the ways a criminal justice student can benefit from the study of subjects such as political science, psychology, and sociology. Now consider subject areas not as closely associated with criminal justice, such as religious studies, English, public health, and, of course, history.

Progress in any form of human endeavor comes only when men and women rise above the performance of routine day-to-day functions, and when they have dared to ask "why" and aspired toward constructive change. While the human intellect and imagination have their limitations, these limitations have hardly been reached in the administration of criminal justice. We are right in striving to improve our system of law enforcement. We are wise to question the rationale and fundamental assumptions that support our penology. We do well to question what crime is and whether it can be prevented. The fact that these are age-old questions does not make them less pressing in the twenty-first century; it proves that they are among the most complex problems facing humanity.

However, progress can be achieved only if an individual or a society has a firm understanding of where it has been and what has been achieved in the past.

Knowledge of history provides a special sort of orientation for the leader of tomorrow. The word "history" has myriad definitions and applications. The definition that best suits the study of this book is "a branch of knowledge that records and explains past events."[1] Too often, the study of history is viewed only as a record of past events, and those who study it do not focus enough attention on the second part of this definition. Without searching for and analyzing causes and explanations for past events, the study of history is confined to the rote memorization of names, titles, and dates. There are several rationales for the study of history.

First, history provides a sound perspective concerning the nature of human growth and development. Change takes place over time, and in most cases the elapsed time between the statement of a new idea or invention on one hand, and its full acceptance on the other, may well be more than one lifetime. Discontent with the slow tempo of change is more easily borne by one who recognizes this peculiarity of individual humans and their societies. By studying the history of criminal justice, one sees the social, economic, political, and philosophical forces that have come together to create the system of justice that currently exists.

Studying history provides another kind of perspective. On any given day, someone may read a newspaper, watch the news on television, or read the news from a news website. If one does this for the first time, he or she quickly may get the idea that the world is in terrible shape and that we are doomed. However, an appreciation of history teaches the news consumer that things have always seemed bad and that the world has always been on a path of destruction. Knowing history provides us with a sense, for better or worse, that the condition of the world only seems worse than it really is. The world is beset by war and strife but, for better or worse, this has always been the case and somehow humankind has survived. When it comes to criminal justice, knowing history tells us that while crime seems to be a huge problem now—and it is—there never has been a golden age of crime and criminal justice, when crime was not a problem. In fact, we may be much better off now than in the past.

Second, historical knowledge brings with it some assurance against "reinventing the wheel." Modern society needs history much more than our ancestors did; the tragedy is that, in most cases, we do not realize it. Human beings badly need a sense of where they and their civilization have been before they can decide where they and their world should try to go. History is in many ways the "memory bank" of humankind. It does not repeat itself very frequently, if at all, but it gives to those who study it with care a very good idea of the mistakes past generations have made. It is only human to make mistakes; it is stupid to repeat them. Viewed in this way, the study of history is the accumulation of experience over time. By studying criminal justice history, one is able to compare current criminal justice practices with those of past time periods and cultures. Those who study and work in the criminal justice system would be well served to understand the origins and development of the various components and institutions of that system, just as anyone in any profession or academic discipline would benefit from knowing their own history. With much of criminal justice history, one discovers that the system that we now have is less the result of a carefully constructed plan and more the result of a series of unplanned historical occurrences and "accidents."

Third, history demands critical analysis and careful thought from its students. One of the worst charges that can be brought against the study of history is that it is the mere memorization of dates. The relationship of historical events, which is the study of cause and effect, is vastly more significant than dates. Historians must struggle with the weighty question of why individuals and societies acted as they did. Why are some historical events so difficult to explain, and why do others seem to lend themselves to easy solutions? Spending time with human history makes the historian inquisitive about the nature and psychology of men and women throughout the ages. Has humankind really changed since the time of the pharaohs? Historians seek to shape their findings into coherent patterns, and to draw generalizations from what people and societies have done at various times and in different places over the course of human existence. In this sense, history is always the application of a comparative method, for it is by comparisons, across time periods as well as across cultural and national experiences, that the general principles of human behavior can be most easily discerned.

This introductory survey of the history of criminal justice deals with the ways in which human beings and their societies have dealt with the serious issues of crime and punishment. Throughout this text, an attempt has been made to engage the reader in his or her own analysis of historical events, and to raise issues from both a historical and a contemporary perspective. Focusing on the American experience, the book nevertheless devotes a substantial amount of space to the coverage of European and British developments, both as an antecedent to our national experience and as a parallel evolution of ideas and practices that have influenced American criminal justice. In addition, the treatment of ancient and medieval history has been included to not only illustrate the antiquity of the issue of crime and punishment, but also to provide the reader with an overview of the earliest developments. At the outset, it will be useful to direct some attention to the nature of crime itself, the general trends in law enforcement, and the various approaches to punishment. These are themes that will recur throughout the chapters and are subjects that will become more clearly defined as the reader proceeds through the book.

CRIME

One of the fastest ways to stop a glib speaker is to ask for a definition; that also works for college professors in the middle of a lecture. The definition of *crime*, supposedly a simple concept, is actually very difficult. *Webster's New Universal Unabridged Dictionary* (New York, 1972) provides us with three useful definitions and one indirect definition:

1. An act committed in violation of a law prohibiting it, or omitted in violation of a law ordering it; crimes are variously punishable by death, imprisonment, or the imposition of certain fines or restrictions.
2. An extreme violation of the law; wrongdoing of a criminal nature, as felony or treason, which affects the whole public and not just the rights of an individual; distinguishable from a misdemeanor.
3. An offense against morality; sin.
4. The acts of a criminal; habitual violation of the law.

If we exclude the fourth, which defines crime as what criminals do and thus defines criminals as those who commit crimes, we are left with two basic positions: (1) crime is defiance of a positive law and (2) crime is a breach of moral law. Henry Campbell Black, the compiler of the most widely used American law dictionary, defined crime as "a positive or negative act in violation of penal law; an offense against the State." He proceeds to discuss crimes that are *mala in se*, that is, evil in themselves or inherently evil, and those that are *mala prohibita*—not basically or morally wrong, but simply wrong because a statute or rule of common law makes them wrong. Placed side by side, it seems the two writers suggest that there is a positive definition that crime is the act or omission that the state condemns, and that there is also a moral or ethical dimension to the definition of crime. Indeed, their definitions and the historical experience of humankind suggest that, in the latter instance, crime may actually be identical with sin. When the ruler was considered the earthly manifestation of a god, such as in pharaonic times, legal compulsion was indistinguishable from moral rules and sanctions.

Even this initial exploration into the accepted definition of crime does little to explain why a given act is a crime and another act, perhaps similar, is deemed acceptable and not punishable as a crime. It is best to approach the subject in terms of how societies in the course of history have decided what conduct should be prohibited. At the most basic level, societal prohibitions of conduct must focus on the relationships between individuals that most need protection. A person's life, the welfare of his or her family, the security of the individual against bodily harm, and the security of his or her possessions are among the basic needs of people in society. By far, the most significant collection of criminal law rules touches upon these basic human requirements. A second level of interest and concern is the need for a society to ensure order, stability, and productivity. Private wars, like family feuds in the American West, are not only costly in life and limb to the individuals directly involved, but they also pose a threat to innocent bystanders. As economic relationships become more complex, private battles and revenge may exact an unacceptable level of waste to the society and the state that depends upon prosperity for its well-being. At a still more abstract and third level of crime prohibition, there is the need for the state to ensure against being weakened by individual action. For example, the ruling monarch, president, or civil magistrate must be protected against violence; the public highways and places of legislative assembly must be given special attention; and places of religious devotion must be made secure and kept inviolate. Individuals perform state-related functions, such as military duty, labor on highway maintenance, and undertaking public office; in appropriate cases, penalties may be prescribed for failure to keep oneself ready for such duties, as well as for failure to accept them gracefully and to perform them acceptably.

Crime as a concept does not emerge full-grown in any society. Quite to the contrary, it develops out of experience and is conditioned by social and cultural attitudes. For example, let us consider the act of killing another human being. In American society, unprovoked homicide committed knowingly and without justification has always been considered wrongful and punishable either as murder or manslaughter. However, in primitive societies, killing prevailed as a way of exacting private retribution, or revenge, upon one who killed a kin member. As we shall see, the killer's state of mind may also alter the criminal nature of the offense. If he or she lacked a certain level of mental capacity or was "insane" at the time the offense was committed, society may accept that as an adequate defense against prosecution. The state, by declaring war, may render legal, in both national and international law, a killing that otherwise could be prosecuted as murder or manslaughter. The further one attempts to define criminal homicide, the more apparent it will become that, over the course of history, "crime" has changed, just as the reasoning that condemns it has changed.

Other evidence of the impact of culture is the degree to which a law applies only to the territory of the tribe or nation that created the law. This ensures that the cultural preferences of that particular region are implemented by the legal system. In the *Dudley and Stephens* case, English criminal law was held to apply because the men were shipwrecked from a British vessel; thus, English courts might try them under Admiralty Law for an offense committed on the high seas. However, had the two who killed the boy been under the same strictures of necessity in a territory ruled by a cannibal king, would they have been free to act as they did? Might it not be argued that even though they were by nationality English, they had the right to act as the law permitted in a land of cannibals: "When in Rome (in this case, in cannibal territory), do as the Romans (or cannibals) do."

Anthropologists tell us that culture is what shapes individuals into a civilization; it is the cement of tribes and nations. It is not surprising that law was once also a matter of belonging to a given clan, tribe, or nation, rather than being in a particular territory. Among nomadic tribes, rules of law applied only within a tribe or cultural group; outside that group, one would be free to act as one pleased. Thus, the rules against killing another human were applied only within the tribe, and no formal action was necessary to permit a tribesman to kill a human being outside the tribal ranks. On the other hand, a tribe might specifically prohibit such homicides if they were found to bring warfare and hardship to the offender's people. Birth into a tribe or nation brought with it the right to appeal to tribal law for both privileges and protection. In the case of one of the graver offenses, an individual might lose this birthright and be "outlawed"; outside of the law's protection, he or she might be injured, robbed of possessions, or even killed without any punishment being imposed on other members of the tribe. Obviously, as interaction between different tribes and cultural groups became more frequent, the system of a tribal law that protected only individuals within the tribe became cumbersome and self-defeating. The need to trade with other tribes required a certain level of physical security to those who came to trade in tribal lands. This recognition of the need to expand beyond a tribal system of law worked two changes in customary law: (1) it broadened its applicability to include friendly strangers; and (2) because it had to deal with strange new customary laws, it gradually was influenced by them and adapted its rules to those more generally accepted by adjacent tribes.

Across cultural boundaries and throughout historical time, there are a few constants that seem applicable to our definition of the term "crime." Despite variants, there is general agreement that taking another person's life is an evil act. Certain rules concerning family life (those prohibiting incestuous marriage, adultery, and other acts detrimental to the marital union) also tend to be common, but not universal. There is also a general tendency to use penal sanctions to uphold the social structure; for example, harsher penalties may be applied to one who kills an overlord or chief than to one who kills an equal on the social ladder. Where societies have placed the father of an extended family in the role of judge and law enforcer within his household (as in republican Rome or in China), there are stronger penalties for patricide. Whenever the political powers are able, the tendency is to suppress blood feuds and revenge killings.

HISTORY TODAY

Definitions and examples of crime vary greatly among cultures. In some cultures, women do not have nearly as many rights as they do in Western culture. In some cultures, a man can legally beat his wife. In some cultures, homosexuality is severely punished. Should we accept this as justifiable under the idea of cultural relativism?

CRIME AND SIN

Sin can be defined at least two ways. First, any action that is believed in violation of the will of God can be called an act of sin. Second, sin is often defined as the basic condition of humankind. Because human beings are not God, they are born with a predisposition to sin and violate the will of God; thus everyone is a sinner from birth, no matter how good a life they lead. Sin is sometimes defined as "missing the mark" of godlike perfection.[2] At the beginning of the previous section, we noted that the definition of crime, by common usage, also includes the idea of sin; lawyers tend to exclude this moral dimension in the discussion of crime and treat crime as something that is either prohibited or required by some rule of man-made law. At the outset of our study of criminal justice, it is important that the two concepts be discussed at some length, and that they be compared and contrasted in such a way that their distinctions and similarities are highlighted. However, at the same time it is important to realize that, historically, the concept of crime had the same roots as sin. Secular rulers, such as the Egyptian pharaoh, Chinese emperor, and even obscure tribal chieftains, were viewed as gods residing on earth, or as emissaries of gods who spoke authoritatively on behalf of the godhead. That being the case, the rules made by leaders had divine sanction as well, and offenses against those regulations might at the same time be considered both crimes and sins.

FEATURED OUTLAW: CAIN

The most influential book in human history is without a doubt the Bible. It is also the most hotly debated, both in terms of historical accuracy and whether its lessons apply to contemporary life. It is one of the few books in human history that has actually generated war. No section of the Bible is debated more than the opening chapters of the book of Genesis (Beginnings), which give the biblical description of how human history began. While many people fiercely maintain that the Bible is to be taken literally and as inerrant, both in terms of divine inspiration and historical accuracy, many biblical scholars maintain that the opening chapters of Genesis are not to be taken literally, but that they nevertheless provide powerful messages about the biblical view of human nature.

The story of Cain provides a window into the Old Testament view of human nature. According to Genesis, Cain was the first-born son to Adam and Eve, the first man and woman. Cain, a farmer, brought offerings to God, as did his younger brother, Abel. For reasons that are not made clear, God approved of Abel's offering, but not Cain's, and God counseled and warned Cain that sin was "crouching at his door" and "sought to devour him." Rather than heeding God's warning, Cain continued to seethe with anger and jealousy. This attitude culminated in Cain murdering his brother.

When God confronted Cain with his crime, Cain sarcastically asked God if he was his "brother's keeper." Rather than striking Cain dead, God banished him from his life with his family, and made him a wanderer or a vagabond. God also cursed the ground that Cain worked, so that his farming efforts would no longer be fruitful.

Whether one chooses to view this story as historical fact or whether one even chooses to learn the lessons that the writers of Genesis were trying to impart, those studying the historical links between criminality and sin can see that the Old Testament view of human nature was not optimistic. The Bible's first naturally born child was a cold-blooded, remorseless murderer, who spurned God and the choice of living a godly life. The lesson is that human beings, without God, are inclined to jealousy, pettiness, and violence.

HISTORY TODAY

Later in the Old Testament, one can cite numerous examples of people being "justifiably" executed for far less serious crimes than the one discussed in the story of Cain. Could not opponents of capital punishment invoke the story of Cain as an argument against the death penalty?

Of course, there is a moral dimension to the definition of crime. One of the most formative influences upon human culture is that of religious belief and practice. Theology, or the way in which men and women understand their relationship to their gods, determines the manner in which they will view society; it has been, and in many societies continues to be, the major source of ethical and behavioral rules. Not surprisingly, when legislators or judges participate in the lawmaking process, they are strongly influenced by their religious beliefs. Every rule of criminal law thus has a moral dimension derived in large measure from cultural views concerning theology.

The early identification of crime with sin meant that offenses against human laws had the added dimension of being transgressions against divine commands. Those who committed crimes were offenders against the divinity, as well as against the state and other inhabitants; condemnation of such individuals who turned their backs upon both man and god was not a particularly complicated matter. The evil impulses of people and societies puzzle theologians and philosophers; essentially, the two major camps divide over whether there is one god who represents good or if there are two contending gods or forces that represent the struggle between good and evil. For the most part, the Judeo-Christian tradition has held the first position: that the evil in the world is due to human nature or to the temptations of the devil, who vainly opposes God and tries to draw men away from allegiance to God and into acts of evil. The society that equates crime with sin can easily judge the convicted felon to be either possessed by the devil or irredeemably evil. Ridding the earth of such a depraved creature makes the earth safer for others and also accords with what is perceived as God's purpose; it assists Him in the heavenly struggle against the forces of evil.

However, when society differentiates crime from sin, it refrains from such a moral judgment and is prepared to move in the direction of reforming, retraining, and rehabilitating the offender. Added to these considerations is the impact of Christian belief in the redemptive power of a loving God; even the most degenerate offender against the laws of society and God might be saved through repentance. As a consequence of these developments through recorded history, criminal law no longer considers the offender a person totally beyond the protections afforded to human beings. In this sense, an individual can never be completely outlawed in a society that believes that divine love and forgiveness is available to the most depraved of humankind. A secular version of this

Christian view of humanity is contained in the Enlightenment philosophy of the seventeenth and eighteenth centuries. Based upon a profound confidence in the perfectibility of humankind and the persuasiveness of reason, the Enlightenment had a profound influence over the development of law enforcement and penology.

Charles Colson, the founder of Prison Fellowship Ministries, argues against the idea that human beings can hope to achieve anything approaching perfection if left to their own devices and abilities. Contrary to the Enlightenment view, Colson argues that only a Biblical worldview, one that includes the belief in the existence of and reliance on God, can save humankind. He argues that Enlightenment thinking that humans can work toward perfection using their own mental abilities, that is, better education, offers false hope to attempts to reform human beings, including the convicted criminal.[3] That is why Colson has been such a strong advocate in recent decades of faith-based prisons, which include a strong emphasis on spiritual development in addition to the normal educational programs that have been a traditional hallmark of the correctional system. According to Colson, intellectual development by itself will not be nearly as rehabilitative as intellectual development coupled with spiritual development.

HISTORY TODAY

Do you agree or disagree with Charles Colson's idea that we cannot educate our way toward becoming more moral? Is education necessarily the most important factor to improving human beings?

The Renaissance of the fifteenth century turned the focus of scholarly activity away from theology and toward the study of humanity. Thereafter, writers undertook the task of explaining why people acted as they did, and the modern social sciences began to take root as one of the primary tools used to understand human beings. As the National Rifle Association states, "Guns don't kill people, people do." That leads to the inevitable conclusion that human psychology is a vital key to the nature and source of crime. In times of despair over the venality of humankind, one is apt to conclude that Charles Darwin's theory of evolution—that human beings are evolved from anthropoid apes—is bound to be wrong. In fact, it is an outright insult to most monkeys, gorillas, and orangutans of our acquaintance. Yet some scientists assure us that humans are truly descended from a small, aggressive (and mean), meat-eating monkey. Even a brief survey of the cruelties of humankind, along with the extent and variety of criminal activities, leads one toward acceptance of such a verdict. Whatever our ancestry may be, humans are extraordinarily attracted to crime.

TIME CAPSULE: WHY DO WE PUNISH?

In examining the reasons given for punishing convicted persons, criminologists have identified five major categories of justification for punishment (each of which has subcategories). These five purposes are not mutually exclusive, nor are they specifically related to particular cultures or time periods. It is, however, often possible when reading contemporary accounts or judicial opinions to discern which reason was primary. As you read this text, ask yourself which purpose was predominant in the Anglo-Saxon period, in medieval England, in the American colonies, and on the western frontier, and which is predominant in the United States today.

1. Retribution
The principle of retaliation is that the person who has caused harm must suffer punishment, be it through physical pain, financial deprivation, loss of freedom, or other hardship. Often included in the concept of retribution is the principle of proportionality (*lex talionis*): the suffering inflicted on the convicted person should be equal to the harm he or she caused.

2. Deterrence
Under this principle, a sentence can be designed to deter the convicted person from committing further crimes (specific deterrence) by convincing him or her that the potential punishment for future violations would be too painful to risk. In an effort to impress this message on other members of the society as well (general deterrence), the sentence can be maximized and dramatized.

3. Incapacitation
The goal of incapacitation is to make it impossible for the convicted person to commit crimes. A death sentence is the ultimate example; other types of punishments severely limit the ability to violate criminal law, such as imprisonment, castration, or revocation of the license to practice medicine or law.

4. Rehabilitation
Based on the idea that the criminal violation resulted from inadequate socialization of the offender, rehabilitation represents an effort to provide counseling and practical training that can aid an offender and thereby weaken or remove the stimuli that led him or her to crime.

5. Divine Will
In societies that believed in an interactive god, divine will was the genesis of criminal law: When a person violated the law, he or she also offended God. The object of punishment was to bring the offender back to right relation to God and to avert the wrath of God against a community if it tolerated violation of divine will. Countries that have established the principle of separation of church and state do not, of course, overtly acknowledge a religious basis for punishment. However, it may continue to be significant in the attempt to rehabilitate offenders.

HISTORY TODAY

In your opinion, which of these rationales should be most important when it comes to dealing with crime? Or should the rationale depend on the individual offender or case? Do these rationales overlap? Should our priority about which rationale is most important change over time?

ENDNOTES

[1]*Encyclopedia Britannica online academic edition*. October 5, 2007.

[2]*Fausset Bible dictionary*, Biblesoft, 1998.

[3]Colson, C. (2001). *Justice that restores*. Wheaton, IL: Tyndale House.

CHAPTER 2

Criminal Justice in Ancient Times

KEY TERMS

Abraham

Archons

Bailee

Code of Hammurabi

Confucianism

Consuls

Court at the gate

Crucifixion

Cutting a neighbor's crop

Dicastery

Eye for an eye

False witness

Flogging

Hesiod

Jezebel

Lex talionis

Magistrate

Mosaic Law

Multiple compensation

Oaths

Phreatto

Platter and loincloth search

Robbery

Socrates

Sodom and Gomorrah

Sycophants

Taoism

Ten Commandments

Vicarious punishment

Yahweh

LEARNING OBJECTIVES

1. Understand the role of religious beliefs in shaping justice practices among the ancient Israelites, Greeks, and Romans.
2. Learn the Ten Commandments and the role they played in ancient Israelite criminal justice.
3. Become familiar with some of the Old Testament patriarchs and the role they played in shaping government and criminal justice.
4. Understand the principle of *lex talionis*, or *"eye for an eye."*
5. Learn some of the methods used by the Israelites, Greeks, and Romans for dealing with various categories of offenses.
6. Learn the formats and settings for judicial actions in the three cultures.

7. Learn the duties of ancient judicial officials and how they obtained their positions.
8. Understand the basic tenets of Taoism and Confucianism as they related to criminal justice in Imperial China.

Table 2.1 Time Line

Israel/Near East	Athens	Rome
1800 BC Code of Hammurabi in Babylon		
c. 1280 BC Exodus from Egypt Ten Commandments		
c. 1000-961 BC Reign of David Cities of refuge established		
c. 961-922 BC Reign of Solomon Two-witness rule established		
	753/752 BC Tenure of magistrates reduced to 10 years	
		713-673 BC Compensation to be paid for accidental killing
	683 BC Tenure of magistrates reduced to 1 year	
	659-510 BC First Age of Tyrants	
640-609 BC Reign of Josiah		
c. 625 BC Deuteronomy text discovered		
Court of priests established	**621 BC** Draco's criminal law code	
	594 BC Solon (Greek) becomes Chief magistrate	
	594/593 BC People gain right to appeal from magistrates	
		578-534 BC Law against patricide
		509 BC *Lex Valeria* limits magistrate's authority in regard to death sentences
	508/507 BC Cleisthenes expands Athenian citizenship	
	487-422 BC Cases tried by jury (*dicastery*)	
		451-450 BC The Twelve Tables, a penal code, promulgated
	410-404 BC Revision of laws by Nikomakhos	
		367 BC *Urban praetor* courts established

Continued

Table 2.1   Time Line—cont'd

Israel/Near East	Athens	Rome
	c. 300-245 BC Evidentiary rules introduced	
		c. 242 BC *Peregrine praetor* courts established
		c. 200 BC *Lex Aquila* establishes punishment for killing slave or animal without justification
		c.190-10 BC *Quaestiones* (jury) court established for trial of crimes
		c. 70 BC Challenge to jurors authorized
		c. 10 BC Police courts replace *quaestiones* courts
		527-565 AD Justinian, as emperor of the eastern empire, orders compilation of Roman law

The roots of Western civilization reach deep into antiquity, as do the problems of crime and punishment. In this chapter we shall be concerned with the experience of biblical Israel, classical Athens (Greece), and republican Rome (Italy); this spans a period of nearly 1200 years. These cultures differed in their stages of economic development and in their fundamental attitudes toward human life, but each formed a vital part of Western civilization. The vast treasury of the Bible provides a rich heritage of history, theology, and philosophy that has had a persistent impact upon modern society. The Greek city-state of Athens provides the ideal of a culture governed by the active political participation of the people in the affairs of government, and the massive edifice of Roman legal and constitutional principles has shaped Western views of government through the ages.

Each of these civilizations left its imprint on recorded history at a crucial stage in its development. Biblical Israel moved from a nomadic existence, based on herding sheep and goats, to an established farming society located in the Promised Land (c. 1200-650 BC) or modern-day Israel. Athens in its classical period (594-404 BC) thrived upon Mediterranean commercial activity, its vast trade providing foodstuff and other necessities of life imported from less advanced territories. With a long history of seeking freedom, Athenians placed a high premium on their city-state's ability to resist the rise of tyrants, although much of Athens' labor was performed by slaves acquired through conquest or purchased abroad. Republican Rome built upon the loyalty of the Roman citizen to erect a constitutional state, ruled by the interplay of aristocratic power in the Senate and plebeian strength manifested in the tribunate. At the time we study Rome (509-25 BC), it triumphed over most of the civilized world. It was heavily dependent upon trade for its necessities and employed a vast army of foreign slaves on its farms, manufactories, and households.

Abraham: Prominent figure in the biblical book of Genesis, considered one of the principal patriarchs of Judaism, Christianity, and Islam.

Biblical Israel's civilization and its criminal justice system, as recounted in the biblical books of Exodus, Leviticus, Numbers, and Deuteronomy, centered upon the fact that the descendants of *Abraham* occupied the unique position of being the chosen people of the great god, *Yahweh*. Rules of behavior, as well as the structure of criminal law and punishments, reflected this profound religious influence. Wrongful conduct was offensive upon two grounds: (1) it destroyed the bonds of society, causing dissension among the people of Israel; and (2) the wrongdoing of any member of God's chosen people could easily bring divine wrath down upon the entire nation.

The foundation for Israelite law and for Israelite life in general was the *Ten Commandments*. Historians cannot agree on precise dates, but it is believed that the Ten Commandments were instituted somewhere around 1400-1200 BC. According to the biblical book of Exodus, God actually carved the Ten Commandments into stone on Mount Sinai in the presence of Moses, the Israelite leader who had led his people out of slavery in Egypt. The first four Commandments deal with human relationship to God; the latter six deal with human relations with each other. The Ten Commandments are the following:

1. I am the Lord your God, who brought you out of the land of Egypt, out of the house of bondage. (In some listings, this is not listed as a Commandment but as a prologue to the Commandments.)
2. You shall have no other gods before me. You shall not make for yourself any carved image, or any likeness of anything that is in heaven above, or that is in the earth beneath, or that is in the water under the earth; you shall not bow down to them nor serve them.
3. You shall not take the name of the Lord your God in vain.
4. Remember the Sabbath day, to keep it holy. Six days you shall labor and do all your work, but the seventh day is the Sabbath of the Lord your God. In it you shall do no work.
5. Honor your father and your mother.
6. You shall not murder. (Some translations use the word "kill" rather than murder.)
7. You shall not commit adultery.
8. You shall not steal.
9. You shall not bear false witness against your neighbor.
10. You shall not covet your neighbor's house; you shall not covet your neighbor's wife, nor his manservant, nor his maidservant, nor his ox, nor his donkey, nor anything that is your neighbor's.

HISTORY TODAY

In what ways are the Ten Commandments still a part of our legal system? In what ways are they no longer part of the legal system? Should they be?

A crime or violation of Israelite law was an offense against God himself. National obedience to God was essential to the survival of a culture so closely tied to its jealous and all-knowing deity. Nowhere is this illustrated more clearly than in the story of Achan, which is told in the book of Joshua, Chapter 7. Achan, a name that means "troubler" (which suggests that his real name is unknown) was a soldier in the Israelite army as they moved to conquer the promised land of Canaan (now Israel). The Israelites, flush with spectacular victories over major armies in Canaan, approached the small city-kingdom of Ai. They were surprised and humiliated at their defeat at the hands of the army of Ai. The reason for the Israelite loss, according to the book of Joshua, was that Achan had looted some items during the previous battle, in direct contradiction of divine command. When his crime was discovered, Achan was put to death, along with his entire family. This example of *vicarious punishment*, that is, punishing someone for crimes committed by another, illustrates the Israelite belief in the reality of divine wrath that could be visited on the entire nation of Israel, even for the misdeed of one Israelite. Unlike the modern American legal system, the rights of the individual were secondary to the welfare of the larger community.

HISTORY TODAY

Should a person be punished for the crimes of others? While the story of Achan seems extreme today, do we not indirectly punish children, wives, and husbands by imprisoning their family members?

Athenians lived by a different code, although there is evidence that some of their criminal laws, derived from an earlier historical period, also sought to prevent divine displeasure. Students of ancient Greek religion, now referred to as Greek mythology, are well acquainted with the ancient Greek view of their gods. The Greek gods were temperamental and suffered many of the same character flaws as human beings, and thus were easily offended. Their experience with harsh rulers had convinced them that democracy (a very limited democracy by modern standards), or the rule of the people, was essential to happiness. As their economic prosperity grew, so did their insistence upon governmental forms that would discourage any citizens from seizing power and establishing a tyranny.

Roman republicans shared the Greek antipathy to kingly rulers, but their government was founded upon the concept of the citizen-soldier as the key to Roman dominance in the world. Conferring special status upon those privileged to be citizens of Rome, their system of criminal justice served to protect the citizen from unjust prosecution and to provide each citizen with a clear understanding of his rights and responsibilities to the state.

HOMICIDE

BIBLICAL ISRAEL

Virtually all Near Eastern (or Middle Eastern) civilizations permitted a murderer or his family to pay compensation to the family of the deceased victim. In a primitive and violent society where labor was scarce, this seemed an adequate penalty for ho-micide while maintaining the labor of the culprit for the sustenance of his family and clan. However, Israelite law demanded that one who killed should be put to death, a relatively harsh principle that developed from the theological connection between the blood of the victim and the spirit of God. Yahweh was believed to pos-sess the blood of a human, which in turn contained the spirit given to the individual by the Creator. In shedding human blood, a murderer took what rightfully belonged to Yahweh, and only the murderer's death and the shedding of his blood was adequate compensation. If a murdered person was found in a field, the nearby village was expected to sacrifice an animal if the culprit could not be found, and domestic animals that caused a person's death were put to death for their offense.

This approach to homicide cases reflected the Israelite reliance on the doctrine of *lex talionis*, or the "*eye for an eye*" principle. The *eye for an eye* doctrine was observed for a number of reasons. One reason was so that rich or powerful victims of crime would not take unfair advantage of poor offenders. All crime should be pun-ished, but poor criminals should be punished no more harshly than wealthy or more powerful criminals. Another justification for observing the *lex talionis* doctrine pertained to homicide cases. Under the *lex talionis* doctrine, blood for blood, not money for blood, was the only just punishment.

HISTORY TODAY

Many people claim we should adhere to the "*eye for an eye*" principle. Is this always possible? How do we inflict the type of psychological trauma experienced by an armed robbery victim? What about drug- or alcohol-related offenses?

Although the Ten Commandments contain an absolute prohibition against kill-ing, certain forms of homicide were permissible. The most obvious exceptions were killings required by warfare. Nonintentional killing was shielded by the existence of cities of refuge, to which a killer might flee to avoid conviction and the immediate imposition of the usual sentence: death by stoning. In a city of refuge, the killer awaited extradition from the place of the homicide, at which time the elders of the refuge city either turned the killer over to the prosecuting authorities or declared him guiltless and free to leave. Issues of criminal intent and proximate cause also played a role in Israelite homicide law, and these mat-ters were so complex that they were removed to the Temple in Jerusalem, where the priests resolved these issues rather than the traditional court of town elders.

ATHENS

Because of its origins well before the classical period of Athenian history, the city-state's homicide law bore some similarity to that of ancient Israel. It was believed that a type of corruption, or *miasma*, attached to the person of a murderer. It also infected homicidal animals, or even a stone statue if it fell upon an Athenian citizen and killed him. Merely being accused of homicide made a person corrupt, and the accused person's movements were sharply circumscribed to keep him away from places of assembly and from sites of religious significance. The punishment for homicide, either intentional or unintentional, was expulsion from Athens and the surrounding countryside. Should the killer return from exile, he was tried at the *Phreatto*, a seaside location where a special court heard the evidence from a boat anchored offshore and then either reimposed exile or ordered death as a punishment. In the case of an unintentional homicide, the exiled culprit might secure a pardon from the victim's family and, thus, obtain permission to return to Athens.

In Athenian law, certain homicides were deemed justifiable. One could execute an exile who had returned without first obtaining a pardon. A citizen was justified in killing another who was attempting to set up a tyranny or to overthrow the democracy. A thief caught at night in the house of the intended victim might justifiably be killed by the householder. Deaths that occurred during brawls, in athletic contests, and in a passion over finding a wife or a concubine in the amorous embrace of another were also justifiable, and thus excused.

ROME

Roman law concerning homicide seems to have provided death as the penalty for intentional homicide and to have permitted the payment of blood money to the victim's family should the homicide be declared unintentional. From the meager evidence that survives, it appears that Roman views of homicide were more primitive than those prevalent at Athens, and we know that life was less valued in Roman society. In the early days of the republic, it was a common practice to expose deformed infants at birth, leaving them to die of exposure. Also, it was long the rule in Rome that a father might discipline his sons, even to the point of inflicting death, without running the risk of prosecution. It is not possible to say whether any special revulsion or religious taboo was involved in republican Rome's punishment of homicide.

HISTORY TODAY

Consider the amount of leeway ancient Rome provided fathers and husbands in administering discipline. Given our concern with domestic violence and child abuse, how much authority should the law give a parent in disciplining their children?

SEX OFFENSES

BIBLICAL ISRAEL

Society and family life in biblical Israel was strongly patriarchal (male-dominated) and heterosexual in its orientation. This preserved the genetic integrity of God's chosen people and also ensured rapid population increase to consolidate Israelite dominance of the Holy Land. Given this emphasis, it is not surprising that the major thrust of law was the punishment of adultery, defined as the sexual intercourse of one person with a married member of the opposite sex. With certain exceptions, both parties were put to death by stoning. Unlike other systems of Near Eastern law, Israelite criminal law did not permit the wronged husband to pardon his adulterous wife, because that would not make the criminal act clean.

Should a free man engage in intercourse with a female slave betrothed to another, he was compelled to pay a fine, but no compensation was given to the betrothed husband of the adulterous slave. Fornication, or the unlawful sexual intercourse of two unmarried persons, was subject to mild sanctions. The father of a seduced virgin might demand the customary marriage present from the culprit, even if she did not marry him.

The Law of Moses, or the *Mosaic Law*, as recorded in the biblical book of Leviticus, took a dim view of homosexuality. Leviticus 18:22 calls sexual relations between men a detestable offense punishable by death. Earlier references to a disapproving attitude toward homosexuality are found in the book of Genesis, in an event that was believed to have occurred long before the writing of the Mosaic Law. Genesis 18 and 19 tell the story of the cities of the plain, more commonly referred to as the story of *Sodom and Gomorrah*. In that instance, four cities (two in addition to Sodom and Gomorrah) were entirely wiped out because of the depravity of the men in those cities. According to Genesis, the men of Sodom were so depraved that they tried to gang rape two men who, according to the Genesis passage, were angels sent by God to see firsthand what Sodom was like. Naturally this story is the stuff of controversy today. Some claim that this is a clear biblical condemnation of homosexuality, while others suggest that this story merely condemns rape, not consensual relations. The modern word "sodomy" has its roots in the biblical story of the men of Sodom.

HISTORY TODAY

The sentiments (arguably) expressed in the story of Sodom do not coincide with contemporary laws or the attitudes of many Americans regarding same-sex relations. Is this an example of outdated Old Testament values? If no, then should we adopt all Old Testament values and practices?

ATHENS

By way of comparison, Athenian punishment for sex offenses seems relatively mild. The rape of a free woman was punishable by a fine to be paid to her father or husband. Seduction was subject to harsher sanctions, presumably on the theory that her mind as well as her body had been corrupted. The seducer caught in the act might be killed outright by the woman's father or husband. If death was not inflicted, the seducer might be imprisoned and tormented. Two forms of torture were preferred: pulling out the culprit's pubic hair or forcing radishes up his anus.

The offenses of incest and fornication existed in Athenian law and usually were punished by compensation to the woman's husband or father, rather than by any physical sanctions. The presence and tolerance of homosexuality in Athenian society required that the laws concerning rape and seduction be applied equally for the protection of men as well as women. Penalties against recruiting free persons into prostitution were also unisex in their application.

ROME

Early Roman legal texts do not deal with sex offenses, but the likelihood is that Greek rules may have provided a pattern for later Roman development. After 100 BC, the offense of *inuria* (a malicious destruction of reputation) was developed by the Roman judges, and included within inuria was the right of a free woman whose chastity had been slandered to recover compensation from the wrongdoer.

HISTORY TODAY

It is not illegal to gossip, even to the point of harming someone or destroying their reputation. At most, some extreme instances of slander might get one sued in civil court. The modern news medium is often vicious in what it says about public officials, celebrities, and even ordinary citizens. Given our concern about free speech, should a person or media professional be held criminally responsible for willfully harming someone through gossip or through malicious words?

THEFT

BIBLICAL ISRAEL

The Ten Commandments prohibit theft in a statement that includes both property-taking and kidnapping. Originally, the sanction of death may have applied to both infractions, but by 620 BC, only kidnapping was punished this severely. Property-taking was punished by fining the thief some multiple of the value of the animal or object stolen. That fine was increased if it appeared that the culprit exercised acts of dominion beyond mere possession: for example, if he either sold or destroyed the stolen animals or goods. This suggests that among a nomadic people whose wealth is in flocks of animals, it was difficult to establish criminal intent by the mere fact of possession. However, either selling or killing another's animal involved the greater likelihood that the culprit knew that he was dealing with the property of another.

Property placed in the possession of a *bailee* (one who held goods for the owner) and subsequently stolen was subject to two rules of law. The taker was punished by *multiple compensation* if he was found. Otherwise, the bailee was put to proof and required to show that he did not take the goods himself. This rule, with increased compensation demanded because of sale or destruction of the stolen property, is an interesting demonstration of the way in which guilt was determined by weighing the probability of wrongful intent. A herdsman was expected to survey his flock regularly to prevent wrongful possession of another's animal. However, the inadequate performance of that duty was not as culpable as singling out an animal that belonged to another and selling it or killing it as if it belonged to the wrongdoer. Similarly, a bailee was responsible for returning the goods, and was subject to sanctions if the property was taken from his possession and he could not identify the thief; indeed, it was presumed that the bailee himself stole the goods unless he could prove the contrary.

Violent seizure of another person's property, known as *robbery* in modern law, does not appear within the offenses enumerated by biblical law. Scholars have suggested that such an offense was outside the communal law of the people, something to be expected only of brigands and foreigners. Consequently, it was a matter to be dealt with by the military authorities and very likely punishable by death.

ATHENS

Athenian views of theft appear to be similar to the Israelite pattern of demanding multiple compensation to the owner. Harsher sanctions were provided for the thief caught in the act of a nocturnal (at night) burglary; if discovered by the owner, he could be killed by the owner. If his activities were later proven, the nocturnal thief would be executed. Stealing from Athens' sacred Temple or its precincts was punishable by death, as was theft from the public treasury or Temple property.

Kidnapping a freeman was also a capital offense. Commercial aspects of life in Athens generated a new group of economic crimes that might be included within the general category of theft. Special courts imposed rules concerning fair prices and the forestalling (or monopolistic hoarding) of goods for profit. Counterfeiting coins and knowingly passing such coins were punishable by death.

ROME

Like biblical and Athenian law, Roman statutes imposed compensation as the penalty in situations of ordinary theft. If the thief was caught in the act, either at night or in possession of a weapon while stealing in the day, he could be killed by the victim and the homicide would be justified. However, such a killing during the day had to be preceded by the owner's shouting, presumably to draw the neighbors' attention to the owner's exercise of self-help. Unarmed thieves caught in the act during daylight hours were scourged and enslaved to the victim if the victim was a free person. Slaves caught in the act during the day, even if unarmed, were sentenced to be scourged and then executed by being thrown from the Tarpeian Rock.[1,2]

Selected for special punishment was the offense of *cutting a neighbor's crops* by night. The offender was sentenced to be "hung up" and then sacrificed (killed)

FIGURE 2.1 The site of the Tarpeian Rock as it appears today. *Courtesy en.wikipedia.org.*

to the goddess Ceres, presumably because the offender offended her as the patroness of the earth's fertility. The use of the term "hung up" in the provisions of Rome's Twelve Tables, a special legal code, suggests that *crucifixion* may have been used as a way of enhancing punishment prior to actual execution. The punishment could be mitigated if the offender was underage, in which case he or she was usually scourged and enslaved to the victim.

HISTORY TODAY

The behavior just mentioned provides an example of a property offense that also constituted a religious offense. Can you think of modern examples of that same application?

Both Athenian and Roman law used a strange rite for the discovery of stolen goods. This was the *platter and loincloth search,* which required the owner of the stolen goods to walk virtually naked through the premises of the suspect, holding a platter in both hands. Presumably this arrangement was to prevent him from touching any object and from carrying incriminating evidence into the house. The rationale was that, if the lost object was present, it would reveal itself to its rightful owner. Clearly, this mode of search would have been most effective if the stolen property was a domestic animal that would recognize its master, even in his nakedness. How it would reveal inanimate objects is unclear.

CRIMINAL PROCEDURE AND SANCTIONS

In all three systems of ancient law, the initiation of a criminal case depended upon the initiative of the person wronged or, if the person had been killed, by his family. Thus, criminal procedure perpetuated the primitive system of revenge, and the state acted not as a prosecutor, but as a weigher of evidence and as a sovereign power dispensing punishment. To a limited degree, the forgiveness of the prosecuting individual or family might serve to lessen the penalties imposed for an offense.

BIBLICAL ISRAEL

The ancient trial court of Israel, and the most common tribunal throughout its biblical history, was the *"court at the gate."* Originating in the authority of each clan's elders to determine controversies within the kin group, the court at the gate came into being with the establishment of towns and cities in the Holy Land. Usually convened in the morning hours, it met at the demand of litigants who waited at the gate of the town, demanding that the elders who passed through on their way to the fields should first stop to do justice.

FIGURE 2.2 Painting depicting the death of Jezebel. *The Death of Jezebel by Gustav Doré/Courtesy of en.wikipedia.org.*

Both civil and criminal actions were tried at the gate, and, undoubtedly, the selection of this place for trial was made to allow the maximum number of people to witness the proceedings. In a criminal case, the accusing party stood to the right of the accused and, in the presence of the elders (who were seated), presented his or her complaint. Although this accusation was usually given orally, it might be written. The accused person might be assisted in his or her defense by a defender, who was in fact a witness for the defense. Each of the elders sitting as a judge acted as an arbitrator in the case and might himself give evidence pertinent to the matter being tried. The accusing witness bore special responsibility for prosecuting the case, and his role was emphasized by the rule that, if the death penalty were imposed, it was he who was responsible for throwing the first stone in execution of the judgment.

FEATURED OUTLAW: JEZEBEL

Jezebel is one of the most intriguing and infamous females in the history of Western civilization. Today, the word "Jezebel" is used to refer to a woman of loose sexual morals, or a conniving female. The real-life Jezebel was not necessarily a woman of loose sexual morals, but she was very conniving, dishonest, and also one of the powerful monarchs of Old Testament Israel, a nation usually dominated by men. In an era and land where women were relegated to second-class status, and where even most queens were not allowed to approach their husband kings without permission, Jezebel was a definite exception.

Jezebel was the wife of Ahab, an Israelite king who ruled during the ninth century BC. As was common for that era among Middle Eastern kingdoms, Jezebel was presented as a gift from the neighboring kingdom of Phoenicia. Giving a bride in this way was a common diplomatic gesture to try to ensure peace between kingdoms.

Jezebel was constantly at odds with Israel's spiritual leaders and prophets, in large measure due to her encouragement of idol worship, a direct violation of the Second Commandment given to Moses. Another example of Jezebel's treachery and moral depravity is found in

FEATURED OUTLAW: JEZEBEL—CONT'D

I Kings 21. Ahab wanted to acquire a piece of land and the vineyard that came with it for his winter home. The owner of the vineyard, Naboth, refused to sell the vineyard. To sell the land would have deprived Naboth's descendants of this property, and it would have been a violation of the Mosaic Law as noted in Numbers 36:7.

Jezebel was enraged at Naboth's refusal to accede to the King's request, and she was equally outraged that Ahab accepted Naboth's refusal to sell. In retaliation, she arranged for Naboth to appear at a banquet. In preparation for the banquet, Jezebel, obeying the letter, though not the spirit, of the Mosaic Law, arranged for two "scoundrels" to appear at the banquet and swear that Naboth had blasphemed, or cursed, both God and the King. This was an offense punishable by death, and required the sworn testimony of at least two witnesses. As a result of the false accusations, Naboth was stoned to death, and so were his sons, who would have been the rightful inheritors of his vineyard.

When confronted by the prophet Elijah, Ahab was penitent, and God spared his life. Jezebel, true to her basic nature, was unrepentant. According to I Kings, she lived for many more years, but, in accordance with Elijah's prophecy, Jezebel was thrown from her balcony by her servants onto the ground, and her corpse was eaten by dogs.

HISTORY TODAY

Compared to other tyrants, is it possible that many people may view Jezebel as especially evil because she was a female? Does that double standard apply today?

False witness, or knowingly lying in a court proceeding (usually referred to today as perjury), was a serious matter in proceedings at the gate. Bearing false witness against a neighbor was specifically prohibited by the Ten Commandments, suggesting that at one time a death penalty may have applied. When a person lied in a prosecution that could end in capital punishment, the rule was that the false witness should be punished as severely as the accused would have been if the false evidence had been accepted. The *lex talionis* (an *eye for an eye* and a tooth for a tooth) was strictly applied in cases of perjury. Aside from outright lies, witnesses might mislead a court by repeating evidence they received secondhand or by repeating unfounded conclusions they may have arrived at independently of their knowledge. Courts at the gate carefully instructed witnesses in capital cases (and most noncapital cases) that they were not to testify from supposition or to give secondhand or hearsay evidence. One should bear in mind that in an era in which the outcome of a judicial proceeding usually depended entirely on the testimony of witnesses (with little fear of being contradicted by scientific evidence), it was of paramount importance to make sure that witnesses were truthful.

HISTORY TODAY

Perjury in criminal cases is seldom prosecuted today. Even if a person were caught committing perjury in a capital punishment case, the penalty would not be terribly severe. Should a perjurer, whether civilian or law enforcement, be given the same punishment as would be given to the defendant?

Biblical courts required that at least two witnesses testify concerning the guilt of the accused. While this requirement may have originally been limited in application to cases of murder and idolatry, it became more general and applied to all criminal prosecutions by the time of King Solomon (circa 970 BC, around four centuries after the leadership of Moses). There is reason to believe that, if a thief was caught in the action of stealing (*in flagrante delicto*), only one witness was necessary to convict. In such a case, the surrounding circumstances might well justify abandonment of the two-witness rule; however, there was wisdom in always having corroboration of a witness's evidence. If the submitted evidence did not provide an adequate basis for a decision, the accused would be asked to take an exculpatory oath, denying his guilt. The accused would call upon God to curse him if the oath was false, and the case would be dismissed.

After the establishment of the Davidic monarchy (circa 1000 BC), named after King David, the religious activities of the nation shifted to the royal city of Jerusalem, where a Temple was raised to Yahweh. Difficult cases that could not be resolved at the gate were taken to the priests and judges at Jerusalem. Once there, additional exculpatory oaths might be used or the issue of guilt could be determined by oral oracular means. The breastplate of the high priest contained two objects for the purpose of determining guilt or innocence; a party wishing to prove his innocence was required to "draw lots," and the success of the accused's case would depend upon which of the two lots he or she drew from the breastplate.

David: One of the principal figures of the Old Testament, regarded as a great though sometimes ruthless warrior and king of the Israelites. As a youth, gained great fame for killing the Philistine giant Goliath in battle; also a great poet, wrote many of the Old Testament Psalms.

Once the priests or judges ascertained guilt, sentencing and execution followed immediately. They usually inflicted death penalties by stoning, with the community casting stones at the convict until death occurred. Provisions of Israeli law that parallel those in the *Code of Hammurabi* (circa 1800 BC) stipulated that burning to death was the appropriate sanction against a priest's daughter convicted of prostitution, as well as against a man who committed incest by wedding both a mother and her daughter. Late in biblical history, perhaps as the consequence of Persian influence (circa 450 BC), *flogging* became a sanction for lesser offenses. Theft was punishable by compelling the convicted thief to make multiple restitution.

Code of Hammurabi: One of the oldest known legal codes, overseen by King Hammurabi of Babylon (probably present-day Iraq), discovered intact during the twentieth century and on display at the Louvre in Paris.

Capital punishment might be rendered additionally harsh by providing that the convict's deceased body be exposed to the elements for a period of time on the day of his death. This could be done by hanging the body from a tree or impaling it in a public place. In both cases, the corpse was to be buried before nightfall. Although similar, the sanction of crucifixion was unknown to Old Testament law; while there is some evidence that it was used among the Persians and the Greeks, especially during the period between the Old and

New Testaments (circa 400 BC to the First Century AD), it became common-place only among the Romans, whose dominance in the Middle East did not come to fruition until a century prior to the New Testament era.

ATHENS

Athenian citizens prosecuting crime relied on self-help in arresting their adversaries, just as victims did in biblical Israel. However, they also had the option of asking a *magistrate* to accompany them to make the arrest; in a number of cases, the prosecution might begin with the simple filing of a complaint and service of a summons on the accused. When the parties were present, the magistrate held a preliminary hearing concerning the charge and then held the matter for the next session of the appropriate court.

Ancient Athenian procedure assigned the trial of homicide cases to a special tribunal composed of the serving magistrates, called *archons*, and all previously commissioned archons. Meeting in the agora (marketplace) or Areopagus (a hill in Athens where the tribunal met), this court tried all premeditated homicides and heard constitutional cases. Portions of the Areopagus tribunal, presided over by an archon, dealt with lesser homicide matters. These quasi-religious courts did not deal with other criminal offenses, which were left to the disposition of individual magistrates.

FEATURED OUTLAW: THE TRIAL OF SOCRATES

Consistent with the Athenian principle of direct democratic rule, the trial of Socrates in 399 BC for impiety and corruption of youth was conducted by lay members of the community rather than by citizens with legal training. Whether the verdict was fair is a question that has occupied scholars ever since.

Ancient Greece is remembered for its famous philosophers, and chief among them was Socrates. Despite the prominence of Socrates in philosophical discussion, he left no written record. The principal source for the events of his trial is Plato, who was present and wrote four dialogues concerning the trial and execution of Socrates (Euthyphro, Apology, Crito, and Phaedo). Two additional contemporary accounts by Xenophon and Aristophanes are supplemented by that of Aristotle, who wrote two generations later. On this slim documentary basis, a mountain of interpretation and controversy concerning the trial of Socrates has developed.

Regardless of Socrates' intention, the trial offers the student of criminal justice history a dramatic example of Athenian prosecution, procedure, and adjudication in the

fourth century BC. Prosecution in Athenian procedure was initiated by citizens; it is known that three men (Anytus, Meletus, and Lycon) raised accusations against Socrates. By bringing the charges, the accusers put themselves at risk. Any citizen could bring an accusation, but as a safeguard against unwarranted or purely malicious attacks, accusers who failed to convince one-fifth of the jury were subject to paying a heavy fine.

The indictment, drawn up by Meletus, was put in writing and taken to the office of the King-Archon, who then forwarded the case to trial. No complete set of the charges leveled against Socrates in 399 BC has survived, but it is recorded that Meletus swore that Socrates was guilty of not recognizing the gods whom the state recognized, of introducing other new divinities, and of misleading the youth of Athens. The charges were vague and apparently did not cite specific violations of the criminal law.

Regardless of the questionable legality of the accusations, there is substantial documentation that Socrates had long antagonized political leaders in Athens. It was well known

Continued

FEATURED OUTLAW: THE TRIAL OF SOCRATES—CONT'D

that Socrates was no admirer of democracy, preferring rule by those of knowledge and ability. Nor, with rare exceptions, did he take an active governmental role.

The characteristics of the court that tried Socrates were quite different from today's criminal courts. Aside from a magistrate whose only duty was to keep order, there were no judges. Nor were there official prosecutors or defense counsel. The decision was to be rendered by jurors chosen from a pool of volunteers and randomly assigned to the court. The exact number of jurors in Socrates' trial is not known, but scholars estimate that there were probably 501. After swearing to judge according to the laws, the jurors heard from the prosecution and defense, each of which was allotted a limited amount of time so that the trial could be concluded before nightfall.

Following speeches by the accusers, Socrates spoke in his own defense. In essence, he argued that in seeking virtue and urging others to value wisdom above material wealth and reputation, he had both served the state well and followed the will of the gods. He saw himself as one who was "like a gadfly to a horse, which, though a large and noble beast, is sluggish on account of its size and needs to be aroused by stinging. I think the god has fastened me upon the State in some such capacity, and I go about rousing, urging, and reproaching each one of you, constantly alighting on you everywhere the whole day long."

As expected from the beginning, the jurors voted to convict Socrates, but by an unexpectedly narrow margin; a shift of 30 votes would have meant acquittal. Under Athenian procedural rules, there was no possibility of appeal from this verdict. The same jurors then heard arguments regarding sentence. Meletus proposed that

Socrates be sentenced to death. It was then Socrates' turn to suggest an appropriate penalty. The jurors had to choose one or the other; no other sentence was possible. Some scholars believe that had Socrates proposed banishment, the jurors would have agreed. At first Socrates suggested that, because he had benefited the state, he should be allocated free meals for life, then backed off and offered to pay a token fine, and finally made the proposal that he pay a substantial fine.

With slightly more votes than for conviction, the jurors sentenced Socrates to death. Death sentences in Athens were carried out immediately. The condemned man was turned over to officials to be executed within 24 hours. At the time of Socrates' condemnation, however, the execution had to be delayed until a sacred boat that had been sent to the shrine of Apollo returned. It was delayed for nearly a month, and during this time Socrates' friends pleaded with him to flee. He chose instead to abide by the legal (if unjust) decision of the court. Once the boat reappeared, the execution ritual began. In the midst of his friends, Socrates drank the cup of hemlock handed to him and died quietly. Tradition has it that his last words concerned a request that his debt of a cock to Asclepius should be paid.

The trial and death of Socrates represents a paradox. The city of Athens, renowned for the principle of freedom of speech, had seen the prosecution, conviction, and execution of a man for words that alienated powerful members of the society.

Sources: Plato. (1963). *The trial and death of Socrates: Euthyphro, Apology, Crito, and Phaedo.* New York: Dutton, Everyman's Library; Stone, I. F. (1989). *The trial of Socrates.* New York: Doubleday.

HISTORY TODAY

Given that many people on death row fight so hard to save themselves, even when they admit guilt of terrible crimes, how does a person like Socrates compare?

Where the magistrates alone decided cases at the trial level, the matter might be appealed to the entire people of Athens for review. When this became cumbersome, Athenian procedure adopted a type of jury drawn from a broad cross section of the people, called a *dicastery*, to serve with the magistrate and render decisions in criminal cases. This could be as many as 50 citizens of Athens. As the practice matured, the panels from which jurors were drawn represented an ever-widening group of Athenian citizens. Unlike modern jurors in the United States, who may be called upon, or "polled" to verbally state their vote, each member cast a secret ballot to determine the guilt or innocence of the accused.

Oaths played a significant role in Athenian criminal prosecution. The accuser and the defendant were both required to take an oath to the accuracy of their pleadings. At an earlier stage in history, an exculpatory oath procedure was available

FIGURE 2.3 Statues of Socrates and Apollo outside Academy of Athens, Athens, Greece. © *Marco Simoni/ Robert Harding World Imagery/Corbis.*

whereby defendants might invoke a curse upon themselves and their families in connection with their denial of guilt. If the "oath-helpers" that a defendant assembled outnumbered those who supported the accuser's oath, the case was dismissed. Later, during classical times, the oath procedures alone no longer disposed of criminal cases, but still gave weight to a party's evidence. The challenge oath was frequently used for the purposes of joining issues and bringing evidence before juries in a particularly dramatic way. It was customarily met with a crosschallenge, in which the respondent asserted that the challenger was a known atheist and perjurer whose oath was worthless. Decreased reliance upon oaths indicated not only a reduction in piety, but also marked an increased emphasis on the reliability and accuracy of evidence; these characteristics were enhanced, in at least some cases, by the solemnity of the oath.

HISTORY TODAY

In past civilizations, oaths were important because the person was afraid of telling a lie after swearing to God they would not. Given our concern about separation of church and state, and the fact that many people do not regard an oath to God as something to fear, does stating "so help me God" mean anything in modern courts?

After the submission of evidence and speeches by the parties in support of their cases, the jury gave its verdict. From this there was no appeal, but the losing party might ask for a new trial within 2 months of the judgment, or ask that the verdict be suspended or annulled for false testimony. The successful prosecutor of a public case was awarded a sum of money for his effort; if he failed to continue the case to conclusion, he was fined for his neglect. If the prosecutor lost a case, he usually escaped a fine unless he failed to obtain more than one-fifth of the jurymen's votes, in which case he would be fined 1,000 drachmas. This fine was instituted to discourage *sycophants*—individuals who made their living by threatening prominent citizens with prosecution for sham criminal offenses. By the end of the classical period, sycophancy was a public nuisance in Athens.

Athenian punishments took a variety of forms. Capital punishment in earliest times was accomplished by throwing the criminal into an open pit; in classical times, death by another means might be followed by an undignified burial in an open pit as an additional sanction. Stoning was the form of punishment most commonly applied in the time of *Hesiod* (circa 800 BC). In classical Athens, strangulation was a common punishment, and impalement on an upright board resulted in death through exposure. More common was death by drinking hemlock; this was the general mode for committing suicide and by far the most merciful form of execution. There is no record of Athenian executions by decapitation or hanging. In noncapital punishment, a variety of forms of *atimia*, or public degradation, were available, ranging from loss of the right to vote to various types of outlawry, or losing all one's rights, including the right to live, in some instances. Physical punishment by flogging was used for slaves but not for freemen; imprisonment was a rare punishment, the usual practice being to sell the convict into slavery.

> Hesiod: Great Greek poet, most significant work was *Theogony*, an insight into Greek culture of that period.

ROME

Rome's republican constitution provided ingenious checks on the unbridled exercise of judicial power. *Consuls*, as the two principal magistrates, shared authority over the major affairs of state; in office for only 1 year, each consul was limited by the need to obtain the consent of his colleague. All magistrates, including the *praetors* and *quaestors*, who were the major judicial officers, had the authority to veto a colleague's action, and this process (called *intercessio*) provided an effective check on arbitrary judicial power.

Criminal judgments against Roman citizens were subject to an appeal. During the Republic, this appeal was to the body of the people, but after Caesar's establishment of the principate in 25 BC, criminal appeals were heard by the emperor. Paul, the Christian apostle who was a Roman citizen, was permitted such an appeal from the adverse decision of Festus, governor of Judea. These appeals from a magistrate's judgments in serious criminal matters were called *provocatio*; they were available at all times except in situations of grave national emergency or civic disorder. A magistrate recognizing the likelihood of an appeal to the people could avoid such a review by bringing the matter before himself and his *consilium*, or council of advisors. Preliminary hearings were held in this forum, then the magistrate transferred the case to the popular assembly, which was responsible for judging the offense and to which the magistrate owed his selection.

Because magistrates were drawn from the senatorial class, the common people (plebeians) soon established their own claim to hold offices similar to those of the magistrates. These were the tribunes who, while not technically magistrates

TIME CAPSULE: CRIMINAL JUSTICE IN IMPERIAL CHINA

Because the modern criminal justice system in the United States was largely derived from European legal and governmental practices, the primary focus of this book is on English and other European criminal justice practices. However, it is worthwhile to at least briefly focus on criminal justice practices in some non-Western cultures. Until long after the beginning of the Christian era, or until the explorations of China by the Italian Marco Polo, China's isolation from the West allowed the development of a legal culture independent of Western thought.

The earliest known written law, Hsing Shu (punishment book) in China dates to around 530 BC. The oldest known Chinese imperial code was the Code of Li k' vei from the fourth century BC. It was revised during the Han Dynasty of the third century BC, and included in the revisions was the abolition of corporal punishment. Unlike the Roman legal codes, the Chinese code was oriented more toward penal law than civil law. There was little focus on laws concerning marriage or commercial issues. Moral impropriety and violence were viewed as disruptions to the social order, and the maintenance of social order was paramount.

Like any legal codes, those of Imperial China were greatly influenced by the prevailing social thinking of the period. The two predominant philosophies in China during this period were Confucianism and Taoism. The Confucianists believed that laws were not necessary if government rulers were just. They believed that human beings instinctively did what was right. Legalists believed in the supremacy of law, trusting more in law than in human nature. The Legalists, influenced by Taoism, argued that strong law enforcement was necessary to maintain the social order. One leading Taoist, Kun-Sun Yang, argued that laws and punishments should be very strict so that no one would dare to break them. In fact, many Chinese viewed harsh punishments for criminals, along with lower taxes, as a sign of a benevolent government, not a harsh or uncaring one. Only a government that cared about its citizens would care enough to mete out harsh punishments to those who violated the social order.

Chinese criminal punishments made no claim at being equal for all. An offender's punishment was partly dependent on their status and that of the victim. A poor person would be punished more severely if the victim was powerful or rich. Capital punishment was routinely handed down, but pardons and amnesties were common. The death penalty could be imposed for adultery (both parties), treason, witchcraft, incest, blasphemy, forgery, and grand theft. Curiously, another capital offense was leveling an anonymous criminal accusation. Even if the accusation proved true, the accuser could be sentenced to death by strangulation. Other methods of execution included being beaten to death, being buried alive, impalement, being cut to pieces, hanging, burning, drowning, and being thrown off a cliff.

Confucianism and Taoism were not mutually exclusive; many Chinese adhered to both philosophies to varying degrees. Unlike many contemporary religions, Taoism and Confucianism are more akin to philosophies that guide a person's life, but they do not demand exclusive obedience or adherence. A person felt free to embrace elements of Taoism and Confucianism at the same time. In time, Confucianism, while still a popular philosophy for guiding one's personal life, became increasingly obsolete as Chinese society became more complex and less communal. More complex societies demanded a more complex codified written code.[3]

Confucianism

1. Man is basically good by nature or at least capable of being taught to be so. Li's teaching, therefore, is preventive, whereas *fa* is punitive.
2. A virtuous government, based on *li*, can win the hearts of its subjects. Law is the tool of tyranny. An unwritten law is flexible and therefore can be adapted to any situation.
3. A stable social order is based on the five major hierarchical relationships: father-son, ruler-subject, husband-wife, older-younger brother, friend-friend. By enforcing uniformity, *fa* obliterates these relationships.
4. *Li*, created by the sages, is of universal and eternal validity.
5. Laws are only as good as those who create and execute them; thus, the moral tenor of the kingdom is determined by the morality of the rulers and officials.

Legalism

1. Most men are motivated purely by self-interest. Therefore, the law must prescribe firm punishments.
2. The impartiality of law is the basis of stable, effective government. *Li*, which is unwritten and subjective, is

Continued

TIME CAPSULE: CRIMINAL JUSTICE IN IMPERIAL CHINA—CONT'D

always open to interpretation, whereas law is precise and fixed.

3. One of the basic principles of social order is that of collective responsibility. Every individual is equally responsible for the wrongdoing of others and equally subject to punishment. A strong state maintains a uniform system of morality; individual standards are to be suppressed.

4. Law must change to suit the times; all human institutions must adapt to changing conditions.

5. Even a mediocre ruler can stand at the head of a strong state if he has an efficient legal framework that maintains a high standard of morality.

Source: Drapkin, I. (1989). *Crime and punishment in the ancient world.* Lexington, MA: Lexington Books.

possessed of the imperium, were early declared sacred in their persons and granted broad governmental powers. The tribunes might present a criminal for trial before their own assembly, the *concilium plebis*, or to the assembly of the entire people, the *comitia centuriata*, which heard capital cases and other matters involving heavy penalties. During the closing days of the republic, prosecutions of unsuccessful generals and politicians before the comitia centuriata were commonplace.

Procedures before republican Roman criminal courts tended to provide a maximum flexibility in the submission of evidence. To the extent that the original procedures were tried before large assemblies, the oratorical ability of advocates played a significant role. Hearsay evidence was included and, frequently, testimony might be admitted in affidavit form even if the witness was readily available. Advocates were given license in their comments upon the evidence, in cross-examination, and in attacking the credibility of witnesses. In any criminal case, the reputation of the accused was a point in issue; therefore, the introduction of character evidence was not only permitted, but it was expected that the accused would take upon himself or herself the burden of proving his good character.

HISTORY TODAY

Very often, our study of history and criminal justice is confined to Western society. Given the fact that we live in a "global" community with cultures so interconnected, should we devote more attention to ancient non-Western civilizations like China?

Sanctions in Roman criminal law varied according to the offense and the status of the accused. An intentional killer, one who gave false testimony, a citizen who incited a public enemy or betrayed a fellow citizen to the enemy, and an official who accepted bribes were subjected to capital punishment, usually by beheading. However, the false witness was thrown from the Tarpeian Rock, and a defendant convicted of intentional arson was burned to death. A person convicted of singing incantations or casting spells and curses was to be clubbed to death. When a Roman citizen was sentenced to death, scourging, or a heavy fine, he was entitled to appeal the sentence to the people and remain at large until their decision was handed down. The result was that most Roman citizens convicted of serious crimes were never punished, but escaped into exile. Slaves, on the other hand, were imprisoned and dealt with harshly; they were perhaps simply thrown into prison and strangled shortly thereafter.

SUMMARY

Despite the cultural and chronological distinctions among the three cultures presented, certain common themes can be discerned. For example, all three placed the heaviest of sanctions on intentional killers and lighter penalties on kidnappers. Athenian and biblical theological positions appear to have added particular revulsion to intentional homicide, and in Roman law it resulted in death or exile, even for a Roman citizen. For the most part, sex offenses were dealt with less severely, but biblical Israel's emphasis on its status as Yahweh's chosen people altered the biblical law. In all three legal systems, theft was generally a matter of compensation; however, aggravating circumstances that made the property offense a possible occasion for physical violence, or that offended religious taboos, may have caused additional sanctions.

Turning to criminal procedure, there was a common pattern of self-help being required from the victims of criminal activities. Each system developed a number of rules of evidence, based upon logical analysis of the value of testimony. Probabilities of guilt or innocence entered into the assignment of burdens of proof. In the Roman and Athenian use of the platter and loincloth search and in biblical Israel's use of lots in the breastplate of the high priest, we see a common thread of superstition and reliance upon the intervention of divine guidance into the evidentiary process.

Running through the organization of courts was a common thread of relying on group decision as being superior to the judgment of an individual. In the cases of Athens and Rome, this was seen as a protection for the individual against the power of magistrates. Judgment at the gate in ancient Israel placed the accused before the elders of his or her town. There was an element of probability present also, for the populace represented by the dicastery, the quaestiones jury, and the council of town elders could not fail to be influenced by the reputation of the accused. Justice may not have been precise, but it tended to reflect public attitudes and judgments. As such, it maintained order, discouraged revenge, and advanced the interests of the community.

REFERENCES

de Vaux, R. (1961). *Ancient Israel, vol. I: Social institutions.* New York: McGraw-Hill; Smith, J. M. P. (1931). *The origin and history of Hebrew law.* Chicago, IL: University of Chicago Press; Goldin, H. E. (1950). *Hebrew criminal law and procedure: Mishnah, sanhedrin, makkot.* New York: Twayne Publishers; Phillips, A. C. J. (1971). *Ancient Israel's criminal law: A new approach to the decalogue.* Oxford: Basil Blackwell; Falk, Z. W. (1964). *Hebrew law in biblical times.* Jerusalem: Wahrman Books; Childs, B. S. (1974). *The book of Exodus: A critical, theological commentary.* Philadelphia: Westminster Press.

Boecker, H. J. (1980). *Law and the administration of justice in the Old Testament and ancient east.* Trans. Moiser, J. Minneapolis: Augsburg Publishing House: Daube, D. (1947). *Studies in biblical law.* Cambridge: Cambridge University Press; Noth, M. (1966). *The laws of the pentateuch and other studies.* Trans. Ap-Thomas, D.R. Edinburgh: Oliver & Boyd.

Andrewes, A. (1967). *The Greeks.* London: Hutchinson & Co., Ltd; Whibley, L. (1963). *A companion to Greek studies* (4th ed), revised. New York: Hafner Publishing Company; MacDowell, D. M. (1978). *The law in classical Athens.* Ithaca: Cornell University Press; MacDowell, D. A. (1963). *Athenian homicide law in the age of the Orators.* Manchester: Manchester University Press; Harrison, A. R. W. (1971). *The law of Athens. Vol. 2: Procedure.* Oxford: Clarendon Press; Calhoun, G. M. (1927). *The growth of criminal law in ancient Greece.* Berkeley: University of California Press; Bonner, R. J. (1905). *Evidence in Athenian courts.* Chicago: University of Chicago Press; Bonner, R. J., & Smith, G. (1930). *The administration of justice from Homer to Aristotle.* 2 Vols. Chicago: University of Chicago Press; Gagarin, M. (1981). *Drakon and early Athenian homicide law.* New Haven: Yale University Press; Plescia, J. (1970). *The oath and perjury in ancient Greece.* Tallahassee: Florida State University Press; Brickhouse, T. C., & Smith, N. D. (1989). *Socrates on trial.* Princeton: Princeton Press; MacDowell, D. M. (1978). *The law in classical Athens.* London: Thames and Hudson; Plato. (1963). *The trial and death of Socrates: Euthyphro, Apology, Crito, and Phaedo.* New York: Dutton, Everyman's Library; Stone, I. F. (1989). *The trial of Socrates.* New York: Doubleday.

Nicholas, B. (1962). *An introduction to Roman law.* Oxford: Clarendon Press; (1972). *An Introduction to Roman Legal and Constitutional History* (2nd ed) Trans. Kelly, J. M. Oxford: Clarendon Press; Jolowicz, H. F., & Nicholas, B. (1972). *Historical introduction to the study of Roman law* (3rd ed). Cambridge: Cambridge University Press; Greenidge, A. H. J. (1901). *The legal procedure of Cicero's time.* Oxford: Clarendon Press.

Drapkin, I. (1989). *Crime and punishment in the ancient world.* Lexington: D.C. Heath; Freeman, K. (1963). *The murder of Herodes and other trials from the Athenian law courts.* New York: W.W. Norton & Company; Maine, H. S. (1963). *Ancient law: Its connection with the early history of society and its relation to modern ideas.* Boston: Beacon Press, first published in 1861; Diamond, A. S. (1971). *Primitive law, past and present.* London: Methuen; Anderson, J. N. D. (1975). *Islamic law in the modern world.* Westport, CT: Greenwood Press; Lippman, S. M., & Yerushalmi, M. (1988). *Islamic criminal law and procedure: An introduction.* New York: Praeger; Ruthven, M. (1997). *Islam.* New York: Oxford University Press.

ENDNOTES

[1]The Tarpeian Rock on Capitoline Hill was named for an early traitoress buried nearby.

[2]Roman statutes were named after the first consul during the year of their enactment.

[3]Drapkin, I. (1989). *Crime and punishment in the ancient world.* Lexington, MA: Lexington Books.

CHAPTER 3

Medieval Crime and Punishment Before the Lateran Council of 1215

KEY TERMS

Abjurer

Benefit of clergy

Bier-right

Blood feud

Botleas

Canon law

Canute II

Circuits

Compurgatory oath

Dooms

Fourth Lateran Council
   of 1215

Gavelkind

Henry II

Islamic criminal justice

Joseph Glanvill

Judicial eyres

King's peace

Nisi prius

Ordeal

Ordeal of hot water

Ordeal of red-hot iron

Outlawry

Psalm 51

Robin Hood

Trial by battle

Urban cohorts

Vengeance

Watchers

Wergild

William the Conqueror

LEARNING OBJECTIVES

1. Learn why the decline of the Roman Empire affected the operation of criminal justice throughout Europe.
2. Understand criminal justice practices in Europe during and after the decline of the Roman Empire.
3. Learn the antecedents of law enforcement put into place by the Romans and the European Germanic kingdoms during this period.
4. Understand the significance of canon law in European criminal justice before 1215.
5. Learn the role of vengeance, wergilds, and blood feuds in European criminal justice.

6. Learn the importance of oaths, ordeals, bier-rights, and torture in European criminal justice.
7. Learn the different types of ordeals employed by European governments.
8. Gain a basic understanding of some aspects of Islamic Law as practiced in the early days of Islam.
9. Understand the "outlaw as hero" theme in the Middle Ages.

Table 3.1 Time Line

Western Empire		Eastern Empire
	318-324 AD	Emperor Constantine recognizes Christianity as a religion within the Roman Empire, and declares himself a Christian
	325, 327 AD	At the call of Constantine, the Councils of Nicaea adopt a credal statement concerning the Trinity
	324-326 AD	Constantine unites the Western and Eastern Empires
Visigoths sack Rome	410 AD	
Vandals conquer Carthage	439 AD	
Pope Leo I asserts primacy of the bishop of Rome; his status affirmed by Emperor Valentinian III	440-461 AD	
	451 AD	Ecumenical Council at Chalcedon clarifies church doctrine concerning the divinity and humanity of Jesus Christ
Odoacer deposes the last Roman Emperor in the West	476 AD	
Clovis, King of the West Franks, becomes a Christian	496 AD	
	527 AD	Justinian becomes sole Emperor of the East
	527-540 AD	Justinian's jurists compile the Corpus Juris Civilis
	535-553 AD	Justinian's general, Belisarius, conquers Carthage, and evicts the Visigoths from Rome, and Justinian becomes Emperor of East and West
Pope Gregory the Great sends Augustine of Canterbury to Christianize England	596 AD	
	633-732 AD	Islamic caliphs conquer Syria, Iraq, Palestine, Libya, Tripoli, Carthage, Spain, and Southern France. Their advance is halted at Tours by Franks

Continued

Table 3.1 Time Line—cont'd

Western Empire		Eastern Empire
Charlemagne, King of the Franks, is crowned Holy Roman Emperor by the Pope	800 AD	
Frankish kingdom divided into three parts, one for each grandson of Charlemagne, by the Treaty of Verdun. The divisions represent the future nations of France, Germany, and Italy	843 AD	
Viking leader, Rollo, granted Normandy by the Frankish king	911 AD	
	1053-1054 AD	The Great Schism divides the Eastern Church (Orthodox) from the Western Church (Roman or Latin)
	1071 AD	Battle of Manzikart; Selijuk Turks take Asia Minor from the Byzantine Empire
	1096-1099 AD	The First Crusade; Jerusalem captured and Latin Kingdoms established in the Holy Land
	1187 AD	Saladin reconquers Jerusalem
Pope Innocent III calls the Fourth Lateran Council, which abolished church participation in ordeals	1215 AD	

DARK AGES, GAVELKIND, AND OUTLAWRY

The principal focus in this chapter is the history of portions of the western empire that, after the fall of Rome in 426 AD, came under the control of a number of Germanic kings and ultimately emerged as the countries we are familiar with today. During this time, criminal justice changed markedly from that of the ancient world. As medieval Europe sank into a period of confusion and illiteracy called the Dark Ages, Christianity became one of the sole unifying factors in Western civilization. Consequently, the Roman Catholic Church was one of the few remaining vestiges of Roman imperial authority. Yet the rapid disruption of ancient Roman systems of transportation (and thus communication) vastly increased the cultural distance between Rome and the rest of Europe. The church gradually fell under the administrative control of powerful local bishops and archbishops, and New Testament Christianity gave way to a special mix of Christian principles and local pagan (nature worship) customs and practices. For example, the midwinter date for Christmas drew upon a pagan festival held during the winter solstice, and it is believed that the "Christmas tree" originated in the practices of Druids, who were known to worship trees. Moreover, the design of the Celtic cross incorporated the traditional symbol of Christianity with an older symbol used by those who recognized the sun as a god.

The declining power of Rome left in its wake a vacuum in political authority filled only in part by the rule of petty kings and would-be Holy Roman Emperors. Localities began to fall back on their own resources for instruments of government and crime control. Economically, it became important for poor farmers and merchants to associate themselves with a powerful lord, thereby securing protection in return for services or taxes paid to their overlord. Crime control was based on kindred groupings; an individual's relatives became his supporters if he was injured by another, and they bailed him out of trouble by paying compensation if he maimed or killed a member of another kindred group. Expulsion from the kindred group deprived one of protection and permitted initially anyone, and ultimately solely the sheriff, to injure or kill the expelled individual through the practice of *outlawry*. Rather than being outlawed, a person could be an *abjurer*, literally a person who recants solemnly, which consisted of wearing a white robe and carrying a cross and being subjected to a type of perpetual vagrancy as an abjurer was not permitted to remain in one place for more than two nights.

Given the widespread illiteracy in Western society during the Dark Ages, historians have limited sources of information upon which to draw, and many conclusions are speculative. However, there is little doubt that this period in history was very important for the development of Western government and society. In the millennium between the fall of Rome and the collapse of Constantinople, as well as the eastern empire, vitally important changes took place in England and Western Europe. One result, as we have noted, was the beginning of modern national states. There was a slow buildup of power in the hands of noble families, on the basis of dynastic alliances and their social standing among those who shared a similar language, culture, and traditions. As territorial magnates consolidated their control, their people found a new sense of cohesion in their differences from neighboring states and nations; this resulted in the rapid decline of pan-European culture that had once been based on Roman principles and the teachings of the Christian church. The other consequence was the proliferation of a new view of humankind based on one's importance as a member of a kindred group, clan, or society. To some degree, at its inception such an ideal was a perpetuation of Israelite, Athenian, and Roman attitudes toward the individuals who formed ancient societies. However, this new view of humankind was founded less on religion or political philosophy and more out of necessity, in a world perceived as increasingly primitive and violent. Chastened by the dangers of weak and uncertain government, Western societies reconstituted a new form of state through reciprocal rights and obligations.

TIME CAPSULE: PERSONAL LAW AND TERRITORIAL LAW IN THE DARK AGES

The New Testament narrative of the life of the apostle Paul introduces us to the impact of personal law. Accused by the Jewish authorities of blasphemy and defiling the Jerusalem Temple, Paul escaped a scourging by claiming his rights as a Roman citizen, a status he inherited from his father. At the time, Roman citizenship might be purchased, but under the Edict of Caracalla (213 AD) it was also awarded to all freeborn inhabitants of the empire. Unfortunately, Paul continued to claim Roman citizenship rights, which included the privilege of being tried in the courts of the emperor; the authorities who might have tried him in Jerusalem observed that, but for his claiming the right to a trial by the emperor, Paul would have been acquitted of the charges. The narrative suggests that trial by the emperor may have been the means he chose to spread the Christian faith to Rome.

Paul claimed a personal law that exempted him from a Judean territorial law. The tension between laws that governed all relationships within a geographical area, and laws that applied only to specific individuals qualified by birth or tribal associations, was typical of the collapse of the Roman Empire in the West after 476 AD. As Germanic tribes moved into Italy and the other provinces formerly held by Rome, they brought customary law with them. In some cases, they eliminated Roman law and applied their own customary law throughout the conquered territory. In many other situations, they continued to allow the use of Roman law by the Romans living in their lands, but applied tribal customs to their own people. The Salic Franks were particularly generous in tolerating the continuance of tribal customs along with the rules of Roman law; as a consequence, France up to the time of Napoleon Bonaparte was governed by Roman law in the south and by a variety of customary laws in the north.

England, on the other hand, was not influenced by Roman law but derived its principles of law on a territorial basis, drawing heavily upon Anglo-Saxon and Norman customary law. The one exception to this rule was the exemption of clergy from the royal criminal law; as in continental Europe, English clergy were allowed the right of trial in church courts according to rules of canon law. As we shall see, these exemptions not only gave rise to the practice of "benefit of clergy," but also encouraged lawlessness on the part of ordained clergy.

There are good and bad aspects of the resort to either territorial law or personal law. In territorial systems, all individuals located within the governed territory, whether they are natives or foreigners, are subject to the same rules. On the other hand, if they wish to break the territorial rules, they may do so with impunity by going to a territory where those rules do not apply. In personal law systems, the rules within a given land differ from each other, because each person may be entitled to a different set of customary laws. However, the person subject to customary law carries his law with him, and thus may be subject to punishment wherever he may be. He may also be punished by his homeland for offenses committed outside its territory. As Professor Simeon Guterman points out, the territorial system has been dominant since the 1648 Treaty of Westphalia. Will the preference for territorial law persist? Modern pressures toward establishing international rules of criminal law may begin to modify this tradition. American federal statutes concerning air piracy, for example, apply to persons subject to U.S. control, regardless of their citizenship or where the offense was committed. Another example may be the modern practice of punishment for war crimes that may not be offenses against the law of the territory in which they were committed, but that violate international law norms or treaty obligations.

Sources: Acts of the Apostles, 22:25-29; 25:6-12; 26:32; Guterman, S. L. (1972). *From personal law to territorial law: Aspects of the history and structure of the Western legal-constitutional tradition.* Metuchen: The Scarecrow Press, MD, pp. 11-13, 17, 18, 22-23, 27, 29; Drew, K. F. (1949). *The Burgundian code: Book of constitutions or law of Gundobad: Additional enactments.* Philadelphia: University of Pennsylvania Press. p. 4.

HISTORY TODAY

Should a person's citizenship or national origin be a factor in how the criminal justice system treats him or her? Should people arrested in other countries, for example, terrorists and drug offenders, be allowed the same due process rights as people born or living in the United States?

Even after the fall of Rome, Western societies and Germanic kings continued to recognize the personal nature of law; that is, individuals who had inherited Roman citizenship (and there were many in the Dark Ages) were entitled to the law of Rome, however imperfect the current understanding of what that law might have been. On the other hand, special tribal laws and customs applied to Germanic subjects of the same kings, resulting in complex rules concerning legal relationships between Romans and Germans. Over time, these differing laws produced a wide variety of local customs and usages. The English county of Kent and the borough of London each had inheritance laws that differed from those in other areas in England.

Kent became famous for the introduction of *gavelkind*, a system of dividing land equally between heirs. What was unusual for the time was that should a person die intestate (without leaving a will) normal practice was that the oldest son inherited all the land. Under gavelkind (the word originates from the Latin word *gabulum*, meaning to rent or have an interest) this was an equal division between the parties and this included consideration of women's interests also.

The northeast of England, dominated for years by the Danelaw designed for the descendants of Viking conquerors, also had unique customs, among which was requiring 12 freeholders to appear in court (A Thing) to swear they would not accuse an innocent man. It was the task of centralizing monarchs and their legal advisers to shape and impose a common law that would minimize both personalization of legal rules and the existence of distinctive territorial law.

One final point must be made concerning the rise of independent kingdoms and the growth of national cultures based on shared languages and traditions. Shortly after the fall of Rome, Western Europe and England enjoyed a common heritage of Roman law, the Latin language, and Christianity.

Roman influence remained in the nature and form of developing criminal justice systems (and continues to be influential today). For example, the Romans introduced city law enforcers known as *Watchers*, 3500 in total divided into cohorts of 500 men, who were located in barracks around the city of Rome with the responsibility for fire and policing. The task of crowd control was assigned to *Urban Cohorts*, somewhat similar to the present day CRS (Companies for Republican Security) of France. Like the specialized CRS of France, the Urban Cohorts were better equipped and armed than the Watchers. Another piece of ancient Roman justice that formed the genesis of a criminal justice system in Europe was the need for a personal accusation before a magistrate to start the criminal process. However, unlike the system that developed between 1000 and 1300 across Europe, in ancient Rome there was no jury deliberation period and up to 80 jurors would cast an immediate vote of guilt or innocence at the conclusion of the trial.

HISTORY TODAY

The Romans would employ up to 80 jurors to try a case. The modern American system uses 12 or in some cases fewer jurors and they deliberate for hours or sometimes several days. Do we use too many jurors or too few? Should jurors be encouraged to deliberate where they might fall victim to being unduly influenced by other jurors in the room? Or should they individually pronounce their decision in open court?

By the year 1000 AD, these remnants of Roman civilization had subsided into a literate subculture loosely clustered around the church. This subculture included newly founded universities. The University of Bologna granted its first degree in 1088 and within the space of 200 years a number of former theological schools had grown into universities: Oxford 1096, Paris 1150, and Cambridge 1209. However, most of these institutions would hardly resemble the contemporary campus. It was not until 1209 that Cambridge University introduced the concept of linked buildings and from these developed the campuses as we know them today and the curriculum was led by what books the university had and consequently all students followed the same courses.

However, the language and customs of the common people and many of their landlords were either of Germanic origin or a barely recognizable version of the ancient Latin speech and culture. England early became subject to this sort of separation from its continental contemporaries. Conquered in 1066 by Norman French nobles, England was drawn into the orbit of the Angevin empire, a family that produced 15 English kings and ruled for 300 years. The Angevins were so named as they originated from Anjou, capital of Angers. They eventually became known as *Plantagenets* because of the genus of plant, the common broom, worn in the cap of Geoffrey V of Anjou. At their height, this family ruled most of western France, England, and Ireland.

However, family dynastic ties could not restrain the pressures that drew England toward isolated nationhood. It is against this background that we must understand the similarities between English and continental European criminal justice in the Dark Ages and it is this factor that partially explains England's departure from continental Europe in its response to the mandates of the *Fourth Lateran Council of 1215* AD.

VENGEANCE, WERGILD, AND DOOMS

Among Germanic peoples, kindred groups were formed by blood relationships. This meant that one's kindred were those who had a close biological relationship; it excluded one's spouse as well as the spouses of one's children. Closely connected to these considerations is the fact that in primitive societies there must have been considerable pressure to ignore the ecclesiastical (church) rules concerning incest. A small population with a limited number of marriage partners might have applied incest rules more loosely, particularly in regard to the upper classes of society, where marriage would frequently be a means of amassing wealth. Nevertheless, *canon law* (church law) prohibited the marriage of first cousins, but great-grandchildren of the same couple (second cousins) could legally marry. It was acceptable that kindred ties might also be created by adoption or by the creation of blood ties through ceremonial means.

The basic relationship for purposes of *vengeance* was the blood relationship, but it was supplemented by other practices. For example, the widow of a murder victim might apply first to her husband's kinsmen (son, father, or brothers) to avenge his death, but if that request did not bring results, it was expected that she might appeal to her own kindred. She did this by a variety of methods, ranging from a simple demand for help to an elaborate ceremony of presenting the head or bloody garments of the deceased to her kinsmen. Women, small children, and elderly men were not expected to take part in the *blood feud* as actual avengers, but they played a vital role as aggrieved parties.

HISTORY TODAY

People in the United States are not allowed to commit a crime for the purpose of avenging a wrong done to a relative. However, many otherwise law-abiding people feel morally justified in doing just that. Should the law recognize the moral "right" or "duty" of a person to avenge harm done to a loved one?

A complex series of rules governed who among the deceased's male relatives were first entitled to seek vengeance, and the very complexity of the rules made it difficult for an accused slayer to pay *wergild* to the proper representative of the family. In the event a wergild agreement was not reached, a blood feud was agreed upon as the way to resolve the conflict. A blood feud developed when families or clans engaged in widespread vengeance over a series of generations because efforts to resolve their differences had failed. It was for the challengee, rather than the challenger, to pick the form of combat. Wergild, sometimes spelled "wergeld," is taken from the Old English words "wer" (man) and "geld" (payment). Wergild was compensation paid to the victim of a serious crime or the family of a victim. The amount of the wergild depended on the victim's status and wealth; the greater the victim's material worth, the greater was the amount of the wergild.

HISTORY TODAY

In a modern civil case, the amount of money granted may depend in part on the person's "worth," how much money he or she made or his or her earning potential. Is this similar to a wergild? In a criminal trial, does the social status or wealth of a victim make a difference as to the punishment a defendant might receive? Should it?

Despite its apparent barbarity, vengeance progressed on fixed rules that tended to limit its scope and ferocity. For example, indiscriminate killing was forbidden; a life could be avenged by the taking of a life from among the kindred of the slayer; exceeding the amount corresponding to the *lex talionis* in ancient law was illegal. Under *lex talionis*, or "eye for an eye," the penalty is the same in kind as the grievance received. Clans and kindred groups were careful to restrain the violence of their members because misbehavior that resulted in injury or death beyond the clan triggered revenge and brought disrepute on the slayer's group.

A rough sort of public opinion operated to discourage taking revenge when the victim's behavior might have justified the homicide. Revenge was dangerous and could erupt into counter vengeance if viewed in an unfavorable light by the opposing kindred group. But once a valid case was established, the results of the feud were frequently put on public display with the body, or body parts, of the defeated party being placed in prominent positions around the village.

Despite the complications inherent in a system of blood feud and vengeance, it formed one of the most significant portions of the criminal law in Scandinavia, Germany, Scotland, and Anglo-Saxon England, as recorded by the Norse Sagas, the Niebelungen Ring legends, and the epic poem *Beowulf*. Further evidence of the history of blood feuds remains within the motto of Scotland *nemo me impune lacessit*, meaning "none shall injure me with impunity." This period in history provides great opportunity for the exercise of historical imagination. For example, one can examine the consequence of having a special law that applies to certain groups and not others living in the same geographical area.

By the time Anglo-Saxon England emerged from the Dark Ages and laws began to appear on record, revenge and the blood feud had given way to a complex form of involuntary compensation for criminal acts, including the payment of money to a slain man's kindred. In the event of a guilty party not being able to pay compensation, slavery was an option.

The earliest recorded Anglo-Saxon laws were those issued by Aethelbert of Kent in 601-604. These proclamations, known as *dooms*, treated theft as an offense punishable by fines that varied widely in magnitude. Stealing from the church or persons in holy orders was punishable by compensation ranging from three times the value of the property to a maximum of 12 times the value of the assets taken. Theft from the king was punishable by a fine of nine times the value of the stolen goods, equivalent to the fine imposed when a priest's property was taken.

HISTORY TODAY

Should wealth, social status, or position in government be a factor in assessing the punishment for a property offense? Should stealing from a church or from the government be regarded more harshly than stealing from someone else?

Canute II (994-1035): Danish king who conquered England and Norway; was able to unify his rule over all of England; most powerful monarch in Europe during his life; kingdom fell apart soon after his death; according to legend, once (unsuccessfully) commanded the tide to halt so as not to wet his feet or clothing.

These dooms evidence the beginning of a custom known as the *king's peace*, a special protection that applied to those in the physical presence of the king, or to those located in a village or assembly area to which the king's protection had been extended. A similar form of peace, enforced by more modest fines, applied to the person and protected areas of an Eorl (nobleman). With practice, the king's peace extended to everyone so that the king's cook had entitlement to peace, the king's stablehand had peace, and so would lords, artisans, and peasants. The king's peace applied to all forms of wrongdoing, and was imposed as an additional fine, supplementing the normal penalties and sanctions for the wrong itself. Aethelbert's dooms imposed a relatively heavy wergild of 100 shillings as the ordinary wergild; it was to be increased in proportion to the dignity of the victim. Similarly, the dooms of Hlothaere and Eadric, issued in 685, perpetuated the wergild compensation imposed nearly a century before, but in the case of a servant who slayed a freeman, the dooms required that the servant be turned over to the victim's family in addition to the payment of the fine by his master. By the time of *Canute II* (c. 1020), some crimes were considered so severe that they could not be satisfied by compensation. These crimes were referred to as *Botleas*, and included arson, treachery to a lord, and murder by poisoning. It was only the king who had authority to pardon Botleas or allow a person to avoid immediate outlawry.

Dooms issued by King Ine of the West Saxons (688-695) reflected a growing determination to control violent behavior, although there remained no distinction between a misdemeanor and a felony until the 1176 Assize of Northampton. Fighting in the house of the king became an offense punishable by forfeiture of all property, and at the discretion of the monarch, the offender might be put to death. A detailed list of fines applied to fighting in the houses of nobles, churchmen, and common householders.

By the eighth century, wergild had extended to offenses of theft, rape, and marrying a widow within 1 year of her husband's death. Tariffs and values were also set more formally through the Angylde. In most parts of England, a sheep had a set value of one shilling, a freeman a value of 200 shillings, and a nobleman's value was 1200 shillings. In the county of Kent, the common value for a cow was one shilling. Under Alfred the Great, the system became even more standardized to the point where a lost ear was valued at 30 shillings and a nose at 60 shillings. A finger was worth just nine shillings and a toe 20 shillings.

Later, Anglo-Saxon dooms reflected the revival of commercial activity in England. By restricting trade to given ports or market towns and requiring witnesses to all sales transactions, the dooms were meant to deter disputes and criminal charges among merchants and the king's subjects. After the ninth century, there was an increased emphasis on bringing criminal charges before the king's officials or courts before resorting to revenge. The dooms of Edgar (946-963) and

Canute (1020-1034) regulated the creation and operation of local courts charged with law enforcement in the hundreds, shires, and boroughs. Saxon England was divided into hundreds composed of 10 things, which in turn were made up of 10 families. The shire, later called a *county*, was a larger division created by the grouping of hundreds. The borough was a walled town, usually incorporated by or possessed of a royal charter of privileges.

While private vengeance and reliance on self-help remained a significant part of English law, by the eleventh century such measures were reserved as a last resort for victims who had exhausted all opportunities for redress in the king's courts.

Canute (Cnut) was responsible for much lawmaking and brought clarity and uniformity to many areas of the law that had traditionally been customary. One such example is his influence on the previously mentioned gavelkind, which under Canute. C. 71 became formalized to ensure that "... the property be distributed very justly to the wife and children and relations, to everyone to the degree that belongs to him."

OATHS, ORDEALS, TORTURE, AND BIER-RIGHT

Once a system of trial was adopted as an alternative to blood feuds, it became necessary to develop means for determining the truth of testimony and other evidence presented to courts. English kings from 668 onward made use of trained clerics. At this time, the common language of the courts was a vernacular of Anglo-Saxon and Latin. It would be another 500 years before the influence of the French nobility made a significant impact on the language of writs and the courtroom.

Initial truth finding was done by means of a *compurgatory oath*, whereby an individual accused of crime might take an oath that he or she was innocent of wrongdoing. If the accused gained the support of a sufficient number of his kindred, or "oath helpers," the individual was acquitted. This procedure by oath has some similarities to early oath-taking modes of proof in Athenian procedure and was a forerunner to the jury system whereby the nobles (Thegns) and the Reeve (Sheriff) swore at the Hundred (Wapentake) Court that they would not accuse an innocent man nor conceal any guilty man. Oath-helping relied on the widespread fear of divine retribution after perjury, and in the case of the medieval oath, the credibility of the party increased the likelihood that he would succeed in obtaining a sufficient number of helpers.

Should the exchange of oaths by the parties and the support of oath helpers not be sufficient to determine the issues of fact, medieval judges had the option of leaving the case undecided or proceeding to what was known as the *ordeal*, which would seek divine intervention to determine guilt or innocence.

The most common ordeal was the *ordeal of hot water*. The ordeal of hot water required that the accused thrust a hand, or an arm up to the elbow, into a kettle of boiling water. When the hand was withdrawn, it was usually bound for 3 days and the divine verdict was determined by whether or not the accused emerged un-scathed. An ordeal by cold water required that the accused be lowered into a body of water. If the accused floated on the surface, it was held that he or she was a sinner or wrongdoer, for it was believed that the spirit of Satan invaded the body of a perjurer, making its weight less than that of water. Careful calculations were, of course, necessary to preserve the life of an innocent party who sank to the bot-tom. Descriptions of the mode of placing accused persons in the water would in-dicate that a rope was attached to the body in such a way that only a short immersion would occur before the vindicated party was removed from the water. At times, divine intervention occurred in unusual ways; it was said that in some cases murderers and other felons were scalded by cold water, the unexplained change in water temperature indicating their guilt to the assembled multitude.

A variant of the hot water ordeal was the *ordeal of the red-hot iron*, which could be accomplished in one of two ways. The first method was to heat a bar of iron to red-hot heat and require the accused to carry it a given distance before dropping it. The alternative was to heat a number of plowshares, ranging from 6 to 12 in num-ber, and require the accused to walk barefoot across them. The variations in the number of plowshares, and the weight of the bar of iron to be carried a given dis-tance, depended on the gravity of the crime. Ordeals by hot iron tended to be fa-vored by nobility, while water ordeals were considered more appropriate among commoners. These two forms of ordeals were common throughout Europe, and were used extensively in Anglo-Saxon England and early Norman England. In En-glish criminal procedure, the ordeal by water or iron was halted by the reforms of the Fourth Lateran Council of 1215, which prohibited the church from playing any role in the administration of ordeals. However, ordeals, particularly the or-deal of water, continued to be used in witchcraft cases into the nineteenth century.

HISTORY TODAY

Is the modern polygraph a successor to the ordeal?

The close connection between the ordeals and the church is noteworthy primarily because it demonstrates the degree to which certain Christian beliefs influenced modes of criminal procedure, as well as evidence produced before criminal courts. Because the ordeal depended on divine intervention to determine guilt or inno-cence, it was not administered in a routine fashion. Quite to the contrary, the ordeal was preceded by an extensive religious ceremony that always included the celebration of the Eucharist (or Mass) and the exorcism of the water or iron to be used in administering the test. Finally, the celebrant delivered a lengthy prayer requesting God's assistance in conducting the ordeal and adjuring the ac-cused that, if he had been guilty of perjury, he should recant and confess any guilt. An interesting ordeal variant was the requirement of an accused to receive the consecrated bread during the course of the communion service, it being widely believed that if one guilty of crime or perjury took consecrated bread into his mouth he would choke or die. Before it was taken, a special prayer that emphasized the danger was recited. The practice of taking the "Sacred Morsel" or Corsned (not a host but a meal of cheese and barley bread) was not exclusively for the clergy as seen in the case of Godwin, Earl of Wessex, who died in 1053 while eating the sacred morsel, having denied playing any part in the death of the king's brother.

Certain vestiges of the ordeals and their related superstitions persisted well after such methods had been eliminated from criminal procedure. *Bier-right* was reportedly used before juries and as an investigative tool well into the seventeenth century. Bier-right was the belief that a corpse approached by its slayer would begin to bleed, regardless of how long ago the time of death might have been. Widely used in the Dark Ages to survey a number of suspected killers, bier-right may well have provided special encouragement for the confession of an accused person. There are reports of such unfortunate persons being immediately put to death on the occurrence of bier-right and in the absence of any other evidence.

FIGURE 3.1 Tortures of the accused in medieval times included "the wheel." © *Bettmann/CORBIS.*

The compurgatory oath, ordeals, and bier-right were integral parts of the law in Anglo-Saxon England before the arrival of Duke William of Normandy (history records him as *William the Conqueror* but his first title was William the Bastard) in the eleventh century. With his arrival came a number of additions to the criminal justice system. William introduced a new form of ordeal called *trial by battle*. He initiated the beginning of a formalized criminal justice system with the Witan courts of Saxon England becoming a king's court or *curia regis*. William also started to reduce the power and influence of the bishops. His first move toward this was to remove the bishops from presiding at the shire courts. William also increased the use of the death penalty for numerous offenses previously punished by mutilation. He also introduced the Manor Court. This court had responsibility for choosing numerous officials within the community including the wine-taster, ale-taster, swine ringer, and the office of *constable*. Under William the term constable came into use. The word is derived from the French phrase "Count of the Stable," denoting a position of great responsibility in Rome and equivalent to Marshal-in-Chief or Marshall of the Stables and subsequently arbitrator of tournaments.

HISTORY TODAY

Today's criminal justice system never employs the ordeal. However, many people believe that right or justice usually wins out, or "what goes around comes around." Is it possible that we cling to some sort of vestige of the ordeal today?

William the Conqueror (1027-1087): Frenchman, first Norman King of England, considered first modern monarch by some; conquered England in 1066 when he saw a power vacuum there, and later conquered Scotland; great legacy is the creation of the Doomsday Book, a comprehensive record of all the lands and property ownership in England at the time, and his careful mixing of the Anglo-Saxon custom law system with continental legal systems; also responsible for greatly increasing the power and scope of the work of the sheriffs; responsible for separating canon law and establishing church courts separate from secular courts; one of the principal figures of European history.

Trial by battle involved the settlement of a legal issue by the combat of two champions (or substitute fighters) selected by the parties. It was used extensively in the trials of early claims to land, but was also available when an individual was privately accused of a felony, from the Latin *fello*, meaning cruel or wicked. The accusing party who brought the complaint (an appeal of felony) was responsible for engaging the accused in a duel or appointing a champion to do so. While this form of private prosecution eventually died out as the state increasingly brought public actions for the punishment of crime, trial by battle remained an option in English criminal law until 1819. During this time, the English Parliament, reacting to a case in which a criminal escaped punishment by offering to do battle, abolished this method of prosecution by statute.

TIME CAPSULE: ADJUDICATION BY BATTLE

In the words of William Blackstone, writing in the eighteenth century, trial by battle was "another species of presumptuous appeals to Providence, under an expectation that Heaven would unquestionably give the victory to the innocent or injured party" (Blackstone IV, 346). Fortunately, Blackstone provided a detailed description of the ritualistic procedures of the duel. The duel in a felony matter was to be fought in a manner similar to that prescribed for civil trial by combat. A person accused of a felony could plead not guilty, throw down his glove, and declare his willingness to defend it by his body. If the appellant took up the glove, they both swore an oath to the truth of their statements and a further oath against sorcery and enchantment:

Hear this, ye justices, that I have this day neither ate, drank, nor have upon me, neither bone, stone, nor grass: nor any enchantment, sorcery, or witchcraft, whereby the law of God may be abased, or the law of the devil exalted. So help me God and his saints.

A piece of ground is then in due time set out, of 60 feet square, enclosed with lists, and on one side a court erected for the judges of the court of common pleas, who attend there in their scarlet robes; and also a bar is prepared for the learned serjeants at law. When the court sits, which ought to be by sunrising, proclamation is made for the parties, and their champions, who are introduced by two knights, and are dressed in a coat of armour, with red sandals, bare-legged from the knee downward, bareheaded, and with bare arms to the elbows.

The weapons allowed them are only batons, or staves of an ell [45 inches] long, and a four-cornered leather-target.... And if the appellee be so far vanquished that he cannot or will not fight any longer, he shall be adjudged to be hanged immediately; and then, as well as if he be killed in battle, providence is deemed to have determined in favor of the truth, and his blood shall be attainted. But if he kills the appellant, or can maintain the fight from sunrising till the stars appear in the evening, he shall be acquitted. So also if the appellant becomes recreant and pronounces the horrible word of *craven*, he shall lose his *liberum legem*, and become infamous; and the appellee shall recover his damages, and also be forever quit, not only of the appeal, but of all indictments likewise for the same offense (Blackstone III, 338-340; IV, 347-348).

Source: Blackstone, W. (1899). *Commentaries on the laws of England* (4 vols). Chicago: Callaghan and Company. pp. III, 338-340; IV, 346-348.

THE FOURTH LATERAN COUNCIL, GLANVILL, AND ROYAL JUSTICES

The clergy's active participation in ordeals long occupied the attention of the Roman Catholic Church leadership, or papacy. Over the course of time, an ambiguous attitude developed that sanctioned clerical participation in some cases and condemned it in others. The accession of Pope Innocent III (1198-1216) did not indicate any substantial change, but the new pope had been educated at the University in Paris and was determined to reform certain abuses that had developed within the church. Among those excesses was participation in ordeals, which brought revenues to local priests and bishops and violated a long-standing prohibition against clerical involvement in blood-shedding judicial proceedings. Ultimately, Pope Innocent III's determination to exert spiritual supremacy over the western church resulted in critical attention being directed against ordeals and their supporting religious rituals. When Innocent III convened his bishops and theologians at the Fourth Lateran Council in 1215, the stage was set for an abrupt curtailment of the ancient system of trial by ordeal.

The absence of records makes it impossible to determine why the ordeal procedure became a matter of pressing concern to Innocent III just 1 year before his death in 1216. His decision to submit the matter to the Fourth Lateran Council undoubtedly reflected his belief that a consensus among his cardinals and bishops would strengthen his action. There is historical conjecture that the origins of Innocent III's preoccupation with ordeals can be traced to his experiences as a young theology student in Paris. During that time, Peter the Chanter was one of the leading theological thinkers in Europe. Peter's interest in the ordeal ceremony was precipitated primarily by the execution of one of his penitents; prior to his execution the man informed Peter that he was innocent of the criminal accusations against him but did not wish to undergo the ordeal. On refusing the ordeal, as suggested by Peter, the man was subsequently executed; this prompted Peter to conduct an exhaustive study of the ordeal process. A series of treatises emerged from his study, pointedly criticizing ordeals in both theological and legal terms. Perhaps, his most effective publication was his extensive collection of ordeal cases that had wrongly resulted in the execution of accused persons; subsequent evidence proved that many of the condemned criminals could not have committed the offenses of which they were accused and cast serious doubt on the infallibility of the ordeal. Peter took special aim at trial by battle, suggesting that if God really helped the champion of the innocent party, why should not one really obtain divine proof by selecting the most decrepit old man to be one's champion?

HISTORY TODAY

The Fourth Lateran Council decreed that the Roman Catholic Church should no longer sanction ordeals. Should modern religious institutions be able to sway the government in ending a criminal justice practice they believe to be unjust, such as the death penalty?

There is no direct known connection between Innocent III and Peter the Chanter, but the future pope studied with a student of Peter and may well have listened to Peter speak or read his treatises. Nevertheless, it is clear that the decree of November 1215 at the Fourth Lateran Council, which prohibited clerical participation in preparations for ordeals, had immediate and significant impact throughout Western Europe. Within Normandy, England, and Denmark, ordeals stopped almost immediately; records as early as 1219 indicate that the practice no longer existed in England, but trial by battle still remained in more secular garb.

In addition to the significant impact of banning the clergy from participating in ordeals, Innocent III also made public his condemnation of the Magna Carta. He also commanded that anyone other than the clergy who was caught reading the Bible should be stoned to death. This allowed the church to control and interpret the Bible and biblical knowledge the way they deemed fit. Innocent III also allowed the development of a practice called *benefit of clergy*. This system allowed clergymen to have criminal matters tried before ecclesiastical (church) rather than secular courts. Initially, this was exclusively available to members of the cloth; however, over time it became commonplace in usage and was used by men and women to avoid the death penalty. When it was introduced, the only members of society who could read and write were clergymen and nobility. Consequently, it was believed that if a man could read and recite from the Bible it was conclusive proof that he was a cleric; Psalm 51 became the standard verse that was recited in court. Psalm 51 became known as the *neck verse*. Over time, many common folk learned the words and then pretended to read them in court. In doing so, they were declared clerics and avoided hanging "By the Neck." The literacy test for benefit of clergy was abolished in 1706. The extent of 'clergyable' offences was also reduced significantly during the early 18th century. Privilegium clericale was finally abolished in 1823.

HISTORY TODAY

Whether and in what form Shari'a law should be applied today is a tremendous controversy, especially in predominantly Muslim countries. Should religion and government be merged in such a way? Many prominent Muslim leaders oppose political Islam but many advocate a strict application of Islamic law.

TIME CAPSULE: PSALM 51

Psalm 51, believed to have been written by the Israelite King David several centuries before the birth of Jesus, presents an example of repentance before God. Biblical adherents believe that David wrote the Psalm after he was confronted for a murderous affair with one of his female subjects, Bathsheba. According to the Biblical account, Kind David had an affair with Bathsheba, impregnated her, and tried to cover his crime by having Bathsheba's soldier husband killed in battle. David was confronted with his crime by the prophet Nathan, and this Psalm followed that encounter.

1. Have mercy on me, O God, according to your unfailing love; according to your great compassion blot out my transgressions.
2. Wash away all my iniquity and cleanse me from my sin.
3. For I know my transgressions, and my sin is always before me.
4. Against you, you only, have I sinned and done what is evil in your sight; so you are right in your verdict and justified when you judge.
5. Surely I was sinful at birth, sinful from the time my mother conceived me.
6. Yet you desired faithfulness even in the womb; you taught me wisdom in that secret place.
7. Cleanse me with hyssop, and I will be clean; wash me, and I will be whiter than snow.
8. Let me hear joy and gladness; let the bones you have crushed rejoice.
9. Hide your face from my sins and blot out all my iniquity.
10. Create in me a pure heart, O God, and renew a steadfast spirit within me.
11. Do not cast me from your presence or take your Holy Spirit from me.
12. Restore to me the joy of your salvation and grant me a willing spirit, to sustain me.
13. Then I will teach transgressors your ways, so that sinners will turn back to you.
14. Deliver me from the guilt of bloodshed, O God, you who are God my Savior, and my tongue will sing of your righteousness.
15. Open my lips, Lord, and my mouth will declare your praise.
16. You do not delight in sacrifice, or I would bring it; you do not take pleasure in burnt offerings.
17. My sacrifice, O God, is a broken spirit; a broken and contrite heart you, God, will not despise.
18. May it please you to prosper Zion, to build up the walls of Jerusalem.
19. Then you will delight in the sacrifices of the righteous, in burnt offerings offered whole; then bulls will be offered on your altar.

TIME CAPSULE: ISLAMIC CRIMINAL JUSTICE

Students may be appalled, and perhaps intrigued, by references in the newspapers to the harsh corporal punishments of Islamic law (Shari'a) still in effect in countries such as Saudi Arabia, Pakistan, and Sudan. In the centuries following Muhammad's death, four major schools of Islamic law have developed— Hanafi, Hanbali, Maliki, and Shafi'i—making it difficult to generalize about criminal law and procedure in the various countries that follow Shari'a. Nevertheless, it may be useful to include a brief explanation of the origin and principles of Shari'a and to indicate ways in which it differs from the civil law and common law.

The criminal law of Islamic countries derives from the revealed word of God; the basic principles of Islamic criminal law are found in the eternal and unchanging word of God expressed in the Qur'an. In addition, explications of these fundamental rules, found in the recorded sayings of Muhammad (hadith or Sunna), consensus (ijma'), and analogical reasoning (qiyas), have offered further guidance and provided the flexibility to deal with contemporary legal problems.

The realm of acts considered criminal is far wider under Islamic law than in Western systems. Because the eternal will of God governs all human acts and is to be obeyed at all times, any transgression is a crime, and in this sense there is no distinction between religious and secular offenses, along the lines of separation of church and state. Classification of crimes is determined by the punishment rather than by the harm caused by the offender, as would be the case in Western law. Shari'a identifies three categories of crime: offenses against God (hudud) for which punishment is prescribed in

Continued

TIME CAPSULE: ISLAMIC CRIMINAL JUSTICE—CONT'D

the Qur'an and Sunna; crimes of physical assault and murder (quesas), which are punishable by retaliation and can be waived for compensation; and offenses (ta'zir) whose penalties are within the discretion of the judge. Included in this roster of offenses are acts such as blasphemy, which Western countries do not punish. In December 2007, the world was reminded that blasphemy punishments are far from extinct. Gillian Gibbons, a 54-year-old British national working as a schoolteacher in the Sudan, was convicted and sentenced to 15 days in prison for blaspheming Islam. Her crime was allowing her 7-year-old students to give a teddy bear the name Mohammed. Although many Muslim men are named Mohammed, giving a teddy bear such a name was viewed as an insult to the Islamic prophet. While Sudanese government officials tried to engage in damage control from the international uproar over Gibbons' situation, thousands of demonstrators in the predominantly Muslim country complained that the punishment was too light and argued that Gibbons should be executed or given 40 lashes. Gibbons had her short sentence commuted by Sudanese President Omar al-Bashir on December 3. The President was responding to immense pressure from the British government, spearheaded in part by two Muslim members of the British House of Lords who had traveled to Sudan to lobby for her release.

The category of crime determines responsibility for initiating prosecution. Offenses against God (hudud) are to be prosecuted by the state. Crimes in the other two categories can be initiated by complaint of the victim or survivor and can be prosecuted by the state. As a protection against false accusation, the complainant can himself be punished if proof is not brought forth.

Penal law of Shari'a is indeed harsh by Western standards, both in regard to the nature of the offense and the severity of punishment. For example, the crime of apostasy (voluntary renunciation of Islam) carries a death penalty. In February 2006, a 41-year-old Afghanistan native named Abdul Rahman, who had been living in Germany for the previous 9 years, was imprisoned for apostasy. Born a Muslim, Rahman had converted to Christianity shortly before moving to Germany. The government of Afghanistan, which had been installed because of the U.S. invasion of the country in 2001, faced enormous pressure from other governments to release Rahman. However, many Afghans, including the prosecutor in the case, demanded

that Rahman be executed. Rahman was also a challenge for Afghan prison officials; he had to be isolated from the other prisoners for his own safety. Rahman was eventually released at the order of the Afghan government. He left Afghanistan for Italy in March 2006.

As is well known, a thief risks the loss of hand or foot, and adulterers can be stoned to death. The potential harshness of Islamic law is, however, modified by stringent evidentiary rules. The doctrines of presumption of innocence and a prohibition against ex post facto charges protect the defendant. In the absence of a confession, the prosecutor must produce two witnesses (usually two male Muslims) with direct knowledge of the offense. The testimony of two women could be accepted in place of that of one man. The Qur'an requires that adultery be proved by eyewitness testimony of four male Muslims or by confession on four separate occasions by the defendant in open court; understandably, few charges result in conviction.

A criminal justice system based on divine law would, of course, contravene the hallowed principle of separation of church and state embodied in the United States Constitution in 1787. Many Muslims oppose a legal system based on puritanical interpretations of the Qur'an. In today's Muslim world, there is great debate over the proper application of Qur'anic principles and how they should be applied today. Some literalists such as the Taliban in Afghanistan (the ruling authority at the time of the September 11, 2001, terrorist attacks on the United States) believe that modern life should be exactly as life was during the time of Mohammed. That is why the Taliban banned modern inventions such as television from homes and movie theaters. Other Muslims maintain that Qur'anic principles should be adapted for modern times. Some critics of Shari'a law claim that modern Islamists lack the tools of "anachronization," or using proper discretion in deciding what aspects of the Qur'an should be literally applied to modern life and what aspects should be considered as components of a past culture.

Sources: Anderson, J. N. D. (1975). *Islamic law in the modern world.* Westport, CT: Greenwood Press; Lippman, S. M., Yerushalmi, M. (1988). *Islamic criminal law and procedure: An introduction.* New York: Praeger; Ruthven, M. (1997). *Islam.* New York: Oxford University Press.

HISTORY TODAY

Although modern legal systems do not employ benefit of clergy, sometimes courts do lessen a punishment—or parole boards may be more inclined to release a prisoner—if the defendant shows an attitude of repentance or claims that he or she has experienced a religious conversion. Should a penitent's disposition make a difference in the treatment of an offender?

The impact of the Fourth Lateran Council should not be underestimated. This does not mean, however, that the monarchs of Europe were not also making considerable changes to legal procedure and practice. *Henry II*, who ruled from 1154 to 1189 is often remembered for his role in the murder of Thomas Becket in Canterbury Cathedral. In reality, this was not of such historical importance as Henry's influence on recording and writing the laws and customs of England. Often referred to as *Glanvill* and written in 1188, it is assumed to have been named after the author. It is the first time in English history where offenses, practices, and customs were recorded in a systematic manner.

> Henry II (1133-1189): First Angevin King of England; tried to fight corruption among local sheriffs in England; tried to incorporate decisions that had typically rested on the whim of the monarch into law; developed the principle of jury inquest, comprised of honest men in each county, the forerunner to the modern grand jury; notable for his role in the creation of the Constitutions of Clarendon in 1164, which asserted the right of king over the church in matters such as the appointment of bishops, excommunications, and appeals to Rome; responsible for the Assize of Clarendon in 1166, which established the procedure of criminal justice, including the creation of jury trials.

In addition to overseeing this important work, Henry also introduced *judicial Eyres or circuits*. Initially the sheriff sat at the Eyre court. Eventually this position was filled by a circuit judge. These royal judges had specific job duties: to perform the role of permanent justice of the peace, to hear and determine, to "Oyer and Terminer," specific offenses, to deliver persons to the gaol (sentence), to hear possessory claims at Assize (the seated courts; *Assize* meaning "to sit" in French), and to effect *nisi prius*. *Nisi prius* meant "unless before then." Some offenses were exclusively justiciable before the king. In addition to these matters, the king had power to summon people before him. Under this ability of *nisi prius*, the king delegated this requirement to the circuit judges who, upon attending the shire court, would act in place of the requirement that a person should attend the king personally.

Previously we have speculated about the origins of the jury system. Under Henry II, at the Constitution of Clarendon we see "Twelve lawful men in each shire shall upon oath present those suspected of murder or theft or present those persons suspected of harboring such persons." This initial establishment of the Grand Jury survived until 1933 in England and continues in numerous states in the United States today. It would not be until the thirteenth century that the petty or trial jury would be in place. Once the grand jury had found that a person was to answer an

Joseph Glanvill (1636-1680): self-described supporter of the Royal Society; defended the reality of witchcraft and the soul; most popular work was *The Vanity of Dogmatizing, or Confidence in Opinions*, in which he famously denounced scholastic dogmatism, and instead advocated a scientific approach to obtain knowledge.

allegation, it was the role of the sheriff to ensure that the suspect was appropriately detained until the circuit court arrived.

But perhaps the greatest influence Henry had over the development of English law was an expansion of the writ system. The writ system was a means of the king sending a sealed message to his sheriffs, usually in the form of deciding his judgment of a case or the punishment of an offender. Henry expanded this significantly and formulated an office, the Office of Chancery, to take responsibility for writing of writs. Over time, the office of chancery became the Court of Chancery or Court of Equity, a court of conscience where matters of inequity or wrongs, that no other court felt capable or equipped to deal with, were addressed. What Henry II and Glanvill achieved was a standardization and organization of English law that became a major influence on the establishment of the Common Law, a legal system that was to become the most widely used in the world.

FEATURED OUTLAW: ROBIN HOOD

Was Robin Hood a real person? Although this question has never been answered definitively, historians and folklorists agree that people like Robin Hood did indeed live in the forests of England during the Middle Ages. The Robin Hood story is probably part fiction, part truth, and part composite of other medieval legends. Many of the outlaws who roamed the forests of medieval England were the descendants of Anglo-Saxons, who had been displaced and disenfranchised as a result of the Norman (France) invasion of the eleventh century. Many of these outlaws had lost their property to the government, and retreated to the forest both to survive and to prey on those unfortunate enough to cross their paths. The idea of benevolent outlaw who robbed from the rich and gave to the poor is a matter of grave doubt.

Today, the label of *outlaw* is usually applied to someone who habitually breaks the law or lives a life totally outside the confines of the criminal law. However, the original definition of outlaw is tied to stories like that of Robin Hood. The term *outlawry* originally applied to a person who had been stripped of his or her civil rights—including the right to participate in government affairs, the right to own property, and the right of inheritance. Therefore, if the English government wanted to confiscate a person's property, they could declare the person an outlaw, because of either legitimate or trumped up charges, and therefore be "justified"

FIGURE 3.2 American actor Kevin Costner on the set of *Robin Hood: Prince of Thieves*. © David James/Sygma/Corbis.

in confiscating the property. Having no real recourse, the newly declared "outlaw" often retreated to the forest to join other people in the same situation, along with some unsavory characters who fled legitimate criminal charges.

FEATURED OUTLAW: ROBIN HOOD—CONT'D

There were numerous outlaw ballads surrounding the forests of medieval England. One was the Hereward legend, the ballad of a man who hunted on property owned (or stolen) by the English monarchy. According to legend, the actions of Hereward prompted the crown to enact Forest Laws, which called for harsh punishment of anyone caught hunting or farming on government-owned land. Another ballad was that of Fulk Fitzwarin, which contains a romantic element. A third ballad is that of Eustace the Monk, who had a long argument with a feudal lord over property rights.

These three ballads contain elements often associated with the Robin Hood story—abuse of government authority to confiscate property, poaching on that same land, a Catholic monk, and a romantic relationship between the primary protagonist and a female companion. There is also a great likelihood that a character named John had a

dispute with the local Sheriff of Nottingham, who was charged with protecting the Crown's property. In medieval England, a sheriff's, or shire reeve's, primary duty was collecting taxes and protecting government interests, not crime detection.

Robin Hood, the original outlaw, has served as the prototypical outlaw hero for several centuries. He has been the subject of endless writings and films. The notion of stealing from the rich to give to the poor is synonymous with the name Robin Hood. The Robin Hood of modern movies is probably a far cry from the real-life character, but the Robin Hood story stimulates the study of subsequent outlaw hero stories, and the outlaw as hero idea is part and parcel of the study of criminal justice.

Source: Wilson Web Biographies, vnweb.hwwilsonweb.com, accessed March 24, 2008.

HISTORY TODAY

Try to think of some examples now or in the recent past in which accused or convicted criminals have been made into heroes by the news media, the movie industry, or certain elements of the larger culture. Try to think of someone you regard as an "outlaw hero." Is it proper to create these heroes, especially for those whose guilt is not in question?

SUMMARY

The ending of church support for trial by ordeal created a void in all European legal systems, and new methods had to be found to determine issues of fact and the guilt or innocence of accused persons. Indeed, those new procedures were already in the process of development both on the European continent and in England. With the action of the Fourth Lateran Council, each separate kingdom was given the opportunity to institute its own substitute for the ordeal. In the vital area of criminal trials, there no longer existed a uniform transnational method approved by and supported by the western church. At this point in history, English and continental criminal procedure came to a fork in the road and went their separate ways.

Abolition of the ordeal may also be seen as a mark of increasing sophistication in judicial fact-finding and of decreased reliance on divine intervention (or miracles) in the affairs of men. In biblical Israel, legal issues were tried by drawing lots from the high priest's breastplate; Athens and Rome used "platter and loincloth" searches. People were beginning to substitute reason and informed judgment for blind reliance on these methods of superstition and chance. The Fourth Lateran Council's eighteenth canon on ordeals effectively ended a system of trial based on superstition and magic. The change left a vacuum that would be filled in continental Europe by the rise of judicial inquisition (a form of investigation) and in England by the rise of the trial jury.

REFERENCES

Pollock, F., & Maitland, F. W. (1968). *The history of English law before the time of Edward I* (2nd ed). 2 Vols. Cambridge: Cambridge University Press; Holdsworth, W. S. (1936). *A history of English law* (4th ed). London: Methuen & Co; Lea, H. C. (1973). E. Peters (Ed.), *The Ordeal*. Philadelphia: University of Pennsylvania Press; Thayer, J. B. (1898). *A preliminary treatise on evidence at the common law*. Boston: Little, Brown and Company; (1960). *Njal's Saga*. Trans. Magnusson, M., & Palsson, H. Hammondsworth, England: Penguin Books; Stephenson, C., & Marcham, F. G. (Eds.). (1972). and trans., *Sources of English constitutional history* (2nd ed), vol. I. New York: Harper & Row.

Esmein, A. (1913). *History of continental criminal procedure with special reference to France*. Boston: Little, Brown and Company; Gummere, F. B. (1892). *Germanic origins: a study in primitive culture*. New York: Charles Scribner; von Bar, C. L. (1916). *A history of continental criminal law*. Boston: Little Brown and Company; Thomas, D. A. (1985). Origins of the common law: Part II. Anglo-Saxon Antecedents of the common law. *Brigham Young University Law Review*; Whitelock, D. (1956). *The beginnings of English society*. Baltimore, MD: Penguin Books.

Windeyer, W. J. V. (1949). *Lectures on legal history*. Sydney: Law Book Company of Australia; Scott, G. R. (1959). *The history of torture throughout the ages*. London: Luxor Press; Sawyer, J. K. (1991). Benefit of clergy in Maryland and Virginia. *American Journal of Legal History, 34*; Ives, G. (1970). *A history of penal methods*. Montclair, NJ: Patterson Smith; McCall, A. (1979). *The medieval underworld*. London: Hamish Hamilton.

Notes and Problems

1. Given the existence of one's personal "law" during this period in history, what did it mean to be placed outside that law, or to be outlawed? Can you see similarities between medieval outlawry and treatment of modern-day offenders who are deprived of certain rights?
2. How well can a system of vengeance and blood feud discourage crime?
3. Is there sufficient evidence in either the Old Testament or the New Testament that God intervenes in human administrations of criminal justice? Did church participation in the ordeal provide an aura of spirituality and legitimacy to a procedure based on magic and superstition?
4. Do we still cling to the idea that the hand of God ensures justice on earth?

ENDNOTE

[1]*Washington Post*. Web site, www.washingtonpost.com, accessed December 9, 2007.

CHAPTER 4

From the Lateran Councils to the Renaissance (c. 1150-1550)

KEY TERMS

Adversarial nature	Gaol delivery	Oubliette
Appeal of felony	Great Collection of	Oyer and terminer
Bastille	Customary Law	Phillipe de Beaumanoir
Bridewell Palace	Heresy	Pleading the belly
Chivalry	Important persons	Queen Mary
Commercial revolution	Inquisition	Robert Colynson
Criminous clerks	Inquisitorial	Thomas Becket
Debtor's prison	Joan of Arc	Turba
Dungeon	Matron's juries	Vikings
Edward I	Ordinance of 1539	William Penn
Equity	Ottoman Empire	

LEARNING OBJECTIVES

1. Learn the significance of suppressing unpopular religious beliefs in the administration of criminal justice.
2. Understand the basics of the inquisitorial forms of justice prominent in Europe during the Middle Ages.
3. Learn how the appellate process began its evolution.
4. Learn some of the reasons that criminal charges could be dismissed or the punishment mitigated during this period.
5. Learn the significance of the commercial revolution in the administration of criminal justice.

6. Learn how prisons and forerunners of prisons functioned in Great Britain and France during this period.
7. Learn a brief history of the Ottoman Empire and its effect on the spreading of Islamic law throughout the Middle East and southern Europe.

Table 4.1 Time Line

England		The European Continent
Rise of accusation by men of the country (grand jury)	c. 1150	
Assize of Clarendon	1166	
	1176-1226	Waldensee and Cathari heretics suppressed through use of inquisitorial procedures
Assize of Arms	1181	
	1215	Fourth Lateran Council prohibits clergy from participating in trials by ordeal
	1229	Church council at Toulouse authorizes Dominican clergy to launch the Holy Office (Inquisition) to stop the spread of heresies
Criminal trials by petit jury common throughout England	1240	
	1260-1295	The Venetians Marco, Nicolo, and Maffeo Polo travel to Bukhara and China to establish trading relationships
	c. 1290	First mention of gunpowder in European documents
	1300-	Use of extraordinary inquisitorial procedure (including torture) expanded in French civil courts
	1347-1377	Bubonic plague, or the Black Death, kills approximately 40 percent of Europe's population
Justice of the peace becomes a local judicial official	1350	
By statute, members of grand jury prohibited from serving on petit juries to try those they indicted	1352	
	1457	Johannes Gutenberg perfects the system for using movable type; his son-in-law prints an edition of the Book of Psalms
	1492	Christopher Columbus, sailing in the service of Spain, reaches islands off the coast of North America
	1494	Treaty of Tordesillas, later confirmed by a Papal Bull, divides the newly discovered world between Portugal and Spain
	1498	Vasco da Gama, sailing in the service of Portugal, reaches India

Continued

Table 4.1 Time Line—cont'd

England		The European Continent
	1513	Nicòlo Machiavelli writes *The Prince*, a manual for statesmen that emphasizes *realpolitik*
	1517	Martin Luther posts his *95 Theses* in Wittenberg, condemning the Church's sale of indulgences
Parliament declares Henry VIII to be Supreme Head of the Church in England	1534	
	1536	John Calvin's *Institutes of the Christian Religion* published in Basle, Switzerland
	1545-1563	Three sessions of the Council of Trent reassert the primacy of the Pope and restate Roman Catholic doctrine

While the abolition of trial by ordeal was the most notable development in thirteenth-century criminal justice, it was but one of many historical trends that caused the separation of English criminal procedure from that of continental Europe. The four centuries from 1150 to 1550 witnessed rapid and fundamental changes in all areas of economic and social life. Not surprisingly, the criminal justice system responded with new initiatives, striving to achieve efficiency in law enforcement and seeking to control mounting violence, spurred on by pressures of urbanization and the upheaval of economic growth and diversification.

Vast changes took place in daily life over the course of these 400 years. They were marked by the decline of feudalism, a political system founded upon relationships between lords and vassals in which the king was, in many cases, no more than the highest-ranking lord in a given territory. The feudal system of government provided a mode of land distribution; along with ownership of lands, feudal nobles were accorded certain judicial powers over their vassals and the farming classes laboring on their lands. In fact, the modern word "felony" is derived from an offense against a feudal lord. When feudalism collapsed, down also went the local baronial court and the administration of justice fell once more into the hands of the kings.

Under feudalism, land holdings were established in self-sufficient economic entities called *manors*. These produced all of the food necessary to sustain the meager diets of Western Europeans and also provided the necessary craftsmen and manufacturing skills needed for the comfort of the manor lord and his retainers. Within the manor, the lord or bishop as manor-owning lord had virtually unlimited authority, both in civil disputes and in criminal justice. Unlike feudalism, manorialism persisted well into the seventeenth century, but its insularity and self-sufficiency were undermined as early as 1000 AD, when a revival of trade caused a growing demand for new products. Small commercial villages and towns attracted excess labor from the manors, and enterprising men recognized that mercantile activity was the path to wealth.

Taken by themselves, these changes were of great magnitude, but they were also accompanied by a growing interest in learning and experimentation known as the *Renaissance*. Seeking to understand the world around them and also to fathom the complexities of human nature and behavior, Renaissance scholars reexamined the relationship between individuals and society. Ancient systems of science, based on classical Greek authors, began to be challenged despite opposition by the Roman Catholic Church. Universities began to flourish throughout Europe and many schools introduced the study of law alongside classics, philosophy, and religion. In England, Edward III established Oriel College, Oxford, and King's Hall (now Trinity College), Cambridge, but these were not homes to the study of law for another 500 years as in England the development of *curia regis* and legal training from the "crib" or well of the court became formalized through the establishment of Inns of Court and a legal apprenticeship system. Ultimately, the Church was unable to restrain this inquisitiveness, and the lines of debate shifted from matters of science and political theory to disputes over religion.

HISTORY TODAY

Throughout history, people have been punished criminally for many types of behavior that were unpopular with various religious leaders and many religious followers. Should people be prosecuted for blatantly insulting the name or personage of Jesus Christ?

From 1150 onward, the Papacy fought a continual battle against *heresies* by criminal prosecutions (the Holy Office, or Inquisition) as well as on the battlefield, and the judicial suppression of heresy provided a background against which a new system of criminal procedure would evolve. A heresy is an opinion or doctrine that runs contrary to the prevailing church belief. Ultimately, theological heresy did not shatter Christian unity in the West. Instead, growing pressure for clerical reform and demands for adjustment in church organization triggered the soul-shaking movement of the Protestant Reformation and the equally vigorous internal reform of the Roman Catholic Church in the sixteenth century.

HISTORY TODAY

In 2005, a Danish newspaper published a satirical cartoon image of the Muslim prophet Mohammed wearing a turban and carrying a stick of dynamite. Some Islamists called for the death of those responsible for publishing the cartoon. Should governments mandate that blatantly anti-religious works such as that of art be banned for inciting violence?

Against this background of chaotic upheaval in the lives of people and nations, we must assess the way in which criminal justice changed, following the story of how English law took a separate path from that of the legal systems of continental Europe. Initially, we will trace the development of the French system of inquisitorial procedure, beginning in about 1150 and concluding with the enactment of the Ordinance of 1539. It will then be necessary to detail the evolution of the English system of jury trials, giving some attention to the ways in which both grand jury and petty (petit, or trial) juries shaped criminal law and procedure. Finally, we shall consider the impact of social and economic change on England and the continent, giving special attention to alterations in the criminal justice systems in rural England and rapidly urbanizing Italy.

THE FRENCH INQUISITORIAL SYSTEM, BURNING AT THE STAKE, AND CRIMINAL TRIALS FOR ANIMALS

The *Vikings* were the ancestors of modern Scandinavians—people from Denmark, Norway, and Sweden. From around 800-1100, they were among the most feared and aggressive seafaring peoples in the entire world, their violent and aggressive lifestyle standing in direct contrast to the largely peaceful and passive inhabitants of those countries today. They were also among the most adventurous explorers and traders of their time; some historians believe that the Vikings were the first Europeans to set foot on the North American continent. The Vikings plundered and killed, often mercilessly, practically everywhere they landed. The Vikings did not restrict their attacking to England and Paris, and lands as far south as Bordeaux were invaded. Protection from such incursions was offered by freelance knights who hired themselves out to villages as protectors, perhaps not entirely dissimilar from current-day Mafia protection racketeers.

Against this backdrop we see a custom of ancient and medieval criminal procedures based on two fundamental premises. First and foremost, the responsibility for accusing an individual of a crime rested not on the state or a public officer, but on the person or group wronged by the accused's alleged criminal activity. In the event that no accuser came forward, prosecution was impossible. In such a situation, criminal cases and private actions to collect damages for wrongdoing tended to become indistinguishable from one another in a generalized customary law. The first attempt at recording all of the customary laws was the *Great Collection of Customary Law* written by *Phillipe de Beaumanoir* in 1283.

> Phillipe de Beaumanoir (c. 1246-1296): French administrator and jurist known for his seminal work *Coutumes de Beauvaisi*, which became an early codification of old French law; believed it was crucial to record the legal rules and customs of a region in order to protect their integrity from the fleeting memories of their creators.

During this period, protection from violence or property damage depended almost entirely on the likelihood that the victim, or the victim's kindred on his or her behalf, would commence litigation. To establish whether a particular action was an established custom there was an inquest or *Turba*. At the Turba,

10 local men sat and determined whether the alleged custom was in fact a custom or not. Local use of a Turba did not cease until formal abolition in 1667. Eventually it was agreed upon that local customs needed to be written down, or codified—a process that, not unlike many facets of French law, took a considerable period of time; in this case, the work started in 1498 and took more than 100 years to complete.

In keeping with the first premise of private accusation, the second characteristic of early criminal procedure was its *adversarial nature*. In other words, the parties were charged with presenting evidence of crime on one side, and counteracting or disproving the evidence of criminality on the other side. Magistrates and triers of fact served as impartial referees of the contest, assuring that the parties followed certain rules in presenting their proofs and, ultimately, deciding between them. Only on rare occasions did a magistrate or fact-finding individual or jury independently develop evidence pertinent to the case.

Whereas England was moving slowly toward what would become an accusatorial system, in France the events of history were leading the country toward a more *inquisitorial* method of determining the veracity of an accused. The inquisitional system originated from the efforts of church courts to discover and stamp out heresies. For example, southern France, beset by a corrupt clerical establishment and immoral behavior by churchmen, erupted into a series of heretical movements, including that of the Cathari (or Albigensees). The Cathari believed that there were not only forces of good (the spiritual side of man) and evil (his physical or material passions), but also that God had two sons, Christ (the good) and Satan (the evil son who rebelled against God). The rapid growth of the Cathari drew the attention of the Third Lateran Council, which authorized a 2-year crusade against the Cathari (1179-1181); despite great bloodshed, the heresy continued to flourish until the arrival of Dominican friars. Authorized by the 1229 Council of Toulouse, the Dominicans began inquiries into the beliefs of accused persons and endeavored to eliminate heresy either by destroying the religious beliefs of the individual or by keeping the suspect from spreading the heresy to others. These investigations were called *inquisitions*. In secular criminal procedure, which began to adopt the church's methods, they became the basis for modern continental criminal justice systems.

HISTORY TODAY

France still uses a variant of the inquisitorial system; Great Britain and the United States use an adversarial system. Given that the excesses of the Middle Ages are a thing of the past, which modern system is best?

There were sharp contrasts between the older adversarial system and the new methods of inquisition. Generally, French lords had limited rights to exercise justice within their manors. Exceptions to this might include authority to administer the death penalty (such authority existed, for example, with the Lords of Flanders and Normandy. The Lord of Normandy of course became the English monarch William I and this might go some way toward explaining his zeal in extending death penalty offenses). Already noted in adversarial procedure was the role of the judge, who was to serve as an impartial referee between two contending parties. Adversarial systems were originally based on the private accuser, who was later replaced by the public prosecutor; consequently, the proof available for the judge's decision was essentially what the contending parties presented at their "battle," or trial. The judge in the inquisition received evidence discovered, not by a private accuser, but by an official investigator. If additional evidence was needed, the judge himself might inquire further into the matter, including a secret hearing of witnesses at which the accused need not be present.

During his first few years as king (1229-1270), *Louis IX* supported the creation of a sophisticated judicial system and, similar to the practice in England, an appeal against a finding of guilt by the Grand Jours (Great days or Assizes) court could be made to Paris before the Chambre aux Plaids (The Pleading Chamber). Louis IX was a popular king and many believed he was just and approachable. Louis IX died August 25, 1270. He is the only French king to have ever been declared a saint. Louis often took a personal role in the administration of justice and popular history. One legend, perhaps a myth, is that Louis would sit under his favorite oak tree in the grounds of the royal palace at Vincennes and listen to cases and pronounce judgment.

> Louis IX (1214-1270): French monarch; achieved peace with England through the treaty of Paris, which formally recognized Henry II as the Duke of Aquitaine; death in Tunis as a result of Second Crusade.

In adversarial litigation, the judge played a passive role, but in the inquisitorial system he was an active participant in the trial process. The adversarial system utilized a trial by the accused's peers (or, earlier, a trial by ordeal), while the inquisitorial system afforded a modicum of protection to the accused by permitting him or her appeal to a higher court or judge. Because the adversarial system presumed that the parties were contending with each other (if only in pleadings and words), it was essential that the parties themselves be present or the trial could not go forward. As we have noted, some significant phases of trial in the inquisitorial system might take place in the absence of the accused.

Both systems sought to determine the truth concerning the events in question, as well as judge the criminal nature of the accused's behavior. Yet their concept of truth, as well as their mode of determining it, differed markedly. The adversarial system assumed that there were at least two sides to every controversy, and it permitted the parties to present their views for the judge and jury's consideration. Truth in the adversarial system was actually a determination of which position was more likely to be correct. Truth was a matter of plausibility, mature judgment, and balancing two versions of a given event against each

FIGURE 4.1 Woodcut of an Outdoor Court Session by Hans Schaufelein, c. 1510. © Bettmann/CORBIS.

other. By contrast, the inquisitorial system demanded that one truth be ascertained by assembling all available evidence. Every effort of reason and all scientific knowledge had to be directed toward finding the truth. Only on such overwhelming evidence, and less on a lack of proof or probabilities of guilt, could an accused be declared innocent or guilty.

This emphasis on the conclusive nature of proof led to the emphasis on confession in the inquisitorial system. This demonstrated to the world that the accused accepted the conclusiveness of the proof against him or her. It exonerated judges and courts from the burden of deciding between conflicting bodies of evidence, and it reassured the public. As the inquisitorial system became more elaborate, it became standard practice to establish levels of proof adequate to convict for certain crimes. For the major crimes, it became almost impossible to obtain a conviction without having the confession of the accused person.

As confessions became a significant part of the state's case against those accused of crime, the methods used to obtain confessions were refined and perfected. Torture, limited by Roman procedure to extracting evidence from slaves, was expanded to all accused persons regardless of rank, and was also used to obtain evidence from witnesses or accomplices. There were few limits on the form that tortures could take, but French law prohibited officials from causing the loss of life or limb through torture and also from using fire in its infliction. The most common method of torture was to stretch the accused naked on a wooden horse, throw water on him, and then pour the water down his throat. After the cessation of this, or some other form of torture, the accused was permitted to regain his strength and then be re-interrogated. If the accused reaffirmed the confession, it was used as evidence, but if he did not ratify the confession previously given under torture, it was invalidated.

In the earliest stages of the French inquisitorial method, a system of ordinary trial was available. This provided an opportunity to hear the testimony of witnesses, to read depositions presented to the court, and to have a general knowledge of the case being presented by the state.

Torture was not permitted in ordinary procedure, except in unusual cases. But it was not the intention of the crown that the life of the citizenry should be worsened by the inquisitorial process and there is much evidence of a conscious effort being made to improve the life of peasants. For example, during the thirteenth century the king took personal oversight of the building of new towns and villages as evidenced through the wonderful small markets and towns established throughout the South of France during this period. Many of these towns are laid out in a checkerboard style with the central emphasis no longer being the church but rather the market square. Under the charter of Montflanquin of 1269, these towns, collectively known as *Bastides*, allowed the townsfolk to hold the right to buy and sell to whomever they chose, and not to have taxes imposed without the authority of the residents of the town, and for the first time residents were permitted by law to decide who they married. In addition, no dueling or battle to redress local feuds was permitted. Adulterers could choose their punishment: pay a fine or run through the town naked. Such pleasantries as decapitation, hanging, burning (for witchcraft, heresy, and sodomy), mutilation, and "breaking the wheel," where the accused was tied to a wheel and the executioner would break his limbs with a hammer and then leave him tied to the wheel to starve to death, remained common sentencing practices for more serious offences than adultery.

After 1300, more and more offenses came within the scope of extraordinary procedure, which did not give the accused any idea of the allegations against him and kept all testimony secret from him and the public. Interrogations and torture were performed in private, and the trial itself took place behind closed doors. By 1400, torture became a fundamental part of French criminal procedure and torture times were directly related to the time it took to recite a prayer such as the Pater Noster.

HISTORY TODAY

Whether a government should allow torture is still an ongoing controversy. Although it is seldom publicly acknowledged, torture is still routinely administered in some countries for a number of reasons—sometimes to exact a confession, sometimes to deter political dissidents, or sometimes merely for the amusement of the police officials, correctional officials, or soldiers who carry it out. Is it ever justifiable to use torture or physical coercion against anyone for any reason, even a mass murderer or terrorist?

By the mid-sixteenth century, the extraordinary method of criminal procedure was the rule in France. The *Ordinance of 1539* provided for a two-stage process, consisting of examination before one judge, followed by formal trial before the entire bench of the court. The law abolished any right to be represented by counsel and prevented the accused from examining the accusations or depositions of witnesses. However, in some instances, several defenses might be accepted: for example, one accused of homicide might obtain release by producing the victim alive. Self-defense and insanity were also available as defenses. All evidence by the accused was permitted only if the court granted the accused person's motion to prove these defenses by means of witnesses.

Trial and punishment were not restricted to humans throughout this period and animals were frequently put on trial alongside their human accomplices. In one instance, in 1494, a pig was on trial for entering a house and attacking a child. Although not subjected to torture, a trial was held, the pig was given a defending lawyer, found guilty, and sentenced to hanging and then strangulation. In Toulouse a man was hanged for the offense of bestiality with a donkey. The donkey was spared the death penalty, however, as it was held that the animal had not been a willing accomplice to the crime.

THE ENGLISH JURY SYSTEM, PRESSING CONFESSIONS, AND BOILING TO DEATH

Abolition of the judicial ordeal in England caused accelerated development of the English jury system, but not the introduction of a new method of criminal procedure. The origins of the grand jury (the body of local citizens who investigated and reported suspected crimes and serious wrongdoing to the royal justices) are unknown, but traces of the institution may be found in Germanic tribal law, Anglo-Saxon dooms, and the Norman Grand Inquest. On the other hand, the trial jury (or petty jury) seems to have evolved from some of the functions of the grand jury, a process that had begun before 1215 and that became a matter of urgency when the trial by ordeal was summarily removed from the law of western Christendom.

To further complicate English criminal procedure, the practice of private accusation persisted in regard to felonies. These prosecutions began by an *appeal of felony* brought by an interested party, and the issue of guilt or innocence was decided by combat. The appeal of a felony was one of the remaining vestiges of self-help. On the basis of the private complaint of a party claiming injury to himself or his family, it had become a mode of harassing those too poor to hire champions and too weak to participate in trial by battle. Long in disuse, the appeal of felony finally disappeared from English law in the nineteenth century. The use of the word *appeal* in this context differs from that in modern law, in which one "appeals" to a higher court against the adverse decision of a lower court. The appeal of felony, in contrast, was a proceeding at the trial court level.

Although the appeal of felony fell into disuse well before 1550, it was technically available as a mode of procedure up to 1819, when the right to claim trial by battle was demanded before the King's Bench in the case of *Ashford v. Thornton*. Embarrassed by its continued existence, the British parliament abolished trial by battle after this case, although one man attempted to resurrect this as an option in a battle against the United Kingdom's Driver License Bureau in 2002. (He failed.)

HISTORY TODAY

The appellate process has undergone many changes and grown much more complex than in the Middle Ages. Has the appeal process in modern courts become too complex?

Under Henry II, the Assize of Clarendon (1166) directed that 12 family heads of each hundred should be placed under oath and required to report all known or accused robbers, murderers, thieves, and accomplices to criminal activity to the King's justices. The term *assize* has had various meanings in English legal history. As used here, it refers to a pronouncement of law by the king, usually in consultation with his counsel, which had binding effect throughout the kingdom. On the basis of such a law, new court procedures might have been introduced and also called assizes. During the reign of Henry II, the central courts began to travel on circuit, and sessions held away from Westminster, particularly those dealing with criminal matters, were also referred to as assizes. The accused were to be tried by the water ordeal, but, even if acquitted by that method, they might nevertheless be outlawed and exiled from the realm if they had poor reputations. Of the 16 articles contained within the Clarendon constitution, most articles confirmed existing practices.

FIGURE 4.2 Artist's impression of Henry II, circa 1620. *Courtesy en.wikipedia.org.*

However, one new clause was the cause of much debate as it concerned *criminous clerks*, that is, criminal priests and members of the clergy. Under the proposed changes, members of the clergy would now be answerable to crown courts, not church courts. Any appeals to Rome, that is, to the Pope, required permission from the king. For many centuries wealth and much social control rested with the church. Perhaps not surprisingly, the church was keen to ensure that its clergymen were protected from the increasing influence of secular law. In 1170, *Thomas Becket*, Archbishop of Canterbury, was murdered; the king was implicated, by rumor, in his death. As a result of this event, the Pope was in a strong bargaining position and was able to force Henry II to rescind the requirement of the Clarendon provision that allowed benefit of clergy.

In the "Time Capsule" below there is a discussion about *"Pleading the belly,"* which called upon women, who were normally excluded from jury service, to serve on a matron's jury to determine whether or not a woman was pregnant. If the accused was with child, then she could avoid hanging until such a time as the child was born. Interestingly, although we have numerous examples of women successfully pleading that they were men, clergymen, there are no recorded instances of men successfully pleading they were pregnant to

> Thomas Becket (1118-1170): Appointed Archbishop of Canterbury, the leading religious position in England, by Henry II, who assumed that Becket would choose loyalty to the monarchy and Henry II as a personal friend; but instead clashed with the king over improper government interference in church affairs; executed by order of Henry II.

avoid the hanging gallows. Pleading the belly, introduced in 1387, was removed from the English law in 1931. The last known successful use of this plea was in 1914 by Ada Williams. Her murder conviction was commuted from hanging to life imprisonment. Williams murdered her 4-year-old child while pregnant.

TIME CAPSULE: MATRON'S JURIES

Until the twentieth century, jury service in England was restricted to men. There were, however, two exceptions to this rule. If a woman sentenced to death claimed to be pregnant, she could "plead the belly" and be granted a reprieve. The judge then would convene a special jury, composed of "twelve matrons or discreet women." The task of the matron's jury was to determine whether the woman was "quick with child"—that is, whether life in the fetus could be detected; merely being pregnant was not sufficient. Various tricks were utilized by condemned women, such as drinking to swell the belly or becoming pregnant during the pretrial period. A positive jury verdict meant that execution could be delayed until delivery or until it was shown that there was no child. A woman could call upon this form of mercy only once; if she became pregnant again, she could be executed before delivery. That pleading the belly could be a successful maneuver is attested to by the tale of *Moll Flanders* written by Daniel Defoe, a man personally acquainted with the jails and criminal justice procedures of England. The second use of a jury of women was to determine whether a woman accused of infanticide had recently given birth. The matron's jury was later replaced by medical examination.

It was not unknown for women to deliberately attempt to become pregnant while in prison awaiting hanging; a feat not so difficult to achieve given that male and female inmates were housed together and that all prison wardens were men. In days when the death sentence was carried out according to the schedule of the visiting executioner, there were often delays of some months between sentence and death. To circumvent this legal loophole, the 1752 Murder Act legislated that all condemned prisoners must be executed within 48 hours of sentence.

Source: Blackstone, W. (1962). *Commentaries on the laws of England, of public wrongs.* Boston: Beacon Press.

HISTORY TODAY

Although laws do not specifically mandate that criminal justice officials be more charitable to a pregnant woman than they would be to others, some police officers, prosecutors, judges, probation officers, and parole authorities may take pregnancy into account when making a decision. Is this fair?

It is clear that the assize directed the use of a form of grand jury to bring criminal activity before the royal judges. Although ordeal was the mode of trial, the very fact that the grand jury had reported the suspect carried with it the inference of bad reputation. While supernatural ordeals might clear the accused of wrongdoing in the case at hand, his poor standing in the community could nevertheless serve as a basis for banishment. In this way, the character of the accused was as much an issue as it had been with the Greek dicastery or the Roman quaestiones jury.

While the criminal procedure system for grand juries might seem to have provided ample basis on which to construct a trial system for petty juries, it took several decades after 1215 to make the transition. At first, the royal judges were simply directed to order the banishment of criminals presented to them by grand juries. This was consistent with the past practice, in which the accused was acquitted by ordeal but was still of suspicious character. However, it did not provide the same verification of the grand jury's finding of probable guilt, and a rational alternative to the supernatural ordeal was needed. By 1240, the trial jury was in wide use; by 1275, it was rare that members of a grand jury would serve on the trial jury of an individual they had helped to present; and by 1352, such an overlapping of personnel was prohibited by statute.

Initially, petty jury trials were sufficiently novel that defendants were given the option of either electing for this trial method or accepting banishment. The alternative of banishment might be appealing because it did not carry with it the penalties of forfeiture of goods and lands attached to conviction before a trial jury. Because many defendants were inclined to take advantage of this loophole in criminal procedure, it was accepted practice to place them under torture to compel them to plead to the case and accept trial by jury. This torture, termed *peine forte et dure*, was also known as *pressing to death*. The accused was placed in solitary confinement, starved, and then stripped naked. His or her body was then subjected to gradually increased weights of iron until he or she either pleaded to the indictment and accepted jury trial or died under the torture. Available until the nineteenth century under English law, pressing to death was ultimately replaced by the automatic entry of a "not guilty" plea on behalf of an accused person, with the resulting "acceptance" of jury trial. The last case of death by pressing in England occurred in 1735 in the market town of Horsham, Sussex.

HISTORY TODAY

In the United States, at least in states that administer capital punishment, the method of imposing capital punishment, in most cases lethal injection, is designed to be as painless as possible. Some death penalty opponents claim that this is merely an attempt to sanitize an inhumane practice. The opposite held true in many societies that practiced capital punishment in the past. If capital punishment is to be administered, should it be administered painlessly?

The availability of *peine forte et dure* in English criminal procedure makes it clear that torture and barbarism were not unique to French and continental criminal justice. Although both practices were reprehensible, the English basis for pressing was to compel the accused to accept what the state had determined to be a rational form of trial. On the other hand, the continental reason for torture during inquisition was to make the accused person admit his or her guilt, thereby eliminating the need for additional proof of culpability. In England, torture could be a precondition of trial; in Europe, it was an integral part of the trial itself.

Almost from the beginning, grand and petty juries proved to be forces for the modification or nullification of law. Early thirteenth-century cases show patterns of petty jury convictions that suggest there was public dissatisfaction with the formal rules concerning murder and simple homicide. When a killing took place as a consequence of an ambush, or at night, or when the accused hid or buried the victim's corpse, conviction was highly probable. However, if the offense occurred in the course of a fight, or in circumstances that might today be considered worthy of a manslaughter conviction, the rates of conviction were extremely low. There is also some indication that early English juries manipulated the facts presented to them and reported to the courts a group of circumstances that justified pardoning the accused either on grounds of self-defense or justifiable homicide.

Modification of formal and unpopular rules of criminal law was not the sole function of trial juries. Their function as determiners of fact had, in many respects, the same finality that had hitherto attached to judgment by ordeal. Absent proof of bribery or intimidation, the jury's verdict could not be attacked nor could the jurymen be punished. Later generations of lawyers would say that there was no appeal from a jury verdict, but even at this early stage judges must have found it frustrating to deal with criminal prosecutions in which the good reputation or popularity of the accused prevented a guilty verdict. At a time when royal justice was becoming increasingly efficient and centralized, the trial jury ensured that the ultimate decisions in criminal prosecutions were still made in the light of local conditions and preferences.

The English jury developed during an era of rapid centralization of English criminal justice. During the latter years of the twelfth century, itinerant royal judges heard cases in each county not more frequently than once every 6 years. By 1230, new systems of judicial appointment, based on commissions of *gaol delivery* and commissions of *oyer* and *terminer*, ensured semi-annual visitations and trials of presented individuals. Commissions of general gaol delivery authorized the royal justices to hear the cases of all individuals held in the jails of the counties of their circuit, whether or not charges had been filed against such individuals being held. Oyer and terminer commissions empowered the justices to hear and determine all cases of treason, felony, and misdemeanor pending in the visited counties.

Edward I (1287-1327), known as "Longshanks" due to his tall, lanky body, made two important contributions to history and particularly criminal justice. First, he was the king who brought the Stone of Scone from Scotland to Westminster and in doing so started the tradition of all British monarchs being crowned on the Coronation Stone. Second, Edward removed the burgeoning legal specialization away from the clergy and firmly placed it with secular judges and what were to become the Inns of Court. This development is particularly important as the judiciary increasingly became recognized experts in legal training and decision making. It was the recording of these decisions that formed the basis of precedent, the rule that requires a lower court to follow the ruling of a higher court, and the establishment of the Common Law.

As early as the early 1100s, English law started to look unique and very different from that of continental Europe. Uniquely the concept of chancery, or *equity* had been introduced to protect farmers from having to undergo trial by battle. The process allowed an aggrieved farmer to present himself before the Court of Chancery and apply for a writ to 12 knights (noblemen) of the Eyre (Grand Assize) and seek an alternative redress from battle. By 1300, the training of lawyers was a practical and courtroom-based 7-year apprenticeship, and by the end of the century the Court of Chivalry, around for most of the fourteenth century, was now formalized. *Chivalry*, the procedure for establishing heritage, nobility, knighthoods, and gentility when formalized into the Court, also took responsibility for the payment of ransoms and exchange of prisoners during wartime. This developed into what we know today as the Courts Martial. In terms of the trial by battle, this court was important as it was from the common courts that the Court of Chivalry determined the time, date, and place for trial by battle. The Court of Chivalry now sits only when convened, the last time being 1954, or for the coronation of a new monarch.

Ultimately, most legal decisions rested with the king. Although delegation to the courts was increasing significantly, the crown reserved the right to intercede in many matters, especially those surrounding sentencing. Royal prerogative can be seen in practice in 1398 when the future Henry IV of England, Duke of Hereford at the time, was about to duel in battle with the Duke of Norfolk. Rather than risk the death of the future monarch, King Richard II stepped in and sentenced Hereford and Norfolk to banishment.

These increasing additions to criminal procedure were not adequate to stem the growing tide of crime; by 1350, a system of royal justices of the peace had been established in each county, designed to try minor cases and to hold offenders accused of serious crimes for the arrival of the royal justices on circuit. By 1361, circuit courts could try all criminal cases at the quarterly sessions and the monthly "petty" sessions dealt with minor offenses such as "eavesdropping with a view to blackmail." There also was an increase in the role and function of the village constable to one of rural constable, a model that continued until the early nineteenth century.

The statutes of Parliament exhibited continuing concern for public safety and crime suppression, but at the same time no effort was made to modify or eliminate the institutions of grand and petty juries, both of which could be used to counteract the effectiveness of criminal prosecution. In a very real sense, the Crown and its judges depended on the cooperation of each county's population for the suppression of local crime. Acceptance of that situation is apparent in the course that English criminal justice took in the years before 1550. Jury trial became the accepted rule, and public trials were insurance against investigative excess and judicial prejudice. Except for *peine fort et dure*, torture never became an integral part of English criminal procedure, and the presence of the

Queen Mary (1542-1587) or Mary, Queen of Scots: Raised in France, practically a monarch her entire life; escaped to England after being forcibly removed as Queen of the Scots but was held as prisoner by Elizabeth I for many years; eventually executed by Elizabeth for plotting against her.

accused in court at all times provided him with information and testimony useful in shaping his defense.

Cruelty was not confined to France. Hanging and burning for heresy were all commonplace sentences in England as well. *Queen Mary* (1553-1558) authorized the burning to death of 300 Protestants during her brief reign. Until its abolition in 1790, burning was also a sentencing option for women found guilty of murdering their husbands or counterfeiting. Beheading was also utilized but reserved for the nobility, the last execution by beheading taking place in 1747 when Lord Lovat's body and head parted under the axe. For less serious matters, the stocks and pillory were often used.

Sometimes, special punishments were created, often by the king. One such example was when the unfortunate cook to the Bishop of Rochester, Richard Roose, managed to inadvertently food poison 17 of the Bishop's dinner guests. Regrettably, two of the guests died. The king intervened and created a special punishment for Richard. He was boiled alive.

Drowning was not a death sentence, but a process for revealing the truth. There were two exceptions, however; anyone who committed murder onboard a royal ship was tied to the deceased victim and thrown into the sea alive to perish alongside the victim. The second opportunity for delivering drowning as a death sentence applied to women found guilty of murder if they resided in the naval city of Portsmouth. The accused was tied to a post at the water's edge and drowned on the incoming tide. As we have seen, by 1500, defining crimes had moved away from the church and become vested with secular courts. But the power of the church had not completely waned. Until the reformation, it retained jurisdiction over matters such as working on feast days and numerous sexual misconduct offenses.

COMMERCIAL REVOLUTION, RISING POPULATIONS, AND RISING CRIME

With the single possible exception of the Industrial Revolution (c. 1700-1850), no economic movement has had a greater impact on Western civilization than the *commercial revolution* that began in about 1200 and has continued into modern times. This was characterized by a gradual reestablishment of trade, not only within Europe and Britain, but also by sea routes in the Mediterranean, the Red Sea, and the Indian Ocean. Throughout this early period in history, transportation followed rivers and navigable waters rather than land routes and, for this reason, the Mediterranean areas of Europe were the first to experience commercial development. Their access by sea to the coasts of the Holy Land and the Near East (demonstrated by the ready transport of armies to fight the Crusades) ensured that the Italian city-states would become centers of wealth and commercial power, while northern Europe and Britain remained locked in an agrarian economic system, and thus had less wealth and prestige than their southern neighbors. Exploiting their advantages as trading centers, Venice, Milan, Florence, and Genoa established industrial activity early. This included specialized craft industries supervised by guild organizations; examples are the goldsmith and silversmith guilds and the more mundane occupations of iron makers, carpenters, shipbuilders, and masons. Other industrial activity, for the most part also under guild control, included cloth-making, rope-making, tailoring, and leather work. These manufacturing processes added economic value to the raw materials that passed through the Italian cities and, as a consequence, added to the wealth of the craftsmen and guilds of those urban centers.

Throughout Europe and Britain, there was related growth in the sense that commercial towns developed for the purpose of trading with Italian cities and for the sale of trade goods to smaller towns and villages in the rural areas of Europe. London served as such a commercial center in England, as did Paris in France. Over the course of the four centuries after 1150, these northern European trading centers became equal in wealth and prestige to their Italian counterparts.

Rising populations in cities caused an increase in theft and other property-related offenses. It is estimated that about 50 percent of the crimes prosecuted in early modern Europe were property crimes, while only 30 percent were violent crimes. Sources contemporary to the period, as well as historical research thereafter, suggest that the growing incidence of property crime is attributable to greater opportunity to participate in theft and other attacks on private property. Unlike modern cities, the trading settlements of the late Middle Ages and the Renaissance were not divided into sectors restricted to the wealthy and other areas designated as ghettos for the poor. The servants and retainers of wealthy nobles and merchants lived in the immediate vicinity of their master's residence, if not within the house enclosure itself. There was ample opportunity to observe the lifestyle and daily itinerary of the well-to-do victim in order to plan a burglary or theft with the advantage of good and reliable information.

Such an environment created a strong incentive to engage in criminal activity. Economic prosperity resulted in a wide disparity between the standards of living of the rich and those of the urban poor. Economic necessity and class-related tensions helped to increase the likelihood of property-related crime. Similarly, cities provided an excellent facility for "fencing" stolen goods. Thefts of jewelry, household paintings, and other valuable personal adornments were encouraged by a ready market for stolen goods. To a lesser degree, this was also true of smaller towns near the cities, but thieves in rural areas were deprived of this urban-centered service. As a consequence, the rural thief concentrated on farm implements, draft animals, and food or clothing for him or his family.

HISTORY TODAY

Do you think it is true that poverty leads to criminality? If so, why do rich people commit crime, and why is it that all poor people do not commit crime?

Commercial growth depended on the maintenance of peace, both between international trading partners and within the cities where trade was to be conducted. As a result, violence was discouraged, and the authorities did their best to ensure the safety of alien merchants and tradesmen. In Italy, they seem to have been less than successful, in large part because of the continuing taste of the nobility for blood vengeance and the degree to which the noble class did violence to individuals of lesser rank. Incidences of sex-related crimes within Venice are a good illustration of this tendency. For example, in Venice, it was common for a nobleman to rape a woman of a lower class, and the penalties were generally so nominal that it was not worth the expense to bribe the judge or purchase the silence of the victim. On the other hand, no noble-woman over the course of nearly 200 years complained of being raped by anyone other than a member of her own class. To some degree, this may have been due to the common practice of secluding unmarried noblewomen, but it was also attributable to the harsh penalties provided for such an offense. Yet even in an environment in which the machismo of noblemen was given relatively free rein, there were limits beyond which the rapist might not go. It was a taboo punishable by death to rape a girl under the age of puberty, and similar harsh punishment was available for those convicted of bestiality or homosexual activity.

The class of *"important persons,"* ranking just below the urban nobility in status, was composed largely of merchants and owners of manufacturing establishments. This urban bourgeoisie was strongly devoted to the ideal of civic peace and tranquility. However, the virtual isolation of the nobility from the violence of the lower classes meant that laboring class resentment found its outlet against the "important persons." These "important persons" were the principal victims of property-related offenses and absorbed more than their share of the violent crimes. Nobles met with violence mainly as a consequence of their duties as leaders of police units charged with enforcing law and order.

Laboring and seafaring classes in Italian cities were the sources of most criminal activity. Most were unfamiliar with local customs and procedures because their population shifted frequently; all were kept at or below a subsistence standard of living. Easy access to the wealth of the upper class was a continuing temptation, as was the aggravating factor of the violence of nobles against the persons, wives, and property of the working man. In this shifting population, it was difficult to identify a person accused of crime, and the conditions of urban existence made crime an easy and relatively safe way of life. It was highly dangerous to move about the cities at night; the lack of any street lighting gave the advantage to criminals bent on robbery or murder. Special patrols were established to keep the streets clear, but could not provide adequate protection in all areas at all times. In Venice, women carefully avoided certain ferries renowned for the number of assaults and rapes committed in the course of a trip across the Grand Canal.

Italian city officials reacted by establishing a police system based on patrols commanded by noblemen. Heavy penalties were imposed for assaults on a member of the patrol, and attacking or killing a nobleman carried an extremely harsh punishment, rarely less than death. Magistrates had broad discretion in sentencing, and penalties ranged widely, depending on the social rank of the accused and the victim, the amount of property involved (if any), and the degree to which the crime disturbed public order. Capital punishment was designed to expiate community feelings of vengeance and deter would-be criminals. The execution ritual required that the condemned man or woman be marched from prison to the place where the offense had taken place. There, he or she would be mutilated by the removal of the offending member (usually a hand in the case of theft or murder). Then the convict was marched back to the place of execution, to be hung if a man or burned alive if a woman. In Florence, the crowds added to the ceremony by urging the official tormenters to keep torturing irons at high temperatures throughout these marches; executioners who failed to keep the convict howling by this method were occasionally killed on the spot by the mob.

HISTORY TODAY

In some countries, mutilation, or amputation, is still employed under some circumstances. Such an idea often finds favor in general conversation, or in moments of frustration, but few if any public officials seriously entertain such an idea. What should be the policy of the United States toward countries that do employ amputation?

FEATURED OUTLAW: ROBERT COLYNSON

One striking thing about English criminality during this period was the intense involvement of clergy in a wide variety of offenses. Violence and theft by lower orders of clergy were common. Nuns were recruited into schemes for prostitution; churches and priories served as places of refuge and refreshment for outlaw bands. Clerical literacy, and the access of clergy to the confidence of royal officials, made forgery of deeds and the counterfeiting of seals a clerical criminal specialty. Among the most enterprising of clerical criminals was Robert Colynson, a fifteenth-century priest who began his career as a confidence man by offering to represent fellow clerics before the Curia courts in Rome. He pocketed the fees they offered and never appeared to defend the cases. Discovered in this fraud, he moved on to obtain the savings of a wealthy widow through his assurances that her soul would never suffer pain while he prayed for her. Frequently visiting convents, he preached strong sermons urging the need for absolution and then collected a shilling from each nun to buy absolution in Rome. He retained the money and repeated the procedure several times before his reputation spread. Colynson lived openly with another man's wife, attempting at one point to kill the woman's husband. He also misbehaved with a young female parishioner and, on another occasion, romantically fondled a boy of 11. Despite all of these lapses, he avoided trial in a church court, was acquitted in royal courts on a charge of treason, and died in possession of the rectorship of Chelsfield in Kent and as the absentee bishop of Ross in Ireland.

Given the derelictions of English clergy in general, it should come as no surprise that the students and faculty at Oxford, who were all either ordained clergy or clerks in orders, were responsible for countless outbreaks of murder, theft, and mob violence. Because of their clerical status, all were entitled to the more lenient procedures of the church courts. As a consequence, the crime rate for Oxford was among the highest in England, and Cambridge was probably not far behind.

While outbreaks of violence are uncommon in today's Catholic clergy, the perception that the Church goes too far in protecting its priests has not gone away. Throughout its history, the Roman Catholic Church has been criticized for protecting those among its clergy who commit crimes. This criticism is still very real today, with revelations in recent years about bishops covering up the crimes of pedophile priests.

England provides a striking contrast to Florence and Venice. No commercial centers were of great consequence beyond the city of London, and royal authority diminished as one moved away from the capital city. Local magnates in outlying areas exercised great influence on the deliberation of judges and local juries; they also maintained their own private armies for revenge and personal protection. In wooded and remote areas, bands of outlawed men preyed upon local residents and plundered merchants attempting to trade with provincial towns. There is reason to believe that the English nobility was less violent in criminal behavior than the Italian urban elite, and the statistics show a much lower rate of involvement in criminal activity. This is not to say that English or French royalty and nobility had lost their taste for mayhem. Quite the contrary, they had been directed into the form of the tournament or jousting, in which many a noble contestant was either seriously wounded or killed under suspicious circumstances. The reign of Henry II of France ended abruptly on July 10, 1559, when a jousting lance entered his eye, a wound that killed him.

MEDIEVAL PENOLOGY, ROYAL PRISONS, AND FRENCH DUNGEONS

The late Middle Ages gave little thought to problems of penology. In a general sense, there was an effort to measure the severity of the punishment by the magnitude and circumstances of the crime, and there was clearly an element of public vengeance in many of the sanctions that were imposed. Perhaps the major change during the four centuries before 1550 was the movement toward imprisonment as a punishment. Hitherto, mutilation had been common, and this form of physical punishment had been followed by economic sanctions. However, fines quite frequently resulted in the offender serving time in prison as a debtor to the state when he or she could not pay the fine. Gradually, it became the rule to impose a prison term in lieu of the fine, leading to the use of imprisonment itself as a form of punishment. Early prisons had served merely as places of detention for those awaiting trial, but now removal from society became an accepted form of sentence. By current standards, prison terms during these times may seem unduly short, but it should be remembered that the prison provided nothing but a place of confinement. Food, clothing, medical supplies, firewood, and all other necessities had to be supplied by friends or relatives, or purchased from extortionate jailers. Privileges to leave a cell or to walk in the prison yard, for example, were also available at a price. For the wealthy, prison was an inconvenience; for the poor, it might easily lead to starvation, disease, and death.

The first prison to be opened in England was a *debtor's prison*. Historians are unable to give an exact date to the opening of this prison but it is known that it was during the twelfth century. It was located in Fleet Street, London, and at one time housed *William Penn* before his departure for America. Fleet Prison, the "Largest Brothel in England" (so named because male and female prisons were mixed together) closed in 1842.

In 1515, a new palace, at a cost of $80,000, was constructed for King Henry VIII. In 1553, the *Bridewell Palace*, named after the St. Brides Inn, which was demolished to make room for the royal residence, was given by King Edward VI to the city of London to house the homeless and "punish disorderly women." After listening to sermons by Thomas Lever and Bishop Nicholas Ridley, the young King Edward VI decided to create an institution to receive the vagabonds and those who were otherwise idle

William Penn (1644-1718): Arrested and tried in England in 1670 for holding a meeting of Quakers; a jury refused to find him guilty and the angered judge held the jury, without food or water, for contempt of court until they found Penn guilty; the jury still refused and the judge convicted Penn of contempt of court for failing to remove his hat when he originally arrived in the courtroom; he soon left England for the American colonies and the establishment of the commonwealth of Pennsylvania.

and destitute. By 1576, it was decreed that bridewell "work" prisons should be established in every county throughout England. Bridewells became not just places of refuge for the homeless or prisons for miscreant females; they also served as places for work training and trade schools. It was always the intention that bridewells would be financially self-sufficient rather than being just centers for punishment. However, as a reminder of punishment the welcome greeting for all women and children was 12 lashes with the whip.

Increasingly, the distinction was made between those who could not work to support themselves and those who, with proper training and the development of habits of industry, could earn a living. By 1576, the distinction was clearly made by parliamentary statute, and the helpless poor were put on the poor rolls of the counties and parishes; the able-bodied poor were assigned to houses of correction, or bridewells, for training.

Early in their confinement, bridewell residents did the simplest and most menial of tasks, but as they showed promise, they were promoted to positions in which they learned skills marketable in the business and industrial communities. Coercion was applied in securing the cooperation of inmates in the work of the bridewell, and the production was such that authorities thought that the bridewells were virtually self-supporting. Cloth-making, weaving, spinning, and ironmongering were among the crafts conducted within these institutions. Unfortunately, overcrowding and a decline in public and official interest had, by 1581, made the bridewells virtually indistinguishable from the prisons. Little actual production took place, and it was not uncommon for individuals who came to the notice of the local justices of the peace to find themselves in bridewells for punishment.

Established on the same basis as the bridewell, the Rasphuis and Spinhuis of Amsterdam (1596) were correctional institutions established for men and women, respectively. Designed to provide vocational training, along with punishment for idleness, both facilities began their inmates working on the simplest tasks and gradually increased their training as their skills became evident. The men's house drew its name from the rasping of wood to make dyes, while the women's was identified with the cloth production of its inmates. Both institutions were visited by European penal reformers, who brought the ideas home to their own countries and were responsible for establishing a number of houses of correction.

HISTORY TODAY

Local jails are still often referred to as *America's poorhouses*, in part because they house inmates who cannot afford to post bail, or offenders who fail to meet court-imposed financial obligations such as restitution, fines, and child support. Are there practical alternatives to such practices?

In France the concept of the *dungeon* was gaining notoriety. The word *dungeon* derives from the French *donjon*, meaning a keep or tower. But the notion of a dungeon as a dark enclosed space is better captured by the word *oubliette*, meaning a forgotten place. Early prisons were often places where the prisoners were incarcerated and literally forgotten. Prisons, rather than dungeons, were first established in France during the fourteenth century. In 1370, the infamous *Bastille*, meaning "fortress," was constructed in Paris. Like the Bridewell Palace in London, the Baston de Saint Antoine was constructed as a residence. It was Louis XIII, known as Louis "The Well Beloved," who converted the Bastille into a prison.

By 1568, French law attempted to treat children separately from adult prisoners and all children under the age of 12 years were spared whipping as a form of punishment within prisons. In both England and France, it was many centuries before women became involved in the supervision of female prisoners. It may be the case that one reason *Joan of Arc* continued to wear men's clothing while imprisoned awaiting trial for heresy was that she wanted to be seen as a male rather than female prisoner and by doing so wanted to avoid sexual assaults that were commonplace against female inmates. However, prison attire or the wearing of a common uniform became normal practice in France and even royal prisoners had to relinquish their fine garments and wear a uniform.

The waning of the Middle Ages resulted in severe adjustments of the social and economic system, and it produced criminal behavior of greater magnitude and greater variety. A rapid increase of population, estimated at about 150 percent for the years from 1450 to 1599, put great urgency on the need to modernize the criminal justice system. Law enforcement procedures exacerbated the class divisions in society, and conflicting opinions of noblemen made constructive change difficult. For a time, at least, the crisis in criminal justice was subordinate to the turmoil of the Protestant Reformation and the religious wars, but it would also be accentuated by those troubled times and, in turn, be shaped by them.

Joan of Arc (1412-1431): An exceptional—because of her gender and age—French military and political leader; once captured by the English; condemned as a heretic for stating that her first allegiance was to God and not the Roman Catholic Church; executed by burning by a government court; posthumously cleared of wrongdoing and made a saint by the Roman Catholic Church; one of the great feminist heroines in world history.

TIME CAPSULE: THE TURKS IN THE GOLDEN AGE OF ISLAM

The eighth to the thirteenth centuries are often referred to as the *Dark Ages*, but this label only makes reference to most of Europe. For Islam, it is referred to as the *Golden Age*, or the *Islamic Renaissance*. Islam experienced a period of growth unmatched since that time, and it represents a period that many modern Muslims strive for today.

The Muslims of those centuries made tremendous strides in mathematics, the natural sciences, architecture, agriculture, literature, philosophy, economics, and science and education in general. Western civilization realized great benefits from these innovations. Many of the early Muslim political and military advances were made by various ethnic groups under the protection and tolerance of Arabs, as Islam has its genesis in the Arab world, but this was also an age that saw Islam spread to Southern Europe, to Africa, and to South Asia.

The political war over who should succeed Mohammed, Islam's founding prophet, pitted followers of Ali, who was Mohammed's cousin and son-in-law, against followers of Abu Bakr, Mohammed's father-in-law. The followers of Ali eventually became known as *Shia Muslims* and the believers in Abu Bakr as Mohammed's rightful successor became known as *Sunni Muslims*. Today, Sunni Muslims greatly outnumber Shia Muslims. Shia Muslims constitute a majority in Iran and Iraq, but in most countries, Shia Muslims are greatly outnumbered by Sunni Muslims.

Among the ethnic groups that embraced Islam were the Turks. The war also resulted in a diminished tolerance for political and cultural pioneers, and as a result many Muslims moved to Anatolia (modern Turkey) and lived under the protection of the Ottoman Empire. During that period, Mevlana Celalleddin Rumi, Yunus Emre, and many other Muslim philosophers lived freely and discussed their ideas without fear of punishment. The Turks established the Ottoman Empire, also called the *Ottoman Caliphate*, which survived and outlasted the Islamic Golden Age. The Ottoman Caliphate lasted from approximately 1300 to the early twentieth century, exercising its greatest influence during the sixteenth and seventeenth centuries. At its peak, the Ottoman Empire encompassed most of Southeastern Europe, North Africa, the Middle East, and much of South Asia. In part because of its strategic location, Turkey is still referred to as a place where East meets West, where Islamic and Asian cultures intersect with Western and Christian cultures.

As Ottoman political and military influence spread during the Golden Age, so did its influence in legal matters. Among the branches of Islamic jurisprudence, one is the Hanafi branch, which was named after its Iraqi Arab founder, who lived in the eighth century. Although Turks do not regard themselves as strict adherents to Hanafism, it was the Hanafi branch of Islamic jurisprudence that held sway in the Ottoman Empire. A legacy of religious tolerance and secularism in government matters is very evident today in modern Turkey, largely because of Turkey's ethnic and cultural diversity. Most modern Turks, while practicing Islam in their everyday life, are strong believers in secular government, although, as is the case in many Muslim countries, this strong secular tradition in legal and government matters is under threat from some Muslim fundamentalists within Turkey.

The Ottoman version of Shari'a (Islamic) Law allowed some degree of religious freedom for other religions. It was intolerant of polytheistic (more than one god) religions, but tolerant to a great degree of "people of the book," namely Christians and Jews. Christians and Jews were subject to a tax, called the *Jizya*. The Ottoman judicial model typically employed separate courts for Muslims and non-Muslims. Muslims would not sit in judgment of non-Muslims and vice versa. Judges were appointed by the government. Judges were educated and trained in Imperial schools. Caliphs established law schools throughout the Ottoman Empire. The civilian judges had their greatest influence in the large Turkish cities. Because of threats to their safety, these civilian judges were not as influential throughout the rest of the empire, where the military typically administered a more authoritarian brand of justice.

While all Muslim cultures enjoy some similarities, Islamic law and criminal justice administration vary among the various ethnicities and nationalities that employ it. In the Ottoman Empire, government leaders relied on more than strict interpretations of the Qur'an in creating laws. They employed their own discretion, which was influenced more by Turkish tradition and culture than its Muslim Arab counterpart. Local custom and tradition blended with Islamic principles in establishing crimes and their punishments. Ottoman rulers claimed that the Qur'an empowered leaders to apply Islamic principles to the application of Shari'a as

TIME CAPSULE: THE TURKS IN THE GOLDEN AGE OF ISLAM—CONT'D

long as it conformed to the basic spirit of Islam. The Ottomans made little claim to the idea of a judiciary independent of the ruling authorities; Ottoman judges largely ruled in accordance with the orders of the governing authorities. Compared to other Muslim governments, the Ottomans were unique in establishing a legal tradition embodied in legal codes called *kanun-name*, which reflected the beliefs of lawgivers, called *Kanuni*. This is similar to the principle of *stare decisis*, or the law of precedent, which is a foundation of common law, on which the American system of law is based. Most of the upper echelon Kanuni, who dealt with cases of significant consequence, were highly educated, but their lower court counterparts were not.

The Ottomans, especially in Anatolia, established an alternative justice system of sorts. Its origins lie in the very early days of the Ottoman Empire. Many Ottomans held this system in higher regard than the one officially administered by the state. This justice system was based on a board of Chamber. This Chamber (*AhiLoncas*) consisted of local craftsmen who had won the respect of the people through mastering their craft. People were deferential to this Chamber, which in some cases included women. Serving much like a modern arbitration or mediation body, the Chamber strove to resolve a dispute to the satisfaction of both sides. Such a chamber was effective with petty crimes and civil cases, but complex and serious crimes such as murder were harder to deal with. In some cases, the Chamber was so successful that they acted as a voice of the people, in defiance of the ruling Sultans. As a result, some Chamber members were killed by soldiers of the Sultans. When such persecutions backfired, the Sultans eventually realized they were better off allowing the Chambers to operate independently, and the two often rival entities operated alongside each other until the fall of the Ottoman Empire.

The Ottoman Empire was the remnant of the Golden Age of Islam, the lone Islamic world power whose influence on the world stage lasted into the twentieth century, only to be dissolved as a result of its disastrous defeat during World War I. During World War I, the Ottoman Empire allied itself with the Central Powers, which included Germany and the Austro-Hungarian Empire. The Central Powers were defeated by the Allies, which included the United States, Great Britain, and France.

As a result of this defeat, the Ottoman Empire was carved into nation-states that in large measure reflected the political and commercial interests of Western Europe, rather than the indigenous peoples of the Middle East. The effects of this breakup are still being felt today. Nation-states in the Middle East and Africa are still striving for a national identity, and an end to border disputes, most prominent among them involving Israel, and the Kuwait/Iraq dispute, which provoked the Persian Gulf War of the early 1990s. Iraqi President Saddam Hussein argued that Kuwait was an illegitimate state created by European economic interests, and that it rightfully belonged to Iraq. Hussein lost the argument by virtue of being defeated in the Gulf War. During the Second Gulf War which started in 2003, he was captured by the U.S. Army and ultimately executed by the new Iraqi government, but the debate about the remnants of the Ottoman Empire remains.

Sources: Drapkin, I. (1989). *Crime and punishment in the ancient world*. Lexington, MA: Lexington Books; Hourani, A. (1991). *A history of the Arab peoples*. Cambridge, MA: Belknap Press. Thanks to Gurson Savut, Dr. Yaprak Savut, and Tolun Savut for their contributions to this section.

SUMMARY

The abolition of the ordeal launched European nations and England on two different courses of criminal procedure. Using methods devised by the church to combat heresy, continental nations such as France developed an inquisitorial system designed to provide an exhaustive investigation seeking the truth concerning an allegation of criminal activity. Gradually, the ordinary methods of inquisition gave way to extraordinary procedure, which stressed denial of information to the accused, isolation from counsel, and the use of coercion (including torture) to secure a confession. In contrast to the inquisitorial method, in which the judge was the principal investigator, the English system retained the adversarial nature of the older procedural system. Drawing upon pre-Lateran Council development of a type of grand jury, the English devised a system of trial through a petty jury that decided issues of fact. The parties themselves provided the evidence to be considered by the trial (petty) jury.

Revival of commerce in southern Europe set the stage for a shift of population to urban areas and an increase in the crime rate due to greater opportunity for property-related crime and increased probability of interpersonal violence. Increasingly, class structure played a role in the administration of criminal justice. The rise of certain privileged classes, such as the nobility in Italian city-states and the clergy in England, had a significant impact on the volume and nature of crime. At this time, there was a clear increase in crimes such as forgery, counterfeiting, and confidence games, all of which depended on the learning or social status of the perpetrator.

REFERENCES

Esmein, A. (1913). A history of continental criminal procedure: With special reference to France. Trans. Simpson, J. Boston: Little, Brown & Co.; von Bar, C. L. (1916). A history of continental criminal law. Trans. Bell, T. S. Boston: Little, Brown & Co.; Mueller, G. O. W., & Poole-Griffiths, F. L. (1969). Comparative criminal procedure. New York: New York University Press; Pollock, F., & Maitland, F. W. (1968). In S. F. C. Milsom (Ed.), (2nd ed). The history of English law before the time of Edward I, 2 vols. Cambridge: Cambridge University Press Plucknett, T. F. T. (1956). A concise history of the common law (5th ed). London: Butterworth & Co.; Green, T. A. (1984). Verdict according to conscience: Perspectives on the English criminal trial jury, 1200-1800. Chicago: University of Chicago Press; Weisser, M. R. (1979). Crime and punishment in early modern Europe. Atlantic Highlands, NJ: Humanities Press; Bellamy, J. (1973). Crime and public order in England in the late Middle Ages. London: Routledge & Kegan Paul; Given, J. B. (1977). Society and homicide in thirteenth century England. Stanford: Stanford University Press; Langbein, J. H. The origins of public prosecution at common law. American Journal of Legal History, 17(4); Oldham, J. C. (1985). On pleading the belly: A history of the jury of matrons. Criminal Justice History, 6; Wrightson, K. (1980). Two concepts of order: Justices, constables and jurymen in seventeenth-century England. In J. Brewer & J. Styles (Eds.), An ungovernable people: The English and their law in the seventeenth and eighteenth centuries. London: Hutchinson; Ruthven, M. (1978). Torture: The grand conspiracy. London: Weidenfeld and Nicolson; Summerson, H. R. T. (1979). The structure of law enforcement in thirteenth century England. American Journal of Legal History, 23(4); Post, J. B. (1986). The justice of criminal justice in late-fourteenth-century England. Criminal Justice History, 7.

Crook, D. (1991). Triers and the origin of the grand jury. Journal of Legal History, 12(2).

Cockburn, J. S., & Green, T. A. (Eds.), (1988). Twelve good men and true: The criminal trial jury in England 1200-1800. Princeton: Princeton University Press; Ruggiero, G. (1980). Violence in early Renaissance Venice. New Brunswick: Rutgers University Press; Wolfgang, M. E. (1956). Socioeconomic factors related to crime and punishment in Renaissance Florence. Journal of Criminal Law,

47; Blanshei, S. R. (1983). Criminal justice in medieval Perugia and Bologna. *Law and History Review*, 1.

Burford, E. J., & Shulman, S. (1992). *Of bridles and burnings: The punishment of women.* New York: St. Martin's Press; Naish, C. (1991). *Death comes to the maiden: Sex and execution: 1431-1933.* New York: Routledge.

Abbott, G. (1991). *Lords of the scaffold: A history of the executioner.* New York: St. Martin's Press.

Harding, A. (1973). *Law courts of medieval England.* London: Allen & Unwin; Moore, L. E. (1973). *The Jury: Tool of kings, palladium of liberty.* Cincinnati: Anderson Publishing Co; Dawson, J. (1960). *A history of lay judges.* Cambridge: Harvard University Press; Barlow, F. (1960). *Thomas Becket.* Berkeley: University of California Press; Butler, J. (1995). *The quest for Becket's bones: The mystery of the relics of St. Thomas Becket of Canterbury.* New Haven: Yale University Press; Pain, N. (1964). *The king and Becket.* London: Eyre & Spottiswoode; Winston, R. (1967). *Thomas Becket.* New York: Alfred A. Knopf.

Notes and Problems

1. Can you accept the adversarial method of trial? Does not the adversarial method incite at least one party to lie?

2. Is a confession obtained under torture more or less valid than one given voluntarily?

3. The English trial jury, along with the Greek dicastery and the Roman quaestiones jury, indicates a general preference for group decision over the judgment of a magistrate or judge. Do you agree with the basic premises upon which these various forms of jury trial depend? Why are juries drawn from the vicinity in which the crime was committed? Are they influenced by public opinion? Should they be?

4. If you were on the ruling council of an Italian city-state, how would you restructure the criminal justice system to combat the new crime wave? Should individuals (such as nobles in Italy and clerics in England) have immunity from prosecution?

5. Should criminal law be structured and administered so that it preserves class status and maintains stability in society? Was the "important person" in Renaissance Italy better protected from violence and more secure from public prosecution than the plebeian citizen of Rome in the late Republic?

CHAPTER 5

Criminal Justice and the English Constitution up to 1689

KEY TERMS

Act of Six Articles

Bible codes

Bushell's case

Declaration of Rights

Glorious Revolution

Glorious Revolution of
1688-1689

Guillame de Lamoigen

Guy Fawkes

Habeas Corpus Act of
1679

Justice of the peace

Levellers

Magna Carta

Martin Luther

Matthew Hopkins

Monmouth's Rebels

Newgate Prison

Oath *ex officio*

Phrenology

Popish plot

Princess Jabirouska

Protestant Reformation

Regicide

Sir George Jeffreys

Sixty-first clause

Star Chamber

LEARNING OBJECTIVES

1. Understand the impact of the Protestant Reformation on the administration of criminal justice.
2. Learn about the igniter of the Protestant Reformation, Martin Luther.
3. Learn how the Glorious Revolution affected criminal justice.
4. Learn about the Star Chamber, one of the ways in which justice was carried out in secret.
5. Learn about the creation of the position of justice of the peace.
6. Understand the role of Levellers in the administration of criminal justice.
7. Understand the Habeas Corpus Act of 1679 as a forerunner of modern *habeas corpus* rights.
8. Read and understand how the Declaration of Rights was a precursor to the American Bill of Rights.

9. Learn about one of the earliest documented examples of serial murder in France.
10. Learn about the creation of Great Britain's Newgate prison.

Table 5.1 Time Line: The English Constitution, 1215-1689

1215	An army raised by the barons defeats King John at Runnymede. During negotiations, the King grants Magna Carta, promising to respect the feudal privileges of the barons, to protect the borough towns and merchants, and to conduct criminal trials in accordance with the "law of the land." The "law of the land" provision is the forerunner of "due process of law" in modern judicial procedure.
	Thereafter, each English monarch at his or her coronation swore to uphold the principles of Magna Carta.
1327	Deposition of King Edward II for failure to uphold Magna Carta.
1485	Henry VII proclaimed King of England by Parliament after his victory at Bosworth Field; establishes the House of Tudor.
1529-36	Henry VIII obtains an annulment of his marriage to Catherine of Aragon, and Parliament separates the English Church from the authority of the Pope. A Parliamentary statute declares Henry to be Supreme Head of the Church in England.
1603	James VI of Scotland succeeds Elizabeth I and establishes the House of Stuart as King James I of England.
1604	At a Hampton Court Conference, members of Parliament and James I disagree about the powers and privileges of the House of Commons.
1611	The "King James," or Authorized Version, of the Bible is published.
1616	James I dismisses Sir Edward Coke from his position as Chief Justice of the Court of King's Bench.
1628	Parliament addresses the Petition of Right to King Charles I, demanding that Parliament be consulted before new taxes are imposed, that similar approval be required before troops can be quartered in private dwellings, and that Parliamentary action be required before military law can apply to civilians.
1629-40	King Charles I begins a period of personal rule, omits calling Parliamentary elections.
1641	Long Parliament abolishes courts of High Commission and Star Chamber.
1642-46	English Civil War. The Royalist forces are defeated by the New Model Army under Oliver Cromwell.
1649	King Charles I executed after being adjudged a traitor.
1653	The Instrument of Government is adopted as the form of Parliamentary government in the English Commonwealth. It establishes a Lord Protector to execute the laws, to be assisted by a council. Parliament to meet at least once in 3 years.
1653-58	Oliver Cromwell becomes Lord Protector until his death in 1658.
1660	Charles II called by Parliament to accept the Crown.
1670	*Bushell's Case* holds that juries may not be imprisoned for their refusal to convict an accused person.
1679	Habeas Corpus Act is passed by Parliament.
1685-88	James II succeeds upon the death of his brother, and attempts to restore England to Roman Catholicism. A coalition of Parliamentary leaders calls William of Orange and Mary, James II's daughter by his first marriage, to the throne. James flees to the Continent.
1689	William and Mary agree to the Bill of Rights, which declares Parliament to be an active force in government and imposes substantial limits on royal authority and the exercise of the royal prerogative.

The *Protestant Reformation* had an unlikely beginning in the austere cell of a German monk, *Martin Luther*, whose theological views were different enough from those of the Papacy that they eventually resulted in his excommunication as a heretic. When Luther nailed his Ninety-Five Theses to the church door in Wittenberg (1517), he launched both a theological and political revolution throughout Europe. Belatedly, the strokes of his hammer were to be felt even in the relatively isolated island kingdom of England.

Under Henry VII's rule (1485-1509), England became increasingly stabilized; a new generation of nobles drawn from mercantile backgrounds gained power, and the nation began to take its place among the great nations of Europe. Given the tumultuous background of England in the fifteenth century, it is not surprising that his successor, Henry VIII, placed special emphasis on the tranquility of his realm. Among other things, England's stability required maintaining close relations with the Roman Church and the vigorous suppression of any trace of Lutheranism. So successful was English policy in this regard that Pope Leo XI conferred upon the English King the title of "Defender of the Faith." The final project in Henry VIII's quest for this title was his authorship of a treatise against Lutheranism published with a large international circulation in 1521.

Ironically, this "Defender of the Faith" would, in less than two decades, lead his people out of allegiance to the Church of Rome and institute a modified form of the Protestant Reformation called the *Church of England*. A fascinating sequence of events led to this remarkable change in Henry's public policies and personal relationships. Perhaps the most significant factor was Henry's need for a male heir. Unfortunately, his marriage to Catherine of Aragon had produced only one surviving child, Mary. Dynastic considerations merged with the King's amorous interest in Anne Boleyn, a lady of the royal court who finally gave in to Henry's advances and became pregnant. The possibility that the baby might be a boy, coupled with Henry's ardent desire to marry Anne, drove him to seek a divorce or annulment from Catherine. It was his misfortune to be frustrated in this effort by events beyond his control. Pope Clement VII, who might otherwise have bowed to English diplomatic pressure, was at the time under virtual house arrest due to Rome's military occupation by the armies of Catherine's nephew, Emperor Charles V. With Anne's pregnancy advancing rapidly, Henry took the extreme measure of declaring himself Supreme Head of the Church in England, and, shortly thereafter, succeeded in obtaining the necessary marriage dissolution from a compliant English ecclesiastical court. Turning his attention to the new Church of England, Henry attempted to create a national church that preserved the orthodox Roman Catholic faith but at the same time was independent of the papacy and politically subservient to the king of England.

FEATURED OUTLAW: MARTIN LUTHER

Martin Luther is without question one of the most significant figures of the last millennium. The idea of being persecuted for publicly expressing disagreement with prevailing religious beliefs would strike most Americans of today as strange. After all, the First Amendment to the United States Constitution and the laws that flow from it guarantee religious liberty. However, this right (which most Americans take for granted) is, relatively speaking, a historical anomaly. Throughout most of the world, both past and present, millions have been and still are severely persecuted for daring to go against the religious establishment in their society.

Martin Luther was one of the most significant religious dissidents in world history. He was born on November 10, 1483 in Eisleben, Saxony (Germany). He was educated at a school operated by the Brethren of the Common Life as a lay monk. Much more educated than many of his contemporaries, due in part to his father's success as a businessman, Luther was awarded a college degree in 1502. Forsaking his father's wish that he enter business, Luther entered the priesthood. He eventually earned his doctoral degree, an extraordinary accomplishment for the time, and taught theology and the Bible.

Luther grew increasingly disenchanted with the corrupt and autocratic practices of the Roman Catholic Church, including the Pope, but when he posted his 95 complaints against the Catholic Church, he intended it to act as the springboard for an academic debate, not a revolution. However, a revolution did come about as a result of Luther's complaints. In addition to his complaints about church behavior, Luther also took the radical step of asserting that salvation could be obtained only through the grace of God. Contrary to the popular teaching of the time, Luther maintained that human beings could not work for their salvation, and, furthermore, that any attempts at achieving perfection were in vain.

Luther was condemned for heresy in 1521, but he enjoyed a strong following among the masses, which led to the Peasant War of 1525. Unlike most theological debates of today, which are more intellectual exercises than anything else, Luther's theological difference held profound political and societal implications. Given the oppression he suffered for expressing his religious beliefs, one would think that Luther would have been indulgent and tolerant of those who disagreed with him, but such was not the case. Luther was just as intolerant of Anabaptists and Jews as the Roman Catholic hierarchy was of him. Luther was condemned and persecuted as heretic and blasphemer; Luther condemned those who disagreed with him the same way. He died February 18, 1546, but his legacy survived him. Most modern Protestants, including the Baptists whom he denounced, claim Luther as one of their founding pioneers. Martin Luther King Jr., the great American civil rights leader of the 1950s and 1960s, bears the name of his father, Martin Luther King Sr., who, like his son, was a minister. The elder King was given the name Mike King at birth, but had his name changed to Martin Luther King in honor of the Protestant pioneer.

Source: Levy, L. W. (1993). *Blasphemy: Verbal offenses against the sacred from Moses to Salman Rushdie.* New York: Alfred A. Knopf.

HISTORY TODAY

Martin Luther was considered an outlaw by many in his time, but millions of modern Christians regard him as a religious hero. Consider today's unpopular criminals; how will history judge them?

These events were codified under the 1534 Act of Supremacy that declared Henry the head of the newly created Church of England. The act required an oath of allegiance and those who could not or would not so swear were prosecuted for treason on the basis of praemunire, serving a foreign dignity, in this case the Pope. Prior to the 1534 legislation, the most famous case of praemunire still involved Henry VIII, this time with his Chancellor, Cardinal

Thomas Wolsey. Wolsey was given the inevitable and perhaps impossible task of trying to convince the Pope to annul Henry's marriage. When he failed, his career was doomed, he was stripped of his office as Lord Chancellor, and forfeited his home, York Palace (now Whitehall), to the king.

For Henry, breaking the ties that bound England to Rome proved easier than fathering a son. Despite the king's exhaustive efforts to produce a son, Anne Boleyn gave birth to a child that would become the future Elizabeth I. Shortly after this disappointment, Anne was tried and executed for treason, after which Henry successively sought other wives and managed to produce only one son, who briefly succeeded Henry as Edward VI in 1547. Similarly, casting the English nation off from the main trunk of Roman Christendom proved to be simpler than shaping a coherent body of doctrine that would be acceptable to all subjects. Henry's insistence upon religious orthodoxy was undermined by Protestant-oriented counselors during the reign of Edward VI. Then, when the Catholic princess Mary succeeded her brother after his death in 1553, she and her consort (Phillip II of Spain) attempted to restore the Roman Church to England.

FIGURE 5.1 Martin Luther nailed his *Ninety-Five Theses* on the church door at Wittenberg, beginning the Lutheran protest that shattered the religious and social unity of Europe, leading to great changes in English constitutional government. *AP-Photo/HO.*

Upon the death of Mary (known thereafter in English history as "Bloody Mary" for her violent purges of Protestants), Elizabeth became queen in 1559. Under her direction, the Church of England was revived to pursue a moderate Protestant path. The advisers of "Good Queen Bess" were quick to equate Roman Catholicism with treason against the Crown, and the long reign of Elizabeth I was marked by suppression of Catholics. Attending a Catholic mass resulted in a 100-mark fine, and for the priest saying mass the penalty was death. The refusal to attend Protestant mass, known as *recusancy*, was punishable with a fine of 20 pounds. In a time when a knight's yearly salary was 50 pounds, this was a severe penalty.

Elizabeth's initial "don't ask don't tell" policy toward Catholics was not to last long. Soon she was hard-pressed to deal with growing Protestant elements within the English church that demanded that the national church be reformed and that its liturgy and theology be stripped of Roman practice and principles. Elizabeth wisely made concessions to these dissenting viewpoints, but undertook no harsh repressive measures.

Catholic judges and justices of the peace were no longer allowed to hold office. But more significant and focused repression was left to Elizabeth's successor, James I. Fresh from struggles against Scottish Presbyterians, this first of the Stuart monarchs embarked on a policy of royal domination of the church and the political affairs of England. The result was a series of constitutional crises, a civil war, and the *Glorious Revolution*, which established Parliamentary supremacy in political matters and religious toleration as a state policy in ecclesiastical affairs.

James I was the first monarch of a United Kingdom. He arrived in London in 1603 already holding the crown of Scotland since 1567, and so his accession to the English throne brought the country of Scotland together with England and Wales. Dubbed "The wisest fool in Christendom" by historian Anthony Weldon, James introduced the concept of the "Divine Right of Kings" and reigned during a golden period of literature and drama with works produced by William Shakespeare, John Donne, Ben Jonson, and Francis Bacon. James I was also responsible for the creation of the King James Bible.

James I was the monarch in 1606 when an event took place that is now celebrated each year by children and adults throughout the United Kingdom. On November 5, 1606, *Guy Fawkes* was arrested while guarding numerous barrels of gunpowder under the Houses of Parliament. Fawkes, a Catholic, had conspired with a number of other prominent Catholics to blow up Parliament the following morning while the king was in attendance. Guy Fawkes was betrayed and tried; his death sentence was hanging and then quartering, a particularly painful process as the method of hanging really amounted to a slow death by strangulation, therefore the disemboweling took place while still alive. Once on the scaffold, Guy Fawkes forced his own quick death and avoided the quartering agony by jumping off the platform and snapping his own neck. This day in history is celebrated as a result of King James decreeing that all citizens should remember the failed attempt and light good fires (bonfires). Over time, the custom has evolved and now bonfires are accompanied by fireworks to symbolize what would have happened if the gunpowder plot had succeeded.

Against a backdrop of religious unrest, James I repealed previous legislation; for example, he reintroduced the death penalty without benefit of clergy for the offense of witchcraft. Under James' reign, numerous heresy trials were held. The period also witnessed the development of specialist witch hunters such as the self-proclaimed witch-finder General *Matthew Hopkins*. Hopkins hanged around 200 people during a 2-year period. His title came about because he offered his services, for a fee, to towns and villages to rid them of the scourge of witches. The greatest challenge to Hopkins' defendants was that because they were in collusion with the devil, and the devil was not likely to confess to heresy, then a human confession prior to trial was the only manner in which to proceed. However, torture was not permitted in law and therefore Hopkins had to devise methods of extracting confessions. One was the swimming test; if the accused floated, it was because the devil could not face the waters of baptism. If the accused drowned, then the accused might die but it meant innocence. In most cases, the accused would be raised from the water before drowning. Hopkins himself was eventually executed on suspicion of witchcraft.

HISTORY TODAY

Modern witchcraft or Wicca is the religion of choice for some. However, it is a far cry from the "crime" of witchcraft known in the Middle Ages, and it is no longer a factor in American or European criminal justice. However, in some other countries, more specifically some African countries, the belief in witches and the belief that witches cause misfortune still exists and some people are punished severely for being witches. Should Western countries work toward changing these practices and attitudes?

Torture was no longer permitted, except for defendants who had to appear before the infamous *Star Chamber*. The Star Chamber, originally a court of appeal under Henry VIII, was given its name due to the stars painted on the ceiling of the room at Westminster Palace. This court became infamous and feared due to its ability to skirt the no-torture rule, as well as impose excessive fines and lengthy prison sentences. Over time, the Star Chamber extended its remit to trying nobles suspected of treason. These trials were conducted in private, which further increased its reputation for a court that worked outside of the law. Parliament abolished the Star Chamber in 1641. The right to debate, amend legislation, and impose taxes had already been granted to Parliament by Elizabeth I. James I, unimpressed by the extended powers given to it by Elizabeth I said of Parliament "I am a stranger, and found it here as I arrived, so that I am obliged to put up with what I cannot get rid of."

HISTORY TODAY

Almost all courtroom proceedings, juvenile cases representing one exception, must be held in public settings and a public record must be kept of what occurs. However, in some cases, such as with accused terrorists, strong arguments have been made for keeping some proceedings private. Based on the experience of the Star Chamber, should there be any other exceptions to the law mandating that judicial proceedings be public?

Against the rich historical backdrop of Tudor dynastic intrigue and growing religious diversity, the seventeenth century emerged as the most important time in England's history for the development of constitutional government. Ancient traditions, dating back to medieval times, were pitted against the Stuart dynasty's attraction for royal absolutism and the Roman Church. The struggle would be waged in Parliament, in the courts, and on the battlefield; from this struggle grew a form of constitutional government that shaped not only the future polity of England but also the thought and law of its colonies in North America. Much of what is distinctive in the English and American systems of criminal law and procedure can be traced to this period in English history.

ENGLISH CONSTITUTIONALISM AND THE DIVINE RIGHT OF KINGS

England's dynastic and religious difficulties of the Tudor (1485-1603) and Stuart (1603-1689) periods prompted the transition of the nation into a modern state marked by a strong central government and an increased concern for the rights of the individual. These were times of immense change in both the criminal law and in the constitution of England. They were characterized by religious persecution; numerous prosecutions for treason and countless lesser crimes, sharp shifts in political power between the Crown and Parliament; and a long, violent constitutional crisis and civil war stretching from 1629 to 1660. Only with the Glorious Revolution (1688-1689) were these matters resolved in a practical subordination of royal prerogative to the political supremacy of Parliament and in the strong affirmation of the traditional rights of Englishmen.

Ancient tradition and the practices of the Tudor monarchs confirmed the subordination of the kingship to law and custom. They also established the principle that matters of state concern required Parliamentary concurrence in royal actions. To deem this "government by consent of the governed" would state the matter too broadly, but it is clear that England in the sixteenth and seventeenth centuries was highly resistant to the novel and then-prevailing concept of the divine right of kings. This political theory, highly attractive to the Stuart kings of England and typified by Louis XIV of France (the "Sun King" who ruled from 1643 to 1715), traced royal power on earth to a direct grant of divine power from God. Anointed kings at their coronation, French monarchs saw themselves as possessing all political and moral authority. Unfortunately, for the similar pretensions of the Stuart dynasty, English constitutionalism raised a formidable barrier to absolute monarchical rule.

The bedrock of English constitutional government is the *Magna Carta* (1215), an old charter of privileges created by King John in 1215. Originally, it afforded John's rebellious barons relief from onerous and extraordinary taxation; it also made certain concessions to the church and provided protection for foreign merchants. Several specific guarantees (at the time closely limited to the protected classes) laid a foundation upon which subsequent rights of the people would be established. Most significant are the 38th, 39th, and 40th articles, which read as follows:

38. No bailiff shall henceforth put any one to his law by merely bringing suit [against him] without trustworthy witnesses presented for this purpose.

39. No freeman shall be captured or imprisoned or disseised [dispossessed of property] or outlawed or exiled or in any way destroyed, nor will we go against him or send against him, except by the lawful judgment of his peers or by the law of the land.

40. To no one will we sell, to no one will we deny or delay right or justice.[1]

From these liberties in the Magna Carta, Englishmen in subsequent centuries gained the rights to trial by a jury of one's peers, to indictment only upon probable cause shown to a grand jury, and to a speedy and honest trial according to the law of the land. Even before the sixteenth century, Englishmen were protected against arbitrary prosecution by the state; individuals could be subjected to criminal prosecution and punishment only in accordance with accepted procedures.

As granted by King John, the Magna Carta's *sixty-first clause* also provided for a committee of barons to police the king's compliance with its provisions. They were specifically authorized to raise a force to oppose him. In addition, the king directed that, if he or anyone acting for him attempted to cancel any of the liberties outlined in the Magna Carta, such attempted revocations would be null and void. Subsequent history demonstrates recurring royal attempts to nullify or circumvent the Magna Carta, just as the rise of a powerful representative legislature (Parliament) made reliance upon a baronial committee unnecessary. However, the sixty-first clause is illustrative of the early emphasis that was placed upon countering power with equal force vested in other hands, something that later generations would call *balancing* (or *separating*) powers. It also shows a primitive form of the constitutional principle that actions or laws that are beyond the traditional scope of governmental activity may be considered null and void, a concept that future generations would call *judicial review* or *substantive due process*.

FIGURE 5.2 King John signed the Magna Carta in 1215, laying the foundation upon which subsequent rights of the people would be established. *Courtesy en.wikipedia.org.*

RELIGION, POLITICS, AND CRIMINAL JUSTICE

This ancient tradition of constitutionalism should not obscure the fact that social and political developments of the fifteenth century permitted the Tudor monarchs to make significant alterations in the criminal law, as well as provide more efficient methods than common law prosecution for its enforcement. For the most part, this was accomplished by expanding the judicial power of the Privy Council (exercised by the Court of Star Chamber), establishing a Court of High Commission to deal with high-level religious issues (1559), and giving additional authority and duties to the local justices of the peace. Although such actions resulted in an increase in royal power, these new courts and officials did not supplant jurisdiction previously exercised by the common law courts. Historically, the English common law courts dealt with a very restricted number of felonies, and the modernization of English society and economic life created a number of other crimes not punishable at common law. English church courts had general jurisdiction in dealing with matters of heresy, blasphemy, illegal sexual activity, fraud, and perjury. Ecclesiastical sanctions were limited to fines, the imposition of public penance, and excommunication. This vacuum in criminal law enforcement permitted the Tudors to expand royal authority and to impose religious conformity throughout England.

From Henry VIII's break with the Roman Church until 1640, the Crown was actively involved in using the criminal law as a means of obtaining conformity with the theology and practices of the Church of England. In November 1538, John Lambert was tried for denying the doctrine of transubstantiation. This doctrine held, in accordance with the accepted belief of the Roman Church, that the physical elements of bread and wine actually became the body and blood of Jesus Christ during Holy Communion. Lambert was tried at Westminster Hall before the Privy Council, with the king himself presiding; upon his conviction of heresy, Lambert was burned at the stake. A year later, in 1539, Parliament passed the *Act of Six Articles*, which condemned as heretical the denial of the doctrine of transubstantiation. It also made heretical, and thus punishable by death, any speech or act that degraded the sacrament and any preaching that advocated altering the mode in which the Church of England administered communion to the people. As Sir James F. Stephens noted in his study of criminal law, writings or speech that earlier might be mildly punished as heretical now became matters of great political concern.[2] Personal religious beliefs that deviated from state policy were now punishable either as treason or one of the many new types of felonies directed against irregular religious practice or belief. This intermixing of political loyalty with religious orthodoxy was characteristic of Tudor and Stuart England. As a result, the Court of Star Chamber (charged with most criminal law enforcement) and the Court of High Commission (charged with the administration of ecclesiastical law and the punishment of heresy) had overlapping jurisdictions.

Prosecutions in the Court of Star Chamber and the Court of High Commission involved the examination of the accused by members of the court. Most frequently, this was done under oath and without the accused knowing the charges against him or her, the identity of prosecution witnesses, or the contents of their statements of evidence. The *oath ex officio* was used as a method to obtain statements from the accused that could subsequently be used to institute formal criminal proceedings against him. Both courts sat without juries and, as might be expected, very few defendants called before them secured an acquittal. Opponents charged these courts with following the harsh inquisitorial methods then in use on the continent. Whether such methods were employed is debatable, but it is clear that the existence of these courts challenged the constitutional traditions of England and, most specifically, weakened the protection of trial by jury.

TIME CAPSULE: ENGLISH CENTRAL COURTS OF THE SEVENTEENTH CENTURY

All English royal courts evolved from the *Curia Regis* of the Norman kings, and began to be centralized in the twelfth and thirteenth centuries. The original and appellate jurisdiction of the House of Lords is also derived from this source, because Parliament at one time exercised some judicial authority and this has in modern times begun the work of the Law Lords. The Law Lords are composed of hereditary peers who have been trained as lawyers, or life peers appointed after distinguished careers as lawyers or judges.

With the rise of the overseas empire, the ancient Privy Council jurisdiction over the King's Channel Islands was expanded to include the American colonies and British India. Within Great Britain, the House of Lords exercised appellate jurisdiction over the Irish courts after 1719.

Admiralty jurisdiction was exercised by vice-admiralty courts in the colonies, subject to appeals either to the High Court of Admiralty in England or to the Privy Council.

Although the Reformation and the English statutes separated the Church of England from the authority of the Pope, the traditional courts of the Church remained in place. These included Archdeacon Courts, the Courts of the Ordinary (bishops), and the Prerogative Courts, which exercised the authority of the two Archbishops. For the level of review previously exercised by the Pope, the English Parliament substituted the High Court of Delegates and the Court of High Commission. The American colonies were considered part of the province of Canterbury until 1696, when they came under the ecclesiastical authority of the bishop of London.

The Figures that follow provide a graphic summary of the English court system as it existed in the seventeenth century. In 1873, the common law courts (King's Bench, Common Pleas, and Exchequer) were made separate divisions of the High Court of Justice. The Chancery court became a separate Chancery Division of the High Court of Justice, and the matrimonial and probate jurisdiction of the Archbishops' Prerogative Courts were united with Admiralty, becoming the Probate, Divorce, and Admiralty Division; this last division is affectionately termed the court of "wives, widows, and wrecks." The appellate jurisdictions of King's Bench and Exchequer Chamber became the Court of Appeal. This Court of Appeal and the High Court of Justice together comprise the Supreme Court of Judicature.

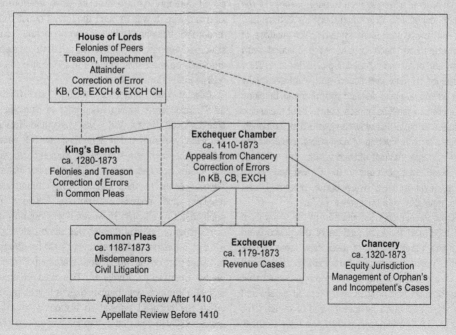

FIGURE 5.3

Continued

TIME CAPSULE: ENGLISH CENTRAL COURTS OF THE SEVENTEENTH CENTURY—CONT'D

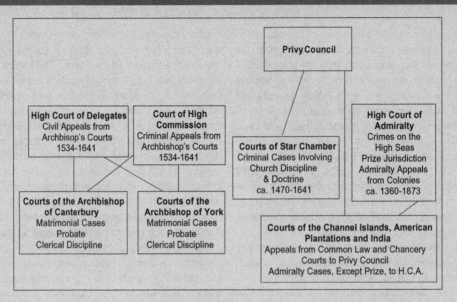

FIGURE 5.4

Although the Tudor monarchs did not originate government by Privy Council or local administration through *justices of the peace*, they were responsible for refining these institutions into relatively efficient law enforcement systems. The justices of the peace, appointed for each county, were charged with maintaining law and order and adjudicating civil disputes. They also acquired minor criminal jurisdiction, and were eventually responsible for preliminary hearings and commitments in felony cases to be tried before the Westminster courts, or at the assize sessions of those courts. In this way, the justices of the peace, either individually or in a meeting of all justices, replaced the sheriffs as the principal judicial officers within the counties. Because they owed their positions to the Crown and not to local magnates, royal interests were better protected, and favoritism to local nobility was less likely to occur.

New economic legislation was common in the years from 1485 through 1603, and the local justices of the peace were burdened with the administration of these new areas of law, frequently with penal sanctions. Participating in general sessions and quarter sessions, the justices made certain that roads were maintained and bridges were kept in repair, and that vagrants were supported by their towns of origin. This growing army of "J.P.s" was supervised by the Privy Council, which exercised virtually all of the executive powers vested in the Crown. The Council's ordinances and orders were as binding in law as statutes passed by Parliament, and it had the added authority derived from its close relationship with the king or queen. It was through the Privy Council that the Tudor monarchs influenced Parliamentary action, calling upon selected members of the Council to stand for election and to articulate government programs in the House of Commons as well as in the House of Lords.

Dissent was dangerous in Tudor and Stuart England. Sir Thomas More, former Chancellor of England and former confidant of Henry VIII, was executed for questioning the validity of the Act of Supremacy (which established the king as head of the Church of England). A vast array of individuals not conforming to Henry's new church followed Thomas More to their deaths. Even minor incidences of religious and political dissent by citizens resulted in punishment by officials. However, it was not only major issues of religious or political dissent that drew official punishment. In 1612, a foreign trader was fined £2000 for grumbling that in no other part of the world were merchants "so screwed and wrung upon as in England." This mild complaint against official corruption was punished by a 6-year prison sentence when the accused refused to apologize to the officers in question. Three years later, two gentlemen were heavily fined and sentenced to a year in prison for expressing doubt about whether a convicted felon was actually guilty.

HISTORY TODAY

In many countries, criticizing the government or its leaders is criminally punishable. What do the experiences in Tudor and Stuart England teach about American's First Amendment rights?

As early as 1612, the common law courts began to assert traditional constitutional precedents in a struggle against the power of these two courts. Attempts were made to use writs of *habeas corpus* to free prisoners condemned to jail by one of the prerogative courts, and, at other times, writs of prohibition were issued to stop proceedings in the Court of Star Chamber or the Court of High Commission. Foremost in leading the common law's opposition to these executive courts was Sir Edward Coke, Chief Justice of the Court of King's Bench.

Sixteenth- and seventeenth-century England was also a battleground for free speech and freedom of the press, for the printing press made political and religious dissent a threat to bishop and king alike. Just as the invention of movable type and the printing press (1423-1450) aided in the spread of the Protestant Reformation, so did this new method of dispersing ideas play a vital role in English constitutional development and criminal law, much as the Internet and satellite television are doing today in the Middle East and Asia. Originally, the Privy Council assumed the authority to issue printers' licenses. As a consequence, whenever objectionable material appeared in print, the printer was arraigned before the Court of Star Chamber or the Court of High Commission. Should it develop that he had not obtained a license, he was *prima facie* guilty of seditious libel and subject to punishment.

TIME CAPSULE: TREASON

The offense of treason, the only act for which one can still be sentenced to death in England today, was clearly defined by Parliament in 1352. The statute passed during the reign of Edward III, although temporarily modified, has remained essentially the same.

Whereas divers opinions have been before this time in what case treason shall be said, and in what not; the King, at the request of the lords and of the commons, hath made a declaration in the manner as hereafter followeth; that is to say, When a man doth compass or imagine the death of our lord the King, or our Lady his Queen, or of their eldest son and heir; or if a man do violate the King's companion, or the King's eldest daughter unmarried, or the wife of the King's eldest son and heir; or if a man do levy war against our lord the King in his realm, or be adherent to the King's enemies in his realm, giving to them aid and comfort in the realm, or elsewhere, and thereof be provably attainted of open deed by the people of their condition. And if a man counterfeit the King's great or privy seal, or his money; and if a man bring false money into this realm, counterfeit to the money of England, as the money called Lushburgh, or other like to the said money of England, knowing the money to be false, to merchandise or make payment in deceit of our said lord the King and of his people; and if a man slay the chancellor, treasurer, or the King's justices of the one bench or the other, justices in eyre, or justices of assise, and all other justices assigned to hear and determine, being in their places, doing their offices.

Source: 25 Edw. III, c.2.

The *Licensing Acts*, which were reestablished in 1662 after royal government resumed, restricted printing in England to firms previously licensed, thus providing strong prior restraint over the publication of opposition opinions. When criticism appeared, it was harshly punished. For example, William Prynne, convicted of seditious libel before the Court of Star Chamber in 1632, was disbarred from the practice of law, deprived of his university degrees, twice placed in the pillory, maimed by the loss of one ear, fined £5,000, and sentenced to "perpetual" imprisonment—the equivalent of a life sentence.

Despite the sanctions available against seditious libel, opposition printers flourished, publishing a vast array of constitutional tracts attacking the excesses of royal government and stressing the constitutional value of trial by jury, the danger of examination by means of the oath *ex officio*, and the theological ambiguities and objectionable liturgical practices of the established Church of England. Dissenters in seventeenth-century England were like the ancient Jews in Egyptian captivity: "the more they were oppressed, the more they multiplied."[3]

REGICIDE, THE CIVIL WAR, AND LAW REFORM (1640-1660)

In 1625 Charles I introduced the Petition of Rights in return for money to pay for his wars. Under this agreement, Charles accepted that there would be no imprisonment without cause, no martial law during peacetime, and no forcing homeowners to accept soldiers for food and lodging. This bill also proposed that taxes would be agreed by Parliament before being imposed on the citizenry. Charles appeared to agree and then dissolved Parliament before implementation.

By 1629, opposition to Charles I became so extreme that he attempted the experiment of ruling England without calling Parliament into session. In normal times, refusing to ask Parliament for the right to tax would have made governing difficult, but Charles was shortly faced with a rebellion in Scotland that placed heavy demands on the royal treasury. When Parliament was finally summoned in 1640, it proceeded to reassert its constitutional prerogatives and ultimately precipitated open warfare with the Royalists. Defeated on the field of battle, King Charles I was tried for treason and executed in Westminster Hall (1649), this being another example of the application of *regicide* in English law.

HISTORY TODAY

Fortunately, in modern Western democracies, the transfer of power from one President or Prime Minister to the next is peaceful. However, in dictatorships, the leader usually has to be forced out and/or killed, or may have to leave the country. What part does the rule of law play in the way leaders in Western democracies transfer leadership?

A series of unsuccessful attempts to reconstitute government on a permanent basis followed. The United Kingdom operated a commonwealth under the Rump Parliament from 1649 to 1653. This was followed by martial law and the Protectorate (1653-1659), established under the quasi-regal authority of Oliver Cromwell. The execution of Charles I left the way clear for the establishment of a republican form of government, and the various parties contended for popular sovereignty, elimination of the nobility, and a variety of other schemes. Ultimately, the army became the ultimate source of power, and England remained under virtual military rule until Oliver Cromwell established himself as Lord Protector in 1653. Thereafter, his government (called the *Protectorate*) closely followed the institutional forms of royal government. Cromwell's death in 1658, along with the inability of Richard Cromwell (Cromwell's son and successor) and a growing dissatisfaction with republican government, led to the restoration of the Stuart dynasty in 1660. In 1660, Parliament formally asked that Charles II resume the throne; the legislation and governmental forms of the Interregnum (a time during which a throne is vacant between two successive reigns) were declared null and void and, with few alterations, royal government resumed on the same constitutional framework as existed in 1649.

FIGURE 5.5 Portrait of Charles I by Anthony van Dyck (1636). *Courtesy en.wikipedia.org.*

For posterity, this period is of considerable legal and constitutional interest, because it contributed new ideas concerning criminal justice that deserve our attention. In the course of the search for a permanent form of republican government, there emerged groups of political theorists known as *Levellers* and Fifth Monarchists. Believing that all law should be subject to rules of reason and conformable to Holy Scripture, they developed a law reform program designed to ensure that English law conformed to biblical practices.

An early product of this emphasis was a 1650 statute that made adultery and incest capital offenses. Subsequently, Leveller pamphleteers suggested that specific rights be guaranteed in criminal trials. These rights included requirements that all charges be based upon the testimony of two or more witnesses, that the accused be permitted to confront his or her accusers, and that both parties be allowed to introduce evidence and examine their own witnesses. Those who brought false accusations were to receive the same penalty that would have been imposed if the defendant had been convicted wrongly. In the case of maiming or other physical injury, it was suggested that the biblical *lex talionis* ("eye for eye, tooth for tooth") would be an appropriate penalty. Considered by Parliament in 1653, these various proposals were referred to a committee for the regulation of the laws, which attempted to revise and codify all English law, shaping it in accordance with reason and the "law of God." However, divisions within the Leveller reform movements and partisan opposition in Parliament resulted in no such legislation being passed.

Contrary to earlier opponents of the royal prerogative, the Levellers took no solace in the protections of the common law. Many of them attacked the institution of jury trials, while others were harshly critical of the legal profession and judges, despite the fact that these groups were most effective in resisting Stuart absolutism. Constitutionally, the Levellers believed that all men should be treated equally before the law. As a consequence, they opposed special privileges such as benefit of clergy, which was available only to male defendants who could read. They also believed that the law should be based upon positive acts of Parliament, easily available to everyone and printed in English so that they could be understood.

This emphasis on a statutory basis for criminal punishment would surface in American legal history, as would a number of the procedural guarantees advocated by the Levellers. The efforts of the 1653 law revision committee, destined to failure in England, were paralleled by similar work in the New England colonies. This produced the *Bible Codes*, which had a significant impact on American criminal justice and constitutional development.

The Levellers sought a higher, or fundamental, law that would limit the supremacy of Parliament and secure the people against excesses of tyrannical government. With the execution of Charles I, political authority shifted to Parliament, limited only by the actual power vested in the army. To the Levellers, this was just as unsatisfactory as the exercise of monarchical power. Because men were considered equal before the law, there was no basis upon which any man or group of men should exert authority over another, particularly in regard to basic rights that they traced back to Anglo-Saxon times. Among the rights Englishmen held most dear was what we would today call *freedom of conscience* in matters of religion. Ultimately, these concepts would find their lasting impact not only in England but also in the newly established North American colonies.

Despite the limited impact of Leveller law reform, as well as the downfall of the Commonwealth in 1660, this troubled time in English history witnessed the permanent abolition of the Courts of High Commission and Star Chamber, which resulted in an increase in the competence of the common law courts in criminal justice. The chaos of revolutionary society and government resulted in the expression of new and seemingly radical ideas that otherwise would have been suppressed. Although the locality of English law reform would shift to the colonial frontier, within the next three decades the constitution of English government would also be transformed.

RESTORATION, GLORIOUS REVOLUTION, HANGING JUDGES, AND SERIAL KILLING IN PARIS

The decline of Cromwell's Commonwealth meant the end to republican experimentation in government and law, but did not end English attachment to well-ordered Parliamentary government or popular support for moderation and Protestantism in religion. It was the misfortune of the restored Stuart monarchs to be either unwilling or unable to adapt to these two political facts of life. When called upon to resume the throne, Charles II agreed with the Convention Parliament that statutes passed between 1640 and 1642 would remain part of English law, but that all other acts of the Interregnum period would be null and void. This meant that the new king agreed to the abolition of the Courts of Star Chamber and High Commission and thus heightened the constitutional position of the common law courts and their hallowed tradition of jury trial.

Known as "The Merry Monarch," Charles restored theaters, public houses, and brothels. Charles II reigned from 1660 to 1685 and during this time he introduced the Clarendon Code, which required all clergymen to use *The Book of Common Prayer*. He forbade nonconformists from attending university. Charles's reign was marked by the Great Plague of 1665 followed the next year by the Great Fire of London. However, not every aspect of these two events was detrimental to the country, and the Great Fire produced a period of expansive building and a new era in British architecture.

Two circumstances made it difficult for common law courts to protect constitutional rights and provide due process to defendants in criminal cases. First, the judges continued to hold their offices at the pleasure of the Crown rather than on the basis of good behavior. Instead of a judge holding office until good cause could be shown for his dismissal, an office held at the king's pleasure was easily manipulated for political purposes. Second, ancient methods for judicial control of juries were revived and reinstituted. These methods included fining jurors who returned verdicts contrary to the wishes of the presiding judge, and even imprisoning them on short rations until they altered their verdicts. Both of these situations made it possible for the Crown and its ministers to influence common law court decisions in vital cases.

Many of the most significant political trials of the day concerned seditious libel and unlicensed printing, and were often characterized by juries unwilling to return guilty verdicts. However, *Bushell's Case* (1670) involved the imprisonment of a jury that refused to convict William Penn (the Quaker and future founder of Pennsylvania) and others of riotous assembly. Edward Bushell, a member of the trial jury, along with his colleagues, was thrown into prison for his resistance to the judge. The Court of King's Bench ordered the release of the imprisoned jury, reasoning that the jury's view of disputed facts did not contradict the manifest weight of the evidence. If it were the function of the judge to pass on the accuracy of the jury's verdict, he would in effect be judge of both the law and the facts of the case. Although this decision did much to affirm the independence of the common law jury, it did not stop Royalist efforts to obtain hanging juries or to coerce the decisions of jurors who resisted the authority of judges.

HISTORY TODAY

Sometimes when jurors render an unpopular verdict, they are criticized by court officials or by people in the media. Is it fair to put laypeople in the uncomfortable position of determining the verdict in a high-profile case?

There is much of value that can be attributed to William Penn, including, on occasion, great wit. He had been arrested for preaching in the street after he was refused entry to a Quaker Meeting Hall. During his trial, Penn asked the judge for clarity over precise law under the Common Law that he was charged with. The infuriated trial judge responded "You are an impertinent fellow, will you teach the court what it is? It is *lex non scripta* that many have studied 30 or 40 years to know, and would you have me tell you what it is in a moment?" William Penn replied "Certainly, if the common law be so hard to understand it is far from being common."

Under Charles II and later by his Roman Catholic convert brother, James II, conformity to the Church of England was enforced by vigorous prosecutions of nonconforming Protestants. These prosecutions took place before common law judges subservient to the interests of the Crown; the most notorious of these was *Sir George Jeffreys*, Chief Justice of King's Bench, who held his "bloody assizes" throughout the realm. "Hanging" Judge Jeffreys was notorious for his conduct and the manner in which he required others to conduct themselves in his courtroom. Whether it is now popular myth or reality, there are numerous reports of Jeffreys arriving drunk and frequently swearing at defendants. He was known for his intimidation, not just of the defendants but all the court staff. He appeared to take a particular pleasure when sentencing defendants: "Hangman I charge you pay particular attention to this woman, scourge her soundly—till her blood runs down." On another occasion he informed a convicted prisoner, "You will be cut down alive and see your bowels burned before you." While presiding at the trial known as *Monmouth's Rebels*, he informed the defendants that a not guilty plea would mean the death sentence. Five hundred pleaded guilty in 1 day. Two hundred fifty convicted prisoners were pickled and their bodies were displayed throughout the county to deter future uprisings.

HISTORY TODAY

Should judges be elected or appointed? Supposedly, making a judge stand for election makes them more accountable in the event they behave as badly as George Jeffreys did. How many of your elected judges can you name? Federal judges are appointed for life and are not accountable to the electorate, but complaints of misconduct are probably more common with elected judges.

George Jeffreys (1645-1689): Known as the "Infamous Jeffreys" and "Hanging Judge Jeffreys"; Chief Justice of the King's Bench in 1683; became involved in several high-profile trials including those of Titus Oats and Richard Baxter, in addition to trying the followers of the Duke of Monmouth during the "Bloody Assize." Jeffreys lost his authority; in a failed attempt to leave England by stealth and was arrested at St. Katherine's Dock in London while attempting to escape to Holland and was imprisoned for his former activities.

James II, during his short reign (1685-1688), took steps to enhance the ability of Roman Catholics to take public office in civilian government and in the military. These measures generated strong opposition among the English gentry and populace and resulted in the positioning of a standing army on the outskirts of London.

The Crown's executive authority was, for the most part, left unaffected by the Restoration settlement; those powers included a sweeping power of arrest, restrained only by the common law writ of *habeas corpus*. The writ of habeas corpus commanded jailors and other individuals holding prisoners to deliver them before the issuing judge. Additionally, such individuals were required to provide some legal basis for holding their prisoners captive. The *Habeas Corpus Act of 1679* regularized these procedures and made them more effectual against the arbitrary use of royal authority. Multiple imprisonments on the same charges were declared illegal once the defendant had been released on *habeas corpus*. The 1679 Act also required that individuals imprisoned for treason or felony (previously beyond the relief afforded by *habeas corpus*) would have to be indicted promptly, or *habeas corpus* would be available. Finally, the statute prohibited the transportation of persons outside of England to Scotland, Ireland, or other dominions of the Crown, where the writ would not be available.

Sir James F. Stephen suggested that "the greater part of the injustice done in the reigns of Charles II and James II was effected by perjured witnesses, and by rigid enforcement of a system of preliminary procedure which made the detection and exposure of perjury so difficult as to be practically impossible."[4] One example of this injustice is the series of treason trials connected with the *Popish Plot* (1678-1680), a supposed attempt to overthrow Charles II and place James II on the throne. The defendants were held in close confinement; ignorant of the evidence against them, they were allowed neither counsel nor an opportunity to confront witnesses. Moreover, they were given no copy of the indictment, nor information concerning the panel of jurors.

The political trials of the Restoration exhibited English criminal procedure very prominently. Countless men and women of modest income and obscure reputation may well have labored for centuries under the same restrictions in defending their lives and property. However, the highly publicized treason trials and the prosecutions for seditious libel and unlawful assembly focused public attention upon the need for law reform. That reform would come as a result of the peaceful overthrow of James II, known as the *Glorious Revolution of 1688-1689*.

Religious and dynastic considerations, rather than matters of constitutionalism or law, brought about the Glorious Revolution of 1688-1689 and the deposition of James II. The rule of Charles II had rested upon a coalition between the established Anglican Church and a Parliament that represented a large Protestant majority. Charles II had followed a policy of de facto religious toleration, dispensing with the enforcement of many pro-Anglican statutes and ignoring others. At the same time, the Test Oaths (which excluded both Catholics and nonconformists from government and the military) and the Corporation Act (which applied similar restrictions to holding city or borough offices) kept Anglicans in political power. What Charles II did not do, and what James II unwisely attempted, was to disestablish the Anglican Church and to substitute Roman Catholicism as the state religion.

It seems that some of the mistakes made by James II that resulted in him bringing about the revolution that Charles II had avoided can be traced in the nature and form of the legislation enacted throughout this period. One example of James's concern about an uprising is seen in the act of 1671 that forbade anyone other than a game warden to "Keep for themselves guns, bowes, greyhounds, setting dogs..." Not wholly dissimilar to the act of 1328 passed by Edward II that banned the carrying of "sword, dagger, or affray of the peace, nor to ride by night or carry such item at any fair, market, or in the presence of justices".

When James's Roman Catholic wife gave birth to a son, thereby displacing the Protestant Princess Mary as heir to the throne, the stage was set for revolution. Mary and her husband, William of Orange, were called to accept the Crown by the Convention Parliament. Both had Stuart blood in their veins (William was a grandson of Charles I); however, their right to rule was founded not upon heredity, but rather upon the invitation of the people of England as expressed in Parliament.

Mary was in a strong position to persuade Parliament to accept her conditions of acceptance. In doing so Mary created a unique situation in that she required that her husband would jointly hold the throne with her. It was and has subsequently been the case with Queen Victoria and the current Queen Elizabeth II that their husbands did not hold the throne jointly. William was very happy with the outcome, as it afforded him the opportunity to cause England to join the League of Augsburg and bring protection to his homeland, The Netherlands. Perhaps of greater long-term significance is that the outcome of this agreement set in motion the law that stipulates that no British monarch may ever be a Roman Catholic.

Because the invitation to William and Mary was conditional, the Glorious Revolution was a significant constitutional event. First and foremost, it recognized the authority of Parliament, and thus was a further step in restricting government by royal prerogative. Second, it provided a bill of rights that restated some traditional rights of Englishmen and established new privileges and immunities for English subjects. The Bill of Rights, also known as the *Declaration of Rights*, was to become of major significance to the United States as the blueprint for its own Bill of Rights. Interestingly, this has often been miscited as a source for the right to bear arms. There is no mention of a right to bear arms under the English version. Third, it established religious toleration for all Protestant denominations as the basis for future government policy and at the same time retained the principle that Roman Catholics were to be excluded from political life. The Anglican Church continued as the established (state-supported) church, but under William and Mary virtually all of the restrictions on freedom of conscience were removed for Protestant dissenters.

FIGURE 5.6 The Glorious Revolution: Depiction of William of Orange landing at Torbay. *Courtesy en. wikipedia.org.*

The impact of the English Bill of Rights upon constitutional and criminal law was of major importance. It provided that no standing army be maintained in England without express consent of Parliament, thereby sharply limiting royal power over the military forces. In addition, the Bill of Rights guaranteed to Protestant subjects the right to bear arms for their own defense and exempted debates in Parliament from criminal prosecution. In criminal law and procedure, the bill made illegal the imposition of excessive fines or the demand for excessive bail (later included in the Eighth Amendment to the U.S. Constitution), while also limiting the royal authority's ability to provide immunity from prosecution. Cruel punishments were also prohibited, and the bill required that jurors be properly returned and empaneled. In treason cases, jurors were required to be qualified freeholders (that is, they had to own land of a set value). Supplementary legislation to the Bill of Rights provided that judges would hold office based on good behavior rather than at the pleasure of the Crown. A new statute made the offense of treason more specific and provided specific procedural protections, which included the right to receive a copy of the indictment and the right to assistance by assigned counsel. Conviction might be had only upon the testimony of two witnesses, but a confession obtained without violence and made in open court could be substituted for the evidence of witnesses.

The abolition of cruel punishments did not ensure a standard of treatment for prisoners that would be close to what we expect in today's society. As we shall see, much of the groundwork for penal reform was to follow during the Enlightenment. English (and European) prisons remained damp, squalid hovels that were little better than the dungeons of the Medieval period.

The infamous *Newgate Prison* in London, first constructed in 1188, was not renovated and then rebuilt until 1770. Until 1783, Newgate was primarily a holding prison, for those awaiting trial and for those awaiting public execution at Tyburn Tree. The last few days of life for prisoners were initially a time of solace with only bread and water to drink. Over time, even the final days improved. Eventually, on the final journey to the place of execution, it became common practice to give the convicted person a bowl of ale as they journeyed to the gallows. Perhaps by design or perhaps by fate, the public house was named The Resurrection Gate Inn.

By the mid-1400s, the behavior of inmates at Fleet and Newgate prisons was near riotous. In fact, the floor of Fleet prison was dubbed Bartholomew's Fair, as it so resembled the actual fair that took place on August 24 each year in nearby Smithfield. Down the road at Newgate prison, galleries were installed where the public could attend and watch the revelry of the last night of condemned prisoners, encouraged no doubt by the gin supplied to them by the spectators. However, by midnight on death's eve, the bellman from the local St. Sepulchre's church would awaken the prisoners with a hand bell and encourage them to make their peace with God. This brought into popular use the phrase "for whom the bell tolls," made even more famous by the twentieth-century Ernest Hemingway novel bearing that title.

Criminal justice underwent huge changes in England throughout the fifteenth, sixteenth, and seventeenth centuries. Mainland Europe was not stagnant either during this period but the magnitude of change to be brought about by the great French philosophers was not to occur until the eighteenth century. Nevertheless, a brief commentary on the laws and crimes of the 1600s provides a context to what followed during the Enlightenment.

In France, Louis XIV (1643-1715) reigned, and during his era many legal reforms were introduced, principally through the work of Jean Baptisste Colbert and *Guillame de Lamoigen*. Colbert was responsible for establishing the Conseil de Justice, and Lamoigen served as the first president of a French parliament. Of the two, Lamoigen was the more productive jurist. He drafted at least 150 pieces of legislation and sought to simplify the entire criminal law of France. This effort culminated in his *1670 Ordinance on Criminal Law* and *Ordinance on Criminal Procedure*. The former defined all crimes and the latter codified criminal procedure and penalties.

Also, during the reign of Louis XIV, Paris experienced its first encounter with serial killings. During a period of 3 months, 26 men—aged 17 to 24—disappeared. Outrage at this eventually reached the ear of the king, who appointed the chief of Paris police, Gabrielle Nicholas De La Reynie, to investigate. The Lieutenant of Police instructed his best detective Le Coq to investigate. Le Coq had a son who was 22 years of age at the time and it occurred to Le Coq that he should use his son as bait. Exupere Le Coq agreed. Exupere had a curious nickname; it was "Wide Awake," given to him as he was considered intelligent and witty. "Wide Awake" toured the fashionable parks of Paris and on one occasion after seeing a beautiful young woman he was approached by her elderly chaperone who invited him to meet with the young female, *Princess Jabirouska,* later that evening. At the appointed time "Wide Awake" met the old woman who then took him on a lengthy tour of Paris. Eventually, they arrived at Rue Cortalon and "Wide Awake" went inside to meet the "princess." He immediately became suspicious and started looking around the premises. He soon found a false wall that he attempted to look behind, but as he did the princess and four male assistants entered the room to attack him. As agreed, the police had followed "Wide Awake," and they entered the premises and arrested the woman and her helpers. Behind the fake wall the remains of 26 young men were found. All had had their heads removed. The fake princess had been abducting men and decapitating them. The heads were being sold in Germany for the emerging science that investigated character and propensity to commit crime, *phrenology,* based upon skull shape. The remains of the corpses were being sold to Paris medical students for research. "Princess" Jabirouska, the old woman, and the four male assistants were hanged.

HISTORY TODAY

Serial murder is not new, nor is the fascination with it. What does the fact that so many people are fascinated with serial murder say about our society?

This event demonstrates how much further ahead France was than England in the establishment of a police force for the capital city. Until the reign of Louis XIV, policing in France had been piecemeal and local. In October 1666, Louis appointed Colbert to design and plan a police organization for Paris. By March

15, 1667, Louis authorized the creation of two new positions, Lieutenant of Police and Lieutenant Civil. This measure effectively separated the police and the law courts in France for the first time in its history.

Apart from the successful investigation of serial murders, the workload of the chief of police was far wider than we would see today. His functions included: oversight of seven districts, the security of Paris, arresting thieves and spies, controlling begging, issuing licenses to wine shops and food stores, firefighting and flood control, providing care for abandoned children and pursuing unfaithful wives, inspecting the jails, and oversight of the public drainage system and sewers.

SUMMARY

The constitutional and religious conflicts of the sixteenth and seventeenth centuries resulted in sweeping changes in English law, giving increased protection against criminal prosecution and confirming the traditional reliance on the common law courts and trial by jury. At the same time, the unsettled environment of revolutionary times permitted men to consider revision of the criminal law. In the case of Interregnum theorists, that reevaluation included modification of secular law to conform to biblical guidelines. Although these substantial departures from common law rules were rejected, they left a legacy of enthusiasm for biblical precedent that would influence American legal development in the seventeenth and early eighteenth centuries. More permanent was the impact of the English constitutional struggle on the legal system of England. By virtue of the Glorious Revolution, Parliament emerged as the preeminent law-giving authority. Within the next century, the doctrine of Parliamentary supremacy would flourish. The constitutional struggle also developed the common law courts as the primary force for upholding the constitutional rights of English citizens against royal power. Ultimately, English governmental practice would subordinate those courts to the supremacy of Parliament, but American constitutional practice would, through judicial review and written constitutions (themselves a legacy from the English Civil War period), subordinate legislative discretion to the moderating influence of constitutional litigation.

Alterations in governmental and institutional power should not obscure the advances made in criminal justice. The rights of accused persons were extended and enhanced by the Bill of Rights that emerged from the Glorious Revolution; the independence of judges was secured by the same document. Judicial decisions strengthened the ability of common law jurors to resist the punishments of corrupt judges. The privilege against self-incrimination arose from deep-seated resentment against the *ex officio* oath of the prerogative courts, and the inquisitorial system fell into extreme disfavor in English law. Finally, England learned the lesson that criminal prosecutions were ineffectual in enforcing religious conformity and that toleration was the only acceptable alternative if a tranquil society was to survive.

REFERENCES

Ashley, M. (1963). *England in the seventeenth century*. Baltimore: Penguin Books; Bindoff, S. T. (1963). *Tudor England*. Baltimore: Penguin Books; Keir, D. L. (1966). *The constitutional history of modern Britain since 1485* (9th ed.). New York: W. W. Norton & Co.

Prall, S. E. (1966). *The agitation for law reform during the Puritan revolution*. The Hague: Martinus Nijhoff, pp. 1640–1660; Shapiro, B. (1975). Law reform in seventeenth century England. *American Journal of Legal History, 19*, 280–312; Warden, G. B. (1978). Law reform in England and New England, 1620-1660. *William and Mary Quarterly, 35*(3d Series), 668–690; Innes, J. (1980). The king's bench prison in the later eighteenth century: Law, authority and order in a London Debtor's Prison. In J. Brewer & J. Styles. *An ungovernable people: The English and their law in the seventeenth and eighteenth centuries* (pp. 250–298). London: Hutchinson; McGowan, R. (1988). The changing face of God's justice: The debates over divine and human punishment in eighteenth-century England. *Criminal Justice History, 9*, 63–98; Bellamy, J. (1979). *The Tudor law of treason: An introduction*. London: Routledge & Kegan Paul; Du Cann, G. G. L. (1965). *Famous treason trials*. New York: Walker and Company.

Stephen, J. F. (1883). *A history of the criminal law of England*. 3 Vols. London: Macmillan & Co; Vols 4 to 6 of Holdsworth, W. (1945 and 1937). *A history of English law*. London: Methuen & Co.

Hay, D. (1975). *Albion's fatal tree: Crime and society in eighteenth-century England*. New York: Pantheon Books; Cockburn, J. (Ed.), (1977). *Crime in England*. Princeton: Princeton University Press. pp. 1550–1800.

Ives, G. (1970). *A history of penal methods*. Montclair, NJ: Patterson Smith; Pike, L. O. (1968). *History of crime in England*. 2 Vols. Montclair: Patterson Smith; Radzinowicz, L. (1948-1957). *A history of the English criminal law and its administration from 1750*. 3 Vols. New York: Macmillan.

Notes and Problems

1. To what extent did the constitutional developments from 1485 to 1689 influence changes in criminal law and procedure?

2. Strengthening the jurisdiction and powers of local justices of the peace and placing them under Privy Council supervision was perhaps good policy early in the Tudor monarchy; did it continue to be an effective means of conducting business after the Court of Star Chamber supervision was abolished in 1641?

3. How did trial by jury change under the Tudor and Stuart monarchs? Was it an effective protection against executive tyranny? Did it help to combine jury trials with an independent judiciary that cannot be removed at the king's pleasure?

4. Was the Glorious Revolution a necessary consequence of the Interregnum? If Parliament already had extensive power, was it necessary to formalize the situation with a bill of rights?

5. To what degree did the events of the seventeenth century and the text of the English Bill of Rights serve as precedents for the American Bill of Rights?

ENDNOTES

[1]Stephenson, C., Marcham, F. G. (1972). *Sources of English constitutional history* (2nd ed), vol. 1. New York: Harper & Row. p. 121.

[2]Stephen, J. F. (1883). *A history of the criminal law of England* (vol. 2). London: MacMillan and Co. pp. 302-303, 424.

[3]Exodus 1:7.

[4]Stephen. *History of Criminal Law* (vol. 1). pp. 369, 383.

CHAPTER 6

Criminal Justice on the North American Colonial Frontier (1607-1700)

KEY TERMS

Body of Liberties
  of 1648
Captain John Smith
Close watching
Codes
County courts
Covenants
Demography
Ducking stool
Duke's Laws of 1665
General court

Indentured servants
Informal system
*Laws Divine, Morall
  and Martiall* of 1611
Massachusetts Bay
Mayflower Compact
Moses: His Judicials
Pamphleteers
Pentateuch
Petit treason
Public humiliation

Riot Act
Salem witches
Samuel Sewall
Slavery
Stocks
Sumptuary laws
Sweat lodge
Vagrant
Virginia Company

LEARNING OBJECTIVES

1. Learn how criminal justice was administered in primitive settings like seventeenth-century Jamestown, Virginia.
2. Examine some of the early attempts at codifying British-style law in the American colonies.
3. Learn of some of the ways and reasons public humiliation was administered in the American colonies.
4. Learn some of the ways that courts were organized in early colonial America.
5. Understand the role that application of biblical principles played in colonial criminal justice.

6. Learn how the institutions of slavery and indentured servitude influenced criminal justice.
7. Read and understand the story of the Salem witch hysteria and become familiar with some of its key players.
8. Learn how the sweat lodge has played a role in the application of criminal justice among Native Americans.

Table 6.1 Time Line: Criminal Justice in North America, 1607-1700

1607	First permanent English settlement at Jamestown, Virginia.
1611	*The Laws Divine, Morall and Martiall*, a military disciplinary code, established for the all-male settlement at Jamestown and surrounding areas.
1619	First meeting of the colonial assembly, called the House of Burgesses.
	The population changes from all white males. Young women are brought to the colony to marry the men and establish homes in the New World, and African laborers arrive and become indentured servants, leading to the establishment of slavery by 1660.
1620	English Separatists (Calvinists wishing to separate from the Church of England) arrive in Plymouth and adopt the Mayflower Compact as their form of political government.
1629-1640	Complete Puritan congregations—men, women, children, and pastors—arrive in Massachusetts Bay. This is the so-called Great Migration, caused by King Charles I's rule without Parliament and by the suppression of reform-minded clergy of the Church of England.
1634	English Roman Catholics establish a colony in Maryland.
1636-1648	To restrain the discretionary justice dispensed by Massachusetts magistrates, the legislature passed a series of "Bible Codes," which provided careful descriptions of what is a criminal defense and what the standard penalty would be if an accused person were convicted.
1636-1638	Anne Hutchinson, accused of teaching the predominance of personal revelation, tried for sedition and banished from Massachusetts Bay.
1652	As a fleet of Commonwealth warships lays at anchor in Chesapeake Bay, Virginia renounces its allegiance to Charles II and acknowledges the authority of Cromwell as Lord Protector.
1660	The Restoration Parliament enacts the Acts of Trade, limiting colonial trade to England and the colonies of England, and requiring trade with the Continent to pass through English ports.
1664	New Netherlands, a Dutch colony, conquered by an English fleet. It becomes a proprietary colony ruled by the Duke of York, who later becomes James II in 1685.
1682-1683	William Penn granted Pennsylvania to serve as a colony for Quakers. Penn's "Frame of Government," published in 1682, is noteworthy for its prohibition of capital punishment.
1689-1692	The Glorious Revolution in England results in disorganization of government in the colonies. New governors are appointed by William and Mary.
1692	Chief Justice Samuel Sewall presides over the trials of witches at Salem, Massachusetts.
1696	Parliamentary statutes provide more rigid enforcement of the 1660 Acts of Trade and establish colonial courts of vice-admiralty for enforcement of trade restrictions in the colonies.

Government institutions do not readily adapt to changed economic and cultural conditions, and criminal law and penology also follow this rule. The establishment of English colonies in North America required that rules of criminal law, methods of enforcement, and modes of punishment be reconsidered and applied in an entirely new geographical, economic, and social situation. It is difficult for us to imagine the cultural shock and disorientation that must have confronted the earliest migrants to the North American colonies of England. It was not only a movement to a different part of the world; in many ways it was also a step back in history, back to a primeval forest, to the economic systems of pre-Bronze Age hunters and farmers, and into a total absence of external legal systems and authority. The highly sophisticated way of life and the system of criminal justice that had developed in western civilization over the course of 1,000 years suddenly became almost irrelevant in the face of primitive conditions in the colonies.

Survival dominated the first years of settlement, and the basic human requirements for food and shelter were paramount. Oftentimes, relations between European settlers and Native Americans were friendly or at least civil. However, very often the colonists found it necessary to deal with hostile and sometimes violent encounters with Native Americans, and vice versa. This made it prudent to restrict settlement to easily defended locations and to increase the number of men available for militia duty. A scarcity of labor discouraged capital punishment and lengthy terms of imprisonment. However, one benefit from the scarcity of population was the advantage it offered for law enforcement. Crimes that in the Old World depended upon anonymity for their success were impossible in the American wilderness. Everyone knew everyone else; in fact, most were related by blood or marriage. Identification of criminals (or strangers who were watched for illegal behavior) was a simple matter, and flight to avoid prosecution meant living a precarious existence among compassionate Indians or being tortured to a slow death by less friendly tribes. In the rough world of seventeenth-century America, every colonist was a police officer, and there was no extradition from the tender mercies or harsh cruelties of the neighboring Indian tribes. It made the would-be criminal think twice.

Much Old World criminal law was practically useless in North America. Many of the old laws were unacceptable to settlers who had fled from governmental imposition of harsh laws to limit religious belief. Both practical and cultural considerations entered into the growth of a new system of criminal law and punishment in seventeenth-century North America. Each colony functioned under unique conditions imposed by nature and by a variety of rules imposed either by the Crown, the corporate owners of the colony, or its feudal proprietor.

Stretching along the vast expanse of the Atlantic Coast, the settlements exhibited great differences in climate, fertility of the soil, and accessibility to trade. Their people had abandoned the relative comfort and security of Old World homes, driven by adventure or necessity to seek a new life in the wilderness. Their reasons for migrating varied, from economic advantage to religious zeal, from the vibrant exuberance of a dreamer seeking personal and national glory to the grim choice of a condemned criminal offered the hard alternatives of transportation to the colonies (banishment) or death by hanging on London's Tyburn Hill.

Yet these colonists were still shaped by their experiences in the Old World. Although largely inapplicable to the situations in which they found themselves, their Old World experiences and culture were nevertheless a part of their outlook and thus shaped their opinions on law and order. Most of the politically influential settlers were of English or Scottish origin, and the events of recent English history had left a permanent mark on their political attitudes. Migrants from other nations brought differing views and cultural preferences. Combined with the harsh realities of colonial life, this diverse European heritage molded a uniquely American approach to crime and punishment.

VIRGINIA UNDER MILITARY LAW

Under the sponsorship of the *Virginia Company* of London, the first *permanent* settlement by the *English* in what is now the *United States* (Previous settlement attempts by the English had failed; Spain already had numerous settlements throughout the country; England had established settlements in what is now Canada.) at Jamestown, Virginia (1607), was intended as a commercial outpost to facilitate trade between England and Native Americans. Failing to find either gold or a quick passage to China or India, the colonists increasingly depended upon agriculture for their livelihood. Commercial viability of the colony was assured when John Rolfe learned the techniques of tobacco farming (1612), and by 1619 the Company extended a modicum of self-government to the settlers and permitted them to make purchases of land from the Company and begin independent farming enterprises.

FIGURE 6.1 John Smith, Englishman who led the founding of the Jamestown Colony in present-day Virginia. *Library of Congress.*

Even before 1619, most of the significant adaptations to American conditions had been accomplished. Many of the first settlers were adventurers averse to manual agricultural labor in the sweltering fields of tidewater Virginia. *Captain John Smith* successfully bullied them into work, alternating threats of starvation with more terrifying sanctions of expulsion from the settlement into the hands of the Natives. To ensure order and to maintain centralized control, the Virginia Company permitted its resident governor to institute a system of military law. This gave maximum authority to the governor and his company-appointed council. It also provided harsh sanctions for those who deviated from the accepted norms of their society. *The Laws Divine, Morall and Martiall* of 1611 imposed harsh punishments for many offenses that might be considered "economic crimes." These punishments included a death penalty for mariners who came to Virginia and sold food and other necessities at prices above those fixed by the governor and council. Death was also prescribed for inhabitants who attempted to leave without permission, and it was also the penalty for stealing crops from a garden one was employed to cultivate.

> John Smith (1580-1631): Englishman who led the founding of the Jamestown Colony in present-day Virginia; captured by the Powhatan tribe, and famously made peace after being saved by the tribal chief's young daughter, Pocahontas.

The spiritual vigor of the inhabitants was reinforced by the penalties for failure to attend services or sermons. The first offense resulted in a loss of a week's rations, the second offense was punishable by loss of a week's rations coupled with a whipping, and the third was punishable by death. Sodomy, rape, sacrilege, trading with or attacking the Natives, larceny, and murder were all punishable by death, as was desertion on the field of battle.

While the imposition of military law may seem an extreme measure, the vulnerability of Jamestown to attack either from Indians or from neighboring Spanish settlements in Florida made military discipline essential. There were few women or children in the colony, and in many ways the male-dominated settlement was more like an army camp than a civilian community. Imposition of a military code, based in part upon the martial rules of continental nations, was evidence of the lack of stability and internal self-discipline within the Virginia colony. The arrival of a substantial number of women in 1619 altered the social and cultural orientation of the Jamestown settlement. With the authority to participate in colonial government through a House of Burgesses, granted in the same year, Virginians ended martial rule and began the difficult task of adapting English laws to American conditions.

THE OLD DOMINION AND ENGLISH LAW

Colonial statutes and court records indicate that Virginia's criminal law was taken almost in its entirety from English criminal law. Treason was punishable by death and forfeiture of property. In some cases, the punishment involved stretching the traitor on a wheel to break his back, disemboweling him while he was still living, hanging him until dead, and then cutting off and exhibiting his head on a pole. The full sentence, derived from a statute of Henry VIII, was rarely used in America except when the convicted traitor was a Native American or an African slave.

The offense of *petit treason*, or the murder of a master by his servant, was of special significance in Virginia because of the growing slave population. It served as the most frequent occasion for the application of the law of treason and the imposition of its heaviest sanctions. Treason—along with murder, burglary,

TIME CAPSULE: NATIVE AMERICAN CRIMINAL JUSTICE: THE SWEAT LODGE

Prior to the arrival of Europeans, the idea of a criminal justice system as it exists today was foreign to Native Americans. There were no police officers in uniform and the idea of prisons and jails was unknown. As most Native Americans did not adhere to the significance of the written word, codified laws as they exist today were practically unknown as well. Nevertheless, like practically all communities and societies in human history, Native American communities had rules and norms of behavior that were generally understood by all of the citizens in that community. Unlike Europeans, most Native cultures relied more on oral tradition than the written.

It would be a mistake to simplistically regard all Native American communities as one monolithic culture. Native Americans populated the entire Western Hemisphere, from Alaska to South America. This geographic dispersion alone accounts for many differences. One commonality among numerous Native American communities was an instrument still in use today, the sweat lodge. Sweat lodges have been used in various Native American communities for centuries. Although they differ in design, sweat lodges essentially are similar in operation to saunas. The Native Americans were not alone in perceiving the potential physical and psychological benefits of intense sweating. Similar practices were common in ancient Rome, Greece, Turkey, and Russia. The Native American sweat lodge was and is often seen as a means of purifying mind and body of toxins and impurities. It is seen as a means of addressing physical ailments and

mental or behavioral problems, including some behaviors that would be labeled crimes today.

Unlike the modern sauna, the sweat lodge included a spiritual element and rituals administered by recognized elders or medicine men of the community. As with the design, the type of ritual varied, but the spiritual element was uppermost in most sweat lodge rituals, except for those that, like most modern saunas, were purely recreational. Sweat lodges were and are used in some cases of suicide prevention, with some participants experiencing spiritual renewal as a result of the sweat lodge.

The treatment of Native Americans in the modern criminal justice system, especially its correctional aspects, is still debated today. Many Native Americans argue that traditional native methods of dealing with offenders are more effective than those in mainstream criminal justice. Some tribal courts and probation officials incorporate traditional methods like the sweat lodge with typical criminal justice practices. The state of California has had sweat lodges in some of its prisons. As the modern criminal justice system continues to evolve and modernize, its officials sometimes learn that searching history provides some answers for modern problems.

Sources: Schiff, J. W., & Moore, K. (2006). The impact of the sweat lodge ceremony on dimensions of well-being. *American Indian and Alaska Native Mental Health Research, 13*(3), 48-69; Ogden, S. (2004). Ex-prisoner pomo woman speaks out. *Social Justice, 31*(4), 63-69.

rape, robbery, and forgery—was punishable by death in Virginia as it was in England; none who committed such a crime received benefit of clergy, which had made its way from Europe to the colonies.

Virginia legislative action seems to have enforced what were termed *sumptuary laws* (regulations prohibiting excesses in dress or home furnishings) and prohibited free political speech through penalties for seditious libel. These libels were punished by fines (which was the most commonly imposed sanction in colonial America, just as it is now), imprisonment, or *public humiliation*. Sitting with feet in the *stocks* (or standing with hands in the stocks) was a common penalty for such offenders.

HISTORY TODAY

Sumptuary laws regulated what people could wear and how they could decorate their homes. American society is much more permissive now in both of these areas than in the early days of the colonies. However, some town ordinances or neighborhood covenants prohibit decorating homes in certain ways. Should this be allowed? Some town ordinances also place restrictions on what people can and cannot wear in public. Should such laws be allowed?

FIGURE 6.2 The ducking stool was a common punishment for women in colonial days. © *Bettmann/ CORBIS.*

A peculiar form of humiliation was reserved for women who spoke irresponsibly of their neighbors. If the convicted woman's husband refused to pay the fine, she was subjected to "ducking" in the *ducking stool*. The process required that the accused woman be placed in a chair that was attached to the end of a long beam; then, while fully clothed, she was lowered into a pond or river in the presence of the community.

As in England, Virginia's early settlers had the morality of their behavior and the nature of their religious practices supervised very closely by civil authorities. Fines and imprisonment were used to discourage blasphemy, failure to attend church, and attacks upon ecclesiastical practices. In this regard, it is helpful to note that Virginia remained loyal to the Stuart kings until a Cromwellian fleet in 1652 demanded its submission to the Commonwealth. Until that time, it was treason in Virginia to claim allegiance to the Commonwealth or to any sovereign other than Charles II, who was then in exile.

Church and state worked together in the colony, seeking to maintain the established Church of England. However, when at the end of the seventeenth century Commissary James Blair attempted to obtain trial of ecclesiastical matters in separate church courts, rather than in county courts, the Virginians successfully resisted this movement toward clerical meddling in judicial matters.

Throughout the seventeenth century, Virginia and its tidewater neighbor, Maryland, remained tied to English forms of justice and followed the procedures of the mother country. About three decades after the initial settlement at Jamestown, it became too cumbersome to continue all legal judicial activity at the provincial capital; separate *county courts* were set up to try virtually all civil cases and to sit as a magistrate's court in criminal matters. Thus, the county courts were responsible for deciding whether the accused person should be held in jail to await trial for a felony. Composed of the leading planters of the various counties, the county courts maintained law and order in their jurisdictions, aided by the sheriff and local constables. All criminal cases involving black slaves were tried before the county courts, as were minor cases involving free persons. Capital cases (which included virtually all felonies) were tried before the *general court*, which met at the Jamestown capital and was composed of the governor and members of his council.

Law enforcement does not seem to have raised a serious problem in early Virginia, but the presence of a growing number of slaves was cause for alarm. The individual master was responsible for the conduct of his slaves, and he was given a fairly free hand in their discipline. Although public opinion was harshly critical of masters who abused their slaves, very few cases, including those involving the deaths of healthy slaves who had been punished too severely, were prosecuted. On the other hand, the harsh penalties for petit treason discouraged slaves from violence against their masters.

PLYMOUTH AND A NEW BASIS FOR GOVERNMENT

In sharp contrast to the settlement of Virginia, the second colony in English North America began with a new form of government by consent rather than with a system of military law. The separatist group that came ashore on Plymouth Rock in 1620 did not have a charter, but intended to settle on lands

TIME CAPSULE: COMPACT GOVERNMENT

When the American colonists declared themselves independent of the English monarchy and turned instead to a contract form of government, they could draw on the experience of their forefathers as well as the theories of political scientists such as John Locke. Europeans who ventured to settle in the New World, far from the seat of government, and who were concerned about the questionable efficacy of distant enforcement power, often voluntarily submitted themselves to a compact that determined the authority structure of a community. In addition to the Mayflower Compact, similar agreements originated in other colonies, pirate groups, and settlements on the frontier in the nineteenth century among members of caravans crossing the American "desert," and in the mining camps and vigilante organizations on the West Coast. Below is an example of prohibitions and obligations included in a pirate ship's articles:

1. Every man shall obey civil command; the captain shall have one full share and a half in all prizes; the master, carpenter, boatswain, and gunner [known as *artists*] shall have one share and a quarter.

2. If any man shall offer to run away or keep any secret from the company, he shall be marooned with one bottle of powder, one bottle of water, one small arm [weapon] and shot.

3. If any man shall steal anything in the company, or game, to the value of a piece of eight, he shall be marroon'd or shot.

4. If at any time we should meet another Marrooner [pirate ship], that man that shall sign his articles without the consent of our company shall suffer such punishment as the captain and company shall think fit.

5. That man that shall strike another whilst these articles are in force shall receive Moses' Law (that is 40 stripes lacking one) on the bare back.

6. That man that shall snap his arms [weapons], or smoke tobacco in the hold without a cap to his pipe, or carry a candle lighted without a lanthorn, shall suffer the same punishment as in the former article.

7. That man that shall not keep his arms clean, fit for an engagement, or neglect his business, shall be cut off from his share and suffer such other punishment as the captain and the company shall think fit.

8. If any man shall lose a joint in time of an engagement he shall have 400 pieces of eight; if a limb 800.

9. If at any time you meet with a prudent woman, that man that offers to meddle with her without her consent shall suffer present death.

Source: Mitchell, D. (1976). *Pirates.* New York: Dial Press, p. 86.

of the Virginia Company farther south. Instead of landing south of Virginia, they landed much farther north, in what is now Massachusetts. Although they had no charter, they possessed a strong Calvinist faith in the value of *covenants*. As a result, while they were still aboard ship, they had entered into a voluntary agreement stipulating that the group would make rules and regulations that would then become binding on all. This *Mayflower Compact* served as the charter for government until the Pilgrim colony was absorbed into Puritan Massachusetts Bay in 1662.

While the Mayflower Compact was unique in asserting that governments might be instituted through the voluntary action of those to be governed, it followed earlier practices. It had been traditional for travelers aboard ships to enter into agreements for the regulation of their affairs in the course of a long voyage. English fishing fleets working the Grand Banks off Newfoundland during the sixteenth century usually submitted themselves to the governance of the captain of the vessel first to arrive, thereby establishing a method for administering both civil and criminal justice.

The government established on the basis of the Mayflower Compact had several advantages. First and foremost, the majority of individuals who landed at Plymouth were members of an English congregation at Scrooby. Harassed by church and royal officials because of their Calvinist criticism of the established Church of England, they fled to Holland and established themselves in Leyden. Dutch religious tolerance provided a safe haven until the group decided that they should settle in the New World, where their English manners and customs, as well as their religion, might survive and prosper.

These shared experiences and common purposes contributed to the success of the Pilgrims and their Mayflower Compact. On the other hand, the original group of Plymouth settlers included individuals who were not members of the Old World

TIME CAPSULE: COMPACT GOVERNMENT II

Another example of the contract form of government is the Mayflower Compact:

> In the Name of god, Amen. We, whose names are underwritten, the Loyal Subjects of our dread Sovereign Lord King James, by the Grace of God, of Great Britain, France, and Ireland, King, Defender of the Faith, etc. Having undertaken for the Glory of god, and Advancement of the Christian Faith, and the Honour of our King and Country, a Voyage to plant the first Colony in northern Parts of Virginia; Do by these Presents, solemnly and mutually, in the Presence of God and one another covenant and combine ourselves together into a civil Body Politick, for our better Ordering and Preservation, and Furtherance of the Ends of aforesaid: And by Virtue hereof do enact, constitute, and frame, such just and equal Laws, Ordinances, Acts, Constitutions, and Offices, from time to time, as shall be thought most meet and convenient for the general good of the Colony; unto which we promise all due Submission and Obedience.

Source: Hall, K. L., Wiecek, W. M., & Finkelman, P. (1991). *American legal history: Cases and materials.* New York: Oxford University Press, p. 11.

congregation and thus were not subject to church discipline and sanctions. For those "nonbelievers," a secular and political form of government was required. The Mayflower Compact thus served two purposes: (1) it provided additional support for discipline within the church, and (2) it supplied a neutral political order to which both Pilgrim and nonbeliever would be required to adhere.

Although Plymouth colony did not survive as an independent settlement to the end of the seventeenth century, its laws and compact form of government had great impact upon American government and constitutional theory. Its larger, but more religiously orthodox, neighbor *Massachusetts Bay* was established by charter in 1629 and settled the following year. Like the Plymouth settlement, Massachusetts Bay enjoyed the advantage of being settled by groups of English dissenters who left the mother country not merely as family groups but also as entire congregations. The people of Massachusetts Bay, like those of Plymouth, shared common goals for their political and religious lives, and they also shared similar views concerning both the civil and the criminal law.

Plymouth colony's form of government by consent, or compact, was to serve as a model for many other English settlements. For example, the Fundamental Orders of Connecticut were drawn up by representatives of the settlers in the Connecticut River towns of Hartford, Wethersfield, and Windsor in January 1639. This agreement established a colony constitution that survived nearly 200 years as the basic governing document. Similarly long-lasting was the Plantation Agreement at Providence, which provided a government for the settlement on Narragansett Bay and which, after incorporation into the royal charter of 1662, would continue as the form of Rhode Island government until well after the American Revolution.

THE SPECIAL SITUATION IN NEW ENGLAND

Homogeneity in population and belief were not the sole distinguishing characteristics of New England systems of law and government. Significantly, all of these colonies were established by groups that, at one time or another, were considered heretics, criminals, or traitors. The English establishment of the Anglican Church, and subsequent efforts by bishops and their ecclesiastical courts to stifle dissent, resulted in a broadly based migration to New England beginning in 1630 and continuing until the execution of Charles I in 1649. Throughout this period, Puritan *pamphleteers* (pamphlet writers), spurred on by the cruelties of the Stuart Court of High Commission and the inquisitions of the Court of Star Chamber, spelled out the constitutional right against self-incrimination. Marked as criminals and traitors solely because of their religious beliefs and practices, these pamphleteers became experts in asserting the ancient rights and privileges of Englishmen. A beleaguered people, they understood the helplessness of the individual citizen accused and prosecuted by powerful agencies of the state. This left those who ultimately migrated to New England with a profound attachment to trial by jury and to procedural rights against unreasonable searches and seizures, compelled confessions, the use of torture, and the activities of all courts based upon the royal prerogative, including the courts of chancery (high courts of equity with common law functions). They also believed strongly that laws should be drawn with sufficient certainty so that individuals would instantly know what was forbidden and what was permitted.

This demand for certainty in the criminal law moved New England officials in the direction of providing all law, both criminal and civil, to the public in a convenient and simple written form. During the earliest years of settlement, the administration of justice was in the hands of local magistrates appointed by the governor. Because the application of English criminal law was by no means required, the individual judge frequently was in the position of deciding what behavior was prohibited, while at the same time concluding whether the defendant before him was guilty of the "offense." This discretion in magistrates and judges was inconsistent with the strict views of criminal law that had been developed by Calvinist dissenters in England. For this reason, the colonists began to voice objections and to demand that the criminal law be set forth in writing and that the full body of prohibited activities be stated with certainty.

Beginning in 1636, Massachusetts Bay approached this problem by drafting various *codes* of law that would establish norms for conduct not only in the criminal sphere but also in matters of civil law. The first of these codes, which were no more than a collection of statutes, was titled *Moses: His Judicials*. This particular code was not enacted into law, but its title suggests the strong influence of the Bible on the drafting of the New England Bible codes. Of all the Massachusetts codes, the most important for historical purposes was the *Body of Liberties of 1648*.

First enacted by the Massachusetts colonial legislature in 1641 and revised 7 years later, the Body of Liberties provided capital punishment for a long list of felonies, including idolatry, blasphemy, witchcraft, murder, sodomy, adultery, kidnapping, bearing false witness, conspiracy, and insurrection. At the same time, it brought into American colonial law a number of provisions for the safety of persons accused of crimes. These provisions included a clause providing that both inhabitants and foreigners in Massachusetts Bay should receive the same justice and law throughout the jurisdiction, a rough parallel to the "privileges and immunities clause" of our federal Constitution today. Specific prohibitions were enacted against double jeopardy, cruel and unusual punishment, and certain forms of torture. Both the clear statement of criminal offenses and the enactment of procedural guarantees were seen as essential to the tranquility and stability of the state.

The Massachusetts Body of Liberties spurred the enactment of similar pieces of comprehensive legislation in many other North American colonies. While many varied in content and some departed from the Bible as a primary source of law, each incorporated the idea that criminal acts should be precisely defined and that persons accused of crime were entitled to particularly stated rights and privileges. After the English conquered the Dutch province of New Amsterdam and renamed it New York, they provided a New England-type code, the *Duke's Laws of 1665*, to govern the newly acquired territory.

Criminal law in Puritan New England moved even further from the English mode than the enactment of Bible codes would indicate. The secondary source of law was held to be not the common law of England, but rather the rules laid down in the Bible's first five books, called the *Pentateuch*. Secondary rules of law constitute the body of precedents and customs upon which a judge may draw in interpreting the positive commands of the written law. Instead of contemporary English common law, the Puritans substituted the more punitive laws of ancient Israel. This demonstrated their deep respect for the continuing value of the Old Testament and, at the same time, showed their profound distrust of the English law under which they had been persecuted. It was, of course, just a few years later when Levellers and members of the English committee on law reform would make their unsuccessful attempt to conform English criminal law to that of the Bible (1653).

TIME CAPSULE: MASSACHUSETTS BIBLE CODES

Discontent with English law in the seventeenth century led to initiatives for change—on both sides of the Atlantic. Given the religious fervor of the times, it is not unusual that the law contained in the Bible was suggested as an alternative to English criminal law. In England, this was an integral part of the program of the Fifth Monarchy party, composed of radical dissenting groups who wished to change all of English law to conform to biblical standards. When Fifth Monarchy members gained a majority of seats in Oliver Cromwell's Barebones Parliament (elected by church congregations), the opportunity for such a reform existed, and a bill making adultery a capital offense was defeated by a narrow margin (1652). More sweeping amendments of the criminal law were proposed but also not enacted, and Cromwell shortly dissolved the Barebones Parliament after realizing that it was not only unrepresentative but also likely to cause serious disruption in the orderly administration of government.

The same checks and balances on Biblicism did not exist in New England during the middle of the seventeenth century. During the earliest period of settlement, Massachusetts towns were governed by magistrates exercising the authority of an English justice of the peace, but also applying law in a discretionary fashion. In response to this autocratic rule, the settlers demanded that their laws be reduced to writing. The first product of this "codification" effort was *Moses: His Judicials*, printed in 1636 but never adopted as law by the legislature. Subsequent redrafting under the guidance of Nathanael Ward resulted in a Body of Liberties that was adopted by the legislature in 1641 and then reenacted in a slightly different form in 1648. Both of these compilations embodied elements of biblical law into the criminal law of the colony, but as we shall see from an examination of the 1641 Body of Liberties, there were significant differences between the criminal law provisions and the biblical originals.

Codification of the criminal law is important for American ideas of due process. It provides a convenient source of information concerning what is criminal activity, and it stipulates what punishment applies to any given offense. In this way, it warns would-be offenders of the consequences of their acts, and serves as a deterrent. As later interpreted in our federal system of criminal justice, criminal prosecutions must be based upon a statute defining the offense before it was committed. In other words, there is no federal common law of crimes in the United States. This represents one of the procedural protections that grew out of the early New England codification movement.

TIME CAPSULE: MASSACHUSETTS BIBLE CODES—CONT'D

The following comparisons between Massachusetts's 1641 Bible Code and the Bible's text are examples of the variations between the two documents. They appear with more extended commentary in Edwin Powers, *Crime and Punishment in Early Massachusetts* (Boston: Beacon Press, 1966), 258, 259, 261, 263, 268-269.

Massachusetts Body of Liberties, 1641	The Bible
Murder	*Murder*
If any person shall commit any willful MURTHER upon premeditate malice, hatred, or cruelty, not in a mans necessary and just defense, nor by meer casualty against his will, he shall be put to death, Exod. 21:12, 13; Numb. 35:31.	He that smiteth a man, so that he die, shall be surely put to death—Exod. 21:12. Moreover ye shall take no satisfaction for the life of a murderer, which is guilty of death: but he shall be surely put to death—Numb. 35:31. Whoso sheddeth man's blood, by man shall his blood be shed: for in the image of God made he man—Gen. 9:16. Thou shalt not kill—Exod. 20:13.
Manslaughter	*Manslaughter*
If any person slayeth another suddenly, in his ANGER or CRUELTY of passion, he shall be put to death, Levit. 24:17; Numb. 35: 20, 21.	And he that killeth any man shall surely be put to death—Levit. 24:17. But if he thrust him of hatred, or hurl at him by laying of wait, that he die; Or in enmity smite him with his hand, that he die: he that smote him shall surely be put to death; for he is a murderer: the revenger of blood shall slay the murderer, when he meeteth him—Numb. 35:20, 21. [See also Numb. 35:22-25].
Sodomy	*Sodomy*
If any Man LYETH with MANKINDE as he lyeth with a Woman, both of them have committed Abomination, they both shall surely be put to death, unless the one party were forced, or be under 14 years of age, in which case he shall be severely punished, Levit. 20:13.	If a man also lie with mankind, as he lieth with a woman, both of them have committed an abomination: they shall surely be put to death; their blood shall be upon them—Levit. 20:13.
Adultery	*Adultery*
If any Person COMMIT ADULTERY with a Married or Espoused Wife, the Adulterer and Adulteress shall surely be put to death, Levit. 20:19; 18:20; Deut. 22:23, 27.	And the man that committeth adultery with another man's wife, even he that committeth adultery with his neighbour's wife, the adulterer and the adulteress shall surely be put to death—Levit. 20:10. Moreover thou shalt not lie carnally with thy neighbour's wife, to defile thyself with her—Levit. 18:20. If a man be found lying with a woman married to an husband, then they shall both of them die; both the man that lay with the woman, and the woman: so shalt thou put away evil from Israel—Deut. 22:22. Thou shalt not commit adultery—Exod. 20:14. [See also Deut. 22:23-30.]
False witness in capital cases	*False witness in capital cases*
If any man rise up by FALSE-WITNESSE wittingly, and of purpose to take away a man's life, he shall be put to death—Deut. 19:16; 18:16.	If a false witness rise up against any man to testify against him that which is wrong; Then both men, between whom the controversy is, shall stand before the LORD, before the priests and the judges, which shall be in those days; And the judges shall make diligent inquisition: and, behold, if the

Continued

TIME CAPSULE: MASSACHUSETTS BIBLE CODES—CONT'D

Cursing or smiting parents

If any Childe or Children above 16 years old, and of sufficient understanding, shall CURSE or SMITE their natural FATHER or MOTHER, he or they shall be put to death, unless it can be sufficiently testified, that the Parents have been very unchristianly negligent in the education of such Children, or so provoked them by extreme and cruel correction, that they have been forced thereunder to preserve themselves from Death or Maiming—Exod. 21:17; Levit. 20:9; Exod. 21:15 (1646).

Stubborn or rebellious sons

If a man have a STUBBORN or REBELLIOUS SON, of sufficient years of understanding (viz.) 16 years of age, which will not obey the voice of his father, or the voice of his mother, and that when they have chastened him, will not hearken unto them, then shall his Father and his Mother being his natural Parents lay hold on him, and bring him to the Magistrates assembled in court, and testifie unto them, that their Son is stubborn and rebellious, he will not obey their voice and chastisement, but lives in sundry and notorious Crimes: such a son shall be put to death—Deut. 22:20, 21.

witness be a false witness, and hath testified against his brother; Then shall ye do unto him, as he had thought to have done unto his brother—Deut. 19:16-19.

Cursing or smiting parents

And he that curseth his father, or his mother, shall surely be put to death—Exod. 21:17. For every one that curseth his father or his mother shall be surely put to death: he hath cursed his father or his mother; his blood shall be upon him—Lev. 20:9. And he that smiteth his father, or his mother, shall be surely put to death—Exod. 21:15.

Stubborn or rebellious sons

If a man have a stubborn and rebellious son, which will not obey the voice of his father, or the voice of his mother, and that, when they have chastened him, will not hearken unto them: Then shall his father and his mother lay hold on him, and bring him out unto the elders of his city, and unto the gate of his place; And they shall say unto the elders of his city, This our son is stubborn and rebellious, he will not obey our voice; he is a glutton, and a drunkard. And all the men of his city shall stone him with stones, that he shall die: so shalt thou put evil away from among you; and all Israel shall hear, and fear—Deut. 21:18-21. [This reference was probably the one intended.]

The comparisons highlight the development of concepts of criminal intent (*mens rea*), premeditation, and conspiracy to commit crime. We also find a stress upon a minimum age, below which criminal sanctions either cannot be imposed or are of a less severe nature.

Children who cursed or rebelled against parental authority did not fare well in either society, but notice that the Puritan code places an age limit on prosecution, and also provides that cruel treatment or unchristian neglect by the parents may be accepted as excuses for cursing or hitting a parent. Rebelliousness carries an age limitation, but the exceptions (which would seem equally applicable to the rebellion situation) do not apply. Gluttony and drunkenness are included in the biblical offense of rebelliousness, but do not find their way into the *Body of Liberties*. Perhaps they are treated adequately elsewhere, but why were they deleted from the Bible Code of 1641? It is possible that Ward, a Puritan clergyman, was a gourmet or a fancier of hard liquor.

When the Body of Liberties was first enacted, it drew criticism that it was not in accord with the laws of England. Dr. Robert Child and similarly minded inhabitants who were not Puritans in religion attacked the colony's leadership for imposing laws that departed from the laws of England (1646). Because England was then moving toward civil war, this colonial dispute did not draw a negative response from the imperial authorities until after the 1660 restoration of royal government in England.

New England justice under the Bible codes appears harsher than that applied to the same offenses in England, but the actual evidence of prosecutions under these codes indicates that maximum sentences were rarely imposed or carried out. Criminal procedure in New England seems to have been less arbitrary than that afforded in Virginia and other Southern colonies which were influenced by English precedents. This aspect of being less arbitrary was evidenced by the refusal on the part of the Puritan colonies to allow the practice of benefit of clergy. Another example of the egalitarianism of New England Puritan justice was its heavy reliance upon the independent judgments of trial juries. The trial jury long had been a strong check upon overzealous criminal prosecutions in England. The continuing vitality of the trial jury in North America is one of the strongest marks of colonial attitudes favoring the retention of certain English legal and constitutional forms.

POLICING SEVENTEENTH-CENTURY AMERICA

Although formal police organizations did not exist in seventeenth-century America, there were at least two systems of law enforcement that operated in colonial society. The first was an *informal system* that had been effective from ancient times and that may still perform a useful role in modern society. This informal system involved the internal controls that exist in a small agricultural community, where virtually all of the inhabitants are related either by blood or marriage. Such a situation discouraged crime for many reasons. Disguise was impossible in a society where everyone was immediately recognized. Those who had criminal records were known and their modes of operation were easily identified. Also, punishment by public humiliation in front of relatives and long-term neighbors was a harsh sanction and a powerful deterrent. This system served the ancient world quite well until it became heavily populated and urbanized. It was revived in medieval Europe, which was intensely local in its politics and similarly provincial in the close economic and family relationships on each manor. From this background the ancient grand jury was drawn, a body of local inhabitants that reported on misdoings based on their own knowledge and their assessment of the probability that an accused person already well known to them might, in fact, be the guilty party. Historians of colonial America have found marked similarities between medieval manorial organization, the towns established in New England, and the plantations in the Southern colonies. Of course, the full-blown manorial and feudal system was not adaptable to American conditions, even though some efforts were made to implement it in New York, Maryland, and South Carolina.

HISTORY TODAY

Public humiliation was a commonly imposed punishment in colonial days. In what ways does the modern justice system impose public humiliation? Think of sex offender Web pages, drunk driving, or sex offenders' pictures in the local paper. Also consider Megan's Laws, which require local law enforcement to inform neighbors of a sex offender's presence in the neighborhood. Are these attempts at public embarrassment effective? Are they counterproductive, and if so, are they as counterproductive as prison?

The key to understanding the informal system of law enforcement in colonial America is *demography*. At the earliest stages of settlement, land was sparsely settled. In the case of New England towns, the original settlers were frequently members of the same English nonconformist congregation. Together they migrated to the New World, bringing with them church organizations and town governments based in part on their English practices and in part on their concept of the political covenant (that men could form governments by mutual consent, as in the Mayflower Compact). While similar religious ideas did not have such a decisive impact on the Mid-Atlantic and Southern colonies, those settlements also began with sparse populations and gradually evolved into established communities governed by a newly established elite. Apparently, social mobility was great at first, and a number of men brought to the New World as *indentured servants* were able to amass considerable fortunes and achieve high political office. Individuals were indentured so that they might work off a debt, which arose either from their passage being paid by their future master, or by judgment of an American court. Frequently young boys were indentured as apprentices to learn a trade or profession. Indentured servants would comprise a large segment of the Georgia colony, as many Georgia transplants had been released from debtors' prisons.

All colonies experienced rapid population growth, which presented difficulties in the distribution of land and dangers in public health, solved in part by the beginning of two centuries of westward migration. Within the settled communities, the crime rate rose rapidly in proportion to population growth.

Population was but one of many demographic factors that influenced crime rates and police systems. Another significant consideration was the rate of change in population, showing the numbers of individuals newly arrived in the community and the sizes of the groups emigrating to other settlements. This turnover in what was initially a static population decreased social control and created problems in identification. In its extreme form, the existence of transient populations caused growing seaport towns to resort to English law enforcement methods: constables, night watches, and special patrols.

Even in the small agricultural towns and villages, the influx of new settlers was cause for great concern. Movement in seventeenth-century America was no simple matter. Just as Elizabethan Poor Laws required that each parish support its own poor, New England towns also took on this burden. *Vagrants* who could not assert a claim to the generosity of a specific town were usually driven out before they could establish residence and claim support. As a consequence, strangers were not only suspect in colonial America, but they were usually received with hostility.

The rule in the American colonies was that everyone was expected to work and everyone was expected to marry. A critical scarcity of labor required that all able-bodied males be profitably employed. The local courts administered terms of apprenticeship and assured that orphaned children received appropriate training in some needed skill or trade. As might be anticipated, judges were reluctant to imprison convicts but quick to assign sentences of hard labor or even to design penalties that would compensate a victim through the labor of the convicted criminal.

HISTORY TODAY

Besides economic reasons, the colonists had a reason for requiring people to work. Those who did not were more likely to get into trouble. There is no legal requirement that men or women be employed today. The criminal justice system does not punish people for being unemployed, but they may suffer economically. However, in many jurisdictions, courts require people under probation supervision to be gainfully employed to the best of their ability. Should a court take into account whether a person has a good employment history when passing sentence or deciding whether to revoke probation?

In a similar vein, the family was viewed as a vital instrument of social control, and strong pressures moved both men and women in the direction of matrimony. Those who remained single were a source of concern to their neighbors, and court records abound of cases in which unmarried individuals of both sexes were involved in a wide variety of sexual offenses. Policing the activities of the unemployed and the unmarried was not difficult in small towns. It was accomplished by *close watching*, a neighborly "sport" designed to identify suspicious activity that might be reported to the local court or grand jury. In New England, this was particularly apparent in the large number of accusations for fornication, adultery, sodomy, and bestiality; the diligence of "close watchers" even resulted in some married couples being prosecuted for fornication after the early birth of their first child.

HISTORY TODAY

Adultery and fornication were taken very seriously in many areas of colonial America. In some states, these laws may still exist but they are seldom, if ever, enforced. In today's complex society, the prevailing attitude is that sex between consenting adults should not be regulated or controlled. To enforce fornication and adultery laws today would be impossible for a host of reasons. Given the damage done to families and communities as a result of adultery and sexual relations outside marriage (unplanned teen pregnancies, etc.), is it possible that colonial Americans may have had more wisdom in this area than we are willing to admit?

CRIMINAL JUSTICE AND SLAVERY

By the middle of the seventeenth century, a new demographic factor of major socioeconomic importance had appeared. African servants, originally imported into Virginia in 1619, increased in numbers and declined in legal status until at some time after 1660 virtually every person of African heritage held the status of a slave, and slavery was not confined to the Southern colonies. As indentured servants, both blacks and whites had the obligation of laboring for a term of years either to repay the cost of their passage to North America or to satisfy their outstanding debts. The assignment of a term of service was made by the local courts if no precise time had been agreed upon beforehand. By mid-century, it was generally accepted that Africans imported into the colonies were bound to servitude not only for their lifetimes but also for the lives of their descendants.

Because of this historic development, control and subjugation of a growing population of slaves became an issue in all of the colonies. For the most part, this was accomplished by giving extensive disciplinary powers to the master and, at the same time, using the plantation and its staff of overseers as the enforcement authority. If a slave committed a felony, he or she was tried before the local town or county court.

Some colonies established special courts charged with hearing criminal cases involving slaves. As a general rule, fewer procedural protections were given to slave defendants, and the sentences were always harsher than those given to whites convicted of the same offenses. Throughout the colonial period, there were outbreaks of rebellion among the slaves. These were invariably put down with great cruelty, which demonstrated the underlying fears of the ruling and slaveholding classes. It is significant that most uprisings occurred not in the small rural communities dominated by plantation agriculture, but rather in the growing towns and seaport cities where itinerant slaves had the opportunity to mingle with free blacks and with slaves temporarily free of their masters' close control.

HISTORY TODAY

Slavery still exists, though not legally, in many countries in the form of human trafficking. People, including children, are trafficked for labor exploitation, sexual exploitation, and other reasons. Conduct some research on human trafficking in your area, in the United States, and in other countries. Are governments doing enough to combat modern-day slavery?

Supplementing this informal system of law enforcement was the traditional English structure of local courts and government. Enforcement of the criminal law was the duty of sheriffs and local constables, aided at their request by anyone within earshot of a call for assistance. All persons were obliged to assist the enforcement officer, but few were eager to risk injury or death in the discharge of the duty.

The role of a sheriff or constable was not a happy one in colonial America, and the arrest of a suspect was frequently delayed or prevented by his or her resistance or by the occurrence of a riot. Riots and unlawful assemblies were subject to prohibition by a single justice of the peace; upon his reading of the *Riot Act*, a gathering became unlawful and was required to disperse. Harsh penalties, which might range as high as the sanctions for treason in opposing the forces of the sovereign, applied.

TIME CAPSULE: SAMUEL SEWALL

Alone among the persons involved in the prosecution of witches in Salem, Judge Samuel Sewall had the following statement read out in the South Meeting House in Boston in 1697 as he stood to acknowledge his penitence:

> Samuel Sewall, sensible of the reiterated strokes of God upon himself and family; and being sensible, that as to the Guilt contracted upon the opening of the late Commission [sic] of Oyer and Terminer at Salem (to which the order for this Day relates) he is, upon many accounts, more concerned than any that he knows of, Desires to take the Blame and shame of it, Asking pardon of men And especially desiring prayers that God, who has an Unlimited Authority, would pardon that sin and all other his sins; personal and relative: And according to his infinite Benignity, and Sovereignty, Not Visit the sin of him, or of any other, upon himself or any of his, nor upon the Land: but that He would powerfully defend him against all Temptations to Sin, for the future; and vouchsafe him the efficacious, saving Conduct of his Word and Spirit.

Source: Russell and Russell, 1963, *Samuel Sewall's diary.* New York: pp. 139-140.

Criminal cases were tried in the town or county courts if misdemeanors were involved. Those same courts heard arraignments of free inhabitants charged with felonies or treason and held the accused for the next meeting of the grand jury. It was customary for felony and treason cases to be tried either by the highest common law court of the colony or by a specially appointed court of oyer and terminer, composed of legally trained persons commissioned by the governor to hear and determine the guilt of the accused.

Judges of American colonial local courts were members of the leadership elite; they were determined to maintain law, order, and the dignity of their class. In theory, they were subject to the same supervision that the Privy Council exercised over their English counterparts. However, the governors of colonial America found that local justices of the peace and county courts were relatively isolated from centralized control. As a consequence, real political power became concentrated in the hands of local officials, and thus in the local gentry elected to represent the counties in the lower house of the colonial legislature.

Throughout colonial America, it was extremely uncomfortable to attract the disapproval of the local gentry. Many persons of blemished reputation were harassed by unwarranted threats of prosecution and decided to leave for other jurisdictions, notwithstanding the hostility of other townspeople to transients. Thus, a distrust of the gentry and the legal officers who upheld the status quo came to characterize the lower social classes, and resistance to the authority of constables and sheriffs was complemented by contemptuous speech directed toward the justices of the peace and magistrates. This formal system of law enforcement, despite its weaknesses and potential for abuse, persisted until the American Revolution.

FEATURED OUTLAW: THE SALEM WITCHES

One of the most fascinating and infamous events in the history of colonial America was the Salem Witch Trials of the 1690s. The story begins in 1692 with tales of several of the town's young women reportedly exhibiting various bizarre behaviors, including screaming, rolling on the ground, and making animal noises. Much of the blame was placed on a slave woman named Tituba. Tituba was a native of South America who had lived in Barbados before being purchased by a minister named Samuel Parris, who took her to New England. (Contrary to popular belief, Tituba was not of African dissent.) Parris's daughter Betty was the first young woman to exhibit bizarre behavior. No doubt influenced by her exposure to voodoo while living in the Caribbean, Tituba made a "witches' cake," which she fed to a dog, with the hope that the dog would reveal Betty's tormentor. Parris beat a confession out of Tituba, a confession she eventually recanted once the witchcraft hysteria subsided. In a successful effort to avoid further trials, Tituba identified two women, Sara Good and Sara Osborne, as witches.

Tales and accusations of witchcraft began swirling around Salem, fueled in part by personal vendettas. Accusations of witchcraft were practically impossible to refute, and several people confessed to witchcraft in order to spare their own lives. Others refused to confess or to name other witches and were executed, usually by hanging. Although most of the accused were women, some were men, including Giles Corey, who experienced the most gruesome execution of all. He was slowly pressed to death with heavy stones as he refused to name other witches. In all, 19 people were executed for witchcraft; more were sentenced to die, but were eventually pardoned as the hysteria died down.

Both the formal system of law enforcement and its unofficial "close watching" system were badly strained by the witchcraft agitations of the late seventeenth century. Beginning with prosecutions of old women in New England, the contagious fear of witches spread throughout the New World, just as it had infected the Old World in the sixteenth and seventeenth centuries. The famous Salem, Massachusetts, witchcraft trials before Judge Samuel Sewall resulted in the conviction and execution of a large number of women accused by hysterical children. Alone among the persons involved in the prosecution of witches in Salem, Judge Samuel Sewall had the following statement read out in the South Meeting House in Boston in 1697 as he stood to acknowledge his penitence:

Samuel Sewall, sensible of the reiterated strokes of God upon himself and family; and being sensible, that as to the Guilt contracted upon the opening of the late Commission [sic] of Oyer and Terminer at Salem (to which the order for this Day relates) he is, upon many accounts, more concerned than any that he knows of, Desires to take the Blame and shame of it, Asking pardon of men And especially desiring prayers that God, who has an Unlimited Authority, would pardon that sin and all other his sins; personal and relative: And according to his infinite Benignity, and Sovereignty, Not Visit the sin of him, or of any other, upon himself or any of his, nor upon the Land: but that He would powerfully defend him against all Temptations to Sin, for the future; and vouchsafe him the efficacious, saving Conduct of his Word and Spirit.

Historians believe that witchcraft cases arose because of instability in society and shifts in political and moral power. At the end of the seventeenth century, the American colonies were experiencing a declining influence of the clergy, a rapidly growing and more diverse population, and an economy that was maturing into a mixture of commercial and agricultural activities. It was a time when the older, informal system of "close watching" no longer worked as a police system, and the formal structure of constables, sheriffs, and local courts was to experience difficulties in restraining crime and disorder.

The Salem Witch Trials brought the term *witch hunt* into the English vocabulary, a term that is still used today. Likewise, modern Salem does not shrink from its association with the infamous witch trials. The witch trials are Salem's most famous legacy and tourist attraction. The town is dotted with shops that sell witchcraft-related items. Tourists flock to Salem to see the location of the witch trials and executions, and many official city vehicles, including police cars, are emblazoned with images of witches.

Sources: Russell and Russell, (1963). *Samuel Sewall's diary.* New York. pp. 139-140. Walker, S. (1998). *Popular justice: A history of American criminal justice* (2nd ed). New York: Oxford University Press; University of Missouri Kansas City School of Law Web site, http://www.law.umkc.edu/faculty/projects/ftrials/salem/ASAL_BI.HTM, accessed January 10, 2008.

SUMMARY

American colonial development in the seventeenth century was extraordinarily rapid, moving by 1700 from primitive settlement conditions to a complex society experiencing some of the ills of overpopulation and urbanization. For this reason, legal and social developments also occurred rapidly. Quite naturally, the settlers found much of value in their European and English traditions, and they reacted strongly to the persecution they had experienced in their home countries. The turmoil of the century and the frontier quality of colonial settlement provided opportunities

WITCHCRAFT AT SALEM VILLAGE.

FIGURE 6.3 The central figure in this 1876 illustration of a courtroom during one of the Salem Witch Trials is usually identified as Mary Walcott. *Courtesy en. wikipedia.org.*

for law reform that were stifled or short-lived in England, but flourished in the colonial wilderness. At the same time, political pressure from the royal authorities in London and the practical demands for effective police methods indicated that further changes would be required in the eighteenth century. American life drew closer to contemporary existence in England. Social mobility and access to cheap land decreased throughout the seventeenth century, and was to prove a serious problem in eighteenth-century America. An initial scarcity of labor softened harsh criminal sanctions in the early days of settlement, but a contrary trend was caused by unemployment and vagrancy in the cities and seaports. Law enforcement, like the law itself, became more formal and more in accord with English models. Experimentation of the early days gave way to the evolution of a mature legal system during the eighteenth century.

REFERENCES

Friedman, L. M. (1985). *A history of American law* (2nd ed). New York: Simon & Schuster; Hall, K. L. (1989). *The magic mirror: Law in American history.* New York: Oxford University Press; Chapin, B. (1983). *Criminal justice in colonial America, 1606-1660.* Athens: University of Georgia Press; Haskins, G. L. (1960). *Law and authority in early Massachusetts: A study in tradition and design.* New York: Macmillan Co.; Rankin, H. F. (1965). *Criminal trial proceedings in the general court of colonial Virginia.* Williamsburg, VA: Colonial Williamsburg; Scott, A. P. (1930). *Criminal law in colonial Virginia.* Chicago: University of Chicago Press; Levy, L. W. (1968). *Origins of the fifth amendment: The right against self-incrimination.* New York: Oxford University Press.

Erikson, K. T. (1966). *Wayward puritans: A study in the sociology of deviance.* New York: Wiley; Sawyer, J. K. (1990). Benefit of clergy in Maryland and Virginia. *American Journal of Legal History, 34*(1), 49–69.

Notestein, W. (1911). *A history of witchcraft in England from 1558 to 1718.* Washington: American Historical Association; Hill, F. (1995). *A delusion of satan: The full story of the Salem witch trials.* New York: Doubleday; Barstow, A. L. (1994). *A new history of the European witch hunts.* San Francisco: Harper; McManus, E. J. (1993). *Law and liberty in early New England: Criminal justice and due process, 1620-1692.* Amherst: University of Massachusetts Press; Geis, G., & Bunn, I. (1991). And a child shall mislead them: Notes on witchcraft and child abuse accusations. In

R. J. Kelly & D. E. J. MacNamara (Eds.), *Perspectives on deviance: Dominance, degradation and denigration* (pp. 31–45). Cincinnati: Anderson Publishing Co.; Richardson, J. T. (1991). *The Satanism scare*. New York: A. de Gruyter; Wilson, N. K. (1993). Taming women and nature: The criminal justice system and the creation of a crime in salem village. In R. Muraskin & T. Alleman (Eds.), *It's a crime: Women and justice* (pp. 52–73). Englewood Cliffs, NJ: Prentice Hall.

Wunder, J. R. (1994). *"Retained by the people": A history of American Indians and the Bill of Rights*. New York: Oxford University Press; Zatz, M. S., Lujan, C. C., & Snyder-Joy, Z. K. (1991). American Indians and criminal justice: Some conceptual and methodological considerations. In M. J. Lynch & E. B. Patterson (Eds.), *Race and criminal justice* (pp. 100–112). Albany: Harrow & Heston; Nielsen, M. O. (1996). *Native Americans, crime and justice*. Boulder, CO: Westview Press; French, L. (1982). *Indians and criminal justice*. Totowa, NJ: Allanheld, Osmun.

Bodenhamer, D. J. (1992). *Fair trial: Rights of the accused in American history*. New York: Oxford University Press; Greenburg, D. (1982). Crime, law enforcement, and social control in colonial America. *American Journal of Legal History, 16,* 293–325.

Notes and Problems

1. Because the first settlers in North America found such primitive conditions, was it wise for them to adopt biblical law as a convenient source of rules for a wilderness existence?

2. It is interesting to speculate upon the interplay of Native American customs with the colonial legal systems. Native Americans did not recognize personal rights to land or possessions; as a consequence, they were frequently prosecuted for "stealing" goods of a European settler or for trespassing on "his" land. Which law should have governed, that of the Indians or that of the newly arrived colonists?

CHAPTER 7

The Enlightenment and Criminal Justice

KEY TERMS

Age of Reason	Farinacius	Montesquieu
Alphonse Bertillon	Franz Joseph Gall	Old Bailey
André-Michel Guerry	Gendercide	Philosophes
Augustin Nicholas	Henry Faulds	Phrenology
Bloody Code	Henry Fielding	Positive law
Bow Street Runners	Henry Goddard	Radical criminology
Cartographic school	Jeremy Bentham	Shogunate
Cesare de Beccaria	John Locke	Sir Robert Peel
Criminalistics	Joseph Ignace Guillotin	Sir Samuel Romilly
Declaration du Roi	Justice	Thief takers
of May 1788	Karl Marx	Utilitarianism
Deterrence	Lambert Adolphe	Voltaire
Enlightenment	Jacques Quetelet	William Blackstone

LEARNING OBJECTIVES

1. Understand the role of the philosophes and the Enlightenment in the administration of criminal justice.
2. Learn some of the contributions made by Beccaria on criminological thought.
3. Become familiar with some of the innovations in criminal punishment.
4. Learn how the London police force was created.
5. Learn about the development of phrenology as a way of explaining crime.
6. Learn about the development of criminalistics and some of its pioneers.

7. Understand the principle of utilitarianism as articulated by Jeremy Bentham.
8. Understand the basics of radical criminology based on the writings of Karl Marx.
9. Learn about criminal justice under the Japanese Shogunate.

Table 7.1 Time Line: The Enlightenment in Europe and North America

1649	The Parliamentary party, having defeated English King Charles I in battle, executes the king for treason and institutes a republican form of government.
1651	Thomas Hobbes publishes *The Leviathan*.
1653-1658	Oliver Cromwell serves as Lord Protector of the Commonwealth.
1660	Charles II, the son of the executed English monarch, is called to the throne by Parliament and reestablishes royal authority in England and Scotland.
1682	Augustin Nicholas, a French judge at Dijon, attacks the use of torture in French criminal procedure.
1689	English Bill of Rights is issued by King William III and Queen Mary II of England, newly called to the throne by Parliament to replace the deposed King James II.
1690	John Locke's *Second Treatise of Government* is published, arguing that political authority is derived from the consent of the governed.
1717	Voltaire is committed to prison in France and charged with writing a seditious poem.
1748	Montesquieu's *Spirit of Laws* is published, setting forth the concept that there should be a separation of powers in governments.
1766	Beccaria publishes *Essay on Crime and Punishment*, urging that punishments should be proportionate to the seriousness of the offense, and that certainty of punishment is more deterring than its severity.
1776-1783	The War for American Independence officially begins with a Declaration of Independence drafted by Thomas Jefferson; it ends with a peace treaty, by which Great Britain recognizes the independence of the former colonies.
1780	The French Estates-General abolishes torture in preliminary criminal procedure.
1787	The Philadelphia Convention drafts the federal Constitution, which is approved by the Confederation Congress and then sent to the states to be ratified by conventions elected by the people.
1789	The new form of federal government, based on the Federal Constitution, begins operation in New York City. George Washington wins the election and is inaugurated as the first president.
1789	On July 14, the French Revolution begins with the storming of the Bastille Prison in Paris. A republic is established, and King Louis XVI is executed in 1793.
1798-1800	The United States becomes involved in an undeclared naval war with France, called the *Quasi-War with France*.
1801	Thomas Jefferson becomes the third president of the United States.
1803	France cedes the Louisiana Territory to the United States.
1803	Chief Justice John Marshall delivers the Supreme Court's opinion in the judicial review case of *Marbury versus Madison*.
1848	Popular uprisings occur in France and Germany, and a brief period of republican governments follows.
1848	Karl Marx and Friedrich Engels publish *The Communist Manifesto*, which advocates a class-based revolution that would lead to the collapse of the political state and to the institution of a utopian society in which wealth would be shared according to individual needs.

THE AGE OF REASON, THE NEED FOR SAFETY, AND FORBIDDEN BOOKS

England's settlement of North America in the seventeenth and eighteenth centuries is eclipsed in significance by the upheavals caused by the *Enlightenment*. The Enlightenment was a philosophical movement that drew its initial driving force from the rise of scientific investigation in mechanical physics (marked by Isaac Newton's publication of *Principia* in 1687) and the application of reason, humanitarianism, and secularism to problems of philosophy and political theory, typified by the publication of *John Locke's Essay Concerning Human Understanding and Second Treatise on Government* (both published in 1690).

> John Locke (1632-1704): among the most referenced of British philosophers; known for his influences in British empiricism and theories of liberal philosophy; outlined the elements of social contract theory, which emphasized natural rights, individual liberty, and justified constitutional law.

Sparked by cynicism and satirical humor, the Enlightenment found ready acceptance in eighteenth-century France. Englishmen were, for the most part, preoccupied with the formidable task of reestablishing a stable and functional government after the upheavals of the seventeenth century. The impact of thinkers such as David Hume, *Adam Smith*, and his Professor of Moral Philosophy at Glasgow University, Francis Hutcheson, was to become more significant in the legal and political thinking of the Founding Fathers than in the establishment of the early colonial history of the United States.

> Adam Smith (1723-1790): Scottish economist and philosopher; known for *Wealth of Nations*, which is among the most influential examinations of economics of all time, criticizes the effects of monopoly and unrestricted free enterprise, and is considered by many as the Bible of capitalism.

In the English colonies, Enlightenment thought ultimately led to the American Revolution and the institution of a republican government in a federal state marked by constitutionalism and limited political power. In France, it fueled seething discontent in the laboring and mercantile classes, generating a series of critical and satirical writings that survived both the censure of the authorities and the imprisonment of the authors. Ultimately, the Enlightenment was to be one of the leading causes of the French Revolution, which shook the old regime to its very foundations and caused a reconstitution of French society and political life. The impact in Britain was less dramatic, but within the first half of the nineteenth century the entire structure of English political power was radically altered by the gradual extension of the electoral franchise to virtually all classes. By 1881, 50% of the U.K. population was living in towns. The ownership of property had expanded vastly. A movement that started with the Charterists' attempts to gain the vote for all men in 1838 finally achieved the vote for most men by 1884.

The diversity of the Enlightenment makes it difficult to identify its main characteristics, but one of the primary aspects of the period was an increased emphasis on the role of reason in the enhancement of human understanding. Just as physical science used observation and measurement as the key to knowledge, so did the philosopher or political theorist study observable phenomena and then use logic to arrive at his or her conclusions. This required extensive research, not only of the variety of contemporary societies, but also of the historical evidence concerning long-dead civilizations. In the course of historical study, the Enlightenment philosophers discovered the ancient world and made it a model for their new view of life. However, they were careful to restrict their enthusiasm to the Athenian and Roman ancestors of Western civilization, ignoring the Jewish experience so readily available in the Bible. To the *philosophes*, who were the Enlightenment philosophers of the eighteenth century, the Bible, along with other religious writings, was a product of superstition and ignorance. In this sense, the Enlightenment was a rejection of a past dominated by Christianity and a "rediscovery" of the secular humanism of the classical authors.

Enlightenment era thinkers, although frequently differing in their conclusions, shared common modes of thought and methods of inquiry. Each sought certainty through objective observation and by the rigorous use of skepticism and logic in analyzing evidence. These philosophers were primarily interested in people and earthly societies; they carefully constructed hypothetical models to explain individual and group functions.

Typical of this sort of reasoning was John Locke's view of government as being based upon the consent of those to be governed. According to Locke's model, humans naturally feel the need to seek security for themselves as well as their property. This seemingly insatiable need for safety is satisfied through the creation of a society designed to protect individuals from criminal activity, as well as restraining them from committing crimes against others. Social and political processes were subjected to precise study, and it can truly be said that modern social science began with the Enlightenment. However, several aspects of Enlightenment era thought processes do not readily lend themselves to objective evaluation. Emotional attachments, sentiments concerning religious faith, and personal loyalties to individuals (and groups) do not fit well into Reason's analytical scheme. As a consequence, most Enlightenment era philosophers treated religion either with hostility or relegated it to a minor role in the affairs of mankind.

Montesquieu, in his *Spirit of Laws* (published in 1748), held two highly controversial views concerning religion. First, he indicated that no given religion was best for all societies and all situations; his detractors pointed out that this relativism undermined the very foundation of Christian missionary activity throughout the world. Second, he subjected religions to the test of utility; they were only as good as the benefit they conferred on the societies in which they existed. Because Christianity had long maintained its centrality as a source of public morality, as well as the fact that political power had been enhanced by religious endorsement for centuries, it is not surprising that Montesquieu was attacked by the politically and ecclesiastically orthodox people of his day. Earthly institutions and societies were no longer to be judged by religious standards; rather, religion was to be measured by the new moral standard of utilitarianism: what good it did for humankind.

The greatest threat to theology and traditional religion was posed by men like Montesquieu, who chose not to attack Christianity but to ignore it. However, Montesquieu is best remembered in terms of his impact on the delineation of the democratic state into the judiciary, legislature, and executive, exemplified in the United States under the separation of powers. According to him: "When the law making and the law enforcement are invested in the same person there can be no liberty." The Roman Catholic Church placed *The Spirit of Laws* on its index of forbidden books in 1751.

HISTORY TODAY

Social and philosophical movements have differed in many ways throughout history. In light of what occurred in the Middle East in 2011, with rebellions being triggered by communication mechanisms such as satellite television, the Internet, and social networking Web sites, is it reasonable to say that communication and technology have triggered an enlightenment of sorts in traditionally poor countries that were isolated from the Western world for centuries?

THE BEGINNING OF THE END FOR SECRET PROCEDURES

Minimizing or ignoring the role of religion in the lives of men resulted in an entirely new approach to crime and punishment. For the first time in the history of Western civilization, it was possible to think about crime as a secular phenomenon—something that had nothing to do with sin or moral standards based on theology. While biblical law represents the high point of religious influence on criminal justice, the connection remained through the ages and was not really challenged until the *Age of Reason*. The Age of Reason originally stressed the importance of observing and measuring physical phenomena. It was expanded into the application of scientific methods and logic to the study of human beings and their society.

Ultimately, this latter phase of the Age of Reason became known as the Enlightenment. The philosophes viewed crime as an earthly phenomenon that had to be studied in a secular framework and explained in a logical way. Wrongful acts were evaluated in terms of their impact on the welfare of individuals and society. Entirely absent from the equation was a need to expiate the wrath of an angry god. Punishment served a utilitarian purpose; it was intended to discourage future criminal activity by both the convicted person as well as those who witnessed his or her chastisement. Social control, rather than divine purposes, became the guiding light of Enlightenment penology.

HISTORY TODAY

Samuel Walker, a prominent criminologist, once argued that many crime control proposals fail because they are based more on faith than on facts. He meant that lawmakers enact legislation that they want to work and not so much what is likely to work based on empirical evidence. On the other hand, a person should not set aside their values and morals when considering crime control proposals. How much of a role do a lawmaker's or criminal justice professional's personal values play in his or her job performance?

When French proponents of Reason turned their attention to the criminal law of their day, they found a repressive system that had not only not changed in its particulars since 1539, but had become much more arbitrary and class-oriented as a result of the Ordinance of 1670, an Ordinance that was to remain effective until the Revolution in 1789. However, still present was the secrecy of extraordinary procedure—the lack of a defendant's right to call or confront witnesses, the denial of defense counsel, and the use of torture to satisfy the need for a sufficient number of proofs of guilt. Practice had expanded the availability of royal pardons and remissions of penalty for those with sufficient influence or wealth to obtain them. On the other hand, the autocratic reign of the Sun King (Louis XIV) increased the use of the *lettre de cachet*, a royal warrant that might commit an innocent person to prison without trial or even an idea of the offense.

The notorious "letters," warrants, were abolished by the Revolution only to be re-introduced by Napoleon Bonaparte in 1790. Such a *lettre*, issued on the false suspicion that *Voltaire* was the author of a seditious poem, condemned him to prison as a young man (1717) and made him an inveterate critic of French criminal procedure. Damaging as this appears to be, we should remember that the French had formalized "innocent until proven guilty" under Johnnes Monachus at the end of the thirteenth century. This legal maxim was widely taught in French law schools throughout the fourteenth century and permeated judicial proceedings.

In 1536, the Parlement of Paris reminded judges that it was illegal to describe a suspect as a murderer or thief in an arrest warrant and by the time of the 1670 Ordinance judges were encouraging trial witnesses to describe suspects not by name or alleged criminal conduct but rather more by a simple physical description. This is exampled by the case of John Calas of Toulouse, who was executed for murdering one of his sons. There was strong criticism from the courts that the investigation had not considered that Calas junior had committed suicide and in failing to take this into consideration the spirit of the law of "innocent until proven guilty" had been offended. Following this line of thinking, priests were not permitted to exclude suspects from taking the sacraments of penance or communion on the basis that they were innocent people until determined otherwise by a court of law. Before leaving this topic (and France), we should consider that, because torture was still commonplace, this did not *de facto* assume guilt, as otherwise the French legal system was torturing innocent people. By the eve of the French Revolution, under the *Declaration du Roi of May 1788* signed at Versailles, the presumption of innocence received royal blessing when Louis XVI referred to it as "[t]he first of all principles in criminal matters." Louis followed this up by banning the wearing of prison uniform, even for those on death row, until the appeal process had been exhausted and the removal of the low stool, the *selette*, that defendants were required to sit on in court and from this time onward defendants sat at the same level and height as all others in the courtroom.

By way of contrast to arbitrary French law, the philosophes looked to England, recently restored to stability after its struggle with Stuart absolutism. They found much to praise in English institutions of criminal law and particularly prized the jury trial that formed such an important part of the liberty of English citizens.

CLARITY IN LAW; EQUALITY IN APPLICATION

The philosophes considered the drafting of penal statutes to be one of the fundamental activities of the legislative power. They carefully distinguished justice and law, viewing justice as a "higher law" that existed even before the establishment of political societies. In this sense, they rejected the political theories of Thomas Hobbes, a seventeenth-century English philosopher who reacted to the disorders of his day by advocating the preeminence of *positive law*, which held that the authority that the sovereign power willed was both legal and just. Montesquieu, in his *Spirit of Laws*, made it quite plain that all laws should conform to natural law ideals. Furthermore, in shaping penal laws, the legislator should be certain to make the letter of the law conform to the nature of the society in which it was to function. Laws should be adapted to the people for whom they were designed to protect, as well as ensure both the health and stability of society.

Following the lead of Voltaire, Montesquieu also insisted that the criminal law be clear and without subtlety. A person of common understanding should be able to comprehend each prohibition of the law and thus be dissuaded from violating any provision of the criminal code. In 1766, *Cesare de Beccaria* pointed out that when law is written in a clear manner and can be universally read and understood, the very fact of its existence will cause a decrease in crime. Clarity in regard to punishment was also desirable, for then the individual contemplating committing a crime might be persuaded to measure the inconvenience of conviction against the momentary pleasures of the crime.

Another benefit of clear and concise criminal statutes was the elimination of judicial discretion, which had regularly facilitated unequal application of the law. According to philosophes of the day, the judge or magistrate should determine the relevant facts of a particular crime as well as the identity of the accused. The definition of the crime, and the elements of proof necessary to convict, should be rigidly established by the written law. Additionally, the principal function of the judge should be to apply the law to the facts of a particular case; at no point were judges to become involved in the interpretation of the law. As previously mentioned, such discretion could result in the unequal application of penal laws that might fluctuate in accordance with the class or reputation of the defendant. In sentencing, the subjective decisions of judges were highly suspect, and Enlightenment commentators preferred precise legislative standards for punishment. As Beccaria phrased it,

> That a magistrate, the executor of the laws, should have a power to imprison a citizen, to deprive a man he hates of his liberty upon frivolous pretenses, and to leave his friend unpunished, notwithstanding the strongest proofs of his guilt, is an error as common as it is contrary to the bond of society, which is personal security.[1,2]

Judges had traditionally possessed a significant amount of discretion in interpreting the law, and in many situations the punishments were finely tuned to the social or political status of the accused. However, the Age of Reason insisted on the equality of individuals before the law. In France, and throughout most of Europe, this new attitude toward criminal law resulted in a precise codification of penal statutes and a sharp limitation on any exercise of judicial interpretation. On the other hand, in Anglo-American law, this quest for certainty and equality has led to the general principle that criminal statutes should not be vague. The United States Constitution, written at the full flush of the Age of Reason, has been interpreted to read that vague penal laws are constitutionally void, that all federal crimes must be defined by statute, and that all accused persons must be afforded both due process and equal protection of the laws.

PROCEDURAL GUARANTEES, ABOLITION OF TORTURE, PUBLIC SPANKING, AND GENDERCIDE

Enlightenment era attitudes concerning criminal procedure sprang from a new view of the relationship between individuals and their society; in the words of Montesquieu, "in moderate governments . . . the life of the meanest subject is deemed precious" and no one can be deprived of honor or property except after a long and careful inquiry during which he or she has been given every possible opportunity to make a defense.[3] This was supplemented by the principle that, in the eyes of the law, every person should be considered innocent until his or her crime had been proven beyond reasonable doubt. Departing from the viewpoint of earlier ages, the Age of Reason was more concerned with the moral injustice of a wrongful conviction than the need for effective policing and control of the masses. The main complaint of the philosophers during this age was against the European systems of inquisitorial procedure. Although the excessive harshness of French criminal procedure was the background against which these philosophers wrote, the general principles of fair procedure and rights of the individual accused were also highly influential in Anglo-American legal development and constitutional thought.

As we have seen, preliminary arrest was one of the widespread abuses of French criminal law, under the infamous *lettre de cachet*. The ordinary course of criminal prosecution utilized imprisonment before trial, leading Enlightenment writers to demand that a system of bail be instituted in noncapital cases. In addition, they suggested that individuals held under preliminary arrest be separated from convicted felons, thereby softening the circumstances of imprisonment and mitigating its dangers.

Proposals for reforming the French system of trials included the demand that all criminal trials be held in public, affording the accused an opportunity to confront any alleged witnesses, and that no person be convicted in a capital case except on the testimony of two witnesses. It was stated that the accused should not be placed under oath and examined in such a way that he or she might accuse him- or herself either by confusion or through compulsion.

Following English practice, it was suggested that the most objective decision in criminal trials could be obtained only by the use of a jury with numerous members. This would provide additional security for the accused and also ensure impartiality in judgment. Where the accused was of a different social class than his or her victim, Beccaria suggested that one-half of the jury should be drawn from the victim's peers and the other half from the peers of the accused.

Central to the philosophes' attack on criminal procedure was a logical and humanitarian critique of torture. By 1780, the vehemence of the effort convinced the French States-General to abolish the use of preliminary torture, a particularly objectionable method of obtaining incriminating evidence. In the seventeenth century, lawyers and judges had spoken out against the use of torture, claiming that it was an uncertain method of obtaining evidence and that more likely than not it would result in the conviction of innocent people. *Augustin Nicolas*, president of the Parlemant of Dijon, penned a powerful attack against torture (1682) that criticized the execution of countless innocent people "upon confessions forcibly extorted by unbearable torments."[4]

FEATURED OUTLAW: VOLTAIRE

Voltaire (1694-1778) was the pseudonym for Francois Marie Arouet, one of the most famous French writers and philosophers in history, and a prominent political and social theorist of the Enlightenment. Voltaire's mother died when he was seven and he was not close to his father. He attended a Jesuit College in Paris with the intention of becoming a lawyer, but abandoned this plan shortly after college, being a bigger fan of literature, poetry, and drama than the law. In fact, his ambition was to be France's premier epic poet.

Voltaire was skeptical of the mainstream religious thought of the day, which branded him as a rebel in college and throughout his life. However, he loved to debate theology and religious doctrine and he wrote about it as well. Voltaire was a vocal advocate of deism, which posits that a sense of morality and religious belief can and should be acquired through human reason rather than divine revelation. Deism was viewed by many mainstream church authorities, both in Europe and the Americas, as heretical and as a threat to mainstream Christian thought. While Montesquieu made his lack of regard for the Roman Catholic Church respectfully and subtly, his contemporary Voltaire drove the matter home with satire and ridicule.

His writings resulted in substantial notoriety, which caused him to run afoul of the law. In 1717, he was arrested and imprisoned for 1 year at the infamous Bastille prison (which in later years would become the symbol of government tyranny in France) for criticizing the Duc d'Orleans. The Duc d'Orleans was a regent, the person who effectively served as head of state when the monarch was a minor, for King Louis XV. Today it would be unthinkable to imprison someone in the United States for merely criticizing the head of state, but this was not the case in eighteenth-century France.

Voltaire's next imprisonment was for something less noble. He fought a man who made fun of his name, was imprisoned in 1726, and was subsequently exiled to England. He returned to France several years later, emboldened and enlightened by prolonged exposure to English literature and philosophy. His next brush with the law came on the heels of his fictional treatise on religious toleration, titled *Lettres philosophiques*. A warrant for his arrest led him to go into hiding in the Champagne area of France.

Subsequent years found Voltaire writing about French matters, both political and religious, but in Switzerland, away from the reaches of French authorities. He moved back and forth between Switzerland and France, constantly dodging legal and church authorities who sought to prosecute him for his heretical writings. Voltaire's main objection to the Roman Catholic Church was its emphasis on the preeminence of its own religious dogma to the exclusion of other ideas, especially human reason. He envisioned the perfect state as one with a strong government, and he even endorsed a monarchical form of government, but not a theocracy. He was also a vocal opponent of torture and what he called "useless punishments." Voltaire died shortly after a triumphant return to Parisian theatre in 1778.

Source: Wilson Web Biographies, http://vnweb.hwwilsonweb.com, accessed March 24, 2008.

By comparison, consider that in Italy unscrupulous merchants were given a good spanking in public and for more than 2,000 years athletes who performed badly were flogged. England was still applying pressure liberally on suspects, and less than a century earlier priests were subject to immediate execution, hanged, drawn, and quartered, if found conducting mass. The Scold's Bridle, last used in 1824, a metal device placed upon the mouth of women to stop them talking, was used frequently in Scotland and south of the border and execution by axe was still used as a means of dispensing with English nobility who were viewed as disloyal.

Nicolas questioned how a judge, faced with deciding the fate of an accused person, could possibly decide in favor of the death penalty without overwhelming evidence; in fact, torture resulted in confessions by the innocent as frequently as it resulted in admissions by the guilty. However, such sentiments were generally ignored until the arrival of Enlightenment philosophers, particularly Voltaire and Beccaria, who launched a full-scale attack on the practice. By 1780, there was an established academy (Chalons sur Marne) dedicated to reform of the criminal law. Among the subjects for discussion and study was the abolition of torture. In fact, torture was used widely across the globe. It was abolished in Sweden in 1734, Prussia in 1754, France in 1788, and Japan finally in 1879.

While Voltaire dealt with the subject of torture at various points in his correspondence and writings, it was left to Beccaria to mount a systematic campaign in his *Essay on Crimes and Punishments* (1766). It was widely accepted that Italian methods of torture had reached the ultimate in cruelty and barbarism. Thus, it is not surprising that Beccaria would be more effective in questioning its legitimacy.

Torture had its origins in twelfth-century efforts to suppress heresy, and its survival in church courts ensured its incorporation into continental legal systems. The abomination of witch hunts throughout Europe had led to the execution of 26,000 in Germany, 10,000 in France, and only four in Ireland. Seventy-five percent of those killed were women, arguably constituting *gendercide*, and the majority were over the age of 50 years. However, 50% of those prosecuted were not executed and 1,300 appeals were heard by the French Parlement.

As Beccaria pointed out, torture shared the defects of the ancient trial by ordeal, long ago condemned by the church and society, for both procedures had no logical relationship to discovering truth. Could it be intelligently believed that truth depended on the stamina of the prisoner? Was truth to be found in the muscles and fibers of the accused? People varied in their physical and emotional ability to withstand pain, but that had nothing to do with guilt or innocence. Indeed, the weaker persons who were innocent of crime were more likely to be condemned than the strong and robust individual who was guilty. Furthermore, it was contrary to logic to use torture as a means to compel the accused to become one's own accuser. It was equally unreasonable to inflict the same amount of pain on an innocent person as on one who was actually guilty. Because punishment was to serve as a deterrent to crime, the use of torture as a part of the criminal process made it clear that one would be tormented not for guilt but, rather, as a simple consequence of having been accused.

As the French Revolution approached, the attacks of the philosophes on criminal procedures and the barbarities of torture began to have their impact. Shortly after the abolition of preliminary torture in 1780, there were a series of criminal prosecutions in which individuals were convicted and executed for crimes later shown to have been the deeds of others. However, prominent lawyers and judges continued to defend the system of criminal procedure, asserting that without torture it would be virtually impossible to convict persons accused of crime.

TIME CAPSULE: BENTHAM'S CALCULUS OF PLEASURE AND PAIN

The term *utilitarianism* is often associated with Jeremy Bentham (1748-1832). He defined utility as the "principle which approves or disapproves of every action whatsoever, according to the tendency which it appears to have to augment or diminish the happiness of the party whose interest is in question; or, what is the same thing in other words, to promote or to oppose that happiness." As a legislator strives for pleasure and avoidance of pain, Bentham argued, it benefited him to understand their nature. As a child of the Enlightenment, Bentham therefore analyzed the values inherent in pleasure and pain as a way of comprehending the hedonistic calculus a person might undertake when contemplating an action.

To a person considered *by him or herself,* the value of a pleasure or pain considered *by itself* will be greater or less, according to the following four circumstances:

1. Its *intensity*
2. Its *duration*
3. Its *certainty* or *uncertainty*
4. Its *nearness* or *remoteness*

These are the circumstances that are to be considered in estimating a pleasure or a pain. But when the value of any pleasure or pain is considered for the purpose of estimating the tendency of any *act* by which it is produced, there are two other circumstances to be taken into the account; these are as follows:

5. Its *fecundity,* or the chance it has of being followed by sensations of the *same* kind: that is, pleasures, if it be a pleasure: pains, if it be a pain.
6. Its *purity,* or the chance it has of *not* being followed by sensations of the *opposite* kind: that is, pains, if it be a pleasure: pleasures, if it be a pain.

And one other; to wit:

7. Its *extent:* that is, the number of persons to whom it *extends;* or (in other words) who are affected by it.

Source: Bentham, J. (1948). *An Introduction to the Principles of Morals and Legislation.* New York: Hafner Publishing Co., pp. 2, 29-30.

FIGURE 7.1 Jeremy Bentham. *Courtesy en.wikipedia.org.*

THE BIRTH OF PENOLOGY, CRIMINAL INSANITY, AND SWIFT EXECUTIONS

The publication of Marquis de Beccaria's *Essay on Crimes and Punishments* (1766) represented the high tide of Enlightenment thought on criminal justice and was also the beginning of the modern science of penology. A true product of the Age of Reason, the *Essay* was influenced by theories of public utility and moderation in the exercise of political power. It not only demonstrated a deep compassion for those convicted of wrongdoing, but also attempted to provide a realistic appraisal of the nature of crime and to suggest methods for its control. Beccaria saw the increase of population, with the consequent clash of private interests, as the reason for the increase in crime. Certain steps might be taken to suppress criminal activity, such as the illumination of the streets at night and the establishment of security guards and street patrols, but the greatest deterrent to crime was the certainty of punishment and not its severity. Indeed, the harshness of penalties might cause the populace to become hardened to cruelty and render punishment less effective as a warning to future offenders.

Public utility was the central focus of Beccaria's system of punishment. He was deeply concerned that the bonds of society be strengthened, not weakened, by the imposition of criminal sanctions. Those bonds he called *justice*, by which he meant the very minimum of behavior necessary to maintain tranquility in society and also the very minimum of punishment necessary to discourage misbehavior. Quoting Montesquieu, Beccaria asserted "Every punishment, which does not arise from absolute necessity . . . is tyrannical."[5,6] Necessity was found in the need to suppress crime, to deter its future commission, and to protect society from criminal behavior. Sanctions that did not serve these purposes were both unjust and counterproductive. For example, Beccaria believed that capital punishment was unnecessarily harsh in the case of convicted murderers. The major concern was the protection of society against a future offense, which could be more humanely achieved through the banishment of the criminal. Because banishment traditionally had been associated with the forfeiture of property rights, Beccaria again applied utility as the measure. The banishment of the murderer, if it were a permanent break with society, might justify some seizure of property. However, forfeiture punished the innocent heirs of the convict, and should it impoverish them to the point of desperation, it might easily cause them to resort to crime out of necessity. Thus, Beccaria noted that the best interests of society would be served by banishment, coupled with very limited forfeitures of family property.

Deterrence was a major factor in Beccaria's penology. To serve as a good example, punishment should be both quick and certain. Penalties were to be fixed by law, not subject to the whim of the ruler, who might pardon the accused or remit the sentence. Swiftness of punishment was a common feature throughout Europe and the period between sentence and execution of punishment was often immediate or at most a couple of days. In cases where an appeal was permitted, the delay might extend to months but once the appellate procedure had been exhausted, then if the death penalty were confirmed most prisoners were executed straight away. In England the deceased was immediately removed to Surgeons Hall, within the walls of the *Old Bailey*, for public dissection and anatomical investigation by surgeons. The joint task of being a barber and surgeon finally ended with two professions. The only remains of this history are the blood intertwined with white on the red and white poles outside of some barber shops. In France, *Joseph Ignace Guillotin* had perfected his execution machine on cattle and sheep. Nicholas Jacques Pelletier became the first Frenchman to be executed by the guillotine in 1792.

Clemency was to be found not in the heart of the ruler but, rather, in the precise provisions of the penal statutes. Prosecutions were to be prompt, thereby ensuring that the public did not forget the nature of the crime before it viewed the extent of the punishment. Sanctions should be graduated to fit the severity of the crime. The troubling issue of how to deal with the insane who committed crime had been problematic for centuries. During the sixteenth century, the Italian jurist *Farinacius* introduced the idea that the insane should be held incapable of criminal intent and accordingly the court should order that they are not guilty and should not be imprisoned. This was apparently too radical for the times and the legislature amended the legal language to show insane but guilty; therefore, imprisonment remained an appropriate sanction.

TIME CAPSULE: DEMOGRAPHY, CULTURE, AND CRIME

The essence of Enlightenment thought was the application of "Reason" to all areas of human knowledge. Given the right data, all human behaviors would also conform to some predictable pattern—or so the *philosophes* thought. Yet the problem of crime has proven to be much more difficult to resolve than Beccaria surmised. Indeed, the complex origins of crime may lie deep within segments of culture and personality that we have yet to explore. On the other hand, we have made a beginning. One interesting case study is that undertaken by Douglas Greenberg, which looks at colonial New York from 1691 to the American Revolution. Virtually alone among the North American colonial settlements, New York was characterized by a wide range of nationalities in its population. There were also a substantial number of slaves, and the colony experienced slave revolts in 1712 and 1741. For most of the seventeenth century, the descendants of the original Dutch settlers were treated with suspicion by the English residents. They, in turn, retained many of their original customs and Dutch was spoken well into the eighteenth century. New York also welcomed Protestants fleeing from religious persecution in Louis XIV's France, and Jews expelled from the Spanish empire also found refuge in the colony. With such a mix of racial, ethnic, and religious groups, New York was the preeminent "melting pot" of colonial North America—and therefore an excellent subject for Greenberg's study.

As we might expect, the largest number (90%) of defendants in New York's colonial courts was of white English men. Only 10% were women, but a higher percentage (16.8%) of city-dwelling defendants were women; Greenberg surmises that this was probably due to New York City being a seaport, with a large collection of brothels. Slaves constituted between 11% and 15% of New York's population, but they were less than 8% of those prosecuted for crime. Perhaps their oppressed condition left them fearful

of the consequences of criminal behavior, and even more likely is the possibility that most slave crime involved theft from masters, who took punishment into their own hands.

Another interesting comparison is the type of criminal activity for which men and women were arrested. For men, the major category (22.6%) was violent crimes against persons, followed by violations of public order (drunkenness, street fighting, etc.). For women, maintaining "disorderly houses" (brothels and bars) was the highest basis for prosecution (40.4%), followed by illegal relations with slaves (usually selling alcoholic beverages) (32.4%) and theft (26.1%).

Among those accused of crime and brought to trial (about 50% of all accused persons), the highest percentage of those convicted (68.6%) applied to slaves, and 51.6% of Indians were convicted. On the other hand the conviction rates of men (48.1%) and women (46.5%) are remarkably similar.

Greenberg provides many thought-provoking speculations, based in part on his evidence. For example, he notes that single women accounted for an inordinate number of prosecutions, and quite likely the same is true for single men. Is the marital status of a population a significant factor in causing criminal activity? Does it alter the nature of criminal activity? We might also wonder whether the eighteenth-century patterns persist even today, or have women become more violent and men more property-oriented in their crime patterns?

Source: Greenberg, D. (1974). *Crime and law enforcement in the colony of New York, 1691-1776.* Ithaca: Cornell University Press.

Question

In light of these statistics, what can you say about sources of crime in colonial New York? Do you believe that Beccaria's view of penology—that is, the way in which punishment will deter people from crime—would have worked in New York? What other factors would you have to consider?

Beccaria intended to ensure that no would-be offender would be tempted to commit a more serious crime simply because it bore the same penalty as a lesser crime. One example of this is the variant treatment he accorded to what American law calls *larceny* (the nonviolent taking of property) and robbery (seizure of property coupled with violence or the threat of violence against the owner). Larceny was to be punished by pecuniary sanctions, either fines or multiple restitution, while robbery was to be subject to these penalties plus corporal punishment, the preferred method being public whipping. In fact, throughout the 1800s the death penalty was still liberally applied, as was mutilation. For example, deserters were commonly subject to the amputation of a foot; hands were removed from thieves; and the tongues of slanderers were cut. Because physical punishment was believed to be a deterrent, amputations, floggings, and executions remained public spectacles for most of the century. In 1786, the Grand Duke of Tuscany, the future Emperor Leopold II, approved legislation that abolished the crimes of suicide, dueling, and *lese majeste* (injuring the name of the monarch or state) and the death penalty. He was successful for a while; however, Italy reinstated the death penalty, mutilation, and torture after his death.

The precise application of punishment was no simple matter. Each crime had to be studied and placed within the scale of severity. Severity, in turn, was a measure of the degree to which a given act undermined society or threatened the security of some individual or group. Matching punishment to crime required a consideration of the deterrent value of the sanction, as well as its effectiveness in protecting society. Finally, it was Beccaria's view that sanctions should be moderate, exceeding the anticipated gain from criminal activity only enough to discourage would-be offenders. Severity beyond that measurable limit was, in his opinion, superfluous and tyrannical.

By modern standards, Beccaria's *Essay* presented an overly optimistic or overly rational view of the potential of penology. Throughout Beccaria's work, there exists a confident assertion that each individual crime can be eradicated from society simply by discovering the "right" penal medicine. One could argue that certainty of punishment is impossible without effective policing and accurate procedures of criminal investigation, both conspicuously absent in Beccaria's day. The *Essay* rested on the basic premise that all criminals will react in similar ways to the same sanction and that criminal activity is itself a rational form of behavior subject to logical deterrence. In this sense, Beccaria overlooked psychological diversity between individuals and the infinitely varied motivations for criminal behavior.[7,8] Beccaria also did not account for the simple fact that many people who commit crime are not rational thinkers, at least at the time the crime is being committed. Drunkenness, mental illness, and occasional irrational or angry behavior among otherwise rational people do not enter into Beccarian ideals.

FIGURE 7.2 Karl Marx.
Library of Congress.

Despite these reservations about its major premises, one cannot deny that Beccaria's masterpiece was a milestone in the history of criminal justice. For the first time, penology was subjected to vigorous and systematic analysis. Crime and its punishment were studied in an entirely secular framework, using public utility as the guideline for judging both the morality and the practical value of sanctions. After publication of the *Essay*, sin was to play a minor role in Western civilization's discussions of penology.

CLARIFYING ENGLISH LAW AND BLUEPRINTS FOR AMERICA

Beccaria called for statutes written in a clear manner that could be easily understood. Over the centuries, however, the English Parliament had passed a succession of statutes that resulted in a collection of criminal laws that were not only contradictory,

TIME CAPSULE: RADICAL AND CONFLICT CRIMINOLOGY

Enlightenment philosophy bore unforeseen fruit in the nineteenth century in the form of communist theory and practice. *Karl Marx* (1819-1883), preeminent among communist thinkers, followed the philosophes in emphasizing the ability of man rationally to form societies based on equitable principles, but he derived a far different concept of criminology, which has come to be known as *radical* or *conflict criminology*.

Analysis of earlier societies convinced Marx and Friedrich Engels (1820-1895) that the principal dynamic of societies was the mode of production. Starting from the premise that labor is the source of all wealth, Marxism found inherent conflicts of interest between the class of persons who controlled the means of production (capitalists) and the class of actual producers (proletariat) who sold their labor to the capitalists. Marx and Engels believed this conflict would generate a series of revolutions. In their *Communist Manifesto* (1848), they wrote that the history of all previous society was one of class struggle. They predicted that the proletariat, which far outnumbered the capitalists, would come to recognize their common cause and rise up to

overthrow their oppressors. Out of this class struggle would emerge a communist society in which the means of production would be communally owned and all persons would be equal.

In the ultimate classless society, the innate goodness of humankind would prevail and individuals and groups would live harmoniously in a community in which the "free development of each is the condition for the free development of all" (*The Communist Manifesto*). The state, being no longer necessary, could then wither away. However, before reaching this final stage, a society would, as Vladimir Lenin argued, pass through a socialist phase led by a dictatorship by the proletariat, which could educate individuals for life in a communal society. It is this dictatorial phase of development that spawned totalitarian criminal justice systems in socialist countries. So far, no nation has claimed to have moved beyond the socialist transitory period into full communism.

Although Marx and his collaborator Friedrich Engels wrote little concerning crime, passages in works such as *A*

TIME CAPSULE: RADICAL AND CONFLICT CRIMINOLOGY—CONT'D

Contribution to the Critique of Political Economy (1859), *The German Ideology* (1845-1846), and *The Condition of the Working Class in England in 1844* (1844), indicate their conclusions regarding the causes of criminal activity, its nature, and possible means of curtailing it. If, as they contended, those who command the means of production can shape other fundamental institutions of a society by controlling the legislature, administrative bureaucracies, police, judicial systems, and prisons, then it is the economic elite who determine the legal definition of crime, the means of enforcement of criminal law, and the nature of sanctions to be imposed. Some of Marx's adherents created a branch of criminology called *conflict criminology*, more specifically *group conflict criminology*, which suggests that the groups with the most power control the legislative and judicial processes in society. Law, in the eyes of a Marxist, is a means of exploitation of the true producers of a society, the proletariat, and therefore an instrument in the class struggle.

Capitalists, who dominated the legislature and judiciary, could shape substantive law. By selecting the types of behavior to define as criminal, the ruling class created prohibitions that enhanced its power while at the same time avoided criminalizing their own transgressions. Therefore, emphasis was placed on "street crime" and property crimes that adversely affected the capitalists. In particular, deviant thought was criminalized, thus stripping political opponents of a claim to legitimacy. The genesis of crime, Marx and Engels argued, lay in the inequitable economic relations of members of society. The capitalist system not only increases the wealth of the owners of the means of production by exploiting laborers, but also fosters a sense of alienation of the worker from the product of his labor by depriving him of a fair share of its market value. Furthermore, when capitalists seek to maximize profits through laborsaving devices, they create an army of unemployed. These processes cause increasing misery among the proletariat, including hunger and homelessness. Some members of the oppressed class resort to illegal means to satisfy their needs. In 1844, Engels wrote, "If the influences demoralizing the working man act more powerfully, more concentratedly than usual, he becomes an offender as certainly as water abandons the fluid

for the vapourous state at [its boiling point]" (*The Condition of the Working Class in England in 1844*).[9] Only in a fully developed communist society could the major economic and social causes of crime be eliminated.

At the lowest level of society, Marx and Engels perceived a parasitic "dangerous class" (Lumpenproletariat) that produces nothing and survives by criminal activity such as theft, prostitution, extortion, and beggary. This class of criminals was denigrated by Marx and Engels as the enemy of the working class, both because they lacked the capacity to aid in the movement toward communism, and because many actively served the capitalist state as police informers.

Marxists were not alone in urging fundamental transformation of the economic relations of man. In part, they drew on the concepts of earlier socialists such as Robert Owen (1771-1858) of England and Charles Fourier (1772-1837), Henri Count de Saint-Simon (1760-1825), and Louis Blanc (1811-1882) of France.

Thus, although Marx, Engels, and other communists followed the Enlightenment method of analysis in utilizing reason to understand societal dynamics and in viewing crime as a secular phenomenon, the model they posited and the goals they sought represented a sharply divergent trend. For them the fundamental causes of crime lay not within the individual but within society. Because individual free will was significantly curtailed by economic forces, solutions to the crime problem involved a radical transformation of economic relationships rather than deterrence of criminal activity or rehabilitation of individual criminals. Moreover, Marxists would not look to existing political systems to guarantee procedural protections for the accused. Where legislatures serve the exploiters, no reforms could be achieved. These concepts, which remained peripheral to the mainstream of Enlightenment thought during the nineteenth century, provided the foundation for repressive criminal justice systems in the former communist governments of Eastern Europe and in the People's Republic of China. In the eyes of many Americans, communism was viewed as the greatest threat to the existence of democratic government and the American way of life in general during most of the twentieth century.

but also lacked a rational gradation of designated harm and punishment. If one were to make a rational choice concerning whether to commit an act, theoretically he would need to know whether it violated a criminal law and what punishment he would be liable for. The lack of a comprehensive explanation of existing English law made this a difficult, if not impossible, task.

In the spirit of the Enlightenment emphasis on reason, *William Blackstone* (1723-1780) undertook the task of providing a broad and logical explanation of the whole of English common law of the late eighteenth century. Blackstone had had a distinguished legal career as a professor at Oxford, a judge in the Court of Common Pleas and in the King's Bench, and as a member of Parliament. Beginning in 1765, he published his Oxford lectures in a series of *Commentaries on the Laws of England*.

Although criticized by some contemporary scholars, Blackstone's *Commentaries* were an immediate success, welcomed for comprehensive coverage and praised for his engaging literary style. Perhaps the most quoted passage is the one in which he stated that "... all presumptive evidence of felony should be admitted cautiously: for the law holds, that it is better that 10 guilty persons escape, than that one innocent suffer."[10,11]

Blackstone is also significant in legal history for bringing the study of law into English universities: he was the first professor of law at Oxford. His *Commentaries* were studied in the United States and American universities also began offering legal courses. The impact that Blackstone had on the formalization and understanding of the common law should not be understated. His commentaries served as a model for the writing of many legal codes, including the 1808 Civil Code of Louisiana. This is perhaps curious, given the significant influence of France on the American nation and particularly the state of Louisiana, but even the French were to concede that the clarity of Blackstone's civil codes was unsurpassed. James Kent (1763-1847), the first professor of law at Columbia College, followed the example of Blackstone and published his lectures in four volumes as *Commentaries on American Law* in 1826-1830.

THE "BLOODY CODE," NEWGATE EXECUTIONS, AND OLD BAILEY

Clarification of the law stimulated efforts to revise statutes to conform to reason and current values. These reform efforts often targeted the death penalty. The eighteenth century saw a rapid increase in the number of capital offenses to more than 200, most of them for property offenses. In the absence of a police force in England, Parliament responded to the pressures of propertied classes anxious to protect their wealth by including ever more acts into the category of capital offenses. It was a capital crime, for instance, to cut down a cherry tree in an orchard. Furthermore, this *"Bloody Code"* also restricted the number of capital offenses for which a person could plead benefit of clergy, a process that would move the case to ecclesiastical courts, which did not have a death penalty; even minor theft was designated nonclergyable.

The level of drunkenness, violence, and crime throughout London was of such proportions that it was inevitable that the late seventeenth century and all of the eighteenth century would see significant enactment of public order and criminal statutes. Class divisions were normal during this period and "gentlemen" who swore in the street were fined five shillings; "commoners" were fined one shilling. *Henry Fielding*, the famous novelist and creator of the *Bow Street Runners*, wrote in 1751 that the area of St. Giles, London, had many inns and boarding houses that were little more than brothels, and often with three to a bed; they were places where gin was sold for a penny a quart. In 1692, highway robbery was of such concern that the "Act for Encouraging the Apprehending of Highwaymen" was introduced. Under this provision, a reward of 40 pounds and retention of the offender's horse and goods was available to anyone who apprehended a highway robber. Effective though this was, it also introduced the concept of professional *thief takers* into the English language. Getting paid to apprehend criminals caught on.

> Henry Fielding (1707-1754): Prominent novelist and playwright; considered the founder of the English novel, including *Joseph Andrews* and *Tom Jones*; after being appointed magistrate for the county of Middlesex, started a newspaper, *The Covenant Garden Journal*, in order to improve relations between the police and public.

Eighteenth-century England had engaged in much of the discussion about the establishment of prisons as an alternative to mutilation, transportation, and the death penalty, but prisons as a place to serve a sentence did not gain universal approval until 1840. London had built its fifth gate into the city in 1218 but it soon became Newgate prison. It was rebuilt in 1770 but a fire prevented the opening until 1775. Before this, it was not uncommon for prisoners awaiting trial to be left to perish. This happened to 11 monks in 1537 when they were simply left to starve. It was another 100 years before England was to establish modern penitentiaries at London's Millbank and Pentonville. In 1877, Newgate stopped being a general prison and was used exclusively to hold prisoners awaiting trial or execution.

Conditions in Newgate prison throughout its history have at times been appalling. For many decades, inmates were required to pay for their food and shelter. Failure to do so resulted in being placed in leg irons. Improvement came slowly and immediate execution was extended to a minimum of 3 weeks between sentence and death. Prisoners on death row were no longer kept in leg irons 24 hours per day, and family and friends were permitted to visit those awaiting execution. Because of the number of executions conducted at Newgate,

FIGURE 7.3 Henry Fielding. *Courtesy en.wikipedia.org.*

the prison employed its own executioners. Those sentenced to death were hanged in groups, with men and women together. Ordinary, nonmurder prisoners were hanged any day of the week, although Mondays and Wednesdays were the busiest. Edward Davis, official executioner at Newgate, 1771-1776, successfully hanged 20 people in one day on February 2, 1785. Once public executions were banned, the death sentence was conducted within the prison yard. A black flag was raised to indicate that an execution had taken place. Most executions were not for murder: between 1800 and 1833, 20% of all hangings were for burglary, 17.5% were for forgery, 13.2% were for highway robbery, and 8.3% were for murder.

On May 6, 1902, George Wolfe became the last person to be executed in Newgate prison. The prison was closed in 1907 to make room for an extension to the Old Bailey. Newgate prison was the execution capital of England. Between 1783 and 1902, 1,169 people were put to death there. Prior to this, hangings were held at Tyburn Tree near Marble Arch in London. Public executions were performed in the lane outside Newgate; this lane is called *Old Bailey*. Of the 1,169 executions, 1,120 were of men and 49 were of women. Three women were burned at the stake. The burnings were for the offense of coining (making fake money from melting down coins), which was classified as treason. Edward Davis, the executioner, would hang the women and then supervise the burning of their bodies.

By 1856, the Central Criminal Court Act allowed prisoners from anywhere in the country to be tried at Old Bailey (the Central Criminal Court), conveniently situated immediately next door to Newgate prison. This act was introduced to allow defendants the opportunity to be tried away from bias that may have existed locally and thereby ensure a fair trial, a far move away from the fundamental concept of being tried by your peers in feudal England. The first person to utilize this opportunity was a poisoner from Staffordshire, William Palmer; he was found guilty at "The Bailey" and returned to Stafford for hanging.

The harshness of death penalty laws could, however, be ameliorated in practice. Historical researchers have attempted to gather statistics regarding the instances of prosecution and conviction for capital offenses and the numbers of death sentences actually carried out in the eighteenth century. Their analyses are limited to specific cities or geographic areas, but the figures suggest that offenders were often unprosecuted and seldom executed. Victims, judges, and juries proved reluctant to invoke capital punishment for a minor crime. When a person was sentenced to death, he could hope for a commutation to transportation to English colonies or for a full pardon from the judge or from the king.

Blackstone condemned the indiscriminate infliction of punishments of unreasonable severity. Much like Beccaria, Blackstone recognized that the disproportion between crime and punishment actually led to a weakening of the application of criminal law. It was much easier, Blackstone wrote, to extirpate than to amend mankind.[12,13] While Blackstone was not against the death penalty for incorrigible persons or for atrocious crimes, he did advocate a gradual scale of punishment keyed to gradations of guilt.

PARLIAMENTARY REFORM AND ROYAL PARDONS

A leading proponent of statutory reform was *Sir Samuel Romilly* (1757-1818), who became a member of the House of Commons after long practice of law and service as solicitor general and judge. His experience in criminal courts led him to deplore the counterproductive severity of punishment, especially for property crimes, as well as the randomness of its application. Romilly believed that certainty of punishment was a greater deterrent than its severity. He contended that disproportionate severity increased rather than diminished crime. Romilly began introducing bills in Parliament to remove lesser crimes from the capital statutes; and in 1808, he succeeded in passage of a bill in the House of Commons that exempted petty theft from the death penalty—only to see it struck down by the House of Lords. Finally, in 1812 Parliament repealed a statute that made it a capital offense for an English soldier to beg without written permission from his commanding officer.

HISTORY TODAY

Was Romilly correct? Does the certainty of punishment matter more than the severity? You may not know the actual penalty for certain offenses, but you know you will be arrested and perhaps punished, and perhaps the certainty of arrest itself is enough to deter you from committing a crime.

Nevertheless, bills to reduce the number of capital offenses were often stifled by opponents such as Archdeacon William Paley (1743-1805) and failed in the House of Lords. Paley presented the principal arguments against reduction of capital offenses. Paley argued that in order to deter crime, the severity of punishment should be proportionate not to the harm it caused, but to the ease with which a crime could be committed. Additionally, Paley postulated that the uncertainty of punishment should increase its effectiveness. Paley acknowledged that while the death penalty was carried out only 10% of the time, the danger of it hung over many. In fact, Paley contended, Parliament never intended for capital punishment to be enforced indiscriminately. Romilly disputed Paley's contentions before the House of Commons in 1810, a speech so cogent that it was published and circulated in pamphlet form.

Despite repeated efforts for legal reform, little change in the criminal law occurred during Romilly's lifetime. The pattern of passage by the House of Commons and rejection by the House of Lords persisted. Then in 1818, at the instigation of

Sir James Mackintosh, a committee was formed in the House of Commons to consider revising the criminal law. The report of the Mackintosh committee recommended repeal of obsolete capital punishment statutes that had not been acted upon for at least 70 years, that all offenses be grouped according to gravity, and that only the most serious be subject to capital punishment. Under the leadership of Home Secretary *Sir Robert Peel* during the 1820s, Parliament removed the threat of a death sentence for many minor offenses. In addition, a statute of 1823 authorized the court to abstain from pronouncing a death sentence if the offender was a fit and proper subject for a royal pardon.

The prerogative to pardon was established in the Middle Ages although it has existed as a concept since ancient Greece. Pardons have often been used in exchange for an agreement to be transported to another land. Under English law, all offenses except one are pardonable. Section 1 of the 1679 Habeas Corpus Act prohibits a pardon for persons found guilty of unlawfully transporting prisoners out of England. Pardons may be granted to more than one person. In 1843, Queen Victoria granted a Royal Pardon to the Pentonville Exiles when 200 men agreed to transportation to Australia in exchange for their release from London's Pentonville prison.

HISTORY TODAY

The power of executive pardon rests with most U.S. governors and with the President (for federal crimes only). Some pardons generate considerable controversy. President Bill Clinton issued some very controversial pardons during his last days in office in 2001, including a pardon for a man who had provided him with gifts and contributions. In 1974, President Gerald Ford pardoned former President Richard Nixon before he could be accused of any crimes stemming from the Watergate scandal that ended his presidency. Despite the outrage generated by these and other pardons, no move has been taken to remove this authority. Should pardoning power be retained, modified, or abolished?

CRIMINAL ANTHROPOLOGISTS

Unlike "armchair theorists" like Bentham and Beccaria, empirical scientists sought factual material to analyze in their search for the roots of criminal behavior. Some looked for physical traits that predicted deviance, while others examined statistical compilations regarding demographic and social environment. The efforts of these early empiricists did not, however, document causes of crime; they merely indicated correlations between certain characteristics or conditions and criminal activity.

Enlightenment emphasis on scientific analysis led some early criminologists to focus on physical characteristics that determined criminal behavior or at least predisposed an individual to commit crimes. A pioneer in the field of criminal anthropology was Gianbaptiste della Porte (1535-1615). He examined corpses of hundreds of prisoners and insane persons, and found correlations between criminals and their facial characteristics (physiognomies), such as small ears, bushy eyebrows, small noses, and large lips.

In the following century, further anthropological examination of criminals was carried out by *Franz Joseph Gall* (1758-1828) and Johann Caspar Spurzheim (1776-1832). Gall studied the head shapes of gifted and insane persons, as well as those of criminals. His empirical research, which he called *cranioscopy*, linked skull contours with abnormal social behavior, thus initiating a field of study later called *phrenology*. A medical doctor in Vienna, Gall hypothesized that different regions of the brain were related to specific psychological traits. His research led him to contend that corresponding bumps in the skull resulted from increased activity and that low levels of activity resulted in depressions. Protuberances could foretell criminal tendencies, such as those in brain regions involved in greed, self-defense, and the carnivorous instinct. Gall did not argue that people were born criminal but that there was an internal struggle between the opposing forces of animal propensities and ethical conduct; children could be trained to overcome their innate criminal tendencies.

Gall's lectures were banned in his native Austria because they were against religion and he was forced to emigrate. Nevertheless, he developed a following among the French, who formed the Phrenological Society of Paris. His phrenological research was extended by his pupil Spurzheim, who gave lectures in England and the Americas. In the United States, some prisons used the results of the research to classify prisoners until the early twentieth century. Phrenology was scorned from the beginning by some scientists as the theory of "lumps and bumps."

The field of phrenology was more significant for the scientific approach employed than for the conclusions reached. Nevertheless, the phrenologists might have taken comfort from recent research, which has demonstrated that mental and emotional activities are indeed localized in the human brain. It should be noted that Gall was a skilled anatomist and has been credited with important and accurate analyses of brain structure and function.

EARLY CRIMINAL STATISTICS AND CRIMINALISTICS

While biological researchers focused on individual characteristics, statisticians examined group characteristics. Following the latter strategy, a French lawyer, *André-Michel Guerry* (1802-1866), and a Belgian mathematician, *Lambert Adolphe Jacques Quetelet* (1796-1874), utilized governmental data in their search for the roots of criminal activity through study of large numbers of crimes and offenders.

Drawing from national crime statistics published by the French government, Guerry analyzed the data to identify correlations between crime and environment. He published his essay on the "moral statistics" of France in 1833. In collaboration with a Venetian geographer, Adriano Balbi, Guerry developed maps shaded to reflect criminal activity, resulting in the label *cartographic school* of criminology. Guerry recognized the difficulties related to his endeavor, which have always plagued researchers in their attempts to study criminal activity. Such data often includes, but is not limited to, statistics regarding known crimes, accusations of criminal acts, and criminal convictions, each of which could potentially yield false results when utilized in scientific study. He was particularly interested in ascertaining correlations between types of crime and economic or educational status. As he refined his analyses, Guerry recognized the complexity of causal factors and adapted his maps to reflect multiple variables. Although he took into account the element of free will, he argued that criminal acts were nevertheless subject to invariable laws that could be derived from "moral statistics."

Quetelet, a contemporary of Guerry, also analyzed aggregate criminal statistics in a search for constants, laws similar to those of the physical sciences. Using demographic data in the French national statistics, Quetelet identified factors that were significantly associated with criminal propensities: age and sex, socioeconomic status, and climate. A high propensity was noted for the poor, for men between the ages of 21 and 25, for violence during summer months, and for property offenses during winter. Quetelet also found correlations with geographic location and drinking habits.

This era also saw significant developments in the area of *criminalistics. Henry Goddard* was building upon the first use of ballistics at the close of the eighteenth century. *Henry Faulds* argued that he (Faulds), not William Herschel, was the father of fingerprint evidence. *Alphonse Bertillon* experimented with body measurements as a credible, albeit temporary, means to identify repeat offenders.

Ballistic evidence is now commonplace largely thanks to the work of a British police officer stationed at Bow Street, London. Henry Goddard was aware of an event that occurred in 1794 when a surgeon removed a piece of paper from a bullet entry wound of a murder victim. Subsequently, when the police arrested the suspect, he was found to be in possession of the other piece of paper that identically matched the paper found on the deceased's bullet entry wound. Goddard utilized this idea when he was called to investigate a house burglary where shots were exchanged between the intruder and the butler. After taking two bullets from the scene, one from the alleged intruder's weapon and the second from the butler's gun, Goddard established that in fact both bullets had the same marks on them and he concluded that they were fired from the same weapon. When confronted with this evidence, the butler confessed that there had never been an intruder and he had discharged both shots from the same gun.

During the same period, Alphonse Bertillon was working for the French *Surete* in Paris. A recurring problem was that repeat offenders were avoiding long prison sentences as they always claimed that their court appearance was a first and that they had no previous convictions. The only way in which a repeat offender was identified was through personal recognition and a number of celebrated cases had shown this to be thoroughly unreliable. Bertillon had always had a keen interest in anthropology, and therefore he devised a system of recording in minute detail all of the body measurements (head, torso, fingers, and feet) of all the men arrested at his police station. Bertillon then kept a file record of these measurements. The next time a similarly aged man was arrested and claimed he had never been in trouble before, Bertillon used his anthropomorphic identification method to successfully show that the offender was well-known to the police and had already been convicted a number of times. Bertillon's system might have survived had it not been for the invention of fingerprinting as a more reliable identification method.

The history of fingerprints has remained disputed for years. Henry Faulds, a British medical doctor, claimed that he was the father of fingerprinting after his experimentation with using thumb prints as a way of identifying illiterate farmers in India during the late 1800s. This is partially correct. However, at the same time, William Herschel and Sir Francis Galton were collaborating in England to use inked fingers as a way of identifying recidivists. Ultimately, the art of inking fingerprints and using the patterns to show that all humans have unique marks became established and recognized, and by the early twentieth century a British jury was prepared to convict a man of murder and sentence him to the gallows on dactylographic evidence alone.

TIME CAPSULE: JAPANESE CRIMINAL JUSTICE DURING THE TOKUGAWA PERIOD

Throughout its history, the island nation of Japan has alternately integrated and isolated itself from the rest of the world, often to very radical degrees. The exact origins of the Japanese are still somewhat mysterious, with some claiming that the original Japanese migrated from China and others claiming that the Japanese were an amalgam of migrants from China, Korea, and Mongolia. Despite this belief that the Japanese were the result of migrations of other cultures, one of the most fascinating aspects of studying Japanese culture, including its criminal justice practices, is that it offers a chance to examine a system that developed largely in isolation from most of the rest of the world, even excluding most of its closest neighbors.

Throughout most of the past millennium, Japan was ruled by a series of *Shogunates*. The Shoguns, similar to Western military generals except the title was usually inherited rather

Continued

TIME CAPSULE: JAPANESE CRIMINAL JUSTICE DURING THE TOKUGAWA PERIOD—CONT'D

than attained by rising through the ranks, headed the Shogunates. The longest reigning Shogunate was the Tokugawa Shogunate, which ruled Japan from 1603 to 1867. The Tokugawa Shogunate was established by Tokugawa Ieyasu, who was 61 years old when he assumed power. For several decades, Japan had observed an influx of outside influences, probably to an unprecedented degree, of Western influence, including Christianity brought to Japan by European missionaries. Throughout his life, Ieyasu was fascinated by Western culture and welcomed its influence. However, convinced by Dutch traders that a Spanish invasion of Japan was imminent, and that Christian missionaries and Japanese Christians were going to side with the invading Spaniards, Ieyasu and his successors began brutally persecuting European missionaries and Japanese Christians, effectively closing Japan off from the outside world in the process and transforming Japan into a police state. This isolation would endure for the next two centuries, but Japan would continue to develop culturally, economically, and militarily even in isolation.

The first criminal law code during the Tokugawa era was written in 1742. The first portion of the code, called the *Kujigata Osadamegaki* (written rules of procedure), established the rules by which police and judicial officials had to abide, similar to procedural due process laws today. The second portion was the *Osadamegaki Hyakkajo* (the hundred written rules), which contained 184 laws or regulations over the citizenry.

Collecting and examining physical evidence of even the most rudimentary kind was practically unheard of in Japan at the time, so convictions almost always relied on the confession of the accused. Therefore, torture was commonly employed to elicit confessions, a practice that no doubt resulted in many false confessions, as many suspects would confess to anything simply to stop the torture.

Prisons or detention facilities were used for people awaiting trial. The more common forms of punishment were execution, banishment, and corporal punishment, which included branding or tattooing.

The Japanese recognized the insanity defense, even though modern psychiatric labels were not in use, and unless the crime was of an extremely serious or violent nature, an insane defendant might have his or her sentence commuted and be remanded to the custody of a relative willing to assume responsibility for his or her care.

Such an example might lead one to believe that the legal system under the Tokugawa Shogunate was egalitarian and beneficent, but this was not the case. There was little respect for human rights overall, and keeping the citizenry in the dark and guessing was paramount. In contrast to modern Western thought, but consistent with European thinking of that time, the Tokugawa motto was "Let the people know nothing, but make them obey."

Source: Drapkin I. (1989), *Crime and Punishment in the Ancient World*. Lexington, MA: Lexington Books.

SUMMARY

The Enlightenment formed a critical point in the intellectual history of Western civilization, just as the national revolutions that followed in its wake transformed the nature of politics and society. As a branch of learning, the study of crime and its punishment was inevitably influenced by the writings of the philosophes, but it was even more profoundly changed by the new worldview espoused by the Age of Reason. Stressing the importance of the individual's freedom of action, the new philosophy readily accepted reduced social control. Both the structure and the mechanics of government were seen as instruments for moving men and nations toward perfectibility; thus, the U.S. Constitution's redundant but characteristic declaration that it sought a "more perfect" union. Past societies in Western civilization had been communal in their orientation; they placed theology in the primary place of academic study. The Enlightenment, however, sought the growth of the individual, and philosophy replaced theology as the central focus of academic training. As the Enlightenment poet Alexander Pope would phrase it, "The greatest study of mankind is man."

In balancing the interests of the individual against those of the state, the philosophes emphasized a view of limited government that had worldwide impact. Questioning the legitimacy of absolute monarchies, they found virtue in political systems that gave the greatest protection to the life, liberty, and property of the citizen. Criminal procedure was viewed as a fundamental guarantor of the freedom of the individual; it was praiseworthy only when it protected the rights of the accused and secured no more than the bare minimum of security for the continuance of the state and civilized society. Basic to the philosophers' respect for every human being was their demand for equality in the application of all laws, not only the penal laws. This reflected their philosophical model of society, in which the consent of each individual was necessary to the legitimacy of the state.

Concern for the condition of human freedom also triggered thoughtful study of Western Europe's social and economic order. As industrialization widened the gap between wealthy capitalists and the laboring poor, socialist thinkers blamed crime on repression of the working class. They viewed criminal law and enforcement as capitalism's instrument to sustain an unjust social order. Thus, they sought revolutionary change within society, and they considered crime to be a byproduct of unjust and inhumane social forces. In this way Enlightenment rationalism generated two fundamentally opposed views of crime: (1) that it originated in human psychology and could be discouraged by reasonable punishment, and (2) that criminal behavior was caused by a repressive economic and social system. While Enlightenment thinkers stressed the autonomy of the individual, socialists analyzed the impact of economic forces on classes within society.

Sparked by the Enlightenment emphasis on reason, legal theorists were led to devise an orderly presentation of existing laws. These efforts revealed deficiencies, inconsistencies, and injustices in the criminal law. Slowly, Parliament responded to the arguments of legal reformers and repealed some of the capital punishment statutes. The eighteenth and nineteenth centuries also saw significant application of scientific methodology in documenting offenses and in seeking the causes of crime.

During the period when Enlightenment thought ran its course, the American colonies of European nations began to assert their political independence. In North America, the colonies of Great Britain rebelled in 1776 and built a new nation based to a large degree on the principles of the Enlightenment. For them, the traditions of English constitutionalism, the rich background of European history, and the philosophy of the Age of Reason combined to provide a bountiful resource for the creation of a new government. The new group of independent states and the federal government were soon to provide the world with ample cause to admire American ingenuity and inventiveness in dealing with the age-old problems of criminal justice.

REFERENCES

Gay, P. (1966). *The enlightenment: An interpretation.* 2 Vols. New York: Alfred A. Knopf; Nicolson, H. (1961). *The age of reason: The eighteenth century.* New York: Doubleday & Co; Morrison, W. (Ed.), (2001). *Blackstone's commentaries on the laws of England,* Vol. IV. London: Cavendish Publishing, Ltd; Radzinowicz, L. (1948). *A history of English criminal law and its administration from 1750: The movement for reform.* New York: Macmillan, pp. 1750–1833.

Esmein, A. (1913). *A history of continental criminal procedure.* Boston: Little, Brown and Co; Beirne, P. (1993). *Inventing criminology: Essays on the rise of "homo criminalis."* Albany: State University of New York Press; Martin, R., Mutchnick, R. J., & Timothy Austin, W. (1990). *Criminological thought: Pioneers past and present.* New York: Macmillan; Cullen, F. T., & Agnew, R. (1999). *Criminological theory: Past to present; essential readings.* Los Angeles: Roxbury Publishing Company.

Carew Hunt, R. N. (1963). *The theory and practice of communism.* Baltimore: Penguin Books; Taylor, I., Walton, P., & Young, J. (1973). *The new criminology: For a social theory of deviance.* London: Routledge & Kegan Paul, Chapter 7; Jenkins, P. (1984). *Crime and justice: Issues and ideas.* Pacific Grove: Brooks/Cole; Rawlings, P. (1992). *Drunks, whores, and idle apprentices: Criminal biographies of the eighteenth century.* London: Routledge.

Notes and Problems

1. Do you agree with the Age of Reason's attitude toward penology, or do you believe that the rights of society deserve greater protection?
2. Can torture ever be justified as a mode of criminal investigation? Is current police interrogation procedure a successor to torture? Why or why not?
3. Montesquieu claimed that crimes against religion should be punished only by religious sanctions, that is, exclusion from the church or from its services and sacraments. Are there any behaviors that violate religious beliefs and should be criminalized?
4. What belief would the philosophes take toward what we today call *victimless crimes*, such as adultery, fornication, seduction, and the distribution of pornography to adults? Would you agree?

ENDNOTES

[1]Charles Louis de Secondat, Baron de la Brede et de Montesquieu. *Spirit of Laws*. Thomas Nugent, trans. D. W. Carrithers (Ed.). Berkeley: University of California Press, 1977, p. 158.

[2]Cesare de Beccaria. *An essay on crimes and punishment*, trans. François A.M. de Voltaire, Fifth Edition revised and corrected. London: J. Bone, 1801, p. 112.

[3]*Spirit of laws*, p. 155.

[4]Quoted in Adhemar Esmein. (1913). *A history of continental criminal procedure*. Boston: Little, Brown & Co., p. 353.

[5]*Essay on crimes and punishment*, p. 19.

[6]*Essay on crimes and punishment*, p. 7.

[7]*Spirit of laws*, p. 159.

[8]Many of these oversights in Beccaria's pioneering work were taken up by Jeremy Bentham, particularly in his *An introduction to the principles of morals and legislation* (1789) and in his later proposals for *Panopticon*, discussed in Chapter 9.

[9]K. Marx, & F. Engels. The condition of the working class in England in 1844, trans. F. K. Wischnewetsky. (1962). *Marx and Engels on Britain*. Moscow: Foreign Languages Publishing House, p. 163.

[10]Morrison, IV, p. 4.

[11]Morrison, IV, p. 283.

[12]Morrison, IV, p. 14.

[13]www.groups.dcs.st-and.ac.uk/~history/Extras/Queteler_crime.html.

The American Revolution and Criminal Justice

CHAPTER 8

KEY TERMS

1731 Jury Act of South Carolina	Executive, legislative, judicial branches of government	North African piracy
Aaron Burr		Pardon
Auburn system	Federal Constitution	Piracy
Bill of Rights	Independent judiciary	Sequestration
Blackbeard	John Adams	Smuggling
Boston Massacre	John Howard	South Carolina Regulators
Captain Thomas Preston	John Peter Zenger	Stamp Act
Constructive treason	Josiah Quincy	Thomas Eddy
Dueling	Jury nullification	Thomas Jefferson
Executive clemency	King George III	Treason
	Manumission	William Gilmore Simms

LEARNING OBJECTIVES

1. Understand the aspects of crime and criminal justice that helped lead to the American Revolution.
2. Understand how the law of constructive treason was used as a weapon against political dissidents.
3. Learn about the role of piracy in the early American economy.
4. Learn about the Boston Massacre and the role of the justice system in that event.
5. Understand the importance of an independent judiciary.
6. Learn about the trial of John Peter Zenger and the importance of freedom of the press.

7. Understand the rationale behind the establishment of the three main branches of government.
8. Learn about some of America's earliest correctional reformers.
9. Learn about and understand the Bill of Rights.
10. Examine North African piracy and the role it played in early American foreign policy.
11. Learn the story of Aaron Burr.

Table 8.1 Time Line: The American Revolution and Criminal Justice

1696	The English Parliament enacts a stricter navigation law, designed to impose stronger controls on colonial trade and eliminate smuggling.
1732	The number of hatmakers in the colonies is sharply restricted by Parliament's enactment of the Hat Act.
1750	Pennsylvania's embryonic iron industry is prohibited by the British Parliament's enactment of the Iron Act.
1754-63	The French and Indian War, triggered by colonial incursions into wilderness territory claimed by the French, involves Britain in an expensive and worldwide war with the French. The 1763 peace treaty awards Canada and lands east of the Mississippi River to Britain.
1761	James Otis of Massachusetts argues that the British statute authorizing colonial courts to issue writs of assistance is unconstitutional. He cites as precedent the seventeenth-century English opinion in *Dr. Bonham's Case* (1610).
1763	A British royal proclamation prohibits American settlement west of the Appalachian Mountain chain.
1764-70	The Sugar Act begins a series of taxation measures passed by Parliament to help pay for governmental expenses and debts incurred during the war. In 1766, the colonies meet in a Stamp Act Congress to devise uniform action against another British tax imposed on newspapers, legal documents, pamphlets, and broadsides. The Stamp Act is repealed, but new customs duties are imposed in 1767 and 1770.
1772	The British customs schooner *The Gaspee* is attacked and set afire; despite an official Commission of Inquiry, the identity of the culprits is never determined.
1773-74	Tea ships in Boston harbor are attacked by Bostonians disguised as Mohawk Indians; all of the tea is dumped into Boston harbor. In retaliation, Parliament passes the Coercive Acts, which suspend civil government in Massachusetts Bay, close the port of Boston to all commerce, and authorize the governor to grant immunity to Crown officials prosecuted in Massachusetts courts.
1775-76	First and Second Continental Congresses attempt to reconcile the differences between the British administration and the colonies. They also coordinate relief measures to assist Boston and surrounding areas.
April 19, 1775	Battles are fought between British troops and Massachusetts militia units at Lexington and Concord; the British march back to Boston without the colonial munitions and gunpowder they were sent to seize.
June 17, 1776	The Battle of Bunker Hill won by the British against 1,600 American defenders. The attacking British force sustains more than 1,000 men killed.
October 17, 1777	British General John Burgoyne surrenders his remaining 5,700 troops at Saratoga, New York.

Continued

Table 8.1 Time Line: The American Revolution and Criminal Justice—cont'd	
March 1, 1781	The Articles of Confederation, the first federal constitution, is ratified.
October 19, 1781	British General Lord Cornwallis, surrounded at Yorktown, surrenders his army of 8,000 troops.
November 30, 1782	The United States, France, and Britain sign the preliminary Peace Treaty at Paris.
1785-1796	Thomas Jefferson's revisions of Virginia criminal law result in lessening of harsh physical punishment for crime. Capital punishment remains for first degree murder and murder through poisoning.
1788	The new federal Constitution, drafted at Philadelphia in 1787, is ratified by the states. A series of individual rights and liberties are proposed by the ratifying conventions, and the first federal Congress sends 12 amendments to the state legislatures for consideration.
1791	Ten proposed amendments are ratified and form the current federal Bill of Rights. Limiting the power of the federal government, the Bill of Rights protects citizens against unlawful searches and seizures, self-incrimination, and violations of due process of law. It also guarantees freedom of speech, religion, and the press, and assures equal protection of the laws.

During the mid-eighteenth-century, the American colonies' relationship with Great Britain gradually became increasingly strained. Many Americans simply desired better treatment from the British government, or believed that they should enjoy the same status as English citizens, because many of them were immigrants from England or of English descent, but these Americans had no desire for independence from Great Britain. In effect, some Americans were contending for what would later (in 1867) become recognized as "dominion status" within the British Commonwealth of nations.

At the same time, the sense of being different from Britain moved other eighteenth-century colonists in the direction of independence. Americans were quick to assert that they were entitled to all of the rights of English citizens, including those obtained by the Glorious Revolution. Indeed, they were willing to press constitutional debate even further, adopting into their rhetoric and thought many of the principles first raised by Leveller pamphleteers during the Civil War and Interregnum. Many colonists, particularly New England inheritors of Leveller ideas, wished to establish republican forms of government that were virtually free of any British imperial control. The prized independence of New England town meetings led to a decentralization of political power within the colonies, and innovations in civil and criminal procedure sharply limited the ability of provincial governments to deal with seditious writings or actions.

Divergence of the English North American colonies from their mother country was not a product of the eighteenth century. This divergence began almost with the first days of settlement and became obvious in the seventeenth century, even though Americans at that time remained dependent on British economic support and military protection. In New England, Bible Codes were instituted, at times in defiance of English protests. Slavery developed in the colonial South as local customary law contrary to the common law of England. Throughout the colonies, Americans faced special problems involving the enforcement of laws across colonial boundaries.

Growth in population and in economic activity brought about change in colonial criminal law. At first, this caused a rapid acceptance of English precedents into colonial procedure and substantive law. During the early days of settlement, the lack of labor and opposition to capital punishment restricted the death penalty to the most serious crimes. By the eve of the American Revolution, death was a widespread sanction for almost all felonies in virtually every colony. Density of population in colonial cities, coupled with a shifting group of seamen and itinerant laborers, resulted in a growing urban crime rate that was aggravated by the rise of political dissent with accompanying riots and other disturbances. Once, in the 1760s, New York City was rocked by a riot started by prostitutes who clashed with a group of seamen, which illustrated an economic grievance more than a political protest.

Faced with the explosive nature of colonial discontent, the royal governors took refuge in the law of *treason*, which was applicable to riots and uprisings that did not disperse at the order of a justice of the peace or a magistrate. One such insurrection took place in Dutchess County, New York, after the repeal of the *Stamp Act*. As a means of protesting the tax imposed by British authority, American lawyers refused to bring cases in colonial courts that required the use of tax stamps on filed papers. Many of those cases involved suits for the collection of rents due from Dutchess County farmers. In 1766, when the courts were reopened (and the stamps were no longer required), a flood of rent collection actions were filed in Dutchess County. Sheriffs and their deputies were beaten when they attempted to serve process, and the governor was forced to restore order by sending royal troops into the county. Suspected organizers of the riots were imprisoned and brought to trial for *constructive treason*, meaning that, while actual identification of the individuals present was not possible, the imprisoned persons were constructively guilty because they either instigated the riot from afar or were very likely present when it took place.

HISTORY TODAY

Very few people enjoy paying taxes, yet we realize that taxes are necessary if we want the government to perform the services we expect. However, is there ever a point when taxpayers are justified in openly rebelling against the government through not paying taxes or violently resisting those who try to collect taxes?

Despite strong arguments by defense attorneys, the suspects were convicted and condemned to a traitor's death of hanging, drawing, disemboweling, and dismemberment. Only a royal pardon prevented their deaths, although it is questionable if the ancient Tudor punishment would have actually been used. This and other examples of the broad application of English treason statutes were destined to make a strong impression on leaders of the American Revolution who, by their opposition to the Crown, ran the risk of similar treason convictions.

Smuggling was a popular and profitable pastime of American business; a seventeenth-century royal governor once referred to *piracy* and illegal trade as the favorite twins of New York merchants. Piracy was not confined to the Mid-Atlantic area. It flourished off the Carolina and Virginia coasts as well. Carolina-area pirates like Edward Teach (or Thach), better known as *Blackbeard*, became the stuff of legend as a result of their piracy activity off the North Carolina coast. In fact, Kenney and Finckenauer refer to piracy off the North Carolina coast as the genesis of American organized crime. The crimes of some pirates, including Blackbeard, were greatly aided by corrupt colonial governors and government leaders, North Carolina colonial governor Charles Eden prominent among them.

HISTORY TODAY

Piracy is practically as old a practice as seafaring itself. Piracy has never gone away, but it has not been viewed as a problem in North America for quite some time. In recent years, piracy has reemerged as a major international problem, especially near Somalia, eastern Africa. In 2010, a young Somali became the first person in more than 100 years to be prosecuted for piracy in the United States; he was sentenced to 33 years for his role in hijacking an American merchant ship. What can history teach governments about the best way to deal with this problem?

Among the more economically repressive British regulations were those designed to regulate colonial trade. Essentially, these regulations prohibited commerce with any of the non-English colonies in the New World and also made illegal any trade with Europe that did not first pass through a British port. The chronic lack of gold and silver in the North American colonies could be relieved only by trade with non-English colonies or non-English nations. In a real sense, illegal trade made it possible for Americans to continue in the British system of mercantilism because their most profitable trade was illegal. Britain's efforts to combat this activity consisted of extensive use of naval forces to stop suspected merchant vessels at sea, and searching on wharves and in warehouses for illegally imported goods.

FIGURE 8.1 James Otis Jr., whose argument against writs of assistance is acknowledged to have galvanized the revolutionary movement in the American colonies. *Image courtesy en. wikipedia.org.*

Searches and seizures became high on the list of abuses colonists attributed to the Crown, culminating in the famous *Writs of Assistance Case* (1761), when attorney James Otis eloquently defended the subject's right to privacy in his home. A Massachusetts Superior Court jury upheld the defense. Of this case, *John Adams* later said that, as he heard Otis speak, he could hear the beginning sounds of the American Revolution. Adams was quite right; from the American colonial experience came not only the motivation to revolt but also the legal and philosophical foundations on which American law and criminal justice would be established.

TIME CAPSULE: CRIME IN THE MEDITERRANEAN: NORTH AFRICAN PIRACY

During the late eighteenth and early nineteenth centuries, crime in other countries, especially non-Western countries far away from American shores, was of little concern to Americans. What happened in faraway lands seldom, if ever, affected Americans, except when it interfered with commerce. However, there was one habitual criminal activity that menaced Americans and sea travelers and traders all over the world. The crime was piracy, and it was a centuries-old institution off the coast of North Africa. While piracy has never been confined to North Africa, especially in the eighteenth and nineteenth centuries, many governments blatantly condoned it and even aggressively sought to profit from piracy, like the government of Tripoli. This government-endowed criminal enterprise eventually led to the first declaration of war against the United States by a foreign power.

Tripoli—modern-day Libya—had profited from piracy committed off its Barbary Coast for centuries. In response, sometimes governments responded in a hostile fashion, but very often foreign governments or businesses would pay the ransom demanded so that their ship, cargo, and/or sailors would be returned. Otherwise, the goods and ship would be confiscated, and the sailors would be forced into slavery or even killed. Sometimes sailors could escape slavery by converting to Islam and assimilating with the rest of the population.

American sailors and merchants fell victim to the Barbary pirates along with Europeans and Middle Easterners. Between 1785 and 1815, approximately 600 Americans were taken hostage by the Barbary pirates. Prior to American independence from Great Britain in 1776, Americans sailing near the North African coast could rely to some extent on protection from the mighty British Navy, although even the British fell victim to the Barbary pirates at times. After winning its independence from Great Britain, the United States, with a Navy consisting of only six warships, found it could not protect its merchants and sailors. At first, the Americans did as the

Europeans did, paid ransom to free its citizens, and occasionally simply bribed Tripoli to leave its ships alone. Gradually, Americans grew disgusted with the demands of Tripoli, and the "gifts" to which Tripoli had become accustomed from the United States stopped. This resulted in a declaration of war by Tripoli against the United States in 1801.

On October 31, 1803, the problems between the United States and Tripoli finally came to a head. The *U.S.S. Philadelphia*, led by William Bainbridge and carrying 307 American Sailors and Marines, accidentally ran aground in Tripoli while trying to enforce a blockade of Tripoli. All of the sailors and marines were taken prisoner, and the *Philadelphia* and its cargo were hailed by Tripoli's Bashaw, Yussef Karamanli, as "gifts from Allah." When word finally reached "Washington City" as the new capital was known at the time, cries for vengeance and rescue were loud and clear. Conflicts with foreign powers, both on land and at sea, had been a persistent problem for the young nation since its inception. Most of those problems stemmed from the imperialistic ambitions of European powers, mainly England, France, and Spain. However, this was a very brazen challenge to the United States from a third-rate power, aggravated no doubt by the racial and religious differences between mostly White Christian America and the Muslims of North Africa. There were cries for action against Tripoli in many quarters. One problem, however, was simple logistics. How could the United States, with a total arsenal of six warships, realistically combat Tripoli through an invasion by sea? The answer, according to President Thomas Jefferson's advisers, was a more clandestine approach, something more akin to a modern operation led by special forces, and one that would involve stealth and diplomacy.

The task of leading the expedition fell to William Eaton, a disgraced former Army Captain, diplomat, and secret agent. Eaton secured the promise of the necessary resources to

TIME CAPSULE: CRIME IN THE MEDITERRANEAN: NORTH AFRICAN PIRACY—CONT'D

conduct the mission, but Jefferson began to have second thoughts about the operation even before Eaton left. Undeterred, Eaton departed for Africa, where he would have to beg for resources from, among others, British merchants and diplomats. Eaton also knew he would have to enlist the assistance of North Africans hostile to the Tripoli regime, most notably the Bashaw's exiled brother and archenemy, Hamet Karamanl. Eaton's intention was to install Hamet and depose Yussef. Instant communication with the United States was not an option, so the entire operation had to be managed on the ground in North Africa, and little help could be expected from faraway Washington. Eaton began his operation after landing in Egypt, and along with some of the other Americans participating in the mission, must have thought that they had landed on another planet. If Western understanding of Muslim and North African culture is scant today, it was absolutely nil in 1803.

Nevertheless, Eaton and his men made the treacherous 500-mile journey from Egypt to Tripoli, trying to enlist assistance along the way and fighting periodic attempts at brigandage as well. However, a serious wrinkle was put in the operation when President Jefferson withdrew official support. Tobias Lear, an American diplomat, was sent to offer a ransom of $60,000, a move that infuriated Eaton, who had not only made a personal vow to deal appropriately with Yussef, but also given word to Hamet that the United States

would not abandon him. Eaton forged ahead, and gathered a force consisting of eight American Marines, some European mercenaries, and some avuncular Arabs and Bedouins hostile to the Bashaw. Eaton and his men successfully took the nearby city of Derne, and forced its inhabitants to surrender. The Bashaw, feeling the very real threat of Eaton's invasion, agreed to the terms of Lear's ransom offer. The hostages were freed, Hamet returned to exile, and the Bashaw raided Derne (after Eaton left) and wreaked havoc on the city as revenge for caving in to the American-led invasion.

This daring exploit to dent the operation of a criminal regime was immortalized in the first verse of the Marine Corps Anthem, although the United States Marines would not be taken seriously as an American military force until World War I. Unfortunately, this operation did not stop Tripoli's participation in piracy, although it did eventually grind to a halt. Americans returned to fight the Barbary Pirates even after the Eaton mission. Eaton returned to the United States to a hero's welcome, but he had made an enemy in President Jefferson by disobeying his orders, and was vilified by Jefferson. Eaton degenerated into a life of gambling and alcoholism, and felt betrayed by the nation he had served. He died on June 1, 1811, at the age of 47.

Source: Zacks, R. (2005). *The pirate coast: Thomas Jefferson, the first marines, and the secret mission of 1805.* New York: Hyperion.

PROCEDURAL RIGHTS IN COLONIAL AMERICA

The eighteenth century was a time for growing conformity between English and American criminal law and procedure. It was also a time for the development of the procedural rights of accused persons. Building on the English Leveller tradition, American lawyers early established the right against self-incrimination. This right was utilized fairly extensively in the defense of patriot leaders during the opening years of the American Revolution and appears to have been generally available throughout the colonies as a defense against coerced confessions and oaths *ex officio*. Significantly,

> John Adams (1735-1826): One of the most influential of America's founding fathers; signed the Declaration of Independence; served as Ambassador to Great Britain and The Netherlands, first Vice President of the United States, and second President of the United States from 1797 to 1801.

a compurgatory oath was used in certain cases of paramount social concern: in prosecutions for selling arms or liquor to the Indians, for entertaining or providing refuge for slaves without a master's consent, and for engaging in certain forms of illegal trade.

American colonial legislatures elaborated on English experience and put their faith in common law juries as a method of safeguarding those falsely accused of crime. Typical of this concern was the *1731 Jury Act of South Carolina*, which specified a complicated method for the random selection of jurors that was designed to eliminate the possibility of bias in selecting a grand or trial jury. The need for establishing jury trials became paramount in the face of two situations. Most commonly, it became an issue when an American was tried before a court of vice-admiralty for smuggling or other breaches of the Navigation Acts. Vice-admiralty courts were established in each colony in about 1696; they sat without juries and increasingly were the tribunals preferred by royal officials prosecuting illegal trade matters.

With the enactment of the Sugar Act (1764), a vice-admiralty court was established at Halifax in Nova Scotia and given jurisdiction over all illegal trade cases that might arise in any of the North American colonies. Not only was a jury trial avoided by such a measure, but American merchants were forced to defend themselves before a court located at a great distance from the scene of the alleged offense. Making provision for the travel of witnesses and the process of employing counsel was vastly complicated. In addition, the judge was unlikely to be influenced by the public uproar that frequently attended smuggling prosecutions in the defendant's home colony. These grievances formed a significant part of the Declaration of Independence's indictment of the administration of *King George III*: that he forced them to stand trial before courts functioning without juries that were distant from their homes and from the scene of the alleged offenses.

King George III (1738-1820): King of England from 1760 to 1820, although he did not always enjoy full power during those years; served as King during the American Revolution; became mentally unstable during his final years.

The other occasion for assertion of the right to jury trial came in a civil case, but it was equally necessary in criminal procedure. *Forsey versus Cunningham* (1764) involved a claim for damages, resulting from an assault and battery, in which the jury had returned an exceptionally high verdict. Shocked by the amount of the jury award, the governor contended that the case should be subject to review (on both the law and the facts) by the appellate court of governor and council. Virtually the entire New York bench and bar opposed the governor in this matter, and when it was finally decided against him by the Privy Council, it was hailed as a victory for individual rights. What the case established was the finality of a jury verdict in civil cases, as well as the independence of a common law jury from subsequent reversal by a higher court. It is an important precedent because it demonstrates the uniformity of American public opinion concerning the need for an independent jury.

Closely connected to the finality of jury verdicts was American colonial insistence on an *independent judiciary*, namely, that judges would not need to kowtow to politicians or other government officials. With the Glorious Revolution, English judges were guaranteed continuance in office during good behavior. This had been the rule concerning colonial judges until the accession of George III in 1760. With the accession of a new monarch, English practice required the reissuance of all commissions in the name of the new sovereign. To the dismay of the colonial legal profession, the new commissions were issued "at the pleasure of the King" rather than during good behavior, thus making the judges more susceptible to gubernatorial and royal pressure. Many judges refused to accept these commissions, precipitating a crisis in colonial affairs. Although the Crown and its advisors did not retreat from their position on the tenure of colonial judges, Americans considered this assault on judicial independence to be subversive of their liberties as Englishmen. New laws and constitutions enacted in the postrevolutionary years were to reflect their concern for a free and independent judiciary.

HISTORY TODAY

An independent judiciary, free from the pressures of legislators, governors, and presidents, is an essential part of American government. Americans are often infuriated and confused when a judge or an appellate court can nullify legislation or action taken by a popularly elected legislature. Nonetheless, why is it important that we have a judiciary that is free to make decisions based on what it views as legal and constitutional, without regard to the objections of other government officials?

Another example of colonial concern for fairness in criminal procedure is to be found in an evolving right to counsel. South Carolina's Jury Act (1731) provided for the appointment of counsel in treason cases and for all persons accused of felonies where the punishment was death. While this extensive grant of right to counsel was unusual, even in colonial America, it did represent a significant liberalization of the English practice that denied assistance of counsel in all felony cases until the beginning of the nineteenth century.

FREEDOM OF THE PRESS

The 1735 trial of New York printer *John Peter Zenger* drew attention throughout the British Empire and resulted in basic changes in the law of seditious libel. More than four decades later, the Revolutionary leader Gouverneur Morris was to term the case the "Morningstar of that liberty which subsequently revolutionized America."[1] The Zenger trial established that truth might be pleaded as a defense to a charge of seditious libel, and it also demonstrated that common law juries could (in appropriate situations) take to themselves the decision of points of law and issues of fact in these cases. After Zenger's acquittal, the colonial press began to flourish as a significant factor in provincial politics, and the censorship authority of royal governors was virtually eliminated.

This *cause celebre* began with a dispute over the salaries and perquisites of the governor's office. After his appointment as governor of New York, William Cosby delayed his departure from England for an extended period, during which the president of the council, a native New Yorker named Rip Van Dam, assumed the powers of the governor and received the salary. When Cosby finally arrived in the colony, he demanded one-half of the salary from Van Dam, who denied that it was payable and also set forth a list of counterclaims against the governor. Political factions within the colony quickly regrouped in support of one or the other contestant. Governor Cosby decided to sue for his salary in the Supreme Court of Judicature, but Chief Justice Lewis Morris was a member of the rival faction. To protect his personal interests, the governor dismissed Morris and appointed James Delancey (leader of the governor's faction) in his place. The threat of removal convinced the other justices that cooperation with Cosby was the only way to ensure continuity in office. They readily decided that they had jurisdiction of the case and, ultimately, awarded the half-salary to the governor.

In the course of these legal proceedings, the *New York Weekly Journal*, printed by John Peter Zenger but written and edited by James Alexander, provided a running critique of the litigation and the governor's machinations. The progovernor newspaper, the *New York Gazette*, replied with biting satire, terming Cosby's opposition baboons, mastiffs, and assorted other insults. When the *New York Weekly Journal* replied in kind, the governor felt himself aggrieved and had Zenger imprisoned on charges of seditious libel. Only with difficulty did the administration obtain an indictment; two successive grand juries refused to return a bill against Zenger.

As the trial began, public sympathy strongly favored the printer. His wife continued to operate the newspaper, receiving at the cell door Zenger's report of his treatment in prison. Zenger's lawyer (and former editor) James Alexander was early held in contempt of court and barred from the courtroom. Andrew Hamilton of Philadelphia carried the case to completion. Arguing that the jury had the right to decide the law of the case, and that truth was a defense to seditious libel, he drew the sharp rebuke of the court. Hamilton pointed out that a free press was the foundation of the liberties of a people, and he made pointed criticisms of the governor's arrogant disregard for the law of the province and the procedures of its courts.

The jury found Zenger not guilty, and he was released from prison. Shortly thereafter, his press was kept busy printing the text of the trial proceedings, edited by James Alexander. A year after the trial, Governor Cosby died in office, still smarting under the humiliation of the jury's verdict.

HISTORY TODAY

Americans have a love/hate relationship with the news media. While we depend on them for information (and sometimes for entertainment), we are often infuriated at their behavior. Government officials and politicians tend to share this view. Nonetheless, what does the Zenger case and those like it, not to mention attempts at controlling the media in countries with dictatorships, teach us about the importance of a free press? What do you think would have been the effect if Zenger had been found guilty?

The Zenger case demonstrated the vulnerability of criminal courts to gubernatorial influence and manipulation, but it also showed that when public opinion was arrayed against the administration it was impossible to secure a conviction for seditious libel. In effect, the New York jury had done what common law juries had done for centuries: it nullified the unpopular rule of law by refusing to apply it to the case at hand. The Zenger case provides an early example of *jury nullification*, in which a jury disregards a law, or the specific application of the law with which it does not agree. The law of seditious libel would subsequently undergo a series of changes until, by 1843, both England and the United States adopted the essence of the Zenger decision. Thereafter, truth would be a defense to seditious libel and, in both countries, the jury was assigned the responsibility of judging issues of law as well as issues of fact.

HISTORY TODAY

Jury nullification occurs from time to time, but it is sometimes difficult to conclude why a jury decides the way it does because jurors are not required to publicly disclose their rationale for making a decision. If you were serving as a juror, and you could plainly see that the defendant was guilty, but you disagreed with the way that prosecutors and police officers had enforced the law, or you thought the law itself was unjust, would you disregard the evidence and vote for acquittal?

While it went a long way toward securing freedom of the press, the Zenger case did not accomplish that result. As historian Leonard Levy has shown, the colonial legislatures were, by far, more effective in suppressing newspaper publication than the courts have ever been. By imprisoning editors and other opponents for contempt, the assemblies were most effective in stifling dissent. It was only as the United States entered the nineteenth century that press freedom was widespread and this necessary foundation for republican government was secure.

FAIR TRIAL IN VIOLENT TIMES

Britain and its North American colonies were on a collision course after 1763. The end of the French and Indian War left Great Britain with a large war debt, and the leaders in Parliament attempted to increase revenues by imposing new taxes on the American provinces. Colonial newspapers and pamphleteers raised verbal challenges to these constitutional innovations, but violence surfaced early as a symptom of opposition. Some of the rioting arose from genuine political causes. Trade embargoes against British goods were enforced by the threat of tarring and feathering pro-British consumers who ignored the prohibitions established by the Sons of Liberty. Boycotting British trade increased the number of unemployed seamen, longshoremen, and warehousemen. British troops garrisoned in colonial cities aggravated the unemployment problem by their moonlighting activities, which displaced other Americans from jobs.

As the Zenger case shows, it was not easy to secure a fair trial even in the best of times, and the approach of the American Revolution created a period of increasing uncertainty and apprehension. By 1774, most royal judges were sufficiently apprehensive of their safety that they did not ride circuit (travel) in the outlying counties of the provinces. When they did so, they spent a substantial portion of their time lecturing the courtroom crowd about their duty of loyalty to the Crown and the need to preserve law and order. Growing popular resentment against royal authority challenged the legitimacy of government and reinforced the growing crime rate. The transition of allegiance from royal to American state government was far from being either instantaneous or orderly. Yet, it was at this time of crisis that Massachusetts lawyers graphically demonstrated their loyalty to the principles of fair trial for all accused of crime.

The trial of the soldiers accused of the *Boston Massacre* grew out of a series of events on March 5, 1770. While the full details of the situation will probably never be known, it is undisputed that a single British sentry was stationed in front of the royal Custom House, or court house. A small crowd had gathered about him. Fearing violence or an attempt to enter the building, the sentry called for assistance. Immediately, he was reinforced by a group of six soldiers, a corporal, and *Captain Thomas Preston*, who took command of the men involved. Shortly thereafter, the soldiers fired shots; three persons were killed instantly, and two others were fatally wounded.

Public uproar was such that the authorities feared the reaction of postponing trial, but at the same time, it was readily apparent that no impartial decision could be reached until tempers cooled. Captain Preston and the men were turned over to the civil authorities and held in the Boston jail. Although there were murmurs that lynching was an appropriate fate for the captain and his men, no effort was made to carry out this plan.

On March 6, 1770, the day after the Massacre, John Adams (who would later become the second President of the United States) was approached on behalf of Captain Preston and the imprisoned soldiers. Would he agree to serve as defense counsel, along with Samuel Auchmuty and *Josiah Quincy*? Adams later recalled his prompt agreement to undertake the burdensome assignment that brought great risk to his personal safety and professional standing: "I had no hesitation in answering that Council ought to be the last thing that an accused Person should want in a free Country."[2] We can guess some of the sacrifices Adams made in handling Preston's defense. His cocounsel, Josiah Quincy, was required to defend his actions to his own father and to point out that no man should be assumed guilty until proven to be so.

Defense counsel were hampered by the circumstances surrounding the Massacre and their need to protect both Captain Preston and his men. When Preston's case came to trial in October 1770, the defense counsel introduced evidence of self-defense that would justify the homicide and require a jury verdict of acquittal. They succeeded in casting doubt on the accuracy of testimony introduced to show that Preston actually gave the order to fire into the crowd.

After 3 hours of deliberation, the jury returned a not guilty verdict, and Preston was free to deal with the numerous civil actions for damages that had been lodged against him. Adams and his colleagues turned to the soldiers' case, which they had separated from the proceeding against Preston. Despite the separate trials of the two cases, defense counsel was presented with a difficult tactical decision. Because Preston had been acquitted, presumably because of doubts relating to the order to fire, would the soldiers be convincing before a jury if they advanced the defense that Preston had ordered them to fire? Preston's acquittal deprived the Boston mob of its demand for blood vengeance. At the same time, it increased public pressure for the conviction of the soldiers. Fortunately for the soldiers, not a single member of the trial jury was a resident of the city of Boston.

The Massacre perpetrated in King Street Boston on March 5th 1770, in which Mess.rs Sam.l Gray, Sam.l Maverick, James Caldwell, Crispus Attucks, Patrick Carr were Killed, six others Wounded, two of them Mortally.

FIGURE 8.2 The Boston Massacre took place March 5, 1770. *Library of Congress.*

The defense of the soldiers depended on moderation in introducing testimony on their behalf. While it was necessary to prove their fear of the mob, it was important that the sensibilities of the jury not be affronted by proof that attacked the peacefulness of the province or the conduct of its people. In part, Adams shifted the blame to nonresidents of Boston, suggesting that the crowd was largely composed of visitors from surrounding areas and perhaps even other provinces or nations. To all but two of the soldiers, the jury returned a verdict of acquittal; the two remaining were found guilty of manslaughter and, after pleading benefit of clergy, were branded on the thumb and released from jail.

The acquittal of Preston and his soldiers and the release of the two convicted men caused considerable resentment in Boston, which, until the Revolution, held a memorial celebration of Massacre Day on March 5. Adams claimed that Preston left Boston almost immediately after the trial of the soldiers and never expressed any gratitude to his defense counsel. However, Adams never doubted that he had done the right thing in accepting a part in the defense.

HISTORY TODAY

John Adams and his colleagues assumed the unenviable task of defending clients who were extremely unpopular with the public, including members of the public whom the three lawyers regarded as friends and compatriots. Adams' career survived this trial and he eventually became a popular patriot, statesman, and eventually a U.S. President, but that is not always the way it ends for some defense attorneys. Imagine you are an attorney. Imagine the worst possible crime you can imagine, and imagine that your client's guilt is not really in question. Also imagine that you may lose friends and even some close relatives are going to be very angry if you represent this defendant. Could you defend this client to the best of your ability?

PATRIOTS, LOYALISTS, AND THOSE "IN BETWEEN"

If international war is hell, then civil war must be the ultimate in torment. The American Revolution was both civil war and a war for national independence. Within the colonies, it divided families against each other, and it gave rise to a number of marauding bands that operated in the wastelands between zones of British and American authority, preying on the civilian populations of both areas. The Revolutionary War novels of *William Gilmore Simms* provide a realistic, although fictional, account of the inhumanity of these outlaw bands as they existed in Revolutionary South Carolina. All phases of life were in disorganization as a result of the war, and numerous opportunities existed for both violent and property-related crimes.

William Gilmore Simms (1806-1870): Poet and writer from South Carolina; strong proponent of slavery, most noted novel was *The Partisan*, about the American Revolution.

Well before the colonies declared their independence on July 4, 1776, the break with Britain had taken place. Military battles had been waged in Massachusetts, Virginia, and North Carolina, and provincial congresses in each of the colonies began the slow process of developing new forms of civil government.

Of paramount concern was the establishment of militia detachments and naval units that would afford some degree of security against the substantial military might of the mother country. A lesser concern was the problem of identifying those supporting the patriot (independence) cause and expelling or imprisoning those who remained loyal to the Crown. This task was assigned to local committees on conspiracy, staffed by patriot leaders, which searched out and punished actions that undermined the authority of the new states.

In the early days of the conflict, it was something of a legal puzzle to determine who owed allegiance to the new states, but the immediate need of suppressing espionage and sabotage obscured the legal issues. Once the states had declared their independence, it was a simple matter to demand that those favoring the Crown make the choice: either leave American territory, and thus reaffirm their allegiance to George III; or remain and run the risk of prosecution for treason, sedition, or espionage if their actions were contrary to the interests of the United States. Those who chose the first alternative frequently found themselves the victims of *sequestration*, a process that seized their real estate and personal possessions, and gave ownership to the American state where the assets were situated.

Not surprisingly, many inhabitants chose to remain neutral, neither supporting the American defense efforts nor assisting the British forces. Some estimates place the number of "neutrals" as high as one-third of the total colonial population. Many within this category were peaceful observers of the suffering and cruelty that were the inevitable consequences of the long and tedious War for Independence, but others were ruthless opportunists who found the chaotic situation a perfect backdrop for all sorts of criminal activity. A vacuum of authority introduced a new crime wave that added to the hardships of the war itself; the war's impact was particularly severe in states like New York and South Carolina, where the British military controlled part of the territory while the remainder was occupied by American forces.

The period from 1760 to the end of the war in 1783 has been identified as a time when American culture became attuned to violent behavior. For many reasons, this is an accurate assessment. Well before the outbreak of the war, colonists living in areas distant from the seaboard centers of authority found it necessary to take law enforcement into their own hands. Noteworthy in this connection were the *South Carolina Regulators*, a group of law-abiding citizens who organized patrols and tried members of criminal bands and others deemed to have committed crimes. Vigilante activity became a necessity because the only available criminal courts in colonial South Carolina were at Charleston, reached by travel over primitive roads and trails. Only after 1768 did upcountry South Carolina obtain its own circuit courts, and it was not until the end of the American Revolution that the courts and law enforcement were fully functional in the area.

HISTORY TODAY

The South Carolina Regulators viewed themselves as defenders of justice in a situation in which they could not count on the government to provide the protection that the citizenry needed. If a group of citizens comes to the conclusion that the government, more specifically the criminal justice system, is not able to do its job, what measures are they justified in taking?

PENOLOGY IN REVOLUTIONARY AMERICA

Patriot leaders of the Revolution were hard-pressed to maintain law and order in the newly independent states. Despite this, there was a growing sentiment for a change in punishments. This was due in part to discontent with the continued use of British criminal law; in part, it was an interest in the new penology advocated by Beccaria and the French philosophes; but it was also a recognition that harsh penal laws do not, in themselves, discourage crime.

In 1768, New York lawyer Robert R. Livingston Jr. (who would become chancellor of the newly independent state) wrote about a woman convicted of petty theft who was under sentence of death. Her execution was delayed because of her pregnancy, but would be carried out shortly after the child was born. Livingston stressed the harshness and inhumanity of a legal system that left the infant motherless. In the same year, a fellow New York lawyer, Peter Van Schaack, contemplated the penal law of the colony and concluded with resignation that, "to preserve Society Individuals must bleed; to secure a reverence for the laws that connect that Society the Violators must suffer."[3] However, both of these young men must have suspected that excessive punishments did not deter crime. A 1767 notice in the *New York Mercury* described a hanging of pickpockets at the public execution ground, and noted that as the hanging took place one man in the assembled crowd had his pocket picked.

Dissatisfaction with English penal laws existed throughout the American colonies and the newly independent states, giving rise to far-ranging reform efforts once the Revolutionary War was safely past. One such reform was *Thomas Jefferson*'s early unsuccessful effort to alter Virginia's system of sanctions. Originally drafted in 1776, his reform proposal was subjected to extensive revision and finally introduced in the Virginia Assembly's session beginning in October 1785. Jefferson proposed to reduce the number of capital offenses to two (treason and murder) and provide terms of imprisonment for most of the other felonies. Specific deterrents were provided to discourage *dueling*, and many property offenses were punishable by a term in prison coupled with multiple restitution. To Jefferson's dismay, the revisers had inserted the *lex talionis* into the revised code, including castration for rape and bestiality, and maiming in retaliation for similar injuries inflicted on the victim. In keeping with Beccaria's view that justice should be equally administered, the bill eliminated benefit of clergy. It also followed a principle of proportionality in the assignment of punishments. Commenting on the failure of the reform bill to pass the General Assembly's consideration in 1785, Jefferson believed that it was the reduction in capital punishment that brought about its rejection.

> Thomas Jefferson (1743-1826): Principal author of the Declaration in Independence; one of the most famous founding fathers; governor of Virginia; United States Minister (Ambassador) to France; first United States Secretary of State (1790-1793); second Vice President of the United States (1797-1801); third President of the United States (1801-1809); founder of the University of Virginia.

In Virginia, as in most of the other states, *executive clemency* and *pardons* were utilized to soften the impact of capital punishment, and gradually the legislative climate became more receptive to penal reform. In 1796, a bill following the general lines of the 1785 proposal was enacted into law. It limited the death penalty to murder in the first degree, which included premeditated killing and murder by poisoning. Other crimes by free persons were punishable by terms in prison. Property crimes were subject to both restitution requirements and prison sentences, proportional to the severity of the offense. Multiple restitution and the *lex talionis* in regard to maiming were absent from the 1796 law, as was the sanction of castration for rape and bestiality.

Historian Kathryn Preyer's study of the fragmented criminal court records of postrevolutionary Virginia suggests that the failure of the 1785 bill may have been due in part to the reluctance of the legislators to reduce punishments in a society that retained a high incidence of violence in its frontier areas. During the intervening decade, it became clear that the harsh sanctions provided by English law were not reducing the rate of crime and, thus, some experimentation with less severe penalties was justified. Another influence, not mentioned by Preyer, was the growing tendency in American jurisprudence to require, as a matter of due process, that the definition of crime and the provision of penalties should be a matter of statutory law. As a result, codification of Virginia's penal law was much more acceptable in 1796 than it was in 1785.

A discussion of revolution-era American penology would not be complete without some mention of *Thomas Eddy*. Eddy was one of the United States' earliest correctional reformers and pioneers, and is sometimes compared to *John Howard*, the Englishman widely regarded as one of the most significant penal reformers in history. Born in Pennsylvania in 1758, Eddy was part of a Quaker family that remained loyal to the British Crown before and during the American Revolution. As a result of being a Loyalist, Eddy, ostracized by many Patriots, did not attend public schools and was largely self-taught. A well-to-do merchant despite his political affiliation, Eddy experienced a formative event in his life during the American Revolution. While traveling to visit his family, Eddy was shot and taken prisoner by a patriot militia in New Jersey in 1780. Suspected of being a Loyalist spy, Eddy spent 10 days in a dungeon, not knowing whether he would live another day, before being released in a prisoner exchange.

> John Howard (1726-1790): English prison reformer; perhaps the most famous prison reformer in European history; traveled thousands of miles to many countries observing prisons and advocating reform; died as a result of contracting typhus from prison visits while in Russia.

Unlike many Loyalists who fled to Nova Scotia after the Revolutionary War, Eddy remained in the United States and achieved great success in a number of business endeavors. His success in business allowed him enough spare time to devote to philanthropic efforts. Remembering his incarceration experience and, like many reformers of his day, revolted by the spectacle of public punishments, Eddy led an effort to have a penitentiary built in New York, following the lead of neighboring Pennsylvania, except that Eddy championed the *Auburn system*, which advocated that prisoners work in groups rather than total isolation. Eddy insisted that prisons be clean, humanely administered, and that the focus be on education, religious instruction, and general moral reform, not torture and deprivation.

HISTORY TODAY

Very often people say that it does not matter whether prisons and jails are humane or clean. Aside from the fact that courts will get involved and force governments to administer humane penal institutions, why should Americans be concerned with the humaneness of jails and prisons? Is it possible that many of us, like Thomas Eddy, would have to experience incarceration firsthand to be able to answer that question?

Although he realized that prisons did not live up to his expectations, Eddy continued to lobby for prison reform in ways that were far ahead of his time. He advocated gender segregation and separate facilities for offenders under the age of 16, more than 75 years before the first juvenile courts were established. He also promoted the idea of having separate facilities for drunks and minor offenders, keeping them away from more serious offenders.

Eddy was also active in freeing mentally ill inmates from prisons, playing a large role in the building of New York's first mental hospital, or, as it was called at the time, a lunatic asylum. He was also involved in the New York Bible Society and the New York *Manumission* Society, which was devoted to the abolition of slavery.[4]

HISTORY TODAY

Aaron Burr was one of the first in a long line of American politicians and statesmen who were held in extremely high regard and were high achievers in public life, before they experienced a tremendous fall from grace. Richard Nixon was elected to a second term as President in 1972 in one of the most lopsided elections in history; but he resigned in disgrace less than 2 years later. John Edwards was one of the most popular young politicians in the United States when he served as the Democratic nominee for Vice President in 2004. An extramarital affair and some questionable financial dealings led to his quick downfall. What do cases like this teach Americans about the importance of an effective system of governance as opposed to devotion to any single person?

THE NEW CONSTITUTIONS AND CRIMINAL JUSTICE

Independence removed the last vestiges of British control over American law. As a result, the several state provincial congresses set about the task of drawing up new forms of government. These governments were based upon written constitutions that carefully balanced the powers allocated to the *three branches of government: the executive, the legislative, and the judicial branches.* Suspicion of executive authority was the result of past struggles against colonial governors. Dependence on colonial assemblies to protect the people against royal authority led the new states to stress the preeminence of legislative power,

FEATURED OUTLAW: AARON BURR

Few criminal trials in American history have attracted the public attention that followed the treason trial of former Vice President Aaron Burr (1756-1836). This sensational court proceeding was held at Richmond, Virginia, from August 3 to October 20, 1807. However, Burr is equally remembered as a participant in the most infamous duel in American history. Despite the fact that Burr served as his Vice President, President Thomas Jefferson and Burr were political enemies. Unlike today, when the President and Vice President run as a team and it is clear which person is to occupy which office, the election procedure of 1800, in a country barely 20 years old, generated a not-so-clear result. Presidential electors, who played a more prominent role than today's Electoral College, were not clear as to which man would be President and which would be Vice President, and the election was bitterly contested in the House of Representatives. Jefferson won the election but the die was cast for a bitter relationship between the two men.

In 1804, Burr, willing to relinquish the chance of being elected to the Vice Presidency, was nominated for the Governorship of New York but was defeated. Burr blamed his defeat in part on Alexander Hamilton, a fellow New Yorker and former Secretary of the Treasury, because Hamilton had circulated unflattering stories about Burr. In keeping with a fairly common practice among "chivalrous" and "honorable" upper-class men of the day, Burr challenged Hamilton to a duel. Against the advice of friends who warned Hamilton that he did not stand a chance against an experienced marksman like Burr, Hamilton accepted the challenge.

Fearing the legal consequences of dueling in their home state of New York, Burr and Hamilton arranged to duel in Weehawken, New Jersey, on July 11, 1804. Coincidentally, they dueled at the same place where Hamilton's son had been killed in a duel previously. Burr killed Hamilton and fled to Philadelphia. Warrants were issued for Burr's arrest, and he was indicted in New Jersey and New York, but he was never convicted in Hamilton's killing. Although this was his ruin in some respectable circles, Burr remained popular in the South and the West.

After shaking off the legal troubles stemming from the duel with Hamilton, Burr embarked on his next infamous endeavor. Burr was charged with having planned a military expedition into the Louisiana Territory with the purpose of starting a rebellion against the authority of the United States.

FIGURE 8.3 Aaron Burr, Vice President of the United States from 1801 to 1805, is shown in a nineteenth-century painting. Burr was indicted for murder by a New Jersey grand jury in 1804 after he killed Alexander Hamilton in a duel in Weehawken, New Jersey. *AP Photo/JSK.*

The charge was based on evidence that he and several others planned the venture, and that an armed force for that purpose gathered at Blennerhassett's Island in the Ohio River, and then embarked in boats bound for the western territories of the United States. However, the evidence indicated that Burr himself was not present on the island when the armed men gathered there, nor when they launched their boats for the trip down the Ohio. President Jefferson, warned of the pending enterprise by Brigadier General James Wilkinson, issued a proclamation condemning Burr's expedition as treasonable, and alerted the territorial authorities to arrest Burr and the men associated with him.

Several individuals associated with the expedition's planning were arrested, and Burr himself was captured by a detachment of U.S. Army troops on February 19, 1807. On orders from President Jefferson, Burr was taken to Richmond to stand trial before the U.S. Circuit Court for Virginia. Blennerhassett's Island was located on the Virginia side of the Ohio River, in what is now the state of West Virginia. This meant that the Federal Circuit Court for

Continued

FEATURED OUTLAW: AARON BURR—CONT'D

Virginia was the appropriate trial court. Under the Judiciary Act of 1789, the U.S. Circuit Courts consisted of one justice of the Supreme Court and the district judges of each circuit. Chief Justice John Marshall was the Supreme Court justice who would preside over Burr's trial.

Arriving at Richmond under arrest on March 27, Burr was charged with treason against the United States. A second charge claimed that Burr and his associates planned to invade the territory of Spain, located beyond the borders of the Louisiana Territory. In committing Burr, Marshall found probable cause to believe that the misdemeanor of waging war on a friendly nation might have been committed, but he refused to commit Burr on the treason charge. Thereafter, on May 28, the Chief Justice refused to accept affidavits as evidence of facts pertaining to the case, and the court awaited the arrival of the witnesses. On June 13, in response to a motion on Burr's behalf, Marshall issued a subpoena duces tecum, ordering President Jefferson to supply the Court with documents in the White House pertaining to the case. In a lengthy opinion, he reasoned that a person accused of crime was entitled to access to all evidence pertaining to his case, and that even the President was not immune from judicial process. After a short delay, Jefferson ordered the documents to be made available to the Court.

On August 18, Chief Justice Marshall issued an opinion concerning the trial agenda. He insisted that evidence of an overt act be provided before the submission of any corroborating testimony or documentation was introduced. Following the testimony of the first group of witnesses, Burr's counsel moved to suppress further evidence, asserting that because Burr was not present at the time of the purported act, it was impossible to prove his participation. Marshall ruled that because Aaron Burr had not actually taken part in advancing armed conflict with the United States, he could not be guilty of treason as defined in the U.S. Constitution. Merely conspiring to oppose lawful authority, or planning to do so, was insufficient to sustain proof of treason. "Levying war," as

required by the Constitution for proof of treason, required that the accused should have been physically present at the acts that represented opposition to the lawful authority of the United States. Mentioning the Supreme Court's earlier opinion in *Ex parte Bollman* and *Ex parte Swartwout* (4 Cranch 75, 1807), Marshall rejected portions of that opinion that implied that one might be guilty of constructive treason if the individual participated in a conspiracy to commit treason but did not actually commit an overt act by levying war. Instead he stressed that to be guilty of treason, the accused person would have to take part in the overt act of treason alleged in the indictment. Following Marshall's opinion setting forth the law of treason, the jury, after a short deliberation, returned a not guilty verdict on September 1, 1807.

The Burr treason trial was followed by a brief jury trial of the misdemeanor charge—that Burr conspired to assemble a body of armed men to attack Spanish territory west of Louisiana. Begun on September 1, the trial ended on September 15 with a not guilty jury verdict. While the government retained the option of prosecuting Burr for events that allegedly occurred in Ohio, Thomas Jefferson and his advisors refrained from taking any further action against Burr. Hounded by creditors, Burr traveled to the northeast and then sailed to Europe, hoping to improve his financial affairs while living abroad. He did not succeed. Burr tried in vain to enlist the aid of the French Emperor Napoleon to plan an invasion of Florida. Burr returned to New York after spending 4 years in Europe, practiced law, married a wealthy widow, committed adultery, and squandered much of her fortune before his death in 1836.

Sources: Kline, M.-J., & Ryan, J. W. (Eds.). (1983). *Political correspondence and public papers of Aaron Burr,* 2 Vols. Princeton: Princeton University Press, Vol. 2, pp. 1017-1046; Hobson, C. F. (Ed.). (1993). *The papers of John Marshall.* Chapel Hill: University of North Carolina Press, Vol. 7, pp. 1-142; Johnson, H. A. *The chief justiceship of John Marshall.* Columbia: University of South Carolina Press, pp. 124-131.

and recognition of the need for an independent judiciary ensured an enhanced place for judges and lawyers in the new American republic. State autonomy, recently won in the battle against the mother country, was jealously guarded, and efforts to establish an effective national government were unsuccessful until 1789.

Criminal law reform might have proceeded slowly, but there was an immediate need to protect the individual rights of the people against governmental oppression. The leaders of the American Revolution were heirs to the traditions of the English Civil Wars and the Glorious Revolution. They were students of the Enlightenment philosophers and knew about the barbarities of continental criminal procedure. They had experienced oppressive searches at the hands of the British customs officers; they valued the right to defense counsel in felony cases and the protections afforded by a common law jury. All of these factors caused these leaders to pay particular attention to criminal procedure and the rights of accused persons. In preparing the new state constitutions, they inserted special clauses extending the most necessary procedural protections, and limiting the power of governments over the lives of citizens. These clauses ensured individual freedom and recognized the dignity of all citizens before the law.

It is significant that all of the states adopted written forms of government, laying the basis for constitutionalism that would emphasize clarity in the distribution of power. Constitutional debates over state constitutions, and over the Federal Constitution in 1787-1788, were directed toward the way in which political leaders could be given effective power without allowing them to oppress the people through tyrannical use of the authority provided. The political thought of Montesquieu was particularly influential in balancing one grant of power with another, as well as separating the powers in such a way that one agency of government checked and neutralized the possible excesses of another. These new republican states rested, in fact as well as in the theory of John Locke, on the consent and support of their people: consent given by their ratification of the constitutional documents, and support demonstrated by their sacrifices throughout the long Revolutionary War.

These proud and autonomous states were reluctantly drawn into a federal union by the realization that a loose confederation was inadequate to provide economic growth as well as sufficient diplomatic power. Ten years passed between the Declaration of Independence and the Mount Vernon gathering (1786) that started American statesmen toward framing a new central government. Fear of a new imperial authority resulted in the creation of a federal government possessed of limited and carefully enumerated powers.

The *Federal Constitution* (ratified in 1788) was sharply criticized because it lacked a *bill of rights* that would secure to defendants in federal courts the same sort of rights they were guaranteed by state constitutional provisions. In spite of Federalist Party arguments that these protections were part of English and colonial common law, the antifederalist opposition succeeded in ensuring that many states did not ratify until guaranteed the passage of a comprehensive federal bill of rights. One of the first matters of business before the Congress that assembled in 1789 was the preparation of a bill of rights to be submitted to the states for ratification. Added to the federal Constitution as its first 10

TIME CAPSULE: BILL OF RIGHTS

During the convention that drafted a constitution for the United States in 1787, the need for a bill of rights was suggested by George Mason and Elbridge Gerry, but the idea was rejected. The absence of a bill of rights, however, became a focus of controversy between the Federalists and Antifederalists, and several states refused to ratify the new constitution until a pledge was made to adopt a bill of rights. In agreement with this promise, in 1791 approval was gained for 10 amendments, referred to as the Bill of Rights. Included were four of particular importance in guaranteeing criminal procedure, which would protect the rights of defendants: the Fourth, Fifth, Sixth, and Eighth Amendments. To ensure that a specific statement of rights would not imply that it was complete, the Ninth Amendment was added. In the ensuing decades, crucial terms in the clauses have been expanded or restricted through interpretation in courts of appeal.

Amendment I Congress shall make no law respecting an establishment of religion, or prohibiting the free exercise thereof; or abridging the freedom of speech, or of the press; or the right of the people peaceably to assemble, and to petition the government for a redress of grievances.

Amendment II A well regulated militia, being necessary to the security of a free state, the right of the people to keep and bear arms, shall not be infringed.

Amendment III No soldier shall, in time of peace be quartered in any house, without the consent of the owner, nor in time of war, but in a manner to be prescribed by law.

Amendment IV The right of the people to be secure in their persons, houses, papers, and effects, against unreasonable searches and seizures, shall not be violated, and no Warrants shall be issued, but on probable cause, supported by Oath or affirmation, and particularly describing the place to be searched, and the persons or things to be seized.

Amendment V No person shall be held to answer for a capital, or otherwise infamous crime, unless on a presentment or indictment of a Grand Jury, except in cases arising in the land or naval forces, or in the Militia, when in actual service in time of War or public danger; nor shall any person be subject for the same offence to be twice put in jeopardy of life or limb; nor shall be compelled in any criminal case to be a witness against himself, nor be deprived of life, liberty, or property, without due process of law; nor shall private property be taken for public use, without just compensation.

Amendment VI In all criminal prosecutions, the accused shall enjoy the right to a speedy and public trial, by an impartial jury of the State and district wherein the crime shall have been committed, which district shall have been previously ascertained by law, and to be informed of the nature and cause of the accusation; to be confronted with the witnesses against him; to have compulsory process for obtaining witnesses in his favor, and to have the Assistance of Counsel for his defense.

Amendment VII In suits at common law, where the value in controversy shall exceed twenty dollars, the right of trial by jury shall be preserved, and no fact tried by a jury, shall be otherwise reexamined in any court of the United States, than according to the rules of the common law.

Amendment VIII Excessive bail shall not be required, nor excessive fines imposed, nor cruel and unusual punishments inflicted.

Amendment IX The enumeration in the Constitution, of certain rights, shall not be construed to deny or disparage others retained by the people.

Amendment X The powers not delegated to the United States by the Constitution, nor prohibited by it to the states, are reserved to the states respectively, or to the people.

amendments (1791), the federal Bill of Rights guarantees freedom of the press, of speech, and of religion; it prohibits cruel and unusual punishments and mandates the use of a grand jury and a petty jury in criminal cases. Unreasonable searches and seizures are prohibited, as are self-incrimination and demanding excessive bail. Echoing the Magna Carta, the federal Bill of Rights protects citizens against being "deprived of life, liberty, or property, without due process of law." Other procedural guarantees include the right to a speedy and public trial, the right to confront witnesses, and access to compulsory process (to compel the presence of defense witnesses). While these protections originally applied only in prosecutions brought under the authority of the federal government, they became the model for similar grants in later state constitutions. Since the ratification of the Fourteenth Amendment (in 1868), there has been a strong judicial tendency to apply many of the Bill of Rights provisions to all criminal proceedings, even those pending in state courts.

HISTORY TODAY

A few years ago, two political commentators, George Will and Sam Donaldson, engaged in a debate about whether a certain law or action was constitutional. Donaldson acerbically accused Will of overemphasizing the importance of that "dried old document," meaning the Constitution. Will replied that nothing is as important as that "dried old document." Who is right and who is wrong in such a debate?

SUMMARY

The era of the American Revolution witnessed the maturity of the colonial legal system and the rise of distinct American views concerning the nature of the imperial constitution. American nationalism and injustices within the British Empire brought on the break in American relations with the mother country, but the newly independent states retained the criminal law of England as well as English modes of criminal procedure. While there was a growing feeling that penalties for crime were too harsh, it was not until the last decades of the eighteenth century that American legislatures altered the English common law of crimes. Constitutionalism in the new states was based upon written forms of government, drafted with due regard to the balance and separation of powers. Virtually all state constitutions and the federal Constitution of 1788 contained bills of rights that set forth an extensive set of procedural guarantees in the conduct of criminal prosecutions.

REFERENCES

Smith, M. H. (1963). *The writs of assistance case.* Berkeley: University of California Press; Younger, R. D. (1963). *The people's panel: The grand jury in the United States, 1634-1941.* Providence: Brown University Press; Ubbelohde, C. W. (1960). *The vice admiralty courts and the American revolution.* Chapel Hill: University of North Carolina Press; Steckley, G. F. (1978). Merchants and the admiralty court during the English revolution. *American Journal of Legal History, 22*(2), 137–175.

Levy, L. W. (1985). *Emergence of a free press.* New York: Oxford University Press; Levy, L. W. (1963). *Freedom of speech and press in early American history: Legacy of suppression.* New York: Harper & Row; Buranelli, V. (Ed.). (1975). *The trial of Peter Zenger.* Westport, CT: Greenwood Press;

Katz, S. N., & Alexander, J. (Eds.). (1963). *A brief narrative of the case and trial of John Peter Zenger, printer of the New York Weekly Journal.* Cambridge: Harvard University Press.

Zobel, H. B. (1970). *The Boston Massacre.* Cambridge: Harvard University Press; Kinvin Wroth, L., & Zobel, H. B. (Eds.). (1965). *Legal papers of John Adams, III.* Cambridge: Harvard University Press.

Brown, R. M. (1983). *The South Carolina regulators.* Cambridge: Harvard University Press; Preyer, K. (1983). Crime, the criminal law and reform in post-revolutionary Virginia. *Law and History Review, 1, ;* Brant, I. (1965). *The bill of rights: Its origin and meaning.* Indianapolis: Bobbs-Merrill Company.

Ritchie, R. C. (1986). *Captain Kidd and the war against the pirates.* Cambridge: Harvard University Press; Black, C. V. (1989). *Pirates of the West Indies.* Cambridge: Cambridge University Press; Winston, A. (1970). *No purchase, no pay: Sir Henry Morgan, Captain William Kidd, Captain Woodes Rogers in the great age of privateers and pirates, 1665-1715.* London: Eyre & Spottiswoode; Friedman, L. M. (1993). *Crime and punishment in American history.* New York: Basic Books.

Chapin, B. (1964). *The American law of treason: Revolutionary and early national origins.* Seattle: University of Washington Press.

Notes and Problems

1. In areas affecting criminal justice, what did American Revolutionary leaders retain from their English heritage? What did they reject, and why?

2. Why are free speech and freedom of the press important? Should they be limited in any way? Should government officials be protected by a law of seditious libel?

3. Why is a grand jury important? A petty jury? How do juries function in criminal cases? If you were John Adams in the Boston Massacre trials, how would you have dealt with jury concerns and emotions? If you were an attorney and were asked to defend very unpopular defendants, could you defend them to the best of your ability?

4. Vigilantism is an interesting phenomenon just touched upon in this chapter. Is there legitimacy in citizens resorting to "self-help" when law enforcement is inadequate or nonexistent in a community? Who determines inadequacy?

5. The Revolutionary War generation was well aware of the perils of constructive treason, an offense at English common law that considered all who had a part in opposing the government to be traitors. Is it wise to limit the offense of treason in this way?

ENDNOTES

[1] Quoted in Buranelli, V. (1975). *The trial of Peter Zenger.* Westport: Greenwood Press, p. 63.

[2] Kinvin Wroth, L., & Zobel, H. B. (Eds.). (1965). *Legal papers of John Adams, III.* Cambridge: Harvard University Press, p. 6.

[3] Van Schaack Papers, Special Collections Library, Columbia University.

[4] Jones, M. (2005). *Criminal justice pioneers in U.S. history.* Boston: Allyn and Bacon.

CHAPTER 9

Early American Penology, European Prisons, and Australia

LEARNING OBJECTIVES

1. Understand the rationale for imprisoning Americans in the early days of the Republic.
2. Learn some of the ways correctional officials managed inmates in early penal facilities.
3. Learn some of the efforts made at dealing with mental illness in prisons and jails.
4. Understand some of the challenges encountered by correctional officials in the early days of American penology.
5. Understand the rationale behind the creation of the American penitentiary.

6. Become familiar with some of the early correctional pioneers in the United States, Ireland, and Australia.
7. Learn the difference between the Auburn and Pennsylvania systems.
8. Learn about the founding of the Australian penal colonies and some of the officials who administered these colonies.
9. Learn the evolution of parole.
10. Learn and understand the story of John Brown.

Table 9.1 Time Line: Early American Penology

1703	Hospice of St. Michael established at Rome as a reformatory for boys.
c. 1715-1774	English felons sentenced to capital punishment are given benefit of clergy or have their punishment remitted on condition that they be transported to the North American colonies. It is estimated that some 50,000 individuals were sent to America under these conditions.
1766	Beccaria publishes his study of penology, *Essay on Crime and Punishment*.
1773	John Howard becomes sheriff of Bedfordshire and becomes an advocate for an improved prison system. His study, *The State of the Prisons in England and Wales*, is published in 1777.
c. 1785	Pennsylvania adopts the solitary system of prison discipline.
1788	New South Wales, Australia, is established as a penal colony.
1791	Jeremy Bentham publishes *Panopticon*.
1813	Elizabeth Gurney Fry makes her first visit to Newgate Prison and begins a lifetime of relieving the distress of female prisoners and their children.
1816	New York's Auburn Prison is established and operates on a "silent" communal system, which encouraged limited conversation but group labor.
1821	Milbank Prison is erected in conformity with Bentham's architectural ideas.
1826	The New York House of Refuge is established for juvenile offenders.
1827	Elizabeth Fry publishes *Observations on the Visiting, Superintendence and Government of Female Prisoners*.
1833	Johann Hinrich Wichern establishes the Rauhes Haus for boys at Hamburg, Germany.
1843	A panel of common law judges provides the House of Lords with a report that establishes the *M'Naghten* Rules to determine insanity in accused criminals.
1840-1848	Royal Navy Captain Alexander Maconochie introduces collective responsibility and early release for prisoners on Norfolk Island off the Australian coast. He publishes *Secondary Punishment, the Mark System* in 1848.
1854-1862	Sir Walter Crofton, director of the Irish prison system, introduces the "progressive stage" system, based upon the discoveries of Maconochie.

American conditions before the Revolution sharply restricted the number of individuals serving prison terms. Most jails and prisons existed for the temporary holding of offenders, either in anticipation of trial or after sentencing and before imposition of capital punishment. Lesser crimes were punished by physical means, such as whipping, branding, and mutilation. It was not uncommon for the culprit to be sentenced to serve his victim, in labor, for a period proportional to the magnitude of the crime. In labor-scarce early America, imprisonment simply was not a wise use of human resources. Burgeoning enterprise eagerly absorbed lesser criminals into the workforce and at the same time managed to absorb the substantial number of English convicts who were exported to the colonies in lieu of capital punishment.

Lack of freedom was not a new situation in nineteenth-century America; the most obvious evidence of this was the existence of *chattel slavery*, that peculiar institution of American life that survived long after its abolition in the British Empire and Europe. Although slavery in one form or another was commonplace in most of the non-Western world, the fact that slavery existed in a nation pledged in its birth to the equality of men generated harsh condemnation and a long and bitter antislavery campaign that ended only in the bloodbath of the American Civil War.

Another restraint on freedom existed in the practice of *debt imprisonment*. Those unable to pay their creditors in pre-Civil War America frequently found themselves thrown into jail until the obligation was satisfied. Once imprisoned, the unfortunate man was deprived of the opportunity to earn money for repayment. Survival depended upon the kindness and aid of others; the prisoner bore the responsibility of securing food, clothing, firewood, and other necessities. Jailers customarily demanded gratuities when these essential supplies were delivered to debtors in their charge. As a consequence, the longer a debtor remained in prison, the larger the debt became.

HISTORY TODAY

Local governments have now recognized, either on their own or by force of court orders, that they are responsible for the welfare of inmates in their custody. Some inmates are able to purchase extra food and other material from the jail if their families supply the money. Should the treatment of local jail inmates depend upon the resources they or their family can supply?

In colonial America, imprisoned debtors were traditionally granted *jail liberty*, which permitted them to seek work within the town limits. However, with the passage of time, this liberality disappeared, taking with it the last hope of earning funds with which to repay the prisoner's obligation. Given the fever of financial speculation that gripped the young American nation, it was common to find prominent people imprisoned for debt. Robert Morris, the "Financier of the Revolution," overextended his trading operations and ended his life in a debtor's prison. An associate justice of the U.S. Supreme Court, James Wilson, got into difficulty while speculating in western Pennsylvania land grants; his death while on circuit prevented an undignified debt imprisonment. In the first three decades of the nineteenth century, there was a campaign to abolish imprisonment for debt. By 1840, virtually every state in the Union had eliminated debtors' prisons.

Robert Morris (1734-1806): American businessman; signer of the Declaration of Independence and the Constitution; U.S. Senator from Pennsylvania; served as Superintendent of Finance during the last years of the Revolutionary War.

HISTORY TODAY

Jail liberty was a forerunner of modern work-release programs operated by many jails and prisons. Should inmates be allowed to work in the community while serving their sentence? Is this a potential threat to public safety? However, should not inmates have some incentive for good behavior?

Local jails were also the depository for the mentally ill, the aged, and vagrants. As the population grew and poverty increased, many people in various conditions huddled together in crowded, unhealthy communal cells. Curious multitudes flocked to pay their penny admission, viewing the degradation of the inmates and the antics of the insane, satisfying their taste for the macabre and their need to feel superior. However, accessibility to the general public was to prove the salvation of these unfortunate inmates. Responsible care through workshops and apprenticeships was substituted for imprisoning vagrants.

Dorothea Dix (1802-1887) took up the cause of the insane, arguing for care and treatment rather than imprisonment and neglect. Private charities assumed the task of housing, clothing, and feeding the aged poor. Dix also advocated prison reform, believing that religious instruction, especially memorization of scripture, and education in general were keys to rehabilitation. She began her efforts in her native New England, particularly in Massachusetts. Dix also worked with the Massachusetts legislature, persuading lawmakers to change laws that were unfair to the mentally ill. She reported tales of ghastly abuse against the mentally ill, including beatings, lashings, and being chained naked in cages.

FIGURE 9.1 Dorothea Dix. *Library of Congress.*

Eventually Dix spread her efforts to other New England states and Canada, usually traveling by stagecoach at night so she could visit jails during the day. As Dix expanded her reach to the Middle Atlantic States, she also forged partnerships with the medical community, encouraging doctors to devote more effort to fair treatment of the mentally ill, and working tirelessly with whoever would listen to divert the mentally ill from jails to medical facilities.

Dix worked very hard throughout her life to improve the lot of the mentally ill, as well as for jail reform and adequate hospital conditions. Strangely, Dix cared little for the plight of black slaves. In fact, she was puzzled that there were so many willing to dissolve the Union and engage in violence over what she viewed as a benign institution, and she maintained that most slaves were content with their situation.

HISTORY TODAY

Dorothea Dix's mission is far from complete. Local jails are still teeming with mentally ill inmates, especially those who are frequently arrested for minor crimes and/or are homeless and have no skills or resources. If someone is accused of committing a serious crime, he or she very often receives an extensive mental health evaluation or treatment, but many minor offenders do not receive much mental health treatment, and if they do, they are often simply released into the community until they are arrested again. What could or should local governments do to address this situation?

Prison reform impulses combined humanitarianism with faith in the *perfectibility of man*. Many of the leaders had strong religious convictions, and all were strongly committed to freedom as a necessary attribute of being American. It was not surprising that reform of the prison system, already under way in England and Europe, should catch the imagination and engage the energies of American reformers. Within a generation, American penal systems became a matter of interest to European penologists, and the New World truly began to lead the Old World in regard to prison discipline and architectural design.

INITIAL STEPS IN PRISON REFORM

Normally, detention in a jail or prison was a method for ensuring the accused person's presence at trial or to hold him or her until the time of punishment. Fines developed as alternatives to physical punishment, and many convicts preferred to pay a fine rather than face the pain and humiliation of physical punishment. Because poor convicts could not afford to pay fines, but were entitled to respite from harsh physical punishment, imprisonment developed as a reasonable alternative. Unfortunately, early governmental administration was not attuned to the prison system. All public servants (such as sheriffs, court clerks, and even judges) were supported by fees paid by litigants or petitioners, and prisons did not readily fit into such a format. Keepers of jails and prisons provided virtually no food or other necessities of life without payment; inmates and their families were constantly coerced for fees and bribes, despite the fact that many of the inmates were imprisoned for poverty in the first place.

Erected as humanitarian alternatives to physical punishment, prisons soon proved to be unsatisfactory. Inmates were kept in large communal quarters; men and women lived together in a state of depravity and degradation. Young offenders consorted with prison veterans, learning new tricks of the criminal trade to be applied when they were released. Overcrowding produced sickness and death. The most virulent disease was *gaol fever*, a form of typhus that decimated prison populations and, at times, threatened all involved in the criminal justice system in the United States and Europe. At the Black Assizes, held at Oxford in 1577, gaol fever claimed the lives of 500 people within a period of 5 weeks. Among the dead was the Lord Chief Baron of the Exchequer, as well as a substantial number of jurors and witnesses.

HISTORY TODAY

Many modern jails and prisons may not have to be concerned with gaol fever, but communicable diseases are still a problem in correctional facilities. Governments are responsible for an inmate's health needs, and an inmate with a communicable disease is a potential risk to other inmates and staff. Health care is very expensive in the United States. How can local governments provide for medical care for the inmates and still avoid their own financial troubles because of rising health care costs?

Rapidly rising crime rates in eighteenth-century England would have overwhelmed the existing facilities if it had not been for capital punishment and exile. Capital punishment became common for virtually all felonies, the harshness of the law being softened to a degree by the existence of benefit of clergy. Taking this benefit saved the lives of first-time offenders, but recidivists stood a good chance of doing their last dance upon the gallows of Tyburn Hill.

In addition to the use of the death penalty, English judges usually gave the condemned criminal the opportunity to select as an alternative the option of being exiled to the colonies. Before 1774, a large number of convicts sentenced to death chose transportation to one of the North American colonies. After the American Revolution halted this involuntary emigration from England, the judges ordered exile to Australia, which remained a penal colony for the first four decades of its existence. (See "Time Capsule: Australian Penal Colonies.")

Despite extensive use of capital punishment and exile to the colonies, English prisons found it difficult to deal with the growing number of inmates. Hunger, nakedness, promiscuity, and violent assault and rape by fellow inmates contributed to a persistent despair and regression to barbarism. Until John Howard was elected sheriff of Bedfordshire in 1773, it seemed that no one in authority was concerned with the inmates' plight. After his first view of the Bedfordshire prison, for which he as sheriff was responsible, Howard went to the local justices of the peace to request funds for the repair of the building and the relief of its inmates. The court demanded that he show that such expenditures from public funds had been made in the past. It was this question that started Howard on a lifetime of inspecting prisons in Britain and Europe. Publishing *The State of the Prisons in England and Wales* in 1777, Howard became the acknowledged expert on the evil conditions prevalent throughout all of Western Europe's penal institutions. Perhaps the most charitable thing that could be said about English prisons was that they did not contain an array of torture instruments as did the institutions in France and Italy.

TIME CAPSULE: AUSTRALIAN PENAL COLONIES

One of the most common conservative-oriented colloquialisms concerning what to do with law violators goes roughly as follows: Find an island somewhere and send all hardened criminals there. Such an idea even captured the attention of Hollywood filmmakers in the 1980s. The setting for the futuristic movie *Escape from New York* was Manhattan, in which the island served as a giant penal colony for America's worst criminals.

The idea of exiling prisoners and political dissidents was on the minds of the British after America declared its independence. Concerned about an increasing street crime problem—it has been estimated that one in eight Londoners were professional criminals—and political dissidence, especially in neighboring Ireland (which was under British control), Great Britain, still under the rule of King George III, sought to rid itself of its crime problem by exporting its criminal population as far from home as possible. The British hoped to accomplish two goals with this experiment. One objective was to rid itself of the "criminal mob" that had overtaken English cities; the other was to expand its empire and profit from Australia's raw materials.

No place was further away from England than Australia. Even today, with the availability of air transportation, Australia is very far removed from the United States and Western Europe. If it is far removed today, when a flight from the West Coast of the United States can last 15 hours, it must have seemed even more remote to the British in the eighteenth century. The first journey carrying prisoners from England to Australia lasted more than 250 days. The route from England to Australia was extremely long by sea. The English had to sail south to the southern tip of Africa and then turn to complete the long journey to Australia.

The first shipment of convicted criminals began on January 6, 1787. It consisted of more than 730 convicted criminals. Approximately 430 had been convicted of minor theft; 93 for breaking and entering; 71 for highway robbery; 44 for livestock theft; 31 for robbery by force; 9 for grand larceny; 8 for fencing; 7 for swindling; 4 for forgery; and 35 for other offenses. The youngest convict was a 9-year-old and the oldest was an 82-year-old woman convicted of perjury; she committed suicide before the ship reached Australia. She was not the only casualty of the long, arduous trip by sea. During the course of the 252-day trip, 48 people died, including 40 convicts, 5 children of convicts, and 3 of the sailors.

Conditions in Australia were extremely harsh. Tools, supplies, and resources were scarce, and most of the convicts had few skills to offer as well. As time wore on, another problem developed. Few, if any, would take on the task of moving to Australia to work with the convicts. Such a move would involve leaving behind their family and entire way of life in Great Britain to live in an untamed wilderness fraught with innumerable dangers, and thus the job attracted very few desirable workers. The hope of making a profit for the English Crown soon evaporated as a result of these realities.

Yet another problem for the British was that Australia was not uninhabited. The Aborigines, or the Iora, had lived in Australia for thousands of years, and most of them were not thrilled with the arrival of the Europeans. Neither the convicts nor most of the British officers got along well with the Iora. Approximately 300,000 Iora lived in Australia in 1787. The Iora population gradually shrank as a result of the diseases imported by the British to which they had no immunity.

The British had an extremely difficult time understanding the Iora and vice versa. Not only did the two groups differ in appearance and language, but the cultures were light years apart. The British were horrified at the Aboriginal custom of abandoning or killing unwanted children at birth—especially children who were sick or deformed—as a form of population control. Because they were a nomadic people, another way of life that was foreign to the British, too many children cut into the food supply and thus became a burden to everyone.

Another cultural difference that caused problems stemmed from the concept of private property. Because the Iora were nomadic, the concept of private property was somewhat foreign to them. They had no qualms about taking British-grown crops or possessions, which made them thieves in the eyes of the British. The result was harsh punishment toward the Iora, who were not above treating the Europeans inhumanely as well.

The great Australian penal experiment ended when the last shipment of convicts came to Australia in 1868. The great experiment led to the establishment of the nation of Australia. It also led to the first experiments in parole: the result of Scotsman Alexander Maconochie's work on the penal colony Norfolk Island, located 900 miles off the coast of Australia. It also resulted in ludicrous complaints about soft treatment of prisoners, a common theme in the history of

Continued

TIME CAPSULE: AUSTRALIAN PENAL COLONIES—CONT'D

correctional reforms worldwide. Many British complained that Maconochie was too soft on his charges, and some complained because the convicts both in Australia and Norfolk Island did not pay taxes.

For most of their history as a nation, many Australians felt a sense of inferiority over their convict history. Robert Hughes, who grew up in Australia and wrote *The Fatal Shore*, the most comprehensive book on the Australian penal experiment, said that Australian schools largely ignored this important aspect of the nation's history, and many generations of Australians remained largely ignorant of it. Many Australians euphemistically referred to their convict ancestors as "government men" rather than convicts. However, in recent decades most Australians have shed this complex and have eagerly embraced their history and ancestry.

Source: Hughes, R. (1987). *The fatal shore: The epic of Australia's founding*. New York: Alfred A. Knopf

Throughout his career, Howard was concerned with the design of prisons, with disciplinary procedures, and with meeting the physical needs of the inmates. Having been held as a prisoner of war by the French in 1756, he knew firsthand many of the difficulties of prison life, but it was only after his inspection of English and Welsh prisons that he reduced his recommendations to written form. He noted that men should be separated from women, preferably in different prisons, but certainly in different rooms. Howard noted that young first offenders should be separated in individual cells during evening hours to provide time for privacy and meditation, and that they should be put to work in communal workrooms during the day to earn their keep and to learn habits of industry. Sanitary conditions made a lasting impression upon Howard; he wrote that the reek of his clothing after a day in prison made it impossible for him to comfortably remain in an enclosed place. His notebooks and papers also smelled of the prison's air. To counter this, Howard recommended that cells be well ventilated, cleaned on a daily basis, and scoured with lime at least twice a year. Howard seems to have had little contact with individual prisoners, and his report is most valuable for the statistics and management recommendations it contains. Yet it is clear that he believed that prisons should not be the cause of unnecessary suffering to the inmates, and that some effort should be made to preserve their lives and to turn them into better citizens.

Expanding his investigations to Europe, Howard came upon workhouses established in the Low Countries (Belgium, the Netherlands, and Luxembourg) for the relief of the poor and the training of petty criminals in useful crafts. During his visit to the Hospice of St. Michael in Rome, he discovered an institution that used labor in silence as a means of ensuring both diligence at work and meditation about past offenses. The hospice was dedicated to the care of young boys convicted of minor offenses who would profit from the training. It was on the basis of his observations at St. Michael that Howard coined the term *penitentiary* to describe an institution that would serve not merely as a place of safekeeping, but also as a training ground in self-discipline and moral meditation.

HISTORY TODAY

Some have argued that penitentiaries produce everything but a penitent attitude. Does prison, or the penitentiary, provide an environment conducive for a person to make penitence—either with God or their conscience—for their crimes?

Three years after Howard's prison report was published, *Elizabeth Fry* (1780-1845) was born into the wealthy Gurney family, which was prominent in English wool manufacturing and banking circles. Raised as a "gay Quaker" (a Quaker who adapted to worldly ways), Elizabeth Gurney married banker Joseph Fry in 1800. His stricter religious views, coupled with her contacts with Quaker preachers from America, converted her to the strict observance of the religious practices and behavioral codes of the Society of Friends (another name for the Quakers). In addition to household duties and caring for 12 children born between 1801 and 1822, she established a school for poor youngsters in her neighborhood and spent many hours instructing them in reading and other basic skills. By February 1811, Fry was recorded as a Quaker minister, giving her words special weight in the Friends' meetings and authorizing her to visit other congregations and to preach to them. At the suggestion of Stephen Grellet, an American Quaker visitor, she first visited *Newgate Prison* in January 1813. In his travel diary Grellet recorded what he and Fry discovered:

FIGURE 9.2 Quaker Elizabeth Fry was an early prison reformer. *Courtesy en.wikipedia.org.*

> I found many very sick, lying on the bare floor or on old straw, having very scanty covering over them, though it was quite cold; and there were several children born in the prison among them, almost naked.[1]

These conditions were appalling even to male prisoners in a separate ward nearby. Fry's immediate reaction was to get flannel cloth, assemble Quaker women to prepare clothing, and deliver children's clothes to Newgate the next day. This initial contact was not to persist, and 4 years elapsed before Fry began her prison visits once more. Against the advice of the keepers, she gained entrance to the women's ward in January 1817 and began to speak to them about the possibility that she could educate the children. With their cooperation, she started a school in a portion of the women's ward, attended by the children of the inmates as well as by juvenile delinquents committed to Newgate. The school was an immediate success, and Elizabeth Fry's commitment to the women of Newgate was firmly established.

Unquestionably, it was the mother-child relationship that made it possible for Fry to so influence the female prisoners. The prisoners themselves were utterly without hope. Maintained on short rations, subject to the ravages of gaol fever, and meagerly provided with clothing for protection against the harsh winters, they were also totally at the mercy of their male keepers and the male prisoners who contrived to enter the women's ward. Into this state of hopelessness, Fry carried the message that their children need not suffer the same fate, but that through education their future might be made more promising. It was thus hope for their children that turned the vicious and depraved female inmates of Newgate into a cohesive community working toward common goals. Their first step was to provide a schoolroom; this was simply one of the sleeping rooms, made available through voluntary acceptance of its occupants into the other rooms.

Passive cooperation escalated into active support when Fry discovered that the Newgate women were willing and anxious to sew clothing for themselves and the children. Organizing the Ladies Newgate Committee, she secured donations of cloth and began training the inmates in sewing. Eventually, she decided that the women's products could be sold commercially, providing funds to buy food and other necessities for the women and their offspring. The prison laundry, used only occasionally during the winter months, was converted into a workroom, and its products were sold in faraway New South Wales (Australia) to prevent any competition with English manufacturers or laborers.

A year after her work began, Elizabeth Fry discovered that force and disorder characterized preparations to transport female prisoners to penal servitude in New South Wales. Placed in heavy chains, the transportees were drawn in open carts through the city of London and placed below decks in the waiting transport ships. The terror of being driven through the gawking and jeering London crowd, coupled with the pain of enduring heavy chains cutting into their ankles and wrists, made the occasion one of anguish and fierce resistance to the keepers. In 1818, Fry succeeded in altering the conditions, persuading the authorities to dispense with the chains and use closed wagons. On the day before the departure, a gathering was held in the women's ward, marked by prayers for a safe journey and an exchange of farewells. From that year onward, the transport of female felons to New South Wales was marked by dignity and restraint. From 1818 to 1843, Fry organized the loading of more than 12,000 women inmates onto 106 ships, and her presence and example caused the preparations to go forward without any violence or unnecessary suffering.

Unlike John Howard, Elizabeth Fry did not begin her work at Newgate with a view toward publishing a report. Rather, she strove to work at the level of individual need within the prisons. However, by 1827 her work was widely known and her advice was sought not only in Britain but throughout Europe. Only then did she record her experiences and recommendations, and her *Observations on the Visiting, Superintendence and Government of Female Prisoners* was published in that year. Her contributions and discoveries are noteworthy.

Moving beyond Howard, she had found that hope for the future was a powerful tool in influencing the behavior of inmates. Dealing with women, she used the mother-child relationship as a means of securing cooperation and acceptance of prison discipline. Even in the case of organizing inmates for transportation, she secured cooperation through avoiding humiliation and unnecessary physical suffering. She ignored the pleas of jailers that the female inmates were degraded beyond the level of humanity and began the process of treating them as individuals who could be inspired by hope, for their children and perhaps even for themselves.

Prison architecture and penal discipline also drew the attention of utilitarian philosopher Jeremy Bentham, who published his treatise, *Panopticon*, in 1791. The book's theme was that prison life should be characterized by continual observation of the inmates. To achieve this goal, cell blocks were to be constructed around a central guard tower from which the keepers could observe inmates at every minute of the day or night. Initially favoring solitary confinement, Bentham was moved by considerations of economy to support the grouping of a small number of inmates in cells, their assignment being guided by the probable influence they would have upon each other. Believing that work should be presented as a pleasurable experience, he opposed hard labor but encouraged the development of workshops in penitentiaries. A man ahead of his time, Bentham suggested that private contractors might be engaged to use convict labor, and that the prisoners be permitted to keep the profits from the enterprise.

Milbank Prison, erected in 1821, incorporated Bentham's architectural ideas. It did not follow his disciplinary system, because there still remained the option of transporting inmates to Australia or Norfolk Island, which lay off the Australian coast. Milbank served as a temporary confinement facility where newly arrived inmates were kept in solitary cells for the first few months of their stay and then gradually integrated into work in association with fellow prisoners. Bentham's proposals, along with the suggestions of Howard and Fry, were fated to have limited application in England because most convicts were either executed or transported to the penal colonies. However, the new principles they proposed were known and in many cases acted upon in the United States.

PENNSYLVANIA VERSUS AUBURN

Established by Quakers in 1681, the colony of Pennsylvania reflected the Friends' strong opposition to capital punishment and harsh conditions of imprisonment. During the colonial period, productive labor was introduced in Pennsylvania jails, anticipating one of the prime components of future penitentiary systems. Shortly after the Revolutionary War, a new form of prison discipline, known as the *solitary system*, or *Pennsylvania System*, was developed. It relied on the total seclusion of one inmate from all others and only occasional silent contact between the prisoner and his or her keeper. The *Walnut Street Jail* in Philadelphia was constructed to provide no visual and little oral communication between the cells. The only opening in cell walls was a small window, far above floor level, designed to let in air and a small amount of light. Prisoners were brought to the jail in silence; once they were processed, a hood was placed on their heads, and they were led blindfolded to the cell where they would spend their entire sentence. They were expected to work at crafts and produce furniture, textiles, clothing, and other products for sale, but all of this labor was performed in the individual's solitary cell.

Each cell was equipped with a Bible and a variety of religious tracts. These were designed to turn the prisoner's thoughts in the direction of reformation and spiritual development. In addition to the keepers, only chaplains were regularly admitted to the cells. The solitary nature of confinement was designed to serve as a punishment, but of equal importance was the emphasis on meditation and repentance. While silence perhaps did not seem harsh to Quakers who used it effectively in their worship services, it caused some frightening reactions in the felons imprisoned at Walnut Street Prison and at its successor institution at Cherry Hill, which was designed by *John Haviland*. After extended periods of confinement, many prisoners began to decline in health and exist in a stupor; others became incurably insane. Despite these developments, advocates of the Pennsylvania System of prison discipline continued to be favored over other, more social forms of punishment.

HISTORY TODAY

Prison and jail inmates cannot be forced to participate in religious activities, but inmates must be allowed the freedom to exercise their religious beliefs, provided they belong to a recognized religion and the exercise of their religion does not compromise the needs of the institution. Local churches or houses of worship are sometimes reluctant to engage in prison ministry. Given that adherence to religious beliefs may pave the way to committing less crime, should correctional officials, especially local jails that cannot afford to hire full-time chaplains, make greater efforts to engage local religious entities?

John Haviland (1792-1852): English-born architect; designed several public buildings and churches in Philadelphia in addition to Eastern Penitentiary at Cherry Hill.

Clearly, solitary confinement with reading of the Scriptures was preferable to indiscriminate imprisonment of men, women, and children in single wards. However, the effects on physical and mental disease indicated that some modification in the Pennsylvania system might be advisable. This modified system was devised by *Louis Dwight* and the Boston Prison Discipline Society. After an initial trial at New York's Newgate Prison (not to be confused with the English prison bearing the same name), an alternative to the solitary system was implemented in the newly erected New York State Prison at Auburn. This was the *silent system*, or Auburn system, as opposed to the solitary Pennsylvania regime. Under the silent Auburn system, the inmates were kept in separate cells at night and required to maintain silence. During the daylight hours, they worked in communal shops but maintained quiet because of a number of behavioral rules. Prisoners were not to communicate with each other except by permission of the keepers; their eyes were always cast down, and when the group moved from one place to another, they did so in lockstep, with the right hand on the shoulder of the man in front. Respectful behavior toward the keepers was emphasized. Breaches of these elaborate rules, which were designed to reduce communication to a minimum, were punished either by banishment to the "dark hole" (a wet, interior, unlighted cell) on a diet of bread and water or by whippings with the cat-o'-nine-tails (a vicious leather whip designed to tear the maximum amount of skin with each stroke).

The Auburn system did not neglect opportunities for religious study and repentance. Chaplains made the rounds of the cell blocks regularly and, gradually, religious services were introduced along with Sunday schools and Bible study classes. As time went on, wardens learned that it was helpful to give prisoners times for relief from the strict discipline of prison life. On major national or religious holidays, a brief time might be allotted for conversation, carefully supervised by the keepers and warden.

European observers of the two American systems frequently confused the two, and even today's literature tends to blur the sharp distinction between silent and solitary imprisonment. "Silence" in the Auburn system was not complete silence, for ample opportunity was provided for essential communication. Solitary imprisonment in the Pennsylvania system meant virtually complete silence coupled with physical isolation from the world.

Alexis de Tocqueville, Gustave de Beaumont of France, William Crawford of England, and Frédéric-Auguste Demetz made extensive studies of the two systems, and all preferred the Pennsylvania system because of its seeming lack of violence. Only *Charles Dickens*, the English novelist who visited the Pennsylvania institutions in 1842, disagreed. While he acknowledged the good intentions of the Quakers, he pointed out that incalculable damage was inflicted upon the inmates subjected to solitary discipline. Indeed, American penologists, except for a few fanatical defenders of the Pennsylvania system, came to prefer the Auburn system even after allowing for the excessive power bestowed upon keepers and the possibility of brutal enforcement of the silent system.

> Alexis de Tocqueville (1805-1859): French political philosopher, most famous for his visit to America during its early years as a nation. His observations were recorded in *Democracy in America*, still a classic of political theory.

> Charles Dickens (1812-1870): One of the most famous novelists in the history of English literature; the most noted English author of his generation; often wrote stories that highlighted the dire conditions of England's lower classes; most famous novels included *Oliver Twist*, *David Copperfield*, *Great Expectations*, *A Tale of Two Cities*, and *A Christmas Carol*, which introduced the world to the famous fictional character Ebeneezer Scrooge.

There were also practical reasons for preferring the Auburn silent system. Penitentiaries stressing silent discipline were cheaper to construct than those with truly solitary cells, and the profits generated by Auburn shops helped to reduce the net cost of prison operations far more than the individualized craft activities of the Pennsylvania system.

In spite of the marked distinctions between the Pennsylvania and Auburn systems, it is abundantly clear that they both represented substantial improvements on the conditions described by John Howard in 1777 and those witnessed by Elizabeth Fry in 1817 when she began her work. Both American systems strove to obtain the inmate's repentance, both provided him or her with useful labor, both were concerned with physical health and well-being, and neither condoned wanton cruelty or neglect. What Elizabeth Fry succeeded in doing with the women in Newgate, American wardens were attempting on a larger scale with all of the prison populations committed to their care. Based on the pioneering work of Howard and Fry, American reformers and prison officials were taking the lead in finding new methods of prison discipline and administration. They were not alone, however; they formed but one part of a growing international movement to provide individualized treatment for prison inmates. They worked along with *Sir Walter Crofton* of Ireland and *Captain Alexander Maconochie* of Norfolk Island in developing new methods for influencing convict behavior.

BRINGING HOPE TO THE PRISONS: MACONOCHIE AND CROFTON

Captain Alexander Maconochie (1787-1860), a retired naval officer whose career had been cut short because of his departures from traditionally harsh naval discipline, relocated to Australia as a civil servant. He soon found himself in command of the penal colony on *Norfolk Island*. British felons were transported to Australia after 1788, but if they were convicted again, they were removed to remote Norfolk Island, where 1,400 of the very worst offenders lived in a state of siege, surrounded by approximately 150 Army troops and flogged at the slightest justification. Riots were frequent, and punishments tended to be brutal and brutalizing.

Maconochie took charge of this settlement and instituted a *mark system*, by which each inmate collected credits for good behavior, exceptionally productive labor, or courageous deeds. Securing a certain number of marks obtained certain privileges, and, ultimately, a convict could reach the point where he had virtual freedom on the island and might qualify for conditional release to Australia. In addition, each prisoner was provided with a small garden plot, along with permission to sell his produce and use his profits to purchase whatever he wished.

This experiment in collective responsibility and early release was begun in 1840 and continued until Maconochie was recalled in 1844. By objective standards, it was highly successful. The convicts immediately set about earning marks and promptly began farming on their own accounts. The military troops maintained on Norfolk Island found little to do because disorder was rare and riots ceased. Among the convicts who left for Australia on conditional releases, very few returned to a life of crime. Most adapted easily to their new life of freedom.

Maconochie's experiment proved to be short-lived. His superiors disagreed with his liberating policies, believing that prisons should exact punishment upon wrongdoers. Ordered back to Australia in 1844, Maconochie watched helplessly as his two successors applied draconian measures to maintain order. In 1846, a prisoners' revolt broke out and was suppressed with great difficulty. In 1848, Maconochie published his book, *Secondary Punishment, the Mark System*, setting forth his methods and their success with the convicts of Norfolk Island. While his experiment was both short-lived and probably limited in application to the conditions on Norfolk Island, it did demonstrate that convicted felons, and even multiple offenders, could be controlled and disciplined by a promised reward. Additional privileges or the possibility of a release before the end of a prison term were both powerful incentives toward cooperation and good behavior.

HISTORY TODAY

Alexander Maconochie was criticized and removed from his position even though his programs demonstrated evidence of success. Whether their ideas tilt toward the conservative or liberal ends of the spectrum, correctional innovators must be ready to endure harsh criticism from the public and from lawmakers for either being "do gooders" or for being inhumane brutes. If you thought your correctional ideas would be effective, would you be willing to try to implement them, realizing you would be strongly criticized?

It remained to Sir Walter Crofton (1815-1897), as director of the Irish prison system, to build Maconochie's rough system of rewards into a comprehensive penal plan. Between 1854 and 1862, Crofton developed what became known as the *progressive stage penal system*. This plan involved an initial period of close, solitary confinement of up to 9 months' duration, followed by a gradual lessening of restrictions and a moderate return to the society of fellow inmates. As imprisonment continued, the convict's tasks increased in complexity, and privileges grew as the inmate progressed in behavior and skills. The key to the inmate's rehabilitation was the intermediate stage of imprisonment, where the tasks assigned were most closely related to gainful employment in society and the convicts worked without supervision. This intermediate stage permitted development of skills and habits of industry, and at the same time provided a test of the convict's self-discipline and ability to deal with freedom.

Each prisoner released from the Dublin penitentiary had been carefully schooled by its teacher, *James P. Organ*, and, upon receiving conditional release, they were assigned to Organ's supervision. Organ not only kept track of the former prisoner's whereabouts and activities, but also was instrumental in finding each of his charges some gainful employment and starting them back on their way to earning a place in society. Sometimes referred to as *ticket of leave*, this Irish system was a forerunner of American parole, which was based on Crofton's system. The word *parole* was derived from the French term *parole d'honneur* (word of honor), which was traditionally assigned to war prisoners who would be released upon a promise not to take up arms again.

Crofton's system was a neat combination of all of the elements of penal discipline. At the initial stages, and with decreasing severity as the term of imprisonment lengthened, it stressed punishment. For a considerable period, the convict was kept away from society, ensuring that the general public was protected from the criminal inclinations of the unreformed inmate. Finally, recognizing that a time for return to freedom was somewhere in the future, Crofton provided for schooling in useful trades and crafts and a gradual social evolution from prison discipline to individual responsibility and independence. In this sense, it was less lenient than the mark system advocated by Maconochie, and it had the additional advantage of detailing the steps by which convicts might safely be conditioned for release without fear of recidivism (repeat offenses).

To a limited degree, American penology anticipated Crofton's methods, even if American reformers did not articulate such a well-defined system. Beginning in 1840, many states had enacted *good-time laws*, which permitted release before the end of a prison sentence if the inmate had a record of good behavior. In addition, Quaker concern for the reintroduction of former convicts into society had caused them to launch programs of aftercare for prisoners, a forerunner of today's aftercare system.

Yet even with these developments and a general knowledge of the work of Maconochie and Crofton, the American states, by 1867, had not fully adopted the Irish progressive system of discipline, much to the regret of *Enoch Wines* and *Theodore Dwight* in their *Report on the Prisons and Reformatories of the United States and Canada*. Recognizing that prison overcrowding prevented application of the individual attention required for Crofton's progressive system, they advocated construction of adult reformatories where the object is to teach and train the prisoner in such a manner that, on his discharge, he may be able to resist temptation and be inclined to lead an upright, worthy life.[2] Their report heralded a new era in American penology, marked by heavy emphasis on reform of the inmate and his or her rehabilitative education.

HOUSES OF CORRECTION AND JUVENILE REFORMATORIES

The Wines and Dwight Report to the New York legislature has significance only because it linked rehabilitation to the situation of convicted adult felons. It had long been the practice, in Europe and America, to use retraining and socializing techniques with youthful offenders. Also, in an effort to reduce vagabondage and unemployment, a number of nations had used a form of vocational rehabilitation with their poor and idle classes. It was the theory that, if adequate training were provided, no individual need be unemployed, and lack of an occupation was considered one of the primary causes of criminal activity.

Closely linked to the rehabilitation of the poor and indigent classes was the question of juvenile offenders. Indeed, the initial impetus for the Amsterdam Rasphuis was the reluctance of the city fathers to commit a youthful offender to the city jail as a felon. European experiments with juvenile delinquents date back to the 1703 establishment of a correctional facility for boys at the Hospice of St. Michael of Rome. The inmates were isolated at night, but during the day they were kept busy in communal work marked by silence and frequent prayer. Punishment for infraction of the silence rules was whipping or solitary confinement.

Gradually, the reformatory inclination of the hospice shifted to punishment, and the boys' house of correction was closed in 1827. John Howard, in the late eighteenth century, commented on the declining effectiveness of the bridewells in England and also upon the penal character of the St. Michael Hospice in Rome. It was left for a new century and a new generation of reformers to take up the task of reforming the treatment of juvenile offenders.

Swiss educators, following the lead of Henrich Pestalozzi (1746-1827), began to reestablish private institutions dedicated to the reform and training of wayward and destitute children. The first of these, Jakob Wehrli (1790-1855), brought the children into his own home, treated them as family, and taught them as much by example as by vocational training. The boys were involved in making decisions concerning the activities of the institution, and they took a part in administering discipline and in the financial management of "family" affairs. Wehrli's principles were applied on a larger scale by Johann Hinrich Wichern (1808-1881), who established the Rauhes Haus ("rough house") at Hamburg, Germany, in 1833. After his marriage in the same year, Wichern expanded his activities to include a girl's school in 1834, named the Mutter Haus ("mother house").

The children lived in cottages, a group of boys spending the entire day and night with a "brother" who was responsible for their work and discipline and who also served as a counselor and confidant. The routine was firmly established and included work interspersed with study and religious devotions. The institutions bore the mark of Pestalozzi's philosophy that love, decency, and happiness should be a natural, daily experience. These methods were so successful that they were instituted on a larger scale in Frédéric-Auguste Demetz's reformatory, Mettray, near Tours, France, and at Charles Lucas's agricultural colony at Val d'Yevre, near Bourges.

HISTORY TODAY

People like Jacob Wehrli take an enormous risk when they treat juvenile delinquents as if they are their own children. Nevertheless, juveniles are not adults and many of them can benefit from adult guidance, but only from adults who are willing to take chances. How much of their personal welfare and safety should juvenile authorities invest in those under their charge?

These European developments did not go unnoticed in the United States. In 1817, the New York legislature condemned the practice of confining youthful offenders in the common jails; by 1826, John Griscom was assigned the task of operating the New York House of Refuge for the reception of juvenile delinquents. The Boston House of Reformation was established in the following year and placed under the leadership of the Rev. E.W.P. Wells, and the Philadelphia House of Refuge was founded in 1828. By 1832, the Massachusetts institution was closed after charges that the discipline was too lax for a penal institution.

It was not until 1856 that the Lancaster Reform School was established in Ohio, putting into practice the family methods of cottage living typical of the Swiss reformatories. However, the concept of correctional confinement, derived from European and English theories and practices, was beginning to have an impact upon American penology when Wines and Dwight prepared their 1867 Report.

Houses of correction for the idle and reformatories for juveniles were characterized by individualized attention. As Mary Carpenter, an English educator and juvenile rehabilitator, phrased it, "treatment should be according to the individual's need rather than being conditioned by the offense he or she committed." The stress was on the quality and adaptability of the offender.

INSANITY, CRIMINAL RESPONSIBILITY, AND PENOLOGY

Closely related to the penal reform movements was the growing need to define the impact of insanity on criminal responsibility and the imposition of punishment. Before Dorothea Dix's successful campaign to remove emotionally disturbed inmates from American prisons, a rational approach to prison discipline would have been impossible. However, segregation of the insane from the convict did not remove the problem of insanity from the administration of criminal justice. The impact of mental disease had to be assessed to determine criminal responsibility, a key ingredient to prosecution for crime. An individual accused of a crime had to be adjudged sane at the time the offense was committed. Otherwise, it would be immoral to punish someone for something he or she did while deprived of his or her reason or free will.

Likewise, it was unfair to prosecute someone who was not sane at the time of trial. This involved the due process consideration that a defendant with an unstable mental condition could not properly assist his or her attorney in preparation of a defense. Finally, a person convicted of a crime could not be imprisoned in accordance with the sentence until he or she regained sanity. Imprisoning a person who was incapable of understanding the conditions of imprisonment or the reason for the punishment was not only futile in a penological sense, but it was also immoral and inhumane.

Criminal law has always experienced difficulty in dealing with the concept of insanity. In 1843, a British prisoner tried on a murder charge was released on a plea of insanity, and in response to public outcry the House of Lords solicited the opinion of 15 common law judges. Their report, setting forth the *M'Naghten* Rules, established the basis upon which future legal development occurred. The *M'Naghten* Rules provide:

1. A man is presumed to be sane and presumed to have a sufficient degree of reason to be responsible for his crime. The defense of insanity must be clearly proved that at the time of committing the act he was laboring under such a defect of reason, or from a disease of the mind, as not to know the nature and quality of the act, or if he did know its nature and quality, that he did not know that it was wrong.
2. That if a man is laboring under a partial delusion, his act must be considered in the same circumstance, as far as responsibility is concerned, as if the facts with respect to the delusion were real.

The first rule set forth a standard based on the reasoning function, coupled with the ability of the accused to bring his or her moral judgment to bear on the nature and consequences of the act. Significantly, it created a presumption of sanity and required that the defense undertake the burden of proving such a defect of reason or moral judgment in order for the offense to be excused.

The second *M'Naghten* Rule established a principle to govern the actions of one who labored under a delusion, which is a belief (opposed to fact) in which the person persisted even after having contrary proof. In applying the *M'Naghten* Rules, the court and jury

Daniel M'Naghten (1813-1865): Scotsman who assassinated an English civil servant named Edward Drummond, whom he mistakenly believed to be Prime Minister Robert Peel; M'Naghten was found to be suffering from mental illness and was delusional.

assumed that the delusion was factually true and then judged the accused's acts accordingly. For example, if A believed that B intended to kill him, but B was innocent of any such intent, A was not insane but had a partial delusion. Given these circumstances, if B walked in the direction of A with a large hunting knife in his hand and A shot and killed B with a shotgun, and if B were, in fact, planning to kill A, A's firing the shotgun would have been justifiable as self-defense. Therefore, A's killing of B was excused, because he was laboring under a delusion.

Virtually all of the American states adopted the *M'Naghten* Rules in deciding issues of insanity. However, as the nineteenth century gained new insights into human psychology, the *M'Naghten* Rules were modified somewhat. Specifically, the emphasis on the cognitive functions of the brain began to be questioned as further study suggested that men and women are not necessarily motivated by reasoned decisions. Was it not possible that, although the accused knew what he or she was doing and knew that it was wrong, the accused nevertheless was so overcome by other emotional factors that he or she could not prevent himself or herself from so acting? This consideration led the Alabama Supreme Court in *Parsons v. State* (81 Ala. 577, decided in 1886) to set forth the *irresistible impulse test*. This added freedom of will to the *M'Naghten* formula, requiring that, in order to be criminal, an act must be both knowing and voluntary. This division of the function of reason on one hand from control of behavior (volition) on the other has fallen to the more recent psychological view that human personality is integrated. Thus, it is unrealistic to separate mental processes into component parts. Only about one dozen American jurisdictions now follow the irresistible impulse test in addition to the *M'Naghten* Rules.

The third test of insanity as an excuse for crime is the so-called *Durham* rule: that an accused is not criminally responsible if his or her unlawful act was the product of mental disease or mental defect (*Durham v. United States*, 214 F.2d 874, decided by the Court of Appeals for the District of Columbia, 1954). The *Durham* rule originated with the 1869 New Hampshire Supreme Court opinion in *State v. Pike* (49 N.H. 339). In *Pike*, the appellate court upheld a jury instruction that if the jury believed there was a mental disease (such as the one that the accused claimed to suffer), if the accused had that disease, and if the criminal act was a product of the disease, they might find him or her innocent by virtue of insanity. In effect, *Pike* treated mental disease as a force working upon the accused and depriving him or her of both reason and volition. However, its focus on whether the accused had a mental disease presented the difficulty of defining the mental disease and then measuring its causal relationship to the criminal act. These complications persuaded the District of Columbia court to abandon the *Durham* rule in 1972 (*United States v. Brawner*, 417 F.2d 969).

The weight of American law seems to incorporate the *M'Naghten* Rules as modified by the irresistible impulse doctrine of *Parsons*. In 1961, the American Law Institute adopted the following rule as section 4.01(1) of the Model Penal Code:

> An accused person is excused by reason of insanity if "... as a result of mental disease or defect he lacks substantial capacity either to appreciate the criminality of his act or to conform his conduct to the requirements of law."

Although mental disease is mentioned, there is no need to determine whether it produces the wrongful act. Rather, the understanding and volition of the accused are key issues, as is the criminality (right or wrong) of the act. The focus is on the mental capability and self-control of the accused, and not the probable manifestations of his or her psychological malady.

FEATURED OUTLAW: JOHN BROWN

Without a doubt, the most controversial social issue of the nineteenth century in the United States was slavery, and no institution was more antithetical to the American concept of freedom and liberty than the barbaric practice of chattel slavery of people of African origin and dissent. Positions on slavery could be roughly divided into six categories. First, many advocated the expansion of slavery, but were willing to work within the existing legal process toward that expansion. Second, some proslavery advocates were violent advocates of their cause. Third, most white Americans, in both slave and nonslave states, had ambivalent feelings about slavery. Although they had misgivings about the humanity of slavery, they were not actively involved as advocates for one side or the other. Fourth, many Americans, including Abraham Lincoln before he assumed the presidency, were content to compromise, to take a "moderate" position on slavery. This "moderate" position suggested that slavery be confined to states that already had it, but that it should not be allowed to spread to any new states being brought into the westward-expanding nation. Fifth, others were abolitionists who advocated that slave states be forced to end slavery within their borders. They were met by those who claimed that what a state did within its borders was not the business of outsiders. Slave owners and nonslave owners alike in Southern states bristled at the idea of someone from industrialized Massachusetts or Pennsylvania telling them to end the institution that aided their primary source of revenue, agriculture. Most abolitionists were content to take any

FIGURE 9.3 John Brown, leader of the historic raid on the federal arsenal and armory at Harpers Ferry, Virginia, is seen in this 1857 picture. Brown and his followers attempted to end slavery in the United States by armed force. *AP Photo.*

legal means necessary to end slavery, but they would not engage in violence; some even opposed the "underground" railroads that aided the escape of slaves to nonslave states.

Finally, there were abolitionists who would stop at nothing to promote their agenda, including violence. John

Continued

FEATURED OUTLAW: JOHN BROWN—CONT'D

Brown (1800-1859) represented the extreme radical fringe of the abolitionist element. He was born and raised in the Northeast in a devoutly religious and antislavery family. Brown's life was marred by personal tragedy, including the death of his first wife during childbirth, and the death of six of his children, including four from his second marriage during a dysentery outbreak. Brown was a stern autocrat in his home, but this was not unusual for that period. Like most fathers, he did not hesitate to administer corporal punishment, but on one occasion, he interrupted the beating of one his sons and ordered the son to beat him instead. The lesson—this is how slaves are treated, punished unfairly and brutally because of the sins of others.

Brown's life was also marked by one failed business venture after another. He never achieved any type of financial or employment stability, due no doubt in part to his fiery and unusual personality and his absolute unwillingness to compromise on any matter that he judged in moral terms. Brown had no use for politics and never sought political office as a vehicle for slavery abolition. He detested the political process because of its tendency to evoke compromise on moral issues, and Brown viewed slavery purely as a moral and religious matter, without regard for any political or economic issues that might be involved.

Unlike most fellow abolitionists, Brown thought it perfectly acceptable, in fact even noble, to kill in the name of a moral principle. Also, unlike many abolitionists who detested slavery but nonetheless viewed blacks as inferior, Brown was unhesitant in accepting blacks as his equals. Despite his own lack of business and farming acumen, Brown assumed the task of training recently freed slaves in farming in New York and lived as their neighbor in the process.

Brown's use of violence in the abolitionist cause came to fruition first in Lawrence, Kansas, in May 1856. As the United States expanded westward, proslavery forces from Missouri sought to expand slavery into new territories and states, while abolitionists opposed them. After proslavery forces killed five abolitionists on May 21, Brown vowed revenge and scoffed at calls for restraint. On May 24, Brown, joined by his four sons, a son-in-law, and several neighbors, dragged five proslavery men from their homes and hacked them to death with broadswords.

Brown continued to move around, spreading his violent antislavery message to anyone who would listen. On May 8, 1858, he assembled a group of black and white supporters in Chatham, Ontario. They made plans to establish a shadow government and an antislavery guerrilla base in the Appalachian Mountains, which would serve as a staging ground for raids on slave-holding plantations, farms, and towns.

Brown returned to Kansas in 1858 and participated in the killing of a slave owner and the freeing of his 11 slaves, who were transported to the free state of Iowa. This was a mere foreshadowing of something Brown had been planning for quite some time, a raid on the town of Harpers Ferry, Virginia (now part of West Virginia), which housed a federal arsenal. Brown had been receiving financial support from numerous antislavery donors in the Northeast for this venture. In the summer of 1859, he rented a farm near Hagerstown, Maryland, from which to stage his raid into Harpers Ferry. On October 16, Brown, accompanied by three of his sons, 13 other white men, and five black men, raided Harpers Ferry, killed several of its citizens, took 60 others hostage, and set the slave population free.

Under the command of Robert E. Lee, a group of Marines raided Harpers Ferry, killing 10 of Brown's men, including two of his sons. Brown and six others were captured. Brown was transported to Charlestown, Virginia, for trial. Far from begging for mercy or retreating from his original stance, Brown eagerly embraced his prosecution and impending execution. He was finally on the brink of martyrdom for his beloved cause. Shortly before he was hanged on December 2, 1859, Brown stated, "Let them hang me, I'm worth inconceivably more to hang than for any other purpose." His final message, which was indeed prophetic, was, "The crimes of this guilty land will never be purged away, but with blood." Brown was correct; the American Civil War, which brought about the end of slavery, began 17 months later.

After his hanging, Brown was praised by the likes of the great American philosopher Henry David Thoreau and French novelist Victor Hugo. He was also criticized by pro- and antislavery forces alike as a lunatic. During his lifetime, many people who knew Brown questioned his mental health. Mental illness ran in his family—both his mother and grandmother suffered mental infirmities. Slaveholders naturally opposed him, but so did Abraham Lincoln, who thought his methods too extreme. In the eyes of history, the abolitionists who refused to compromise on the question of slavery's existence were right, and those who advocated compromise were wrong. However, John Brown serves as a discussion point on the morality of employing violence to achieve even a noble cause, and this is a question that still exists today.

Source: WilsonWeb, www.hwwwilsonweb.com.jproxy.lib.ecu.edu, accessed February 10, 2008.

HISTORY TODAY

Historians are still divided on whether John Brown was mentally ill, simply fanatical, or a brave and religiously idealistic hero, but assume for the sake of discussion he was not mentally ill. In any case, no matter how he was viewed during his life, there is little doubt that he was on the right side of history regarding slavery. Is there any cause for which you think it is justifiable to risk your own life, employ violence against others, or intentionally kill others, or innocent people who may happen to get in the way of you killing someone?

Conflicting views concerning what constitutes insanity are inevitable when the definition may relieve an accused person of criminal responsibility. Psychology does not recognize insanity as a medical condition, but it does classify a variety of mental aberrations that are adjudged abnormal. Some of these disrupt a person's reason and volition enough to appropriately be identified as conditions precluding the existence of criminal responsibility. On the other hand, crimes are behaviors that are so disruptive to society that sanctions are imposed to prevent their occurrence and to punish perpetrators of those acts. In a very real sense, all criminal behavior is aberrant, and thus might be viewed as insane. Understandably, the courts are hard-pressed to define insanity with enough precision that all crimes do not fall within its protection. Most men and women are criminally responsible for their actions; if they were not, civilized society would collapse. At the same time, there are a limited few whose mental disabilities make it impossible for them to have framed the criminal intent essential for guilt.

HISTORY TODAY

Many people who commit serious crimes are indeed mentally ill. Should the fact that a person suffers from some form of mental illness mitigate their punishment?

SUMMARY

Reform of the penal system began with concern for the health and physical well-being of prisoners. As such, it was vitally concerned with prison architecture and the institution of a discipline that would maintain order but also ensure continued health and sanity. Slowly, prison industries began to develop, but before the American Civil War it was only in the area of juvenile reformation that work was seen as a method of rehabilitating inmates. Individual penologists experimented with individualized treatment of prisoners. Systems of early release, increased privileges, and gradual acclimatization to release into society were implemented. At a time when the science of psychology was in its infancy, substantial strides were made in positively influencing human behavior, and efforts were made to provide legal standards to determine criminal responsibility in light of current psychological knowledge. Yet for all their reformatory zeal, penologists already were struggling against rapidly growing prison populations and popular sentiment favoring retributive punishment. Reformers after the American Civil War campaigned through national and international prison reform societies, drawing on a growing body of scientific knowledge and statistics concerning criminal behavior and prison discipline.

REFERENCES

Tyler, A. F. (1944). *Freedom's ferment: Phases of American social history from the colonial period to the outbreak of the Civil War.* Minneapolis: University of Minnesota Press, reprinted New York: Harper & Row; Erikksson, T. (1976). *The reformers: An historical survey of pioneer experiments in the treatment of criminals.* Trans. Djurklou, C. New York: Elsevier; McKelvey, B. (1977). *American prisons: A history of good intentions.* Montclair, NJ: Patterson Smith; Grunhut, M. (1948). *Penal reform: A comparative study.* Oxford: The Clarendon Press, reprinted Montclair, NJ: Patterson Smith; Ives, G. (1914). *A history of penal methods.* London: Hutchinson Publishing Company, reprinted Montclair, NJ: Patterson Smith.

Barnes, H. E. (1927). *The evolution of penology in Pennsylvania: A study in American social history.* Indianapolis: Bobbs-Merrill & Co, reprinted Montclair, NJ: Patterson Smith; Carpenter, M. (1872). *Reformatory prison discipline as developed by the Rt. Hon. Sir. Walter Crofton in the Irish convict prisons.* London: Longmans, Greeb, Reader & Dyer; Carpenter, M. (1853). *Juvenile Delinquents: Their condition and treatment.* London: W. & F. G. Cash, reprinted Montclair, NJ: Patterson Smith; Howard, D. L. (1958). *John Howard: Prison reformer.* London: Christopher Johnson; Howard, J. (1777). *The state of the prisons in England and Wales.* Warrington, England: William Eyres, reprinted Abingdon, England: Professional Books; Johnston, N. (1973). *The human cage: A brief history of prison architecture.* New York: Walker; David Lewis, W. (1965). *From Newgate to Dannemora: The rise of the Penitentiary in New York, 1796-1848.* Ithaca: Cornell University Press; Whitney, J. (1937). *Elizabeth Fry: Quaker Heroine.* Boston: Little, Brown & Co; Wines, E. C., & Dwight, T. W. (1867). *Report on the prisons and reformatories of the United States and Canada made to the legislature of New York.* Albany: Van Benthuysen & Sons, reprinted New York: AMS Press, Inc.(1973).

Hermann, D. H. J. (1983). *The insanity defense: Philosophical, historical and legal perspectives.* Springfield, IL: Charles C. Thomas; Fingarette, H. (1972). *The meaning of criminal insanity.* Berkeley: University of California Press; Fingarette, H., & Hasse, A. F. (1979). *Mental disabilities and criminal responsibility.* Berkeley: University of California Press; Roesch, R., & Golding, S. L. (1980). *Competency to Stand Trial.* Urbana: University of Illinois Press.

Linebaugh, P. (1992). *The London hanged: Crime and civil society in the eighteenth century.* Cambridge: Cambridge University Press; Zedner, L. (1994). *Women, crime, and custody in Victorian England.* Oxford: Oxford University Press; *Victorian prison lives: English prison biography: 1830-1914.* New York: Methuen & Co; Campbell, C. (1994). *The intolerable hulks: British shipboard confinement, 1776-1857.* Bowie, MD: Heritage Books; Children and their offenses in history. Binder, A., Geis, G., & Bruce, D. (Eds.), (1988). *Juvenile delinquency: Historical, cultural, legal perspectives.* New York: Macmillan Publishing Company.

Kealey, L. (1986). Patterns of punishment: Massachusetts in the eighteenth century. *American Journal of Legal History, 30,* 163–186; Rothman, D. J. (1971). *The discovery of the asylum; social order and disorder in the new republic.* Boston: Little, Brown & Co; Hirsch, A. J. (1992). *Prisons and punishment in early America.* New Haven: Yale University Press; Pisciotta, A. W. (1981). Corrections, society, and social control in America: A metahistorical review of the Literature. *Criminal Justice History, 2,* 109–130.

McGarrell, E. F. (1988). *Juvenile correctional reform: Two decades of policy and procedural change.* Albany: State University of New York Press.

Notes and Problems

1. Can imprisonment be made rehabilitative and restorative without arousing public hostility on the basis that it is too lenient?

2. Is it possible to influence behavior once a convicted felon has served his or her time and been returned to society? Clearly it is possible through hope for early release, and through granting or withholding privileges, to greatly control conduct while in prison. But what will happen after release if there is no ongoing control in the terms of a conditional release or a parole system?

3. The nineteenth-century advocates of houses of correction, juvenile reformatories, and penitentiaries argued that gaining skills would make convicts employable. Is that true, even in a high unemployment area of the country?

4. Compare and contrast the Pennsylvania and Auburn systems of prison discipline. Is solitude preferable to violence from fellow prisoners? Can either of these systems be considered rehabilitative?

ENDNOTES

[1]Quoted in Whitney, J. (1937). *Elizabeth Fry: Quaker Heroine*. Boston: Little, Brown & Co., p. 184.

[2]Wines, E. C., & Dwight, T. W. (1867). *Report on the prisons and reformatories of the United States and Canada, made to the legislature of New York*. Albany: Van Benthuysen & Sons, reprinted New York: A.M.S. Press (1973), pp. 72–73.

CHAPTER 10

Early Nineteenth-Century Law Enforcement

KEY TERMS

1792 Middlesex
  Justices Act
Allan Pinkerton
Bifurcated legal
  system
Billy the Kid
Bobbies
Brigade de Sûreté
Charlies
Copper, cop
Denmark Vesey
François Eugéne
  Vidocq
Freeholders
Gendarmerie

Howard Vincent
Intendants
Interpol
Jean-Baptiste
  Colbert
Jonathan Wild
Joseph Fouche
Metropolitan
  Police
Napoleon
  Bonaparte
Napoleonic Codes
Night watchmen
Patrick Colquhoun
Plantation discipline

Robert Peel
Samuel
  Pennypacker
San Francisco
  Association
Scotland Yard
Slave patrol
Stipendiary
  Magistrate
Thames Police Act
Thief-catcher
Vigilante
William Pitt the
  Younger

LEARNING OBJECTIVES

1. Learn how centralized law enforcement was developed in France under Napoleon and French monarchs.
2. Understand the role and profit motive of thief catchers.
3. Learn about the development of the London Police force under the leadership of Robert Peel.
4. Learn about the development of advanced private and public criminal investigation.

5. Learn about the development of some early police agencies in the United States.

6. Understand the role of slave patrols in southern law enforcement.

Table 10.1 Time Line

England	Europe	North America
	1066 Local hundreds (towns, villages) responsible for policing	
Justices of the peace and constables appointed for law enforcement duties	**1285** France continues Roman system	
Charles II restored to the English and Scottish thrones	**c. 1660** Centralized royal policing under Louis XIV	Justices of the peace (magistrates) police the colonies
	1699 Royal Lieutenants-General of police established for French cities	
	c. 1700	Southern colonies establish slave patrols
Bow Street magistrate's post occupied by Sir Thomas DeVeil and Henry Fielding	**1730-1754**	
	1776	U.S. Declaration of Independence
Thames Police Act passed	**1800**	
	1808-1810 French Codes of Criminal Instruction and Penal Code adopted under Napoleon I	
	1815 Congress of Vienna formalizes the end of the Napoleonic Wars	
London Metropolitan Police ("bobbies") established	**1829**	
	1832 Francois Vidocq becomes head of Sûreté, or detective bureau	
	1845	New York City adopts the Municipal Police, a London-style police department

Continued

Table 10.1 Time Line—cont'd

England	Europe	North America
	1846	Charleston, South Carolina, City Guard reorganized into City Police, known as *Paddy Miles' Bull Dogs*
	1848 Marx's *Communist Manifesto* published	
	1848-1852 France a republic for 4 years; the popularly elected president, Louis Napoleon, becomes Napoleon III	
	1852	Boston establishes a London-style police department
	1857-1870	New York City policed by two rival police departments
	1861-1865	American Civil War

The nineteenth century was the century of change, innovation, and development for criminal justice in the United States, the United Kingdom, and France. The impact of this century in terms of framing the future of criminal justice should not be understated. In the United States, city police departments were established in major cities; in rural America sheriffs and constables worked alongside vigilantes and local citizens in an attempt to establish a method for enforcing the law. Many regions started the path toward the establishment of a statewide police presence. At the federal level the U.S. Marshals Service and the Secret Service were introduced. Reform and revised legislation became commonplace and the judiciary responded with new rules and protocols for the presentation of cases that came before the bench. The impact of Enlightenment thinkers was felt in every facet of the criminal justice system but perhaps nowhere more so than in the prison system. The United States followed Europe in the creation of a prison service that sought to rehabilitate offenders rather than incarcerate them pending either public humiliation or execution. New prisons were built at Walnut Street, Philadelphia (1790), Auburn, New York (1817), and then across the nation. The focus was self-sufficiency of the institution and rehabilitation of the offender. Finally, society recognized that *lex talionis*, an eye for an eye, was not the only way of compensating society for the wrongdoing of others and that, perhaps by making offenders recognize for themselves that their actions were wrong and harmful, they might not offend so readily in the future. In keeping with this movement and also following the lead in Europe, executions in the United States became a private rather than public affair after 1834.

Policing was also about to go through a major period of expansion and modernization. Across Europe and the United States, cities were growing at a massive rate and the old night watchman system was woefully incapable of dealing with modern city crime. London had experimented with a force of thief takers from Bow Street, and Paris had had a royal police force for more than 200 years, but the events of the French Revolution were to change policing and the entire criminal justice system forever in France. The French Emperor *Napoleon Bonaparte* was personally instrumental in a complete revision of all laws in France. He authored the codification of the criminal and civil law, a codification that was so well-written that it is still utilized today, not just in France but in many countries across the globe. Bonaparte was a military man and knew the value of a strong military presence within France while he was abroad expanding the empire. He extended the range and role, as well as the size, of the military police force, the Gendarmerie, and he was the architect of the civil police force that was to police all the major cities of France, the Police Nationale.

> Napoleon Bonaparte (1769-1821): Or Napoleon I; French emperor regarded as one of the greatest military leaders in world history; conquered much of southern Europe and Egypt; waged war against the English and invaded Russia, the latter invasion resulting in his downfall; final loss was at the battle of Waterloo in Belgium; died in exile.

Police reform initiated by Napoleon Bonaparte was extended by Louis Napoleon during his reign in the middle of the nineteenth century. Napoleon III was elected president of France on December 10, 1848. It was his intention that he be crowned Emperor of France. He came to power at a time when France was experiencing internal unrest and many citizens supported the establishment of a socialist republic. Napoleon used the police to stamp out the socialist movement. His heavy-handed methods cast the police in a role from which they have never recovered in the eyes of the French public. The French police, whether the military Gendarmerie or the civilian Police Nationale, came to be viewed as a limb of the government in a police state. In 1851, Napoleon III decided to crush the "Red Threat" of socialism and orchestrated a coup d'etat. This move was strongly supported by the police, Gendarmerie, and the military. In the aftermath, the general police became the *Surete Generale* and the Gendarmerie that had glowed under Napoleon Bonaparte now gleamed brightly under Napoleon III.

Louis Napoleon was to utilize his extensive powers once again during his career and again it confirmed in the minds of the public that France had devolved into a police state. In 1858, Felice Orsini, an Italian who lived in London, and two accomplices attempted to assassinate Napoleon. Eight died and 150 were wounded in the bombing. Napoleon escaped unhurt. This event was the catalyst for Napoleon to give the Surete 2 years of police state powers.

It was also enough to persuade most of Europe and particularly England and the United States that, if ever they considered adoption of the French model of policing, this was proof enough that it should never happen (for now at least).

Over time, the Surete became the Police Nationale and the Gendarmerie, with a continuous history dating back to the tenth century. The National Gendarmerie remains the primary police response within France today and has now been copied in more than 20 countries across the globe.

Across the English Channel, or, as the French say, La Manche, Robert Peel had created a French-style police presence in Ireland, which was under English domination, with a constabulary that looked much like the French Gendarmes. For London Peel needed something a little more English and so he created the Metropolitan Police force. Within 50 years, all of the country was required by law to have a constabulary of paid, full-time police officers.

Increased concern with law enforcement went hand in hand with prison reform in both Western Europe and the new American republic. The emergence of national states centralized efforts for the prevention, detection, and prosecution of crime. At the same time, long-established cultural influences shaped the way in which police forces were established and how they functioned. In this chapter, two European systems will be examined, those of France and England. We will then focus upon the variety of American policing systems that functioned in various sections of the United States. Clearly, American practices were based upon, but did not duplicate, those of England, and many characteristics of the French system were influential in the United States. Criminal law enforcement in today's Western democracies still reflects the divergence of French and other European systems from those of Britain and the United States.

LEGAL REFORM AND CODIFICATION ACROSS EUROPE

Enlightenment ideas fused legal philosophy and law reform. Nation states had started to take considerably more responsibility for criminal law so that it moved progressively away from individuals and families to a central government matter. Penalties increased, the range of offenses increased, laws were constantly revised or reformed, and political crimes were increasingly punished most harshly. Enlightenment ideals brought reforms and a more rational approach; reliance upon the principles of the Roman Law decreased across Europe; and the criminal law started to take on broader social responsibilities such as justice, equality, and the social contract.

In the course of 100 years, the words of trial judges at the Old Bailey in the early eighteenth century would be unthinkable because they were so draconian and extreme. On January 13, 1721, Thomas Philips and William Spigget stood trial for highway robbery. The two refused to enter a plea until the property that they had allegedly stolen (money, horses, and goods) was returned to them. An infuriated trial judge ordered the two "Be laid on bare ground without any straw or litter and without any garment about them and be spreadeagled across the floor and so much iron be placed upon them every day until through a combination of starvation and hydration and pressing they die." Upon arrival at the pressing room in Newgate Prison, the two requested to be returned to court. They entered a plea of guilty and were hanged.

The codification of laws was born out of a desire to bring together the best of social reform and legal philosophy and to create a legal system that was based upon natural laws with man as an equal, rational-thinking partner on earth as opposed to a legal system that had for centuries been based upon class, privilege, and birth rights. A code was needed to articulate these legal principles; Louis XVI started the movement but it was the French Revolution that handed the blueprint to Napoleon Bonaparte, who in 1800 instructed four senior law practitioners—Tronchet, Bigot-Preameneau, Portalis, and Maleville—to write a code that would respect previous legal history while at the same time produce a code that was modernized and would last. Napoleon took a great personal interest in the project and sat at 57 of the 102 draft discussion sessions. In March 1804, the *Code Civil des Francais* was published in three books with 2,281 articles. It was reissued as the *Code Napoleon* in 1807. The style of the code is simple and clear, with one code for criminal procedure and a second for criminal law, the *Code D'Instruction Criminelle* and *Code Penal*, respectively.

Codification of laws swept across the world, not just to the reaches of the French empire, which included Belgium, The Netherlands, Algeria, Lebanon, Syria, Morocco, Indo-China, and parts of Sub-Saharan Africa, but also numerous other European countries: Bavaria, Prussia, Austria, and later Germany, Italy, Romania, Yugoslavia, Hungary, Czechoslovakia, Croatia, Switzerland, and Slovenia.

NATIONALIZED POLICING, ROYAL SPIES, AND A THIEF WHO BECAME CHIEF OF THE PARIS POLICE

The seeds of the centralized French police system were planted during the reign of *Louis XIV*. Capitalizing on the doctrine of the divine right of kings, Louis XIV sought to overcome the patchwork of customary laws and lax police administration that had existed in France for centuries. Because of traditional aristocratic privileges and immunities, the first two estates (the clergy of the Catholic Church and the nobility) exercised considerable police power independently of the king and often to the disadvantage of the bourgeoisie, peasants, and urban workers. To subordinate the nobility and the Catholic Church, Louis XIV boldly modified their role in law enforcement. The traditional right of the nobility to enforce the law and to hold manorial court was undermined by a series of royal decrees during the 1660s. Additionally, Louis XIV separated the operations of high courts of France (the *parlements)* from those of the police, and appointed royal judges to serve in feudal courts.

> Louis XIV (1638-1715): Also known as *The Sun King*; king of France from 1643 to 1715; extended France's eastern borders in a series of wars between 1667 and 1697; was also responsible for the revocation of the Edict of Nantes, which had previously guaranteed French Protestants freedom of worship.

Domestic tranquility was further enhanced by placing military forces under royal control, and developing an organized system of police authorities. To subordinate the army to his will, Louis XIV transformed the old military system, which had relied on feudal levies and privately generated troops, into a modern army paid by the royal government and owing allegiance only to the king. One immediate civil benefit was the military police (provost corps), who were utilized to provide security along highways in rural areas of France. Although members of the army could not always be counted on to be loyal to the king, the army proved to be an effective instrument for maintaining civic order in times of domestic crisis, such as the series of revolutions that shook France over the next century. These reforms placed policing directly under royal authority and established a police system that was separate from the judiciary and independent from the control of other political leaders.

The edict by which Louis XIV established the office of Lieutenant of Police resulted in a rather broad meaning of the term *police*, an office that had a range of responsibilities that were never adopted in England and continue to distinguish the French term from its narrower use in the context of English policing. Responsibilities of the lieutenant of police included, in addition to the usual law enforcement roles, diverse activities such as supervising markets, inspecting food and wine, press censorship, repairing municipal drainage, constructing roads, establishing hospitals and schools for poor children, surveillance of foreigners, arresting blasphemers and sorcerers, directing firefighting, coping with natural disasters, monitoring marketplaces, and inspecting prisons. This comprehensive issuance of police power encompassed virtually all of the functions of modern local government in the United States. However, in Louis XIV's France, the power was not shared, but entrusted to one man.

In addition to extensive duties regarding public welfare, the Lieutenant of Police of Paris and certain police officials served as criminal judges in the Châtelet, the center of royal police authority until the revolution. Friday was court day and proceedings commenced at 3:00 p.m. and concluded at 6:00 p.m. Two classes of cases were heard, those for which a fine was suitable, Police Ordinaire, and prisonable or banishment cases, Police Extraordinaire. The workload was massive, and on May 25, 1759, 200 cases were heard in the 3-hour court period. Forty-five women and 16 men were sentenced that day. Sentences were severe and swift. For example, Benjamen Dechauflour was prosecuted for sodomy against a number of young men on May 24, 1726. The trial concluded the same day. Dechauflour was found guilty and sentenced to death. He was burned to death the following morning.

Senior police officers had considerable power in France and they were not averse to making claims about their abilities to ensure fame and longevity of service. Perhaps not unlike some of the large claims made about Compstat in New York during the 1990s, claims that may have helped rather than hindered political careers, there is evidence of such puffery in Paris when in 1746 Inspector Pousset claimed he had performed a miracle. The circumstances were that the police arrested a man wrapped in clothes as though a leper; he was panhandling at the time. Inspector Pousset saw an opportunity for fame and glory and therefore, rather than disclose that the leprosy was a ruse, he claimed that he had done no less than perform a miracle on the man and cured him of his disease. Inspector Pousset was to feature again in 1750. During this period, the prison system of France, much like most of Europe, was going through a period of reflection and review. Prisons were categorized along the lines of criminal offenders and poor. The poor were either "good poor" or "bad poor." "Bad poor" were frequently imprisoned alongside mainstream criminal offenders (who wore brown uniforms and were mostly lifers) and the poor served time in hard labor at a *Maison de force*. In 1750, there was a prison uprising in Paris and Inspector Pousset investigated. He struck a deal with the rioting inmates; they could elect to be shot or hanged rather than endure more time at La Force.

Throughout the rest of France, royal supervision was exercised by the *Intendants*, who had been established by Cardinal Richelieu in the reign of Louis XIV's predecessor. In each of the 30 provinces of France, an Intendant of Justice, Police, and Finance linked the crown and local government.

Jean-Baptiste Colbert (Minister of Finance under Louis XIV) nationalized the local police forces of France. Municipalities that previously had self-rule charters now had established police forces; however, in 1699, the office of Lieutenant-General of Police was instituted by royal decree for each of the major cities. Because the policies of the Lieutenant-General of Paris were binding for municipal lieutenants, there was a certain degree of hierarchical organization to the policing system. Later, Louis XIV established the position of Police Commissioner, which granted appointees limited judicial power and allowed them to serve under each of the municipal Lieutenants-General.

HISTORY TODAY

The United States has no national police force. There is no single agency that exercises jurisdiction in all criminal matters throughout the country. This is more an accidental product of history than a carefully designed plan. Given the fact that there are so many ways of committing crimes that cross state lines, because of ease of transportation, the Internet, and the need for law enforcement agencies to share information, should the United States consider creating a national police force?

As Lieutenant-General of Police, Marc-René Levoyer de Paulmy, Marquis d'Argenson, developed an effective espionage network in France and in the French colonies. He and his successors supplied the king with daily reports containing information garnered by domestic and foreign spies; in fact, Paris' inmates and prostitutes were among their best informers. The extent of domestic surveillance and the omnipresence of informers in France is legendary. An often-quoted (but perhaps untrue) claim made to Louis XV by Gabriel de Sartines (Lieutenant-General of Police from 1759 to 1774) was that, wherever three persons spoke to one another on the street, one of them was sure to be his spy.

FIGURE 10.1 Napoleon Bonaparte, military leader and emperor of France. *Library of Congress.*

The history of the Paris police in the period before the Revolution indicates that this was a well-organized body of officers with a range of responsibilities far beyond those that the United Kingdom and United States were about to create in the nineteenth century. Paris had introduced street lights in 1667, 150 years before London. By 1780, this single police responsibility accounted for 15 percent of the entire police budget. By 1716, officers wore blue uniforms; they walked a beat and were the only citizens of Paris permitted to carry a firearm. In 1730, another responsibility was added to their extensive portfolio; they were required to report cases of venereal disease. In the period of Lent, the 40 days of abstention for Catholics before Easter, police commissioners ordered a focus upon visiting restaurants to ensure the public were not consuming meat; officers also visited butchers to ensure that they were not working during the Lent period. Public order became an increasingly large part of police responsibilities, and by 1784 the police were responsible for operation of a curfew in Paris and ensuring that all bars were closed by 11:00 p.m. in summer and 10:00 p.m. in winter. By 1788, there was one police officer for every 193 residents. This ratio of police to citizenry has never been repeated in Western society. Currently, France and England have ratios of two officers per 1,000 population. The world average is three officers per 1,000 population. This high ratio needs contextualizing though, as we should remember the vast array of responsibilities the police undertook, including operating as the fire service for Paris. In the year of the Revolution, 1789, 200 officers were permanently attached to the police fire department.

With the accession of Napoleon Bonaparte as First Consul in 1799, the trend toward centralization of police was reinvigorated. Following his accession, there were literally hundreds of legal systems (including Roman and Frankish elements) operating throughout the country; statutory law consisted of accumulated legislation, ordinances, and edicts from previous regimes. Voltaire is reputed to have quipped that a person traveling in France had to change laws about as often as he changed horses. The *Napoleonic Codes*, which represented the first successful compilation of French law arranged in logical order, were drafted by a commission appointed by Napoleon in 1800. The codification provided a uniform, organized body of law applicable to all French citizens. A tripartite civil code appeared in 1804, a code of criminal instruction in 1808, and a penal code in 1810. Some of the libertarian principles of the French Revolution were incorporated, but the criminal codes also retained some of the harsh penalties of the revolutionary period.

For police control of rural areas, Napoleon augmented the *Gendarmerie*, a quasi-military force that was utilized by the Bourbons and accountable to the Ministry of Defense. Under the first Inspector-General, Adrien de Moncey, the Gendarmerie were used as both combat troops as well as military police domestically. Napoleon had great respect for the ability of the Gendarmerie to keep order and valued their precise reporting. A significant part of their mission was to protect the regime from subversion. In this activity, they sometimes resorted to disguises, but this was resented by the French, and after the collapse of the First Empire, the Gendarmerie were ordered to carry out their tasks in military uniform. This military aspect of policing is one of the principal characteristics that distinguish the French system from the English system.

Historians concur in designating Napoleon's Minister of General Police, *Joseph Fouché*, as the architect of France's modern national police system. By decree, the prefect of the Paris police was made subordinate to Fouché; additionally, in each of the 12 districts of Paris, police commissioners reported to the prefect. Napoleon refused, however, to follow Fouché's suggestions that would have placed the Paris police commissioners and those of all the administrative departments of France directly under Fouché's authority. Instead, the local commissioners were placed under the supervision of the prefects of the 98 departments of France. The principal responsibility of the departmental prefects, who were nominated by Napoleon, was maintenance of law and order, and they were required to make regular reports to the Minister of Interior. Therefore, local policing was under the authority of the Ministry of Interior rather than the Minister of Police.

It was during the period of Napoleon that one of the most dramatic figures in police history came to the fore: *François Eugéne Vidocq*. Vidocq, the friend of eminent novelists like Honoré de Balzac (*La Comedie Humaine*), Alexandre Dumas (*The Count of Monte Cristo*), and Victor Hugo (*Les Miserables*), was known to embellish his tales, and historians have difficulty separating fact from fiction in his accounts. It is, however, agreed that he initiated a detective unit in Paris that came to be called the *Brigade de Sûreté*. A key to Vidocq's success was his extraordinary ability to observe and remember detail, a talent that enabled him to disguise himself effectively. He was also a pioneer in detection techniques. Not only did he utilize handwriting, paper, and ink analyses to solve cases, but he also foresaw the day when fingerprints would be used to identify suspects.

The basic structure of the national police system instituted by Napoleon I, despite some modification during the administration of the Bourbon Restoration, survived the ensuing political disruptions of the July Revolution in 1830, which replaced King Charles X with King Louis-Philippe, and the revolutions that ushered in the Second Republic in 1848. The degree of centralization in the police system varied with the political shifts. During periods when liberals held power, an element of democracy in the form of election of lower police officials prevailed, only to yield to the practice of nomination and appointment when conservatives regained control. In 1851, the elected president of the Second Republic, Louis Napoleon Bonaparte, succeeded in making himself Emperor as Napoleon III. In implementing a centralized administration, he could call upon the French constitution of 1852 as a basis for executive power. Also, Napoleon III utilized principles of centralization that had been established by Napoleon I, claiming that his selection by the populace constituted a mandate to exercise general police powers in the name of general security. Authority over police was located in the Ministry of Interior, where it has remained despite a brief revival of the office of Minister of General Police (1852-1853).

The development of the police system of France did not proceed in a steady fashion. The bureaucratic structures initiated by the Bourbons, Napoleon I, and Napoleon III were not uniform in all urban or rural parts of France; nor was centralized authority over policing as effective in practice as it might appear on paper. Furthermore, the personal characteristics of those who ruled the nation and those who served in high police office determined in part how far along the libertarian-totalitarian scale the policing system would move one way or the other.

By 1825, the police of Paris kept crime statistics and comprehensive records of criminals. The role of the *police commissaire* was expanding, not just in the capital but across France. Manuals were written and officers received legal training.

They were regularly deployed across the country, and the police started a process of transformation into an extension of the state and central government rather than a local provision. The career policeman had arrived in France. Officers initially drawn from the military were now recruited from educated blue-collar ranks. Although professionalized, policing was and remains a blue-collar job, in France, England, and the United States. What professionalization did was to open up opportunities for those from the French working classes to rise, to a limited extent, up the social ladder. *Commissaire* recruits joined a profession, albeit they were never held to be professionals; they were and remain *petite bourgeoisie*.

By the end of the nineteenth century, however, it was evident that the nature of policing in France differed greatly from that in England. First, political security and public order were accorded greater value than the rights of individuals against invasive police action. In France, throughout the period being examined, rulers used police to suppress opposition, and there was an extensive system of surveillance of individuals. Second, there was a clear hierarchy of authority within the police bureaucracy from the minister in Paris down to the smallest commune. Third, the duties and responsibilities of police included social services and enforcement of regulations, which fell within the realm of administration in England. Fourth, France developed a bipartite structure of policing in which military units (Gendarmerie) policed rural areas and small towns under the authority of the Ministry of Defense and civilian units (National Police) policed municipalities under the authority of the Ministry of Interior.

The period saw the development of highly professional detective police forces (Brigade de Sûreté) that had been initiated by Vidocq. The Sûreté was institutionalized as a separate agency and achieved international renown. Its careful gathering of information and penetrating analysis are seen as a model for major investigation units of today, such as *Interpol* (International Criminal Police Organization). The effectiveness of the French detectives caught the attention of an English barrister, *Howard Vincent*, in the late nineteenth century. He went to France to examine the system and provided a report to authorities who were investigating corruption in Scotland Yard. As a result, he became head of the new Criminal Investigation Department in 1878, a unit that reflected the organization and operations of the Sûreté.

Respect for French methods and attempts to emulate some of them did not, however, encourage the English to incorporate French administrative principles. Despite claims by the French that a citizen in Paris was far safer than a citizen in London, concern about potential abuse of police power ensured the continuance in England of a decentralized, nonmilitary, and largely nonprofessional police force.

FROM CHARLIE TO BOBBY: THE LONDON STORY

By the eighteenth century, the traditional justice/constable system was hopelessly inadequate to deal with the law enforcement requirements of the London Metropolitan area. The justice/constable system was organized around a group of constables appointed by the local justices, who patrolled the streets of their respective parishes by day. Limited in power, these constables were also delinquent in the exercise of their duties; this was understandable considering that, when they raised the traditional hue and cry against a fleeing criminal, bystanders were more likely to ridicule the constable than come to their assistance in making an arrest. Parish boundaries were also matters of great consequence; pursuit beyond the parish area was rare, and constables from adjourning jurisdictions neither helped each other nor exchanged information.

At night, not only did opportunities for criminal activity multiply, but the *night watchmen* were even less vigorous than their daytime counterparts. Charged with the duty of patrolling deserted streets and maintaining street lamps in good order, night watchmen were more likely to be found in a local pub or eating place. A critic of the times described a night watchman as a "person hired by the parish to sleep in the open air."[1,2] The butt of popular and theatrical jokes well before William Shakespeare's time, the London constables after the reign of Charles II were known as *Charlies* because they were reorganized and reinforced by a statute passed during the Restoration period.

A key issue for the sprawling city was crime and, particularly, how to deal with the increasing number of cases being brought before the courts. By the late

TIME CAPSULE: PEEL'S PRINCIPLES

A major step toward professionalization of police was taken when Sir Robert Peel, member of Parliament and Home Secretary, achieved passage of the Metropolitan Police Act of 1829. Peel's 12 principles of reform in the nineteenth century are still pertinent in the twenty-first century.

1. The police must be stable, efficient, and organized along military lines.
2. The police must be under government control.
3. The absence of crime will best prove the efficiency of police.
4. The distribution of crime news is essential.
5. The deployment of police strength both by time and area is essential.
6. No quality is more indispensable to a policeman than a perfect command of temper; a quiet, determined manner has more effect than violent action.
7. Good appearance commands respect.
8. The securing and training of proper persons is at the root of efficiency.
9. Public security demands that every police officer be given a number.
10. Police headquarters should be centrally located and easily accessible to the people.
11. Policemen should be hired on a probationary basis.
12. Police records are necessary to the correct distribution of police strength.

1700s and into the 1800s, there was a significant increase in the number of matters brought to summary justice, that is, before a magistrate with limited powers of sentencing rather than having a case brought before a trial judge and a jury. Minor offenses were delegated to the magistrates courts and along with this came the division of the legal profession into barristers, who had a right to appear at all courts, and solicitors who had a right to appear at the lower magistrates courts but not the higher trial courts or appeal courts. This division, referred to as a *bifurcated legal system*, remains in place even today in England, but the division is no longer as acute as it was in the 1800s. Many solicitors now have rights to appear at the higher trial courts and the appellate courts.

Another legal player was introduced around this time by the passing of the *1792 Middlesex Justices Act*. This act brought into effect the position of *Stipendiary Magistrate*. Regular magistrates are not legally qualified and are not paid. They are members of the public in good standing who serve for a few days each month as a magistrate (a sort of modern-day version of being tried by your peers). When a legal issue arises in the courtroom, there is always a magistrates clerk available to give guidance to the magistrates. The clerk is either a solicitor or barrister. Stipendiary magistrates are legally qualified persons, a barrister or solicitor, who, due to their professional legal standing, may sit in court and hear cases without the need for a magistrates clerk. Stipendiary magistrates, as the term implies, are paid a stipend for their service.

History has given much acclaim to the roles played by Henry Fielding and Robert Peel in creating the modern police. Without denying their importance, it should be remembered that local, ordinary people were often the driving force behind change and this is certainly true with regard to the development of a police force for London. Consider how important it would be to a small-time merchant, or a butcher, or a fishmonger to have the streets of London free of criminals, prostitutes, and beggars, as none of these three could be considered good for trade. It has often been the case that it is the desire for a better society, for better living and business conditions, that merchants and working people have been instrumental in bringing about the pressure that has led to social reform or, in this case, the formalization of a police response to a complex city. Arresting prostitutes, beggars, and pick-pockets creates a safe environment that is good for business.

HISTORY TODAY

One of the most popular concepts in modern policing is the "broken windows" idea. It suggests, in part, that ridding neighborhoods of panhandlers, prostitutes, graffiti artists, and other minor criminals enhances the quality of life, helps businesses grow, and reduces crime. London police officials had a similar idea in the nineteenth century. However, detractors claim that such practices merely force the practitioners of these offenses to move to other locations, and that it ignores the underlying causes of such crimes. Where do you stand on this question?

In addition to establishing the stipendiary magistrate, the 1792 Act created a police office for London. In fact, there were a number of police offices, all rather similar to the Bow Street police office which had been functioning for 30 years. This is perhaps another example of how time and history have muddied our view of the significance of Robert Peel, because this 1792 legislation did create a paid police force across the metropolis. But this Act did not create one unified force, but rather a number of wards with one officer responsible for a number of houses within the ward. Huge discrepancies existed; for example, the officer in charge of Bread Street Ward was responsible for 28 houses, while the constable for Farrington Without Ward had 267. What this Act also achieved was the formalization of the role of the constable and the erosion of the role of City of London Marshall and the Beadle, both of whom had responsibilities for supervising night watchmen, driving out beggars and vagrants, and reporting on newcomers into the wards of the City of London.

During the eighteenth century, with rare exceptions, thieves and other criminals had moved about the streets of London with impunity, with the constables and watchman providing only momentary sport to a truly dedicated felon. Merchants and other residents of London were left to their own resources to protect themselves from robbery, theft, assault, battery, and even murder. The well-to-do, of course, had servants and retainers to shield them from the so-called criminal classes, but no such private protection was available to poorer citizens. In the event of a theft, it was customary to hire a *thief-catcher*, usually a veteran constable well acquainted with the underworld and able to secure the return of the stolen goods. In this case, free enterprise proved to be a mixed blessing. While it inevitably resulted in the return of all or a portion of the booty, it did so at a considerable price to the owner. Not infrequently, the thief-catcher withheld some of the property as an unauthorized supplement to his fee. The most notorious thief-catcher of all, *Jonathan Wild*, operated his profitable business for 7 years before his racket was discovered. Not content with tracking down goods that had been stolen, Wild found it worthwhile to employ a veritable army of thieves who stole on demand. Wild was then paid a commission to "find" the thief for the owner, and duly returned the property. Highly successful in this activity, Wild advertised himself as "Thief-taker General" of London and lived in luxury from his commissions until he was executed.

Thief-taking undermined the criminal justice system in two ways. It always provided anonymity for the criminal, who was required only to return the stolen goods without penalty. Crime always paid under these circumstances, and prosecution simply provided a sanction that forced the felon to disgorge a portion of the profit he would have made if he went undetected. Second, it developed a group of thief-takers who operated on the very edge of the law, at times holding back some of the ransomed property for their own profit, or who, like Wild, actually encouraged thieves for the purpose of increasing their own business. It wasn't a good system, but it was the best that eighteenth-century England had to offer.

HISTORY TODAY

The story of Jonathan Wild suggests that there are problems when law enforcement officials have a profit motive for solving crimes. Thief-catchers like Wild gave priority to people and businesses that would reward them financially. Is it possible that some modern police officers may give priority to businesses or people that reward them with gratuities such as discounts on food, beverages, or rent?

Even within this flawed system of indolent constables, sleepy watchmen, and venal thief-catchers, there was a glimmer of hope for a more efficient system of law enforcement. Sir Thomas DeVeil was appointed magistrate for the Bow Street district in 1730, and in the ensuing 17 years he established his police office as one of the most effective within the metropolitan London area. In 1748, DeVeil was succeeded as Bow Street magistrate by the novelist Henry Fielding who, somewhat to the surprise of his associates, took a serious interest in improving the function of his police office. These changes included the establishment of the Bow Street Runners, a group of highly skilled thief-catchers who received modest salaries for their work. Fielding also turned his literary talents to good purpose. Beginning with *An Enquiry into the Cause of the Late Increase of Robbers* (1748), he published five pamphlets on crime and its prevention before his death in 1754. Working on the assumption that the collection of good intelligence was essential to the detection of crime, Fielding also established the *Covent Garden Gazette*, which specialized in publicizing descriptions of criminals and their modes of operation. Advertisements inserted in the regular dailies asked citizens to report the descriptions and activities of suspected criminals to the Chief Magistrate of Bow Street, as Fielding described himself. Premature death did not halt Fielding's work in law enforcement. The chief magistracy of Bow Street and the campaign for an effective police force was carried on by his half-brother and successor, Sir John Fielding. Sir John remained Chief Magistrate until 1779, and during his tenure the famous Bow Street Horse Patrol was established to maintain order on the highways leading into the metropolis.

FIGURE 10.2 Bow Street Magistrate's Court, London. *Courtesy en.wikipedia.org.*

By 1800, the Bow Street Police Office was recognized as the leading law enforcement agency in London. A historian of English criminal law, Sir Leon Radzinowicz, described it as:

> the headquarters of a closely knit caste of speculators in the detection of crime, self-seeking and unscrupulous, but also daring and efficient when daring and efficiency coincided with their private interest.[3]

Within the framework of the old justice/constable system, the Bow Street Police Office represented the most that could be realized, and its runners were simultaneously "the most perfect creation and ultimately the most complete travesty of the system of incentives."[4]

Even if the evils of the justice/constable system had been eliminated from Bow Street Police Office operations, no local jurisdiction could combat the rising crime wave throughout London. Efficient patrol and thief-catching in one parish simply caused the felons to relocate their activities to adjacent areas that might be totally devoid of any law enforcement. A patchwork system of law enforcement left entire segments of London's population to their own devices. Realizing the need for a universal control of law enforcement throughout the metropolitan area, Prime Minister *William Pitt the Younger* introduced a bill for a police force to be established throughout the city (1785). Defeated because of widespread fear that such a constabulary would undermine the liberties of Englishmen and lead to militarism, the bill nevertheless served as a prototype for the legislation that established the *Metropolitan Police* in 1829. While fear of police-state suppression of liberties doomed Pitt's bill to failure, English statesmen recognized the need for a new police organization. In 1786, the Irish Parliament authorized the Royal Irish Constabulary, which followed the general outline of Pitt's bill. Significantly, Sir Robert Peel, later the founder of the London Metropolitan Police, was Chief Secretary for Ireland from 1812 to 1818.

Patrick Colquhoun (1745-1820), a Scottish-born merchant who spent some early years in Virginia, succeeded to leadership of the police reform efforts in 1790. Appointed a magistrate shortly after his removal to London, he began a painstaking study of law enforcement. His book, *A Treatise on the Police of the Metropolis*, was published anonymously in 1795 and went through numerous editions and reprintings before 1800. Estimating the indigent classes of Britain at more than 1,500,000 individuals, he claimed that more than 50,000 inhabitants of London composed a class of habitual criminals whose lives were spent in crime or in prison. Colquhoun estimated that approximately £12,000,000 per year was lost because of their activities. As a result, Colquhoun argued that a combined effort to deal with the problem of indigence and to discourage crime by effective police activity was essential. He went so far as to suggest that the French police, widely viewed in England as subversive of French liberties, were a model for Britain to follow; to Colquhoun, effective police were perhaps even more important than the British constitution itself.

In a certain sense, Colquhoun was correct. London and other cities in Great Britain were on the brink of criminal anarchy entering the nineteenth century. It was this widespread disregard for property rights and human life that rendered the constitution highly vulnerable. A highly complex and interdependent city that relies upon trade and commerce for its livelihood cannot tolerate extensive criminal activity. That fact was shown by the passage of the *Thames Police Act* (1800), which established a plenary police jurisdiction to cover the river itself and the adjacent land areas. Crossing numerous parish boundaries, the Thames Police Office soon proved an effective institution against the violence and property-related offenses of the waterfront. Most thieves in this area had developed highly sophisticated methods of operation. For example, as a method of removing whiskey and other liquids from wooden casks, a thief would move a barrel hoop from its location on the cask, drill a hole on one side to remove the contents and a hole on the other side to equalize the air pressure. When an adequate amount had been withdrawn, the barrel was plugged on one side and filled with water. The remaining hole was replugged, the hoop replaced, and the barrel sent on to its unsuspecting purchaser.

Patrick Colquhoun's 1800 treatise on the need for a marine police jurisdiction for the Thames was at least partially responsible for the establishment of this new and more effective police office. Yet, despite its author's reputation, it was no more successful than his earlier works in stimulating an overhaul of the entire law enforcement system in London. That would have to wait for the outbreak of a new wave of crime in the 1820s and the decision by Sir Robert Peel to seek a Parliamentary reform of the London police system in 1829.

The necessities of the time, emphasized by the crime wave and frequent riots, created the stage for London police reform; however, little could have been accomplished without the political skills of Sir Robert Peel. It was the identification of the Metropolitan Police with Sir Robert that resulted in the police officers being called *bobbies*. (An earlier popular designation, *peelers*, has been dropped from the vocabulary.) The jurist Sir William Blackstone (supplemented by the influential writer on moral philosophy, William Paley) saw a police force as detrimental to constitutional liberty. Following this viewpoint, most Englishmen opposed the adoption of more efficient systems of law enforcement. It was the utilitarians, led by Jeremy Bentham and supported by Patrick Colquhoun and Edward Chadwick, who were willing to view police activities in the context of efficiency rather than political theory.

Coloring the entire discussion was the example of an efficient and repressive system of police in France, where extensive intelligence networks caught ordinary criminals as well as those who spoke and acted in ways that undermined the stability of the regime holding political power. Such a use of police to buttress unpopular government was contrary to England's concept of free and constitutional politics. Peel's approach to this conflict was to advocate a moderate approach to police activity. He stressed preventative measures, such as the establishment of regular patrols by uniformed police, the collection of intelligence concerning criminal activity only, and the centralization of all law enforcement activities within the London Metropolitan area. Mindful of the strong opposition, which the financial district of London had mounted to the 1785 reform effort, Peel was careful to remove the ancient City of London from the provisions of his proposal. As passed by Parliament, the bill retained this exception, but the separate City of London force very quickly copied the Metropolitan Police, making the exception a mere matter of political expediency that did not hamper the centralization.

Given the precarious political compromise that resulted in the passage of the Peel Act, it was clear that the image of the Metropolitan Police was a critical factor in determining whether the new force would survive. The two men chosen as justices, later named commissioners, were ideal leaders in the attempt to institute an efficient police system that would be free of repressive political behavior, but at the same time be an effective force to prevent and prosecute crime. Charles Rowan was a retired military officer with experience as a magistrate in Ireland, the home of the Royal Irish Constabulary; barrister Richard Mayne contributed both legal skills and political dexterity. Together, they developed a uniform that made their growing force of patrolmen visible, but at the same time they avoided any color or decoration that suggested military dress. The hats of the patrolmen were flat-top hats, designed with steel reinforcements that permitted the officer to stand on the headgear and peer over high walls and fences.

Preventative policing meant knowing what was going on throughout the London metropolitan area. On his beat, the bobby was expected to become familiar with the populace, to extend help as needed, and to remain alert at all times to indications that crimes were about to be committed. At the same time, it was felt that an officer should not be overly familiar with the residents of his beat. This was achieved by appointing officers drawn from other cities and from rural areas surrounding London; the few bobbies who were native to the city were assigned patrol duties well away from their home neighborhoods. As a result, the bobby was known in the area he patrolled primarily as a representative of the state and of the police commissioners. Officers were carefully trained in respectful behavior toward all classes and groups. Violent police behavior was discouraged in both training and in a policy that allowed officers to carry only truncheons (clubs made of birch wood), but no edged weapons or firearms.

Wilbur Miller, noting the tense political situation at the time the Metropolitan Police force was established, found little resentment toward the officers on the part of the laboring classes.[5] There were complaints that Metropolitan Police were more vigorous in administering law against working-class offenders than against members of the governing class. Marxist newspaper editors after 1850 were sharp in their condemnation of the officers as mere instruments for the oppression of the masses. However, as Miller explained, police commissioners were generally successful in maintaining a reputation for restraint at a time when the English nation was sharply divided along class lines over the issue of extending the right to vote. Bobbies were forbidden participation in political activities, and, in later years, when the right to vote was broadened, they were still denied the right to vote.

The Metropolitan Police did not formally establish a detective office until 1842, at which time carefully selected patrol officers were assigned to such work. The close connection to the patrol force meant that detectives were assured the cooperation of their uniformed colleagues; it also provided an incentive for the bobby on the beat to perfect his skills of observation and crime detection. The new detective office also benefited from the reputation of the uniformed force for courteous and restrained behavior.

Although the establishment of a detective force was progressive in some respects, it also located policing in a style that was to take more than 100 years to break away from and that is an overreliance upon reactive detective work as detection always occurred after the commission of a crime. Curiously, the *Scotland Yard* detective became the gold standard for the world. Detectives worked from the main office of the Metropolitan Police in Old Scotland Street; this gave rise to the investigative section being identified as Scotland Yard.

The genesis of this office may in fact have been in Bow Street, where the establishment of a rank known as Principal Officer remained active long after the disbanding of the Bow Street Runners. Principal Officers have established a reputation as excellent detectives and were often called in by local communities; remember, the legal requirement for the formation of constabularies across the entire country did not happen until 1839 and Met detectives were not created until 1842. Between 1829 and 1839, Principal Officers were the *de facto* detective force of the Metropolitan Police and "for hire" to local communities outside of London as and when needed. The detective "for hire" did not restrict himself to the public domain either, and he was available for investigative work to cities as well as individuals or industry, a point not lost on *Allan Pinkerton* (a native of Scotland) in the United States when he decided to form an investigative agency. The success of the Principal Officers was probably their demise, as the British Parliament was concerned that London had a police force of 3,000 officers but needed paid ancillary detectives to solve its crimes. In 1839, 90 years after its creation, the Bow Street Principal Officer was formally disbanded to be replaced three years later by the Metropolitan Police Detective Branch.

Restraint in routine law enforcement as well as political matters did not spare the Metropolitan Police of problems concerning riot control between 1830 and 1850. It was discovered that, while police officers were helpful in the initial stages of disorder, they were unable to stop the activities of a large and determined mob. For that purpose, the Home Secretary (under whom the Metropolitan Police were organized) found that it was necessary to employ regular Army troops. On the other hand, the use of the armed troops usually escalated the casualty rate in any riot situation, and it was understood that bobbies were the preferred option in the case of minor disorders. Closeness to the inhabitants of the community, coupled with respect and confidence, made the Metropolitan Police the first line of defense.

FIGURE 10.3 Born in Scotland, Allan Pinkerton founded the first detective agency in the United States. *Courtesy en.wikipedia.org.*

Once established, the London Metropolitan Police created a law enforcement standard that would be widely emulated. Within England, bobbies were frequently sent on temporary duty to other cities and counties to help in establishing a "new style" police force. Their effectiveness in small-crowd control made them the obvious choice to assist in law enforcement activities outside the boundaries of London, and they were frequently assigned to these tasks. American police reformers, witnessing the transformation of law enforcement in England, sought to import the new system into American urban police organizations.

FROM BOBBY TO COPPER IN NEW YORK CITY

Much like Europe, the United States was experiencing massive growth within its cities. The rudimentary and imported model of night watchman, sheriffs, and constables was insufficient to deal with evolving and complex patterns of criminality. The paid night watchmen introduced by the Dutch into New York in 1648 and copied in Boston in 1663 had long ago been disbanded due to costs. Throughout the eighteenth and early nineteenth centuries, America made do with local responses better suited to Anglo-Saxon villages than a burgeoning world force.

In 1807, Boston created police districts, and in 1823 a Harvard graduate was appointed the first City Marshall. In 1845, New York City abandoned its earlier system of constables and watchmen and instituted the first London-style police department outside the British Empire, with the appointment of 100 Marshalls and 1,000 part-time constables. But even by outward appearances, there was a sharp distinction between the two forces. Initially, the New York City policemen did not wear uniforms, because of a combination of both official indifference and the individual officer's opposition to appearing in what he termed "subservient livery." Only after pressure from above, coupled with the commissioners and commanding officers wearing the uniform to social events, did the policemen accept the uniform, and even then it was customary to wear the heavy woolen coat only in inclement weather. For their mark of authority, the New York policemen relied upon a simple copper badge mounted on a leather circle; from this they gained the popular name of *copper*, later shortened to *cop*. Originally, the new police force, called the *Municipal Police*, carried only a truncheon, and for a brief time these officers were known as *leatherheads*, but by 1850 the policy against firearms was weakened by the number of officers killed or seriously injured by armed criminals.

The London emphases on careful patrol, familiarity with the community, careful supervision, and provisions for adequate salaries were evident in New York's Municipal Police. However, the differing political and social situation in America produced a remarkable variation from the London Metropolitan Police format. Politically, the New York policeman was vulnerable to the "spoils system" that prevailed during and after the presidency of Andrew Jackson (1829–1837). This emphasized a democratic demand that public officers, both elected and appointed, should be accessible to all citizens. Indeed, the most significant factor in police appointments was loyalty to the party that was victorious in the most recent election coupled with support for local landowners, industry leaders, and paid allegiances to business leaders. As a consequence, New York police officers were subject to immediate removal upon the failure of their party to win reelection or police according to the dictates of industry leaders rather than societal needs. By contrast, the London bobby was insulated from changes in political office, not only because of his political neutrality but also because he reported directly to the central government and what would ultimately become the Home Office. Appointed by the elected alderman who represented a particular ward, the New York patrolman usually found himself working in the neighborhood in which he was raised or where he had lived for many years. Closeness in community relations was assured, but the image of the policeman was less that of an objective official and more that of an old friend. Because the officer's job depended on the success of his political party, he was strongly tempted to ensure the continuity of political power.

New York City politics was not divided along class lines, but rather in terms of native versus immigrant elements and, to some degree, ethnic lines. The selection of policemen by wards meant, to a considerable degree, that they represented the majority of the people within their wards. Thus, Irish policemen patrolled Irish wards; Germans dealt with German ward police problems, and Anglo-American officers predominated in the established middle- and upper-class neighborhoods. Political domination of police appointments eliminated the possibility of neutrality in the Municipal Police, but it did ensure acceptance of the individual officer within his native ward. Organization by wards meant that decentralization was the mark of the Municipal Police, and uniformity in deciding which crime should be prosecuted was vested not in the police but rather in politically elected district attorneys.

One matter that New York City residents agreed on was the prohibition of alcoholic beverages. A majority of residents openly flouted the prohibition law of New York State, and their violation of the state "dry law" was widely ignored by the Municipal Police. This defiance, encouraged by the Democratic leadership of the city, caused the Republican and prohibitionist governor to secure passage of a state statute. This law abolished the Municipal Police and substituted a Metropolitan Police Force to be commanded by state-appointed commissioners (1857). Initially, the two police forces worked side by side, despite their conflicting sources of authority and attitudes toward prohibition. Ultimately, growing disorder brought the situation to a crisis, and an open battle broke out between rival police agencies. The Seventh Regiment of the New York National Guard (a militia under state control) established order at the point of the bayonet. Subsequently, the Municipal Police Force was disbanded, and the Metropolitan Police Force exercised police jurisdiction in the city until 1870, when home rule was reinstituted and a new municipal Police Force was established.

The exercise of police power in New York City was substantially different from what had occurred in London. London Commissioners Rowan and Mayne carefully created the image of a politically neutral and institutionally controlled policeman, familiar with the activities of his community while at the same time detached from them. A series of regulations defined the activities and limited discretion of the individual patrolman. By contrast, the New York City Municipal Police (and the Metropolitan Police from 1857 to 1870) depended on the prestige of the individual officer. Conferring a great deal of discretion on individual officers, American practices limited the policeman's authority at the ballot box, where he and his superiors were either indirectly or directly answerable. The New York City policeman's standard of behavior was essentially to react as one of his fellow citizens would in the same situation.

While some police efficiency was gained when the Municipal Police was established in 1845, the political manipulation of the force was such that it verified the fears that had earlier impeded the reform of English police institutions.

After 1848, American law enforcement became increasingly involved in the application of the controversial and inflammatory fugitive slave laws. Public sentiment grew against the increased political power and economic impact of immigrant laborers. Religious animosity between immigrant Roman Catholics and native Protestant groups caused conflict and violence. New York City police officers were not insulated from such disorder, but their political identification with fellow citizens made it unlikely that resentment would be turned against them. Just as their prototypes in London could not effectively control riots, the New York City Police were ineffective in restoring order during the New York City draft riots of 1863.

Adapting the English Metropolitan Police model to American realities meant discarding virtually all of the institutional restraints that were so typical of the London police. Instead, the New York City police were marked by individual discretion and amenability to political influence. It was as if an excessively democratic spirit had sapped the Metropolitan Police model of all of its virtues, leaving only the simple outline of operations. This outline included improved methods of patrol and intelligence, and to that extent New York City was better served than it had been during the colonial past. However, in the future, citizens would at times wonder whether the operation of the city's police was as much a source of crime as a means for its prevention.

The city of Boston, after rejecting a proposal to follow the London police model in 1837, made extensive changes in its police organization in 1852. These changes included uniting the constables and the night watch into a single law enforcement body. Patrols were established, and such activity was monitored by superior officers. In 1855, the newly constructed station houses were connected by telegraph lines, facilitating the rapid transmission of information and the quick assembly of police forces where they were most needed. Between 1855 and 1857, the force was placed in uniform, causing more jeers from the general public than genuine opposition from the men themselves. Boston's ideal for police was simply stated: "The police, while it should be argus-eyed, seeing all things, should be itself unseen and unheard." In this sense, it closely paralleled the London Metropolitan Police and also represented the London ideal of detachment. Few, if any, Boston policemen were drawn from the city; most were from rural New England.

HISTORY TODAY

Should the fact that a police officer may (or may not) have grown up in the town where he or she aspires to work play a role in police department hiring? What about small rural locales where the officer has many relatives and he or she may be lifelong friends with many of the residents? Could this compromise the officer's judgment? On the other hand, could the fact that the officer knows the community weigh in their favor?

SOUTHERN POLICE METHODS

In contrast to London and northern American cities, the South found little incentive to change its traditional police systems until the very eve of the Civil War. In his comparative study of criminal justice in Massachusetts and South Carolina, historian Michael Hindus illustrates how such contrast between North and South came about. Already at the vanguard of American industrialization, Massachusetts resorted to increased state regulation in all areas of economic and social activity, while South Carolina retained a traditional laissez-faire (hands-off) approach toward governmental power and economic regulation. Massachusetts strengthened law enforcement as a method of securing property rights and encouraging commercial activity; South Carolina was concerned with preventing violence in a slave-holding society dominated by racial fear and tension.[6] These general terms of distinction may suffer from some oversimplification, but they accurately portray the wide divergence between the urban North and the agrarian South.

Southern states relied upon *slave patrols* as a method of combating crime and preventing slave insurrections. All able-bodied white men aged 18-50 were subject to duty on the patrol, and female heads of household were also subject to call, even though they were expected to hire a substitute to perform the duty for them. Once every 2 weeks, the patrol inspected roadways and inns, checking for passes that authorized blacks to be away from their master's plantation after the curfew hour. Those found abroad without such documentation, in addition to those found to be acting suspiciously or boisterously, were taken into custody and held for the court of magistrates and *freeholders*. This was a special court composed of one local justice of the peace and two to five landholders. The court had complete jurisdiction in all criminal matters concerning slaves and might impose capital punishment in appropriate cases. The usual penalty for being abroad without a pass was that the slave be flogged and given a passport for his unhindered return to his master's plantation.

While on the plantation, slaves were subject to the discipline of the master or his overseer, and punishments were inflicted for a wide spectrum of offenses ranging from assault, battery, and theft to breaches of etiquette and surly mannerisms. This punishment usually involved legally controlled flogging, but occasionally punishments were carried to excess and slaves died under the lash. In other instances, planters starved their slaves, but in most cases the master's investment compelled him to deal with them in a more humane fashion. Excessive punishments that violated the mores of white society might cause the local justices of the peace to intervene, and there are instances of slave owners being executed for the willful murder of their slaves. Yet white society, for the most part, was willing to let planters manage and discipline slaves as they saw fit.

If a South Carolina slave committed a felony, the case had to be brought before the magistrate and freeholder's court. The defendant was expected to be in court and could present witnesses on his or her behalf. Frequently, counsel was provided; however, conviction rates in the magistrate and freeholder's courts were much higher than those in the higher courts charged with trying white defendants. South Carolina's penal laws made most felonies punishable by death, while other offenses that would be considered minor if committed by a white man were capital offenses for blacks and slaves. Lesser penalties, such as flogging, sale outside the state (and thus separation from family and relatives), or walking the treadmill at the Charleston workhouse, were also imposed. When it was necessary to execute a slave as punishment for a crime, his or her master received either all or part of the fair market value of the slave, established on the basis of a jury verdict.

A mutual fear dominated racial relations in the South. For blacks, even those freed from slavery, there was the constant fear of white violence. Blacks were expected to behave in a deferential fashion; city ordinances in Charleston required them to walk in the gutters and salute every white person they passed. It was a felony to strike a white person, even in self-defense or after extreme provocation. If a master was being attacked by another white, a slave could not act to defend them, except at his master's order. Slaves had no standing before the law and could not bring a lawsuit; additionally, neither they nor free blacks could testify in court against a white person. Slaves were subjected to a rigid curfew law, restricted to social gatherings that did not exceed a certain number, and were always kept under the surveillance of the white community.

In 1830, the city of Charleston had a population of 30,289, of which 17,461 were blacks. Fear of slave uprisings governed the conduct of business, the architecture of houses, and the administration of the criminal laws. Curfews kept blacks off the streets in the night hours, and severe penalties were imposed for selling intoxicating liquor to blacks. Houses in the white community were strongly secured against entry after dark; few, if any, permitted easy access from the slave quarters that were situated in the yards of the mansions. In administering the criminal law, it was the custom that no white man could be flogged. Such a demeaning punishment toward a member of the white race was believed to be an incitement to slave rebellion.

Fear of slave rebellion was not a figment of a white man's imagination. In the 1790s, the black population of Haiti rose up and massacred virtually the entire white population of the island; those who survived fled to the American South, and shared their experiences with slave owners all too ready to apply the lesson to themselves. When in 1822 a freedman named *Denmark Vesey* was caught in the process of organizing a widespread uprising in the city of Charleston, the need for greater control became apparent. One initial step was an abortive attempt to prevent any black seamen from coming ashore at Charleston. This effort brought the city fathers into conflict with the federal government, and while they succeeded in restricting the freedom of seamen, they did not eliminate them from the transient population. More effective steps were taken to restrict the movements and activities of the free black residents of Charleston and the rest of South Carolina. Free black residents were required to obtain the protection of a white "guardian" who would vouch for their good behavior; failing that, free blacks were required to emigrate from the state.

Operating on military lines of organization, the Charleston City Guard was charged with patrolling the city after dark. Privates in the guard were equipped with a musket, bayonet, and cartouche (gun cartridge) box; sergeants, lieutenants, and captains wore swords; and the entire force was arrayed in blue uniforms. Guardsmen on patrol carried rattles, used to call for help and notify their officers of their location; five men and a sergeant patrolled each of the city districts. Given the dangerous state of the streets and alleys late at night, and the desperate nature of the criminals they apprehended, an individual rarely became separated from the main body of the patrol. In 1846, the city guard changed its name to Charleston City Police, and patrolling officers were charged with identifying newcomers on their beats and observing suspicious circumstances that might lead to crime.

By 1856, the city police were in need of reorganization and expansion, a task that was undertaken by Mayor William Porcher Miles. Thereafter, the police force consisted of 1 chief, 2 captains, 6 lieutenants, 4 ordinary sergeants, 4 patrol sergeants, and 150 privates. Taking to the streets in June 1856, the new force was known as Paddy Miles' Bull Dogs. Derision from the white residents was matched by fear from the blacks, particularly freedmen, who in 1857 were further restricted by a city ordinance requiring them to wear a numbered badge for purposes of quick identification. The city police patrolled both night and day, displaying their uniforms and weapons. Some Charlestonians explained their presence as being the consequence of an unruly group of seamen; one of the more forthright and candid privates of the guard told a foreign visitor that the guard was for "keeping down the niggers."

From the little that is known about the Charleston City Police, it seems apparent that, while there may have been some effort to follow the London form of organization, the requirements for policing the "Holy City" were quite unique. Control of blacks, both slaves and freedmen, was of paramount importance. Trading with blacks, particularly selling alcoholic beverages, was strictly forbidden by ordinance but blatantly practiced. Blacks were essential to city life: they were craftsmen, household servants, longshoremen, and seamen. The presence of a large percentage of free blacks, viewed as focal points of insurrections, was troublesome to the inhabitants, but the skills of blacks were in demand. For the blacks, this contact with the white community provided a degree of protection against police harassment. Social control was the primary function of police in Charleston and the surrounding countryside. While there might be crime in the white community, it was of little consequence to authorities concerned with suppressing black crime and assuring black subservience.

HISTORY TODAY

In public opinion surveys of American institutions, police rank high in popularity, but much lower among African-Americans than other racial groups, even though law enforcement agencies employ many more African-Americans than in times past. Given the fact that policing in the south was created primarily to control the slave and free black population, should such results be surprising? What are some steps that law enforcement agencies can take to improve black perceptions of police?

Urban Charleston, with its large black population and a growing number of itinerant black seamen from other American and Caribbean ports, cannot be considered typical of the rural areas of the South, which relied upon *plantation discipline* to control both the slave and free black populations. For the most part, the traditional system of passes and frequent slave patrols kept blacks from planning criminal activities and escaping from servitude. Urbanization and commercial growth rendered these informal methods of law enforcement inadequate, and popular sentiment supported the creation of an efficient military organization to control the black population. Public safety superseded any fear that southern leaders might have had of a military coup. This provides an interesting contrast to the situation in London and New York at that time, where the establishment of a new style of police force was seen as a threat to individual freedom and a step in the direction of a military dictatorship. The establishment of the city guard also removed slave discipline from the master, substituting an impersonal and public system of law enforcement that grew in repressiveness as northern abolitionists attacked the institution of slavery and the growing black population of Charleston increased the fear of insurrection.

LAW AND VIOLENCE ON THE AMERICAN FRONTIER

Americans have long been fascinated with the westerly movement of the frontier, that "cutting edge" of Western civilization where a thin line of settlers stood between the fierce Indian and the ravages of nature on one side and the rapidly changing culture of the United States and Western Europe on the other. It was on the frontier, some historians believe, that the true character of America evolved. That character included rugged individualism, staunch independence in political and economic affairs, incorruptibility at the ballot box, and a simplicity of manners and behavior that lent republican dignity to American life. Others saw the frontier as a time and place where the deeply embedded culture of Western civilization was forced into adaptations to primitive conditions. Recently, a debate has evolved about frontier responsibility for the violent tendencies in American history. It is this last aspect of frontier historiography that holds the most interest for the student of criminal justice.

Crossing the great expanse of the North American continent is quite an experience, even with today's conveniences. It was a monumental endeavor for those who attempted it in the nineteenth century. For a brief period, Indian hostility took its toll in lives, but ultimately it was the geography of the continent that was the most formidable obstacle. From the banks of the Mississippi and Missouri Rivers, the land sloped upward, and with each foot of altitude it became more arid. Many perished of thirst or hunger on the Great Plains even before coming within sight of the next hurdle, the Rocky Mountains, where high passes tested the stamina of man and beast and fierce storms decimated wagon trains that risked the climb in late autumn or winter. Beyond the Rocky Mountains was a vast dry desert bordered on the west by the Sierra Nevada and Cascade mountain ranges. It was in the Sierras that an unlucky party found itself marooned in the Donner Pass and resorted to cannibalism before the ordeal was over. Arrival in Oregon or California provided a more hospitable climate, but did not give peace, for the institutions of government were only recently established and law enforcement was thinly spread. At times, only a handful of federal marshals policed an entire territory that today might include several of the western states.

Lack of effective law enforcement was not the only factor that produced crime on the frontier. Numerous studies have shown that the American West was the place of refuge for those reluctant to remain within settled eastern communities. Also, the sheer geographical expanse of the regions created its own problems even when states attempted to provide a public police response. The modest $15 per month offered to the first 10 Texas Rangers to roam across its massive deserts did not stimulate an excess of applicants for the positions.

Certainly, many migrants sought adventure or wealth, but others found it expedient to "move on" from the East before they were arrested for unpaid debts, to avoid supporting families, or to escape criminal prosecution. There was a certain anonymity in westward migration; systems of communication were slow and unreliable, and it was not difficult to alter one's identity and begin a new life. In the colonial period, Americans complained about the English practice of transporting convicts to the colonies. Undoubtedly, many upright settlers in the West saw the same exportation of undesirables occurring in the nineteenth century; however, where the colonists at least knew something of the convicts' backgrounds, the honest westerners were left to learn by experience.

John Reid spent several years studying the experience on the westward over-land trail in his "Elephant" articles.[7] Pioneers on the trail referred to the con-tinent as the "Elephant," and risked their fortunes and lives in an effort to see or conquer the Elephant. Elaborate agreements governed the management of wagon trains and "messes" of individuals who joined together for the over-land trip. Roughly approximating joint ventures (a simple form of business organization), these agreements provided for common ownership of equip-ment, and constituted a sort of insurance that the group would remain to-gether until the end of the journey. These agreements also represented a pooling of the capital and resources of the individual pioneers and their fam-ilies. Medical doctors frequently entered into contracts to provide care to the group, in return for food and protection during the journey. Crossing the con-tinent exposed the pioneers to conditions far more life-threatening than they had ever encountered before. Prices of goods rose as the number of wayside vendors decreased, and starving men at times arrived at a solitary trading post without sufficient funds to purchase food. However, even in such distress, it was uncommon for theft or robbery to occur. From their backgrounds, the pioneers brought a thoroughly instilled respect for the right of private prop-erty. Beyond the restraints of traditional law, far removed from policy or law enforcement agencies and thousands of miles from the nearest courts, they conducted themselves in an orderly and law-abiding fashion. Reid's findings say much about the manner in which human behavior is controlled by early conditioning and self-discipline.

Selecting companions for the overland journey was a matter of great importance. It was also the key to maintaining order on the trail. When the settlers reached their journey's end (such as the gold fields of California or the rich farmlands of Oregon), such selectivity was no longer possible. Competition for land or mining claims was intense, supplies were expensive, and neighbors were usually strangers. California experienced a rapid expansion of its population as gold speculators poured into the Bay Area, and its admission as a state in 1850 did little to alleviate the growing pains. Disorder and crime began to threaten stabil-ity and property rights, and in 1856 law-abiding citizens launched a vigilante movement. The *San Francisco Association*, like many before and after it, insisted on holding "trials" of the accused persons and, thus, approximated formal court procedures. However, the defendants were always convicted and inevitably sentenced to death, with execution immediately following the trial.

Richard Maxwell Brown, who has studied this and other *vigilante* movements, attributes much of American violent behavior to the vigilante tradition.[8] He finds that Americans are a people inclined to resort to violence even when legal pro-cedures are available; violence has thus achieved a neutral quality, with a percep-tion that there is "good" violence (vigilantism) and "bad" violence (crime and banditry). Brown argues that there is a degree of admiration for the violent outlaw, enshrined in legends about a wide assortment of gunslingers, train robbers, and other felons. Indeed, the American fascination with leading criminals has resulted in Al Capone and Billy the Kid sharing the national pantheon with George Washington, Abraham Lincoln, and Robert E. Lee.

HISTORY TODAY

Do you agree with Brown's suggestion that vigilantism is an American attribute? Are Americans more inclined to vigilantism than people in other countries?

Reid and Brown illustrate two contradictory aspects of law enforcement on the frontier. On the overland trail and when social cohesion was vital, pioneers relied heavily on their concepts of legality. Without lawyers or judges, they made their arrangements for the mutual good of all, and for the most part they abided by their agreements, living up to the pledge of their honor that they would do so. It was in the more permanent, but less demanding, circumstances of frontier

FEATURED OUTLAW: BILLY THE KID

Nineteenth-century outlaws of the American West have assumed a large prominence in American history and folklore. Hollywood films have played a role in romanticizing the Western outlaw. The truth about American outlaws has often been overshadowed by the romantic image presented by the entertainment media. Among the most infamous of the Western Outlaws was Billy the Kid. Billy the Kid's real name is in doubt. His birth name is believed to have been Henry McCarty, and it is believed that McCarty was born in New York City (or Brooklyn) in 1859 or 1860 to Irish immigrant parents. Some writers believe his real name was William Bonney, Jr., which was the name he used while he was committing the crimes that would make him a legend. In any case, McCarty's (or Bonney's) family moved to Kansas during his childhood, where his father died. Sometime later, McCarty moved to Colorado where his mother remarried before moving to Silver City, New Mexico Territory. McCarty's stepfather was named William Henry Antrim, and at times the young McCarty lived under the name Henry Antrim. McCarty was nicknamed "the Kid" as a teenager but did not assume the moniker of Billy the Kid until a few months prior to his death.

A minor brush with the law landed McCarty in jail as a teenager, and he escaped to Arizona, which set him on a criminal lifestyle. Like many wayward youth today, McCarty became involved in gangs, who spent much of their time robbing and stealing throughout the Southwest and Northern Mexico. Contrary to popular perception, Billy the Kid was never a recognized gang leader; he was simply an occasional member. Horse thievery, the nineteenth-century counterpart to auto theft, was one of his specialties.

McCarty is most noted for being a leader in the 1878 Lincoln County cattle war. Two rival companies were fighting for control of the county's economy. One group, known as the *Murphy-Dolan faction*, which had dominated the cattle business in Lincoln County for some time, sought to suppress a threat from an upstart faction known as the *Tunstall-McSween faction*. McCarty joined forces with the Tunstall-McSween faction as a member of their armed faction, known as the *Regulators*. One of McCarty's crimes was the murder of Lincoln Sheriff William Brady on the town's main street, a crime that involved several Regulators in addition to McCarty. On one occasion, McCarty took part in a classic Western shootout that resulted in the death of the Murphy-Dolan faction. McCarty's involvement in the

Continued

FEATURED OUTLAW: BILLY THE KID—CONT'D

War ended on July 19, 1878, when he and his fellow Regulators were barricaded in the McSween house. The Army, ostensibly neutral but in fact on the side of the Murphy-Dolan faction, raided the house along with members of the Murphy-Dolan group. McCarty and several others escaped but some remaining behind were killed.

After the Lincoln County War, McCarty resumed cattle rustling in the New Mexico/Texas border area. At one point, he was offered amnesty for his involvement in exchange for testifying against his cohorts, but the deal fell through because McCarty continued to rustle cattle. McCarty was captured in December 1880 by Sheriff Patrick Garrett, his famous nemesis, and charged with the murder of Sheriff Brady. He was tried in April 1881, found guilty, and sentenced to execution by hanging. McCarty escaped from jail on April 30, killing two deputies in the process. Sheriff Garrett led a search team to find McCarty. Garrett shot and killed McCarty in the bedroom of a ranch in Fort Sumner, New Mexico, on July 14, 1881. Billy the Kid was 21 or 22 at the time of his death.

The exact number of people McCarty killed is in doubt, with some estimates at 27 and other claims that the actual figure was as low as 4, and that he was a participant or involved in 6 more. One popular myth is that he killed 21 men, one murder for each of his 21 years of life. McCarty is believed to have committed his first murder at age 12 but this is in doubt. In fact, some sources suggest that he was a normal youth until his mid-teens. Billy the Kid was a legend before his death, and was the object of popular fascination, and much like the Depression-era robbers and murderers 50 years later, he acquired a Robin Hood image, although it was never seriously suggested or proved that McCarty possessed any altruistic or charitable qualities. Some have suggested that Billy the Kid lived much longer under the name Ollie (Brushy Bill) Roberts, and that he lived the rest of his life in Mexico and Texas until his death in 1950, but the greater consensus is that Billy the Kid died in 1881.

Sources: Billy the kid. (2008). In *Encyclopaedia Britannica*. Accessed February 17, 2008, from Encyclopaedia Britannica Online: http://search.eb.com/eb/article-9079214; Robert M. Utley. "Billy the Kid"; http://www.anb.org/articles/20/20-00069.html; *American National Biography Online* Feb. 2000, retrieved February 17, 2008.

settlement that disorder developed. The lack of law enforcement created a severe vacuum that was filled by the private organization of vigilante groups. In a very real sense, both initiatives can be seen as similar in motivation and in execution. There was an abstract ideal of how societies should function and how individuals should behave toward one another. In the small, self-selecting group setting out on the overland trail, consent by all established a little government with common views and a shared trust in the integrity of one another. In the large, diverse, and fluid society of frontier cities, farms, ranches, and mining areas, such a consensus was impossible to achieve. Those in the community who owned property and sought a stable life free of violence joined together to provide a mechanism to restrain violence and protect property rights and life itself. Expulsion from a wagon train for noncompliance with the rules laid down by the company was a harsh sanction, as was summary justice at the hands of a vigilante committee.

The American frontier experience suggests that there cannot be a vacuum in law enforcement, nor can there be a situation in which there is no applicable law. Group consensus or community pressure establishes standards of conduct and methods for their enforcement. Vigilantism and other similar forms of self-help law enforcement arise because criminal activity cannot be allowed to threaten the existence of any society. The methods chosen for such informal police activities may be excessively violent and completely arbitrary by any legal standard, but their principal recommendation is that they work. By way of a corollary, police institutions must always be adequate to protect society. Failure in this vital task will cause the development of parallel extralegal organizations created to supplement, or even to replace, regular police activity.

While many historians identify the frontier as the source of American democratic virtues and self-reliance, others trace violence and disorder in national life to the frontier experience. Resorting to self-help law enforcement encourages violence and the likelihood of revenge killings. Widespread access to and use of firearms in the nineteenth century may well reflect how frontier attitudes penetrated the settled areas of the East. There is evidence that American individualism surfaced frequently in physical attacks that ended in mayhem or death.

The picture of the establishment of policing across the United States is complex. In part, the influence of the Metropolitan Police of London is clear. But an older regime also moved into place as the West developed, and the sheriff assisted by local homeowners is closer in style to the shire reeve and "hue and cry" than what Peel established for London. We should also not ignore the influence of France, a country that remodeled its own police after the Revolution, retaining the military Gendarmerie but also creating a new police entity, the civilian force for the cities, the Police Nationale. How close a fit is the Police Nationale to the municipal police of America?

As the century progressed and President Abraham Lincoln signed into effect the establishment of the Secret Service on the day of his own assassination, a question was posed: is there any European model for federal policing or is this entirely and uniquely American construct? In 1850, as he established the first private detective agency office in Chicago, Alan Pinkerton referred to himself as "The Vidocq of the West." By the end of the nineteenth century, unemployment was at 20 percent, and more than 600 banks had closed. Unions started to become a force in U.S. employment and this contributed significantly to the impending transformation of U.S. policing into generalist public and specialized (industry) private. As the nineteenth century ended, it was the United States that embraced the establishment of private policing alongside local, state, and federal agencies, and it would take Europe another 70 years before it created federal, Euro-wide police agencies and outsourcing to private security companies.

However, the links are there. Bobbies, cops (coppers), and flics (as the police are referred to in France) have all exchanged styles and origins whether the politicians of the day have embraced the idea or not. Peel would probably have introduced a Gendarmerie to London if he believed it was not political suicide, and it is difficult to argue that he did not introduce a Gendarmerie to Ireland, a military styled constabulary that lives in barracks outside of the towns they police, armed, with military ranks, and required to police communities where local officers might feel compromised due to local allegiances and relationships—this sounds like a Gendarmerie. If one accepts this position, then the United States got a Gendarmerie also. In 1905, as a result of strikes by coal miners in Pennsylvania, the culminating event being The Great Anthracite Strike of 1902, Governor *Samuel Pennypacker* sought help in creating a police force that would be prepared to break the picket lines. His problem was that local police officers were uncomfortable with arresting local men they knew and in some cases were related to. The solution was the creation of a state police force that would be available to move around the state as needed and a force that was not attached to a local community

TIME CAPSULE: BRITISH LAW ENFORCEMENT IN INDIA

The imprint of the British Empire is still present in many respects in many of their former colonial territories, including law enforcement. The British imposed their law enforcement methods while trying to make allowances for cultural differences in the countries under their dominion with varying degrees of success. A prominent Briton in the history of colonial India's law enforcement history is Sir Charles James Napier (1782-1853). A career military man in an era when the military often acted as civilian law enforcers in British colonies, Napier began his career in Ireland, which was also under the dominion of the British at the time.

Napier was sent to India in 1841 to take over the Sind province in Western India (present-day Pakistan). He succeeded in taking over the Sind province and ruled as its military administrator, often usurping the territory of traditional rulers in the area. He established a police agency based on the Royal Irish Constabulary, while trying to take into account some of the differences between British and Indian culture. Napier took the unusual step of separating the civilian police force from the military, something that was slowly taking hold in Great Britain at the time. However, because the primary job of civilian police was order maintenance as opposed to crime detection and investigation, the civilian and military agencies sometimes merged, which

was especially necessary at times given that the British were viewed with hostility by many Indians, who viewed them as occupiers. Despite the fact that most Indians wanted to rid themselves of British occupation, Napier reportedly was a more benevolent administrator than those who had preceded him.

Napier divided the province into three districts and he divided the police into three different units. Each district had a mounted division, which was primarily used for patrol. Each district also had a rural unit, whose main job was guard duty and general support for various government functions. Finally, each district had an urban unit, whose main task was crime detection and prevention, an idea that was rather advanced for the time.

Napier was a very competent administrator and a skilled organizer. His methods of organizing law enforcement were copied throughout the British Empire, which, whether fortunately or unfortunately, helped enable the British to maintain their hold on their colonies throughout the nineteenth century.

Source: Axelrod, A., Phillips, C., & Kemper, K. (1996). *Cops, crooks and criminologists: An international biographical dictionary of law enforcement*. New York: Facts on File.

and consequently had allegiances to that community that prevented effective policing. This solution copied the model of policing that was in Ireland, one that we have suggested actually closely resembled the French Gendarmes. Therefore, Governor Pennypacker created a statewide constabulary for Pennsylvania in 1905. It was modeled upon the Irish constabulary. This new statewide force consisting of 228 officers was divided into four troops across the state.

So, perhaps there are clear examples of the influence of the French police in the United States, alongside twelfth-century shire reeves, Metropolitan police officers, Principal Officers from Bow Street, and a French criminal called Vidocq who became a model for private investigations, as well as numerous detective police departments.

SUMMARY

Examination of the policing systems that developed in France and England during the seventeenth, eighteenth, and nineteenth centuries reveals fundamental differences. France, prior to the Norman Conquest, already manifested tendencies toward a national policing system in the Roman tradition, whereas England continued to rely on the principle of community self-policing that had prevailed in the Anglo-Saxon period. Although cause cannot always be distinguished from effect, it is likely that the chronic political instability in France was responsible for the invasive, even repressive, police characteristics of this period. Unlike English police, whose main duty was enforcement of criminal law, French police were also accorded a wide range of responsibilities that included matters left to the administrative realm in England. In the geographic area that became the United States, predominance of English institutions meant that the narrower definition of police power became the principle followed in American policing.

While a wide variety of circumstances were responsible for the institution of organized police departments in London, New York, Boston, and Charleston, it is clear that each of these institutions reflects the society that gave it birth. Each is a product of the historical forces at play when it was organized; and each reflects public attitudes toward crime, the liberties of citizens, the maintenance of order, and the necessary conditions for the stability of urban life. Because the cities were in the forefront of economic and social change, they were the first to alter the old justice/constable system of law enforcement. Only after the middle of the nineteenth century did provincial towns and rural areas begin to follow the lead set by urban areas, but those law enforcement agencies faced different challenges and responded to crime in very different ways.

American diversity in law enforcement between the North, South, and West reflected the regionalism that would tear the nation apart in the four decades after 1860, first with the North-South conflict in the American Civil War, followed by the bitter Reconstruction period and, subsequently, by a farmers' movement that pitted the West against the financial East. Prison reform was a northern problem; slave discipline preoccupied the South; and the establishment of normal governmental and policing institutions was a continuing concern in the West.

Early nineteenth-century experience with police organization indicates that traditional forms of law enforcement change only when there is a pressing need for reform. Crime waves, new challenges to social stability, changing attitudes toward violence, and new emphasis on the security of property all play important roles in law enforcement reform. Different cultures place varying importance on police protection, but none is willing to do without a system of law enforcement. Where public police organizations are absent or inadequate, private initiative will supply either a consensual basis for orderly government or a forceful vigilante movement to enforce popularly accepted standards of behavior. A creation of the people, the police also depend heavily on the people. Each successful police reform dealt with public opinion. Each measured its actions by the popular acceptance of its programs, and each recognized that, while a people may give police organizations power to enforce the law, the gift is given grudgingly and with suspicion.

REFERENCES

Ascoli, D. (1979). *The queen's peace: The origins and development of the metropolitan police, 1829-1979.* London: Hamish Hamilton; Critchley, T. A. (1978). *A history of police in England and Wales* (2nd ed). London: Constable & Co; Melville Lee, W. L. (1901). *A History of Police in England.* London: Methuen, reprinted Montclair, NJ: Patterson Smith; Radzinowicz, L. (1971). *A history of English criminal law and its administration from 1750.* 5 Vols. London: Stephens. pp. 1948-1986, Smith, P. T. (1985). *Policing Victorian London: Political policing, public order and the London metropolitan police.* Westport, CT: Greenwood Press; Tobias, J. J. (1979). *Crime and police in England, 1700-1900.* New York: St. Martin's Press; and good materials comparing London and New York police forces are found in Miller, W. R. (1977). *Cops and bobbies: Police authority in New York and London, 1830-1870.* Chicago: University of Chicago Press.

Richardson, J. F. (1974). *Urban police in the United States.* Port Washington, NY: Kennikat Press; Emsley, C., & Weinberger, B. (1991). *Policing West Europe: Politics, professionalism, and public order, 1850-1940.* New York: Greenwood Press; Skolnick, J. H., & Gray, T. C. (1975). *Police in America.* Boston: Education Associates; Astor, G. (1971). *The New York cops: An informal history.* New York: Charles Scribner's Sons; and in the more scholarly Richardson, J. F. (1970). *The New York police: Colonial times to 1901.* New York: Oxford University Press; Lane, R. (1967). *Policing the city: Boston, 1822-1885.* Cambridge: Harvard University Press; Cantwell, E. P. (1909). *A history of the Charleston police force.* Charleston: Daggett Printing Co Yearbook, 1908, City of Charleston; Henry, H. M. (1968). *The police control of the slave in South Carolina.* New York: Negro Universities Press reprint ed; Hindus, M. S. (1980). *Prison and plantation: Crime, justice and authority in Massachusetts and South Carolina, 1767-1878*. Chapel Hill: University of North Carolina Press; O'Neall, J. B. (1848). *The Negro law of South Carolina*. Columbia: John G. Bowman; Wintersmith, R. F. (1974). *Police and the black community*. Lexington: Lexington Books.

Brown, R. M. (1975). *Strain of violence: Historical studies of American Violence and Vigilantism*. New York: Oxford University Press; McGrath, R. D. (1984). *Gunfighters, highwaymen, and vigilantes: Violence on the frontier*. Berkeley: University of California Press; Nielsen, M. O. (Ed.), (1996). *Native Americans, crime, and justice*. Boulder, CO: Westview Press.

Nieman, D. G. (1991). *Promises to keep: African-Americans and the constitutional order, 1776 to the present*. New York: Oxford University Press; Gard, W. (1949). *Frontier justice*. Norman: University of Oklahoma Press; Nolan, P. B. (1987). *Vigilantes on the middle border: A study of self-appointed law enforcement in the states of the upper Mississippi from 1840 to 1880*. New York: Garland; Cresswell, S. (1991). *Mormons, cowboys, moonshiners, and klansmen: Federal law enforcement in the South and West, 1870-1893*. Tuscaloosa: University of Alabama Press; Culberson, W. C. (1990). *Vigilantism: Political history of private power in America*. New York: Greenwood Press.

Shapiro, B. M. (1993). *Revolutionary justice in Paris, 1789-1790*. Cambridge: Cambridge University Press; Fouché, Arnold, E. A. (1979). *Napoleon, and the general police*. Washington: University Press of American; Forstenzer, T. R. (1981). *French provincial police and the fall of the second republic: Social fear and counterrevolution*. Princeton: Princeton University Press; Cobb, R. C. (1970). *The police and the people: French popular protest, 1789-1820*. Oxford: Clarendon Press; Galtier-Boissiére, J. (1938). *Mysteries of the French secret police*. London: Stanley Paul & Company; Canler, L. (1976). *Autobiography of a French detective from 1818 to 1858*. New York: Arno Press; Stead, P. J. (1983). *The police of France*. London: Collier Macmillan Publishers.

Edwards, S. (1977). *The Vidocq dossier: The story of the world's first detective*. Boston: Houghton Mifflin Company.

Notes and Problems

1. A recurring theme throughout this chapter is the need to balance efficiency in law enforcement against the danger that police will destroy the liberties of a free people. When comparing patterns of policing in France and England, consider whether there is a link between political instability and repressive police policies. Is that fear realistic?

2. How did nineteenth-century reformers attempt to deal with public fears? To what degree did each police department owe its existence to the need for control of an "out group" in society, such as political opponents, immigrants, slaves, or disenfranchised English workingmen?

3. Public acceptance and cooperation are essential to police work. What means were taken by the French police authorities of the nineteenth century to assure these prerequisites? What means were taken by the English and American police authorities?

4. Does psychological distance between a patrol officer and civilians on his or her beat work better than close familiarity? In this regard, compare the London and New York police departments.

5. What functions do uniforms play in police operations and administration? Why did the London police wait until 1842 to place their detectives in plain clothes? Why did New York policemen resist wearing uniforms while Charleston police seem to have glorified in their uniforms and weaponry?

6. Much ado was made in the nineteenth century about the need for a "preventive" police function, where the visibility of the police force made crime less likely because

it put fear in the hearts of would-be criminals. This, of course, was the beginning of an emphasis on patrol; but the night watchmen and constables also patrolled. Is it just that there were more law enforcement officials on the beat, or was there a qualitative change in the way in which the individual patrolmen acted as a first line of defense against criminal activity?

7. To what extent was preventive patrolling a product of the idea that identifiable "lower classes" or "criminal classes" are responsible for crime? This can be seen in London police practice, which placed a larger number of policemen in the areas where middle-class homes bordered on working-class districts. Of course, that did not restrict crime in working-class areas, which tended to have fewer police if they were isolated from "respectable" parts of town. On the other hand, "respectable" areas out of the reach of the "criminal class" were not heavily patrolled. The question arises "What happened when public transportation made all parts of a city accessible to the 'criminal classes'?" Did all this contribute to the rise of the suburbs?

ENDNOTES

[1]The justice of the peace and constable system is discussed in Chapters 5 and 6.

[2]Quoted in Melville Lee, W. L. (1971). *A history of police in England.* London: Methuen, 1901; reprint, Montclair, NJ: Patterson Smith, p. 184.

[3]Radzinowicz, L. (1948-1986). *A history of English criminal law and its administration from 1750, 5 vols.* London: Stephens, vol. 2, p. 263.

[4]Radzinowicz, A History, 263.

[5]Miller, W. R. (1977). *Cops and bobbies: Police authority in New York and London, 1830-1870.* Chicago: University of Chicago Press.

[6]Hindus, M. S. (1980). *Prison and plantation: Crime, justice and authority in Massachusetts and South Carolina, 1767-1878.* Chapel Hill: University of North Carolina Press.

[7]Reid, J. P. (1976). Dividing the elephant: The separation of mess and joint stock property on the overland trail. *Hastings Law Journal, 28,* 73; (1977). Sharing the elephant: Partnership and concurrent property on the overland trail. *University of Missouri, Kansas City, Law Review, 45,* 207; (1977). Tied to the elephant: Organization and obligation on the overland trail. *University of Puget Sound Law Review, 1,* 139; (1977). Paying for the elephant: Property rights and civil order on the overland trail. *Huntington Library Quarterly, 41,* 9-64.

[8]Brown, R. M. (1975). *Strain of violence: Historical studies of American violence and vigilantism.* New York: Oxford University Press.

CHAPTER 11

Turning Points in Criminal Justice (1787-1910)

KEY TERMS

1833 Nullification Controversy

Abraham Lincoln

Allan Pinkerton

Andrew Johnson

Captains of industry

Charles Bonaparte

City machine

Draft riots

Dred Scott

Equal protection

Federal income tax law

Fourteenth Amendment

Fugitive Slave Act

Henry Wirz

Impeachment

Interstate Commerce Commission

Jefferson Davis

John Wilkes Booth

Mann White Slave Traffic Act

Monopoly

Peculiar institution

Posse Comitatus Act

Pure Food and Drug Act of 1906

Robber barons

Robert E. Lee

Roger B. Taney

Secret Service

Sherman Anti-Trust Act

State interposition

Suspension of the writ of *habeas corpus*

Tammany Hall

Theodore Roosevelt

Third Department

Ulysses S. Grant

Underground Railroad

Watering of stock

William Marcy Tweed

William McKinley

William P. Wood

LEARNING OBJECTIVES

1. Learn some of the conflicts that occurred as a result of the assertions of states' rights.
2. Understand how slavery intersected with criminal justice.
3. Understand the facts and implications of the *Dred Scott* case.
4. Learn about the Fourteenth Amendment and its significance.

5. Learn some of the ways in which the Civil War affected criminal justice.
6. Understand the implications of unbridled capitalism as exercised by the robber barons.
7. Learn about the creation and early mission of the Secret Service.
8. Learn some of the ways in which the federal government's role in crime control expanded.
9. Learn about the assassination of Abraham Lincoln.

Table 11.1 Time Line: Turning Points in Criminal Justice (1787-1910)

1787-1789	A convention of delegates from each of the states meets in Philadelphia to prepare a Constitution of the United States. The Constitution is ratified by state-ratifying conventions held from 1787 through 1789.
1812, 1816	The United States Supreme Court declares that there are no federal common law crimes; all federal crimes must be established by the enactment of a congressional statute.
1819, 1824	Opinions of the U.S. Supreme Court declare the supremacy of the federal government in matters committed to it by the Constitution.
1820	The Missouri Compromise, adopted as a federal statute, divides the Louisiana Territory into "slave" and "free" sections. It was declared unconstitutional in 1857 by the *Dred Scott* case.
1833	South Carolina "nullifies" the 1828 federal tariff; President Andrew Jackson threatens to use federal troops to enforce the law, if necessary. The state finally agrees to compromise tariff measure, but passes an act "nullifying" the President's authorization to use the army to enforce the 1828 tariff.
1850	The Compromise of 1850 establishes popular sovereignty in the territory ceded to the U.S. by Mexico in 1848. It also abolishes the slave trade in the District of Columbia, and strengthens the administration of the fugitive slave laws.
1856	Civil war breaks out in Kansas Territory, fueled by disagreements between slave-owning settlers and "free soil" proponents.
1857	The U.S. Supreme Court announces its decision in *Dred Scott v. Sandford*, declaring that the Missouri Compromise was unconstitutional because it deprived southern slave owners of their property without due process of law. The case also defined state citizenship as primary and a prerequisite for U.S. citizenship. For this reason, blacks could not become citizens of the United States unless the state in which they resided recognized them as citizens.
1859	John Brown, having murdered five proslavery settlers in Kansas in 1856, stages an attack on Harper's Ferry, Virginia, intending to start a slave insurrection. He fails in gaining support, and his small band of abolitionists are defeated and captured by federal troops. Brown is convicted of treason and hanged in October 1859.
1860	In the 1860 presidential campaign, Abraham Lincoln defeats Stephen F. Douglas, and southern political leaders begin to speak out for secession.
1860-1861	South Carolina's legislature passes an ordinance declaring the state's secession from the Union.
1861	Southern state delegates adopt a provisional constitution for the Confederate States of America; U.S. military installations and post offices were seized, and Jefferson Davis was elected President of the Confederacy.
1861-1865	The Civil War is fought, primarily in the south, with Confederate military incursions repulsed at Antietam, Maryland, and Gettysburg, Pennsylvania. General Robert E. Lee surrenders at Appomattox Courthouse in April 1865, but some scattered Confederate military units continue to fight in Texas until August 1865.

Table 11.1 Time Line: Turning Points in Criminal Justice (1787-1910)—cont'd

1863	President Lincoln signs the Emancipation Proclamation, declaring that Blacks held in slavery in territory occupied by the Confederacy are free.
1863	Five days of racially charged rioting against draft laws leave 11 blacks dead in New York City.
1865	The Thirteenth Amendment, abolishing slavery throughout the United States, is ratified.
1866-1871	"Boss" Tweed gains political control of New York City and, through manipulation of city contracts, becomes wealthy and controls access to public office. Convicted in 1871, he serves 4 years in prison before his death.
1867	The U.S. Secret Service, an agency within the Treasury Department, is authorized to investigate fraud against the U.S. government. It subsequently is assigned duties for the protection of the President, and to investigate the activities of the Ku Klux Klan.
1868	President Andrew Johnson is impeached by the House of Representatives for violation of the Tenure of Office Act of 1867. He is acquitted by the Senate on May 16, 1868.
1868	The Fourteenth Amendment is ratified. It grants U.S. citizenship to all persons born or naturalized within the U.S., and requires that these citizens be recognized as citizens by the states in which they reside. It prohibits states from denying due process or equal protection of the law to U.S. citizens.
1887-1918	The federal government implements a stronger enforcement of its power to regulate and, in some instances, prohibit the flow of interstate commerce.
1907	The Bureau of Investigation of the Department of Justice is established. In 1932, it becomes the Federal Bureau of Investigation.

Perhaps the greatest dividing point in U.S. history is the Civil War. The war between the industrial and immigrant North, and the agrarian and nativist South permanently altered the history of the United States. No student of criminal justice can afford to ignore the Civil War because it changed the way the nation was governed, and it profoundly altered the way men and women looked at law and social issues. For nearly 90 years, Americans had thought of themselves as citizens of a given state or geographical region; that provincialism carried with it a preference for long-established ways of life and an isolation from new ideas and political concepts. Police systems in the three major regions differed markedly and, to a degree, reflected local development and cultural preferences.

Prewar America was modeled on the preferences of the men who drafted the federal Constitution in 1787. Strongly influenced by the Enlightenment and resistance to British imperial policy, American Revolutionary leaders sought to restrict political power and thus ensure individual freedom and liberty.

One essential principle was the vesting of most coercive power in the states and restricting the authority of the federal government. That was particularly so in the case of criminal law and its enforcement. It was felt that the exercise of criminal justice was best retained by the states. There its abuse could best be controlled by the people, who, through close surveillance of an officeholder and control of the ballot box, would protect individuals against the abuse of law enforcement authority.

Early in the history of the republic, the United States Supreme Court held that there could be no common law crime against the United States. All federal crimes had to be clearly set forth in a congressional statute, giving warning to all would-be offenders. In addition, there was a belief that all federal law enforcement had to be tied to one or more of the express legislative powers delegated to Congress by the Constitution. Thus, penalties might be established for counterfeiting coins of the federal government, for bribing customs officials, or for violating trade restrictions in oceanic commerce, but the federal government could not prosecute an individual for murder or theft because no express congressional power related to those offenses.

If the states appeared to be the dynamic and active agencies of American government, that was exactly what the founding fathers intended and what their descendants preferred. However, such a compartmentalization of law into state jurisdictions did not entirely serve the broad purpose of the federal Constitution. The initial impulse toward drafting the Constitution came from the need to increase trade between the various states, thereby rendering them less dependent on European nations and creating an economic common market.

These relationships between the states required some modification of states' powers. This was particularly the case in regard to fugitive slaves, runaway indentured servants, and criminals who fled from one state to another to avoid either arrest or imprisonment. Trade requires the easy transportation of goods between one place and another, and this frequently necessitated crossing state boundary lines. The collection of debts in other states, the preparation of contracts between merchants of different states, and the recognition of the statutory law and the court judgments of sister states all formed a part of the legal apparatus upon which American economic prosperity depended.

The 1787 Constitution also erected a government that, while federal in its domestic politics, was a single nation in its conduct of foreign relations. The President and Congress (more specifically, the Senate) dealt with diplomatic affairs, a power denied to the various states. The supremacy clause of the Constitution provided that treaties entered into by the United States were to be the supreme law of the land. It also provided that congressional statutes passed in accordance with the powers granted by the Constitution would be superior to state laws and that state laws in conflict with federal statutes would be of no effect.

This balance between state and federal power existed tenuously, if at all, in the years from 1789 to 1833. At the latter date, a strong nullification movement on the part of South Carolina threatened to wreck the Union on the rocks of state sovereignty. South Carolina called upon its concept of state power to reject, or nullify, federal law that it viewed as unfair to its state. Thus was born the principle of *state interposition*, that a state government might shield its people from the force of a federal statute. The *1833 Nullification Controversy* ended in a standoff between President Andrew Jackson and South Carolina authorities, but the real issue was one of state sovereignty against national power in dealing with slavery. This also had been touched upon in the federal Constitution, but by way of silence. Despite the vast hordes of blacks held in slavery, no provision in the Constitution contained the word *slave*. Certain "persons" were to be enumerated for electoral purposes as being three-fifths of a person, and individuals who fled their states to avoid "servitude" were subject to extradition.

Either unable or unwilling to deal with the issue of slavery, the founding fathers had retained the status quo, and the law of slavery remained the law of the several states in which the institution survived. The expediency of this solution is apparent in the fact that before 1848 slavery was, for all intents and purposes, a matter of state law. Well entrenched in the South and insulated from federal intrusion, the *"peculiar institution"* flourished in the balmy climate of state sovereignty.

Success in the Mexican War (1846-1848) brought new territories into the federal Union and revived the issue of slavery in America's new western territories. Southern planters awoke to the need to expand westward into more fertile lands, taking their slaves with them; at the same time, the activities of abolitionists and the success of the *underground railroad* (a series of shelters to aid slaves fleeing north to freedom) triggered interest in a strengthening of the federal fugitive slave laws. In many respects, it was not slavery that brought on the Civil War but the southern demand for expansion of slavery into the territories and an equally strong southern insistence that blacks fleeing slavery should be subject to arrest and extradition from northern nonslave states.

HISTORY TODAY

The Underground Railroad is an example of people willfully breaking the law because they were answering a higher calling, from their conscience or from God. Is there any cause that might lead you to feel justified in breaking the law?

This summary of the constitutional situation before the Civil War provides nothing more than an inkling of the complexity of the constitutional and legal issues that preceded the conflict. It does suggest that neither the North nor the South was particularly consistent in its support of states' rights or national power. Each was willing to use constitutional theory for its own economic and political purposes; thus, each contributed to new modes of legal thought and constitutional principles.

That the Civil War occurred is of primary importance; that it happened when it did is also of historical relevance. Urbanization and industrialization began to alter the North and require the institution of formal police organizations modeled on that of London.[1] Economic growth and diversification was moving the United States toward a position in world power that could not be evaded even by traditional American methods of cultural isolation. The United States experienced a burgeoning enthusiasm and national pride in the mid-nineteenth century that, although deflected somewhat by the painful war years, pressed on to explore the great riches of the North American continent and to build the United States into one of the great nations of the world.

Elimination of the institution of slavery from southern life meant a major restructuring of that regional society and its economic system, but it also meant that southern entrepreneurs shared in the values of their northern industrial counterparts. Relieved by the Confederacy's surrender of the need to debate slavery in the territories, southerner and northerner alike got on with the serious business of making money in the mines, farms, and grazing lands of the West.

To say that the United States was not a nation in 1789 is incorrect, for there were high points of national power even in the orientation toward states' rights. However, it is accurate to view the nation as one that was governed primarily by state agencies and institutions. The Civil War, both in its inception and in its conduct, challenged the primacy of the states and confirmed the growing power of the federal government. Yet the inexorable growth of the American economy and the transcontinental expanse of the national territory created new demands for federal authority that might well have surfaced independently of the Civil War.

CONSTITUTIONAL ISSUES AND CRIMINAL LAW

FIGURE 11.1 Roger B. Taney, Chief Justice of the United States. *Library of Congress.*

The identity of citizen and state works well in the context of a centralized political unit, but is beset with difficulties when forced to operate in a federated government where sovereignty is divided between constituent states and a central government. The problem was most starkly presented in the *Dred Scott* case (19 Howard 393), decided by the United States Supreme Court in 1857. Scott, a slave belonging to an Army officer, traveled with his master to the free states of Wisconsin and Illinois. Scott claimed that, because the law of those jurisdictions did not recognize slavery, he was, in fact, a free man even after the two of them returned to Missouri, a slave state.

The *Dred Scott* case clearly presented a question of status; Scott could not sue in the federal courts unless he was a citizen, and his citizenship had to be based upon his residence in a free state. Led by Chief Justice *Roger B. Taney*, the Court held that citizenship was a matter of state law and that each state had the right to determine who was entitled to citizenship. In other words, when Dred Scott moved from Wisconsin to Missouri, he could not take his citizenship with him. There was no national citizenship in prewar America, only state citizenship, which carried with it (almost as an afterthought) federal citizenship. Although the Supreme Court may have thought it was deftly using the *Scott* case to avoid conflict, the effect was just the opposite. Many antislavery forces saw the *Dred Scott* case as the last straw—the final attempt to use the law to end slavery. The schism between North and South was not helped by the *Dred Scott* decision; it was deepened.

HISTORY TODAY

Almost all Americans would agree that the Supreme Court made the wrong decision in the Dred Scott case. Consider some Supreme Court rulings from more recent years or ones that you will hear about in the years to come. How do you think history will judge these rulings? Will there be any rulings that will be as universally derided as Dred Scott?

The Civil War began in 1861 and officially ended in 1865. In the years immediately following the Civil War, it was deemed necessary to protect free blacks against actions by state governments that would deprive them of their civil rights, and the *Fourteenth Amendment* was ratified as the instrument to ensure the citizenship of free blacks wherever they might choose to reside:

> Roger Taney (1777-1864): Maryland native; part of a slave-owning family; served as Attorney General of the United States under President Andrew Jackson in the 1830s; nominated to U.S. Supreme Court by President Jackson; never recovered from the criticism he received over the *Dred Scott* decision, which helped lead the U.S. into Civil War; died during the Civil War.

> All persons born or naturalized in the United States, and subject to the jurisdiction thereof, are citizens of the United States and of the State wherein they reside. No State shall make or enforce any law which shall abridge the privileges or immunities of citizens of the United States; nor shall any State deprive any person of life, liberty or property, without due process of law; nor deny to any person within its jurisdiction the equal protection of the laws.[2]

As a result of the Fourteenth Amendment, U.S. citizenship was primary, and state citizenship resulted whenever a federal citizen chose to reside in any given state.

Furthermore, the Amendment recognized privileges and immunities of citizens of the United States, wherever they might reside, and protected them against state action. Also forbidden were state deprivations of life, liberty, or property, except through the use of due process of law. Finally, persons were guaranteed *equal protection* of the laws and states were forbidden to deny equality in the application of their laws. These are sweeping guarantees for the security of the individual against state action.

Originally, the U.S. Supreme Court seemed inclined to limit their application to the specific situation of freed blacks, but ultimately the Fourteenth Amendment has become the focal point for the exercise of federal control over state criminal procedure. It applies to all citizens, male or female, and of all racial backgrounds; in certain cases, it has also been held to apply to resident aliens, minor children, and individuals who are mentally disturbed, retarded, or unable to act for themselves.

The due process of law provision earlier appeared in the Fifth Amendment to the federal Constitution, adopted in 1791. It had been held to restrict federal action that took a citizen's life, liberty, or property, but not to inhibit the states in their criminal procedures or property seizures. Ironically, it was the Fifth Amendment's due process clause that Chief Justice Taney invoked to reason that, to the extent that the Missouri Compromise (which divided the Louisiana Territory into free and slave sections, making Wisconsin a free state) freed Scott from slavery, it took his master's property without due process of law. As such, it was unconstitutional, null, and void.

The same phrase was inserted in the Fourteenth Amendment to protect individuals against harsh or irregular procedures on the part of state authorities. Subsequent legal development would expand the due process clause into two significant protections for individuals: Procedural due process requires that state (and federal) governments follow preestablished and fair procedures in taking criminal or civil action against a person. Substantive due process goes even further. It asserts that, even if all the proper procedures are followed, there are limits beyond which a government may not go without unconstitutionally violating the rights of its citizens.

GOVERNMENT AT FLOOD TIDE

The Civil War itself added a new dimension to governmental power. With few exceptions, the administration of federal power was nearly invisible in prewar American life, and when it emerged, resistance by the states or among the people tended to blunt federal initiatives. One example was the enactment of the *Fugitive Slave Act* provisions of the Compromise of 1850, which were designed to use federal officials and special procedures to secure the extradition of slaves from free states. Mob violence and state obstruction severely hampered the implementation of this law, exhibiting the dearth of coercive power in the central government and serving only to heighten northern antipathy to the growing pro-southern policy of the presidents and Congress. For the most part, Americans were lightly governed. They liked it that way and reacted strongly when federal officials attempted to introduce unpopular practices into the various states.

Abraham Lincoln (1809-1865): Sixteenth President of the United States; served as President and Commander-in-Chief during the Civil War; practiced law; served in the Illinois legislature and the U.S. House of Representatives before election as President; personally opposed slavery but was willing to tolerate slavery if it meant holding the Union together.

Various southern states, usually led by South Carolina, had threatened to secede from the United States at various points throughout the history of the young American republic. For South Carolina, the election of *Abraham Lincoln* to the Presidency in the fall of 1860 was the final trigger. South Carolina seceded in December 1860; other southern states eventually followed. But the secession of the southern states did not automatically trigger war. Many in the North were content to let the South secede, until the Confederate attack on the United States military installation at Fort Sumter, South

FEATURED OUTLAW: CAPTAIN HENRY WIRZ

At the end of the Civil War, in a precedent-setting case, Captain Henry Wirz was tried and executed for war crimes. In March 1864, Captain Wirz of the Confederate Army had been assigned the post of keeper of the inner prison at Andersonville, Georgia, and remained until the prison closed in April 1865. Soon afterward, Wirz was arrested and arraigned on charges of war crimes and murder. Wirz was accused of combining, confederating, and conspiring together with John H. Winder, Richard B. Winder, Isaiah H. White, W. S. Winder, R. R. Stevenson, and others unknown, to injure the health and destroy the lives of federal soldiers held as prisoners of war. He was also charged with 13 specific murders "in violation of the laws and customs of war."

There was no dispute regarding the egregious condition of federal prisoners in the Confederate prisoner of war camp known as Andersonville; they suffered, and many died, from malnutrition, dysentery, and other diseases and from inadequate shelter and sanitation. The press fanned hatred of Wirz with labels such as fiend, savage, barbarian, and bloodthirsty monster. In his defense, Wirz claimed that he had struggled to provide humane conditions for the federal prisoners but was unable to do so. He cited the lack of supplies in a government that faced critical shortages of food, medicine, and housing for its own military and civilian personnel, and he also pointed to a lack of cooperation by government officials. The plight of the prisoners was exacerbated by the refusal of the federal government to exchange prisoners and by the policy of listing medicine as contraband.

On August 23, 1865, Wirz was brought to trial before a military tribunal. In the words of one historian, "Wirz was a dead man from the start" (Marvel, 1994: 243). Serious questions were raised then and later concerning the degree to which Wirz had a fair trial. At the time, critics protested trial by court-martial rather than civilian court. The testimony of government witnesses was in part internally contradictory and in part did not conform to known facts; furthermore, some key witnesses had received rewards from the government. Persons who wanted to testify in Wirz's defense claimed they were unable to do so. Whether Wirz deliberately and maliciously mistreated prisoners remains in dispute.

Wirz's superior officer at Andersonville, General John H. Winder, had died prior to the trial and none of the named conspirators was tried. Nevertheless, Wirz was found guilty of conspiracy. He was also found guilty of 11 of the specified murders, even though he was on sick leave at the time four of them occurred. An appeal for clemency was denied and he was executed in November 1865.

Bitter controversy surrounded the trial and it has continued to prompt analysis. Contemporaries and historians have questioned whether the demonization of Wirz and his execution were designed to serve the political purpose of forcing Confederates to face their responsibility for having caused the misery of war. Jefferson Davis rose to the defense of Wirz as a martyr to a cause through adherence to the truth, and the United Daughters of the Confederacy managed to have a monument erected in Wirz's memory.

Source: Marvel, W. (1994). *Andersonville: The last depot.* Chapel Hill: University of North Carolina Press.

Carolina. The Civil War officially began with that attack, which occurred in April 1861, 5 months after South Carolina seceded. Many in the North were outraged at the attack, and the War was on.

HISTORY TODAY

Today, the term *war criminal* is part of our vocabulary. The World Court in The Netherlands has tried numerous former government leaders for crimes against humanity or war crimes. The United States deals with the issue of war criminals, including citizens of other countries, and crimes committed by American military personnel. Given that war is by definition organized killing, and given that government leaders usually are the initiators of wars, how easy is it to decide whether a soldier or government leader is a war criminal?

FIGURE 11.2 Keeper of the inner prison at the Andersonville, Georgia, prisoner of war camp for federal soldiers, Henry Wirz was charged with war crimes and was convicted of conspiracy. *Library of Congress.*

The control of internal dissent, with the related task of combating espionage and sabotage, was a primary concern of Lincoln's administration. The task was complicated by the fact that disloyal activities were not prohibited by any federal statute. In retrospect, it might seem obvious that the South and the North were clearly divided with one group on one side and the other group on the other side. However, the truth was more complex. There were divided loyalties within states, within cities, and even within families. In addition, several slave states, Maryland (the most proximate state to the nation's capital) among them, had many residents who were sympathetic to the Confederacy.

The sanctions for treason applied to the northern supporters of the Confederacy, and the constitutionally defined offense of treason was one that had been narrowly construed and subject to stringent standards of proof. Lincoln and his advisers resorted to *suspension of the writ of habeas corpus* (thereby permitting military retention of civilian offenders without the privilege of recourse to civilian courts) and a series of emergency actions designed to maintain order, even as the Union army took form for the long struggle that awaited it. Ultimately, a series of federal statutes made provision for the prosecution of disloyalty in the form of espionage, sabotage, and resistance to the government.

HISTORY TODAY

President Lincoln suspended the writ of *habeas corpus* during the Civil War. Such an action would probably be overruled by the courts today. President George Bush and the United States Department of Justice were criticized for some of the actions taken after September 11, 2001, when thousands of Americans were killed in a terrorist attack. President Bush and his supporters claimed that every measure they took was necessary to protect the United States from terrorism. What does the action taken by President Lincoln teach us? Although the writ was reinstated after the war's end, be mindful that neither President Lincoln nor anyone else knew how long the Civil War would last when the writ was suspended.

Given the threat to Lincoln's government, it is remarkable that harsher methods were not employed, but necessity drove Congress into wartime measures that were unheard of prior to the bombardment of Fort Sumter. One example was the enactment of a law permitting *conscription*, or the draft, the forerunner of the modern Selective Service System. When it became impossible to obtain enough voluntary enlistments to fill the ranks of the Union army, the *draft bill* provided for the induction of all men capable of bearing arms.

Among its provisions was a clause that permitted wealthy draftees to pay some-one else to take their place in the ranks. It was the coercive aspects of the con-scription law that triggered *draft riots* in New York City and other metropolitan areas. Of all the riots of that era, the New York City draft riots which were depicted in the movie *Gangs of New York*, not only rank as some of the worst of the 1860s, but among the worst in American history.

The Civil War was not popular among all people in the northern states. Even after the attack on Fort Sumter, many northerners opposed war as a means of reincorporating the southern states into the Union. Even those who supported the war, at least those in the lower and working classes resented the fact that the wealthy were allowed to buy their way out of military service. New York City in particular was a hotbed of Confederate sympathizers, and it was also a hotbed of racist sentiments toward blacks. Some northerners resented the idea of losing loved ones in a war that was being fought, at least in part, to liberate black slaves. Therefore, racist attitudes toward blacks were virulent among many in New York City.

New York newspapers inflamed racist tensions, criticizing the draft as part of an unpopular "n_____' war" being waged by President Lincoln.[3] Part of this ha-tred was based on the fear that the emancipation of slaves would bring an influx of blacks to New York City, and that these newly freed blacks would take jobs from working-class New Yorkers. The Emancipation Proclamation had been signed in January of that year. Hatred of blacks was further exacerbated by the fact that blacks, who were not considered legal citizens, were exempt from military service in a war that included the aim of freeing black slaves.

TIME CAPSULE: THE IMPEACHMENT AND ACQUITTAL OF PRESIDENT ANDREW JOHNSON

The process of impeachment is established by the Constitution of the United States, and in the case of a number of senior federal officers, it is the only method to remove them from office. Frequently, removal from office is a precondition for subsequent prosecution for criminal acts committed while in office. The Constitution provides that the U.S. House of Representatives must make charges against the federal officer, and this presentation of charges is called an *impeachment*. Once charges are presented to the Senate, the Senate proceeds to try the case and either acquits or convicts the individual of the impeachment charges. When the President of the United States is tried, the Constitution provides that the Chief Justice of the U.S. Supreme Court will preside at the trial. Only two Presidents have been impeached by the House and tried by the Senate—Andrew Johnson in 1868 and Bill Clinton in 1998. Both cases raise interesting questions for students of criminal justice, despite the obvious political overtones present in each trial.

Army occupation of the defeated southern states proved to be the flashpoint for an explosive 1868 impeachment trial of President Andrew Johnson. As the successor to President Lincoln, who was assassinated on April 14, 1865, Johnson

Continued

TIME CAPSULE: THE IMPEACHMENT AND ACQUITTAL OF PRESIDENT ANDREW JOHNSON—CONT'D

became Commander-in-Chief of the Army and thus responsible for the military government of the South. Within the chain of command was his Secretary of War, Edwin Stanton, who had been appointed by Lincoln and who sympathized with the members of Congress who looked forward to black citizens voting in the southern states. The Commanding General of the Army was Ulysses S. Grant, the national hero who led the Union to victory and accepted General Robert E. Lee's surrender at Appomattox Court House, Virginia. General Grant was generally viewed as a likely Republican candidate in the 1868 presidential election campaign. He was also allied with the "radical" congressional group that advocated delaying readmission of the southern states to the federal Union until the voting rights and freedom of black freedmen was assured.

Because of the assassination of Abraham Lincoln, President Johnson, in 1865, became the third Vice President to assume the Presidency due to the death of his predecessor. As if assuming the Presidency at that time in history were not difficult enough, Johnson had other political and personal obstacles before him. Johnson was not particularly popular before he became President. He was a southerner and a Democrat who opposed secession and sided with the Union during the Civil War; therefore he was distrusted by southern Democrats. He was also distrusted by some northern Republicans because he was from the south. Johnson reportedly was an alcoholic; some believed he was drunk the day he was inaugurated as Vice President. Supposedly, Johnson had a prickly personality, which did not endear him to much of the Washington political establishment.

President Johnson favored prompt readmission of the southern states, and was generally opposed to federal power being used to gain substantial social changes in the conquered states. He had been generous in granting pardons to former Confederate leaders, and he used his influence to gain recognition of newly elected state governments in the South. Some historians of the period have termed Johnson a racist, while others picture him as a champion for the constitutional powers of the president who stopped, or at least delayed, congressional domination of the federal government. There is no lack of evidence that President Johnson acted with determination to remove "radical" military officers from command of the military districts through which the former Confederate states were governed. These generals

were replaced by others who believed in a more benign approach to the South's newly emergent white supremacists. Ultimately, he discharged Secretary of War Stanton from office, having prevailed upon General Grant to accept an interim appointment as Secretary of War. Unwisely, he delivered speeches and gave press interviews attacking the "radical" faction of the Republican Party in Congress.

Earlier, Congress had passed a Tenure of Office Act, which required that, before the President might dismiss a governmental officer who had been appointed with senatorial approval, he was required to obtain the advice and consent of the Senate to the removal. There was an immediate but premature reaction to the President's action. The House of Representatives considered but rejected a motion to file impeachment charges in December 1867. However, 1 month later, the Senate refused to concur in Secretary Stanton's discharge and General Grant, persuaded that Stanton was thus restored to office, vacated the War Office to Stanton. Within 2 weeks of these events, the House voted to file impeachment charges against the President, and formal charges were presented to the Senate on March 4, 1868.

The impeachment trial began on March 23, and proved to be the social event of the Washington season. Ladies crowded the Senate gallery, rustling in taffeta and crinolines, as the opposing counsel debated the constitutionality of the Tenure of Office Act and whether President Johnson had conspired with others to violate the laws of the United States. By the time testimony concluded and the lawyers had finished their closing arguments, it was the first week in May and the Senate, as the Court of Impeachment, adjourned for 10 days. When the senators reassembled, they voted on the least controversial article of the charges, and it was discovered that there was one vote less than the two-thirds majority required for conviction. A similar fate met the charge that President Johnson had violated the Tenure of Office Act by dismissing Secretary Stanton. Seven Republican senators voted with the Democratic Party senators, resulting in the President's acquittal. Having lost on these matters, the House managers of the prosecution withdrew the remaining charges.

Several reasons have been suggested for Johnson's acquittal. One is that the members of the Senate disliked and mistrusted the president *pro tempore* of the Senate, Benjamin F. Wade,

TIME CAPSULE: THE IMPEACHMENT AND ACQUITTAL OF PRESIDENT ANDREW JOHNSON—CONT'D

who would have become President if Johnson had been convicted. Wade advocated women's rights, high tariffs, and permitting black Americans to vote. While these positions were in accord with the wishes of the radical Republicans, it alienated many of their moderate Republican party associates. Another factor was the legislative history of the Tenure of Office Act, which clearly showed that Secretary Stanton was removed from its protective provisions before it was passed by Congress. In addition, a number of senators felt that conviction should occur only if the accused's actions made him subject to a criminal indictment. Finally, the American people appeared to have lost their enthusiasm for radical reconstruction of the southern states prior to the time President Johnson's impeachment was tried.

Johnson eventually recovered from the trauma of being impeached, at least to some degree. He was elected to the U.S. Senate in 1875, a few months before his death. Like many other impeachments, the trial of President Johnson may be seen as meaning many—and contradictory—things. At least in the short run, it meant that the "radical"

Republican wish to establish black majority governments in the South would be delayed. It also vindicated the executive branch's control of the Army, even though the Tenure of Office Act continued on the statute books and was not held unconstitutional.[4] On the other hand, the election of General Grant to the Presidency in November of 1868, and the growing power of Congress in the direction of southern state reconstruction, both suggest that President Johnson won but a short-lived victory. Most historians agree that the Presidency entered a period of declining power following this aborted impeachment effort, not to be reversed until the dynamic presidential leadership of Theodore Roosevelt (1901-1909).

Sources: There is a well-written study of the Johnson impeachment by Smith, G. (1977). *High crimes and misdemeanors: The impeachment and trial of Andrew Johnson.* New York: William Morrow & Co; equally well-written, but more scholarly in focus, are Trefousse, H. L. (1999). *Impeachment of a president: Andrew Johnson, the blacks, and reconstruction* (2nd ed). New York: Fordham University Press; Benedict, M. L. (1973). *The impeachment and trial of Andrew Johnson.* New York: Norton.

HISTORY TODAY

Since Andrew Johnson's term, only two Presidents have faced impeachment. In 1974, President Richard Nixon resigned from office when it became clear that he was about to face impeachment from the House of Representatives and when it became clear that the Senate would convict him. President Bill Clinton was impeached in 1998 after being accused of lying about an extramarital affair while under oath in a noncriminal proceeding. He was acquitted by a wide margin by the U.S. Senate. Based on what you may read or know about these three cases, did the writers of the Constitution devise the right process for impeachment, or should it be easier to remove the President from office?

Racism in the United States reached the boiling point and exploded in July of 1863. The draft began in New York City on July 11. Recent Irish immigrants, most of whom were poor or working class, who had especially borne the brunt of the war, poured into the streets and attacked residents (especially black residents), the police, and buildings, especially draft headquarters. Property damage was estimated at approximately $1.5 million, an enormous sum for the time. More importantly, an estimated 11 black men were brutally lynched during the riots, which lasted for 5 days. White landlords, fearing their properties would be attacked, drove black residents away; the "Colored Orphan Asylum" was burned down, and thousands of blacks fled New York City, although many fled to the Harlem area of New York City, soon to become the city's predominant black neighborhood. After the riots were suppressed by the police and the Army, the draft resumed as scheduled in August.[5,6]

Protection of railroad and telegraph lines into the city of Washington was another vital concern that led to the use of federal troops and military trials to prevent disruption of communications with the capital city. The Civil War caused the enactment of the first *federal income tax law*; it established procedures for military contracting that persist to the present day; and it started the federal government on its long and controversial career as a printer of paper money, called *greenbacks*, in the inflationary years ahead.

Union army success in the field introduced still another area for expanded government activity. Generals charged with the control of southern populations recently reclaimed for the Union were faced with the vast problem of maintaining law and order, while at the same time dealing with the human suffering and despair produced by the war and Confederate defeat. Dealing with blacks after the Emancipation Proclamation was a special problem delegated early to the Freedman's Bureau, which had the monumental task of educating, training, and sustaining former slaves as they made the difficult transition from perpetual servitude into a wage-earning labor system.

EFFECTIVE POLICE AND BURGEONING NATIONAL ENTERPRISE

In April of 1865, Confederate General *Robert E. Lee* officially surrendered to Union General *Ulysses S. Grant* near Appomattox Courthouse, Virginia. Fighting continued for a short period following the surrender, in part because word of the surrender did not reach the battlefields as quickly as it would today, and in part because *Jefferson Davis* (the Confederate President) and his cabinet did not join in the surrender but fled, hoping to sustain the Confederacy from a location other than Richmond, Virginia, the Confederacy's capital city. Nonetheless, the Civil War was over and so were the southern concept of states' rights and the idea that secession could be done peacefully.

Robert E. Lee (1807-1870): Virginia native and graduate of the United States Military Academy; served in the United States Army and fought in the Mexican-American War in the 1840s; opposed secession by southern states but resigned from the U.S. Army and joined the Confederate Army after Virginia seceded from the Union; led the Confederate Army in the Battle of Gettysburg.

The Union was one and indivisible, but it was also a different Union than had existed in 1860. The foundation for growing federal power existed in the post-Civil War amendments, which altered the position of the states and the federal government. But even more than this took place in the bustle of the war years. Americans discovered that government was capable of undertaking a wide spectrum of tasks hitherto left to private enterprise or not done at all. The lessons of the Civil War remained after Appomattox as guides for the evolution of a new bureaucracy at both the state and federal levels.

Gradually, increased economic activity altered the criminal law, both at the federal and state levels. *Robber barons*, who are sometimes more sympathetically called *captains of industry*, set forth to establish vast personal fortunes in the construction and operation of railroads (Cornelius Vanderbilt and Colis P. Huntington), steel works (Andrew Carnegie), and oil refineries (John D. Rockefeller). Their leadership and daring established new levels of achievement in American business, but their methods led to the establishment of governmental agencies at the federal and state levels designed to limit the worst aspects of free competition, and to prevent economic competition from victimizing large segments of the population.

> Ulysses S. Grant (1822-1885): Ohio native and graduate of the United States Military Academy; fought in the Mexican-American War; resigned from the Army in 1854 in part because of alcoholism; rejoined the Army and was one of the Union's most accomplished generals during the Civil War; elected eighteenth President of the United States.

> Jefferson Davis (1808-1889): President of the Confederate States of America during the Civil War; former U.S. Senator and U.S. Army officer prior to the War.

The first federal regulatory agency was the *Interstate Commerce Commission* (1887), created by Congress to regulate railroad rates for goods carried in interstate commerce. A favorite speculative device of the robber barons was to issue shares of a corporation's stock that represented assets far beyond those in its possession. This *"watering" of stock* was a trap for the unwary. At first it was considered a shrewd, but otherwise unobjectionable, bit of sharp dealing. Eventually, both state governments and the United States Congress found it necessary to legislate controls over security markets and to impose penal sanctions on those who traded upon public naïveté.

Another competitive technique was to establish business combinations or pools that gave one company, or a group of companies, a *monopoly* in a critical field. Called *forestalling* by an earlier generation, such practices were traceable to ancient Greece. In 1890, Congress passed the *Sherman Antitrust Act*, the first federal law dealing with the problem. Supplemented by newer legislation to deal with later forms of monopolistic organization, the Sherman Act remains one of the primary statutes for the enforcement of fair competition today. It provided for civil remedies to competitors wronged by a monopoly, and it also contained criminal sanctions by means of fines against convicted corporations, their officers, and their directors. Investigation and prosecution of offenses involving securities regulation or monopolistic practices required a very special expertise. In these fields and many others, specialized skills, such as accounting and knowledge of marketing practices, were essential. Law enforcement became more complex and more demanding in terms of professional training for its personnel.

HISTORY TODAY

Today, as much as ever, the American dream is about making money. A capitalist economy encourages entrepreneurship. But when wealthy people, especially bankers and those who use the stock market, use dishonest or illegal means of making money, there are cries for the government to keep a tighter rein on capitalistic institutions, and people in the business world claim that government is standing in the way of economic progress. How do we strike the proper balance between controlling and preventing the excesses of dishonest entrepreneurs and still allow people to pursue financial prosperity?

A rapidly expanding national economy and an increasingly mobile population made it difficult to enforce law at the state level and, gradually, federal legislation was enacted based upon the constitutional power granted to Congress by the Interstate Commerce Clause. Originally expounded in the 1824 case of *Gibbons v. Ogden* (9 Wheaton 1), the full potential of the Interstate Commerce Clause was not realized until late in American history. It was the events of the second half of the nineteenth century that triggered the enactment of statutes that imposed penalties on those who conducted illegal activities across state boundaries. These statutes included the *Mann White Slave Traffic Act* of 1910, which made it a federal offense to transport women across state lines for immoral purposes, and the *Pure Food and Drug Act* of 1906, which imposed federal standards for foodstuffs and medicines carried in interstate commerce.

During and after the Civil War, counterfeiting paper money became a major federal problem. The United States *Secret Service* was organized in the Treasury Department on July 5, 1865, with *William P. Wood* as its first chief. A personal friend of Secretary of War Edwin Stanton, Wood had been active in Union spy and detective work during the war. Originally, his agency was restricted to the investigation of counterfeiting and was assigned 10 operatives for that purpose. In 1867, the Secret Service was given statutory authority to investigate cases of fraud against the federal government.

As the only investigative agency of the United States, the Secret Service was prevailed upon to expand its authority whenever a vague provision in federal statutes permitted. Thus, it was assigned to investigate the Ku Klux Klan in the South during Reconstruction, and during the Spanish-American War (1898-1900) and First World War (1917-1918) it served as the primary agency for gathering intelligence as well as preventing espionage and sabotage.

In 1876, agents of the Secret Service uncovered a plot to steal President Lincoln's body from his burial vault and to hold it ransom for the release of counterfeiter Ben Boyd from Joliet Federal Prison. Prompt action prevented success of the plan, and the culprits were turned over to state authorities for prosecution. Also beyond the agency's statutory authority was the job of protecting the president. In 1894, agents of the Secret Service foiled an attempt on President Grover Cleveland's life, but public opinion was alarmed when it was discovered that its agents guarded President *William McKinley*'s private residence in Massachusetts (1898). The assassination of McKinley in 1901 created growing support for statutory approval of Secret Service protection, but not until passage of the Sundry Civil Expense Act of 1907 did Congress finally act in the matter.

FIGURE 11.3 Theodore Roosevelt, later elected President of the United States, is pictured in 1895 while he was serving as New York City Police Commissioner. *Courtesy en.wikipedia.org.*

Ironically, the bureau, originally established in 1907, was itself a product of the Secret Service; eight agents transferred from the older agency formed the initial personnel of the Justice Department's infant Bureau of Investigation. Since America had become a nation, many Americans had opposed the creation of a national police force, fearing that such a centralization of power in the hands of the federal government would lead to the sort of abuses perpetrated by European monarchies and dictatorships. Crime control and law enforcement, so the thinking went, was best delegated to state and local governments, who could better understand the needs and sensitivities of local populations.

Theodore Roosevelt, who served as President from 1901 to 1909, had proposed the idea of a federal law enforcement agency to Congress, only to have his idea dismissed. In 1907, while Congress was out of session, Roosevelt and his Attorney General, *Charles Bonaparte*, secretly created the Bureau of Investigation. The thought of creating such an entity in secret, and having no one discover what has happened until after the fact, may seem strange today, but 1907 was in an era that did not have 24-hour news coverage, or even television or radio at all, so actions such as this could be taken outside the eye of the media and therefore outside the eye of Congress as well when they were not in session.

Theodore Roosevelt (1858-1919): Twenty-sixth President of the United States; prior to Presidency served as Police Commissioner in New York City, Assistant Secretary of the Navy, Colonel and recognized hero of the Spanish-American War, Governor of New York, and vice president under William McKinley; youngest man ever to serve as President of the United States.

When they returned into session, Congress was outraged at Roosevelt and Bonaparte, and they promptly scheduled hearings at which Bonaparte was the unwilling star witness. Congress feared that the Bureau would become a political spy force and that agents would be employed to police political enemies more than actual criminals. The fact that Roosevelt created the Bureau secretly and without congressional authorization only bolstered their argument. The Roosevelt

TIME CAPSULE: CZARIST RUSSIA AND THE THIRD DEPARTMENT

Prior to the Communist Revolution of 1917, Russia had been ruled for several centuries by a monarchy known as the *czars* (or tsars). As in most European countries, the Russians had little control or say about governmental affairs under the czars. Given the long reign of the czars, it is natural that they varied in terms of effectiveness and brutality. Catherine the Great, who ruled from 1762 to 1796, was one of the country's most able leaders; the last czar, Nicholas II, who ruled from 1894 to 1917, was one of its weakest and least capable. Alexander I, who ruled from 1801 to 1825, was one of the most liberal and popular czars, but his brother and successor, Nicholas I, who ruled from 1825 to 1855, was one of its most brutal. The last czar family was the Romanovs, who ruled Russia from 1613 to 1917, until they were overthrown during the Communist Revolution. The entire Romanov family, including Nicholas II, was killed on July 17, 1918. One tragic legacy of the Romanov dynasty was its prisons and its virtual enslavement of the country's working and lower classes. Medieval serfdom thrived in czarist Russia, with most peasants at the virtual mercy and rule of ruling landowners who were friendly to the state and some "state peasants" who were practically state property, whether they actually were imprisoned or not.

The subjugation of the Russian working class was so dominant under some of the czars that there was a gray area between imprisonment and life in the outside world. Many of those not in prisons worked as virtual slaves for the monarchy. One of the most oppressive czars was Nicholas I. His control over the Russian people was complete, and his decisions, whether related to domestic or foreign policy (He sought the virtual elimination of the Polish nationality and engaged in wars with Armenia, Iran, and the Ottoman Empire.) were unquestionable. Nicholas's autocratic tendencies also extended to the criminal justice system. In a country where the notions of democracy and individual liberties were practically nonexistent, the government did not hesitate to employ any means available to suppress dissent and spy on its citizens. Nicholas made liberal use of secret police, formerly known as the *Third Section of the*

Imperial Chancellory (Tretiye Otdeleniye), not to apprehend and investigate conventional crimes but to spy on and terrorize people perceived as unfriendly to the monarchy. Nicholas I authorized the creation of the Third Department, which was administered by Count A. Kh. Benckendorff. The Third Department conducted surveillance on the citizenry in an era prior to the availability of electronic forms of surveillance. Political and religious dissidents (the czar also functioned as the effective protector of the Russian Orthodox Church) and foreign nationals living inside Russia were the primary targets of the Third Department. Censorship of theater plays was another specialty of the Third Department. The Third Department had a well-organized network of spies throughout the vast Russian empire, and they worked with the Corps of Gendarmes, a wing of the Russian military. The Third Department also targeted those suspected of counterfeiting, as it was an offense against the monarchy, and those suspected of creating and spreading fraudulent government documents.[7] Those found to be "state criminals" were either killed or banished to remote prison camps in cold locations, usually Siberia, with little or no procedural due process.

Nicholas I died on February 18, 1855. Some have maintained that he poisoned himself after learning of a disastrous defeat at the hands of the Ottoman Empire and its European allies during a key battle of the Crimean War. The Third Department was abolished in the 1870s. Unfortunately for the Russian population, the Communists under the leadership of Vladimir Lenin (1870-1924) and later Joseph Stalin (1879-1953) were no better and were arguably much worse than the czars. Spying on the citizenry, brutal imprisonment, and deaths in prison did not abate during the first two decades of Communist rule; they became worse. Joseph Stalin, a Georgian who ruled the 15-nation Union of Soviet Socialist Republics (of which Russia was the most dominant member country) for almost 30 years, has gone down in history as one of the twentieth century's most brutal dictators and mass murderers, his alliance with the United States and Great Britain during World War II notwithstanding.

administration's case for a Bureau was not helped by the fact that Attorney General Bonaparte, although he was a career advocate for civil service reform, was the grand-nephew of the French Emperor Napoleon Bonaparte, even though Charles Bonaparte had practically no personal ties to the Bonaparte family in France.

HISTORY TODAY

Theodore Roosevelt is remembered as one of America's greatest Presidents. Yet he probably injured his position with the back door method he used to create the Bureau of Investigation, a move that he saw as in the country's best interests. If a contemporary U.S. President were to do something like this (which is rather unlikely given the constant media presence today), how would the public react?

The evolution of federal law was doubtless the most significant criminal justice event from 1865 to 1910, but substantial segments of crime remained entirely within state jurisdiction. The major violent felonies, such as murder, rape, and robbery, remained punishable only by state law, as did property offenses such as larceny, arson, and burglary. After 1876, Union troops were withdrawn from the former states of the Confederacy, and during a period of extreme violence and terrorism, blacks gave up their right to vote and were held in subjection to white political authority. One lasting legacy of the military occupation of the South is the *Posse Comitatus Act* of 1883, which continues to provide criminal penalties against any army officer or enlisted person who engages in civilian police activities.

HISTORY TODAY

Two of the primary challenges facing the United States today are terrorism and control of the borders, especially the border with Mexico. Some have argued that these two issues are not merely criminal justice issues but are issues of national security, and that military means are justified and may be necessary to control them. Would you favor having soldiers—who are trained to fight wars rather than act as police—patrolling the Mexican border or U.S. entry points alongside civilian law enforcement officers?

If the new United States was an arena for building fortunes, it was also a society in which there were serious disparities in living conditions. The heavy influx of European immigrants after the war resulted in a surplus of labor and a resulting reduction in wages. Desperate workers sent their wives into sewing factories and their children into industrial enterprises, attempting to secure enough through joint labor to support their large families. Housing was limited and expensive, causing urban workers to live cramped into apartments without light or ventilation. Disease flourished and men and women grew violent. Those who formed the "respectable" members of society became alarmed at the growing crime rate, the dangerous state of public health, and the human suffering that surrounded them. Never in the history of the United States had there been such a wide gap between the rich and the poor, and never had there been so many at the poverty level.

Farmers also felt the economic crunch. Dependent upon railroads to transport their goods to markets, they were forced to pay high rates at a time when crops were bringing modest returns, and money was scarce and expensive to borrow. From these conditions arose labor organizations in the industrial areas and farmers' political and cooperative groups in the countryside. To protect their property, businessmen employed a growing number of private police forces, the most prominent being that established by *Allan Pinkerton*. Generally sympathetic to business interests, public officials at the state and federal levels tended to place their emphasis on maintaining law and order and protecting private property. It was during these years that the United States came closest to a full-scale class struggle between the interests of capital and those of the farmer and working class.

Allan Pinkerton (1819-1884): Scottish native; founded the Pinkerton Detective Agency after immigrating to the U.S., still one of the most well-known private detection agencies in the world, which served as the intelligence-gathering arm of the Union during the Civil War.

HISTORY TODAY

Allan Pinkerton was both an entrepreneur and a criminal investigator. The private sector is involved in law enforcement in a number of ways, from providing security at shopping malls, to loss prevention in department stores, to providing sophisticated security at major events. What is the proper role for private entities in modern law enforcement?

AN "OPEN SPOT" IN GOVERNMENT: POLITICAL CORRUPTION

Rapid social and economic growth leaves institutions in a state of disarray. Old bureaucratic methods are abandoned before new techniques can be developed and applied to changing needs. The American Civil War and the Reconstruction period were times when this disorientation was highly visible, and the confusion left a number of "open spots" for ambitious and unscrupulous individuals to exploit. A general decline in public morality characterized the years from 1865 to 1900, and corruption of the political process stalked the land.

As a consequence of the war itself, southern politics became dominated by an unlikely combination of illiterate freed blacks, southern scalawags (those who remained loyal to the Union throughout the war), and northern carpetbaggers (adventurers who moved south to seek their political fortunes). All southern whites who had served in Confederate civil or military positions were barred from office by virtue of the strict rules of Congress, which required clear proof of continued loyalty during the war. "Reconstructed" southern legislatures remained in control of the once-rebellious states until they were readmitted to the Union and until presidential pardons restored the political rights of former Confederates. Despite their inexperience and vulnerability to bribery, the Reconstruction legislatures did yeoman work in caring for the needs of their devastated states. Public schools were established for the first time, new railroad lines were built, and economic recovery began as a free labor system was implemented. However, there were numerous instances of extravagant expenditures; solid gold fixtures were purchased to decorate the legislative halls of southern states whose inhabitants were in imminent danger of starvation.

Although the irresponsibility of southern reconstruction legislatures was strongly criticized, it was a pale reflection of the moral decay in northern political life. It was generally accepted that state legislatures were closely allied with the economic interests of expanding commerce and industry. Monopolies were granted to the corporations or individuals who offered the highest bribes to the legislators. At the national level, Congress deemed the people's interest best served by vast grants of the most valuable lands in the West to railroad entrepreneurs. The administration of the Union war hero, President Ulysses S. Grant, was shaken by a series of scandals involving theft of whiskey tax revenues and bribery in the disposition of Indian trading post privileges. Crime was becoming nonviolent, was directed toward the acquisition of substantial property interests, and frequently involved some form of theft from the government.

This period in American history is best exemplified by the rise of the *city machine*, a political organization that operated on the premise that the path to office was to provide jobs or other valuable services to a majority of the voters. The machine was itself the result of growing complexity in the American system of government. As more immigrants flooded into the United States and became naturalized citizens, politics became the only way in which they could gain relief from their difficult financial situations. Many needed jobs and found themselves appointed police officers by the aldermen of their local wards. Others started small businesses and benefited from the influence of their political ward leaders in obtaining contracts from city governments and institutions. In turn, they loyally voted for the politicians who provided these economic rewards. Many foreign-born citizens merely adapted old ways of conducting business to the American scene. They had previously enjoyed the protection of nobles or gentry in exchange for their labor or political support. It was easy to make similar arrangements with native-born political leaders in the United States. From the American politician's standpoint, the new voters were to be preferred for their reliability; they were not likely to be dissuaded from their allegiance by reformist attacks upon the ward bosses.

This arrangement gave birth to such colorful characters as *William Marcy Tweed*, reputed in history as the "Boss" of New York City from 1866 to 1871. Beginning as the foreman of a volunteer fire company, Tweed became a prominent figure in Democratic Party politics and a member of *Tammany Hall*. Tweed's initiation into political life began with his election as an alderman for New York County in 1851. After serving one term, he was elected to the House of Representatives but found the office uninteresting. By 1856 he was back in New York City, having been elected to the Board of Supervisors, and shortly thereafter he was to play a major role in the erection of the New York County courthouse, authorized by legislative act in 1858. A physical monument to political corruption, Tweed's courthouse was projected to cost no more than $150,000. When construction was stopped by reforming newspaper editors and irate citizens in 1871, the estimated expenditures for the partially completed building ranged from $3,200,000 to 8,224,000. The inflated costs were, for the most part, attributable to the self-dealing of the Tweed Ring and a fraudulent but profitable system of contracting. When the city needed goods or services, a contract would be issued to a favored firm, which inflated its cost estimates by at least 50 percent. The difference between the fair price and the amount paid by the city was divided between the fraudulent contractor and the politician who awarded the contract.

As an indication of the law's inadequacy, it should be noted that Boss Tweed served only 1 year in prison, convicted of the misdemeanor of failing to properly audit the city's accounts. The remaining 3 years he spent in prison before his death were caused by his inability to raise bail and obtain release from arrest in civil actions pending against him to reclaim the city's funds. While imprisonment for debt was a thing of the past, demands for high bail in politically sensitive cases were still very much available.

The Tweed case also provides a glimpse into the informality of prison discipline in the case of favored inmates. While he was held at the Ludlow Street Jail, it was Tweed's practice to take a ride with the warden and keepers to Central Park, where he was permitted to walk with his son. After their promenade, the entire group went to Tweed's residence, where dinner was served to the prison officials and the entire family. After the cigars were finished, Tweed and his jailers returned to the jail. But in December 1875, when the warden, keepers, and family relaxed downstairs, Tweed slipped out the back of the house and headed for parts unknown. He was later discovered in Spain, identified by Spanish police officials who recognized him through one of Thomas Nast's cartoons.

One final matter must be noted; New York City aldermen controlled the appointment of municipal police officers within their wards. While this was not of great financial consideration, it did mean that police officers owed their positions and their continuity in office to Tammany Hall. Professional police activity was subject to direction from the same political groups that engaged in widespread graft and theft; as a consequence, selected criminals might enjoy protection for a price paid into the party's pocket, or into a politician's private treasury.

FEATURED OUTLAW: JOHN WILKES BOOTH

The United States has an unfortunate habit of romanticizing and making celebrities of people accused or convicted of violent and heinous crimes, political assassins among them. The first celebrity assassin in the United States was a celebrity before he committed his most infamous crime. John Wilkes Booth (1838-1865) was one of the most acclaimed and famous stage actors of his day. Booth belonged to a famous family of actors, with both his father and brother being acclaimed actors in their own rights. He also goes down in history as the first person to assassinate a United States President. His murder of Abraham Lincoln assured his place in history, helped make Lincoln an iconic figure, and left historians pondering the unanswerable question of how American history would have been different had Abe Lincoln lived to complete his second term.

John Wilkes Booth lived in Maryland, a slave state that did not secede from the Union like most of the other slave states. Booth was an unapologetic believer in the inferiority of blacks, something that was not unusual even in Union and nonslave states at the time. Although he lived in Maryland, his sympathies concerning the war clearly lay with the Confederacy. As the war ground to a halt and with the South lying in ruins, Booth, like many other believers in slavery, was both sad and enraged at the prospect of blacks joining whites as equals. Booth also despised President Lincoln and his top officials, both because of their stance on slavery and because he perceived the Lincoln Administration as haughtily lording the Union's triumph over his beloved but vanquished Confederacy.

The plot to assassinate President Lincoln involved at least six coconspirators, of whom Booth was chief. The plot not only targeted Lincoln but several other top Lincoln Administration officials as well, and all of the assassinations were scheduled to take place at approximately the same time on Good Friday, April 14, 1865. Booth and his coconspirators laid the plans for the multiple assassinations at a boarding house owned by Mary Surratt, the mother of one of his friends. The plan was for Booth to assassinate Lincoln at Ford's Theater, for George Atzerodt to assassinate Vice President Andrew Johnson at his home, and for Lewis Powell to assassinate Secretary of State William Seward at his home. When the time came for the assassinations, Atzerodt backed out and did not make the attempt on Vice President Johnson's life. Powell fulfilled his attempt on Secretary Seward, stabbing him repeatedly at his front door before running away, but Seward survived.

Booth had no intention of backing out and no intention of leaving any possibility of failure. Sometime late in the afternoon or early evening he entered Ford's Theater. Presidential security at that time was a far cry from what it is today. Although he had tried to secure the job of protecting the President, Allan Pinkerton, the head of the Pinkerton Detective Agency, was turned down. The Secret Service had not yet been created, and would not be handed the task of protecting the President for several decades to come. The job of protecting President Lincoln fell to the Washington, D.C., Police Department, who were woefully inept, and, like most other Americans, simply could not conceive of an American President being assassinated.

Booth came and went freely throughout Ford's Theater, something that aroused no suspicion, given Booth's fame, the fact that he had performed at the Theater many times previously, and the paucity of presidential security. When President Lincoln entered his seating box at 8:30 p.m. along with his wife, Mary, Major Henry Rathbone, and Rathbone's fiancée, Clara Harris, the cast of *My American Cousin* stopped performing and, with the audience turned, gave an ovation to the President as the band played "Hail to the Chief," 1 month after his inauguration to a second term as President and only 5 days after the surrender of the Confederacy.

John Parker, the Washington police officer assigned to guard the President, had left his post—possibly to have a drink at a nearby bar—so Booth entered the Presidential box unimpeded. He shot the President in the head at close range, and after struggling with and stabbing Major Rathbone, leaped from the box onto the stage, fracturing his left fibula in the process. In keeping with his natural flair for drama, even in such a highly stressful moment and in great pain, Booth reportedly yelled the state motto of Virginia, "Sic Semper Tyrannis" (Thus Ever to Tyrants) as he limped off the stage toward the theater's back door, where he made his escape on horseback.

President Lincoln was carried across the street to the home of William Petersen, where he died the next morning. His leg broken, Booth went south to Virginia, to the house of Dr. Samuel Mudd, who treated his leg. The anger directed at Dr. Mudd gave rise to the now famous saying, "Your name is Mudd," when someone is in deep trouble.

Continued

FEATURED OUTLAW: JOHN WILKES BOOTH—CONT'D

The hunt for John Wilkes Booth, recounted in James Swanson's *Manhunt: The 12-Day Search for Lincoln's Killer*, went on for 12 days, until Booth was tracked to a farmhouse near Bowling Green, Virginia, belonging to Richard Garrett. Vowing to never be taken alive, and that he had "too great a soul to die like a criminal," Booth died on April 26 at Garrett's farm, shot either by the posse that was pursuing him or by his own hand, as the farmhouse in which he stood was going up in flames. Four other conspirators, Mary Surratt (whose culpability was in doubt), Lewis Powell, George Atzerodt, and David Herrold, who had accompanied Powell to Seward's house, were tried, convicted on June 30, 1865, and hanged on July 7, 1865. Five others, including Samuel Mudd, were eventually convicted for taking part in the plot or the protection of the conspirators and sentenced to prison.

For better or worse, Booth became the first in a considerable list of assassins and would-be assassins of famous political figures in the United States. Unlike many subsequent assassins, who were either deranged or disenfranchised loners seeking fame through their assassination attempts, Booth was handsome, famous, intelligent, and a well-known public figure before the assassination. The fact that Booth already possessed a flair for self-promotion and drama contributes to the public fascination with him.

Sources: Sullivan, W. (2000). Abraham Lincoln. In M. Beescloss (Ed.), *American heritage illustrated history of the presidents*. New York: Crown Publishers, pp. 188-207; Donald, D. H. (1995). *Lincoln*. New York: Simon and Schuster; Oliver, W. M., & Hilgenberg, J. F., Jr. (2006). *A history of crime and criminal justice in America*. Boston: Allyn and Bacon; Swanson, J. L. (2006). *Manhunt: The 12-day search for Lincoln's killer*. New York: William Morrow.

HISTORY TODAY

Assassinations draw attention to the people who perpetrate them. In fact, one trait that most high-profile assassins share is narcissism. Those who study and report on assassinations inadvertently fulfill the assassin's wish to draw attention to them. How do we strike the proper balance between studying and learning from an assassination without encouraging other would-be assassins by making celebrities out of people like John Wilkes Booth?

SUMMARY

Post-Civil War America passed through several decades that were undoubtedly the darkest area of national history, and criminal justice was heavily influenced by the political corruption of the day. While many explanations have been suggested, the most plausible would seem to be that the nation had grown well beyond its earlier political simplicity. Economic growth outstripped governmental control, leaving only a system of favoritism and bribes. The tremendous expansion of government during the war had created opportunities for profiteering that were the foundation for later political corruption and economic exploitation. The changing nature of the electorate, which now contained large numbers of immigrants and recently freed blacks, required new techniques of political leadership and manipulation, and gave rise to a new type of professional politician who dealt in favors and took payment in votes.

A wide divergence between the wealthy and the poor laborer meant that the law was more rigidly enforced against the impoverished. Politicians elected by the votes of the poor were quick to accept financial favors or bribes from the rich. If political office was bought by patronage, it was also a capital investment that yielded good profits in terms of bribes and business advantage. In a very real sense, the politicians of Boss Tweed's era were brokers of economic and political power; in the spirit of the times, they made more than adequate commissions on their services.

Those years also marked a time of divergence in American cultures. Temperance agitation succeeded in imposing prohibition in many of the states, but it could not stamp out alcohol in cities dominated by hard-drinking immigrant majorities who held political control. States like New York would stretch their constitutional powers to the ultimate (and take over the city police), just as the Confederates and Union antagonists did before and during the Civil War. However, state political power was inadequate to deal with the complex interstate problems of economic control and regulation that faced the United States. Problems of interstate flight of criminals and the exchange of information on crime became more acute. Crime itself became infinitely more complex and subtle, leading to the rise of white-collar crime. It was difficult to tell the criminal from the upright citizen, and easier to suspect everyone's motives and attribute all action to greed.

REFERENCES

McPherson, J. M. (1982). *Ordeal by fire: The Civil War and reconstruction.* New York: Alfred Knopf; Randall, J. G., & Donald, D. (1969). *The Civil War and reconstruction* (2nd ed) (Revised edition). Lexington, MA: D.C. Heath; Randall, J. G. (1951). *Constitutional problems under Lincoln* (Revised edition). Urbana: University of Illinois Press; Hyman, H. M. (1975). *A more perfect union: The impact of the Civil War and reconstruction on the Constitution.* Boston: Houghton, Mifflin Co; Hyman, H. M., & Wiecek, W. M. (1982). *Equal justice under law: Constitutional development 1835-1875.* New York: Harper & Row; Patrick, R. W. (1967). *The reconstruction of the nation.* New York: Oxford University Press.

Josephson, M. (1962). *The Robber Barons: The great American capitalists, 1861-1901.* New York: Harcourt, Brace & World; Hacker, L. M. (1968). *The world of Carnegie: 1865-1901.* Philadelphia: Lippincott; Hawke, D. F. (1980). *John D.: The founding father of the Rockefellers.* New York: Harper & Row; Livesay, H. C. (1975). *Andrew Carnegie and the rise of big business.* Boston: Little, Brown & Co; Nevins, A. (1940). *John D. Rockefeller: The heroic age of American enterprise.* 2 Vols. New York: Charles Scribner's Sons.

Hicks, J. D. (1959). *The populist revolt: A history of the farmer's alliance and the populist party.* Lincoln: University of Nebraska Press; Yellen, S. (1956). *American labor struggles.* New York: S.A. Russell; Hofstadter, R. (1955). *The age of reform: From Bryan to F.D.R.* New York: Alfred Knopf; Pollack, N. (1962). *The populist response to industrial America: Midwestern populist thought.* New York: W.W. Norton.

Bowen, W. S., & Neal, H. E. (1960). *The United States Secret Service.* Philadelphia: Chilton Co; Melanson, P. H. (1984). *The politics of protection: The U.S. Secret Service in the terrorist age.*

New York: Praeger; Lipson, M. Private security: A retrospective. *The Annals of the American Academy of Political and Social Sciences*, 498(7), 11-22; Hofstadter, R. (1984). *Social Darwinism in American Thought* (Revised edition). New York: G. Braziller.

Bales, W. A. (1962). *Tiger in the streets*. New York: Dodd, Mead & Co; Callow, A. B. Jr., (1966). *The Tweed ring*. New York: Oxford University Press; Hershkowitz, L. (1977). *Tweed's New York: Another look*. Garden City, NY: Anchor Press; Lynch, D. T. (1974). *Boss Tweed: The story of a grim generation*. New York: Arno Press; Mandelbaum, S. J. (1965). *Boss Tweed's New York*. New York: John Wiley and Sons; Callow, A. B. Jr., (December 1965). The house that Tweed built. *American Heritage*, 16, 65–69.

Hall, K. L. (1989). *The magic mirror: Law in American history*. New York: Oxford University Press; Hall, K. L., Wiecek, W. M., & Finkelman, P. (1991). *American legal history: Cases and materials*. New York: Oxford University Press; Friedman, L. M. (1993). *Crime and punishment in American history*. New York: Basic Books.

Notes and Problems

1. Should the Constitution be "suspended" in times of war?
2. What impact did the Civil War have on criminal justice?
3. Should government attempt to regulate business enterprise? If it does so, should it resort to criminal sanctions? How do you imprison a corporation? Do economic offenses fit into the usual definition of criminal activity?
4. Was Tweed's ring, and like organizations, the only practical system of governing a large and culturally diverse city?

ENDNOTES

[1] See Chapter 10.

[2] Constitution of the United States, Amendment XIV, sec. 1.

[3] Harris, L. M. (2003). *In the shadow of slavery: African-Americans in New York City, 1626-1863*. Chicago: University of Chicago Press.

[4] These involved the acceptance of bribes by Interior Secretary Albert B. Fall and other high-ranking officials in the Harding administration, which resulted in the lease of federal oil reserves to a number of private oil companies. Uncovered after Harding's death in 1923, the corrupt practices resulted in a series of trials that did not end until 1928.

[5] Walker, S. (1997). *Popular justice: A history of American criminal justice* (2nd ed). New York: Oxford University Press.

[6] Subsequently, the U.S. Supreme Court has held that the President may legally discharge a postmaster without obtaining senatorial approval; however, when an official is appointed by joint action of Congress and the President to serve on an independent commission, the consent of the appointing authorities must be obtained. *Myer v. United States*, 272 U.S. 52 (1926); *Humphrey's Executor v. United States*, 295 U.S. 602 (1935).

[7] Third Department. (2008). In *Encyclopaedia Britannica*. Accessed February 24, 2008, from Encyclopaedia Britannica Online: http://search.eb.com/eb/article-9072140; Hingley, R. (1970). *The Russian secret police: Muscovite, imperial Russian and Soviet political security operations*. New York: Simon and Schuster.

Corrections in Modern America

LEARNING OBJECTIVES

1. Understand the importance of the Cincinnati Congress in American penology.
2. Learn about Zebulon R. Brockway's innovations at Elmira Reformatory.
3. Learn about the development and significance of indeterminate sentencing.

4. Understand the significance of Lombroso's research on prison inmates.
5. Learn some of the methods used to make profit from prison labor.
6. Learn about the creation of the Federal Bureau of Prisons.
7. Examine some attempts at inmate self-governance.
8. Learn about the development of probation in America.

Table 12.1 Time Line—Corrections in Modern America

1841	Peter Oxenbridge Thacher and John Augustus conduct initial experiments with probation.
1859	Friends of Penal Reform meet in Philadelphia.
1867	Enoch Wines and Theodore Dwight's *Report on the Prisons and Reformatories of the United States and Canada* published, urging that rehabilitation be the goal of American prisons.
1870	The first National Prison Congress meets in Cincinnati.
1877	New York State establishes a reformatory at Elmira, with Zebulon R. Brockway as its warden.
1886	Elmira Reformatory begins publication of its local newspaper, *The Summary.*
1890	An English translation of Gabriel Tarde's *Penal Philosophy* is published by the American Institute of Criminal Law and Criminology.
1894	New York Constitution amended to abolish contract prison labor.
1896	Volunteer Prison League organized under the leadership of Maud Ballington Booth.
1899	Cesare Lombroso's *Crime: Causes and Remedies* published.
1899	Juvenile courts introduced in Denver, Colorado, and Chicago, Illinois.
1908	The Borstal system adopted in England as a means of combating juvenile crime.
1913-1920	Mutual Welfare League implemented by Auburn (New York) Prison, attempting to give prisoners responsibility for their discipline and communal life.
1914-1918	The First World War is fought in Europe; the United States enters in April 1917.
1929	The Federal Bureau of Prisons is established.
1929-1941	The United States suffers a major economic crisis, known as the *Depression.*
1939-1945	The Second World War is fought in Europe and Asia; the United States joins the Allied powers in December 1941.
1939	A survey of 25 U.S. states reveals that one-third of all persons convicted of crime were placed on probation.
1939	Federal Prison Industries established.
1941	California adopts the American Law Institute's Draft Youth Correctional Authority Act.

During the American Civil War (1861-1865), American interest in penology did not disappear, but it occupied a minor place in the public consciousness. When the Friends of Penal Reform held a national meeting at Philadelphia in the autumn of 1859, only eight states and three prison societies were represented. Yet the basis for postwar developments was being laid. In 1862, young Enoch Wines was appointed secretary of the New York Prison Association, bringing new and enthusiastic leadership to that group. In association with Theodore Dwight, Wines undertook an ambitious survey of penal institutions in the northern United States and several Canadian provinces, leading to their 1867 publication of the *Report on the Prisons and Reformatories of the United States and Canada*, which was submitted to the Legislature of New York in January 1867. This work restated, in emphatic and expansive terms, the New York Prison Association's firm commitment to rehabilitation within prison walls. Widely read and enthusiastically received, the *Report* launched New York State into a program of reformatory discipline that culminated in the construction and operation of the *Elmira Reformatory*, completed in 1877.

Throughout the nation, a number of states awoke to the need for centralized administration of their penal institutions, a step in the direction of insulation from political appointments and also toward the encouragement of the new cadre of professional prison administrators. These reforms came in the wake of a growing number of prison commitments immediately after the Civil War and went hand in hand with problems generated by overcrowding and budgetary restraints.

THE NATIONAL PRISON CONGRESS OF 1870

The new era in penology was ushered in by the first *National Prison Congress* held in Cincinnati in 1870. A gathering of wardens, prison officials, and interested academics working in the area of penology, the *Cincinnati Congress* promulgated a Declaration of Principles that stressed the need for a professional prison civil service under centralized control of a state board. It asked for the institution of a progressive form of prison discipline, echoing the Dwight-Wines report of 1867, with its basis on the Crofton, or Irish, system.[1]

The declaration was based upon a paper by *Zebulon R. Brockway* titled "The Ideal of a True Prison System for a State," which caught the attention of the Congress. The young prison warden from Detroit advocated a reformatory program that would prepare inmates for release and reduce the crime rate. Stressing that the central aim of a true prison system should be the protection of society against crime, and not the punishment of criminals, Brockway argued for *indeterminate sentencing* (meaning that the time served would depend in part on an inmate's behavior) and for the creation of an impartial board that would decide when it was safe to return inmates to society. While in prison, the inmates were to be provided with a simple but adequate lifestyle. Each would have a separate room for sleeping, with access to a dining hall that operated as a restaurant. A library and public hall would permit reading and other forms of entertainment, as well as a room for religious services. Industrial and agricultural departments would be established, as appropriate to the location of the prison, and these would be run as efficient business organizations, returning profits to the institution and providing training in craft skills to the inmates.

The speech catapulted Brockway to the leadership of his profession. When New York State established its new reformatory at Elmira in 1877, the state chose Brockway to preside over the operations of this new and expanded facility for rehabilitation.

Yearly meetings of the National Prison Congress provided an opportunity for the exchange of information and new ideas in penology. Many meetings were graced by observers and speakers from Britain and continental Europe who were anxious to obtain the latest details of American work in reformatory prison discipline. Largely through the initiative of Wines, who continued to serve as Secretary of the New York Prison Association, an *International Congress on Prison Reform* met in London in July 1872. It drew the participation of 22 nations, including the United States, and resulted in a number of foreign prison reform programs based upon Brockway's proposals. For the next 20 years, American innovations drew worldwide attention; international meetings on penology continued to devote time and study to American experiments with reformatory discipline.

Meetings of the National Prison Congress, designated the American Prison Association after 1908, attracted participation from more states and offered progressively richer programs. The Seattle meeting of 1909 attracted delegations from 34 states. This widespread participation by professional penologists and prison staff encouraged thorough discussion of new programs and facilities. Western states developed reformatory prison systems at an unusually rapid rate, drawing their inspiration and guidance from the more heavily populated and industrialized states in the Northeast and Midwest. California and Colorado, which had only recently entered the Union, became regional leaders in reformative prison discipline.

FIGURE 12.1 Cesare Lombroso (1836-1909)—Italian physician and psychiatrist—argued that there were "criminal types" distinguishable by physical characteristics. *Courtesy en.wikipedia.org.*

After 1908, the international penology movement began to divide sharply into two opposing factions. The Anglo-American group continued to support rehabilitation as the primary goal of penology. Continental Europe, on the other hand, came under the influence of the *positivist school*, headed by *Cesare Lombroso*, a medical doctor from Turin, Italy, who broke new ground with a theory of criminology that stressed heredity as one of the major sources of crime. Positivism moved European prison reform in the direction of providing harsh sanctions in the case of habitual offenders but, at the same time, toward more lenient treatment and extensive aftercare provisions for those who were first offenders.

THE RISE AND FALL OF PRISON INDUSTRIES

The foundation of the penitentiary movement was productive labor by the inmates. This served the function of familiarizing inmates with the discipline of work and providing them with useful skills. At the same time, to the extent that prison industries made a profit, they reduced the cost of the institution to the taxpayers. Industrial work was seen as a way of reducing the crime rate, because it was widely believed that poverty was one of the primary causes of crime.

Initially, some early efforts, such as those of Elizabeth Fry,[2] attempted to use only institutional resources in developing an industrial program. However, it soon became apparent that there were profits to be made in making outside arrangements with private industrial concerns. *Contract labor* was a system that made convicts available to entrepreneurs for work within prison walls or on prison-run farms or camps. Under this arrangement, the lessee or contractor provided machinery, trained the inmates, and supervised their work. An alternative method was the *piece-price system*, in which the outside firm provided only the raw materials and was obligated to pay a fixed price for each unit of goods produced by the prison inmates. This arrangement required the prison to make capital investments for machinery, and it also placed the management burden on prison officials.

Because prison industry competed directly with manufacturers that employed free labor, it was highly vulnerable to political attack as private entrepreneurs grew in number and achieved more political influence. In the case of Britain, the first threat to prison industry was posed by the Reform Act of 1832, which, for the first time, extended the right to vote to the substantial population of the industrial midlands. Within the United States, where industrialization was not as extensive as in Britain, the challenge to prison industrial programs was not mounted before 1850 and did not become a matter of concern until after the Civil War. Then, for the first time, industrial production began to equal agricultural production.

Faced with the need to answer manufacturers' complaints, prison administrators initially turned to the *lease system*, whereby convicts were supplied to a businessman for labor on his premises rather than in the prison. This shifted the responsibility for safekeeping to the lessor. It also relieved the pressure on overcrowded penitentiary facilities. However, it did not lessen the charge that favored individuals were given the benefit of using convict labor. Ultimately, penitentiary wardens fell back on the *state-use system*, which employed convict labor within prison walls, setting them to tasks that either served specific state needs or produced goods that did not compete with products of free labor. For example, after the introduction of motor vehicle licensing, many prisons were assigned the task of manufacturing license plates. Other prisons used their convicts to provide janitorial services in public buildings. In a number of states, convicts worked on road and bridge construction projects.

American prisons met their strongest opposition from the young but rapidly growing labor movement, born after the Civil War and attaining national strength with the establishment of the Knights of Labor in 1878 and the American Federation of Labor in 1886. The use of convict labor at a fraction of free labor cost resulted in decreased wages in the industries. The voice of organized labor combined with the voices of manufacturers unable to acquire convict labor. This resulted in growing pressure to limit the use of prison industry.

By 1873, American prisons were no longer able to "pay their way," or to cover their operating expenses, through the profits from inmate labor. Contract labor also drew the criticism of the National Anti-Contract Labor Association, which in 1883 met in Chicago and went on record as opposing all forms of contract labor. The New York State legislature, despite its recognition of the reformatory value of labor, imposed sharp restrictions on private contractors' use of inmate labor, but this partial eradication of contract labor did not dispel denunciations of the practice. In 1894, the state constitution was amended to abolish contract prison labor. By 1897, all of New York prison industry was limited to the production of goods required under the state-use formula. In only a few instances did individual states manage to survive this rapid contraction of prison industries. Minnesota, having established a cheap source of binder twine (used in threshing), had a form of prison labor that met the needs of voting citizens in the farming industry. As a consequence, this particular form of prison industry proved virtually unassailable by organized labor.

American prison administrators adapted as well as they could to the changed political times. At the urging of Brockway, the National Prison Association adopted the piece-price system as an alternative to contract labor. By 1887, New York State had adopted piece-price as its preferred system of dealing with inmate labor. When strict provisions were imposed by state law on all forms of contract labor, Brockway was ready with a plan for military training of the most advanced inmates. Within 14 hours of receiving notice of the anticontract labor laws, he had a system for military drill in place, defusing the danger of resentment and avoiding discipline problems that would arise from enforced idleness. Later, wardens in the Midwest pioneered the idea of organized sports programs, and the idea spread to the Northeast and Far West within a short period (1910-1915).

From 1900 to 1930, there were rapidly decreasing opportunities for the use of convict labor. A survey of 27 penal institutions in 1928 revealed that 2 had more than 50% of their inmate population idle, 3 had unemployment rates ranging from 30% to 50%, and 6 had from 20% to 30% of their inmates without work. The bad situation changed for the worse when Congress passed the *Hawes-Cooper* legislation (1929), permitting states to exclude convict-made goods carried in interstate commerce. The one bright spot was the creation of the Federal Prison Industries, Inc., in 1939. Established through the efforts of *James V. Bennett* (director of the Federal Bureau of Prisons) and *Eleanor Roosevelt*, the new corporation capitalized on the state-use premise by requiring federal agencies to procure supplies (whenever possible) from Federal Prison Industries. In 1939, the corporation reported a profit of $568,000. With the outbreak of World War II and an influx of federal agency orders, the future of Federal Prison Industries, Inc., was secure.

Eleanor Roosevelt (1884-1962): Wife of President Franklin Roosevelt; First Lady from 1933 to 1945; served as U.S. delegate to the United Nations after her husband's death; strong advocate for women's issues, civil rights, and numerous liberal and humanitarian causes.

While emergency measures and arrangements helped to provide alternatives to prison industries abolished through political pressure, the rehabilitative functions of prison labor were threatened. In the early 1870s, prison labor helped support the prisons, but it also provided training in craft and trade skills that would be useful upon an inmate's release. Recourse to military drill on one hand or the state-use system on the other provided prisoners with few skills that could be adapted to industrial use outside prison walls. To this extent, the rehabilitative goals adopted at Cincinnati in 1870 were victim to the hostile political climate of the 1880s.

HISTORY TODAY

Many people argue that prisons should be self-supporting. But the lessons of history demonstrate that such an ideal is not always possible to fulfill. Few prisoners have more than minimal vocational skills. It is difficult to supervise inmates while they are working without encountering security problems, and prisoners may be taking jobs that members of the public and some labor union members may need. Is there a realistic way today for prisons to help foot their own bills?

Organized labor exerted a minimal political influence in the South, where states were in the initial stages of recovery from the Civil War. For the most part, they were free to deal with their growing prison populations through a variety of leasing arrangements. Responsibility for prison discipline was shifted to those who leased convict labor, and lessors found profit in operating southern penitentiaries.

The inmates, who were disproportionately African-American, survived harsh conditions in prison camps established near road and canal construction projects, or in isolated areas where logging operations were conducted. Many were shackled with chains during night hours, and a few performed their daily labor shackled together in chain gangs. The absence of secure sleeping quarters led many lessors of convict labor to use heavy wooden wagons as mobile cells, crowding inmates into wagons and supplying them with a minimum of ventilation, food, and water. It was common to use open pits, caves, or mine shafts as sleeping facilities. Statistics provide partial verification of the harsh conditions faced by southern convicts. Rough estimates of death rates in northern and southern prisons, prepared in 1888, show that three times as many deaths occurred among southern prisoners than in the case of their northern counterparts.

Southern prison conditions did not improve until the populist political parties began to take control of state governments in the 1890s. Throughout the nation, populism represented the growing complaints of farmers against the financial interests of the North and East, but southern populism can also be seen as the product of regional grievances against wealthy and influential politicians (known as *Bourbons*), who used their political influence for private gain.

One aspect of that favoritism was the provision of prison labor for use on the farms and in logging camps of Bourbon (probusiness Southern Democrat) leaders. So strong was the resentment that white southern farmers joined black farmers in electing populist candidates to office. When they succeeded in gaining office, the end of convict leasing was at hand, and there was increased resort to state-use activities. In 1893 Louisiana made an effort to establish a reformatory penitentiary system. Although the attempt was short-lived, it was quickly followed by the development of *plantation prison farms*, operated by the state under conditions far superior to those under the convict leasing system. Mississippi ended the convict lease system by the 1895 constitutional amendment.

Southern experiments with plantation prison farms were to prove the new direction of prison labor. A general need for road construction, reforestation, park development, and state-use agriculture led states in the North and the West to follow the southern example. In 1906, Colorado began an honor-camp program for prisoners approaching parole. The inmates were assigned road-building tasks and supervised by a single unarmed guard. Although there were escapes, they did not detract from the excellent record and accomplishments of these prison camps. During World War I (1914-1918), prison labor camps were used extensively in both the United States and in Europe, relieving the shortage of labor due to wartime conditions. The camps were recognized as a legitimate alternative to penitentiary commitment. From 1915 to 1920, the American Prison Congress paid particular attention to road construction camps and farm camps, and as late as 1959, surveys showed that most rehabilitation took place in rural prison camps.

HISTORY TODAY

Farming and industry are not relics of the past in the United States, but they are not as prevalent as they used to be. Technology and the information revolution have transformed America's workforce. How can correctional administrators devise ways for inmates to work at jobs more in tune with the work done by most of America's workforce? If they can think of ways to put inmates to work in useful positions, might this not help them when they are released, more than might be the case with simple manual labor?

REFORMATORY PRISON DISCIPLINE AT ELMIRA

With the 1877 establishment of the Elmira (New York) Reformatory, American penology had an opportunity to put its rehabilitative theories into practice. Central to the initial success of the effort was the first General Superintendent, Zebulon R. Brockway, who spent 20 years at Elmira, working with the prisoners on a highly individualized basis. The newly arrived inmate, usually a male first offender between the ages of 16 and 30, was given a general explanation of the prison discipline system. He also received an interview with Brockway, who tried to determine the new arrival's psychological makeup and potential for reform. Brockway's extensive notes on each inmate indicate that most were from poor, but not impoverished, homes; most lived at home when their offense was committed; almost all read with difficulty or were illiterate; and a large majority were common laborers or partially trained mechanics.

It was Brockway's usual practice to place the newcomer in the second (or intermediate) grade in the reformatory's three-tier ranking system. This provided a limited number of privileges, which could be withdrawn by Brockway and eventually result in assignment to the third grade. At the same time, behavior and job performance that met established standards would earn advancement to the first grade, from which prisoners were eligible for parole or early release.

Throughout an inmate's time at the Elmira Reformatory, the general superintendent was readily available. Each evening brought an opportunity to raise grievances or to discuss other matters with Brockway, and it is estimated that with interviewing new arrivals and dealing with inmates in the evening, he spoke to between 40 and 50 men per day. By this extraordinary effort to become familiar with each inmate, Brockway developed a close individual relationship with his charges; observers noted that he was, at the same time, "friend, minister, and prisonmaster."[3] His personal acquaintance with the prisoners meant that he was in a particularly strong position to assess punishments. It was the rule that only the general superintendent could withhold an inmate's privileges or order punishment.

Discipline at Elmira was firmly based on a refinement of the mark system of progressive prison discipline popularized by Captain Alexander Maconochie and the Irish prison director, Sir Walter Crofton. However, Brockway found it necessary to establish more clear-cut differentiation between the grades, and to provide a more detailed method for assigning marks. Keepers were required to submit weekly reports on the progress of each inmate, giving Brockway an assessment of the individual's behavior, willingness to work, and quality of performance. Nine marks could be assigned per month: three for demeanor, three for labor, and three for progress in the prison school. A half-year distinguished by nine marks in each month entitled the prisoner to promotion to the next grade.

Promotion to the higher grade was an achievement rewarded by improved eating arrangements, more distinctive clothing, and greater freedom within the reformatory walls. Those prisoners in the third, or lowest, grade were denied the privilege of having visitors, of writing or receiving letters, or of borrowing books from the library. Inmates in this grade were served meals in their rooms by inmate waiters, and they were not permitted tea or coffee. Their uniform was made of a dark red cloth, and they wore no caps. Those in the second grade were permitted visitors and allowed to write and receive letters; they could also borrow books from the library. Although they were required to eat meals in their rooms, they were permitted tea and coffee. Second grade prisoners wore a civilian style suit of dark colored material and wore a scotch cap. First, or highest, grade inmates were permitted all of the privileges of the other two grades. In addition, they were permitted to eat in the dining hall, and they wore a distinctive blue uniform with a navy cap. Distinctions in grade were also shown in assignment to work details, with the lower grades being assigned more menial tasks while the first grade inmates were provided with jobs that would improve their skills and opportunities for employment when they were released.

Educational advancement was one of the unique contributions of Brockway's system at Elmira. Undoubtedly, the meager educational achievements of his incoming prisoners caused him to make a connection between criminal activity and lack of education in his young charges. He proceeded to make educational attainment part of the mark system for promotion, and at the same time he retained public school teachers, attorneys, and college teachers on a part-time basis, establishing a vigorous multilevel curriculum. By 1891 Elmira Reformatory's library had 3,970 volumes on its shelves and a collection of 650 periodicals for inmate reading. In 1886 a prison newspaper, *The Summary*, was instituted to provide coverage of local, national, and world news that would otherwise be unavailable in the reformatory. This rich resource of reading material and skillful instruction provided ample opportunity for inmate education, just as the promise of promotion in grade and possible early release gave ample incentive for diligence in study.

A New York statute permitted the managers of Elmira Reformatory to establish the term of imprisonment; for all intents and purposes this provided a system of indeterminate sentences. In the first 25 years of operation, more than one-third of the young men committed were released on parole within 15 months, and another one-third were released on parole between 15 and 24 months after their arrival at Elmira. The other third were paroled in less than or slightly more than 3 years. Parole lasted 6 months, during which time the prison officials played an active role in finding employment for the parolees and in locating them in permanent residences.

Symbolic of the high point of rehabilitative imprisonment in the United States, Elmira Reformatory fell victim to two external threats to prison reform: (1) the abrupt cessation of prison industry in response to pressures from organized labor; and (2) the rapidly growing incarceration rate, which overwhelmed prisons and reformatories alike and made rehabilitation extremely difficult (if not impossible). Built with 500 cells to house an equal number of inmates, Elmira by 1899 had an average population of 1,500 prisoners. Its workshops, subjected to a slowdown by successive antiprison labor statutes, were unable to provide 8 hours of work per day for inmates skilled in glass blowing, chair making, and the production of tobacco pipes.

Even Zebulon R. Brockway, its great reformer, was not absolved of old-fashioned abusive conduct. He admitted to using corporal punishment as a disciplinary measure against young inmates. A German visitor to Elmira in 1927 criticized the lack of adequate housing, the absence of productive labor, the lack of full-time teachers, and the long nightly lockup from six in the evening until six the following morning. What had once been a sterling example of successful application of rehabilitative techniques had become, over the course of time, simply another prison with all of the problems that have plagued administrators and frustrated reformers over the long history of prisons and the movements to reform them.

FEATURED OUTLAW: ROBERT STROUD

Robert Stroud is one of the most famous prison inmates in American history. However, unlike many famous inmates, Stroud never made a name for himself for anything he did outside prison walls. A gifted, self-taught ornithologist, he became known as the *Birdman of Alcatraz* for his scientific research and publications on birds while in prison, but the title is misleading. Most of the work he did that made him famous was conducted at Leavenworth Prison in Kansas, not Alcatraz, the infamous Federal Prison near San Francisco (now a popular National Park tourist attraction).

Robert Franklin Stroud was born in 1890 in Seattle, Washington. He ran away from home at age 13. At age 18 he was living in Juneau, Alaska, working as a pimp. He killed a bartender for allegedly failing to pay for services rendered by his prostitute girlfriend. Stroud pleaded guilty to manslaughter on August 23, 1909, and was sentenced to 12 years in prison. He began serving his time on McNeil Island in Puget Sound. Never well-liked by staff or his fellow inmates, Stroud was a problem prisoner, assaulting a staff member on at least one occasion. After stabbing a fellow inmate, Stroud was transferred to the more secure prison in Leavenworth, Kansas. It was there that he

FIGURE 12.2 One of the best-known inmates of Alcatraz is Robert Stroud, the *Birdman of Alcatraz*, who spent 53 of his 72 years behind prison bars. Stroud was permitted to keep birds in his cell and maintain a laboratory during his prison terms. © *Bettmann/CORBIS*.

Continued

FEATURED OUTLAW: ROBERT STROUD—CONT'D

began taking university extension courses and studying ornithology, usually on his own, in large measure because he was a loner and did not get along well with his fellow inmates there, either.

It is often argued that increased knowledge and education are key ingredients to rehabilitation, but Stroud's life counters that notion. By 1916, Stroud, who had a third grade education, had become very knowledgeable and expert in the field of ornithology, but he was still a vicious criminal. On March 26, 1916, he stabbed and killed a correctional officer—in full view of hundreds of witnesses—who had denied Stroud an opportunity to visit with his brother. He was eventually tried and sentenced to hang, but his death sentence was commuted to life in prison by President Woodrow Wilson in 1920. He was ordered to spend an indefinite sentence of solitary confinement because of his violent history.

Over the next 20 years, Stroud sharpened and increased his knowledge and expertise in ornithology. Because most of his time was spent in solitary confinement and because most of his fellow inmates despised him anyway, Stroud had plenty of time to devote to his studies. He kept birds, mostly canaries, in his cell along with lab equipment needed to conduct his research. He developed medicines for birds, as well as writing on diseases and proper treatment. Forbidden by prison officials to publish his work, Stroud managed to get some of his writings smuggled outside prison walls and published. *Stroud's Digest on the Diseases of Birds*, published in 1943, was regarded as an important work in the field. Prison officials also discovered that Stroud was using some of the lab equipment to manufacture moonshine.

In 1942, shortly before his most important work was published, Stroud was transferred to the infamous federal prison on Alcatraz Island in the San Francisco Bay. Rehabilitation was not part of the mission of Alcatraz officials; in fact, when it opened in 1934, the United States Attorney General said that Alcatraz was set aside to isolate the worst inmates from those who had a chance at rehabilitation. Stroud was disallowed from further publishing and from keeping birds in his cell, but was allowed to continue his research while at Alcatraz. However, his fame flourished at Alcatraz and he was able to secure his place in history while serving his time there.

In 1958, Thomas Gaddis released a book on Stroud, titled *Birdman of Alcatraz*. The book sold well and made Stroud famous. In 1962, acclaimed film director John Frankenheimer directed a movie based on Gaddis's book, with equally acclaimed actor Burt Lancaster in the title role. Much to the incredulity of those who knew and hated Stroud, Lancaster portrayed Stroud very sympathetically, and prison officials as inept. If Lancaster's portrayal of Stroud is to be believed, Stroud, once he matured and immersed himself in his bird studies, was a kind, gentle, and misunderstood grandfather figure, and the moviegoer would have trouble believing that any person so kind should be in prison. The film did not reveal Stroud's more sadistic and perverted side. Even as he advanced in age, Stroud was incorrigible, spending his spare time harassing inmates and staff alike, and employing his artistic talent to draw child pornography. The one redeeming aspect of Stroud's experience at Alcatraz, which was portrayed by Lancaster, was his role in helping to quell an inmate uprising at the prison in 1946, which left three inmates and two officers dead, and many others wounded. Lancaster received an Academy Award for his pious portrayal of Stroud. Stroud reportedly was never allowed to view the film, but he knew of its success and how celebrated his name had become.

Experiencing the effects of age and poor health, Stroud was transferred to the Medical Center for Federal Prisoners in Springfield, Missouri, in 1959. Vain and utterly narcissistic to the end, Stroud hoped that his death would be front page news across the country, but that was one wish that did not come true. He died November 21, 1963, 1 day before the assassination of President John F. Kennedy, a death that greatly eclipsed Stroud's in terms of public attention.

Sources: Adams, J. M. (2000). Alcatraz. *Biography*, 4(5), 48-49; Oliver, W. M., & Hilgenberg, J. F., Jr. (2006). *A history of crime and criminal justice in America*. Boston: Allyn and Bacon; Johnston, W. (1999). *Alcatraz Island prison and the men who lived there*. San Francisco: Douglas/Ryan Communication; Stroud, Robert (2008). In *Encyclopaedia Britannica*. Accessed February 25, 2008, from Encyclopaedia Britannica Online: http://search.eb.com/eb/article-9070000.

HISTORY TODAY

Burt Lancaster's portrayal of Robert Stroud was, by credible accounts, inaccurate to the point of unrecognition. The film industry has always taken great license with the truth when trying to reenact a historical event or the life of a famous person; sometimes filmmakers simply invent their own version of the truth. Such a practice did not begin or end with the Birdman of Alcatraz. Hollywood's principal job is to offer entertainment, not a history lesson. What does this say to students who rely on the entertainment media to educate them?

CRIMINOLOGY AND PRISON REFORM

As the noble effort at Elmira was being overwhelmed by unemployment and high incarceration rates, European penologists became skeptical about the American emphasis on rehabilitation. To a degree, the declining success of Brockway's program was responsible for this change in attitude, but the main reason was the rise and popularization of positivism, a new school of criminology based on the work of an Italian medical doctor, Cesare Lombroso. A surgeon by training, Lombroso worked for some time as a medical officer in the army. During that early phase of his career, he noticed that soldiers who had been tattooed were more likely to engage in criminal activities. Later, Lombroso worked in prison hospitals, giving him access to a large number of criminals and providing him with the opportunity to observe and measure facial, cranial, and physiological features, many of which he identified as being typical of a genetic criminal type.

Publishing his major work *Crime: Causes and Remedies* in 1899, he argued that there was a specific "criminal type" that could be distinguished from noncriminal individuals through a number of physical characteristics. The criminal subspecies was a throwback to an earlier stage of evolution; in the male it was characterized by physical violence, and in the female it was typified by promiscuity. Because there was a biological basis for criminal behavior, it followed that rehabilitative efforts would fail whenever they were directed at *born criminals*. Lombroso and his followers contended that either capital punishment or life imprisonment was the only way to treat born criminals. For noncriminals found guilty of criminal acts, the usual graduation of penalties, coupled with rehabilitative techniques, was appropriate.

Lombroso's new approach to criminology launched a series of investigations into the causes of crime, all based on the biological characteristics of convicted individuals and the recidivism rates of born criminals. Positivism was to result in European penology abandoning rehabilitation in the case of confirmed criminals, dividing the mainstream of Anglo-American penology from these new developments on the European Continent.

HISTORY TODAY

Lombroso's work was discredited by others; he even admitted late in his career that criminals could not be identified by their physical appearance. However, does a person's biological or genetic makeup predispose him/her toward committing certain crimes? There are those who do not want to allow inquiry into that possibility because such biological determinism could be abused. Should we encourage scientists to investigate whether physical makeup and crime are linked?

Lombroso had a minimal impact upon American and British thought concerning crime and its punishment. More influential was the work of the sociological school of criminology, which viewed crime as a product of individual personality coupled with a number of societal factors. *Gabriel Tarde's Penal Philosophy*, translated into English and printed by the American Institute of Criminal Law and Criminology in 1890, argued that, even though the individual was morally responsible for his or her criminal acts, slums, the existence of a criminal underworld, and depravity within prison walls all conditioned people to a life of crime. Tarde also developed a law of imitation, which asserted that individuals were drawn into crime through their association with others engaged in criminal activity. Those who are inferior in age, social class, or intelligence will imitate the behavioral patterns of their superiors.

American penologists were first exposed to Lombroso's theories by Professor Charles R. Henderson when he addressed the St. Paul meeting of the National Prison Association in 1894. Stubborn opposition to positivist criminology was almost immediate, based upon the strong feeling that all people were responsible for their acts and, if sane, reformable by penological methods. Ironically, the American evidence assembled by Richard Dugdale concerning the *Jukes* family,[4] then in its fifth American edition, contained more evidence of hereditary criminality than emerged from Lombroso's statistics. Dugdale stated that the Jukes' primary characteristics were "great vitality, ignorance, and poverty." According to Dugdale, the name Juke "had come to be used generically as a term of reproach."[5]

What American penology could not ignore was the gradual incursion of scientific analysis into the study of crime, its prevention, and its cure. As early as 1851, Henry Mayhew, an English playwright and journalist, described the social background of crime and explored the impact of various forms of punishment. Social origins of criminal behavior, being popularized by Tarde and others, had earlier been the subject of the French philosopher Adolphe Quetelet in the 1830s, and a classic statistical study of the causes of crime was in the course of preparation by the English scholar Charles Goring.[6]

Rejection of Lombroso's predestination concept of crime did not lead American penologists to oppose scientific methods of dealing with inmates, their discipline, and their correction. As the twentieth century opened, a new era began in which the impact of science on prison reform was much more pronounced than was the influence of religion in the first three-quarters of the nineteenth century. Reformers recognized that psychological methods, including group therapy sessions, could be valuable additions to the prison's educational and reformatory programs. By the 1930s, F. Lovell Bixby and other psychologists were actively working in group therapy among young offenders who had been convicted of serious crimes (1932-1945), and numerous social workers as well as volunteers from religious organizations participated in counseling sessions for inmates. As Max Grunhut commented, "even in prison the obligations of man to man still exist."[7]

One of the most significant contributions of social science to penology has been the recognition of a specific kind of infrastructure among the inmates of a prison. Donald Clemmer[8] described a process by which a prisoner, through fear of guards and relationships with other prisoners, seeks out a small protective group and thereafter becomes progressively more hostile to the correction program. Clemmer termed this phenomenon *prisonization*, and it has become a recognized aspect of any scientific approach to prison sociology. Recent work in penology and prison sociology has provided valuable insights into the complex web of human relationships present in every prison and reformatory. For the most part, it establishes once more the value of Brockway's approach of individualized attention and patient encouragement in the direction of readjustment and eventual release.

THOMAS MOTT OSBORNE AND MIRIAM VAN WATERS

Never has inmate infrastructure come under closer public scrutiny than it did during the *Mutual Welfare League* experiment (1913-1920). This concept was developed by researcher *Thomas Mott Osborne* after he spent a week living with the inmates of New York's Auburn Prison in September 1913. Although Osborne's identity was known to the inmates, he was nevertheless able to observe their relationships and concerns. From this, he became convinced that prisoners should be made responsible for group discipline and for decisions concerning their communal life.

Previously, similar experiments had been tried. In 1887 Colonel Gardiner Tufts, superintendent of the Concord (Massachusetts) Reformatory, established societies and clubs for prisoners who had advanced to the first grade and thus were approaching parole. In 1896, Maud Ballington Booth developed the Volunteer Prison League, which brought evangelical Christianity to the prisons and organized inmate converts into league units. However, never before had self-government been attempted on such a broad scale as that proposed by Osborne in the Mutual Welfare League.

Subsequently, Osborne instituted the Mutual Welfare League at Auburn Prison during his time as warden there and on later assignments as warden at New York's Sing Sing Prison at Ossining and the U.S. Naval Prison at Portsmouth, New Hampshire. League officers were elected by prisoners and were responsible for supervising prison workshops and assigning punishments for infractions of the league's rules. Any failure to obey the rules or submit to league discipline immediately placed the prisoner back in the charge of prison officials and subject to the old prison routine.

While the league was in full operation, it achieved some notable results. Escapes, mental problems, and injuries from fights all decreased markedly. Over a period of 5 years under Mutual Welfare League operations, shop production at Sing Sing almost doubled. Like many innovations, the league prospered under the leadership of its originator, and Osborne was widely credited with substantial success; few other wardens were able to duplicate the program and its achievements.

By 1920, however, public resistance, legislative opposition, and inmate misgivings began to undermine the league. A highly publicized criminal trial in which Osborne was accused of sexual misconduct with some of the male inmates also damaged his efforts at reform, even though he was acquitted.[9] Thereafter, it survived as a useful organization for planning athletic activities and inmate social events. Abroad, the idea was adopted in the German province of Thuringia, and from 1923 to 1933 it was used as a mode of discipline with prisoners at the probationary stage immediately preceding their release.

HISTORY TODAY

There are different approaches to managing prison inmates. Some prison administrators do not recognize any inmate groupings, that is, gangs or other forms of banding together. Typically under this approach, there is no inmate self-governance allowed. Some administrators believe that prison officials should let inmates organize and be allowed to appoint spokespersons for their groups. Which approach is better—to act as if groups within prisons do not exist, or to acknowledge that inmates should have some sort of input into the way a prison is run?

Another prison reformer who experienced both the triumphs and frustrations of prison reform was *Miriam Van Waters*. Van Waters viewed the female imprisonment experience as being much different from that of the males. Van Waters believed that the separation from family was the greatest deprivation that a female prisoner could experience and that training for family life was the best thing a prison could do to prepare female inmates for life after release. Toward that end, Van Waters, a West Coast native who had worked in Oregon and California, tried to create such a model when she assumed control of the Massachusetts Reformatory for Women in Framingham in March 1932.

Van Waters tried to model her facility more along the lines of a home than an institution. Women were trained in domestic duties and parenting skills, as few women worked outside the home during that era, and many women found themselves in trouble with the law in part as a result of domestic problems. Van Waters encouraged the inmates to develop close, intimate, familial relations with each other, and she did not discourage staff members from developing these same relationships with inmates. In fact, Van Waters shared her living quarters with former inmates from time to time, something that was unthinkable at the time, and is equally anathema for prison officials today.

Like Osborne, Van Waters endured both high praise and sharp criticism for her methods and ideas. She was praised for her innovation and for trying to make a prison as effective as possible at preparing inmates for life after release. She was criticized for being too soft on prisoners and for being too close to the prisoners on a personal level. Also, as with Osborne, charges of sexual misconduct and sexual brutality arose involving the inmates, staff, and Van Waters herself. Van Waters was never convicted of any charges stemming from the scandal, but the damage to her reputation and reform efforts was significant, and was not helped by the fact that unlike Osborne, who was never definitively identified as a homosexual, Van Waters was as open as one could afford to be during her era. Whether Van Waters ever engaged in sexual relations with current or former inmates was never known, but that she enjoyed at the least a nonsexual intimacy with her charges was well-known. Even today, Van Waters' letters to her female companions are the subject of study and fascination in gay literature.[10]

HISTORY TODAY

Should we have more penal reformers like Miriam Van Waters, who try to create a family atmosphere in the prison? Or are people like Van Waters simply naïve, even to the point of being dangerously naïve?

PAROLE

Essential to the success of a parole, or early release, program was maintaining a system that would provide aftercare to released prison inmates. In Europe, this function was performed by government agencies, but in the United States private charitable groups were almost entirely responsible for the welfare of paroled inmates. Most prominent in this work were the *Salvation Army's Prison Gate Movement*; the Volunteers of America (a successor to Booth's Volunteer

Prison League); and the Central Howard Association, established in Chicago to provide parole services wherever another agency was not involved in assisting parolees. During the calendar year 1944, the Salvation Army handled more than 10,000 former prison inmates, providing a sizeable supplement to the limited amount of government activity with paroled convicts.

By 1898, about 25 states in the United States had a parole law in operation, but the slow development of indeterminate sentencing and the assignment of arbitrary minimum and maximum penalties hampered flexibility in administering the law. The organized bench and bar, intent upon the need for certainty and for protection against judicial inconsistencies, preferred definite terms of sentencing. Law schools reflected the new scientific attitudes and stressed standardization, rather than individualization, in criminal law administration. Legal professionalism and lack of sympathy for the aims of prison rehabilitation did much to limit the effectiveness of parole in the states.

Throughout the first quarter of the twentieth century, parole continued to grow, and studies of the systems of early release and parole stressed the need for more vigorous supervision of parolees. Parole boards instituted systems of psychological testing and interviewing, aimed at identifying inmates who were likely to harm society if released on parole. The growing pressures of overcrowding resulted in a general release of most inmates after they had served the minimum time of their sentence. In 1915, Wisconsin launched a *work release* program designed to release inmates for work outside the prison during daylight hours but requiring them to return to spend the night behind bars. This system of work release spread to North and South Carolina in the 1950s and to most of the other states in the 1960s.

PROBATION

Probation also played a significant role in reducing prison overcrowding in the United States. In fact, most people under correctional supervision in the United States are actually under probation supervision. Where parole is early release from prison, and is usually controlled by people appointed by the executive branch of government, probation is a sentence handed down by a court in lieu of a jail or prison sentence. Like parole, remaining in the community under probation supervision is contingent upon following conditions that are spelled out, and failure to abide by the conditions can result in further sanctions, including incarceration.

Judge *Peter Oxenbridge Thacher* and *John Augustus* (1784-1859) were two of the principal actors in the creation of American probation. Thacher hit upon the scheme of releasing young offenders on a recognizance; this was a legal procedure by which a judge could avoid placing a criminal or vagrant in jail pending trial. He stretched the rule somewhat in using the procedure to defer trial as long as the young delinquent behaved himself or herself. Judge Thacher's method would later be copied in modern methods for diverting first-time offenders from the full penalties of the criminal justice system.

John Augustus was a Boston shoemaker who observed the worst aspects of the city's street life. Augustus was also active in several of the temperance (antialcohol) organizations in the Boston area, and he was convinced that alcohol abuse, along with lack of adherence to Christian values, was the core problem afflicting Boston's urban underclass. In 1841 Augustus began visiting Boston's city courts and interviewing defendants as they were led into the courtroom. After speaking with the defendant and if convinced of his or her willingness to reform, Augustus would speak to the court on the defendant's behalf. Augustus would offer to post bail for the defendant or stand good for the bail amount. He would then assume supervisory authority of the defendant and try to get them sober, gainfully employed, and in church. After 30-60 days, Augustus would return to court with the defendant (assuming the defendant had not fled the area) and attest to the defendant's progress while under his supervision. If the judge was convinced that the defendant had made an earnest effort to reform, he would dismiss the case, suspend sentence, or release the defendant upon payment of court costs (which would usually be paid by Augustus).[11] When the work became too much for one man, the Boston Children's Aid Society, headed by prison chaplain Rufus R. Cook, took over Augustus' juvenile caseload.

Although he is associated with the genesis of probation supervision, Augustus actually practiced pretrial supervision because most of his charges had not been convicted of a crime prior to his working with them, unlike most contemporary probation cases where the defendant has been convicted prior to the beginning of supervision. Nevertheless, Augustus helped to set in motion the practice of supervising offenders in the community, and it led to the creation of the first probation law, which was enacted in Massachusetts in 1878. Although John Augustus is considered the first probation officer, he only worked on a volunteer basis, and in fact he volunteered so much of his time and money that he eventually went bankrupt shortly before his death. *Edward Savage*, a Boston police captain, became America's first paid probation officer in 1878.[12]

Probation became commonplace only from 1912 to 1933. During that time, the number of probation officers in the nation increased from 200 to 4,000. The federal government hired its first probation officer in 1927 so that federal courts could use probation. When 25 states were surveyed in 1939, it was found that about one-third of all persons convicted of crime were placed on probation. Only 30% of those placed on probation were later sent to prison, either for violation of probation or for some subsequent offense. With Mississippi officially adopting probation in 1956, all states utilized probation.[13]

HISTORY TODAY

John Augustus's idea behind what is now called *probation* was to select minor offenders whom he deemed receptive to intervention efforts and to try to help them. Today, more than two-thirds of the American population is under probation supervision for both minor misdemeanors and serious felonies. Was this what Augustus had in mind? Or does that even matter? What would he think of the law enforcement outlook that many probation officers in the United States have now?

JUVENILE DELINQUENCY

Increased study of the origins of crime pointed to the influence of environmental and social factors on juvenile delinquency, or criminal activity of juveniles. The response of the criminal justice system was to establish a special court for the trial of youthful offenders and special correctional programs for their rehabilitation. The cities of Chicago and Denver in the United States were among the first (1899) to use juvenile courts designed to provide a separate system of criminal justice for young offenders, as well as to provide social services and aftercare to young men and women committed to reform schools or houses of refuge.

Several studies undertaken from 1930 to 1950 focused on the causes and remedies for juvenile delinquency. They found that young men and women were led into criminal activity through a combination of social factors and emotional instability. Among a group of 111 families living under adverse conditions, 45% of the children were delinquent, and within that group 91% were found to be under some form of emotional stress. More than adult crime, juvenile delinquency was found to be group-conditioned. One of the innovative suggestions that emerged from this period was the *American Law Institute's Draft Youth Correctional Authority Act* (1940), which proposed that juvenile delinquency matters be removed from the court system and placed under the supervision of a *Youth Correctional Authority*, which would have available to it all the facilities of social work and psychological counseling needed for an effective youth correction program. Adopted by California in 1941, the Draft Youth Correctional Act has served as a basis for a number of similar programs in other states.

American developments in the control of juvenile delinquency have paralleled British establishment and operation of the *Borstal* system, which provided a group of correctional facilities for youth and stressed rehabilitation through vocational training. Formalized by the Prevention of Crime Act of 1908, the Borstal system originated through the efforts of Sir Evelyn Ruggles-Brise at Borstal in Kent. It made special training available to young offenders ranging in age from 16 to 21. Girls were trained in domestic work and boys were assigned to labor parties. Eventually, both young men and women progressed to workshops where they learned skills that would be useful upon their release. The Borstal system relied upon a group of more than 1,000 paid and volunteer associates who worked with those discharged from the training facilities, finding them jobs and otherwise easing their adjustment to society.

Criminal activity among young people has occupied an increasing amount of law enforcement time since the 1950s. During and after World War II, juvenile delinquency became a subject for state, national, and international study. In practice, it has resulted in the development of a large and expert bureaucracy devoted to the study of youthful crime and the evolution of techniques for its control and correction. To a considerable degree, this work has occurred outside the scope of American prison reform, and thus it has lacked the formative influence that earlier efforts with youthful offenders had on the reform of adult correctional procedures.

RECENT DEVELOPMENTS IN AMERICAN PENOLOGY

It is difficult to fully appreciate the impact of the *Federal Bureau of Prisons*, which was established in 1929. A succession of outstanding directors, including *Sanford Bates* and James V. Bennett, spearheaded the United States' effort to provide prisons for a large number of offenders. For the first time, the federal government ended its reliance on state prison facilities to maintain those who violated federal criminal laws. The Great Depression of the 1930s caused an increase in federal convictions, particularly for violation of the *Volstead Act* and related laws created to enforce the *Eighteenth Amendment* to the Constitution which banned alcohol (Prohibition). As a consequence, the Federal Bureau of Prisons became one of the leading agencies in operating a classification system for a wide spectrum of inmates requiring imprisonment at the maximum security level, as well as for individuals who could safely be placed in minimum-security camp-like facilities.

The federal prison constructed at Lewisburg, Pennsylvania, in 1930 provided a variety of confinement facilities within one institution, ranging from medium security to maximum security. Beyond being an outstanding model for differentiated treatment of inmates, the Federal Bureau of Prisons pioneered new and innovative methods of rehabilitation and parole. Its establishment and operation of Federal Prison Industries, Inc., gave

FIGURE 12.3 Sanford Bates, former director of the Federal Bureau of Prisons. *Library of Congress.*

encouragement to state prison officials in their efforts to make effective use of the state-use method of prison industry.

A growing concern with recidivism (or repeat offenses) generated interest in methods of identifying prisoners. In the 1890s, a method of identification based upon the Bertillon measurements of facial characteristics was used in obtaining positive identification. In use since 1883, the Bertillon system of identification resulted in a centralized file for the nation, maintained at Sing Sing Prison after 1892. In 1901, New York prison authorities adopted the fingerprint methods developed by Scotland Yard, and by 1907 the federal government established a centralized clearinghouse for fingerprints in its newly established Bureau of Investigation.

Careful statistical analysis was applied to prison records in the years after 1930, giving rise to a wide variation in findings concerning recidivism. In 1930, Sheldon and Eleanor Glueck published *Five Hundred Criminal Careers*,[14] based upon their study at Concord (Massachusetts) Reformatory, where they discovered a repeat offense rate of 80%. Thirty-five years later, Daniel Glaser[15,16] surveyed the federal prison rates and reported a 31% recidivism rate, attributable, in his opinion, to the Federal Bureau of Prisons' recourse to early release programs. Despite the wide disparity in these findings, it is clear that repeat offenses are common in spite of extensive efforts at inmate counseling and rehabilitation. At the same time, American penology continues to seek a method of individualized treatment that will effectively neutralize the criminal tendencies of prison inmates.

Outbreaks of prison violence, both before and after World War II, demonstrate that concern for the conditions of imprisonment is essential if any rehabilitation is to take place. Staff must be competent, adequately paid, and able to engage inmates in useful and challenging activity. There is a growing tendency to rely upon specially trained correctional officers rather than on prison guards provided with a minimum of training and professional pride. Riots and prisoner rights movements have alerted prison management to the need to give serious consideration to inmate complaints and to rectify the difficulties long before they rise to the point of crisis and confrontation.

Two centuries after the reform effort was launched by John Howard, penal institutions continue to provide a fertile ground for study and new programs. The social sciences have provided insights into prisoner psychology and the causes of crime that enlighten prison officials and guide law enforcement authorities in their work. The key to successful rehabilitation of criminals continues to elude Anglo-American penologists. At the same time, they have steadfastly, on the basis of religion and morality, refused to accept Cesare Lombroso's conclusion that there is a subspecies of humans that commit crime and cannot be reformed. American penology continues to hope for, and work toward, a better program for the rehabilitation of criminals and the betterment of our society.

SUMMARY

The National Prison Congress of 1870 restated in emphatic terms an earlier emphasis on rehabilitation as the primary aim of penitentiary sentences. Inspired by the keynote address of Zebulon R. Brockway, the 1870 meeting instituted an era of expanded prison industry, increased educational opportunities within prison walls, and the systematic use of the progressive system of prison discipline, originated by Sir Walter Crofton and applied by Brockway at the New York State Reformatory at Elmira. Unfortunately, prison industry, one of the vital parts of the rehabilitative system, was vigorously opposed by competing industrialists and organized labor. This caused the virtual elimination of prison industry, except for state-use items, by 1890.

Later developments in penology included the establishment of the federal prison system, providing a much larger group of inmates and greater opportunity for classification and the establishment of prisons with graduated security. Thomas Mott Osborne's Mutual Welfare League sparked studies of inmate infrastructure and illustrated the need to avoid disciplinary problems and riots through communication between inmates and wardens. Southern prison systems, largely unaffected by late nineteenth-century penal reforms, moved from extensive leasing of convict labor to a new and widely copied institution of prison farms. The farms provided a healthy method of using labor to support the penal system and have become one of the more effective systems of inmate rehabilitation throughout the United States. Parole and probation have provided partial solutions to the problem of prison crowding, but private charitable organizations have played the major role in implementing postrelease programs. With the rise of juvenile delinquency immediately before and after World War II, there has been a general effort to provide special facilities for young offenders, and substantial study has taken place concerning the sources of juvenile crime and techniques for its punishment.

The 1870 National Prison Congress initiated a period of international influence for American penology that lasted until the turn of the century, when Cesare Lombroso, the Italian criminologist, changed the focus of European penology with his theory that criminal behavior is hereditary, and rehabilitation, in many cases, is impossible. While American criminologists and penologists have examined possible hereditary origins of crime, the major emphasis of American penology has continued to be rehabilitation along with modification of environmental and cultural factors that tend to breed criminal activity.

REFERENCES

Grunhut, M. (1948). *Penal reform: A comparative study.* Oxford: Clarendon Press, reprinted Montclair, NJ: Patterson Smith; McKelvey, B. (1977). *American prisons: A history of good intentions.* Montclair, NJ: Patterson Smith; Erikkson, T. (1976). *The reformers: An historical survey of pioneer experiments in the treatment of criminals.* Trans. Djurklou, C. New York: Elsevier.

Winter, A. (1891). *The New York state reformatory at Elmira.* London: Swan Sonnenschein & Co; Brockway, Z. R. (1912). *Fifty years of prison service: An autobiography.* New York: Charities Publishing Co.

Mannhein, H. (Ed.), (1972). *Pioneers in criminology.* (2nd ed). Montclair, NJ: Patterson Smith; Lombroso, C. (1911). *Crime: Its causes and its remedies.* Trans. Horton, H. P. (1968). Boston: Little, Brown & Co, reprinted Montclair, NJ: Patterson Smith; Ferri, E. (1898). *Criminal sociology.* New York: D. Appleton & Co.

Pillsbury, S. H. (1989). Understanding penal reform: The dynamic of change. *Journal of Criminal Law and Criminology, 80,* 726–780; Fogel, D. (1982). *We are the living proof: The justice model for corrections.* Cincinnati, OH: Anderson Publishing Co; Cullen, F. T., & Gilbert, K. E. (1982). *Reaffirming rehabilitation.* Cincinnati, OH: Anderson Publishing Co; Durham, A. M. III (1994). *Crisis and reform: Current issues in American punishment.* Boston: Little, Brown & Co; Wilson, J. Q., & Herrnstein, R. J. (1985). *Crime and human nature.* New York: Simon and Schuster; Murray, C., & Herrnstein, R. J. (1994). *The bell curve: Intelligence and class structure in American life.* New York: The Free Press; Shichor, D. (1995). *Punishment for profit: Private prisons/public concerns.* Thousand Oaks, CA: Sage Publications; McDonald, D. C. (Ed.), (1990). *Private prisons and the public interest.* New Brunswick, NJ: Rutgers University Press; Logan, C. H. (1990). *Private prisons: Cons and pros.* New York: Oxford University Press.

Notes and Problems

1. Prison industries provide gainful employment, contribute to the cost of prison maintenance, and can serve a rehabilitative purpose. In light of opposition by organized labor, how can prison officials sustain this vital aspect of prison management?

2. Is it possible that Dugdale's work on the Jukes and Lombroso's concept of the born criminal have merit, and that there really is a genetic defect that causes criminal behavior? Should we alter our view of crime and punishment in light of this proposition?

3. Indeterminate sentencing provides correction officials with a powerful stimulant for good behavior and rehabilitation. At the same time, it tends to remove the responsibility of judges and juries to impose sentences in proportion to the serious nature of the crimes. We have seen that the bench and bar tended to resist indeterminate sentencing laws. Were they correct in terms of constitutional law, procedural rights, and protecting the interests of the public? Should correctional officers or parole boards be permitted to second-guess judges and jurors in this area of great concern to public safety?

ENDNOTES

[1] See discussion in Chapter 9.

[2] See Chapter 9.

[3]Winter, A. (1891). *The New York state reformatory at Elmira.* London: Swan Sonnenschein & Co, p. 37.

[4]Dugdale, R. (1891). *The Jukes: A study in crime, pauperism, disease and heredity* (5th ed). New York: G. P. Putnam's.

[5]Dugdale, R. (2004). The Jukes: A study in crime, pauperism and heredity. In J. Jacoby (Ed.) *Classics of criminology* (3rd ed). Prospect Heights, IL: Waveland Press, pp. 132-139.

[6]Goring, C. (1913). *The English convict: A statistical study.* London: H.M. Stationery Office.

[7]Grunhut, M. (1948). *Penal reform: A comparative study.* Oxford: The Clarendon Press, reprinted Montclair, NJ: Patterson Smith (1972), p. 250.

[8]Clemmer, D. (1940). *The prison community.* Boston: Christopher Publishing House.

[9]Chamberlain, R.W. (1936). *There is no truce: A life of Thomas Mott Osborne: prison reformer.* London: Routledge.

[10]Freedman, E. B. (1998). *Maternal justice: Miriam Van Waters and the female reform tradition.* Chicago: University of Chicago Press; Jones, M. (2005). *Criminal justice pioneers in U.S. history.* Boston: Allyn and Bacon.

[11]The American Probation and Parole Association. *A Report of the labors of John Augustus.* Lexington, KY: 1984 [1852]).

[12]Jones, M. (2004). *Community corrections.* Prospect Heights, IL: Waveland.

[13]Ibid.

[14]Sheldon and Eleanor Glueck. (1930). *Five hundred criminal careers.* New York: Knopf, reprinted Millwood, NY: Kraus Reprints (1975).

[15]Glaser, D. (1964). *The effectiveness of a prison and parole system.* Indianapolis: Bobbs-Merrill.

[16]Foucault, M. *Discipline and punish.* New York: Pantheon (1977), pp. 248, 252-254.

CHAPTER 13

Law Enforcement Professionalism and the Establishment of a Criminal Justice System

KEY TERMS

Al Capone

Albert Schneider

Alice Stebbens Wells

Alphonse Bertillon

August Vollmer

Ballistics

Boston Police strike

Brown v. Board of Education

Charles E. Waite

Chicago Eight

Christopher Commission

Civil rights

Civilian review board

Cold War

Criminal justice professional

Daryl Gates

DNA

"Dream Team"

Due process revolution

Earl Warren

Espionage

European Convention on Human Rights

Europol

F. Lee Bailey

Federal Bureau of Investigation

Federalism

Fred Kohler

Golden rule policy

Great Depression

Incorporation debate

International Association of Chiefs of Police

J. Edgar Hoover

John Jay College of Criminal Justice

Johnny Cochran

Juge d'Instruction

Keystone Cops

Lola Baldwin

Louis Daguerre

Martin Luther King, Jr.

National Crime Agency

National Motor Vehicle Theft (Dyer) Act

National Prison Association

New Deal

O. J. Simpson

O. W. Wilson

Omnibus Crime Control and Safe Streets Act of 1968

Paddy wagon

Pearls of Policing

Police fraternal organizations

Progressive Era

Robert Shapiro

Rodney King

St. Valentine's Day massacre

Sunrise court

Teapot Dome Scandal

Televised trials

Texas Rangers

Vietnam War

Warren Court

Wickersham Commission

William Burns

LEARNING OBJECTIVES

1. Learn how criminal justice is evolving into a profession and about some of the people who have affected that evolution.
2. Learn the effect of the Great Depression on criminal justice.
3. Understand how the Cold War between the United States and the Soviet Union affected criminal justice.
4. Learn about some of the ways in which the American civil rights movement affected criminal justice.
5. Understand the impact of the Warren Court.
6. Learn about some of the female pioneers in American policing.
7. Learn some of the technological innovations that improved law enforcement.
8. Understand how social issues such as the Vietnam War and race relations created and affected celebrated criminal justice cases.

Table 13.1 Time Line

1879-1883	Identification by anthropometry is developed, but shortly replaced as a means of identification by fingerprinting.
1901	National Police Chiefs Union meets in Chicago; becomes International Association of Chiefs of Police in 1915.
1901-1940	Experiments in blood testing permit classification into four types, and the identification of the Rh factor.
1903	Chief Fred Kohler of the Cincinnati Police Department institutes sunrise court and a system for rehabilitating juvenile delinquents.
1905	Lola Baldwin of the Los Angeles Police Department becomes the first female law enforcement officer appointed in an American police department.
1906	Chief August Vollmer recruits college students into the Berkeley (California) Police Department.
1907	Bureau of Investigation established in U.S. Department of Justice.
1915	University of California at Berkeley establishes a 3-year course for training police officers.
1918	J. Edgar Hoover becomes head of General Investigations Division, Bureau of Investigation.
1918-1933	Prohibition of the sale of alcoholic beverages begins as a wartime measure and is adopted as the Eighteenth Amendment to the Constitution; it was repealed by the Twenty-First Amendment in 1933.
1919	Boston Police Strike triggers state legislation prohibiting the unionization of police forces.
1922-1929	Ballistic evidence becomes an accepted form of proof in criminal courts.
1923	"Zone" schools established to provide regional training for law enforcement officers.
1924	Hoover becomes head of the Bureau of Investigation.
1929	A stock market crash forces American participation in a worldwide recession.
1930	San Jose State University (California) establishes a 2-year police training curriculum.
1931	Wickersham Commission report on crime is published.
1933	Franklin D. Roosevelt inaugurated as President. The New Deal brings the resources of the federal government to bear on measures to stimulate economic recovery. These include the construction of new local courthouses and jails.

Continued

Table 13.1   Time Line—cont'd

1935	Justice Department's Bureau of Investigation becomes the Federal Bureau of Investigation. FBI Academy established.
1935	Medical examiners introduced in large cities, replacing coroners who served without any significant medical training.
1939-1945	The United States enters World War II in December 1941. Postwar reforms of military justice result in the enactment of the Uniform Code of Military Justice in 1951.
1950-1951	Kefauver Committee hearings on interstate crime televised; officials in the Internal Revenue Service, Treasury Department, and Justice Department removed from their positions.
1953-1954	McCarthy Committee hearings on "un-American" activities broadcast nationally.
1954	U.S. Supreme Court orders desegregation of elementary schools in *Brown v. Board of Education*.
1964-1975	American involvement in Vietnam incites violent confrontation between police and student protesters.
1966	The United States Supreme Court hands down the *Miranda v. Arizona* decision.
1968	Assassination of Rev. Dr. Martin Luther King heightens racial tension and causes unrest in urban areas.
1968	Law Enforcement Assistant Administration (LEAA) established by congressional statute.

ENTER THE NATION STATE

In the twentieth century, law enforcement professionalism took place alongside the continuing shift from personal and family-focused retribution to a public entity of centralized government control. During the past 1,000 years in Europe and the past 400 years in the United States there had been a progressive move toward the creation of a public criminal justice system that affected social values, culture, politics, and the essence of the human community. The *criminal justice professional* became, and remains, a significant force in interpreting how the state wishes its citizens to behave and conduct themselves.

HISTORY TODAY

Some people do not view criminal justice employees as professionals, especially correction officers and officers in some departments. What are some ways in which various criminal justice workers can enhance their image as professionals?

The millennium witnessed a progression toward trading out personal watch-keeping responsibilities to paid professionals and thereby exchanging some personal freedoms for a collectivity that is interpreted for the citizenry, initially by kings and then by the nation-state. Citizens in democracies no longer rely on the local village constable for their safety and protection. Instead, they are dependent on an extension of central government. Much of this movement started in the eleventh and twelfth centuries as lords and later kings transitioned societal dependence away from the church to the secular state. It was the age of knights and chivalry that supported and then became a voice of legal reform. The extension of the right of kings and the nobility as the origins from which ownership and power evolved transformed from the tournament field to the courtroom. The knight in armor battling for the good name of another became the professional jurist and the lawyer became the vehicle that ensured the constant supply of litigants and criminals to the tournament (courtroom). Inevitably, the tournament expanded and needed other actors: the police and prison system for the public sector and private security and detective services for the private and business sectors.

To effect successful policing in the rapidly changing New World, new methods of operation and investigation were needed. American policing needed to take the best that Europe had established and modify it to suit the challenges of a vast new country. Having set the scene in the nineteenth century, the twentieth century became the era of modification, modernization, and reform. The result has been another exchange but this time not East to West, but rather the reverse. It is at this point that the United States leads in many ways, so much so that England and France have now started to adopt American models for their criminal justice systems.

In June 2007, the *Pearls in Policing* conference in The Hague, The Netherlands, emphasized the importance of universal norms and values for police organizations. The future of policing may be divided between delivering the traditional values of policing by consent and public accountability and the need to effectively police global terrorism. It is certain that we can expect a greater use of emergency powers in the future. The language and values of terrorists do not conform to societal norms and much of the legislation implemented in haste at the close of the twentieth century may return for the long term. Terrorism has become a local law enforcement issue for most Western nations. Countering this may inevitably lead to domination of the criminal justice system by national and international agencies and far greater centralization, as has been the case in France, Spain, and Italy. The United States has historically had a decentralized police system, perhaps the most decentralized in the world, and the American public may resist greater centralization. While the twentieth century was a period of reform, the twenty-first may become the century of centralization.

THE RISE OF THE PROFESSIONAL

The quickening pace of twentieth-century historical change resulted in the dramatic alteration of criminal justice professions. Early decades of the century witnessed the introduction of new inventions, such as the telephone, radio, automobile, and airplane, which predictably improved systems of police communication and facilitated increased mobility of police units. More recently, political and social developments have also made their mark. Constitutional limitations on investigative activity have occurred through federal court decisions as well as congressional and state legislative action. Rising demand for equal opportunity by women and racial minority groups has altered the composition of police and correctional units. Further, the growing complexity of governmental regulatory activity has placed new demands on the criminal justice system.

The period between American involvement in the two world wars (1919-1941) was a period of malaise, during which national energy and reform impulses waned, materialism reigned supreme, and criminal activity became commonplace in American life. The *Great Depression* period (1929-1941) significantly decreased national confidence, and resulted in many Americans challenging the validity of capitalism and free enterprise. To counter the impact of the Depression, President Franklin D. Roosevelt instituted the *New Deal*, a pragmatic effort to reestablish confidence in the business world, create regulatory safeguards against excessively harsh competition, and develop legal foundations for a stable national economy.

HISTORY TODAY

The Great Depression serves as a poignant example of how factors external to criminal justice can drastically affect the operation of the criminal justice system. Suddenly, the criminal justice system was dealing with a host of problems it had not dealt with prior to the Great Depression. Why is it important for people who work in the justice system to be attuned to other events and factors in their community, state, and nation that are not directly related to criminal justice?

During the *Cold War* (1948-1991), the growing power of the Union of Soviet Socialist Republics (the Soviet Union), and its apparent success in assembling a group of satellite nations along with the People's Republic of China, had a significant impact on American life and policing activities. Increased emphasis on internal security measures designed to limit *espionage* (spy activities) characterized this period, along with continuing efforts to regulate business practices and strengthen national defense. These broad national and international concerns did not diminish efforts in the criminal justice field, where federal, state, and local police agencies conducted a continuing battle against rapidly increasing criminal activity.

Franklin D. Roosevelt (1882-1945): Governor of New York (1928-1932); thirty-second President of the United States (1933-1945); served longer than any President in American history; President during the Great Depression of the 1930s and during most of World War II.

In addition to economic and foreign policy concerns, *civil rights* dominated the domestic scene throughout the late 1950s and 1960s, ushered in partly by the Supreme Court's 1954 decision in the school desegregation case of *Brown v. Board of Education* (349 U.S. 294). Ultimately, the Supreme Court's opinions undermined the political foundation of racial segregation throughout the United States, and its efforts were supplemented by a series of federal statutes guaranteeing civil rights to all citizens. Coupled with concern for civil rights was a growing awareness of racial distinctions in the administration of criminal justice, as well as a reevaluation of due process and equal protection guarantees for all persons accused of crime.[1] The criminal justice system itself was subjected to careful study and evaluation, encouraged to some degree by the passage of the Federal Law Enforcement Assistance Act (LEAA) of 1968.

THE DUE PROCESS REVOLUTION

FIGURE 13.1 Earl Warren, Chief Justice of the United States from 1953 to 1969. *Library of Congress.*

One of the *Warren Court's* most notable legacies was the *Due Process Revolution*. Under the Warren Court, so named after *Earl Warren*, who served as Chief Justice of the United States Supreme Court from 1953 to 1969, the Court used its opinions to implement new concepts of *federalism* (applying federal control in the field of criminal procedure). The Court applied federal standards on a case-by-case basis to state police methods and court procedures. The result was that virtually all provisions of the federal Bill of Rights (Amendments I through VIII) were held applicable to the states.

This settled the *incorporation debate* that had been argued ever since the adoption of the Constitution. For 160 years prior to the Warren Court, some had argued that the provisions of the U.S. Constitution applied only to the federal government, but a gradual shift had occurred, starting with the adoption of the Thirteenth and Fourteenth Amendments enacted shortly after the Civil War ended. The Warren Court settled the incorporation debate for good; the U.S. Constitution was the supreme law of the states and the federal government. The following are among the more significant cases that directly impacted law enforcement and the criminal justice system:

Earl Warren (1891-1974): Chief Justice of the United States Supreme Court (1953-1969), Governor of California (1943-1953), Republican candidate for Vice President in 1948, Attorney General of California (1939-1943), and Alameda County District Attorney (1925-1939); nominated to Supreme Court by President Dwight Eisenhower; known as a strong conservative advocate of law and order before serving on the Supreme Court, but his name became synonymous with civil liberties, civil rights, and other liberal causes as Chief Justice.

- *Mapp v. Ohio* (367 U.S. 643, 1961): evidence illegally obtained is inadmissible; the "exclusionary rule" applies to the states.
- *Wong Sun v. United States* (371 U.S. 471, 1963): evidence derived from an illegal police act, or "fruit of the poisonous tree" is inadmissible.
- *Escobedo v. Illinois* (378 U.S. 478, 1964): a person charged with a serious offense is entitled to counsel while in a police station.
- *Miranda v. Arizona* (384 U.S. 436, 1966): information and confessions obtained from a suspect undergoing custodial interrogation are inadmissible unless the suspect understood that he or she had certain rights.

- *United States v. Wade* (388 U.S. 218, 1967): a suspect has the right to the presence of an attorney during a lineup.
- *Kent v. United States* (389 U.S. 347, 1967): electronic surveillance that is an invasion of privacy constitutes a search and is subject to the rules pertaining to illegal searches.

THE FBI: PARADIGM AND PARADOX

No police agency has been more controversial than the *Federal Bureau of Investigation (FBI)*, and none has made a greater impression on the law enforcement profession in the twentieth century. Established in 1907 as the Bureau of Investigation of the Justice Department, the FBI was active in countering German espionage before and during World War I. On the eve of America's entry into that conflict, a young law school graduate, *J. Edgar Hoover*, began his professional career as a law clerk in the Department of Justice. Known for his ability and diligence, Hoover was made head of the General Investigation Division in 1918. As head of this division, Hoover was in charge of the prosecutions of espionage agents, as well as the investigations of Communist and Socialist groups. With the close of the war in November 1918, a series of strikes and terrorist attacks generated strong public opinion against the Communist Party and its affiliated organizations. During the Red Scare (1918-1922), a number of aliens residing in the United States were deported after their Communist associations were verified by the Department of Justice. Hoover played an active role in these prosecutions, becoming a recognized authority on the Communist Party and its American operations.

> J. Edgar Hoover (1895-1972): Born and raised in Washington, D.C.; Director of the FBI from 1924 to 1972; great innovator in law enforcement; created the Uniform Crime Reports, the public enemies list, and developed the FBI into one of the elite law enforcement agencies in the world; vigorous anticommunist; later found to have conducted unauthorized surveillance on hundreds of liberal public figures including Martin Luther King Jr. and John Lennon; grew increasingly eccentric and erratic in final years before his death.

Despite its commendable investigative work during the war, the Bureau of Investigation was riddled with political appointees, standards of conduct were low, and police work tended to be shoddy. In addition, the bureau's intervention in a steel strike led by William Z. Foster (later head of the Communist Party USA) enhanced its reputation for being antilabor and an instrument for strikebreaking. It was against this background that President Warren Harding, in September 1921, appointed *William J. Burns*, owner of the large strikebreaking private detective agency, to be director. Almost simultaneously, Hoover was named assistant director and was kept busy with the extensive investigation and prosecution of the Ku Klux Klan resurgence in the southern states. Hoover learned by bitter experience how difficult it was to secure convictions from southern juries and how deeply racism and violence marked southern society.

William J. Burns (1861-1932): Founder of Burns Detective Agency; renowned but sometimes ethically questionable investigator; investigated numerous high-profile crimes including the terrorist attack on the *Los Angeles Times* headquarters; served with U.S. Secret Service before creating his own agency.

Hoover's eventual elevation to the directorship was a direct result of the *Teapot Dome Scandal*, in which high-ranking officials in the Harding administration were found to have conspired to sell valuable oil leases on government lands in return for extensive bribes from oil drilling companies. Although the Bureau of Investigation was innocent of any implication in the scandal, it was discovered that its agents had cooperated with Director Burns in a plot to discredit Senator Burton K. Wheeler of Montana. Wheeler was chairman of the Senate Committee assigned to investigate Teapot Dome, and exposure of this Justice Department attempt to embarrass the Senate investigation led to public outrage. President Calvin Coolidge, who succeeded to office at Harding's death, inherited the Teapot Dome scandal and the related illegal practices in the bureau and Department of Justice.

Harlan F. Stone, Coolidge's new attorney general, named Hoover to be bureau director. Hoover's acceptance on May 10, 1924, was on the condition that Stone would guarantee him freedom from political influence, sole authority to deal with discipline within the bureau, as well as a rigid chain of command in which he would be responsible only to the attorney general, and that FBI employees would channel their complaints to Hoover and be answerable only to him. Thus began an association between the Bureau of Investigation and Director J. Edgar Hoover that for better or worse would dominate federal law enforcement from that time until Hoover's death on May 1, 1972.

The limited scope of federal criminal law at that time is evidenced by the 1928 report on bureau activities. By far the largest numbers of cases prosecuted were the 2,549 indictments and 2,055 convictions under the *National Motor Vehicle Theft Act*, or the *Dyer Act*. Next in magnitude were the 923 cases involving fugitives from justice apprehended by the bureau. Carrying women across state lines for immoral purposes, prohibited by the Mann Act of 1910, was the basis for 602 indictments and 469 convictions. These were followed by investigations involving violation of the bankruptcy laws, embezzlements under the National Bank Act, and larceny of goods being carried in interstate commerce.

Congress gradually extended federal criminal law, relying on constitutional grants of power to the federal government and reacting to the rapidly unfolding national economy and the nationwide scope of criminal activity that was based on exploitation of gaps between state and federal criminal law. Expanded bureau jurisdiction came not only from statutory authorization, but also resulted from a willingness on the part of Hoover and his superiors to use existing federal statutes as vehicles for authorizing necessary expansion of bureau activity. For example, using FBI agents for counterintelligence work before World War II was on the basis of an obscure statute permitting the State Department to conduct such investigations in support of its diplomatic activities.

In the first 5 years of Hoover's directorship, the Bureau of Investigation assumed greater responsibility, while simultaneously being subjected to a steady reduction in personnel. This may have been due to Hoover's intention to eliminate any individuals who did not have either law degrees or accounting degrees from his ranks of special agents. It also demonstrated his preference for a small, highly productive, and cost-effective agency. As such, the management of the bureau appealed to economy-minded members of Congress.

The bureau, renamed the Federal Bureau of Investigation (FBI) in 1935, was the focus of public attention in the 1930s, as its agents tracked down and secured the imprisonment of such legendary underworld characters as George "Machine Gun" Kelly (who named the FBI "G-Men"), John Dillinger, "Ma" Barker, Alvin Karpis, and Bonnie Parker and Clyde Barrow. This was part of the astuteness of J. Edgar Hoover. He was skilled at manipulating and feeling the pulse of public opinion, at least until his later years (when he seemed to lose touch with reality), and he was equally skilled at putting a face on crime. He developed the "public enemies list," which led to the posting of infamous wanted criminals in post offices and federal buildings around the country. By catching or killing a "bad guy," Hoover was able to give the public a sense of closure that one more crime problem had been handled by the FBI. Hoover ignored the social problems that might have been at the root of much crime, laboring under the idea that there were good people and bad people, with bad people being equated with being unchristian and un-American.

The post-World War II years and the beginning phases of the Cold War were also marked by a rapidly rising crime rate, attributable in large degree to illegal behavior by individuals below the age of 18. The FBI estimated that 43 percent of the crimes reported were attributable to persons in this age group and that more than half of the juvenile delinquents were under the age of 15. In response to this challenge, Hoover established a Juvenile Delinquency Instructor's School to assist state and local police agencies in the prevention and investigation of juvenile crime. Responding to the increase of crime among adults, Hoover criticized growing liberality in granting parole and probation. He referred to leading correctional theorists as "gushing, well-wishing, mawkish sentimentalists,"[2] which drew their sharp counterattacks. In his defense, it should be pointed out that many of the FBI's most-wanted criminals were released from prison on parole after having served the bare minimum time for their sentences. These were hard-core criminals who had taxed bureau resources greatly and who had been put behind bars at great risk to Hoover's agents in the field.[3,4,5,6,7]

J. Edgar Hoover and his FBI attracted harsh criticism from the press during their time, and to a degree they remain controversial today. While some of the criticisms are justified, critics often overlook the magnitude of the bureau's contributions to twentieth-century American law enforcement.

The contributions made to law enforcement by Hoover's FBI include the following:

Personnel and management. There was virtually complete freedom from political influence in the appointment of special agents and other employees in Hoover's FBI. Discipline was tight, and all personnel were expected to conduct themselves with dignity and decorum, even when off duty. The smallest lapse might be brought to the attention of the director, and attempts to appeal outside bureau channels or to secure political support were dealt with harshly. For the most part, FBI disciplinary measures did not draw public or political attention, but a few agents who were disciplined or discharged by Hoover wrote books critical of him and the bureau. Special agents were carefully selected from among graduates of law schools or graduates of accountancy programs; they were trained extensively both in formal schools and on the job by their veteran colleagues. Both agents and clerical employees were loyal to the "company," the euphemism used in daily discourse to deflect public curiosity about the individual's work. Management of field offices was marked by decentralization of authority to Special Agents in Charge, but each office was inspected at irregular intervals to ensure that bureau directives and procedures were being followed. Advancement, like appointment, was kept free of political influence. Personnel procedures were outside the normal federal civil service system, giving the director and his subordinates broad discretion in disciplining and rewarding personnel.

Investigative practices. FBI investigative work was thorough, persistent, and results-oriented. It earned the bureau a reputation for always apprehending its criminal, no matter what resources and time were required to do so. Agents were trained to use the most advanced scientific techniques to solve crimes. The FBI Laboratory was then, as now, the leading forensic and identification facility in the nation. Meticulous intelligence files were maintained, both in regard to criminal activity and in the counterintelligence field; these raw files were carefully cross-indexed and provided a treasure of materials concerning individuals who had come to FBI investigative attention. With all of this attention to investigative procedures, the FBI became a leading police agency in extending procedural rights and guarantees to suspects. Long before the Warren Court began its enumeration of protections guaranteed to accused persons, the bureau had implemented those rules in its operations manuals.

Law enforcement liaison and training. The FBI Academy, established in 1935, was designed to provide training for state and local government police officials, a function it has performed with distinction for many years.

The bureau also publishes a *Law Enforcement Bulletin* for circulation among academy graduates and chiefs of police throughout the nation. Its laboratory and the central fingerprint identification bureau (established in 1924) provided invaluable support to police activities nationwide. The bureau served as a model for countless federal law enforcement organizations and activities. For example, when the United States Air Force found itself in need of an investigative agency in 1948, it organized its Office of Special Investigations (1951) along bureau lines, drawing its first director from the ranks of the FBI.

To a lesser degree, the bureau has influenced police and investigative activities at state and local levels. FBI investigative jurisdiction is limited to federal crimes; most of the violent felonies and capital crimes have remained within the jurisdictions of state and local police. Obviously, the bureau has no responsibility for street patrol and traffic control; nor does it deal with riots and public disturbances. In these and many other areas, state and local officials must look elsewhere for their models of good police practices.

HISTORY TODAY

Very few Americans have enjoyed as much power for as long a period of time as J. Edgar Hoover did as FBI Director from 1924 to 1972. Is it possible for any person to hold that amount of power for so long, be virtually unaccountable to anyone, and not abuse that power at some point?

FEATURED OUTLAWS: THE CHICAGO EIGHT

The 1960s was one of the most turbulent decades in American history. The baby boom generation, those born in the decade after World War II, was coming of age, and many of America's youth were in full rebellion against everything their parents' generation held dear—patriotism, devotion to the military, respect for authority figures (including the police and the courts), and allegiance to the idea of law and order. In addition, the civil rights movement, much of which was spearheaded by leaders adhering to the ideals of nonviolence but often accompanied by violence for various reasons, was in full swing and at its height. Although the 1960s is remembered as the decade of protest for a number of causes, including environmentalism, drug legalization, and women's rights, the two issues that provoked the greatest amount of social unrest were civil rights for African-Americans and the military conflict in Vietnam.

1968 was probably the most turbulent year of this decade. It was marked by several significant and tragic events, starting with the assassination of civil rights leader Dr. Martin Luther King Jr. on April 4 in Memphis, Tennessee. Not only was King's assassination a sad event in the history of race relations and civil rights, but it also presented a tremendous challenge for law enforcement when rioting broke out in numerous cities across the United States. Police in most cities were largely unprepared, ill-equipped, and ill-trained for such rioting. On June 6, the country witnessed another tragic political assassination when Robert Kennedy, a United States Senator from New York, brother of the recently assassinated President John Kennedy, and frontrunner for the Democratic nomination for president, was assassinated in Los Angeles.

By the summer of 1968, when the Democratic Party came to Chicago for its Presidential nomination convention, the United States was at a boiling point, and the Democratic National Convention proved to be the point where much of this frustration boiled over and exploded in front of the entire world. With Robert Kennedy dead, the Democratic nomination fell to Hubert Humphrey, a Minnesotan who was serving as Vice President under Lyndon Johnson. Johnson, the architect of the fiasco that was unfolding in Vietnam, was especially hated by antiwar protesters. He also served as the focal point of anger for much of the civil rights community, despite his monumental contributions to the civil rights cause. The fact that so many young African-American men were dying in Vietnam negated many of his civil rights accomplishments. Ironically, Johnson did not even attend the convention. Humphrey was linked to

Continued

Johnson and supported much of his agenda, including his course in Vietnam. In addition, antiwar protesters and various civil rights protesters, especially the more radical (and violence prone) civil rights advocates, knew that the Democratic convention would be a forum for their protests.

The Mayor of Chicago at the time, Richard J. Daley, was probably the worst possible person for the job during this period in time. Daley was an old-school Chicago Democratic machine politician, who liked to think he ruled the city and its police force with an iron fist. Some of the more moderate-minded protesters requested that Daley might accommodate their desire to carry out peaceful antiwar and civil rights protests, but some protesters went to Chicago to pick a fight with Daley's Chicago Police force. In addition, Daley was determined to be completely uncompromising toward any protesters, and he was determined to show the Democratic Party, the city of Chicago, and the rest of the nation that he, not a bunch of rabble protesters, ran Chicago.

To the surprise of no one, the 10,000 demonstrators and the police clashed. Chicago's police officers had little interest in the causes being promoted by the demonstrators. All they knew was that they had been thrust onto the front lines of battles over issues much larger and more complex than mere conventional crime. In full view of television cameras from throughout the world, Chicago Police were shown beating protesters. To the television-watching world, Chicago literally looked like a war zone. The police were flailing their weapons at bloodied and beaten protesters. There seemed to be no order to police actions; the scene outside the convention hall was pure bedlam and chaos. It looked as if America was literally witnessing a political revolution. Inside the convention hall, the situation was not violent but was very ugly, nonetheless. A convention designed to unite the Party was splitting it instead. From the speaker's podium, Senator Abraham Ribicoff accused the Chicago police of using Gestapo tactics. Photographers and television crews captured Mayor Daley screaming anti-Semitic obscenities at Ribicoff, who was Jewish.

The Chicago Police Department and its local justice system were eager to punish the protesters, who were viewed as largely responsible for the convention fiasco. Toward that end, eight prominent protest leaders were arrested and charged with violating the Rap Brown Statute, which forbade traveling across state lines to incite a riot. The eight men were acquainted with each other, but not all of them were close. They represented a cross section of America's counterculture: Rennie Davis and Tom Hayden from Students for a Democratic Society; Dave Dellinger of National Mobilization against the War; two teachers named John Froines and Lee Weiner; Abbie Hoffman and Jerry Rubin of the Youth International Party; and Bobby Seale of the Black Panther Party, a militant African-American organization.

If the city of Chicago had aspirations of humiliating the protesters, they badly miscalculated. Bobby Seale represented himself at trial. The other seven, led by attorneys Leonard Wineglass and William Kunstler, a flamboyant, frequently obnoxious, but very skilled defense attorney who delighted in taking on unpopular cases, demonstrated as much contempt for the presiding court as they did for the police officers in the street. They were purposely rude, loud, and did everything possible to disrupt the trial and show disrespect for the entire proceeding, not caring about the potential consequences. The low moment of the trial occurred when the presiding judge ordered that defendant Bobby Seale be bound and gagged in the courtroom, in full view of the jury. This scene continued for 3 days. This move not only played into Seale's hands by forcing a mistrial in his case, thus reducing the Chicago Eight to the Chicago Seven, but also reinforced the already virulent hatred that many antiestablishment types, including African-American radicals, had for the American criminal justice system. The trial was a fiasco. The City of Chicago was further embarrassed and the protesters merely enhanced their reputation among those who viewed them as heroes. After Seale's mistrial, five of the remaining defendants were convicted—the two teachers were acquitted—and all seven remaining defendants and their attorneys were sentenced to jail for contempt. All of the convictions and contempt citations were overturned on appeal.

What did police officials learn from the Chicago convention? Most police departments in cities that host major political conventions now go out of their way to accommodate protesters and they have also done a much better job training and preparing line-level officers in riot control and prevention, including emphasizing better communication skills with those who have certain social agendas that they wish to promote. Even Chicago learned its lesson from 1968. The Democratic Party held its convention in Chicago again in 1996, and there were protests, but this time, thanks to the compromising and cordial actions of both the protesters and the police, the convention was conducted without incident and violence was practically nonexistent. Coincidentally, the Mayor of Chicago in 1996 was Richard M. Daley, the son of Richard J. Daley.

Sources: Evans, H. (1998). *The American century.* New York: Alfred A. Knopf, Jones, M. (2005). *Criminal justice pioneers in U.S. history.* Boston: Allyn and Bacon, Kunstler, W. M., & Isenberg, S. (1996). *My life as a radical lawyer.* Seacaucus, NJ: Carol.

HISTORY TODAY

Public protests, provided they are done legally, are recognized as a legitimate form of political and social expression in the United States, yet police departments seldom enjoy protests and they do not like most protesters. Most protesters are upset at the status quo in some way, and police officers typically represent the status quo. What are some ways that police departments can improve conditions to the point where protesters and police are not natural enemies? (Some departments have already accomplished this.)

STATE AND LOCAL LAW ENFORCEMENT

Absent any useful federal model, and given the similarity of law enforcement activities throughout the United States, police executives have recognized the value of exchanging police intelligence, as well as comparing their programs and operating procedures. As early as 1871, the National Police Convention met at St. Louis to discuss the impact of new scientific discoveries on law enforcement. After noting the use of photography, telegraphy, and scientific investigative techniques, the group disbanded, resolving to establish a National Police Association. However, the new association did not materialize and no similar meetings were held until 1893, when the National Police Chiefs Union met in Chicago in conjunction with the Columbian Exposition. This group devoted most of its meeting time to organizing, and it was not until 1901 that it became a strong force in the professionalization of American law enforcement. Under the presidency of Major Richard Sylvester, chief of the Washington, D.C., Police Department, the union instituted a strong program of educational meetings and publications. It was renamed the *International Association of Chiefs of Police* (IACP) in 1915 and has been a strong influence in law enforcement activities since the second decade of the twentieth century.

Twentieth-century police reform served two major functions. The primary function was an increased emphasis on efficiency in law enforcement, which has drawn police leaders to direct their attention towards modern management theory, the study of personnel selection and methods of training, and ways of improving methods of command and control. During the *Progressive Era* (1901-1920), this effort was carried out in conjunction with the view that law enforcement officers should also be enlisted to provide certain social services that are not available elsewhere.

Police efficiency depended on strong leadership, the elimination of political influence, and the improvement of personnel through careful recruiting and enhanced standards of training. After 1900, local police organizations became centralized under a single administrative head, who reported either to a city manager or a city commissioner who was responsible for public safety. This

Chief August Vollmer
circa 1925

FIGURE 13.2 August Vollmer, a leader in the development of the field of criminal justice; known as the *father of modern law enforcement. Courtesy en. wikipedia.org.*

centralized responsibility was a large step toward limiting political influence in the appointment of officers and the supervision of their work. Many new police executives were inexperienced in law enforcement and were selected for their knowledge of management techniques; others were veteran law enforcement officers, elevated to command because of their demonstrated effectiveness and abilities.

A cadre of nationally known police executives formed the nucleus for a growing police bureaucracy that would dominate modern police history. Typical of this group was *August Vollmer*, chief of the Berkeley Police Department from 1905 to 1932, who ended his career as a professor of police science at the University of California. Vollmer's disciple, *O. W. Wilson*, after a time as chief of the Berkeley Police Department, joined the University of California faculty as professor of criminology and then became the reform superintendent of the Chicago Police Department.

The police executive who took office in the first three decades of the twentieth century found himself confronted with a serious management problem. Although these were times of significant change, instituting effective street patrols still posed a significant problem. Because patrol officers were few in number, their beats were typically long. Initially, a two-shift system was implemented, requiring 12 hours on the beat for each shift. It was difficult to exercise supervision, even after the introduction of police call boxes; in fact, a 1915 Chicago study suggested that the patrolmen spent most of their time in saloons. Street sergeants charged with ensuring performance of duty found it difficult to locate their men. Most lieutenants did not move from the station house to provide guidance to the sergeants and patrolmen of their platoon.

With the introduction of the three-platoon system (that is, three shifts of 8 hours each), beats became more manageable and patrolmen less fatigued. This change was pioneered in Cincinnati by Chief Phillip M. Dietsch (1886) but did not become commonplace until after it was instituted by the Philadelphia Police Department in 1912. The Philadelphia authorities estimated that under the old two-platoon system of patrol (two shifts of 12 hours each), every patrolman spent 65 hours per week on the streets and an additional 42 hours per week on station duty or in reserve.

The development of motor vehicles, the two-way radio, and the public telephone resulted in major changes in patrol methods. A patrol officer in an automobile could cover greater distances in a shorter period. The radio was an efficient mode of command and control, permitting the station house to concentrate police forces wherever and whenever they needed. The telephone permitted the public to report criminal activity immediately to the station house, which could dispatch aid to the scene or alert its patrol cars to the emergency. Under a system of foot patrol, arrests had been limited to those deemed absolutely essential because the patrol officer had to carry or drag the prisoner back to the station house. A call on the call box produced a horse-drawn patrol wagon or one of the newer motorized *paddy wagons*.

The expense of constructing radio facilities resulted in the development of shared communications nets by neighboring police departments. Progress in adopting radio communication systems was rapid. The Detroit Police Department set up the first publicly owned police radio system in 1928, and by 1939 there were 700 municipal police radio stations. By 1959, virtually every police agency had some form of radio communication system. However, the adoption of radio communication did not solve problems of command and control. The number of authorized channels was limited at the outset, and as police communications systems multiplied, it became impossible to assign a channel to each independent department. This factor, coupled with the cost of transmitting equipment, created a need for the sharing of facilities by neighboring police departments. Shared radio facilities, in turn, resulted in a more efficient patrol and crime suppression system, especially as more advanced means of transportation had made it possible for criminals to pass quickly from one police jurisdiction to another.

Selection and training of police personnel underwent a dramatic change from 1870 to 1940. In 1870, political appointments meant frequent rotation in office, and few patrolmen expected to make police work their lifetime career. By 1940, more than 81 percent of those leaving police departments did so due to death or retirement. This new occupational longevity created a force that began to develop its own distinct subculture in American life. It created cohesion among the rank and file, but also imposed new demands for physical training, periodic retraining, and a need for employee benefits (including pensions). Most police administrators, following the lead of the FBI, tried to exclude their departments from civil service regulations. They reasoned that patrolmen protected by tenured appointments would be resistant to discipline. Despite this management view, in 1915 more than half of the 204 largest police departments were included in civil service systems; by 1959, almost three-quarters of municipal police departments made their appointments through civil service.

The connection between law enforcement and higher education was made early in the twentieth century when Chief August Vollmer recruited college students into the Berkeley Police Department (c. 1906). California institutions of higher education pioneered college-level courses in police subjects. A 3-year police training program was instituted at the Berkeley campus of the University of California in 1915; a major in criminology was offered in 1933, and in 1951 a School of Criminology offering graduate degrees was established. San Jose State College began a 2-year law enforcement curriculum in 1930, and Michigan State College offered a 5-year course in police administration in 1935. Traffic management programs, supported by grants from the Kemper Insurance Company and the Automobile Manufacturer's Association, were begun at Northwestern University (1932) and Harvard University (1936). Taking advantage of the free tuition at City University, the New York City Police Department initiated programs at the Baruch School of Business and Public Administration (1955), leading to Bachelor of Business Administration and Master of Public Administration degrees. By 1959, more than 1,150 students were enrolled in the undergraduate program and 100 officers were taking courses toward the graduate degree. Subsequently, this program would be moved to the *John Jay College of Criminal Justice*, established in 1965. Emphasis on formal education as a qualification for police recruits resulted in more than half of the city police departments in the nation requiring a high school diploma from an applicant by 1959.

Vocational training and research in practical police problems came somewhat later. Zone schools, designed to provide regional police training within each state, began in 1923. The George-Dean Act (1936) provided federal grants-in-aid for vocational training, and in the 1939-1940 fiscal year, more than 9,000 police officers were enrolled in programs funded under that legislation. The Works Progress Administration (WPA) funded 101 police-related projects in the period 1934-1938, allocating $1,275,000 for this purpose and establishing a precedent for federally funded police research. In addition to the FBI National Academy, designed for training police executives, FBI field schools were established in state, local, and "zone" locations beginning in 1959. Education in these vocational programs focused on and was enhanced by two manuals describing skills and training required in police activities (*Job Analysis of Police Services*, published in 1933 by the California State Education Department, and *Training for Police Service*, published in 1938 by the United States Department of the Interior).

Rising standards of law enforcement were also enhanced by the establishment of state police agencies. The *Texas Rangers* (1835), Massachusetts District Police (1879), Arizona Rangers (1901), and New Mexico Mounted Police (1905) were early manifestations of this new move to create police agencies with wide jurisdiction and statewide authority. The Pennsylvania State Constabulary (1903) and New York State Police (1917) were responsible for introducing rigid physical and mental recruiting standards and imposing demanding training and strict disciplinary rules on all officers. Because of their centralized direction, these state police agencies were relatively free from political pressure at the local level. Promotions were on the basis of merit and there were many opportunities for promotions to command area headquarters and substations.

SOCIAL SERVICE AND PUBLIC RELATIONS

At its 1870 Cincinnati meeting, the *National Prison Association* approved a report to its Standing Committee on Police that endorsed a crime prevention role for the police, on the basis of social work principles and designed to reinforce the rehabilitative goals established in accordance with Zebulon Brockway's plan. One year later, the National Police Convention at St. Louis followed their lead. There, police administrators analyzed social evils and how they influenced criminal behavior. They considered problems of juvenile delinquency, as well as debated how prostitution could be effectively controlled or eliminated. Theoretical discussion did not materialize into action before the turn of the century, but thereafter police departments became deeply involved in social work activities.

When *Fred Kohler* became chief of police in Cleveland in 1903, he was disturbed by the high arrest rate for minor offenses such as vagrancy, public intoxication, and disorderly conduct. For the otherwise well-intentioned citizen, arrest and imprisonment could mean the loss of a job and begin the vicious spiral decline of an honest person into a life of crime. Caught between enforcing the law and protecting the innocent, Kohler arranged to convene a *sunrise court* that would process the cases of all honest working people before they were due to report for work the next day. In 1908, Kohler initiated a *golden rule policy*, which operated on the premise that no juvenile should be confined in a jail or prison; it also directed officers to reconcile differences between individuals and to issue reprimands in lieu of arrest whenever the circumstances dictated such a course. In effect, Kohler's sunrise courts and policy-restricting arrests diverted minor offenders out of the formal criminal justice system, relieving court dockets and allowing time to prevent and investigate more serious crimes.

The beginning of the policewomen's movement occurred in 1905 with the appointment of *Lola Baldwin* to the Portland, Oregon, Police Department for service with juvenile offenders apprehended at the Lewis and Clark Exposition. For the next 20 years, women were added to police departments for special assignments involving juveniles, the protection of women and girls, and to assist in interrogating female offenders. These pioneering policewomen were required to meet much higher educational standards than their male counterparts. They also suffered discrimination in receiving lower pay than male officers, and none were assigned to street patrol or to any of the routine police functions of the force. An International Association of Policewomen was organized in 1915 with *Alice Stebbins Wells* as its president, but with the declining interest in women police officers after 1925, the association soon lost membership and became inactive.

HISTORY TODAY

Lola Baldwin and Alice Stebbins Wells were pioneers in the field of policing, notwithstanding the fact that they did not do the same work as their male counterparts. They entered an overwhelmingly male-dominated environment, no doubt receiving a mixed reception from their colleagues and the public alike. How much has policing changed in this regard? Is policing still a predominantly male-centered environment or have women gained enough critical mass in policing to change the culture?

Chief August Vollmer of the Berkeley Police Department was a strong advocate of police participation in social work. Building on his belief that every patrol officer should be a practicing criminologist, Vollmer thought that police should strive to provide better schools, recreational facilities for the poor, and better housing for those likely to fall into criminal activity. Various departments accepted the challenge and became active in raising money for the relief of the poor and destitute. They organized boy police clubs, worked with school safety patrols, and ran clinics to help young people stop smoking.

All of these activities enhanced police-public relations that had been badly neglected, causing public misunderstanding of police functions and capabilities. For years, the police had been the object of wry humor. However, by 1915 the jokes wore thin, and the International Association of Chiefs of Police became worried about the way police were depicted in the new motion pictures; the *Keystone Kops*, with their awkward antics, were not the ideal model. The term *Keystone Kops* is still a euphemism for incompetent police work. Further harmful to the image of police was the *Wickersham Commission's* 1931 multivolume report; its most dramatic disclosure was the extent and brutality of the "third degree," as practiced throughout most American police departments.

SCIENTIFIC CRIMINAL INVESTIGATION

The twentieth century has produced phenomenal growth in the scientific aspects of detective work. August Vollmer recognized this as early as 1916 when he, as chief of the Berkeley Police Department, joined with *Dr. Albert Schneider* to establish the first crime laboratory in an American police department. Earlier times witnessed some work in forensic science, which deals with the application of the physical and biological sciences, as well as social science, to the investigation of crime. As early as 1248, a Chinese handbook appeared on the subject of forensic medicine; between 1510 and 1590, Ambroise Pare of France and two Italian anatomists, Fortunato Fidelis of Palermo and Paolo Zacchia of Rome, were active in the field. However, the scientific revolution of the seventeenth and eighteenth centuries formed a necessary foundation on which to base a truly definitive science of forensic medicine. Specifically, the modern disciplines of physiology, anatomy, physics, and chemistry came into their own, and they collectively provided highly effective instruments for the detection of crime and the identification of criminals. While much of the testing fell to the scientists retained by police departments, it was the responsibility of police investigators to become aware of the methods of preserving physical evidence and to exercise good judgment in determining which scientific investigations were appropriate.

Criminal justice professionals had long needed a method for identifying individuals engaged in criminal activity. Investigation frequently involves matching similar modes of operation in otherwise unrelated crimes; prison officials need means of determining recidivism, and judges need to identify repeat offenders. The first step in providing certainty in identification was taken by a clerk in the Sûreté Archives in Paris. *Alphonse Bertillon* came from a family dominated by medical doctors, naturalists, and mathematicians, but his unassuming air and lack of personal grace resulted in his being assigned an obscure job as assistant clerk in the record room. It was his task to file identifying data on all criminals apprehended and convicted throughout the nation, and this tedious task was rendered distasteful by his realization that virtually all of the descriptions were so vague that they were useless. In 1879, he decided, on the basis of his observations and knowledge of science, that no two people could have exactly the same physical measurements. If enough measurements were taken, a high degree of individuality could be developed for each person contained within a police agency's files. Within a few years, he was given permission to begin his measurements and was provided with a small staff of technicians to process persons to be calibrated. By February 1883, his technique proved successful and was reported in the newspapers as anthropometry or "bertillonage." Bertillon's methods gained immediate attention. In the United States, they were widely adopted and a central file of measurements was developed at Sing Sing Prison for the purpose of identifying multiple offenders.

Ironically, Bertillon's fame was destined to be short-lived, for anthropometry was rapidly replaced by the use of fingerprinting. Fingerprinting seems to have originated in Asia. Henry Faulds, a Scottish physician working in Japan, noticed the practice of identifying pottery and sealing documents through the use of handprints and fingerprints. William Herschel, a British official in India, discovered that he could prevent his employees from drawing a second salary by requiring them to place the inked impressions of two forefingers of the right hand opposite their names in the payroll records. The two men noticed the similarity of their discoveries when Faulds published an article on fingerprinting in *Nature* magazine on October 28, 1880. In 1892, Sir Francis Galton published *Finger Prints*,[8] a book-length monograph that contained a basic system of classification.

American fingerprinting efficiency was increased in 1924 when federal prisoner identification files, maintained at the Federal Prison at Leavenworth, were combined with the files formerly maintained by the International Association of Chiefs of Police at Sing Sing. The consolidated fingerprint bureau, later to be relocated to the FBI in Washington, proved invaluable not only for criminal investigation but also for the identification of the victims of accidents and natural disasters. Emphasis on law and order in the years 1935 and 1936 led to a short-lived campaign for a universal fingerprinting system that would bring all Americans into the FBI fingerprint files. Although that particular effort was far from successful, the passage of time and growing practices of fingerprinting persons wishing to get married, enter professional practice, or join the armed forces have provided virtually complete coverage for identification purposes. Because a variant form of classification (i.e., depending on the characteristics of each finger, rather than all 10) is used for criminal investigative work, the identification files are, for the most part, inaccessible for forensic purposes. A new development in fingerprint analysis involves the microscopic comparison of pores within the ridges of fingerprints, permitting identifications when only a portion of a fingerprint is available for comparison.

The origins of modern forensic medicine predate fingerprinting by about a century, having their inception with the work of Johann Ludwig Casper, Mathieu J. B. Orfila, and Marie G. A. Devergie, all of whom made major contributions during the first half of the nineteenth century. In the 1870s, a Frenchman, Albert Florence, developed a definitive chemical test for the presence of human semen, and in the same decade Ambroise Tardieu discovered dot-like blood spots under the pleura that were characteristic of death by rapid suffocation. In 1882, an Austrian, Eduard von Hoffmann, discovered that persons burned alive had soot in their windpipes and lungs and carbon monoxide in their blood. A 1931 study by John Glaister of Glasgow provided a wealth of information about human hair and its value for investigative work.

Supporting anatomical work was a vastly expanded technology concerning human blood. A German physician, Paul Uhlenhuth, developed a test with blood serums in 1901 that permitted the scientist to distinguish one species of animal blood from another and, thus, made it possible to identify human blood stains and distinguish them from the blood of most other animals. A year earlier, his countryman, Karl Landsteiner, had discovered that human blood cells could be grouped into what came to be known as *A*, *B*, and *O* types.

In 1927, Landsteiner, in conjunction with other scientists, developed 12 additional typing characteristics of human blood and isolated the Rh factor in 1940. In connection with this theoretical research, other scientists devised methods for dissolving blood stains into solutions that could be analyzed in the laboratory. More recent advances in blood chemistry make it possible to positively establish paternity, using a number of tests to determine genetically related human leukocyte antigens.

Closely related to blood typing is the use of *DNA* (deoxyribonucleic acid) matching in criminal investigation. DNA is located in all human cells, and its precise configuration is determined by heredity. First used to establish paternity, the reliability of the test is such that it is now accepted as extremely persuasive evidence in criminal prosecutions. While blood is the most common material subjected to DNA comparison, virtually any cellular material can be used. Recently, DNA testing established that a woman who claimed to be Anastasia, the lost Grand Duchess of Russia, could not possibly have been the child of Nicholas II and his wife, Alexandra. All of the parties were dead at the time the test occurred, the bones of the royal parents having recently been exhumed in Russia. This shows the degree to which DNA testing has advanced the science of identification and forensic investigation.

Dentistry, forensic odontology, long recognized as a system of identification, has become an invaluable part of forensic science. During the early years of life, the growth of primary teeth and their replacement by permanent teeth aid in establishing the age of a corpse; this can be confirmed by measuring the specific gravity of the teeth, which changes with increased age. The size, alignment, and color of the teeth vary with the race of an individual, as do the arch of the mouth and the shape of the jaw. Abnormal functions of the jaw may provide telltale scratches or indentations on the teeth, as may the deceased's occupation; tailors tend to chew pins, and carpenters mar their teeth by chewing nails. When teeth are subjected to professional care, their fillings, crowns, and dentures provide clues to the region or nation in which the dentist received his or her training, and some dentures may even have the Social Security Number of their owner impressed in the supporting material.

Because teeth are virtually unique, bite marks are useful for investigative purposes. Whether on the body of a victim or inflicted on the accused by the victim, bite marks can link a suspect to the crime. Bite marks may fade quickly and lose many of their identifying characteristics shortly after the bite occurs, or they may vary according to the angle and pressure of the bite. To deal with certain variables, an impression can be taken of the biter's teeth and a set of teeth cast and mounted on an apparatus that revolves and can be subjected to varying pressure. An infinite number of bites can be simulated in an attempt to reproduce the bite inflicted at the crime scene.

Toxicology, or the study of poisons, is another area in which science has provided continuing assistance in police work. Arsenic, one of the foremost causes of death by poisoning in the early nineteenth century, formed the subject of extensive research by Mathieu J. B. Orfila, a French forensic scientist. Orfila developed several tests for the identification of arsenic in the bodies of victims, but in 1932 James Marsh, an English researcher, provided a definitive method for isolating arsenic from organic compounds. Through the Marsh method, arsenic in body organs could be detected even if it was only 1/1,000th of a milligram. The identification and isolation of organic poisons such as nicotine, aconine, and morphine proved to be more difficult, but Jean Servais Stas, one of the leading French forensic scientists, succeeded in doing this and in developing a number of confirming tests. By 1955, there were more than 30 different methods of testing for morphine poisoning. When it was impossible to isolate the poison, its presence in body organs could be demonstrated by injection into laboratory animals; this method was developed by Ambroise Tardieu in 1863. Tranquilizer poisons became a threat after the Second World War, and extensive research has been necessary to allow their isolation or identification by laboratory means.

Ballistics is another field in which scientific investigation has long provided assistance to detectives. For nearly a century, the value of ballistics evidence was known to police investigators. Marks on bullets and cartridges, along with analysis of powder and its deposits on the victim's skin, were all accepted as useful forms of evidence. However, it was the misuse of ballistics evidence that brought *Charles E. Waite* into the systematic study of firearms, ammunition, and powders. A dimwitted farmhand in upstate New York was prosecuted and convicted of killing his employer with a .22 caliber pistol; only the concerned interest of a prison warden and a volunteer social worker saved the man from execution. Waite was asked to review the evidence, and discovered that the man's pistol could not have fired the fatal shots. Waite, horrified at the possible miscarriage of justice in future cases, began to assemble technical details and samples from prominent American gun manufacturers (1920-1922) and then, learning that two-thirds of American firearms were imported, supplemented his collection with foreign sources. By the time of his death in 1926, Philip O. Gravelle and Dr. Calvin Goodard had joined him in the enterprise, and between them they were responsible for establishing the Bureau of Forensic Ballistics in New York City. Careful attention to maintaining a centralized file of ballistics information proved worthwhile in 1929, when police investigators were able to use ballistics evidence to identify a machine gun used in the famous *St. Valentine's Day Massacre* of seven gangland leaders by members of a rival Chicago gang, headed by *Al Capone*.

Al Capone (1899-1947): Notorious Chicago-based gangster of the Prohibition Era; multi-millionaire bootlegger; eventually sentenced to Federal Prison for income tax evasion; eventually died of symptoms from syphilis.

Countless other scientific advances have contributed to the efficiency and accuracy of criminal investigation. Belgian law enforcement officials used photography just 4 years after its invention by *Louis Daguerre* in 1839, and Alphonse Bertillon was responsible for establishing standards of crime scene photography by the Sûreté. Advanced techniques of physical and chemical analysis have permitted the examination of textile fibers, dust and dirt, automobile tires, and ash residues in investigative work. Handwriting patterns have long been a method of identifying blackmailers, kidnappers, and other literate wrongdoers, and with the development of typewriters, centralized files were established that permitted the recognition of manufacturer and model. With some degree of luck, imperfections in the typeface actually permitted the investigators to determine whether a given machine prepared a certain document. The development of computers as word processors has virtually eliminated such accuracy in identifying documents produced by a given individual. However, access to a computer, coupled with word content analysis,[9] may provide circumstantial evidence of authorship. Computerized access to information, along with the popularity of communication by e-mail, provides more promising methods for tracing individual involvement in criminal conspiracies or acts of terrorism. The forensic opportunities and investigative challenges presented by cyberspace have yet to be fully explored, but they reemphasize the fact that science is a critical component of law enforcement activity.

Rapid expansion of scientific methods of investigation has placed special demands on the training and financial resources of police agencies. Use of these sophisticated techniques requires a high level of formal education, a comprehensive knowledge of modern science, and the ability to work with highly trained professionals in anatomy, physiology, chemistry, and physics. Under this pressure, the old American system of elected coroners began to give way to trained medical examiners after 1935, and the work of the police detective soon became a matter of coordinating the investigations of many professional scientists and applying their discoveries for the solution of the case at hand.

HISTORY TODAY

Virtually all of the advances in crime detection have been created by people whose expertise is in some field other than criminal justice. What does this say about the need for criminal justice students to at least have some appreciation of other disciplines, including the natural sciences?

SUBCULTURE, POLICE RIOTS, AND UNIONISM

From the middle years of the 1960s to about 1975, the United States passed through a series of domestic upheavals, generated by racial tension, the growing unpopularity of the war in Vietnam, and the uncomfortable prospect of

Martin Luther King Jr. (1929-1968): Atlanta-based minister, civil rights leader, and Nobel Prize winner; advocate of nonviolent but active means of effecting social change; assassinated in Memphis, Tennessee, in April 1968.

declining economic opportunities for American youth. Beginning with the Free Speech Movement (1964) on the Berkeley campus of the University of California, students exhibited a growing tendency to demonstrate their opposition to university, state, and national policies. The civil rights movement, long restrained by *Martin Luther King Jr.*'s emphasis on nonviolent protests, began to meet with violent opposition that generated a series of riots in major American cities.

One of the most spectacular ghetto uprisings occurred in Washington, D.C., in the wake of King's 1968 assassination. Despite sincere efforts on the part of leaders from both racial groups, tension and violence persisted, leaving cities highly vulnerable to widespread disorder and looting. Caught in the crossfire (in regard to both university-based violence and urban ghetto disorder) were the police departments. As one African-American leader pointed out, police officers on the beat were the personification of white society maintaining order, and this made them the most convenient scapegoats for American racial injustice.

Racial tension was not the only cause of conflict between police organizations and society. The escalation of the *war in Vietnam* after 1964 caused a growing peace movement, concentrated for the most part among young, middle-class college students. As demonstrations became increasingly violent, university authorities abandoned their traditional system of self-discipline and called on municipal and state police forces to restore order on their campuses. Historically, there has always been some animosity between "town and gown," but the arrival of tactical patrol forces in riot gear was unprecedented. The inevitable confrontations, resulting in injury and some deaths, focused public attention on law enforcement methods and resulted in some telling criticism of police management.

The new and unwelcome notoriety drove police professionals of all ranks further into the protection of their unique subculture. For nearly a century, the "new police forces" slowly evolved into a distinctive organization, a unique social pattern, and a characteristic mindset that sociologists have identified as a subculture in American life. Initially, this was the product of wearing a distinctive uniform, reinforced by authorization to carry and use firearms. Police officers were required to enforce a broad spectrum of laws, ranging from the apprehension and arrest of felons to breaking up tavern brawls, mediating household fights, and suppressing prostitution, excessive drinking, and disorderly behavior. All in all, the police were expected to impose on the civilian population a standard of conduct dictated by principles of Victorian morality that they, in many cases, did not practice themselves. To avoid inconsistency between official and private behavior, police officers and their families became isolated in their social lives, congregating with other officers and their families.

With the advent of the automobile, officers were charged with administering rules of the road. This also brought about the introduction of automotive patrol, which increased the isolation of police officers from the public. Under street patrol conditions, the local patrol officer met the citizens who lived on his beat. It was the essence of walking patrol that he prevented crime by knowing all the inhabitants of his territory and by noticing changes in individuals and circumstances that might be suspicious. The patrol car precluded familiarity with the honest residents and accentuated the feeling that, outside the car itself, the world and its inhabitants were all suspicious.

The social origins of police recruits also had a bearing on the development of the police subculture. While there were a small number of college graduates in police work before World War II, the postwar period saw a return to high school graduates as the norm. Studies have shown that recruits tend to be drawn from working-class (blue-collar) families and that they are motivated toward upward mobility. For the most part, they are conservative in their political and social views, and by background and training, they place a high premium on orderly behavior. They are quick to resent challenges to their authority, and are impatient and harsh in their views of middle-class college and university students who, by their standards, behave improperly. The "town-gown" polarizations of the Vietnam era have decreased markedly since the end of the Vietnam conflict in 1975. As college graduates increasingly enter the law enforcement field, it seems less likely that such attitudes will persist in professional law enforcement. However, economic and social unrest in ghetto communities has triggered a new form of mob violence that has ominous racial overtones. Efforts to recruit minority law enforcement officers seem to have had a limited impact on the frequency of these urban uprisings. However, techniques of crowd control have been substantially improved, and law enforcement managers are increasingly aware of the need to maintain good community relations.

Police officers develop strong bonds with each other and their departments. In part, this can be attributed to the fact that all levels of authority, from patrol officer to precinct chief (and, in some cases, even police chief or commissioner), started at the entry level. Unlike the military services, there is no division between officers and enlisted men in terms of career progression. Leadership is exercised by officers who have long years of experience and, thus, perhaps great empathy with the circumstances of the patrol officer on the beat or the detective in the squad room. Except at the very highest levels of command, there is virtually no opportunity for transfer from one department to another. An intricate relationship of competition and camaraderie develops among the officers in a given precinct or division. Police officers are highly protective of each other, and entire organizations can be aroused by the injury or death of one of their members.

This brief summary of academic study concerning police subculture provides a basis on which to examine the student riots and racial violence of the 1960s and 1970s. At the outset, it is helpful to recall that the Metropolitan Police of London in addition to the Municipal Police of New York and other American cities have faced difficulties in controlling riotous behavior. However, those who have studied the violence of the 1960s and 1970s conclude that regular army units were most effective in dealing with rioting. National Guard troops were less effective, although vastly superior to police, even when police were specially trained and organized into riot control units.

The key seems to be in the nature of police work and the additional skills needed for the suppression of a riotous assembly. Police officers are trained to act either alone or in small groups. In fact, police work is one of the few activities in which individual discretion increases as one moves down the chain of authority. Police deal with individuals, monitoring suspicious behavior and reacting aggressively to challenges to their authority. They aim to make arrests and determine blame. Control of a riot, on the other hand, requires the concerted, disciplined use of gradually increasing force, which is designed to disperse the disorderly crowd and restore order. Military troops acting under a strong command that stresses dispersal and disengagement are conditioned to work as a team and to use only the weapons and anticrowd methods authorized by their officers. However, American federal law prevents the use of federal troops in most riot situations. In recent years, National Guard units have received expanded training in crowd control techniques; yet the first line of defense remains the local or state police departments. Realistically, a decision must be made about whether riot control will remain with the police; if it does, extensive retraining will be required.

Lack of police training, serious mistakes in tactical application of force, and perhaps even overpreparedness by political leaders and police officials generated serious citizen-police clashes in the student riots and ghetto uprisings of the 1960s and 1970s. Charges of police brutality were given increased credibility by established incidents of police officers breaking into riot themselves, beating innocent bystanders and using tear gas indiscriminately. A substantial portion of police misbehavior can be explained by the clash of student and ghetto cultures with the police subculture. Poor police leadership may also have been involved. In the face of overwhelming hostility and physical injury to themselves or their colleagues, police officers broke ranks, venting their fears and frustrations on any person in the vicinity of the riot.

In the aftermath of the 1960s, professional police officers have taken two significant steps. First, they have begun to realize the need to organize politically in order to protect their interests against hostile forces. An example of their success was the 1967 defeat of New York City Mayor John V. Lindsay's proposed *civilian review board*. This board was intended to reduce police involvement in disciplinary procedures regarding complaints against officers accused of brutality and excessive force. The Patrolmen's Benevolent Association (PBA), representing an overwhelming majority of city police officers, successfully launched a public attack on the civilian review board, securing its rejection by the voters. In a number of other cities across the United States, similar political action by police groups reasserted police independence and professionalism and rejected the contention that outside surveillance was necessary.

HISTORY TODAY

The effectiveness of civilian review boards is still debated. Find out if your local law enforcement agency has a civilian review board and try to ascertain the effectiveness of the board.

Second, the reluctance of officers to join police labor unions has gradually begun to decline. Since 1919, American police officers and city governments have lived in the shadow of the *Boston Police Strike*. Historians differ concerning the degree to which crime increased during the time that Boston was without police protection. Indeed, there are some that suggest law enforcement has never been a major part of police work, and that most police activity involves the rendition of social services such as bringing habitual drunkards into a station house cell for a night's sleep, and similar noncrime-related services.

Whatever the truth may be concerning the Boston Police Strike, it is clear that, thereafter, unionism was considered contrary to public safety and a threat to command and control of police departments. The Boston situation and subsequent efforts at unionization after World War II were generated by the stagnation of police salaries in a rapidly inflating economy. However, the new wave of union enthusiasm among police officers is based not only on economic concerns, but also on the perception among police officers that they have lost the support of the public and that their political superiors and the courts are determined to hinder them in their work. A confrontation between penologists and criminologists on one hand, and J. Edgar Hoover and police professionals on the other, was a recurrent theme of the 1960s and 1970s. Understandably, the police officer who has risked his or her life in apprehending a dangerous felon does not take kindly to the culprit's receiving a light sentence or probation.

Police organizations have, in the past, centered on *benevolent or fraternal organizations*. The New York City Patrolmen's Benevolent Association, founded in 1892, successfully lobbied in 1900 and 1901 for an 8-h workday. Other local police clubs were organized in Buffalo, Rochester, and Milwaukee before 1915, when the Fraternal Order of Police (FOP) established its first lodge in Pittsburgh. By 1941, the FOP had 169 local lodges, and that number increased to 194 by 1959. In 1969, the FOP boasted 733 affiliated lodges and 80,000 members. The International Conference of Police Associations in 1972 reported more than 100 local and state affiliated organizations comprising more than 158,000 members. To date, these growing police organizations have been active in working for the welfare of their members in the political arena and in serving as bargaining agents concerning conditions of employment. They have the potential to lobby for police benefits and increased wages and perhaps even to resort to strikes to attain these objectives. Police organizations present police concerns to voters and can provide powerful arguments for increased emphasis on law and order. They also continue to have increasing control over the command and personnel policies and decisions of their respective departments.

Police agencies throughout the United States have also been profoundly affected by the establishment of the Law Enforcement Assistance Administration (LEAA), chartered by the *Omnibus Crime Control and Safe Streets Act of 1968*. The LEAA provided a method for channeling federal assistance to state and local law enforcement agencies. A series of block grants provided police administrators with opportunities to experiment with new methods of management and operations, and many departments secured new and otherwise unattainable equipment. However, perhaps the most significant impact was in facilitating the elevation of educational standards for police officers. The Law Enforcement Education Program (LEEP) provided federal grants for the establishment of criminal justice education programs in institutions of higher education. It grew rapidly, serving 20,602 students in 1969 with an expenditure of $6.5 million; by 1974, more than 100,000 students were enrolled in a program funded in excess of $44 million.

Reviewing the variety of educational offerings in its 1975 report on the LEAA, the Twentieth Century Fund suggested that many programs merely moved vocational training into university classrooms. Classes on interrogation techniques, they suggested, belonged in departmental or zone schools, but future police officers should be exposed to the challenges of a broad liberal arts education. Fortunately, many programs provided a general education in addition to attention to police-related subjects that were suitable for university discussion. A growing number of police professionals took advantage of LEAA-sponsored criminal justice programs and earned undergraduate and graduate degrees in off-duty hours. Two benefits of such education are obvious. The insularity of police subcultural influences may well be softened by educational contact with other segments of contemporary society. Further, police professionals will be better equipped to deal with the highly sophisticated investigative techniques of the twentieth century. At the same time, they will be sensitive to the delicate balance that must be achieved if police activity is to be both effective and publicly acceptable in our multiracial and rapidly diversifying society of the future.

THE RODNEY KING EPISODE

By the 1990s, it had become clear that most police officers in the United States were better trained, educated, and technologically equipped than at any other time in the history of policing. However, the *Rodney King* incident showed that American policing still had several obstacles to overcome when it came to use of force and race relations. One of the ironies of the Rodney King episode is that it involved misconduct on the part of several members of one of the world's premier police departments (Los Angeles, California) and one of its most acclaimed chiefs, *Daryl Gates*. The Rodney King incident revealed that race relations were still one of America's foremost social problems.

On March 4, 1991, in Los Angeles, California, a private citizen captured the beating of Rodney King, a small-time criminal, at the hands of four police officers—Laurence Powell, Timothy Wind, Theodore Briseno, and a sergeant, Stacey Koon—while other officers looked on without intervening. King had led police officers on a high-speed chase and reportedly refused to comply with their instructions, thus precipitating some justifiable force, but nowhere near the amount actually used against King. King was struck a total of 56 times about the head and body. The video was replayed repeatedly on television stations around the world; a group of white officers pummeling an African-American crystallized attitudes about race relations and police use of force in general. It seemed to buttress the complaints of African-Americans throughout the country, especially in Los Angeles, that there were innumerable instances of police officers physically abusing African-American suspects that went unreported. The Rodney King beating would have never entered the public eye had it not been for George Holliday's fortuitous taping; in fact, several of the officers were not truthful when writing reports about the beating.

All of the officers involved were well-trained, educated, and experienced. The Los Angeles Police Department was world renowned for its professionalism; however, it was also frequently criticized for its militarism and poor relations with minorities. Its chief was Daryl Gates, a smart, macho, tough-talking, 42-year veteran police officer who had worked his way through the ranks of the Los Angeles Police Department. He was credited with such innovations as the DARE (Drug Abuse Resistance Education) program and alternately praised and criticized for bringing militaristic concepts such as SWAT (Special Weapons and Tactics) to civilian policing. The day of the King beating, Gates, the toast of the law enforcement community, was in Washington, D.C.,

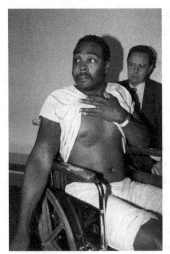

FIGURE 13.3 Rodney King, 25, shows a bruise on his chest during a press conference at the Los Angeles County Jail on March 6, 1991. King was the subject of a videotaped and nationally televised beating by officers of the Los Angeles Police Department. *AP Photo/ Kevork Djansezian.*

attending a presidential forum on crime prevention at the invitation of the Attorney General of the United States. Thirteen months later, Gates would resign in disgrace.

The actions of the officers were quickly condemned by police and public officials around the country, including Chief Gates, but the damage had been done. Led by Mayor Tom Bradley, a long time Gates foe, a commission was appointed to investigate the Los Angeles Police Department. The *Christopher Commission*, named after its chair, future Secretary of State Warren Christopher, placed a large measure of the blame on Gates, who was criticized for failing to deal with instances of excessive force within his department and not disciplining the officers involved. Despite his fame, few people in the law enforcement community or the general public came to Gates' defense; and thus, he had become a law enforcement pariah.

The officers were fired and prosecuted, but a bad situation turned incredibly worse on April 29, 1992, when an all-white jury virtually acquitted all of the officers. Unprepared for the aftermath of an acquittal, the Los Angeles Police Department could only go into retreat mode as Los Angeles exploded in riots. Public officials and police departments throughout North America were shocked when rioting erupted in their cities as well. Much of the Los Angeles rioting was captured on live television, which included vicious assaults by African-Americans in South Central Los Angeles against unprepared Asians, Hispanics, and whites. One particularly vicious event was the savage assault on Reginald Denny, a 29-year-old truck driver who was struck with a piece of medical equipment, then several times with a claw hammer, and finally on the head with a slab of concrete. Damian Williams, a Crips gang member who hit Denny with the concrete, was caught on camera by a television news helicopter dancing over the prostrate Denny and flashing a gang sign. Others threw beer bottles, laughed, and spat at Denny; others took his picture; and a man named Anthony Brown was filmed rifling through Denny's pockets. Just as whites around the country condemned the King beating, most African-Americans—with the exception of a few such as Jesse Jackson and Congresswoman Maxine Waters—condemned the rioters; in fact, many African-Americans came to the rescue of non-African-American riot victims, including Reginald Denny. Those involved in the Denny beating were practically exonerated by the courts, as a payback for the officers' acquittal.

The officers originally involved in the King beating were eventually tried in federal court for violating King's civil rights; this time they were convicted and sentenced to prison. The Los Angeles riots lasted 6 days. Millions of dollars in damage were done in cities throughout North America, as a result of vandalism, arson, and looting. Worst of all, 53 people died in Los Angeles alone.[10]

The Rodney King incident haunted law enforcement throughout the 1990s and cast a pall on American race relations in general.

HISTORY TODAY

In your opinion and on the basis of your observations or what you have read, to what degree is mistreatment based on race still a factor in police work?

THE O. J. SIMPSON TRIAL

Not long after the Rodney King incident, one of the most infamous trials in American history occurred; this time, the issues involved were even more numerous and complex than the King case. *O. J. Simpson* was one of the most admired professional athletes of the twentieth century. Both a college and professional football star, he followed up his hall of fame career by becoming an NFL television commentator, successful actor, and commercial pitchman.

On June 12, 1994, his ex-wife, Nicole Brown Simpson, and Ron Goldman, a Los Angeles waiter who was visiting her to return some items she had left at his restaurant, were found murdered at Nicole Simpson's home. Police investigators usually look first to those closest to the murder victim as the most likely suspects; as a result, O. J. Simpson quickly became the focus of the investigation. The Los Angeles Police Department, at that time in the hands of Chief Willie Williams, Daryl Gates' successor, once again found itself in the spotlight. If there were any thoughts that replacing Gates with an African-American chief would signal better relations with Los Angeles' minority community, the Simpson case dashed those hopes.

The Simpson case became a media circus, and the detention and questioning of Simpson was a media "event." When a warrant for Simpson's arrest was issued, his lawyer told police that Simpson would turn himself in. Instead, Simpson was seen riding in a Ford Bronco being driven by his friend, Al Cowlings, in nearby Orange County. In one of the most bizarre events in television history (to the point of being broadcast live on cable news channels, and simulcast alongside the NBA finals), television helicopters and a dozen police vehicles chased Cowlings and Simpson for 60 miles until Cowlings finally returned Simpson to his home, where he was arrested. Simpson was found with $8,750, a gun, disguise gear, and a passport, clear indications that he originally intended to flee the country, perhaps hoping that Cowlings could take him to Mexico. The police officers chasing Simpson were in frequent contact with him, eventually talking him into ending the chase and surrendering. The Los Angeles Police Department made the arrest, but came across as almost incompetent in the process.

The pretrial proceedings and the trial itself created a group of celebrities. Every witness, attorney, and even the presiding judge became celebrities as a result of the Simpson case. Every moment of the long trial was broadcast live on television. Despite overwhelming evidence pointing to Simpson's guilt, he was acquitted of all charges. The families of Goldman and Nicole Brown Simpson filed civil suits against Simpson, and won damages against Simpson, who relocated to Florida so that his assets would be immune from seizure for the civil verdict. (In 2008, Simpson was sentenced by a Nevada court to 33 years in prison for armed robbery and kidnapping offenses that occurred in 2007.)

The Simpson case brought many issues to light, some directly related to criminal justice and some that transcended the world of criminal justice. The issue of *televised trials* also came into play as it became evident that several of the parties involved in the trial were playing for the television cameras. The presiding judge in the case, Lance Ito, came under almost unanimous condemnation for relishing his own spotlight and losing control of the proceedings. The question of whether a verdict could be bought was also raised, because Simpson assembled

> F. Lee Bailey (1933-): One of the most famous criminal defense attorneys in American history; involved in notable cases including the Boston Strangler (Albert DeSalvo) and newspaper heiress Patricia Hearst.

a group of high-profile, millionaire defense attorneys (nicknamed the "*Dream Team*") consisting of *Johnny Cochran* (lead counsel), who became the star of the trial, along with *Robert Shapiro* and *F. Lee Bailey*, the latter being the most famous criminal defense attorney of his era. Jury nullification—meaning that the jury had ignored the evidence, was also a hotly debated topic once Simpson was acquitted.

The Los Angeles Police Department was also placed on display in the trial. Much to the department's dismay, some of the investigating officers were portrayed to the public as inept at gathering and processing physical evidence. One of the central police officers in the trial was Detective Mark Fuhrman, who was accused of "planting" evidence to frame Simpson. Although there was no evidence that he had done so, Fuhrman's credibility as a witness was destroyed when, contrary to his earlier sworn statements, it was revealed that he had used racial slurs against African-Americans. Fuhrman would eventually plead no contest to perjury and be sentenced to probation. Thanks to his interrogation by F. Lee Bailey, the phrase *n word* came into being as part of the American vocabulary. Another unfortunate term emerged from the trial, and that was the word *testilying*. Alan Dershowitz, a Harvard Law professor who worked as a consultant for Simpson, brought *testilying* into popular use, despite a public announcement by Chief Willie Williams that Dershowitz was a liar.[11] Nevertheless, Simpson's attorneys succeeded in challenging the credibility and competence of several police witnesses, resulting in the Los Angeles Police Department, and the entire police profession, suffering another black eye.

HISTORY TODAY

There were many social and criminal justice-related issues tied to the O. J. Simpson case, including domestic violence, interracial marriage, the treatment of celebrities by the justice system, being able to hire attorneys who would achieve an acquittal, and race relations in America in general. Another issue that was brought under examination was televised trials. The entire Simpson trial was carried on television for several months. Cable channels often show snippets of courtroom scenes, especially when violence erupts or some other bizarre behavior is being exhibited. Court TV is a popular cable channel now and television cameras are brought into many courtrooms, but not federal courts. What are the advantages and disadvantages of allowing television cameras in courtrooms?

REFORM AND MODERNIZATION IN ENGLAND AND FRANCE

In July 2010, the government of the United Kingdom produced a report titled *"Reconnecting Police and the People."* The U.K. government recognized that much had changed since Robert Peel and 1829, not all for the good. This report stated that the mission of Peel had not changed but that central government had grown and local policing and local priorities had gotten lost. The intention in commissioning this report was to restore the connection between the public and the police, and to put the public back into the driver's seat of policing in England and Wales. In effect, the power to police would be transferred back to the people.

Clearly, France and the United Kingdom, through economic partnership in the European Union and the sharing of police officers that takes place under various Euro-wide protocols and initiatives, continue to have a very different view of the role of the police in society. Perhaps, somewhere between these two lies the United States—over-bureaucratized and overwhelmed by increased central demands, burdened by reduced resources and greater efficiency demands and direction since 2001, but still with fundamentally local responses to local issues with a state and federal framework over this to respond to more challenging aspects of criminality.

Reform has raised a fundamental question in the United States, the United Kingdom, and France. In the United Kingdom, there is a move to create a national framework for local policing. The United Kingdom now has a *National Crime Agency*; no one is bold enough it seems to call it an "FBI" and the country implements a National Intelligence Model to establish at an early stage who deals with what. With organized crime costing the United Kingdom $80 billion per year, much of the work of the National Crime Agency is focused on international organized crime as well as terrorism. In France, the policing response continues to be national and highly centralized, but there are moves toward greater efficiencies and the merging of certain activities between the *Police Nationale* and the Gendarmerie.

More profound than the proposed merging of some policing responses has been the proposal by the French President Nicholas Sarkozy to eliminate what Balzac called "the most powerful man in France," the Investigating Magistrate or *Juge d'Instruction*. Unlike the United Kingdom and United States, France developed a cadre of professional judges who perform specific tasks within the criminal justice system. The judge who has historically had the most direct involvement with the police and criminal investigations is the Examining or Investigating Magistrate, J.I. The J.I. is a qualified judge and should not be confused with the English term *magistrate*.

France operates an Inquisitorial criminal justice system whereas the United Kingdom and United States operate adversarial systems (knights in armor doing battle that has developed into lawyers doing battle). Under the Inquisitorial system the court is actively involved in fact finding and questioning witnesses and the defendant. The French courtroom has trial judges who ask questions, prosecutors who are also judges, and defense lawyers who are advocates, members of the bar. Students from a common law jurisdiction would be surprised to see the bench ask questions during the trial and as well as surprised by the youthfulness of the actors. Judges are professional appointees, who have cleared a competitive national exam and then attended judge training school, the result of which is that a judge can be appointed at 26 years of age. The J.I., who, like his trial and prosecutorial colleagues, is a professionally trained judge, has responsibility for conducting the investigation into all serious crimes. He is assisted by the police in this effort. It is the J.I. who has the authority to decide whether a criminal case is established and whether that defendant should stand trial. It is the prosecutor judge who then conducts the prosecution at trial and at this time the J.I is prohibited from any further involvement in the case.

The J.I. position was created by Napoleon Bonaparte and has been contested many times over the past 200 years, usually over personal mistakes resulting in miscarriages of justice. The most frequent and damaging to the J.I. came out of an investigation into an alleged pedophile ring where a young J.I., Judge Burgaud, imprisoned 13 suspects for 3 years before trial. Eventually all 13 had their convictions overturned and the former President of France, Jacques Chirac, sent a personal letter of apology to the wrongly convicted parents and family members. This infamous *Outreau* (named after the village where the alleged incident occurred) seemed to be the final nail in the coffin for the J.I, until the association for professional judges got into the fight and President Sarkozy encountered opposition to his abolition proposals. The principal objection was that if the J.I. positions were eliminated then the prosecuting judge would take responsibility for case investigations, much like the district attorney in the United States and increasingly so with the Crown Prosecution Service in the United Kingdom.

Other reforms in France have included the writing of a new criminal code, *Code Penal*, introduced in 1994 and effective as of July 10, 2000, with new sections covering offenses such as ecological terrorism, sexual harassment, and crimes against humanity. Maximum prison terms increased to 30 years. The jury was abolished in France in 1941 under Vichy government (under German occupation) reforms to the entire criminal justice system. Despite recent reform considerations, the format is for a panel of professional judges except in the serious criminal trial court, Cour d'Assize, where there is a jury of nine laypersons and three professional judges, *jury populaire*. A two-thirds majority is needed for conviction. Sensitive cases such as terrorism are heard by seven judges without a jury. Children are deemed incapable of forming criminal intent and thus *doli incapax* until 13 years of age.

Unlike the British and American legal systems, inquisitorial law does not embrace the concept of binding precedent. Criminal justice reform also reviewed the categorization of prisons, and France now has four categories: *Maison d'Arret*, remand centers and for those serving sentences of less than 12 months; *Centres de Detention*, where the emphasis is on social rehabilitation; *Maison Centrales*, for lifers and those serving repeat sentences, where the emphasis is on security; and *Centres de Semi-Liberte*, halfway houses where those about to return into society are housed during the latter part of their sentences. This category also includes day prisons.

Somewhat incredibly after two world wars, liberal democracy has survived in Europe. The *European Convention on Human Rights*, built on the back of the creation of the United Nations, has set a standard of behavior and guidelines for how the European Union state treats its citizens. The Treaty on European Union created the European Community and it provides the platform for states to work collaboratively in establishing Euro-law. This law is increasingly significant to all European Union member countries and has had a profound effect on every aspect of the criminal justice system across Europe. In principle, any criminal law that transcends a national boundary offends national sovereignty. However, in November 2005, 12 Euro-wide criminal offenses were established. These *droit communautaire* are effectively federal laws for Europe; they include offenses such as drug trafficking, human trafficking, and counterfeiting car parts, toy parts, and the Euro currency.

HISTORY TODAY

The United States and other Western countries constantly emphasize the importance of human rights. However, they are forced to do business and maintain friendly relations with governments that regularly commit human rights abuses. Is this hypocritical or is it simply reality?

Policing Europe presents many jurisdictional challenges such as "hot pursuit" policy. To help negotiate these legal obstacles *EUROJUST* was created to link lawyers across nations within Europe. *EUROPOL*, a Euro-wide policing response initially started to counter drug trafficking in Europe, comprises officers drawn from all European Union member countries who work together on multi-national task forces. CEPOL is the European Police College, which operates under a common curriculum for senior police managers throughout a number of European Union countries.

Traditional police powers have been extended in times of emergency and significantly since 2001. These new stop and search powers have done little to change the minds of the French public about France being a police state. In 2002, President Sarkozy announced a partial merger of the *Police Nationale* and *Gendarmerie Nationale* under the Homeland Security (Orientation and Programming) Act to create a joint terrorist police force. Despite the numerous reforms throughout France's history and some indication that France is considering a more British style of policing, the police of France are highly centralized and, common to most civilian law systems, have a stratified entry system with direct entry into the officer classes.

The twentieth century was not exclusively the time for the rise of professionalism in the United States. It was also a time for a return to professionalism for European criminal justice agencies, particularly in the post-World War II era. Social service responsibilities have gained renewed attention and in all three jurisdictions, the United States, the United Kingdom, and France, these needs compete with the need to secure borders and combine resources for offending that transcends national frontiers. In the United States, many local agencies are now being asked to deal with criminal terrorist activities that would have been a federal issue before September 11, 2001. Just as we saw a move toward community policing in the later part of the twentieth century, so we are seeing a greater emphasis on policing of terrorism in the twenty-first century. Reform has become refocus and refinance.

During the last two centuries, policing in England has undergone a major ideological transition from reactive security provision to proactive presence. The United States did not have such a long history of tradition to break away from. Consequently, pressures brought to bear upon policing in the United States during the nineteenth century that resulted in the reform movement of the twentieth century are unique to the United States. Nevertheless, we should not forget that the reason for the creation of a unified police response for society is born out of the same class structures in each country, that is, the desire of the ruling and business classes to ensure the passage of legislation and police response that supported the continuation of the class divide. By the end of the nineteenth century every major city in Europe and the United States had a functioning police force, criminal courts, and an established penal system. For the first time, it could be argued that there was truly a criminal justice system functioning across Europe and North America.

TIME CAPSULE: POLICING IN PAKISTAN

Pakistan was created in 1947 when India, which had just gained its independence from Great Britain, split into predominantly Hindu India and predominantly Muslim Pakistan, on India's western border. East Pakistan, also predominantly Muslim, was located more than 1,000 miles from Pakistan. In 1971, East Pakistan declared its independence and became the nation of Bangladesh. Because India, Bangladesh, and Pakistan had been under British colonial rule for many decades, it is natural that those countries adopted British practices and traditions in many areas of government and education, including policing. However, police on the Indian subcontinent also had to be adaptive to the culture of those countries.

Throughout its colonial history, police on the Indian subcontinent were viewed by the populations as the muscle behind a political and social order whose primary aim was to suppress dissent against the British and against the Indian and Pakistani government officials who supported the British. Police were not respected but were feared as bullies, and viewed as corrupt and detached from the populace. Such is the nature of policing under a nondemocratic form of government in a country without a democratic tradition. Martial law is not an unusual occurrence in Pakistan, especially when a change of power occurs, and police officers have been called upon to enforce such an odious order on the population they are supposed to serve.

Ever since it became a nation, Pakistan has been beset by political turmoil. In contrast to most Western countries, political assassinations and military coups are more the norm than free, fair elections and peaceful transfers of power. Where have the police been in all of this turmoil? Are police services affected by periods of national political unrest? In countries like Pakistan, police often find themselves having to maintain and prop up an unpopular political order, and their alliances experience frequent and somewhat radical shifts sometimes.

Unlike policing in the United States, police officers in Pakistan, as in several other former British colonial countries, are trained in schools or colleges set up and administered along the lines of American military academies like the United States Military Academy or the Naval Academy, or a military college like the Citadel. One of the most prominent police colleges was the Police Academy in Sardah. Until Bangladesh declared its independence, police cadets from both West and East Pakistan attended the academy at Sardah, now in Bangladesh.

It may be difficult for even older American police officers to relate to what policing was like in Pakistan from the 1940s to the 1980s. As late as the late 1960s, one Pakistani province had only three vehicles, and two of these vehicles were reserved for the exclusive use of the Superintendent and Deputy Superintendent. All other officers had to share one pickup truck. There were no police radios or means of instant communication. When officers went to Pakistan's rural areas, they were totally cut off from anyone on the police force. Most officers were on horseback, and if a message had to be relayed to them, it would have to be via another officer on horseback. Sometimes officers would not receive a message from headquarters for several days. Even today, there is practically no formal policing in Pakistan's tribal areas along Pakistan's border with Afghanistan, an area only recently infiltrated by the country's army, brought about primarily as a result of Western pressure to fight Al Qaeda, Osama bin Laden's terrorist organization believed to be hiding in the tribal areas. The tribal areas of Pakistan have been largely self-governing—but not, as the Western media often says, "lawless"—for centuries with practically no input or authority from the central government. This may change eventually, as the tribal areas come under increasing control by Pakistan's central government.

Pakistan has a long tradition of feudalism. Throughout its history, especially its early history, Pakistan's police officers

Continued

TIME CAPSULE: POLICING IN PAKISTAN—CONT'D

tended to side with feudal landowners, perpetuating the plight of the country's poor, and exacerbating already poor relations with the social underclass. With few exceptions, police officials in Pakistan, at least until the 1980s, received very little exposure to other countries' police methods. Police officers had tunnel vision, and understood only one way—the traditional Pakistani way—of conducting police operations.

Television did not come to Pakistan until the mid-1960s, and very few Pakistanis even owned televisions. It was not until the 1980s that Pakistanis got a view of the outside world, with the advent of satellite technology and worldwide cable news networks like CNN. Over the past three decades, Pakistanis in general have become more knowledgeable about the outside world. They are also more attuned to basic human rights, those that people in other countries take for granted, and that an increasing number of ordinary Pakistanis are now demanding. The status quo in policing, in which police officers were primarily trained muscle that supported government repression, is no longer acceptable. Pakistani police are gradually acquiring greater exposure to Western methods and attitudes toward policing, and have begun to adopt a more citizen-centered mode of policing. Pakistan's current population is approximately 159 million. The country has nuclear capability and is a key ally in current United States efforts to combat terrorism, especially Al Qaeda, and other variants of Muslim extremism. Therefore, the United States and Western countries have a vital interest in the internal political affairs of Pakistan; the police and the military are key players in the future of Pakistan.

Source: Jones, M. (2006). Interview with Abdul Qadir Haye, Inspector General of Police (Retired) Pakistan. In Das, D., & Marenin, O. (Eds.), *Comparative problems of policing: Interviews with nineteen police leaders from different nations.* Lewiston, NY: Edwin Mellen Press, pp. 185-200.

SUMMARY

With its emphasis on strong management, organizational discipline, and scientific investigative techniques, the FBI has had a formative influence on twentieth-century police activities. Long identified with J. Edgar Hoover, its late director, the bureau has encouraged cooperation between police agencies and the role of the federal government in providing training for police leadership. State police agencies established during the first two decades of this century have served similar coordinating and training functions within their states.

Modern inventions, particularly the automobile and radio, have revolutionized the system of street patrol and permitted rapid improvement in the command and control of police units. Scientific methods of criminal investigation, proliferating rapidly since 1880, have placed a premium on training police officers to coordinate and evaluate scientific procedures and findings.

Social service responsibilities have become a growing part of police activities. There is a growing emphasis on eliminating the sources of crime and increasing efforts to build public confidence and pride in the police. Through the use of the sunrise court and the golden rule policy, minor offenders are diverted from the formal criminal justice system, leaving more time for the prosecution of major criminal activity.

A number of factors in modern life have contributed to the rise of a unique police subculture, which imposes limits on the efficiency of local and state police in dealing with riots. At the same time, strong antipolice attitudes on the part of some segments of the public and efforts to impose popular control over police disciplinary procedures have generated solidarity among professional law enforcement officers. The traditional fraternal organizations have gained new power, and a long-standing antipathy to police unionization may give way to pressures for unionization. Most recently, the Law Enforcement Assistance Administration's grants have resulted in a higher level of education among police officers and, thus, a greater level of interaction with and understanding of the needs and attitudes of the general public.

The rise of the voice of working people, suffrage, and the establishment of fundamental human rights for all led inevitably to review, reform, and greater accountability. As the twentieth century progressed and social, educational, and health conditions improved, due process progressed at a pace unseen in previous centuries. The criminal justice system responded with reforms at every level. Police officers became better equipped and trained. Police leaders participated in leadership development and management training and the relationship that had started in the eighteenth century now formalized into partnerships between academics and criminal justice agencies. By 1939, five major American universities had criminology programs. Theories flourished and wars on crime were announced. This resulted in *Miranda* warnings, crackdowns, zero-tolerance policing, "Broken Windows" theory (1982), a return to foot patrol, and Community-Oriented Policing—COPS.

By 2001, 12,000 of a total 19,000 law enforcement agencies in the United States had applied for COPS grants. In the early 1990s, William Bratton and Jack Maple introduced the world to COMPSTAT, a computer statistics generated model to identify crime in a given area and then hold precinct leaders responsible for effectively dealing with that crime pattern. Amazingly, crime declined, not just where COMPSTAT had been utilized in New York, but across the United States generally. In truth, no one is sure why, but just as we were all patting ourselves on the back and praising COMPSTAT, as well as any other theory we had that looked plausible for reducing crime, along came September 11, 2001. COPS money was redirected and policing in America and then Europe followed. We are now in the new world of intelligence-led policing, fusion centers, predictive policing, and technology-directed policing. The reform period was just that, a period. Necessary, but over. Where we are now is the subject of contemporary debate.

REFERENCES

Whitehead, D. (1956). *The FBI story*. New York: Random House; de Toledano, R. (1973). *J. Edgar Hoover: The man in his time*. New Rochelle, NY: Arlington House; Theoharis, A. G. (1981). The presidency and the Federal Bureau of Investigation: The conflict of intelligence and legality. *Criminal Justice History, 2*, 131–160; Collins, F. L. (1943). *The FBI in peace and war*. New York: Books, Inc; Lowenthal, M. (1950). *The Federal Bureau of Investigation*. New York: William Sloane; Turner, W. W. (1970). *Hoover's FBI: The men and the myth*. Los Angeles: Sherbourne Press.

Monkkonen, E. H. (1981). *Police in urban America, 1860-1920*. Cambridge: Cambridge University Press; Walker, S. (1977). *A critical history of police reform: The emergence of professionalism*. Lexington, MA: Lexington Books; Bopp, W. J. (1971). *The police rebellion: A quest for blue power*. Springfield, IL: Charles C Thomas; Juris, H. A., & Feuille, P. (1973). *Police unionism: Power and impact in public sector bargaining*. Lexington, MA: Lexington Books; Price, B. R. (1977). *Police professionalism: Rhetoric and action*. Lexington, MA: Lexington Books; Vollmer, A. (1936). *The police and modern society*. Montclair, NJ: University of California Press Berkeley: Reprint. Montclair, NJ: Berkeley: Patterson Smith (1971).

Thorwald, J. (1964). *The century of the detective*. Trans. Winston, R., & Winston, C. New York: Harcourt, Brace & World, Inc; Osterberg, J. W., & Ward, R. H. (2000). *Criminal investigation: A method for reconstructing the past* (4th ed). Cincinnati, OH: Anderson Publishing Co; Saferstein, R. (1998). *Criminalistics: An introduction to forensic science*. Englewood Cliffs, NJ: Prentice-Hall; Moenssens, A. A., Starrs, J. E., Henderson, C. E., & Inbau, F. E. (1995). *Scientific evidence in civil and criminal cases* (4th ed). Westburg, NY: The Foundation Press.

Skolnick, J. H., & Grey, T. C. (Eds.), (1975). *Police in America*. Boston: Little, Brown & Co; Stark, R. (1972). *Police riots: Collective violence and law enforcement*. Belmont, CA: Wadsworth Publishing Co; Wilson, J. Q. (1968). *Varieties of police behavior: The management of law and order in eight communities*. Cambridge, MA: Harvard University Press; Westley, W. A. (1970). *Violence and the police: A sociological study of law, custom and morality*. Cambridge, MA: The MIT Press; Wilson, J. Q. (1975). *Thinking about crime*. New York: Basic Books; Juris, H. A., & Feuille, P. (1973). *Police unionism: Power and impact in public-sector bargaining*. Lexington, MA: Lexington Books; Bopp, W. J. (1971). *The police rebellion: A quest for blue power*. Springfield, IL: Charles C Thomas; *Law enforcement: The federal role*. New York: McGraw-Hill Book Co. (Report of the Twentieth Century Fund Task Force on the Law Enforcement Assistance Administration) 1976.

Smith, D. C. Jr. (1971). Some things that may be more important to understand about organized crime and the Cosa Nostra. *University of Florida Law Review, 24*(1), 181-185; Hobsbawm, E. J. (1965). Mafia. In *Primitive rebels: Studies in Archaic forms of social movement in the 19th and 20th centuries*. New York: Norton and Company, pp. 90-98.

Geller, W. A. (Ed.), (1985). *Police leadership in America: Crisis and opportunity*. New York: Praeger; Kappeler, V. E., Sluder, R. D., & Alpert, G. P. (1994). A history of police deviance: The forging of an occupation. In *Forces of deviance: Understanding the dark side of policing*. Prospect Heights, IL: Waveland Press, Inc; Sherman, L. W. (1978). *Scandal and reform: Controlling police corruption*. Berkeley: University of California Press; Knapp Commission (New York City), (1972). *Knapp Commission report on police corruption*. New York: George Braziller; More, H. W., & Unsinger, P. C. (Eds.), (1992). *Managerial control of the police: Internal affairs and audits*. Springfield, IL: Charles C Thomas.

Notes and Problems

1. Has police professionalism increased since 1850? What factors have been most significant in this development?

2. Assume that you are a university official charged with designing a proposed criminal justice degree program that would award a bachelor's degree to candidates for

police or correctional appointments. What subjects would you include and why? How would you balance vocational skill enhancement with traditional liberal arts subjects? If your college or university has a criminal justice program, how well does it match your requirements? Should it be changed?

3. A number of scholarly writers on police rioting and violence have suggested (with a battery of statistics to support them) that violence is a way of life for the patrol officer assigned to law enforcement activities. If we accept that viewpoint as correct, what steps could be taken to control excessive use of force? Is this not an important factor in retaining public support, which in turn is an essential ingredient in law enforcement?

4. How should officials plan to assure public safety against rioting and looting? If police units are to be utilized, how must their training be conducted or supplemented?

5. Does patrol perform any useful purpose other than giving the public some assurance that the police are available if trouble should develop? Is the expense of patrol worth the minimal public relations benefits that it gives?

6. Should police be expected to shelter lost children, help the habitual drunk, and help the person who locks his or her keys in his or her car? If they stop, who will take their place? If their duties are sharply limited to law enforcement and crime prevention, will a different type of officer be attracted to police work, and would that be desirable?

7. How different is police administration from business administration and other aspects of public sector management?

ENDNOTES

[1] Jones, M. (2005). *Criminal justice pioneers in U.S. history.* Boston: Allyn and Bacon.

[2] Ibid.

[3] Walker, S. (1997). *Popular justice: A history of American criminal justice* (2nd ed). New York: Oxford University Press.

[4] Cray, E. (1997). *Chief justice: A biography of Earl Warren.* New York: Simon and Schuster.

[5] Oliver, W. M., & Hilgenberg, J. F. (2006). *A history of crime and justice in America.* Boston: Allyn and Bacon.

[6] To be discussed at length in Chapter 14.

[7] Quoted in de Toledano, R. (1973). *J. Edgar Hoover: The man in his time.* New Rochelle, NY: Arlington House, p. 261.

[8] Galton, F. (1892). *Fingerprints.* London: Macmillan Co, reprinted, New York: Da Capo Press (1965).

[9] Word content analysis uses mathematical probability theory to match a questioned document with a control document authored by an individual. Identification of an author is on the basis of the likelihood that any individual is likely to use the same words and phrases when discussing a given subject.

[10] Christopher, W. (Ed.), (1991). *Report of the independent commission on the Los Angeles Police Department.* Darby, PA: Diane Publishing; Jones, supra; Gates, D. F., & Shah, D. K. (1993). *Chief: My life in the LAPD.* New York: Bantam Books.

[11] Geis, G., & Bienen, L. B. (1998). *Crimes of the century.* Boston: Northeastern University Press.

CHAPTER 14

Criminal Justice and Terrorism: The Era of Homeland Security

KEY TERMS

1993 World Trading Center Bombing

Afghanistan

Al Qaeda

Ali Mohmed al-Megrahi

American Airlines Flight 11

American Airlines Flight 77

American embassy in Tehran

American Federation of Labor

Anarchism

Anwar al-Sadat

Arab nationalism

Archduke Franz Ferdinand

Asymmetrical warfare

Austro-Hungarian Empire

Ayman al-Zawahiri

Balfour Declaration

Bill Clinton

Clarence Darrow

Cold War

Crusades

Egyptian Islamic Jihad

Emma Goldman

Fusion centers

Gamal Abdel Nasser

Gavrilo Princip

George W. Bush

Guerilla warfare

Hasan al-Banna

Hezbollah

Homeland Security

Iranian Revolution

Irish Republican Army

Islamism

Jerusalem

Jihad

June 28, 1914

Khaled Sheikh Mohammad

Khobar Towers

Leon Czolgosz

Mecca and Medina

Menachem Begin

Michael Collins

Mohammed

Munich Massacre

Muslim Brotherhood

Nairobi, Kenya; Dar Es Salaam, Tanzania

October 1, 1910

Omar Abdul Rahman

Organized labor

Osama bin Laden

Ottoman Empire

Palestine Liberation Organization

Pan Am Flight 103

Qur'an

Ramzi Yousef

Ruhollah Khomeini

Saddam Hussein

September 11, 2001

Serbian Black Hand

Shah Reza Pahlavi

Sinn Fein

Solomon

Taliban

Terrorism

Timothy McVeigh	United Airlines	Yasser Arafat
Tom Ridge	Flight 93	Zionist terrorism
United Airlines	*USS Cole*	Zionists
Flight 175	William McKinley	

LEARNING OBJECTIVES

1. Understand some of the events and historical forces that helped create modern terrorism.
2. Learn and understand some of the factors that have created tension and warfare in the Middle East.
3. Gain a brief understanding of how and why terrorist actions occur.
4. Learn the role of radical labor groups, anarchists, and other disgruntled political groups in American terrorism.
5. Learn about some of the major terrorist events and actors in European terrorism.
6. Know the events of September 11, 2001.

Table 14.1 Time Line: Terrorism and Homeland Security

1790	Edmund Burke, British political philosopher, describes the French Revolution as a "reign of terror."
1807-1814	During the Peninsula War, the term *guerilleros* (irregulars) is used to describe the tactics of asymmetrical warriors.
1901	President William McKinley is assassinated in New York by an anarchist terrorist.
1910	The office of the *Los Angeles Times* is blown up, killing 21.
1914	The heir to the throne of the Austro-Hungarian Empire is assassinated by a Bosnian Serb terrorist in Sarajevo, igniting World War I.
1917	The Balfour Declaration declares support for a Jewish state in the land of Palestine.
1918	The end of World War I signals the end of Ottoman rule of the Middle East, and countries' boundaries are carved out by European colonial interests.
1919	Michael Collins assumes control of the militant wing of the Irish Republican Army and organizes attacks against occupying British forces in Ireland.
1921	Ireland gains independence from Britain, but Northern Ireland remains part of the United Kingdom, propelling future terrorist acts by Protestant and Catholic militants.
1928	The Muslim Brotherhood is founded in Egypt.
1946	Members of the Irgun, a Zionist terrorist organization, blow up the King David Hotel in British-occupied Palestine, killing 91.
1946-1991	The Cold War pits American interests versus those of the U.S.S.R., resulting in the covert funding of terrorist activities allied with both nations' interests.
1948	The nation of Israel is established; the culmination of 70 years of gradual Jewish migration to Palestine.
1948	Egyptian Prime Minister is assassinated by the Muslim Brotherhood.

Continued

Table 14.1   Time Line: Terrorism and Homeland Security—cont'd

1949	Hassan al-Banna, the founder of the Muslim Brotherhood, is killed by Egyptian government.
1964	The Palestine Liberation Organization (PLO) is founded.
1969	Yassir Arafat assumes control of the PLO.
1972	Israeli athletes are murdered by Palestinian terrorists at the summer Olympics in Munich.
1979	A revolution in Iran installs a radical Shiite government, and results in the storming of the American embassy in Tehran, with American personnel being held hostage for 444 days.
1979	The Soviet Union invades Afghanistan, triggering an American supported Muslim Jihad against the Soviets.
1981	As retaliation for his peace overtures toward Israel, Egyptian President Anwar Sadat is assassinated by soldiers allied with the Muslim Brotherhood and Egyptian Al-Jihad.
1982	Israel invades Lebanon, which results in the creation of Hezbollah.
1983	241 American Marines are killed by a Hezbollah-led suicide bomber in Beirut, Lebanon.
1988	Pan Am Flight 103 explodes over Lockerbie, Scotland, killing all passengers and some on the ground; a Libyan agent is eventually convicted of the bombing. He is sentenced to prison in Scotland, and released in 2010.
1989	The Soviet Union withdraws from Afghanistan, paving the way for the takeover by the Taliban and the establishment of Al Qaeda, led by Osama bin Laden.
1993	Terrorists bomb the World Trade Center in New York City, killing six.
1995	A bomb destroys the Murrah Federal Building in Oklahoma City, killing 168 people; two right-wing American extremists are convicted of the bombing.
1996	Terrorists bomb the Khobar Towers in Saudi Arabia, killing 19 Americans and one Saudi.
1998	Osama bin Laden declares war on the United States, and names any American as a potential target.
1998	Al Qaeda terrorists bomb the American embassies in Kenya and Tanzania, killing over 200.
2000	Al Qaeda suicide bombers attack the *USS Cole* in Yemen, killing 17 sailors.
2001	Al Qaeda terrorists crash four commercial airliners into both towers of the World Trade Center, the Pentagon, and in a field in Shanksville, PA, killing over 2,700 people.
2001	The Office of Homeland Security is created.
2001	The United States invades Afghanistan, deposes the ruling Taliban, and scatters Al Qaeda.
2003	An American-led coalition invades Iraq and deposes Saddam Hussein.
2004	Al Qaeda-inspired terrorists blow up a train in Madrid, Spain, in retaliation for Spanish involvement in Iraq.
	Chechen Islamic extremists attack a school in Beslan, Russia, and take hostages. The siege lasts 3 days; more than 300, including many schoolchildren, are murdered.
	Anwar al-Awlaki, an American-born Muslim cleric, returns to his ancestral country, Yemen, where he becomes a leader in Al Qaeda of the Arabian Peninsula.
2005	Al Qaeda-inspired terrorists attack London's transportation system, killing 52.
	Al Qaeda-inspired terrorists blow up three American-owned hotels in Amman, Jordan, killing 57.
2008	Terrorists attack several known landmarks and hotels frequented by Westerners in Mumbai, India, killing 190 people, including five Americans.
2009	Dr. Nidal Malik Hassan, a U.S. Army psychiatrist of Palestinian descent, kills 13 and wounds many others after opening fire at Fort Hood Army Base in Killeen, Texas. He was guided by Anwar al-Awlaki and Al Qaeda in the Arabian Peninsula.
	A Nigerian man is thwarted in an attempt to ignite explosive material concealed in his underwear, following directions from Al Qaeda, while traveling from Amsterdam to Detroit.
2011	Osama bin Laden is killed by U.S. Navy Seals during a raid on bin Laden's compound in Abbottabad, Pakistan.

THE ROAD TO 9/11: A BRIEF HISTORY OF TERRORISM

One of the most worn-out clichés in recent years is, "The events of *September 11, 2001* changed America forever." Even though it is a cliché, it is true. Anyone old enough to remember can recall where they were and what they were doing when they heard the news of the September 11 terrorist attacks on New York City and Washington, D.C. Many people in the United States separate their lives into the pre- and post-9/11 eras, just as the World War II generation did with the December 7, 1941, attack on Pearl Harbor by Japan. Many aspects of American foreign and domestic policy are divided the same way. Because September 11, 2001, was the catalyst for so much change, those who remember it and are living in its aftermath would do well to understand the events that led up to it.

The roots of modern Islamic *terrorism* are complex and tied to issues other than the ones now associated with such terrorism, namely extremist Islam, sometimes called *Islamism*. Arab nationalism, European colonialism, pride in Islamic history, and other factors have contributed to the current state of Islamic terrorism which for many Americans seem to have come from nowhere. The events of 9/11 were (in part) the culmination of several centuries of events that took place both inside and outside the Arab and Muslim worlds.

Understanding the Middle East, let alone dealing with its problems, has never been simple. The Middle East has been a source of frustration not only for its own leaders, but for those in Europe and the United States as well. In part because three of the world's major religions—Judaism, Christianity, and Islam, sometimes collectively called the *Abrahamic religions*—had their beginnings in the Middle East, fervent religious beliefs, combined with racial, ethnic, and tribal conflicts, coupled with the fact that the Middle East is a source of important natural resources and is a primary transit point connecting all points of the world, have added to this complexity.

Part of the problem when dealing with the Middle East is that almost every ethnic or religious group residing there lays claim to a past glory, or believes that it has a historical or divine claim to the disputed territory. Modern Israelis believe that the nation of Israel should exist either by divine right or historical inheritance, and that the world's Jews need a homeland they can call their own. Those who claim divine right point to the glory of the Old Testament kingdoms of David and *Solomon*, and to the entire Old Testament, which depicts the Jews as God's chosen people.

Solomon: Prominent figure in the biblical Old Testament; son of King David; regarded as one of wisest men of the Old Testament; credited with writing several Old Testament books; regarded as one of Israel's greatest kings despite his shortcomings and his numerous wives and concubines.

Christians in the Middle East, as well as many Christians throughout the world, see the Middle East, especially Israel, as a sacred site as well. Modern-day Israel was the place where Jesus lived. Apocalyptic (end of world) prophecies center on the Middle East as the place where the world will come to an end.

The Arabian Peninsula was the birthplace of Islam, and Saudi Arabia is home to Islam's holiest cities, *Mecca* and *Medina*. It was from modern-day Saudi Arabia that the prophet *Mohammed* and the early disciples of Islam, most of whom were Arabs, set about spreading Islam to the rest of the world. The seventh through the sixteenth centuries are often referred to as the *Golden Age of Islam* because they witnessed the spread of the Islamic faith. During the Golden Age of Islam, the Muslim religion spread to non-Arabs as far east as Indonesia, as far south as Eastern Africa, as far west as Northern Africa, and as far north as Bosnia and Spain. Not only do many Muslims long for a return to the Golden Age of Islam but many also believe that the Middle East is theirs by divine right.

> Mohammed (570-632): The founding prophet of Islam, native of what is now Saudi Arabia; wrote the Qur'an (Islam's holiest book); regarded by Muslims as a prophet from (Allah) God, the last true prophet of God who restored true monotheism (one God) to the world; helped spread the Islamic faith throughout the Arabian Peninsula during his lifetime, by diplomatic, written, and military means.

Another Islamic holy city is *Jerusalem*, which is also a holy city to Jews and Christians. During the twelfth and thirteenth centuries, European armies, with the blessing of the Roman Catholic hierarchy, sought to reclaim the Middle East for Christianity and to rid Christianity's holy land of the "infidel" Muslims who had dominated it for several centuries. The *Crusades* rank among the bloodiest and most bitter conflicts in human history. To this day, some Muslims derisively refer to all Westerners who seek influence in the Middle East as "crusaders," realizing that the term still resonates with Middle Eastern Arabs and Muslims who have learned of the Crusades by studying Islamic history.

HISTORY TODAY

There are many ethnic groups that aspire to have their own homeland within their current country or countries of residence. These groups include the Basque in Spain, the Kurds who reside in Turkey, Iraq, and Iran, the Palestinians in Israel and Jordan, and the Chechens in Russia. Native Americans have similar nationalistic grievances throughout North and South America. All of these groups claim they have a right to their own homeland for their own safety and because the land rightly belongs to them. Does the fact that an ethnic group once ruled their territory entitle them to rule that territory now?

TERRORISM'S ORIGINS

To some degree, terrorism is an offshoot of *guerrilla warfare*. The term *guerrilla* is rooted in the early nineteenth century with the French occupation of the Iberian Peninsula. The occupying French forces were far superior to the Portuguese and Spanish insurgents, known as *guerrilleros* or *irregulars*, so the Spanish and the Portuguese *guerrilleros* employed hit-and-run tactics and made a practice of keeping the French off-guard.[1] This type of *asymmetrical warfare* has been employed very often when a smaller or less well-equipped force encounters superior conventional forces. American patriots used it against the far superior British forces during the American Revolution; it was used against Americans during the Vietnam conflict.

Whether a person or organization should wear the label of terrorist is fiercely debated. There are many who bristle at the idea of comparing modern terrorists with any sort of soldier, be it guerrilla or any other kind. While a person who engages in acts of violence or killing may be called a *terrorist* by one person, that same individual or organization may be called a *freedom or resistance fighter* by someone else, regardless of how cruel their actions may seem. Like the typical guerrilla warrior, a terrorist may see him- or herself as having to resort to unconventional means of warfare such as targeting civilians, because they cannot win through conventional warfare. A group of 19 individuals like the September 11, 2001, hijackers could not possibly hope to compete directly with the United States military in a conventional battle, but that same group of people could change the course of history if they are willing to commit an act as dastardly as crashing a commercial civilian airliner into a building filled with people who are completely defenseless. No matter how one views the events of September 11, 2001, one cannot deny that it was a date that changed history. Tom Friedman of the *New York Times* states that it was nothing less than the beginning of World War III, which is still unfolding.[2] By no means did terrorism originate on September 11, and by no means has it ever been the sole province of Islamic militants. Many other causes, ideologies, and personality types have been at the root of terrorist behavior for more than 100 years.

ANARCHISM AND LABOR MILITANCY

In the eyes of many Americans, the image of the modern terrorist is an angry young Islamist, but this was not always the case, nor is it accurate. Most of the world's Muslims do not endorse terrorism, let alone participate in terrorist activities, and it is unfortunate that people of Middle Eastern or South Asian extraction live with this stereotype. In fact, Muslims have been the victims, whether targeted purposely or not, of Islamist terrorists as often as Westerners. However, at the beginning of the twentieth century it was not Muslims who wore the face of the terrorist. Instead, the image of the terrorist was a (sometimes) hooded or masked Irishman or Eastern or Southern European. The ideology connected to these terrorists was not Islam, but socialism, communism, *anarchism*, and/or a strong allegiance to *organized labor*.

The dawn of a new century always brings with it the hope that it will be more peaceful than the last, but this hope seems never to become reality. On September 6, 1901, a notorious act of terrorism occurred at the Pan-American Exposition in Buffalo, New York. *Leon Czolgosz*, a self-described anarchist, shot and mortally wounded President *William McKinley*, who died 8 days after the shooting. Buffalo authorities treated Czolgosz roughly and he was nearly lynched by Buffalo crowds. Despite some reservations about his mental state, Czolgosz was tried and convicted of the President's murder. He was executed at Auburn Prison on October 20, 1901, less than 2 months after McKinley's death.[3]

> William McKinley (1843-1901): Twenty-fifth President of the United States (1897-1901); former Congressman from Ohio; served as President during the Spanish-American War; assassinated several months after his election to a second term as President.

Although Czolgosz was not intellectually or socially skillful enough to serve in a leadership capacity in any organization, the image of the anarchist terrorist as a madman, already at the forefront of American images of terrorism, was greatly reinforced.[4] This image was reinforced when *Emma Goldman*, a leader in the anarchist movement who had met Czolgosz but did not participate in the McKinley murder, praised Czolgosz for following the dictates of his ideals. One of Goldman's associates, Alexander Berkman, had attempted to assassinate Henry Clay Frick, a prominent Pennsylvania businessman, in 1892, so the image of the Eastern European anarchist assassin was well-planted in the minds of the American public even before the murder of President McKinley.

> Emma Goldman (1869-1940): Lithuanian immigrant to the United States; a principal spokesperson for the anarchist movement in the United States, staunch foe of capitalism, and a strong advocate for socialism and for women's issues; eventually abandoned advocacy for violence as a means of changing social order; deported from the United States in 1919.

TERRORISM AND LABOR MILITANTS

The McKinley assassination was only one example of left-wing radical terrorism in the twentieth century. In many respects an offshoot of communism and anarchism, labor unions, while now mainstream, were viewed by opponents as subversive to American capitalism while it was in its infancy. One of the worst mass killings at the hands of terrorists in American history occurred on *October 1, 1910*, in Los Angeles, at the hands of organized labor militants. Early that morning, a dynamite explosion at the *Los Angeles Times* headquarters caused 21 deaths and many more injuries. At the time, the *Los Angeles Times* was a vociferous opponent of organized labor.

Local police departments, even those in large cities like Los Angeles, lacked the expertise to investigate complex crimes as well as the resources to conduct interstate investigations. The bomb was an instrument of war, not of crime, and police agencies were not qualified to conduct a proper investigation of such a sophisticated weapon. The only federal law enforcement agency that could have become involved was the recently created Bureau of Investigation, but it was hampered by poorly qualified agents and few resources. In addition, in marked contrast to the modern era, the federal government was not likely to get involved in what was viewed as a state or local matter; therefore, the administration of President William Taft did not feel obligated and was not pressured to offer any appreciable assistance to the Los Angeles investigation. Crime, even on this scale, was simply a local matter and was not viewed as being within the purview of the federal government.

George Alexander, the Mayor of Los Angeles, contacted William Burns, head of the Burns Detective Agency, who was already investigating a similar crime that had occurred at a railroad office in Illinois. Burns was awarded a contract from the local government to fund the investigation. Burns' investigation began with much promise but met some political roadblocks; namely, his funding was cut off as a result of a dispute with the Los Angeles District Attorney. Despite having to use his own funds (he eventually received a $200,000 reward for solving the case), Burns investigated the bombing. Three labor militants, Ortie McManigal, James McNamara, and John McNamara, all of whom later told Burns they would blow up the whole country if it meant obtaining worker rights, were charged with the bombing.

Clarence Darrow (1857-1938): Ohio native regarded by some as one of the greatest criminal defense lawyers in American history; impassioned and articulate courtroom orator; participated in high-profile cases such as the Scopes Monkey Trial, where the teaching of evolution was put on trial in Tennessee, and the Leopold and Loeb case, in which two wealthy young men were convicted of killing a little boy in hopes of committing the perfect crime.

The *American Federation of Labor* hired famed criminal defense attorney *Clarence Darrow* to defend the trio. Despite impassioned and nationally publicized accusations of a capitalist conspiracy against organized labor, the case went to trial. While the trial was being conducted, the three defendants changed their plea to guilty and were sentenced to long prison terms. The trial was rife with accusations of tampering on both sides. Burns was indicted for kidnapping in Indiana, where he had gone to apprehend the bombers to forcibly transport them to California. He was not convicted. Darrow was eventually charged with attempting to bribe the jurors but was acquitted as well.[5]

WORLD WAR I

One of the most notorious acts of political assassination/terrorism occurred on *June 28, 1914*. Bosnia, which contains a large population of ethnic Serbians, was under the dominion of the *Austro-Hungarian Empire*. Many Bosnian Serbs were seeking independence from the Austro-Hungarian Empire and wanted a separate Serbian state within Bosnia; the same issue provoked the mass killings in Bosnia in the 1990s. Among those seeking this independence was a group called the *Serbian Black Hand*, and a group they supported called *Mlada Bosna*, or *Young Bosnia*, which counted among its members 19-year-old *Gavrilo Princip*.

Despite prior warnings by the Serbian ambassador to Austria of a potential assassination attempt, *Archduke Franz Ferdinand*, the Crown Prince and heir to the Austrian throne, accepted an invitation from the Bosnian governor to visit Sarajevo, Bosnia, and inspect his army troops. While riding through Bosnia, another member of Mlada Bosna named Nedelijko Cabrinovic threw a grenade at the Archduke's car. The Archduke survived, but rather than getting out of Sarajevo as quickly as possible, he decided to visit the local hospital to visit those wounded in the assassination attempt. After the visit, while still in Sarajevo, his driver took a wrong turn and happened to drive by Princip, who had given up his planned attempt to kill the Archduke when the grenade attack went awry. Princip took advantage of the Archduke's fortuitous reappearance, and shot and killed the Archduke and his wife.[6]

Although the assassination generated big headlines in much of Europe, it went relatively unnoticed in the United States. However, over the next few weeks, a series of threats were exchanged, ending with a declaration of war by Austria-Hungary and Germany (an Austrian ally) against Serbia, a traditional Russian ally. Before long, other countries aligned with one side or the other joined the fray, and World War I, also referred to later as *The Great War* or *The War to End All Wars*, began.

Three years later, the United States entered the war on the side of Serbia and its allies, which included Great Britain and France, as well as Italy and Japan, two countries that the United States would square off against 24 years later in World War II. Princip, a low-level soldier in a ragtag group of young radical terrorists, pulled the trigger that resulted in the deaths of approximately 20 million people and a reordering of the entire world order.

Part of the new order brought about by World War I's end was the breakup of the *Ottoman Empire*. Once the most powerful empire in the Middle East and Southern Europe, the Ottoman Empire had been in gradual decline prior to World War I. The Ottomans lost most of their European possessions in the First Balkan War of 1912-1913. World War I brought the official end to the Ottoman Empire, and dominion over its territories was divided among Russia, Great Britain, France, and Italy. The Middle East was divided to suit the economic and political interests of the victorious Europeans, with little regard for the ethnic and tribal divisions within those countries. To this day, many Middle Easterners do not define their identity with the nation in which they live. They identify themselves with their ethnic, tribal, or religious affiliation more than they do with nationality, to the delight of those fighting against Middle Eastern governments.

The creation of these somewhat artificial nation-states is still a bone of contention throughout the Middle East, as was an announcement by Arthur Balfour, the British foreign minister, with respect to Palestine. The *Balfour Declaration*, as it came to be called, expressed sympathy for the idea of creating a sovereign Jewish state in Palestine. For several decades Palestine had witnessed a gradual influx of Jewish immigration, along with calls for the creation of a Jewish state. The Balfour Declaration also called for equal treatment of non-Jews in Palestine, namely Palestinian Arabs.[7] Over the next three decades, Jewish immigration to Palestine would increase and so would Jewish influence in Palestine, and the calls for the creation of a Jewish state would become louder, especially as persecution of Jews throughout Continental Europe escalated in the 1930s.

MICHAEL COLLINS AND THE IRISH REPUBLICAN ARMY

The seeds of modern terrorism did not take root exclusively in the Middle East or the European Balkan countries like Serbia and Bosnia. While the Middle East was undergoing its forced political evolution, so was another traditionally British-dominated country, Ireland. Given their revulsion of the West, including its politics, culture, and religion, it would seem unlikely that modern Islamic terrorists would draw inspiration or learn lessons from an Irish Catholic. Yet *Michael Collins*, whether knowingly or not, stands as one of the important figures in twentieth-century terrorism. Born on October 16, 1890, in Clonakilty, Ireland, Collins grew up amid rather unremarkable circumstances. There were few indications in his early life that Collins would be viewed alternately as a merciless terrorist and as the voice of Irish patriotism in the early twentieth century. Collins worked rather anonymously in the British civil service from 1906 to 1916, although he joined Irish nationalist groups in 1908 and 1909. Ireland had lived under complete British domination since 1800, and the two countries had endured extremely poor relations for hundreds of years.

Collins participated in the Easter Rising in 1916, a disastrous (for the rebels) uprising against the British at the height of World War I. He was imprisoned for his role in the uprising and released in December 1916. Like many terrorists or resistance fighters, Collins was convinced by the Easter Rising that the opposition, which in this case was the British, could not be defeated or forced to negotiate Irish independence by either diplomacy or conventional warfare. Collins was elected to the Irish Assembly in 1918, representing *Sinn Fein* (Ourselves Alone), the political wing of the Irish Volunteers, which was the precursor to the *Irish Republican Army*.

Michael Collins assumed command of the Irish Republican Army in 1919 and orchestrated attacks against the British, employing guerrilla tactics, bombings, and assassinations of British officials, intelligence agents, soldiers, and police officers as a way of forcing the British to the negotiating table. For a time, Collins was at the top of Britain's most wanted list, with a 10,000 pound bounty on his head. Collins studied the methods used by Russian revolutionaries in the late nineteenth century.[8] On the basis of his studies of the Russians, Collins thought that bombs, ambushes, and assassinations of British soldiers and officials and their Irish supporters would be successful weapons in Ireland's quest for independence.

Whether it was a result of the Collins-led IRA terror campaign or international pressure, the British sat down at the negotiating table with their archenemy in the fall of 1921. Collins and other IRA negotiators persuaded the British to grant independence to most of Ireland, but the country's Ulster region, which consisted of six counties and a sizeable Protestant population, would remain under British control and as part of the United Kingdom, as it does today. While the treaty was greeted enthusiastically by many of the Irish, a substantial minority, including most of the IRA leadership, were outraged by the Northern Ireland compromise and called Collins a traitor.

Collins was killed on August 22, 1922, at the age of 31. He was killed in an ambush by opponents of his efforts, although Collins biographer Peter Hart suggests that Collins was not intentionally targeted. Since his death, Collins has been the subject of admiration, fascination, and revulsion. He embodies the debate about whether one person's terrorist is another person's freedom fighter. His life and methods of operating, which he gleaned by studying Russian revolutionaries, were studied and copied by left-wing and Islamic extremists alike. Although he has been dead for more than 85 years, and could not have foreseen the impact his life would have on terrorist and nationalist movements beyond his native Ireland, Collins simultaneously wore two faces—the embodiment of Irish nationalism and the epitome of modern terrorism.[9]

HISTORY TODAY

Was Michael Collins a cold-blooded murderer or a visionary agent of a legitimate political revolution? It took several bloody and violent decades before peace finally came to Ireland and then to Northern Ireland. There are still many in Northern Ireland who want a united Ireland under the Irish flag. These people may still maintain that they were sold out by people like Collins and some of Collins's successors, most notably Gerry Adams, the leader of Sinn Fein who negotiated an agreement with the British in the 1990s. Who is right and who is wrong in their assessment?

The fact that not all of Ireland was unified as a result of the 1921 treaty meant that the IRA continued to exist, even though it was officially outlawed by the new Republic of Ireland, and it continued to stand as one of Great Britain's worst enemies. For the rest of the twentieth century, the IRA was a major thorn in the side of the British, and untold numbers of lives were lost on both sides as a result of IRA bombings and assassinations, as well as British reprisals and crackdowns against the IRA. In addition, many killings in Northern Ireland are attributable to radical Protestant groups who favor the union with the United Kingdom and oppose the IRA. Currently, both the United Kingdom and the United States State Department list remaining branches of the IRA as terrorist organizations.

Listed below are some of the most notorious acts of terrorism attributed to the IRA over the past four decades:

- 1972—At the Aldershot headquarters of the British Parachute Regiment, an IRA bomb killed seven, none of them British soldiers
- 1973—IRA car bombs in London killed one and injured 180
- 1974—An IRA bomb killed 11 British soldiers and family members
- 1974—An IRA bomb in Guildford killed two soldiers and three civilians and injured 50 others
- 1974—An IRA bomb at a pub in Birmingham killed 21 (This bombing formed the basis for the movie *In the Name of the Father*.)
- 1979—Louis Mountbatten, a British admiral, statesman, and uncle to Prince Philip, was assassinated by the IRA in Ireland
- 1984—At the British Conservative Party gathering in Brighton, an IRA bomb killed five, including a prominent Conservative Party leader
- 1993—In Warrington, an IRA bomb killed two boys, ages 3 and 12, while they were shopping with their families[10]

While the IRA was waging its campaigns, other terrorist groups with other agendas waged campaigns of their own. The IRA formed unlikely partnerships with some of these groups despite their significant religious and ethnic differences. Throughout the twentieth century, the IRA and radical Arab governments shared resources and expertise in training their members.

THE MUSLIM BROTHERHOOD

One of the seminal events in the history of modern Islamic terrorism is the establishment of the *Muslim Brotherhood*. In fact, most Muslim extremism and terrorism can be traced to the establishment of the Muslim Brotherhood in Egypt. The Muslim Brotherhood was founded in 1928 by *Hasan al-Banna*, a 22-year-old schoolteacher. The Brotherhood and its radical Islamic idealism quickly spread to North Africa and the Middle East.

At first, the Brotherhood was primarily a religious organization with little involvement in politics; they were primarily a social activist organization rather than a political movement, even though many of their members were active opponents of European colonial influence in their countries. The Brotherhood advocated a lifestyle of strict adherence to the principles spelled out in the Muslim holy book, the *Qur'an*. Al-Banna and the Brotherhood wanted to reduce or eliminate the influence of Westerners, Christians, and non-Muslims in the Islamic world, especially in the Arab domains of the Middle East and North Africa.

During the late 1930s, the Brotherhood began to assume a more active posture on political matters, advocating not only a Muslim lifestyle, but a theocratic government based on Islamic principles as well, which included application of Shari'a, or Islamic law; in short, a political Islam. Like many other Egyptians, the Brotherhood wanted to end the British occupation of Egypt, and they had little use for the ruling monarch, King Farouk. In December 1948, a member of the Brotherhood assassinated Egypt's Prime Minister, Mahmoud an-Nukrashi Pasha, after the government launched a crackdown on the Brotherhood. Hasan al-Banna, the founder of the Muslim Brotherhood, was assassinated in retaliation in February 1949.

The Brotherhood survived al-Banna's death, but it quickly found an enemy in the secular government headed by *Gamal Abdel Nasser*. Although Nasser was an observant Muslim in his personal life and, like the Brotherhood, a vehement opponent of the nation of Israel, he detested the idea of political Islam. The Brotherhood attempted to assassinate Nasser in 1954, which led to a severe crackdown on the Brotherhood. During the 1950s and the 1960s, the Brotherhood's influence was eclipsed by Arab and Muslim leaders who adopted an ideology often referred to as *Nasserism*, or *Arab Socialism*.[11]

The Brotherhood experienced resurgence in the 1970s and 1980s, spurred on by the Iranian revolution of 1979 and disillusionment with secular Nasserism. Although several thousand Brotherhood members were killed in a 1982 uprising by President Hafez Assad's government in Syria, the Brotherhood's influence widened. Even though it is still officially outlawed in Egypt, the Brotherhood has representatives in both the Egyptian and Jordanian governments.[12]

The establishment of the Brotherhood stands as an important event in the history of twentieth century terrorism because it was a pioneer in the use of violence to impose a strict, some would say perverted, version of Islamic government in Islamic countries. Some of their adherents have been instrumental in trying to spread this ideology to non-Muslim areas as well, including Western Europe and North America.

In early 2011, the Muslim Brotherhood was thrust back into the world spotlight. Anti-government protesters forced the resignation of Egyptian President

Hosni Mubarak, who had ruled Egypt with an iron hand since the 1980s. The protesters who led the revolution acted out of various motives. Many were young people who simply wanted a better way of life along with more freedom of expression and the right to have a say in the affairs of government. Through satellite television, but especially because of the Internet and social networking, they saw what life was like in more prosperous Western countries, and they wanted a similar life. In addition, the protesters who toppled Hosni Mubarak were emboldened by a similarly successful effort in another of its North African neighboring countries, Tunisia. Although the Muslim Brotherhood did not start the protests that led to Mubarak's downfall, they readily seized on the opportunity to make headway into Egyptian government. Perhaps never before had a revolution been captured by constant television exposure like the Egyptian revolution of 2011, and the Muslim Brotherhood became better known as a result of that exposure.

HISTORY TODAY

The Egyptian and Tunisian Revolutions of 2011 might correctly be labeled "Facebook" revolutions. Many of the people who launched the revolutions in those countries were spurred on by social networking with each other and with people outside their country. Through Facebook, the Internet, and satellite television, they saw how the rest of the world lived, and they wanted those same freedoms and privileges that they could not have living in a dictatorship. It is very doubtful that Facebook founder Mark Zuckerburg could have foreseen his innovation toppling governments in North Africa. How much influence will social networking have in the coming years?

THE ESTABLISHMENT OF ISRAEL

For several decades prior to World War II, there was a growing movement to establish a stronger Jewish presence in Palestine, or the Jewish ancestral land of Israel. From the 1880s through World War II in the 1940s, the number of Jewish immigrants to Palestine increased gradually.

The European Holocaust of the 1930s and 1940s, which cost millions of Jews (and other ethnic groups) their lives, led many Jews and non-Jews alike throughout the world to believe that a Jewish homeland was necessary. During and after World War II, many Jewish refugees found themselves without a nation and with nowhere to go. In addition, the financial and political devastation of World War II signaled the beginning of the end of European colonial domination of Africa and the Middle East. The time was ripe for *Zionists* to seize control of Palestine and establish a Jewish state.

Using a combination of diplomacy and violence (see "Time Capsule: Zionist Terrorism"), the Jews in Palestine and their allies around the world brought the British, who had been occupying Palestine under a mandate, to the negotiating table, and the issue of Jewish statehood came before the United Nations. The United Nations voted to partition Palestine into two independent states, one for the Jews and one for the Arabs, but only one independent state emerged, and the nation of Israel was established in 1948. Ever since its inception, Israel and the countries that support it, including the United States, have been the target of terrorist attacks of all types, including Muslim militancy, left-wing terrorists, and right-wing terrorists.

TIME CAPSULE: ZIONIST TERRORISM

There are some places in Israel (and the disputed territories in the West Bank, an area referred to by most Israelis as *Judea* and *Samaria*) even today where Arab schoolchildren must sometimes be escorted to school under armed guard. The reason is that some Jewish extremists want all Arabs off what they see as Jewish land. The Arabs are not alone in the use of violence and terrorism in Israel to further their agenda. In fact, the only Prime Minister in Israeli history to be assassinated was Yitzhak Rabin, who was killed on November 4, 1995, not by an Arab but by a right-wing Jewish extremist who opposed Rabin's peace overtures toward Yasser Arafat and the Palestine Liberation Organization. The assassin had links to EYAL (Fighting Jewish Organization), an outlawed and now-defunct Israeli-based terrorist group. On February 25, 1994, a Jewish terrorist who belonged to the (subsequently outlawed) Kach organization, which was an offshoot of the U.S.-based Jewish Defense League, killed 29 praying Muslims in Hebron before the surviving worshippers killed him. In addition to Arab terrorist groups, the Israeli government also concentrates attention on a few Jewish extremist groups as well, including Kahane Chai, an offshoot of the Kach and Jewish Defense League. Kahane Chai calls for the total elimination of Arabs from all Jewish lands and the establishment of a Jewish theocracy akin to the Old Testament kingdoms of David and Solomon.[13]

Terrorism and political assassination in the name of Jewish nationalism is not new. During the New Testament era when Jewish Palestine was being ruled by the Romans, a Jewish group called the *Sicarii* (dagger) instilled terror in Roman authorities and Jewish collaborators by carrying out assassinations in crowded places, often in broad daylight, and then disappearing into the crowd. This same group initiated a disastrous revolt against the Romans around

65 A.D. that led to the virtual destruction of the city of Jerusalem and the Jewish Diaspora, when the Jews were permanently scattered.[14]

From the time that the Zionist movement to resettle Israel as a Jewish homeland began in earnest in the late nineteenth century, some Zionists used violence to further their agenda. The principal Zionist terrorist organization was the Irgun Zvai Le'umi (National Military Organization). The Irgun's principal targets were Arabs and the British soldiers and officials who occupied Palestine during the British Mandate period of the 1930s and 1940s.

During the struggle for Israeli independence in the 1930s and 1940s, opinions of the Irgun among Jewish Zionists were split. Many Zionists favored diplomacy over force and despised the Irgun; the Irgun responded that most modern nations, including the United States, could not have been established without the use of force, and that no ethnic group could compare to the Jews when it came to persecution. The Irgun claimed that force was the only mechanism that would bring the British to the bargaining table for independence. They also claimed that some of their attacks were in retaliation for similar acts of violence perpetrated against Jews by Arab terrorists.

The Irgun leadership included men who some modern Israelis regard as heroes; chief among them was *Menachem Begin*, the last leader of the Irgun prior to the establishment of the state of Israel in 1948. During his time as head of the Irgun, from 1943 to 1948, Begin ordered and participated in a number of acts of violence, the worst of which was the bombing of the King David Hotel on July 22, 1946. The King David Hotel served as headquarters for British government, military, and police officials. However, not all of the deaths were military or government officials. The bombing killed 91, including many

Continued

TIME CAPSULE: ZIONIST TERRORISM—CONT'D

civilian employees at the hotel. The Irgun claimed that they provided advance warning of the bombing, but this did little to appease the feelings of those who were outraged by the bombing. Menachem Begin ordered the bombing, and a bounty was placed on his head by the British authorities.[15]

In a prototypical example of a terrorist-turned-statesman, Begin, a Polish-born Jewish immigrant to Palestine, eventually became one of the most prominent statesmen in Israeli history. He served as Prime Minister from 1977 to 1983, the first Israeli Prime Minister from the traditionally hard-line Likud Party. Given his ultra-Zionist and Likud background, it is ironic that Begin, one of the most fervent Israeli nationalists in history, shared the 1978 Nobel Peace Prize with Egyptian President Anwar Sadat, his former archenemy, as a result of the Camp David Peace Treaty brokered by U.S. President Jimmy Carter. Even many years since his 1992 death, Begin's legacy is mixed among Israelis and non-Israelis alike.

HISTORY TODAY

In 1960, a film titled *Exodus* was released in theaters. The film, based on a novel by Leon Uris, contains fictional characters, but the movie was based on the real-life events that immediately led up to the creation of Israel in the post-World War II 1940s. The film features two brothers, both of whom favor the establishment of a Jewish state. One brother, Barak Ben-Canaan, favors diplomacy to achieve this goal; his brother, Akiva Ben-Canaan, is a leader of the Irgun. When asked to justify his violent tactics, Akiva Ben-Canaan states that practically all modern countries were established through violence. This is true of the United States. Can violence be justified using this fictional character's rationale? If so, what is to be said about terrorists killing in the name of establishing a homeland?

TERRORISM, THE COLD WAR, AND ARAB NATIONALISM

The *Cold War* that pitted Western capitalism against Soviet Communism played an important role in the picture of terrorism from the end of World War II until the dissolution of the Soviet Union in the early 1990s. After World War II, much of the world, including almost all of Europe, parts of Southeast Asia, the Korean Peninsula, parts of Africa and the Middle East, and some countries in the Western Hemisphere, was essentially divided into two camps, those who supported Western-style capitalism and democracy, and those who supported Soviet-style Communism or one of its variants.

While the United States and the Soviet Union never confronted each other in battle during the Cold War, many countries served as locations for proxy wars between the two superpowers. In the cases of Korea, Vietnam, and Afghanistan, American or Soviet forces were directly involved in the fighting. In other cases, the two superpowers competed against each other by supporting a side in the conflict most aligned with them ideologically or most willing to accept their influence and assistance, with Nicaragua serving as one example.

This war by proxy between the two superpowers was also played out in the Middle East. The United States, which had been the first country to recognize Israel as an independent nation (followed shortly by the Soviet Union), was a strong supporter of the Jewish state during the Cold War. Some Arab countries enjoyed relatively cordial relations with both superpowers and some were aligned with the United States. The Soviet Union, which had a long tradition of Jewish persecution, forged a loose alliance with several of the Arab countries, including Egypt, Iraq, and Syria. Some of the countries in the Eastern European Soviet bloc, especially Czechoslovakia (now the Czech Republic and Slovakia), also aided the Arabs. The Soviets also espoused sympathy for the Palestinians, the Arabs who had been displaced and in many cases exiled as a result of the establishment of Israel. Along with other Arab governments, the Soviets supplied the Palestinians with tools needed to stage terrorist attacks against Israel.

Religion was not at the heart of Arab-led terrorism during the Cold War; rather, it was Palestinian and *Arab nationalism* and unity, often referred to as *Pan-Arabism*. Israel was seen as an example of Western imperialism planted directly in the heart of the Arab world. The existence of a sovereign Jewish state also exacerbated the centuries-old rivalry between Jews and Arabs. Fighting against Israel was a fight against Zionism and a fight against Western imperialism. The Palestinian Arabs, thousands of whom were displaced as a result of the Jewish state, viewed the land of Israel as rightfully theirs. However, many world governments saw the existence of the nation of Israel as a haven against Jewish persecution, and many of the world's Jews and Christians saw the Jews as possessors of divine and historical claims to the land of Israel.

As much as many of the Arab states and the Palestinians detested Israel's existence, they eventually realized that the Jewish state was far superior to them in conventional warfare. With American and Western European backing, Israel quickly established itself as the top military power in the Middle East. A series of humiliating military defeats, starting in 1948 when Israel was attacked by armies of Syria, Iraq, Egypt, Lebanon, and Jordan, led the Arabs to this conclusion. In almost every instance of direct conventional warfare, Israel single-handedly defeated several Arab armies at once. The Israelis defeated the armies of Egypt, Jordan, and Syria in the Six Day War of 1967, and they defeated Egypt and Syria in the 1973 Yom Kippur War, even though Egypt was able to claim some success. No full-scale direct Arab military attack has occurred since.

In 1958, under Gamal Nasser's leadership, the nations of Egypt and Syria merged to form the United Arab Republic, but the partnership did not last; Syria withdrew in 1961, but Egypt referred to itself as the United Arab Republic until 1971. Pan-Arab nationalism began to fail in the 1970s in part because of the 1970 death of its founder, Egyptian President Gamal Nasser. Arab unity was not achievable for many reasons, tribal and regional differences among them, and because Arabs have never been one unified group.

Among the Arab leaders to recognize the failure of Pan-Arabism and to officially acknowledge the existence of a Jewish state was *Anwar Sadat*, President Nasser's successor. Sadat severed Egypt's relations with the Soviet Union, embraced the United States as a partner, and in 1977 made the radical step of making peace with Israel, personally visiting Israel, and opening up formal diplomatic relations with the Jewish state. While Sadat's gestures toward Israel earned him worldwide acclaim and a Nobel Peace Prize, it infuriated many radical Muslims, including some in his own country, such as the Muslim Brotherhood, which included a physician named *Ayman al-Zawahiri*, who would be a principal founder of another terrorist organization called *Egyptian Islamic Jihad*, and would later serve as second-in-command to Osama bin Laden and Al Qaeda.

THE PALESTINIANS

Meanwhile, the nationless Palestinians, because they lacked the infrastructure to mount an open military campaign against Israel, and because their leadership included a substantial number of corrupt hacks and cold-blooded brutes, used terrorism to attract attention to their cause. With aid from their fellow Arabs and the Soviet Union, the word *Palestinian* became synonymous with *terrorism*. Like most of their Arab brethren, most Palestinians are Muslims, but it was nationalism, not religion, that was the primary motive for acts of terrorism.

Even though many Arab leaders publicly voiced support for the Palestinian cause, this did not always translate into friendly relations between Arab governments and Palestinian leaders. Some of the bloodiest incidents in the Middle East during the Cold War were the result of rivalries between Palestinians and Arab leaders like King Hussein of Jordan and President Haffez Assad of Syria, both of whom were probably responsible for more Palestinian deaths than the Israelis, and both of whom were distrustful of Palestinian leaders who operated in their territory.

One of the major obstacles to peace in the Middle East is the question of the Palestinians, who claim rights to the land of Israel on the basis of historical and religious grounds. Displaced and disenfranchised by the establishment of the Jewish state, and often treated as second-class citizens by their fellow Arabs, Palestinians were effectively without a voice for the first decade of Israel's existence. The strongest and most prominent voice of Palestinian nationalism came in the person of *Yasser Arafat*.

Yasser (or Yasir) Arafat was born in 1929, probably in Cairo, Egypt. A civil engineer by training, Arafat joined the Muslim Brotherhood and was president of the Union of Palestinian Students as a young man. He served in President Nasser's Egyptian Army in the 1950s. Later, he journeyed to Kuwait where he established a business and founded Fatah, which would later become the military wing of the *Palestine Liberation Organization* (PLO), and which remains in force today. Although Arafat's name is associated with the PLO, Arafat was not its founder. The PLO was founded in 1964 under the sponsorship of the Arab League. Its first chair was Ahmad Shuqeiri, a Palestinian diplomat. Arafat assumed control of the PLO in 1969.[16] For the next 25 years, Arafat and the PLO would be seen as the face of Middle East terrorism. Hijackings and attacks against Israelis of all sorts were trademark PLO tactics.

The 1972 Olympics marked the arrival of Palestinian terrorism on the world stage. On September 5, 1972, eight Palestinian terrorists invaded the Olympic village in Munich, West Germany, and stormed the building housing the Israeli Olympic contingent. One Israeli athlete and one coach were killed in the raid. The terrorists demanded the release of 200 Palestinian prisoners in Israel. Nine other Israelis were taken to the airport as hostages. A botched rescue operation headed by the West Germans resulted in the merciless slaughter of all of the Israeli athletes, and the killing of a West German police officer and five of the terrorists.[17,18]

The *Munich Massacre* was planned to generate as much media attention as possible. The entire world watched the massacre unfold on television as media sources were already on hand in plentiful supply to cover the Olympics. In fact, the person who broke the news to Americans watching the event unfold on television was not a news journalist, but Jim McKay, an ABC sports journalist. The Munich Massacre brought the problem of Arab terrorism and the Palestinian cause into the living rooms of people throughout the world, not just the Middle East.

HISTORY TODAY

Security has been a seminal issue at the Olympic games ever since the 1972 Munich massacre. Eric Rudolph, a lone right-wing American terrorist, bombed an event at the 1996 Olympics in Atlanta. Is it possible that the day will ever come when such mass international gatherings cannot be held because of fear of terrorist attacks?

THE REVOLUTION IN IRAN

Although it is difficult to rank events that created modern terrorism in any specific order of importance, the *Iranian Revolution* in the late 1970s stands as one of the most important events, if not the most important event, in the history of twentieth-century terrorism. Iran was under the rule of *Shah Reza Pahlavi*, part of a monarchical dynasty that had ruled Iran for most of the twentieth century. Reza Pahlavi himself had ruled since his teen years. The Shah's regime grew increasingly out of touch with the Iranian populace. He was also unpopular because of human rights abuses, close ties to the West, and a feeling that his regime did not reflect true Islamic governing principles.

In 1953, while the young Shah was in the twelfth year of his rule, the United States assisted in the overthrow of Mohammad Mosaddeq, an ardent Iranian nationalist who opposed Western intervention in Iran. Mossaddeq's overthrow was another blow to Iranian-Western relations. Coupled with the perception that Western values were increasingly encroaching on Iranian and Muslim culture in general and corrupting Muslim women and the youth, many Iranians nursed a strong hatred of the West and the United States, in particular as the decades wore on.

One of the key figures of the twentieth century was *Ruhollah Khomeini*, an Iranian Shiite Muslim "Ayatollah" who was a dedicated foe of Iran's Shah and what Khomeini viewed as Western, and especially American, interference and corruption of Islamic culture. Khomeini and those who followed him were vocal advocates of government by his interpretation of pure Islamic law. Khomeini came to be synonymous with fundamentalist Islamic government. Unlike some other leading figures identified with Muslim militancy, Khomeini did not identify with communist-like beliefs and had almost as much disdain for the Soviet Union, Iran's longtime enemy, as he had for the United States, which he labeled "The Great Satan." Not being an Arab, and in fact looking askance at Arabs in general, Khomeini and his supporters did not identify with the gradually deteriorating Pan-Arabism that was so dominant in previous decades.

Khomeini and his fellow mullahs came to power in 1979 with the overthrow of an ailing, cancer-ridden Shah Palavi. When the former Shah went to the United States to seek medical treatment, a group of Iranian militants stormed the *American embassy in Tehran* on November 4, 1979, taking all of those in the embassy hostage. For 444 days, the United States and President Jimmy Carter were humiliated on the world stage, an embarrassment exacerbated by a failed rescue attempt on April 24, 1980. Most of the African-American and female hostages were released a few days after the takeover; one hostage was released a few months later for health reasons.

The remaining 52 hostages remained in captivity until January 20, 1981, the day Ronald Reagan was inaugurated as President. Despite condemnation from governments around the world, Iran relished its role as a new power broker in the Middle East and the Muslim world, and it was emboldened to expand its influence and hegemony in the Middle East, Europe, Africa, and Southern Asia.

The Islamic government of Iran, headed by Ruhollah Khomeini, became emboldened by the American failure to deal with the hostage crisis of 1979-1981. For centuries, Iran, which is predominantly Persian, had a contentious relationship with its western neighbor, Iraq, which is predominantly Arab. When Iran was attacked by *Saddam Hussein*'s Iraqi army in September 1980, many, including Saddam Hussein, believed that the new, unstable Islamic regime would not be able to hold the government together and that Iraqi influence and territory would expand as a result. However, the Iran-Iraq War, which lasted until 1988, did not produce a clear winner, but it did demonstrate to the world that the Iranian government could function while under attack from hostile forces, and the Islamic government not only continued to function but also became motivated by their successful resistance against their ancient Arab enemy.

> Saddam Hussein (1937-2006): President of Iraq from 1979 to 2003; part of the (purportedly) socialistic Baath party which was prominent among Arab governments in the twentieth century; waged wars against Iran in the 1980s, and against Kuwait in the 1990s—which resulted in the First Persian Gulf War and the expulsion of Iraq from Kuwait—and was dethroned in 2003 by an American-led coalition during the Second Gulf War; executed by hanging in December 2006.

During the 1970s and 1980s, Soviet influence experienced a decline in the Arab and Muslim worlds, in part because of its invasion of the Muslim nation of *Afghanistan*, which is discussed in the next section. While the Cold War was gradually winding down, and while Soviet influence on and support for their Arab allies were slowly evaporating, the popularity of fundamentalist Shiite Islamic extremism, the kind practiced in Iran, was spreading. Some secular Arab leaders like Saddam Hussein of Iraq and the PLO's Yasser Arafat, who in years past had seldom demonstrated any sense of devotion to Islam as part of their leadership philosophy, began wearing a religious façade in public, making it a point to be seen praying, attending mosques, and speaking with noted religious leaders, even though they were adherents of the Sunni branch of Islam, unlike most Iranians, who are Shia Muslims. Despite their ethnic and religious differences, Yasir Arafat and the PLO managed to forge friendly ties with Iran. Even though Saddam Hussein hated his non-Arab Iranian neighbors, he was beginning to see that fundamentalist Islam, not Arab socialism, was key to attaining influence in the Middle East and the Arab and Muslim worlds.

THE SOVIET INVASION OF AFGHANISTAN

On December 24, 1979, the U.S.S.R., or the Soviet Union, shocked the world by invading Afghanistan and installing a pro-Soviet government. Since its inception, and especially after World War II, the Soviet Union had aggressively sought to expand its influence throughout the world, especially in or near its bordering countries, but most of the world's governments assumed that the days of brazen Soviet expansionism by military means was a thing of the past.

The Soviet Union in and of itself was an artificial confederation of states dominated by Russia. The Soviet Republics shared few cultural commonalities, so many Soviet citizens, especially those in predominantly Muslim republics such as Kazakhstan, Uzbekistan, and Turkmenistan never felt a strong sense of allegiance to the Soviet Union. The Warsaw Pact, which bound the Soviet Union into a forced alliance with its satellite countries in Eastern Europe, was unpopular in most of those countries too, especially Czechoslovakia, Hungary, and Poland. Much of this Soviet aggression was the work of a series of World War II-era Communist leaders, who, by the early 1980s, were beginning to age and die, which was symptomatic of the Soviet empire itself.

The invasion of Afghanistan signaled the unraveling of the Soviet empire. Muslims from around the world, especially the Middle East and South Asia, and some of the member Soviet Republics, came to Afghanistan to assist in the *jihad* against the "infidel" Soviets. Afghan rebels and their non-Afghan Muslim allies received considerable assistance from other governments, including some of the Arab countries, and also from Pakistan and the United States. After years of fighting, with the Soviet empire and its economy crumbling, its population weary of war, and its Cold War leadership dying and being replaced by younger and more pragmatic leaders like Mikhail Gorbachev, the Soviets withdrew from Afghanistan in February of 1989.

Mikhail Gorbachev (1931-): The last head of state of the Union of Soviet Socialist Republics (Soviet Union) before its collapse in 1991; in marked contrast to his predecessors, he advocated more openness in Soviet society and politics; viewed with considerable admiration in many Western countries for his willingness to end the Cold War and the Soviet dominance of its neighboring countries.

The successful although bloody victory over a superpower at the hands of a rebel force was viewed by many Muslims as a miraculous victory for Islam over the infidels. Afghan rebel forces and their non-Afghan Muslim allies were emboldened by the withdrawal of Soviet forces from a Muslim country.

Unfortunately, much of the foreign assistance that was so helpful to the defeat of Soviet forces dried up after the Soviet withdrawal, creating a huge power vacuum in Afghanistan and leaving the country with virtually no centralized government. This vacuum opened the door for a bloody takeover of the Afghan government by a religious group called the *Taliban*, a group of ignorant, uneducated Islamist fanatics who knew little about governing, but who were determined to impose a strict, reactionary form of Islamic law on the population of Afghanistan. Many of those supported by the United States against the Soviets now turned their animosity toward their former benefactors, including the United States, other Western governments, and secular Muslim governments that enjoyed good relations with the West, including Saudi Arabia, Jordan, and Egypt.

THE SADAT ASSASSINATION

While Muslims were fighting the Soviets in Afghanistan, Egyptian President Anwar Sadat paid the ultimate price for making peace with Israel and increasing Egypt's ties with the United States. On October 6, 1981, Sadat was assassinated by soldiers in the Egyptian army (who were allied with the Muslim Brotherhood and Egyptian Islamic Jihad) while he sat in a reviewing stand. More than 300 defendants were tried for the Sadat assassination, including Ayman al-Zawahiri, the eventual second-in-command in Al Qaeda, and *Omar Abdul Rahman*, a blind Egyptian cleric who would later be involved in the *1993 World Trade Center bombing.*[19]

Although the Sadat assassination was viewed as a tragedy in the West and in the United States, many in the Arab and Muslim world celebrated his death. Sadat was viewed by most of his fellow Arab leaders as a traitor; in fact, only one Arab government sent an official representative to his funeral. Sadat's assassination also motivated Muslim extremists, who had just begun fighting the Soviets in Afghanistan and were about to increase their presence in Lebanon.

ISRAEL INVADES LEBANON

Since its creation, the nation of Israel has been surrounded by hostile neighbors. Even though the governments of Israel have enjoyed a relatively peaceful relationship with its southern and eastern neighbors, Egypt and Jordan, Israel still faces threats from many in those countries. Israel has long had an openly hostile relationship with its northeastern neighbor, Syria, and for decades Syria and Iran have been dominant forces in the government of Lebanon, Israel's neighbor to the north. From its inception, Israel has had to deal with threats from Lebanon, whether outright military confrontation, infiltration of terrorists from Lebanon into Israel, or having to contend with bombs and rockets launched into Israeli territory from Lebanon. In 1982, Israel invaded Lebanon in reaction to attacks from Lebanese territory. The objective was to neutralize hostile forces in Lebanon and to create a buffer zone sufficient to shield northern Israel from encroachments and rockets launched from Lebanon.

The Israelis succeeded in creating the buffer zone, occupying southern Lebanon for more than 20 years. However, the invasion of Lebanon brought an unintended consequence. Palestinian attacks from Lebanon had always enjoyed the approval of many Arab and Muslim countries, and this support only increased with the Israeli incursion into Lebanon. Iran, buttressed by its humiliation of the United States because of its takeover of the American embassy, increased its support to the Palestinians in southern Lebanon. With aid from Iran and Syria, *Hezbollah* (the Party of God) came into being and still lives on as an important player in Middle East politics and as a nemesis of Israel. Although some countries, including the United States, Canada, and Israel, classify Hezbollah as a terrorist organization, other countries, especially Arab and Muslim countries, view Hezbollah as a legitimate resistance organization. Hezbollah officially assumed a strong voice in Lebanese government during the first decade of the twenty-first century.

Hezbollah not only is a menace to Israel and its political opponents in Lebanon, but also was responsible for one of the deadliest attacks against Americans in the 1980s. President Ronald Reagan had ordered a contingent of Marines to be stationed in Beirut, Lebanon, as part of an international peacekeeping force. On October 23, 1983, a car bomb driven by a suicide bomber rammed into the Marine barracks in Beirut, Lebanon, killing 241 American service personnel. The Marine bombing was one of many incidents that occurred in Beirut during the 1980s that defined the city as one of the most unsafe places on earth. At that time, Hezbollah established a presence, which remains to this day, in Lebanon's Bekaa Valley.

HISTORY TODAY

Hezbollah is viewed as a terrorist organization by the United States government, but it has official representation in the Lebanese government. If an organization is officially represented in government, is "terrorist" the proper label or is another term more appropriate?

INTERNATIONAL COOPERATION IN THE SUPPRESSION OF TERRORISM AND PAN AM FLIGHT 103

On December 21, 1988, *Pan Am Flight 103* exploded in the sky above Lockerbie, Scotland. All the passengers and crew, totaling 276 persons, were killed, and the village of Lockerbie lost residents as airplane fragments crashed to the ground. At the time, it was known that Pan Am Flight 103 originated in Malta, and had made intermediate stops at Frankfurt and London before it took off for New York City. Forensic evidence indicated that the bomb particles were of Libyan origin, and further investigation led to the identification of *Ali Mohmed al-Megrahi* and Al Amin Khalifa Fhimah, and implicated them in the placement of the bomb.

After the imposition of economic sanctions against Libya, the government of Colonel Quaddafi agreed to deliver the two men to international authorities, provided that they would be tried in the Netherlands before Scottish judges. The trial lasted 9 months and was held at Camp Zeist, a former NATO base in the Netherlands. Understandably, after 12 years the evidence against the defendants was limited, and their identification as persons involved in the preparation of a bomb and its placement in Flight 103 was uncertain. Nevertheless, the court found al-Megrahi guilty and sentenced him to life imprisonment, which was mandatory under Scottish law. After imposing the sentence, the judges told Megrahi that they would recommend that he be eligible for parole in 20 years. This was the strongest penalty that was available to the court. He was released in 2010, supposedly on compassionate grounds: Megrahi was reportedly stricken with cancer. However, there is strong speculation that the Scottish government and British Petroleum struck a deal with the Libyan government to secure his release. On his return to Libya, Megrahi was greeted as a hero by the Libyan government and by thousands of Libyans who greeted him as his plane landed.

HISTORY TODAY

Ali Mohmed al-Megrahi was released from a Scottish prison, supposedly on "compassionate" grounds, that is, cancer. Should convicted murderers or terrorists be released from prison for any reason?

The second defendant was acquitted, the only evidence against him being diary entries indicating a meeting with Megrahi and his acquisition of suitcase luggage tags. Unlike the record on Megrahi, there was no connection established between Fhimah and the Libyan intelligence service. Two prosecution witnesses, a Libyan secret service informant and a Swiss electronics firm owner, were considered to have given unreliable and untruthful testimony that the judges discounted. On the other hand, Megrahi had dealt with the Swiss electronics firm Mebo, and it was a Mebo timer that triggered the Lockerbie bomb. Within the suitcase that held the bomb, investigators found clothing very likely purchased by Megrahi at a clothing store in Malta.

TIME CAPSULE: THE CONTINUING ROLE OF INTERPOL

Among the international organizations involved in global law enforcement, few are as active as the International Criminal Police Organizations, known since 1956 as Interpol. Established in 1923 as a private organization of senior police officers in Europe, the International Criminal Police Commission served as an informal place for the exchange of information concerning criminals who conducted their activities across national borders. With the fall of the Austrian Republic into Nazi control in 1938, the commission ceased to function at the international level and many of its records were apparently destroyed. At the end of World War II, the commission's headquarters was established at Paris, and with the aid of a French government loan, Interpol moved into a new building at Saint-Cloud in 1967.

Shortly after Interpol was situated in its new headquarters, the outbreak of the Cold War resulted in the withdrawal of Eastern Bloc nations from membership. The United States,

Continued

TIME CAPSULE: THE CONTINUING ROLE OF INTERPOL—CONT'D

represented by the Federal Bureau of Investigation, withdrew from membership after 1950. This was in protest of Interpol's identification of individuals who hijacked a Czechoslovakian airliner for a flight to freedom in 1949. The United States resumed membership in 1958, with the Treasury Department and its Secret Service being the main participants in Interpol activities.

Throughout its history, Interpol has been reluctant to serve as a channel for distributing information concerning "political" crimes. Most controversial has been its refusal to assist in the location of Nazi war criminals, many of whom had been convicted in absentia at Nuremberg. On the other hand, Interpol's refusal to assist communist Cuba in searching for President Fulgencio Batista's regime leaders has been widely acclaimed by Western nations and the United States. In 1988, Interpol reviewed its policy concerning Nazi war criminals and has since been active in assisting nations seeking to apprehend them. Interpol had also refrained from participating in the investigation of terrorism, deeming terrorist activities "political crimes." However, the 1984 Luxembourg General Assembly of Interpol members agreed to assist in investigating terrorist acts, but provided that the decision to participate would be made on a case-by-case basis.

Unfortunately, the degree of national cooperation with Interpol, as well as compliance with Interpol requests for information, is shaped by the member nations' divergent concepts of criminal law enforcement and by their assessment of the appropriate scope of police activity. In the past two decades, growing international law enforcement needs have increased the value of police cooperation across departmental and national boundaries. That is particularly the case in regard to drug trafficking, as many nations (including the United States) have stationed police officials in

other nations, hoping to halt the illegal trade in drugs. Interpol has exercised a growing role in the exchange of police intelligence, in the capture of most-wanted criminals, and in the location of missing persons. Cross-national efforts to control drug trafficking, solve terrorism cases, and enforce laws against smuggling have also increased the frequency of using the extensive files maintained by Interpol. The organization has thus expanded from a European institution to a police intelligence activity that has global recognition and impact.

Policing international criminal activities has a long way to go before it will proceed without disagreement and tension. Professor Malcolm Anderson points out that without a harmonization of criminal law procedures—such as the United States-British common rules concerning drug trafficking and policing this threat—there is a limited amount of success that can be achieved through international organizations such as Interpol. There is also strong American and British skepticism concerning the centralized police systems of Europe, which place inordinate emphasis on the assembly of large dossiers of information on all citizens, not only those who have criminal records.

The reluctance of Interpol to deal with terrorism prior to 1984 has resulted in the rise of other institutions for the exchange of international police information. Under the category of European Political Cooperation activity, sponsored by the European Union, three so-called Trevi groups have emerged as focal points for inter-European cooperation in law enforcement. Trevi 1 was organized in 1975 to establish a secure communications system that would relay information concerning terrorists and their activities. Trevi 2, established later, is dedicated to the exchange of information on police methods and systems, and Trevi 3 deals with approaches to serious crime other than terrorism.

The conclusion of the Camp Zeist trial provides insight into the utility of criminal justice systems as instruments to combat terrorism. Newspaper comments of the day suggested that formal rules of evidence and procedure make it difficult to secure justice against accused terrorists. Others argued that the measured use of military force is a more appropriate and more effective response to discourage nations that adopt terrorism as a national policy.

Undoubtedly, the sparsity of the evidence and documentation, coupled with Libya's initial refusal to surrender those accused of this crime, was partially responsible for the acquittal. On the other hand, one of the accused was tried, found guilty, and sentenced to life imprisonment with a possibility of parole after 20 years.

AL QAEDA AND OSAMA BIN LADEN

One of the Arab foreigners who came to Afghanistan to fight the Soviets was *Osama bin Laden*. Born in 1957 in Saudi Arabia to a family of Yemeni immigrants, bin Laden was raised amid a life of privilege.[20] His father, the father of 57 children (Osama bin Laden was his seventeenth), was a millionaire construction magnate in Saudi Arabia. Osama bin Laden graduated from King Abdul Aziz University in 1979 with a degree in civil engineering and, like many other young Muslims from around the world, went to Afghanistan to join the fight against the Soviets.[21]

At least one account of the Soviet-Afghan conflicts states that bin Laden's role in the conflict has been greatly exaggerated by bin Laden and his minions. George Crile states, "It is ironic that a man who had almost nothing to do with the victory over the Red Army, Osama bin Laden would come to personify the power of the jihad."[22] Whether deserved or not, bin Laden emerged from the war a hero in the eyes of many Muslims, and he used this reputation to build his organization and his power base far beyond Afghanistan. After the Soviets withdrew from Afghanistan, bin Laden worked toward solidifying his control over the remnant Muslim factions that had worked together in Afghanistan. He had his chief partner, an Egyptian named Abdallah Azzam, assassinated on November 24, 1989, leaving him in complete control of his emerging network of Muslim fighters, which by this time had acquired a name, *Al Qaeda*, or *the base*.[23]

On August 2, 1990, Iraq invaded Kuwait, its tiny oil-rich neighbor to the south. Iraqi President Saddam Hussein announced that Iraq was annexing Kuwait, claiming that Iraqis had a legitimate claim to the tiny emirate, and that Kuwait was an illegitimate nation created to serve Western oil interests. Kuwait and the Western countries, including the United States, had enjoyed a mutually beneficial relationship for many years. Almost immediately, U.S. President George H. W. Bush announced, along with the leaders of many other countries, that the Iraqi occupation of Kuwait would not be tolerated. World leaders became even more nervous when it was feared that Iraqi forces would invade Saudi Arabia. Soon after it became apparent that Iraq would not withdraw from Kuwait, the United States and other countries, including Great Britain, began to amass forces to prepare to extract Iraqi forces from Kuwait, while President Bush recruited other countries into its coalition. Most notable was the fact that Egypt and Syria, two Arab countries, joined the coalition against Saddam Hussein.

By now back in his native Saudi Arabia, and regarded by many there as a war hero, bin Laden and his followers saw that Saudi Arabia, or as he called it, the "Land of the Two Holy Sanctuaries" (Mecca and Medina), was under siege by Iraq. He let it be known to the Saudi monarchy that he and his forces were ready and able to go to war against Saddam Hussein's forces.[24] Bin Laden viewed Saddam Hussein's government as non-Islamic and as too secular, a by-product of Gamal Nasser's Arab Socialism. In fact, he often referred to Iraq and Syria as "communist" countries.

Bin Laden also saw the Iraqi invasion as an opportunity to expand his own influence in the Muslim world. In bin Laden's view, Muslim rebels, under divine inspiration and guidance, had succeeded in ridding Afghanistan of the Soviets; therefore, they would be able to extract the Iraqis from Kuwait and protect the "Land of the Two Holy Sanctuaries" from Hussein's aggression. According to bin Laden, ridding the Arab world of Saddam Hussein's menace was a task best left to fellow Arabs.

Bin Laden was incensed when the Saudi monarchy turned to Western governments to help them with their battle against Iraq. He was outraged even further when the Saudi government allowed Western military forces to establish operations in Saudi Arabia from which the invasions of Kuwait and Iraq would be launched. In bin Laden's view, Saudi Arabia was sacred ground reserved for Muslims only. The Saudi monarchy, which was charged with guarding and protecting Islam's holiest cities, committed the ultimate act of apostasy by allowing infidel Western forces on its soil. This was compounded when Saudi Arabia allowed foreign forces to remain there after the brief war's end.

THE 1993 WORLD TRADE CENTER BOMBING

The devastation of September 11, 2001, was so enormous that it has eclipsed the first attack on New York City's World Trade Center. On February 26, 1993, terrorists detonated a car bomb beneath the North Tower of the World Trade Center. The objective was to create enough of an impact to cause both towers to fall, which would have resulted in thousands of casualties. The terrorists did not succeed in bringing down the towers, but six people were killed and more than 1,000 were injured.

Several men were eventually convicted of the World Trade Center bombing, including *Ramzi Yousef*, the nephew of *Khaled Sheikh Mohammad*, who would also be the chief architect of the September 11, 2001, attacks. Also convicted was Omar Abdul Rahman, who had been tried and eventually released in the assassination of Egyptian President Anwar Sadat several years earlier. Despite the successful prosecution and prison sentences imposed on many of the perpetrators of the World Trade Center bombing, the first attack was merely a trial run for the much more devastating attacks that followed 8 years later.[25]

FEATURED OUTLAW: TIMOTHY MCVEIGH

On April 19, 1995, a truck bomb exploded at the Murrah Federal Building in Oklahoma City. The final death toll was 168 and thousands were injured. Some of the dead were preschool children who had been dropped by their parents at the building's day care center. Suspicions immediately abounded that the bombing had all the earmarks of Middle Eastern terrorism. Many Americans were surprised when, a few days later, a decorated U.S. Army Persian Gulf War veteran was linked to the bombing. Timothy McVeigh was stopped by an Oklahoma State Trooper for driving without a license plate; he was also found to have an illegal weapon. He was in jail for these offenses when evidence was discovered that linked him to the bombing.

McVeigh and a co-defendant, Terry Nichols, were charged with the bombing. Both had loose affiliations with right-wing anti-government militia groups in the Midwest, but the leaders would claim no formal affiliation with McVeigh or Nichols. McVeigh was angered about an event that occurred in Texas 1 year earlier. In February of 1994, Alcohol, Tobacco, and Firearms agents raided the Waco compound of a religious cult called the *Branch Davidians*, who were maintaining a cache of illegal weapons; they were suspected of other crimes as well. On April 19, when federal agents attempted another raid, the compound was burned to the ground, killing all those inside. The Waco incident, and the federal government's involvement in it, proved to be a lightning rod for right-wing opponents of the federal government. Exactly 1 year after the Waco raid, the Oklahoma City bombing was carried out in revenge.

McVeigh was also influenced by an underground novel called *The Turner Diaries*. Written under the pseudonym Andrew Macdonald, *The Turner Diaries* was the work of William Luther Pierce III, who had formal ties to several white supremacists and right-wing groups throughout the Midwest, including the American Nazi Party. Pierce, who had earned a Ph.D. from the University of Colorado, was a former physics professor at Oregon State University. In his novel, which had been circulating in non-legal circles for almost 20 years, Pierce's protagonist, Turner, was involved in the blowing up of FBI headquarters, the killing of non-whites and Jews, and the persecution of white women who had had sex with non-whites.

McVeigh and Nichols were convicted of the bombing. McVeigh was sentenced to death and executed on June 11, 2001. Nichols was convicted and sentenced to life imprisonment. Michael Fortier, a former Army buddy of McVeigh's who had prior knowledge of the plot, testified against the pair and received a 20-year prison sentence.

The Oklahoma City bombing reminded Americans that terrorism was not just a radical Muslim phenomenon. Right-wing terrorism was neither created nor did it die with Oklahoma City, but no right-wing terrorism of this scale had ever been perpetrated. In fact, until 2001, the Oklahoma City bombing was the deadliest terrorist attack in U.S. history on American soil.

Sources: White, J. R. (2006). *Terrorism and homeland security* (5th ed). Belmont, CA: Thomson Wadsworth; Macdonald, A. (1996). *The Turner diaries* (2nd ed). Fort Lee, NJ: Barricade Books, original publication date 1994; Wilson Web Biographies, http://vnweb.hwwilsonweb.com.jproxy.lib.ecu.edu, accessed March 5, 2008.

FIGURE 14.1 Timothy McVeigh is escorted by law enforcement officials from the Noble County Courthouse in Perry, Oklahoma, April 21, 1995. The April 19 bombing of the Alfred P. Murrah Federal Building claimed the lives of 168 people. McVeigh was convicted Monday, June 2, 1997, of blowing up the Oklahoma Federal Building. *AP Photo/David Longstreath.*

THE 1996 KHOBAR TOWERS BOMBING

By 1994, bin Laden's activities brought him under the watchful eye of the Saudi government, and even many members of his family had disassociated themselves from him. Bin Laden was expelled from Saudi Arabia in 1994 for subversion. He went to Sudan, where he organized terrorist training camps. Bin Laden was expelled from Sudan in 1996 and went to Afghanistan, where his wealth and popularity enabled him to stay as the "guest" of the ruling Taliban.[26] Al Qaeda was not the only entity that opposed the American presence in Saudi Arabia. An eight-story building in *Khobar*, Saudi Arabia, which housed foreign (including American) service personnel and their families, was the target of a truck bomb on June 25, 1996. Nineteen American service personnel were killed, as was one Saudi. Hundreds of soldiers of different nationalities were injured.

More than a dozen men were indicted for the bombings, but the exact identity of those behind the Khobar bombing is still unclear. Suspicion has centered on Hezbollah, who receives assistance from Syria and Iran, on high-level Iranian government officials, and on Al Qaeda.[27] Given the animosity between the Shia Muslim government of Iran and the Sunni Muslim-dominated Al Qaeda, it is unlikely that there was a partnership between the two.

AL QAEDA ACCELERATES: THE 1998 EMBASSY BOMBINGS AND THE *USS COLE*

In February 1998, bin Laden and Ayman al Zawahiri, by now bin Laden's second-in-command, arranged for a fax to be sent from Afghanistan to an Arabic newspaper in London. In the fax, they claimed that the United States had declared war against God and his messenger (the prophet Mohammed). Bin Laden stated that it was the duty of all Muslims to kill any American anywhere on earth. Bin Laden declared war on the United States, and that any and all Americans were fair targets because by paying taxes they supported the actions of the U.S. government. In May 1998, in an interview from Afghanistan with ABC Television's John Miller, bin Laden stated, "We do not have to differentiate between military or civilian. As far as we are concerned, they are all targets."

Bin Laden proved true to his word less than 3 months after his interview was broadcast. On August 7, 1998, car bombs exploded at the United States Embassies in *Nairobi, Kenya* and *Dar Es Salaam, Tanzania*. The attacks were practically simultaneous. The Nairobi bombing claimed 212 lives, most of them Kenyans, and the Tanzania bombing claimed 11 lives.

More than a dozen members of Al Qaeda were indicted for the bombings, including Osama bin Laden and Ayman Al Zawahiri. Some have been killed; some were sentenced to life in prison; some were held in prisons outside the United States; and others, including Zawahiri, are still at large as of this writing.

Al Qaeda's attacks against the United States were growing bolder and more deadly. In response to the East African bombings, President *Bill Clinton* authorized Operation Infinite Reach, in which cruise missile attacks were launched in Sudan and Afghanistan. The Sudan raid demolished a pharmaceutical plant, but little real damage was done. In fact, many have argued that the token response by the United States military only demonstrated that America was a paper tiger, lacking the will or capability of crippling Al Qaeda. Bin Laden's fame grew; he even earned praise from the Iraqi government that he despised, and from the ruling Taliban in Afghanistan, who had welcomed bin Laden as their "guest." Taliban hospitality was motivated in large measure by Al Qaeda money.

Despite the sometimes prickly relations between the Taliban and Al Qaeda, the two entities enjoyed a symbiotic relationship. Al Qaeda needed a safe haven for its operations and the Taliban needed Al Qaeda's money, and neither entity could rid itself of the other.

> Bill Clinton (1946-): Forty-second President of the United States (1993-2001), and former Governor of Arkansas (1979-1981 and 1983-1992).

Al Qaeda was not finished. On October 12, 2000, the *USS Cole* was docked in the port of Aden, Yemen. Yemen has long been a hotbed of anti-Americanism, radical Islam, and virtually lawless tribal bands. On October 12, suicide bombers aboard a small boat rammed the *Cole*. The attack killed 17 American sailors and wounded 39 others. The alleged mastermind of the *Cole* bombing was killed on November 4, 2002, by a predator drone operated by the CIA.

HISTORY TODAY

A very difficult question is whether the Presidents who preceded George W. Bush did enough to deal with Islamist terror organizations between the 1970s and 2001. Did President Jimmy Carter's administration deal firmly enough with Iran during the Iran hostage crisis? Did President Ronald Reagan's administration deal firmly enough with Iran and Libya after the attacks linked to those governments? Did President Reagan and President George H. W. Bush's administration allow Afghanistan to become a breeding ground for terrorism? Did President Clinton respond strongly enough during the 1990s to Al Qaeda attacks against New York City and American interests abroad? Or are such accusations simply the benefit of "20/20 hindsight"?

SEPTEMBER 11, 2001

On the morning of September 11, 2001, there was nothing to suggest that the day would be eventful. Before the morning was over, this would change drastically. At 8:46 a.m., a plane crashed into the North Tower of New York's World

FIGURE 14.2 New York Police tell people to move as they make photos of the wreckage of the World Trade Center, Wednesday, September 19, 2001, in New York. The public is now able to get a view of the destruction from some vantage points *AP Photo/ Kathy Willens.*

Trade Center, killing everyone aboard and many people in the North Tower instantly. At first, many assumed that the crash was simply the result of pilot error, and that the plane was probably a small private jet. However, questions arose about the likelihood of such an error, given that the weather on September 11, 2001, in New York City was clear and sunny, a typical late summer day.

Unbeknown to all but a few, the plane that crashed into the North Tower was *American Airlines Flight 11*, with 92 passengers and crew aboard. The flight had taken off from Boston and was bound for Los Angeles. It had broken off contact with the FAA a few minutes after takeoff. Even though the FAA knew that American Airlines 11 was inexplicably headed toward New York City, and even though they suspected that a hijacking was in progress, they were unsure if the plane that had crashed into the North Tower was indeed Flight 11. Within minutes, the worldwide media had arrived to cover the crash, still unsure as to its nature.

Any doubt as to the cause of the crash was put to rest when at 9:03 a.m., a second plane crashed into the South Tower of the World Trade Center, in full view of a worldwide television audience. The second plane was *United Airlines 175* with 65 crew and passengers aboard. It too was a Boeing 767 jet traveling from Boston to Los Angeles.[28]

The situation worsened as the day wore on. At 9:37 a.m., *American Airlines Flight 77* (a Boeing 757), traveling from Dulles Airport in Washington, D.C., to Los Angeles, and carrying 62 passengers and crew, crashed into the Pentagon near Washington, D.C. Like the two Boston-based flights, it had been selected by the hijackers in part because cross-country flights carry more fuel than short flights, thus maximizing the damage inflicted by a crash.

At 10:02 a.m. a Boeing 757, *United Airlines Flight 93*, originating in Newark, New Jersey, and bound for San Francisco and Tokyo, crashed into a field near Shanksville, Pennsylvania. The plane carried 44 passengers and crew. Hearing of the World Trade Center crashes through phone calls to friends and relatives on the ground, United 93 passengers had attacked the hijackers and stormed the cockpit, causing the plane to crash. It was determined later that United 93 was probably headed for either the White House or the United States Capitol. United 93 failed to reach its intended target because it had taken off 25 minutes late, which threw off the hijackers' timing, allowing time for passengers on board to get word from the ground about what had happened in New York City and at the Pentagon.[29]

Ben Sliney was assuming his first day as Director of FAA Operations on September 11. After the World Trade Center attacks, he ordered all commercial air traffic halted, and he ordered the grounding of all planes already in the air. The military was alerted and presidential authorization was given to shoot down any plane that would not comply with the order to land or that was thought to be hijacked.[30] Fortunately, this order did not have to be carried out.

To many Americans, life in the United States seemed surreal. Major League Baseball ordered all games postponed, in large measure because teams could not travel, but also because there was a fear of terrorist activity in large gatherings. News outlets covered the incident nonstop for days. Commercial air traffic was completely suspended for three days. Not since World War II had Americans experienced such an emotional and psychological jolt, and no event as traumatic and deadly had occurred on the soil of the American mainland since the Civil War. Even those who compared 9/11 with the Pearl Harbor attack noted that as horrible as the Pearl Harbor attacks were, at least the Japanese had targeted a military installation, rather than thousands of unsuspecting civilians of all ages.

FIGURE 14.3 President Bush's Chief of Staff Andy Card whispers into the ear of the President to give him word of the plane crashes into the World Trade Center, during a visit to the Emma E. Booker Elementary School in Sarasota, FL, Tuesday, September 11, 2001. *AP Photo/Doug Mills.*

At the time of the World Trade Center attacks, President *George W. Bush* was in Sarasota, Florida, speaking to a group of schoolchildren. When he was notified of the first crash, Bush was told that it may have been an accident. When he was notified of the second crash by Chief of Staff Andrew Card, Bush wore the same look of shock and chagrin as many Americans; he knew that America was at war. After a day of being flown to several different airbases because it was believed that the White House might come under attack, Bush returned to the White House that evening, where he delivered a televised address, in which, referring to the Taliban, he stated that the United States would make no distinction between terrorist entities and the governments that supported them.

Nineteen hijackers carried out the 9/11 crashes. Fifteen were Saudi Arabian nationals and all were Middle Eastern or North African Islamists. Attention turned immediately to Osama bin Laden, Ayman al-Zawahiri, and Al Qaeda. The attacks of September 11 claimed over 2,700 lives.[31] It thrust the United States into a shadow war against an enemy without official ties to a sovereign government, and it established the course of American foreign and defense policy for years to come. The attacks also had a profound effect on domestic issues in the United States, many of which are criminal justice-related.

The attacks of September 11 had been in the planning phases for at least 5 years. The hijackers spent several years simply traveling by airplane from place to place, acquainting themselves with the layout of various planes, the habits and nuances of flight crews, and the security systems at various airports. The hijackers each had his own role to play and had received extensive training in the role he was scheduled to play in the attacks. Some acted as muscle men, whose primary job was to take over the plane and immediately kill or subdue enough passengers and crew to cow the other passengers into submission. The primary weapons were box cutters, which the hijackers carried aboard the plane legally. One hijacker would attach a fake bomb to his chest, thus deterring the passengers from fighting back. The hijackers led the passengers to believe that the plane was merely headed to an airport. Thinking that the hijackers would release them pending some sort of ransom demand, the passengers aboard the New York City and Pentagon flights did not know that they were part of a suicide mission. Every plane had at least one hijacker designated to pilot it once the crew was removed or killed. These hijackers had received training at flight schools in the United States, amid a degree of curiosity from some in the flight schools when they learned that some of these individuals wanted to learn how to pilot a plane but not how to land it.

Although many terrorist experts had predicted that some sort of terrorist attack against American interests was in the planning stages, including the possibility of using commercial airliners as weapons, and Osama bin Laden had unabashedly stated in 1998 that he had declared war on the United States, the attacks of September 11, 2001, still caught America by surprise. Terrorism was not new to Americans, but mass murder on such a brazen and massive scale perpetrated on American soil by foreign interests shocked Americans to the greatest extent since the bombing of Pearl Harbor.

Shortly after the September 11 attacks, President George W. Bush's administration requested that the ruling Taliban in Afghanistan either expel Osama bin Laden and his top lieutenants or turn them over to American authorities. There was little optimism about this request and, as expected, the Taliban failed to comply. In October 2001, the United States and other allied nations invaded Afghanistan and deposed the Taliban, but its main leader, Mullah Mohammad Omar, eluded the allies' grasp, as did Osama bin Laden and Ayman al-Zawahiri. All three were believed to have taken refuge, although probably not together, in Pakistan or the borderless tribal regions between Afghanistan and Pakistan. Prior to the 9/11 attacks only three countries had formal diplomatic ties with Afghanistan, which was effectively a nation without a functioning government. Those three countries—Saudi Arabia, Pakistan, and the United Arab Emirates—severed relations with Afghanistan after 9/11.

TIME CAPSULE: WHY DO THEY HATE US?

"Why do they hate us?" was one of the most frequently repeated questions in the aftermath of September 11, 2001. There is no simple answer. Thomas Friedman of the *New York Times* states that many pockets of the Muslim world, especially the Arab world, feel humiliated by the Western world, left behind in technological advances, democratic advances, and quality of life in general.[32] Many Arabs and Muslims see the existence of the nation of Israel as a symbol of that humiliation. In addition to the historic enmity that has existed between Jews and Muslims, many Islamic extremists and even some moderate Muslims blame Western Europe and the United States for the existence of Israel. Some believe that it is Western guilt over the Holocaust and over the persecution that Jews suffered in Europe for centuries that resulted in the establishment of Israel. In other words, today's Palestinians are paying the price for Western guilt over treatment of the world's Jews. In addition, the perception is that most Israelis enjoy a democratic government and live lives of comfort, at least in relation to the vast majority of Arabs and Muslims who live in abject poverty under the oppressive thumb of dictatorial governments supported by Western oil money, a situation that began to change as a result of the 2011 uprisings in Egypt and Tunisia.

Another reason offered for the enmity between the Muslim world and the West is religious. Some fundamentalist Islamists believe that modern culture is simply not compatible with Islamic teachings, thus the Taliban's insistence on the banning of televisions, radios, mirrors, and anything that is not specifically endorsed by the Qur'an. Shmuel Bar refers to this as lacking the tools of anachronization, the inability to distinguish what was right in a bygone time versus what is right or wrong in modern times, with the only solution being to try to make life as much like it was in the time of Mohammad as possible.[33]

There are a few in the Muslim world, especially among the Shia, who are awaiting or trying to facilitate the appearance of the "hidden Imam," which is akin to Christian apocalyptics who are awaiting the return of Jesus Christ to earth. This hidden Imam will bring Allah's kingdom to earth and vanquish the world of Allah's enemies. This belief, coupled with Qur'anic commands to wage war against the enemies of Allah who refuse to convert to Islam, provides the theological justification for hatred of non-Muslims, although many Muslims view such an interpretation as a perversion of the Qur'an. Whatever the motive, non-Muslims and moderate Muslims would be wise to remember that the most fanatical Islamists see themselves as operating on "God's timetable." The global jihad, or holy war, will last as long as the world is not completely surrendered to the will of Allah, a period that will last far beyond the life of anyone now living on earth. If the jihad must last 1,000 years, so be it.

THE PRESENT AND THE FUTURE: HOMELAND SECURITY

On May 1, 2011 (May 2 local time in Pakistan), U.S. President Barack Obama announced on television that the U.S. military had killed Osama bin Laden in a raid on his compound in Abbottabad, Pakistan. The raid was led by a team of U.S. Navy Seals. Bin Laden had been living in a walled multi-story compound in Abbottabad, a city located near the Pakistani capital of Islamabad. Abbottabad houses a Pakistani military academy, located approximately one mile from bin Laden's safe haven. Fearing that bin Laden might be given advance warning, Pakistani officials were not given advance warning of the raid, and its brazen success deeply embarrassed the Pakistani government and its intelligence service, the ISI, which had been duplicitous in its dealings with Al Qaeda and the United States. After observing proper Islamic burial rituals, bin Laden was buried at sea, so there would be no burial site to serve as a shrine to his minions.

The death of Osama bin Laden notwithstanding, what implications does terrorism have for criminal justice today and in the future? Prior to September 11, 2001, most terrorist attacks in the United States were investigated and prosecuted much like any other crime. If American interests in other countries were attacked, they were sometimes dealt with militarily, sometimes through the civilian criminal justice system, and sometimes with a combination of military and civilian means.

In his nationally televised address to a joint session of Congress on September 20, 2001, President George W. Bush introduced a term that was new to many Americans, but has become a household term since that night. The term was *homeland security*. So many Americans were swept up in both the fear and patriotic euphoria generated by 9/11 that they probably could not grasp the future significance of this portion of President Bush's speech:

> Today, dozens of federal departments and agencies, as well as state and local governments, have responsibilities affecting homeland security. These efforts must be coordinated at the highest level. So tonight, I announce the creation of a Cabinet-level position reporting directly to me, the Office of Homeland Security. And tonight, I also announce a distinguished American to lead this effort, to strengthen American security: a military veteran, an effective governor, a true patriot, a trusted friend, Pennsylvania's *Tom Ridge*. He will lead, oversee and coordinate a comprehensive national strategy to safeguard our country against terrorism and respond to any attacks that may come.[34]

Tom Ridge became the first Director of the Office of Homeland Security in October 2001. Following Congressional approval, the Office of Homeland Security was granted cabinet-level status, and on January 24, 2003, Ridge became the first Secretary of the Department of Homeland Security (DHS). Tom Ridge stepped down as DHS Secretary in February 2005 and was succeeded by Michael Chertoff, a former federal appellate court judge and prosecutor. On his election to the Presidency in 2008, President Barack Obama appointed Janet Napolitano as DHS Secretary.

The attacks of September 11, 2001, altered the structure of the federal government; they affected state and local governments as well. Numerous state and local agencies began competing for DHS funds and lined up behind DHS directives to secure their localities against the threat of terrorism. In law enforcement circles, police agencies began implementing training for their officers, both in counterterrorism, recognition of terrorism indicators, and first responder training. Perhaps most significantly for the criminal justice system, the issue of information sharing was addressed. It turned out that numerous

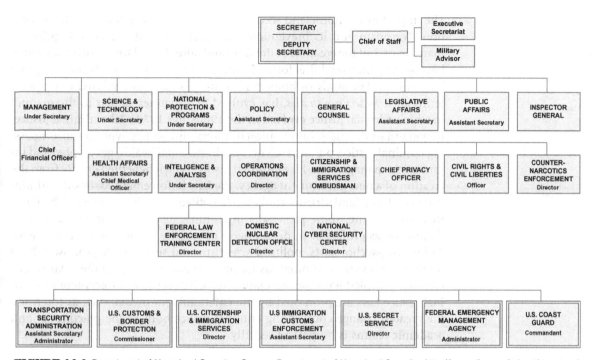

FIGURE 14.4 Department of Homeland Security. *Source:* Department of Homeland Security. http://www.dhs.gov/xabout/structure/editorial_0644.shtm. Accessed September 5, 2010.

agencies had assembled information on some of the 9/11 hijackers and some of them were on terrorist watch lists both in the United States and other countries, but no mechanism existed so that these agencies could pool their information, and allow some centralized information specialists to "connect the dots" and foresee the plot. At least three of the hijackers had been stopped for traffic offenses not long before the 9/11 attacks. One was stopped twice in Florida in July; another was stopped in Virginia in August for speeding; a third was stopped in Maryland on September 9 for speeding.[35] Had the Maryland police officer had access to the information that the federal government had on this individual, namely that he was on terrorist watch lists in several countries, he might have been able to at least detain one of the hijackers, which might in turn have thwarted the entire operation.

DHS was assigned the monumental task of assembling information from the vast number of federal, state, and local agencies that may have information related to terrorism. *Fusion centers*, which operate throughout the country, are being used as one such means for assembling information. Information specialists have become front-line soldiers in the United States anti-terrorism fight just as much as soldiers, sailors, and law enforcement officers.

The impact of the homeland security focus has also been felt in higher education. Terrorism and its prevention have been areas of academic inquiry for many years, but the creation of the DHS and other homeland security initiatives have greatly increased this focus. In fact, an entirely new academic discipline has evolved. The study of homeland security, sometimes referred to by other terms such as *security studies*, has evolved in a manner similar to the manner in which criminal justice evolved in the 1960s and 1970s. Like criminal justice, homeland security is a combination of several disciplines, typically encompassing criminal justice, political science, environmental health, geography, and information management. Like criminal justice, which benefited greatly from the creation of a new government agency, the Law Enforcement Assistance Administration, homeland security study has benefited from the creation of the DHS. In years to come, some professors in criminal justice departments may find themselves as professors in departments of security studies, much as many sociologists, psychologists, political scientists, and social work professors have found themselves in criminal justice departments rather than their native disciplines. Coupled with the fascination for whatever law enforcement or criminal justice fads are promoted by the entertainment media, such as forensics, the greatest change confronting criminal justice both in the practitioner and academic realms is homeland security.

Discussion Questions

1. What are the historical events and forces that led to the terrorist attacks of September 11, 2001?
2. What are the implications of labeling efforts to combat terrorism a "war" on terrorism? When can Americans be assured that the end of the "war" is in sight?
3. To what degree is the current war on terrorism a criminal justice effort versus a military effort?
4. The Department of Homeland Security has been assigned duties in addition to preventing terrorism, such as assisting in border security and with natural disasters. Should these functions be a part of Homeland Security's mission?

ENDNOTES

[1]Medhurst, P. (2002). *Global terrorism*. New York: United Nations Institute for Training and Research.

[2]Friedman, T. L. (2003). *Longitudes and attitudes: The world in the age of terrorism*. New York: Anchor Books.

[3]Buffalo History Works Web site, http://www.buffalohistoryworks.com, retrieved March 2, 2008; Young, D., & Cooper, J. M., Jr. (2000). William McKinley. In M. Beschloss (Ed.), *American heritage illustrated history of the presidents*. New York: Crown Publishers, pp. 304-313.

[4]Young, D., & Cooper, J. M., Jr. (2000). William McKinley. In M. Beschloss (Ed.), *American heritage illustrated history of the presidents*. New York: Crown Publishers, pp. 305-314.

[5]Caesar, G. (1968). *Incredible detective: The biography of William J. Burns*. Englewood Cliffs, NJ: Prentice Hall; Jones, M. (2005). *Criminal justice pioneers in U.S. history*. Boston: Allyn & Bacon.

[6]Medhurst, P. *Global Terrorism*.

[7]Stein, L. (1961). *The Balfour declaration*. New York: Simon and Schuster.

[8]White, J. R. (2006). *Terrorism and homeland security* (5th ed). Belmont, CA: Thomson/Wadsworth.

[9]Hart, P. (2005). *Mick: The real Michael Collins*. Viking Press.

[10]Alonso, R. (2007). *The IRA and armed struggle*. New York: Routledge.

[11]Aburish, S. K. (2004). *Nasser: The last Arab*. New York: St. Martin's Press.

[12]Hourani, A. (1991). *A history of the Arab peoples*. Cambridge, MA: Belknap Press of Harvard University Press; Muslim Brotherhood. (2007). In *Encyclopaedia Britannica*. Accessed November 11, 2007, from Encyclopædia Britannica Online: http://search.eb.com/eb/article-9054456.

[13]MIPT Terrorism Knowledge Base, www.tkb.org, retrieved November 10, 2007.

[14]Jones, M. (2006). *Criminals of the Bible: Twenty-five case studies of biblical outlaws* . Grand Haven, MI: Faithwalk Publishing.

[15]Medhurst, P. *Global Terrorism*.

[16]Nassar, J. R. (1991). *The Palestine Liberation Organization: From armed struggle to the declaration of independence*. New York: Praeger.

[17]Garner, J. (2002). *We interrupt this broadcast: The events that stopped our lives—from the Hindenburg explosion to the attacks of September 11*. Naperville, IL: Sourcebooks.

[18]Halberstam, D. (1993). *The fifties*. New York: Villard Books.

[19]Gerges, F. A. (2006). *Journey of the Jihadist: Inside Muslim militancy*. Orlando, FL: Harcourt.

[20]Ibid. p. 178.

[21]Osama bin Laden. (2007). In *Encyclopaedia Britannica*. Accessed November 11, 2007, from Encyclopaedia Britannica Online: http://search.eb.com/eb/article-9343571.

[22]Crile, G. (2003). *Charlie Wilson's war: The extraordinary story of the largest covert operation in history*. New York: Atlantic Monthly Press, p. 522.

[23]National Commission on Terrorist Attacks upon the United States. (2004). *The 9/11 Commission Report: Final report of the National Commission on Terrorist Attacks upon the United States*. New York: W.W. Norton.

[24]Gerges, *Journey of the Jihadist*, p. 178.

[25]National Commission on Terrorist Attacks upon the United States. *The 9/11 Commission Report*.

[26]Gerges, *Journey of the Jihadist*; National Commission on Terrorist Attacks upon the United States. *The 9/11 Commission Report*.

[27]National Commission on Terrorist Attacks upon the United States. *The 9/11 Commission Report*.

[28]Ibid.

[29]Ibid; also, the "docudrama" film *United 93* presents an account of this incident.

[30]Ibid.

[31]Ibid.

[32]Friedman, T. L. *Longitudes and Attitudes*.

[33]Bar, S. (2006). *Warrant for terror: The Fatwas of radical Islam and the duty to Jihad*. Lanham, MD: Rowman and Littlefield.

[34]*Washington Post* Internet Web site, www.WashingtonPost.com, accessed November 10, 2007.

[35]National Commission on Terrorist Attacks upon the United States. *The 9/11 Commission Report*.

CHAPTER 15

Epilogue

No single volume can provide a comprehensive coverage of the history of criminal justice in the Western world, but the chapters of this book provide sufficient basis for drawing tentative conclusions concerning crime, modes of law enforcement, and methods of punishment both in the United States and some of the countries whose governments most influenced the creation of the American style of governing.

In retrospect it becomes apparent that there is a "layering" process of criminal justice knowledge and practice. Practically all societies, even those that have not employed writing as we know it to codify criminal laws, have had rules or normative behaviors which were generally understood by its citizens, and all societies devised ways of sanctioning those who violated those norms. As societies have grown increasingly complex and diverse, they have formed new stages in the history of crime and punishment and provided succeeding generations with a stronger basis on which to construct still another "layer." Through examining a number of cultural histories, it is possible to trace the transfer of ideas and crime control methods across societal lines.

Criminal justice systems are social institutions that respond to the cultural requirements of each distinct human society. However, at the same time, humankind does not exist within hermetically sealed social and cultural enclaves. There are constant cross-cultural exchanges of ideas, moral preferences, and techniques of social and political control. Even in the midst of great diversity, humankind is one, and individual societies do not hesitate to borrow from others the institutions that offer solutions to pressing human problems. This is increasingly prevalent given the advent of instant worldwide communication. Since the first edition of this book was published in the 1980s, much has changed regarding communication. Satellite television, the Internet, e-mail, social networking, cell phones, and cell phones with cameras and videotaping capability, are all developments that have brought instant communication with the world to an unprecedented degree.

Society's attitude toward antisocial behavior has been remarkably altered over the past three millennia. Ancient societies, perhaps because of their recent emergence from systems of group property, did not worry about most property-related crime, except to the extent that it might result in physical violence. Growing commercial activity changed that, raising the protection of property to a high priority in criminal law. It also spawned a new group of economic crimes, such as counterfeiting, use of false weights, and monopolizing necessary goods in the marketplace. Opportunities for fraud and theft presented themselves to medieval clerics and nineteenth-century American politicians, but their societies reacted slowly to penalize behavior that preyed upon the gullibility of the devout or the weaknesses of American municipal government. Today, criminal law is hard-pressed to deal with the burgeoning possibilities for larceny through computer systems or identity theft. Social and technological changes inevitably lead to new forms of antisocial behavior, and gradually a culture's definition of what is criminal must expand to forbid these activities.

Definitions of crime change constantly, usually to include offenses previously tolerated as being beneath notice by the criminal law. Traditional prohibitions against violent crime (murder, rape, robbery, assault, and battery) and those against property-related crime (larceny, arson, and burglary) tend to persist through time periods and across cultural lines. However, sanctions against what have become known as *victimless crimes* vary over time and between cultures. Prosecutions for prostitution, adultery, fornication, bigamy, sodomy, and excessive use of alcohol or habit-forming drugs all fall within this category. For most of America's history, the notion that a man might be found guilty of raping his wife was unthinkable, as the marriage contract carried with it the implication that a man could force his wife to engage in sex at any time. Likewise, the criminal law has made its way into other family areas as well, as parents are more likely to be held criminal for excessive discipline of children now than in times past.

Law enforcement systems also demonstrate cross-cultural and chronological layering. Emphasis on self-help was natural to a culture that was not differentiated into vocational groups and in which there was an absence of formal police and judicial institutions. At its best, self-help was limited by the relative physical prowess of the victim and the accused, and at its worst it led to vengeance and the blood feud. The transfer of police responsibility to the community eliminated some of the defects and temptations of the self-help system, but inefficient justices of the peace and lethargic constables provided little security. Their shortcomings as detectives led to the rise of the professional thief-catcher, available for hire by the victim. By the early nineteenth century, law enforcement was sorely in need of change. The newly established modern municipal police forces emphasized protective patrol and public investigations of criminal activity. However, the modern urban police system has found an increasing number of tasks assigned to it. The invention and widespread adoption of the automobile as a means of transportation has required police supervision of traffic and enforcement of rules of the road. Reformers, anxious to eradicate the supposed social origins of crime, have called upon police departments to institute social action programs. Politicians, businesspeople, and even university presidents call upon police officials to supply officers trained in crowd control. Sociologists have estimated that a very small portion of modern police activity deals with the prevention or investigation of crime. Much more time is involved with traffic patrol and providing a warm cell for drunks to sleep off their evening on the town. Indeed, if police officers were not available for these tasks, where in modern society could one find a substitute service?

It may very well be that the community service activities of police organizations are needed to bring police officers out of a subcultural pattern that may separate them from the society they serve. Police officers bear a heavy responsibility when they are given a virtual monopoly of violence in their jurisdiction. Better armed and equipped to deal with crime, better prepared now than in the 1960s to deal with student riots and ghetto uprisings, they nevertheless need the confidence and full cooperation of the people if they are to be effective agents for law and order. Advanced education will provide a broader perspective of the needs of society and the role that the criminal justice system should play in the community. It will facilitate the adoption of new systems of communication, transportation, and criminal investigation. Hopefully it will bridge the gap between law enforcement officers on one side and the criminologists and penal reformers on the other. Allied agencies in the war against crime should not waste resources fighting each other.

The prison system is of fairly recent origin in the history of criminal justice, but it reflects the full spectrum of historical attitudes toward crime. In its retributive aspects, the prison inflicts pain on the convict through deprivation of freedom, through hard labor, and through other coercive means. Crime must be adequately punished by the state; if the prison is not sufficiently punitive, a system of private revenge will arise to supplement it. Since the eighteenth century, reformers have paid increasing attention to rehabilitation. This recognizes the social need to reclaim criminals and return them to the ranks of the law-abiding. A tremendous task of restructuring human behavior has been undertaken by the rehabilitative prison and, not surprisingly, recidivism rates there is little hope for success. The idealism of nineteenth-century prison reformers has degenerated into valiant attempts at retaining educational and vocational training in the face of budget cuts and public hostility.

The public, fearful of a rising crime rate, demands longer and harsher sentences but refuses to supply the expanded prison facilities required to meet those demands. One manifestation of this need to "warehouse" offenders, and thereby to protect society, has been the establishment of mandatory minimum sentences for certain violent crimes. The use of probation and other forms of diversion continues to increase and is effective in some respects, but community-based sanctions must be able to present offenders with the threat of incarceration to act as a deterrent. Parole for good behavior has been sharply restricted, limiting the use of parole and early release as rewards for exemplary behavior behind bars. Recidivism has become a matter of public concern, and some states have enacted three-strikes laws under which any three felony convictions can result in a life sentence without the possibility of parole. Unfortunately, lawmakers have enacted many of these increased sanctions into law without giving adequate attention to the degree to which they will influence plea bargaining, prison discipline, or jury behavior.

There is a serious need for professional penologists to realistically reassess their goals and to provide the general public with accurate cost estimates for a program of long prison sentences. The activism of the federal courts in examining the physical conditions of state prisons and the growing judicial interest in humane systems of prison discipline promise to have a major impact on prison administration in the years ahead. In addition, the federal judiciary has made a concerted effort to equalize the application of sanctions imposed in United States courts. This effort has provided sentencing guidelines for federal district courts exercising criminal jurisdiction. Although this initiative has eliminated much of the individual judge's discretion in imposing punishment, it also provides a less flexible system of penalties. As such, sentencing guidelines may also assist in prison overcrowding.

Ultimately, increasing the severity of imprisonment may find its limits not in public compassion, but rather in the economic realities of costs. In the past, penology has found ways to conserve costs through the use of minimum-security prisons for offenders who have not been convicted of violent crimes or whose rehabilitation is more likely to occur in less restrictive confinement. Public reaction to these practices and increased demands for harsh prison terms may well accelerate costs beyond what society is willing to pay.

There is an even more pressing moral issue, raised by growing evidence that prosecutorial and evidentiary systems are unable to prevent wrongful convictions of crime in death penalty cases. To a large degree, the recent development of DNA evidence has heightened public awareness of these miscarriages of justice, but reversals of death sentences based on other evidence have also become increasingly common. International pressures for abolishing the death penalty in the United States reinforce this moral demand for its suspension and ultimate abolition.

A less alarming issue is raised by the much larger number of sentences that do not involve the death penalty. If wrongful, these convictions unjustly deprive the individual of months and years of freedom. They may decisively foreclose career choices; they may make parenthood unwise or impossible; they may, through length or vigor of confinement, undermine physical, mental, or spiritual health. Even without the shadow of capital punishment, these are catastrophic losses that no system of compensation, no matter how generous, can reimburse or justify. Time is not money—it is far more precious. The intentional disenfranchisement of convicted offenders must also be examined. Should a person carry the scars of a felony conviction after their sentence has been completed or even for their entire life?

Criminology must ultimately confront the problem of what causes crime within society. The historical record suggests that crime may be inevitable, but there is also a powerful societal need for order, security, and justice. This is the force that sustains not only the formal criminal justice system, but also the basic cultural values that support modern life.

Students of criminal justice search for methods to combat crime, and they doubtless will find new and more effective ways of preventing, investigating, and punishing criminal activity. But when they attempt to eliminate the causes of crime, they must look beyond the criminal justice system and examine society itself. People turn to crime for a variety of reasons, and painstaking study has begun to provide insight into those basic causes of criminal behavior. Certainly we cannot dismiss Lombroso's suggestion that genetics may condition one to crime, but it seems clear that heredity plays a minor role. The link of criminal activity to young men belonging to what society deems an "underdog" social group should suggest that the vibrant, rebellious energy of youth, combined with resentment against real or imagined slights, is an explosive mixture that frequently results in crime. And we must wonder too about the clerics of fourteenth-century England, exempted from criminal prosecution by their status, and the nobility of Renaissance Italy, licensed to rape inferior class women by a criminal justice system that overlooked such sexist activities. Can it not be said that exemption from prosecution and punishment is a strong incentive to commit major offenses against society?

Crime is an integral part of our society. It will continue to exist as long as two human beings walk the face of the earth. Criminals are not an isolated or special group, but even in their most deviant behavior they are shaped by the society and culture they share with the general population. Seeking to understand the "criminal mind," we must first look within ourselves to find the emotions and states of mind that could lead to antisocial behavior, and also to discover the social and psychological inhibitions that deter us from criminal or even unacceptable actions.

Finally, with respect to the root causes of crime, there must be some mention of addiction. Crime is not only related to academic disciplines such as law, sociology, and political science, but it must also be viewed within the paradigm of medicine and public health. If one peruses university catalogs, one cannot help considering the academic disciplines that touch crime in some way: Health Education, Rehabilitation Studies, Psychology, Nutrition, Social Work, Psychiatry, Family Relations, and Child Development, to name a few. Professionals within all of these disciplines must often concern themselves with addiction and the results of addictive behavior. On any given day, a large majority of courtroom dockets and jail cells are filled with people whose crime is directly or indirectly related to the disease of addiction, be it alcohol, other drugs, gambling, or other addictions. If the medical profession were to somehow devise a cure for addictions, crime as we now understand it would decline drastically. Criminologists in the coming decades must be able to look beyond the issues that have traditionally dominated the field and join the medical and allied health professions if they are serious about reducing crime.

Index

Note: Page numbers followed by *b* indicate boxes, *f* indicate figures and *t* indicate tables.

9781437734911